Paul-Éric Dumontier
Jennifer McMorran
Lorette Pierson
Pierre Longnus

ULYSSES
TRAVEL PUBLICATIONS
Travel better... enjoy more

Series Director
Claude Morneau

Project Supervisor
Pascale Couture

Research and Composition
Southern British Columbia
Paul-Éric Dumontier
Rocky Mountains
Lorette Pierson
Alberta
Jennifer McMorran
Northern British Columbia
Pierre Longnus
Portrait
Claude-Victor Langlois

Editors
Tracy Kendrick
Jennifer McMorran

Translation Rockies and British Columbia
Tracy Kendrick
Eric Hamovitch

Page Layout
Isabelle Lalonde

Graphic Layout
Alain Rondeau

Collaboration
Joël Pomerleau
Marc Rigole

Cartography
André Duchesne

Artistic Director
Patrick Farei
Atoll Direction

Photography
Cover page
Courtesy of Via Rail
Interior Photos
Pierre Longnus
Calgary Convention Visitors Bureau
Jennifer McMorran

Distributors

AUSTRALIA:
Little Hills Press
11/37-43 Alexander St.
Crows Nest NSW 2065
☎ (612) 437-6995
Fax: (612) 438-5762

GERMANY & AUSTRIA:
Brettschneider Fernreisebedarf GmbH
Hauptstr. 5
85586 Poing bei München
☎ 08121-71436
Fax: 08121-71419

NETHERLANDS:
Nilsson & Lamm
Pampuslaan 212-214
1380 AD Weesp (NL)
☎ 02940-65044
Fax: 02940-15054

SPAIN:
Altaïr
Balmes 69
E-08007 Barcelona
☎ (34-3) 323-3062
Fax: (3403) 451-2559

CANADA:
Ulysses Books & Maps
4176 Saint-Denis
Montréal, Québec H2W 2M5
☎ (514) 843-9882, ext.2232
Fax: 514-843-9448

GREAT BRITAIN AND IRELAND:
World Leisure Marketing
9 Downing Road West
Meadows, Derby
UK DE21 6HA
☎ 1 332 343 332
Fax: 1 332 340 464

SCANDINAVIA
Scanvik
Esplanaden 8B
Copenhagen K
DK-1263
☎ 33.12.77.66
Fax: 33.91.28.82

SWITZERLAND
OLF
P.O. Box 1061
CH-1701 Fribourg
☎ 41.37.83.51.11
Fax: 41.37.26.63.60

BELGIUM:
Vander
Vrijwilligerlaan 321
B-1150 Brussel
☎ (02) 762 98 04
Fax: (02) 762 06 62

ITALY:
Edizioni del Riccio
Via di Soffiano 164 A
50143 Firenze
☎ (055) 71 63 50
Fax: (055) 71 33 33

SOUTH-EAST ASIA
Graham Brash
32, Gul Drive
Singapore 2262
☎ 65.86.11.336
Fax: 65.86.14.815

U.S.A.:
Seven Hills Book Distributors
49 Central Avenue
Cincinnati, Ohio, 45202
☎ 1-800-545-2005
Fax: (513) 381-0753

Other countries, contact Ulysses Books & Maps (Montréal), Fax: (514) 843-9448

Canadian Cataloguing in Publication Data
Dumontier, Paul-Eric
    Western Canada   (Ulysses travel guides)
    Translation of: Ouest Canadien
    Includes index.
    ISBN 2-89464-007-2
1. Canada, Western - Guidebooks.   I. Pierson, Lorette, 1963- II. McMorran, Jennifer, 1971- III. Title   IIII. Series.
FC3203.D8513 1996   917.1204'3   C96-940409-3   F1060.4.D8513 1996
© April 1996, Ulysses Travel Publications
All rights reserved

"Then the locomotive whistle sounded again and a voice was heard to cry: 'All aboard for the Pacific.' It was the first time that phrase had been used by a conductor from the East... The official party obediently boarded the cars and a few moments later the little train was in motion again, clattering over the newly laid rail and over the last spike and down the long incline of the mountains, off towards the dark canyon of the Fraser, off to broad meadows beyond, off to the blue Pacific and into history."

                                        Pierre Berton
                                        The Last Spike

TABLE OF CONTENTS

PORTRAIT 11
    Geography 11
    History 14
    The Canadian Political System .. 19
    The Economy 20
    The Population 21
    The Amerindians 21
    Language 22
    Culture 22

PRACTICAL INFORMATION 25
    Entrance Formalities 25
    Embassies and Consulates ... 26
    Tourist Information 28
    Customs 29
    Finding Your Way Around 29
    Airports 34
    Time Difference 35
    Business Hours and Public
        Holidays 35
    Mail and Telecommunications . 36
    Money and Banking 36
    Climate and Clothing 37
    Health 38
    Shopping 38
    Accommodations 39
    Taxes and Tipping 40
    Restaurants and Bars 40
    Wine, Beer and Alcohol 41
    Advice for Smokers 41
    Safety 41
    Children 41
    Weights and Measures 41
    General Information 42

OUTDOOR ACTIVITIES 43
    Parks 43
    Summer Activities 46
    Winter Activities 48

VANCOUVER 51
    Vancouver today 51
    A brief history 52
    Finding Your Way Around 56
    Practical Information 59
    Exploring 60
    Parks and Beaches 73
    Outdoor Activities 75
    Accommodations 76
    Restaurants 78
    Entertainment 81
    Shopping 82

VICTORIA 85
    Finding Your Way Around 86
    Practical Information 89
    Exploring 90
    Parks and Beaches 95
    Outdoor Activities 95
    Accommodations 96
    Restaurants 98
    Entertainment 99
    Shopping 100

VANCOUVER ISLAND AND THE
GULF ISLANDS 101
    Finding Your Way Around 102
    Practical Information 104
    Exploring 105
    Parks and Beaches 112
    Outdoor Activities 114
    Accommodations 116
    Restaurants 118
    Entertainment 120
    Shopping 120

SOUTHERN BRITISH COLUMBIA ... 121
    Finding Your Way Around 121
    Practical Information 124
    Exploring 126
    Parks and Beaches 146
    Outdoor Activities 147
    Accommodations 152
    Restaurants 157
    Entertainment 160
    Shopping 160

NORTHERN BRITISH COLUMBIA ... 161
    Finding Your Way Around 162
    Practical Information 166
    Exploring 168
    Parks and Beaches 189
    Outdoor Activities 191
    Accommodations 192
    Restaurants 198
    Shopping 202

THE ROCKY MOUNTAINS 203
    Geography 203
    History 208
    Economy 209
    Finding Your Way Around 209
    Practical Information 213
    Exploring and Parks 214
    Outdoor Activities 238

Accommodations 252	Exploring 284
Restaurants 265	Parks 331
Entertainment 271	Beaches 338
Shopping 272	Outdoor Activities 338
	Accommodations 340
ALBERTA 275	Restaurants 352
Finding Your Way Around 278	Entertainment 360
Practical Information 282	Shopping 365

Help make Ulysses Travel Guides even better!

The information contained in this guide was correct at press time. However, mistakes can slip in, omissions are always possible, places can disappear, etc. The author and publisher hereby disclaim any liability for loss or damage resulting from omissions or errors.

We value your comments, corrections and suggestions, as they allow us to keep each guide up to date. The best contributions will be rewarded with a free book from Ulysses Travel Publications. All you have to do is write us at the following address and indicate which title you would be interested in receiving (see the list at end of guide).

**Ulysses Travel Publications
4176 Rue Saint-Denis
Montréal, Québec
Canada H2W 2M5**

Thanks to: Stephen Puddister and Maria Greene (Tourism British Columbia); Heather Chapman (Tourism Vancouver); Chrsitine Sommers (Tourism Victoria); Maureen C. Cumming (BC Ferry Corp.); Connie Rabold and Tara Woolley (Whistler Resort); Diane Lamoureux (Alberta Economic Development and Tourism); Wendy McGee (Alberta Community Development); Roy Klassen (Association des Canadiens Français de l'Alberta); Johane Biron; Catherine Boivin; Meredith and Paul Vaillancourt; Carol Wood; Stephen Darling; Jean-Louis Hérivault.

LIST OF MAPS

Alberta	p 279
Tour B: Southern Alberta	p 295
Tour C: Central Alberta	p 309
Tour E: Northern Alberta	p 325
Banff	p 217
Banff National Park	p 215
British Columbia	p 50
Calgary	p 285
Calgary Centre	p 287
Dawson Creek	p 172
Edmonton	p 317
Edmonton Centre	p 319
Fort St. John	p 175
Icefields Parkway	p 226
Jasper	p 231
Jasper National Park	p 229
Kananaskis Country, Kootenay and Yoho National Parks	p 234
Lake Louise and Surroundings	p 222
Nanaimo	p 106
Northern British Columbia	
Tours A, B, C, D, E and F	p 163
Penticton	p 137
Prince Rupert	p 184
Prince George	p 169
Queen Charlotte Islands	p 187
Rocky Mountains	p 211
Southern British Columbia	p 123
Southern British Columbia	
Tours A, B and C	p 127
Southern British Columbia	
Tours D and E	p 143
Stanley Park	p 74
Vancouver	p 57
Tours A, B, C and D	p 61
Tour E	p 67
Tour F	p 69
Tour G	p 72
Vancouver Island	p 103
Via Rail Lines in Western Canada	p 9
Victoria and Surroundings	p 87
Tours A, B, C and D	p 91
Waterton Lakes National Park	p 332
Where is Western Canada?	p 8

TABLE OF SYMBOLS

≡	Air conditioning
bkfst	Breakfast
⊗	Ceiling fan
tv	Colour television
☉	Exercise room
⇄	Fax number
½b	half-board (lodging + 2 meals)
hw	Hot water
C	Kitchenette
≈	Pool
pb	Private bathroom
ps	Private shower
ℝ	Refrigerator
ℜ	Restaurant
△	Sauna
#	Screen
sb	Shared bathroom
☏	Telephone number
⊛	Whirlpool

ATTRACTION CLASSIFICATION

★	Interesting
★★	Worth a visit
★★★	Not to be missed

HOTEL CLASSIFICATION

Unless otherwise indicated, the prices in the guide are for one room, double occupancy, in high season.

RESTAURANT CLASSIFICATION

$	less than $10
$$	$10 to $20
$$$	$20 to $30
$$$$	more than $30

Unless otherwise indicated, the prices in the guide are for a meal for one person, excluding tip and drinks.

Western Canada
Alberta and British Columbia

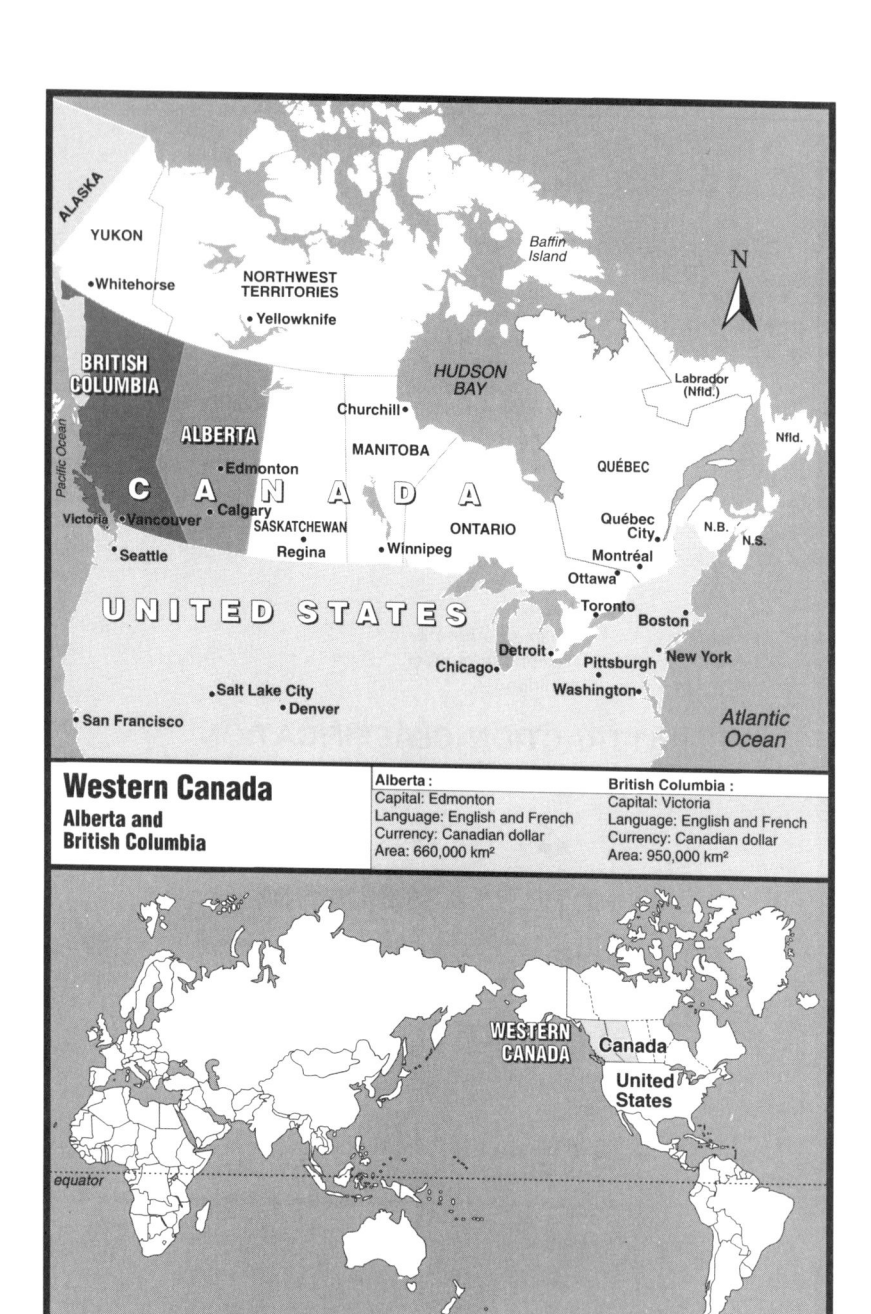

Alberta:	British Columbia:
Capital: Edmonton	Capital: Victoria
Language: English and French	Language: English and French
Currency: Canadian dollar	Currency: Canadian dollar
Area: 660,000 km²	Area: 950,000 km²

© Ulysses Travel Publications

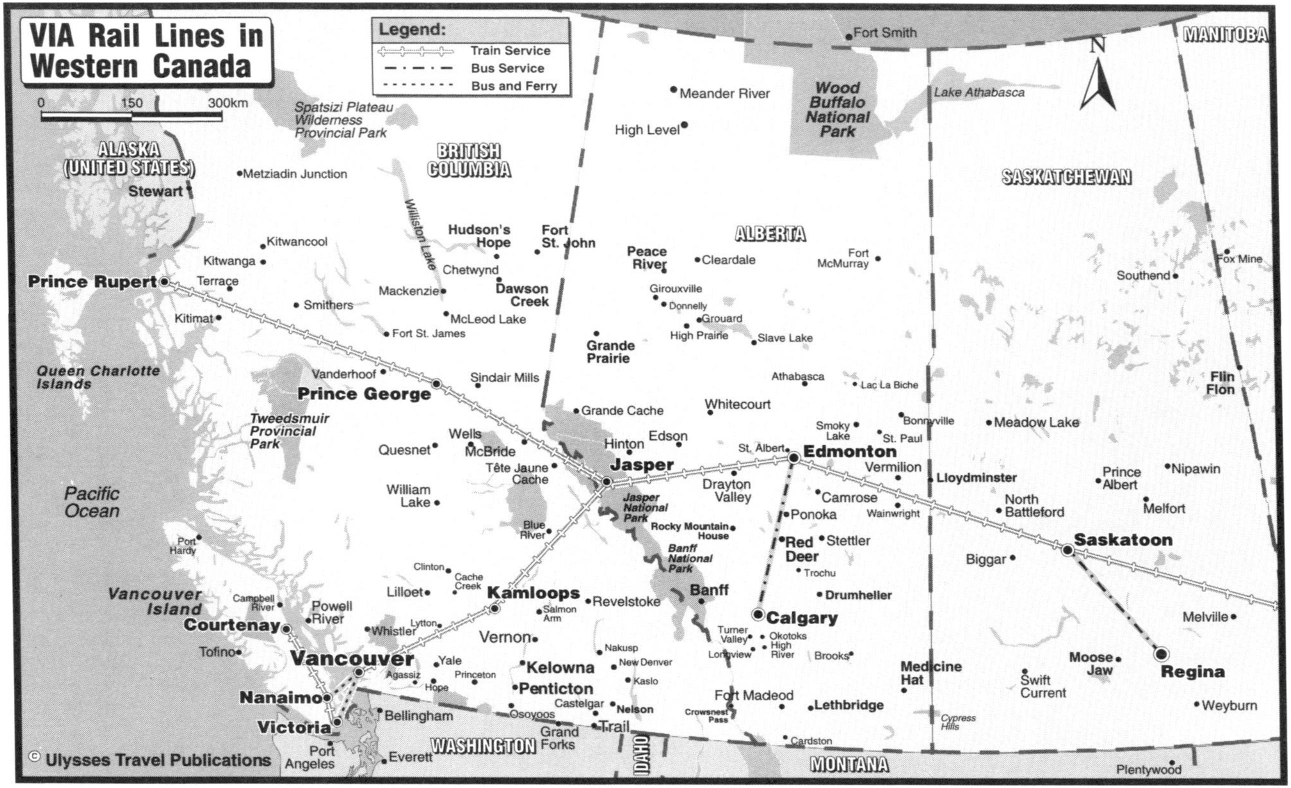

VIA Rail Lines in Western Canada
Legend:
Train Service
Bus Service
Bus and Ferry
0
150
300km
N
ALASKA (UNITED STATES)
BRITISH COLUMBIA
ALBERTA
SASKATCHEWAN
MANITOBA
WASHINGTON
IDAHO
MONTANA
Pacific Ocean
Queen Charlotte Islands
Vancouver Island
Spatsizi Plateau Wilderness Provincial Park
Tweedsmuir Provincial Park
Wood Buffalo National Park
Jasper National Park
Banff National Park
Lake Athabasca
Williston Lake
Fort Smith
Meander River
High Level
Stewart
Metziadin Junction
Kitwancool
Kitwanga
Terrace
Prince Rupert
Kitimat
Smithers
Hudson's Hope
Fort St. John
Chetwynd
Dawson Creek
Mackenzie
McLeod Lake
Fort St. James
Vanderhoof
Prince George
Sindair Mills
Peace River
Cleardale
Fort McMurray
Girouxville
Donnelly
Grouard
High Prairie
Slave Lake
Grande Prairie
Athabasca
Lac La Biche
Grande Cache
Whitecourt
Smoky Lake
Bonnyville
St. Paul
Meadow Lake
Hinton
Edson
Wells
McBride
Quesnel
Tête Jaune Cache
Jasper
St. Albert
Edmonton
Vermilion
Lloydminster
Drayton Valley
Camrose
Wainwright
William Lake
Ponoka
Blue River
Rocky Mountain House
Red Deer
Stettler
Trochu
Drumheller
Port Hardy
Clinton
Cache Creek
Lilloet
Kamloops
Revelstoke
Salmon Arm
Banff
Calgary
Campbell River
Powell River
Courtenay
Whistler
Lytton
Vernon
Tofino
Vancouver
Yale
Agassiz
Hope
Princeton
Kelowna
Penticton
Nakusp
New Denver
Kaslo
Castelgar
Nelson
Trail
Osoyoos
Grand Forks
Nanaimo
Victoria
Bellingham
Port Angeles
Everett
Turner Valley
Okotoks
High River
Longview
Brooks
Fort Madeod
Crowsnest Pass
Lethbridge
Cardston
Medicine Hat
Cypress Hills
North Battleford
Biggar
Saskatoon
Prince Albert
Nipawin
Melfort
Southend
Fox Mine
Flin Flon
Melville
Moose Jaw
Regina
Swift Current
Weyburn
Plentywood
© Ulysses Travel Publications

PORTRAIT

The region covered in this guide has only been known to Europeans for the last 200 years. In fact, the sons of the French explorer La Vérendrye did not set eyes on the Rocky Mountains until the end of the 18th century, and England's George Vancouver only explored the Pacific coast and Columbia River in the last decade of the same century. White settlement of the region is even more recent, going back just over 100 years in Alberta, which has existed as a province for only 91 years. Amerindians have inhabited this territory for at least 11,000 years, but never in large numbers; there were only 220,000 of them in all of Canada when explorer Jacques Cartier arrived in 1534.

Geography

This guide covers the two most westerly provinces of Canada, British Columbia, located on the Pacific coast and occupied essentially by vast mountain chains, and Alberta, which begins on the eastern slopes of the Rocky Mountains and extends into the vast Canadian prairies to the border of Saskatchewan. British Columbia and Alberta are bordered to the south by the United States (the states of Washington on the coast, then Idaho and Montana inland). British Columbia shares a frontier with Alaska to the northwest and the Canadian Yukon to the north. The Northwest Territories, also under Canadian jurisdiction, border northern Alberta and the northeastern part of British Columbia.

British Columbia is the largest of these two provinces with an area of 950,000 km², while Alberta covers 660,000 km². Together, these two provinces cover a territory slightly larger than Alaska, more than twice the size of Texas and about one and a half times the size of Ontario. The United Kingdom would fit seven times into the area they cover.

Carved out by countless fjords and dotted with hundreds of islands, British Columbia's jagged Pacific coast is 7,000 km long, not counting the shores of the islands. The largest island is Vancouver Island, about the size of the Netherlands and home to the provincial capital Victoria. Despite its name, the city of Vancouver is not on the island but rather lies across the Strait of Juan de Fuca, on the mainland. The Queen Charlotte Islands lie to the north. Despite the maritime nature of the territory, three quarters of the province lies an average of more than 930 m above sea level, and a 3,000 m high barrier of mountains is visible from the coast. A whole series of mountain ranges stretch from west to east, all the way to the famous Rocky Mountains, whose summits reach up to 4,000 m. The bare and rocky eastern slopes of this chain earned it its name.

During the Precambrian era, the Pacific Ocean covered most of Western Canada. Over a period of about 500 million years, the ocean advanced and receded, depositing sediment on the Precambrian rock of the Canadian Shield, one of the oldest rock formations on earth. Microscopic organisms in the sea died, creating enormous amounts of decaying organic matter, at the source of Alberta's huge oil deposits. By the Cretaceous period, some 75 million years ago, the Arctic Ocean had flooded most of Alberta, creating a vast inland sea known as the Bearpaw. Dinosaurs thrived along the shores of this subtropical sea and the rivers that emptied into it. They lived there for millions of years, until about 70 million years ago when the Pacific Plate collided with the North American Plate and was forced upwards, forming the mountain ranges of present-day British Columbia and Alberta. This gradually altered the climate, cooling things down and eventually killing off the dinosaurs around 63 million years ago. Then, about a million years ago, four polar ice caps advanced across the plains, and as tehy receded, carved out the rivers and lakes that make up Alberta's present landscape.

These rivers divided the province into regions. The Mackenzie, Peace and Athabasca Rivers make the land arable as far as the Boreal forests of the north and eventually empty into the Arctic Ocean. The North Saskatchewan and Red Deer Rivers provide most of the irrigation for Alberta farms, and empty into Hudson Bay, along with the South Saskatchewan, Oldman and Bow Rivers.

■ **Flora and Fauna**

There is a section devoted specifically to the flora and fauna of the Rockies at the beginning of the chapter describing that region (see p 205).

Despite the limited extent of the plains in British Columbia, 60% of the province's territory is covered by forest. The forest growing along the coast, on the Queen Charlotte Islands and on the west coast of Vancouver Island is so lush that it is called the northern rain forest, the counterpart of the tropical rain forest. Douglas firs and western red cedars abound, as does the Sitka spruce. The Douglas fir can grow to up to 90 m in height and 4.5 m in diameter. This forest receives up to 4,000 mm of rain per year and many of its trees are more than 1,000 years old, though most of the ancient Douglas firs were cut down in the last century. Much higher and drier, the province's interior is home to vast pine, spruce and hemlock forests.

Larches grow in the subalpine forests found at higher altitudes. The larch is the only coniferous tree in Canada that loses its needles in the fall, after they turn yellow. They grow back in the spring.

Sheltered by Vancouver Island, the southern Gulf Islands have a relatively dry, mild climate, you'll even find certain varieties of cacti here, including the prickly pear. Flowers bloom in this area all year round, especially in the months of April and May.

Southeastern Alberta, the hottest and driest place in the province, is a vast expanse of prairies. Grasses cover the land, except along the rivers, where cottonwood and willows trees grow. Cacti can even be found in the south. The prairies rise and get hilly as you head west into the foothills, where aspen, white spruce, lodgepole pine and Douglas fir trees grow. Beyond these foothills, the Rocky Mountains reach altitudes of 3,700 m, and the vegetation gets sparser the higher you go. A belt of aspen parkland acts as a transition zone between the grasslands of the south and the Boreal forest of the north. Aspen and grasslands cover most of this area. Beyond this, more than half the province is covered with Boreal forest dotted with lakes and bogs. White spruce, lodgepole pine and balsam fir are the most common trees. Finally, parts of this region are strewn with bushes bearing raspberries and saskatoon berries.

Warmed by the Japanese current, the waters of the Pacific maintain a higher temperature than those of the Atlantic which are cooled by the Labrador current. As a result, this region features very distinctive marine life. For example, this is the only place in Canada where sea otters are found, even though they were almost completely exterminated by hunting. Sea lions are also indigenous to the Pacific coast. The Northern sea lion is often the subject of fishermen's griping, since it is the main predator of salmon. It is true that some sea lions can weigh up to a tonne and never seem to stop eating, but many other animals feast on the abundant salmon on the coast and in the rivers where they spawn. Grizzly bears, for example, gather for a feast when the rivers are teeming with salmon, and gourmets that they are, eat only the roe and the head! Wolves, black bears, raccoons, gulls and bald eagles eat the leftovers. Speaking of bald eagles, the Pacific coast is home to Canada's largest population of these majestic birds, which have all but disappeared from the Atlantic coast.

Countless orcas inhabit the waters around Vancouver Island and are commonly spotted from the ferries that link this island with the mainland. They are the only marine mammals that eat warm-blooded animals like seals, belugas and other smaller whales, which probably explains their more common appellation, killer whales.

With the arrival of fall, certain marine mammals like the grey whale, migrate from Alaska to Baja California in Mexico. They make their way back up to Alaska in the winter.

Raccoon

Large numbers of cougars (see description on p 206) inhabit British Columbia's forests, particularly on Vancouver Island, where they feed on Columbia blacktail deer. The cougar attacks by jumping on the deer's back and biting its neck, killing it instantly.

An impressive variety of birds and mammals inhabit Alberta. Some of the more noteworthy winged species are bald eagles found around the northern lakes, prairie and peregrine falcons, which can often be seen in and around the plains either diving for prey or waiting patiently on a fence post by the highway. Finally, the migratory path of the trumpeter swan passes through Alberta.

To the delight of anglers, Alberta's lakes and rivers are teeming with countless fresh water fish, these include eight different varieties of trout.

History

In 1670, the territory now known as the prairies, made up of the provinces of Manitoba, Saskatchewan and Alberta, was ceded by the British Crown to the Hudson's Bay Company (HBC), which took over the economic and political administration of the region.

The HBC controlled trade in Rupert's Land, which encompassed all land that drained into Hudson Bay, therefore covering much of present-day Canada. In 1691, Henry Kelsey, an employee of the company was the first to set sight on the eastern boundary of Alberta. HBC traders, however, had competition from French fur trappers, known as *voyageurs*, who headed inland to the source of the fur instead of waiting for the natives to bring the pelts to the trading posts. Ultimately it was Anthony Henday, an independent trader, who became the first white man to trade in Alberta in 1754-55. Encouraged by favourable reports, independent fur traders in Montreal formed the Northwest Company in 1787, and then founded the first trading post in Alberta, Fort Chipewyan, on Lake Athabasca.

These trading posts eventually came to serve as bases for exploration and in 1792 Alexander Mackenzie crossed Alberta by the Peace River, becoming the first man to reach the Pacific overland. The trading companies' sole interest in the West lay in the fur trade, which continued unabated, even receiving a boost when the Northwest and Hudson's Bay Companies merged in 1821. By the late 1860s, however, beaver stocks had begun to dwindle, and merchants turned their attention to buffalo. After only ten years of buffalo hunting and trading, there were almost no more of these majestic animals which had once roamed wild throughout the province. This had dire consequences for the Amerindians, who depended on the buffalo for their survival and were ultimately left with no choice but to negotiate treaties with Canada, give up their land and move onto reserves.

The fur trade being the principle activity of the HBC, the Company did all it could to discourage colonization in the region, which explains why the population had only reached 12,000 by 1871. At the time, the United States had just ended its civil war and was clearly interested in conquering the British part of North America, present-day Canada. They had purchased Alaska from Russia in 1867, and in 1868, Minnesota drew up a resolution favouring the annexation of the Canadian prairies. These vague American impulses were enough to worry the leaders of the fledgling Canadian Confederation (1867) who negotiated with Great Britain and the Hudson's Bay Company to acquire the Northwest Territories (which at the time included present-day Alberta, Saskatchewan, Manitoba and the Northwest Territories) in 1868 without so much as consulting the people who had settled there, for the most part French-speaking Métis. These people resisted and prevented the governor appointed by Canada from taking power. Pressure from the Americans, who were just waiting for a reason to intervene, the difficulty of taking military action against the well-organized Métis in a region so far from the central government, fear the Amerindian nations would back the Métis and finally Québec' support for the Métis forced the federal government to negotiate. It consented to create the province of Manitoba, giving it a minuscule territory, smaller than Belgium, and granting it most of the powers that the other provinces enjoyed, except those related to natural resources and the development of the land. These circumstances have influenced negotiations between the Canadian government and what would become the three prairie provinces (Manitoba, Saskatchewan and Alberta) up to the present.

Unlike the prairies, which were simply annexed to the Canadian Confederation in 1868, British Columbia was already a British colony and was thus able to negotiate its entrance into confederation. Isolated on the Pacific coast, British Columbia's principal trading partner was California. As its population grew with the gold rush of the 1850s, certain residents even dreamed of creating an independent country. But these hopes were dashed at the end of this prosperous period, when in 1871, British Columbia's population had dropped to only 36,000. Great Britain had already joined its colony on Vancouver Island with British Columbia in anticipation of their eventual integration into the new Canadian Confederation.

With a promise from Canada that a pan-Canadian railway would reach the coast by 1881, British Columbia accepted to join confederation in 1871. However, all sorts of problems delayed the construction of the railroad, and in 1873, as a severe recession gripped Canada, causing major delays in the railway, British Columbia threatened to separate. It wasn't until November 7, 1885 that the railway from Montréal to Vancouver was finally completed, four years late.

As the railway expanded, more and more farmers settled in the region known as the Northwest Territories, which had no responsible government on the provincial level. You will recall that Canada had annexed the prairies without giving them provincial status, except for a small parcel of land, which became the province of Manitoba. Inevitably, Canada had to create the provinces of Alberta and Saskatchewan and enlarge the province of Manitoba in 1905. The province of Alberta, therefore, as it is covered in this guide, has only existed for 91 years.

Life in Western Canada was hard around the turn of the century. For example, the coal mines of Alberta and British Columbia were the most dangerous in the Americas: by the end of the century there were 23 fatal accidents for every million tonnes of coal extracted, while in the United States there were only six. In British Columbia, a strike by 7,000 miners looking to improve their working conditions lasted two years, from 1912 to 1914, and finally had to be broken by the Canadian army. For the farmers who came here to grow wheat, the high cost of rail transport, lack of rail service, low wheat prices and bad harvests, along with duties too high to protect the fledgling industry in central Canada, all came together to make for miserable and desperate times. Certain arrangements improved the situation, like the establishment in 1897 of the Crow's Nest Pass rate for grain transport. The First World War created a temporary boom from 1914 to 1920, causing a rise in the price of raw materials and wheat. The workers remained dissatisfied, though, and in 1919, the workers' unions of the West created their own central union, the One Big Union. As supporters of Russian Bolsheviks, the union's goal was to abolish capitalism. However, a general strike in Winnipeg, Manitoba quickly created a rift between the workers with respect to their objectives, and demonstrated Canada's determination not to let the country fall into the Marxist ideology. The 1920s again proved prosperous for the West, and Alberta, at the time an essentially agricultural province, was able finish clearing its territory.

The great crash of 1929 had a profound effect on Western Canada, in particular the Prairie provinces, which saw their agricultural revenues drop by 94% between 1929 and 1931! And the fact that their farms specialized almost exclusively in wheat made the situation even worse. This period was marked by the evolution of two Western Canadian political movements, both of which remained almost exclusively local, the Social Credit and the Co-operative Commonwealth

Federation (CCF). The doctrine of the Social Credit, which supported the small farmers' and workers' stand against the capitalist ascendancy by providing interest-free credit, reached its height under William Aberhart, who was elected premier of Alberta in 1935. His government dared to defy the capitalist system like no Canadian government ever had before (or has since). In 1936, Alberta refused to redeem any bonds, unilaterally cut the interest it was paying on its loans in half, started printing its own money, prohibited the seizure of assets for non-payment and even went so far as to force provincial newspapers to print the government's point of view. One by one, these Albertan laws were voided by the federal government or the supreme court of Canada, but Aberhart was so successful in making the population believe it was the victim of a conspiracy involving the federal government and capitalists that he was re-elected in 1940. He died in 1943 and was replaced by Ernest Manning, elected in 1944. Manning managed to bring some legality to the party and eliminated all the anti-capitalist rhetoric from the party line. He dealt with all the controversy surrounding Alberta's debt, enabling the province to benefit once again from investment capital. In 1947, large oil deposits were discovered, and from then on the province enjoyed unprecedented prosperity thanks to royalties and foreign investment in the gas and petroleum industries.

The CCF, for its part reached its pinnacle in 1933 when it became the official opposition in British Columbia. An outgrowth of the Socialist Party, workers' unions and farmers' associations, the party was never elected to power, but nevertheless influenced the political agenda and gave rise to the New Democratic Party (NDP).

These two western parties, the Social Credit and the CCF, never came to play an important role in federal politics. The arrival of John Diefenbaker, the first Canadian prime minister from the West, as leader of the federal government in 1957 only further marginalized the two parties. Under Diefenbaker, a true representative of the West, as well as under the leadership of his successor, Lester B. Pearson, who truly understood the need to give the provinces more powers, the demands of the West almost seemed a thing of the past. They came to the fore once again, however, during the seventies, when world markets reeled during the oil crisis. Residents of oil-rich Alberta took particular offense at Prime Minister Trudeau's various attempts to weaken the provinces by imposing unpopular policies such as the transfer of control over natural resources to the federal government.

At the end of the seventies, the oil boom, combined with an economic slowdown in Ontario and Québec, gave Alberta almost total employment and made it the province with the highest revenue per capita. This record performance cost Alberta some credibility when it came to its demands for larger control of its oil and gas. The split between the province and the central government widened, and in the 1980 federal elections none of the deputies elected in British Columbia and Alberta were members of the Liberal Party, the party in power. The Liberals thus lead the country until 1984 without any representation from these two provinces. The sense of alienation in the West culminated with the National Energy Program, put on the table by the Trudeau government

> **Kim Campbell: First Female Canadian Prime Minister**
>
> A native of British Columbia, Kim Campbell was elected leader of the federal Progressive Conservative Party of Canada in June 1993 and thus became the country's first female Prime Minister. Unfortunately, Campbell found herself the leader of a party in turmoil. Confronted with a slow economy and Canadians' desire for change, the Conservative Party suffered a huge defeat in the next election, which took place just a few months later, in October of the same year. Campbell was ultimately replaced as head of the Progressive Conservative by the party's present leader, Jean Charest. She now works in the private sector.

in 1980. Under this program, the federal government was to claim a greater and greater share of the price of Canadian oil and natural gas, leaving only a very marginal amount of the profits generated by the explosion of the world markets for the provinces and producers. This appropriation by the federal government of natural resources that had been regulated and private since Confederation was strongly repudiated by Alberta and was one of the reasons, along with the repatriation of the Constitution without the consent of Québec in 1982, for the federal Liberals' defeat in the 1984 election. In the early eighties, separatist movements in Alberta succeeded in gaining the support of 20% of the population and in electing a deputy to the Alberta parliament in 1981.

Pierre Trudeau's Liberal government, which had lead Canada almost uninterruptedly for 17 years, was succeeded by the Progressive Conservative government of Brian Mulroney, which did away with the much hated National Energy Program. Mulroney was unable, however, to maintain the support of westerners beyond his second mandate. The reasons for this are the same ones that cost him the federal elections of 1993: an inability to reduce the deficit left by the Trudeau government, large-scale corruption and an inability to convince the population of the advantages of many of his major decisions, including free trade with the United States and the Meech Lake constitutional accord. Drawing on Albertan separatist sentiment and the extreme-right's disappointment with the weakness of the Mulroney government, Preston Manning, an Albertan, had founded the Reform Party in Vancouver in 1987. This party advocates, among other things, the reduction of federal expenditures, including the elimination of bilingual services where the demand can not justify the cost. Westerners massively supported the Reform Party during the 1993 elections. At the same time, Quebecers massively supported the Bloc Québecois party, which favours an independent Québec. The Bloc actually became the official opposition in the federal parliament, closely followed by the Reform Party. This election and the parliamentary distribution that resulted illustrates the regionalism that exists in Canada and the potential risk of disintegration.

> **Preston Manning: Western Politico**
>
> Preston Manning, son of Ernest C. Manning, Premier of Alberta for 25 years, was born and raised on a dairy farm east of Edmonton. After working as a research and management consultant, Preston Manning founded the Reform Party in 1987 and lead it to an overwhelming success in the West in the 1993 federal election. With a platform based essentially on cost-cutting, Manning found tremendous support among westerners, who have always felt neglected by Ottawa and were fed up with federal overspending. Many easterners find the Reform Party's *raison-d'être* to be divisive and not conducive to solving the country's constitutional crisis. Furthermore, its desire to cut funding for bilingual services certainly hasn't made Manning many friends among French-speaking Canadians.

Once again, the West found itself being marginalized by the federal government, just like in Trudeau's times.

At the provincial level, Alberta is presently being lead by the most right-wing government in Canada, Ralph Klein's Conservatives. They have yet to infringe too heavily on civil liberties, but rather have chosen to concentrate on cutting the deficit, and so far the population is grateful that at least Alberta's debt has stopped growing. The government has even gained a certain amount of admiration in the rest of Canada, where debt and chronic deficits have reached such high levels that any optimism with respect to the country's economic future seems to have disappeared. British Columbia is also expected to swing to the right in the upcoming elections in May 1996, though at this point it's still anybody's race and the Liberals or the New Democratic Party could conceivably win. The latter party, which has traditionally been very leftist, has just appointed as its new leader and Premier, Glen Campbell, who is known to swing right. Observers even give the Reform Party a slim chance of winning.

The Canadian Political System

The constitutional document that forms the basis of the Canadian Confederation of 1867, the British North America Act, established a division of power between the two levels of government. This means that in addition to the Canadian government, located in Ottawa, each of the 10 provinces has its own government capable of legislating in certain areas. The Confederative Pact originally allowed for a decentralized division of powers, however, over the last fifty years, the Canadian government has tended away from this decentralization in areas traditionally within the jurisdiction of the provinces, thereby creating tensions between the two levels of government.

Based on the British model, Canada's political system, like those of the provinces, gives legislative power to a

> ### Svend Robinson: Canadian Parliament's First Openly Gay Deputy
>
> Elected as deputy for the first time in 1979, at the age of 27, Svend Robinson of the New Democratic Party was the first Canadian parliamentary deputy to discuss his homosexuality openly. This did not stop the constituents of his Burnaby-Kingsway riding near Vancouver from re-electing him twice after he called a press conference in 1986 because a student had told him he could never have a political career because he was gay!
>
> Svend Robinson was in the news again in 1994, when he represented Sue Rodriguez, a woman suffering from Lou Gehrig's disease (ALS) who petitioned the court to end her own life. Though the Supreme Court ruled against her, she nevertheless went through with it, assisted by an anonymous doctor.
>
> In 1995, Svend Robinson almost became the leader of the federal New Democratic Party, but lost in favour of a virtual unknown. Some say certain people were simply not ready to accept him as a leader, despite the tolerant attitudes that leftist parties like the NDP are supposed to express...

parliament elected by universal suffrage according to a single ballot vote with a simple majority. This method of voting usually leads to an alternation of power between two political parties. Besides the House of Commons, the federal government also consists of an Upper Chamber and the Senate, whose real powers are presently being curtailed and whose future remains uncertain.

The Economy

Alberta and British Columbia are the richest provinces in Canada, with a gross domestic product (GDP) of $30,000 and $27,000 per resident, respectively, compared to $22,200 for all of Canada, $22,950 for Québec and $26,700 for Ontario. However, because of their smaller populations, their total GDP is less that Ontario's, even when added together. The unemployment rate of both provinces is lower than Canada's (11%), British Columbia's is at 9.4%, while Alberta's is the lowest in the country at 8.6%.

Alberta is an important grain producer (the three prairie provinces produce almost all Canadian wheat), but it is also the province with the most cattle ranches. Some 4 million head of cattle represent the largest portion of Alberta's agricultural output. These ranches are concentrated in the southern half of the province and in the foothills of the Rockies, where dry conditions and steep slopes make for poor farming conditions.

Although the oil boom is over, the petroleum industry is still vital to Alberta's economy, representing more than 10% of the GDP. Tourism, natural gas, coal, minerals, forestry and agriculture complete Alberta's economic pie.

In British Columbia, only 2% of the territory is used for agriculture, but this is carried out very effectively. Dairy and poultry farms make up the majority of the province's agricultural production, while the cultivation of small fruits, vegetables and flowers represents an important share as well. Orchards fill the Okanagan Valley, while vast sheep and cattle ranches stretch across the centre of the province.

Forestry remains British Columbia's most important economic activity, representing more than 30% of the province's GDP. Mining is next, and tourism now occupies third place.

The Population

British Columbia has 3 million inhabitants, more than half of whom live in Greater Vancouver; over 90% of the province's territory belongs to the provincial government.

The majority of Alberta's 2.6 million inhabitants live in the southern part of the province, while 20% of the population lives in rural areas. Greater Edmonton, has more than 800,000 residents, about 630,000 of whom live in the city itself; Calgary has 750,000 residents.

The Amerindians

Alberta's first human inhabitants are believed to have arrived at least 11,000 years ago when the Wisconsin glacier receded, though they may have arrived on the American continent earlier. These people found large numbers of buffalo and other game animals here, as well as berries and roots. They did not waste any of these resources, using hides for clothing, storage and shelter, bones as tools, horns for spoons, antlers for handles, plants for medicines, sinew for thread and clay for pottery.

Early records from the 1700s indicate that southern Alberta was inhabited by the Blackfoot, Blood, Peigan and Gros Ventre tribes, who had only recently displaced the Shoshoni, Kootenay and Crow Indians. Sarcee Indians were found near the North Saskatchewan River, while the Beavers and Slaveys occupied the area to the north.

The arrival of traders in Hudson Bay introduced items like metal tools and weapons to Alberta natives before they had even laid eyes on a single European. The horse was unknown to Alberta natives, and its arrival in the early 1700s following the Spanish conquest of Mexico changed their hunting methods forever. The traditional buffalo jump, during which buffalo were herded over a cliff to their death, thus became obsolete.

Under Treaty No. 6, the Crees, Assiniboines and Ojibwas surrendered all lands in central Alberta. The next year, in 1877, the Blackfoot, Blood, Peigan, Sarcee and Stoney tribes signed Treaty No. 7, surrendering all lands south of Treaty No. 6. The northern lands of the Beaver, Cree, Slavey and Chipewyan Indians were surrendered in Treaty No. 8, signed in 1899. For the most part, the size of reserves was based on a five people per square mile rule. Today, more than 35,000 natives live on reserves, representing about 60% of the province's total native population.

In 1725, the coastal regions of what was to become British Columbia were occupied by Nootka, Coast Salish, Kwakiutl, Bella Coola, Tsimshian, Haida and Tlinkit. Tagish, Tahltan, Testsaut, Carrier, Chilcotin, Interior Salish, Nicola and Kootenays occupied the interior. Slavery seems to have been practised among the Interior Salish, who had three social classes. Today British Columbia is home to nearly 100,000 Amerindians divided among 200 bands. More than half live on reserves.

Language

The huge majority of Albertans and British Columbians, some 94%, are English-speaking, leaving only 6% who can express themselves in Canada's other official language, French. In Alberta 0.1% of the population is unilingual French, while in British Columbia the percentage is 0.04%.

A larger percentage of Alberta's francophones are of older stock, while those from British Columbia are much more recent arrivals, having moved here from Québec or French-speaking Europe.

Culture

Many Canadians have ambiguous feelings when it comes to their American neighbours. American popular culture is omnipresent in their everyday lives. It is fascinating, but also troubling, and much time and energy is invested in defining just what distinguishes Canadian culture from that found south of the border. Nevertheless, countless extremely talented artists of all kinds have gained international renown and have established cultural trends that are uniquely Canadian.

The Canadian Radio-television and Telecommunications Commission (CRTC) supervises all types of broadcasting in Canada, ensuring among other things Canadian content. For example any non-Canadian songs are limited to 18 airplays per week. Though this may seem restrictive, it has gone a long way to promoting Canadian music and television in all its forms and languages, and to ensuring that Canadian artists get a fair chance in an area that is all too often dominated by the sleeping giant to the south.

In the following pages we have identified some of the distinctive elements of the culture of this young region, in the hopes that travellers will be tempted to learn more during their visit.

■ Amerindian Culture

Totemic culture is perhaps the greatest legacy of Canada's Amerindians. This culture reached its height at the middle of the last century, and it is easy to imagine the wonder that the sight of 30 to 40 totem poles along the rivers leading to each Amerindian village must have engendered in the first Europeans to settle in British Columbia. The totems were not revered like idols but featured elements relating to Amerindian beliefs. The celebrated British Columbian painter Emily Carr (see below) visited many Amerindian villages, and some of her most beautiful paintings were inspired by the totemic culture. Unfortunately, like most of what has been produced by Amerindians, the totem poles do not stand up well against the ravages of weather, and the only ones that have survived to this day are those that have been preserved in parks and museums. Amerindian art has always been linked to native beliefs, which were consistently viewed with suspicion by European missionaries, who did all they could to convert the Amerindians. This ultimately led to a loss of interest in native art among natives themselves. Efforts were made in the sixties and seventies to revive Amerindian culture in northwestern British Columbia with KSAN project, centred in the village of Hazelton (see p 182).

■ Visual Arts

At the beginning of this century, Emily Carr, who had travelled extensively throughout British Columbia, produced magnificently beautiful paintings reflecting the splendid landscapes of the Pacific coast and revealing certain aspects of the Amerindian spirit. Her blues and greens capture the captivating atmosphere of British Columbia. Several rooms at the Vancouver Art Gallery (see p 65) are devoted exclusively to her work. A pioneer of the west coast art scene, she was followed by such great artists as Jack Shadbolt and Gordon Smith, whose work illustrates the unique vision that all inhabitants of this region have of the landscapes that surround them.

■ Literature

One of the earliest pieces of Albertan literature is *David Thompson's Narrative of his Explorations in Western North American 1784-1812*. Earle Birney was born in Alberta, and was brought up there and in British Columbia. His belief that geography links man to his history is evident in his poetry and its attempts to define the significance of place and time.

Born in 1920 in the Yukon, which was overrun by gold-diggers in the 19th century, to a father who participated in the Klondike gold rush, Pierre Berton lived in Vancouver for many years. He has written many accounts of the high points of Canadian history including *The Last Spike* which recounts the construction of the pan-Canadian railway across the Rockies all the way to Vancouver.

Renowned for her powerful paintings of Canada's Pacific coast, Emily Carr wrote her first book at the age of 70, just a few years before her death. The few books she wrote are autobiographical works, which vividly portray the atmosphere of British Columbia and exhibit her extensive knowledge of the customs and beliefs of the Amerindians.

Robert Kroetch and Rudy Wiebe are two of Alberta's most well-respected writers. Kroetch is a storyteller above all, and his Out West trilogy offers an in-depth look at Alberta over four decades. *Alberta* is part travel guide, part wonderful collection of stories and essays, and captures the essence of the land and people of Alberta. *Seed Catalogue* is another of his excellent works. Rudy Wiebe is not a native Albertan but spent most of his life there. He was raised as a Mennonite, and the moral vision instilled in him by his religious background is the most important feature of his writing. *The Temptations of Big Bear*, for which he won the Governor General's Award describes the disintegration of Amerindian culture caused by the growth of the Canadian nation.

Nancy Huston was born in Calgary and lived there for 15 years. More than 20 years ago, after a five-year stay in New York City, she decided to relocate to Paris, where she finished her doctoral studies in semiology under the tutelage of Roland Barthes. After winning the Governor General's Award in 1993 for her novel *Cantique des Plaines* she became a major contributor to French-language literature. Since then she has published, among other things, *Tombeau de Romain Gary*, another brilliant work.

The writings of Jane Rule, an American who has lived in British Columbia since 1956, reflect a mentality that is typical of both the American and Canadian west. However, she is better known for her efforts to bridge the gap between the homosexual and heterosexual communities. Other notable western writers include poets Patrick Lane from British Columbia and Sid Marty from Alberta. More recently, however, Vancouver can be proud of its native son Douglas Coupland, who in 1991 at the age of 30 published his first novel, *Generation X*. His work coined a new catch-phrase that is now used by everyone from sociologists to ad agencies to describe this young, educated and underemployed generation. Coupland's latest novel *Microserfs*, has proven just as sociological, but this time it is the world of young computer whizzes that he is describing, with sweeping generalizations about American popular culture that are both ironic and admiring; interestingly paralleling English-Canadian sentiment about the United States.

Vancouver playwrite George Ryga's play *Ecstasy of Rita Joe* marked a renewal for Canadian theatre in 1967. This work deals with the culture shock experienced by Amerindian societies, inherently turned towards nature yet existing in a dehumanized western society. Albertan Brad Fraser's powerful play *Unidentified Human Being Remains or the True Nature of Love* analyzes contemporary love in an urban setting. The play was adapted for the cinema by Denys Arcand under the title *Love and Humain Remains*.

■ Music

Western Canada is a cultured place with orchestras, operas and theatres. In the case of Alberta, however, country music is perhaps more representative of the culture. This music has recently experienced a revival, entering the mainstream and moving up all sorts of country charts as well as pop charts. Wilf Carter, from Calgary became famous in the United States as a yodelling cowboy. More recently k.d. lang, of Consort, Alberta became a Grammy-winning superstar. In her early days with the Reclines she was known for her outrageous outfits and honky-tonk style, but of late, her exceptional voice and blend of country and pop are her trademarks. A rarity in show business, she has always had the courage to be open about her homosexuality.

British Columbia, and more particularly cosmopolitan Vancouver prefers a little more variety and has produced some significant mainstream stars. Bryan Adams was actually born in Kingston, Ontario, but eventually settled in Vancouver. This grammy-nominated rock and roll performer is known the world over.

PRACTICAL INFORMATION

Information in this section will help visitors better plan their trip to Western Canada.

Entrance Formalities

■ Passport

For a stay of less than three months in Canada, a valid passport is usually sufficient for most visitors and a visa is not required. American residents do not need a passport, though it is the best form of identification. A three-month extension is possible, but a return ticket and proof of sufficient funds to cover this extension may be required.

Caution: some countries do not have an agreement with Canada concerning health and accident insurance, so it is advisable to have the appropriate coverage. For more information, see the section entitled "**Health**" on page 38.

Canadian citizens who wish to enter the United States do not need a visa, neither do citizens from the majority of Western European countries. A valid passport is sufficient for a stay of less than three months. A return ticket and proof of sufficient funds to cover your stay may be required.

■ Extended Visits

Visitors must submit a request to extend their visit **in writing** and **before** the expiration of their visa (the date is usually written in your passport) to an Immigration Canada office. To make a request you must have a valid passport, a return ticket, proof of sufficient funds to cover the stay, as well as the $65 non-refundable filing-fee. In some cases (work, study), however, the request must be made **before** arriving in Canada.

Embassies and Consulates

■ Abroad

Australia
Canadian Consulate General
Level 5, Quay West
111 Harrington Road
Sydney, N.S.W.
Australia 2000
☎ (612) 364-3000
⇄ (612) 364-3098

Belgium
Canadian Embassy
2 Avenue de Tervueren
1040 Brussels
☎ 735.60.40
⇄ 732.67.90

Denmark
Canadian Embassy
Kr. Bernikowsgade 1,
DK = 1105 Copenhagen K,
Denmark
☎ 12.22.99
⇄ 14.05.85

Finland
Canadian Embassy
Pohjos Esplanadi 25 B,
00100 Helsinki, Finland
☎ 171-141
⇄ 601-060

Germany
Canadian Consulate General
Internationales Handelzentrum
Friedrichstrasse 95, 23rd Floor
10117 Berlin, Germany
☎ 261.11.61
⇄ 262.92.06

Great Britain
Canada High Commission
Macdonald House
One Grosvenor Square
London W1X 0AB
England
☎ 258-6600
⇄ 258-6384

Netherlands
Canadian Embassy
Parkstraat 25
2514JD The Hague
Netherlands
☎ 361-4111
⇄ 365-6283

Norway
Canadian Embassy
Oscars Gate 20,
Oslo 3, Norway
☎ 46.69.55
⇄ 69.34.67

Sweden
Canadian Embassy
Tegelbacken 4, 7th floor,
Stockholm, Sweden
☎ 613-9900
⇄ 24.24.91

Switzerland
Canadian Embassy
Kirchenfeldstrasse 88
3000 Berne 6
☎ 532.63.81
⇄ 352.73.15

United States
Canadian Embassy
501 Pennsylvania Avenue, N.W.
Washington, DC
20001
☎ (202) 682-1740
⇄ (202) 682-7726

Canadian Consulate General
Suite 400 South Tower
One CNN Center
Atlanta, Georgia
30303-2705
☎ (404) 577-6810 or 577-1512
⇄ (404) 524-5046

Canadian Consulate General
Three Copley Place
Suite 400
Boston, Massachusetts
02116
☎ (617) 262-3760
⇄ (617) 262-3415

Canadian Consulate General
Two Prudential Plaza
180 N. Stetson Avenue, Suite 2400,
Chicago, Illinois
60601
☎ (312) 616-1860
⇄ (312) 616-1877

Canadian Consulate General
St. Paul Place, Suite 1700
750 N. St. Paul Street
Dallas, Texas
75201
☎ (214) 922-9806
⇄ (214) 922-9815

Canadian Consulate General
600 Renaissance Center
Suite 1100
Detroit, Michigan
48234-1798
☎ (313) 567-2085
⇄ (313) 567-2164

Canadian Consulate General
300 South Grande Avenue
10th Floor, California Plaza
Los Angeles, California
90071
☎ (213) 687-7432
⇄ (213) 620-8827

Canadian Consulate General
Suite 900, 701 Fourth Avenue South
Minneapolis, Minnesota
55415-1899
☎ (612) 333-4641
⇄ (612) 332-4061

Canadian Consulate General
1251 Avenue of the Americas
New York, New York
10020-1175
☎ (212) 596-1600
⇄ (212) 596-1793

Canadian Consulate General
One Marine Midland Center
Suite 3000
Buffalo, New York
14203-2884
☎ (716) 852-1247
⇄ (716) 852-4340

Canadian Consulate General
412 Plaza 600
Sixth and Stewart Streets
Seattle, Washington
98101-1286
☎ (206) 442-1777
⇄ (206) 443-1782

■ In Western Canada

U.S. Consulate General
1095 West Pender
Vancouver, BC
V6E 2M6
☎ (604) 685-4311

615 Macleod Trail SE
Suite 1000
Calgary, AB
T2G 4T8
☎ (403) 266-8962

Australian Consulate
999 Canada Place
Suite 602
Vancouver, BC
V6C 3E1
☎ (604) 684-1177

Honorary Consulate of Belgium
Birks Place
Suite 570
688 West Hastings
Vancouver, BC
V6B 1P4
☎ (604) 684-6838

British Consulate General
10250 101st St.
Edmonton, AB
T5J 3P4
☎ (403) 425-0184

111 Melville St.
Suite 800
Vancouver, BC
V6E 3V6
☎ (604) 683-4421

Consulate General of Germany
1220 ManuLife Place
10180 101st St.
Edmonton, AB
☎ (403) 422-6175

World Trade Centre
999 Canada Place
Suite 704
Vancouver, BC
V6C 3E1
☎ (604) 684-8377

Consulate General of the Netherlands
10214 112th St.
Edmonton, AB
T5K 1M4
☎ (403) 428-7513

Consulate General of Switzerland
999 Canada Place
Suite 790
Vancouver, BC
V6C 3E1
☎ (604) 684-2231

Tourist Information

This guide covers two provinces, British Columbia and Alberta, each of which has a Ministry of Tourism in charge of promoting tourism development in its respective province. British Columbia is divided into nine tourist regions while Alberta is divided into 14. At press time the Alberta Tourism Partnership was undertaking a major reorganization of the tourist regions. Thus as of spring 1996 there should only be six regions, though the more popular regions will maintain their offices. Tourist information is distributed to the public by regional offices. You can obtain various information on the sights, restaurants and hotels in the region. Besides these numerous information centres, most large cities also have their own tourism associations. These offices are open year-round whereas the regional offices are generally only open in the high season. The addresses of the various regional tourist information offices are located in the "Practical Information" section of each chapter.

■ **Before leaving**

British Columbia's and Alberta's provincial tourism offices will gladly send you general information on their province by mail.

Tourism British Columbia
Ministry of Tourism
Parliament Building
Victoria, BC
V8V 1X4
☎ (604) 663-6000 or from Canada or the United States 1-800-663-6000
⇄ (604) 387-1590
Internet:
http://www.city.net/countries/canada/british_columbia/

Alberta Tourism Partnership
3rd Floor, Commerce Place
10155 102nd Street
Edmonton, AB
T5J 4L6
☎ (403) 427-4321 or from Canada or the United States 1-800-661-8888
⇄ (403) 427-0867
Internet:
http://www.city.net/countries/canada/alberta/

Customs

If you are bringing gifts into Canada, remember that certain restrictions apply:

Smokers (minimum age is 16) can bring in a maximum of 200 cigarettes, 50 cigars, 400 g of tobacco, or 400 tobacco sticks.

For wine and alcohol the limit is 1.1 litres; in practice, however, two bottles per person are usually allowed. The limit for beer is 24 355-ml size cans or bottles.

Plants, vegetation, and food: there are very strict rules regarding the importation of plants, flowers, and other vegetation; it is therefore not advisable to bring any of these types of products into the country. If it is absolutely necessary, contact the Customs-Agriculture service of the Canadian embassy **before** leaving.

Pets: if you are travelling with your pet, you will need a health certificate (available from your veterinarian) as well as a rabies vaccination certificate. It is important to remember that the vaccination must administered **at least** 30 days **before** your departure and should not be more than a year old.

Tax reimbursements for visitors: it is possible to get reimbursed for certain taxes paid on purchases made while in Western Canada (see p 40).

Finding Your Way Around

■ **By Plane**

From Europe

There are two possibilities: direct flights or flights with a stop over in Montreal, Toronto or Calgary. Direct flights are of course much more attractive since they are considerably faster than flights with a stopover (for example expect about nine hours from Amsterdam for a direct flight compared to 13 hours). In some cases, however, particularly if you have a lot of time, it can be advantageous to combine a charter flight from Europe with one of the many charter flights within Canada from either Montréal or Toronto. Prices for this option can vary considerably depending on whether you are travelling during high or low season.

At press time, five airline companies offered direct flights from Europe to the major cities of Western Canada.

From Europe

Air Canada offers daily direct flights during the summer from Paris to Vancouver and from London to Vancouver and Calgary. There is a direct flight from London to Edmonton twice a week. Air Canada also flies three times a week from Frankfurt to Calgary and twice a week from Frankfurt to Vancouver.

Canadian Airlines also offers direct flights from London to Vancouver and from London to Calgary, as well as direct flights from Frankfurt to both Vancouver and Calgary.

KLM offers a direct flight from Amsterdam to Vancouver three times a week and from Amsterdam to Calgary two times a week.

Lufthansa offers a daily flight in partnership with Canadian Airlines from Frankfurt to Vancouver and Calgary.

British Airways offers daily non-stop service from London to Vancouver.

From the United States

Travellers arriving from the southern or southeastern United States may want to consider **American Airlines** which flies into Vancouver, Calgary and Edmonton through Dallas.

Delta Airlines offers direct flights from Los Angeles to Vancouver and Calgary, as well as a flight with a stopover from Los Angeles to Edmonton. Travellers from the eastern United States go through Salt Lake City.

Northwest Airlines flies into Vancouver, Calgary and Edmonton via Minneapolis.

From Asia

Both **Air Canada** and **Canadian Airlines** offer direct flights between Vancouver and Hong Kong.

Within Canada

Air Canada and **Canadian Airlines** are the only companies that offer regular flights to Western Canada. Daily flights to the cities of Vancouver, Victoria, Edmonton and Calgary as well as many other cities are offered from all the major cities in the country. Flights from eastern Canada often have stop-overs in Montréal or Toronto. For example Air Canada flies to Vancouver, Calgary, Edmonton and Victoria 14 times a week. During the high season, the aforementioned flights are complemented by many flights offered by charter companies, including Air Transat, Royal and Canada 3000. These flights are subject to change with respect to availability and fares.

Air Canada's regional partner **Air BC** offers flights within Alberta and British Columbia, as does Canadian Airlines' regional partner, **Canadian Regional**.

■ By Train

Travellers with a lot of time may want to consider the train, one of the most pleasant and impressive ways to discover Western Canada. Via Rail Canada is the only company that offers train travel between the Canadian provinces. This mode of transportation can be combined with air travel (various packages are offered by Air Canada and Canadian Airlines) or on its own from big cities in Eastern Canada like Toronto or Montréal. This last option does require a lot of time however, it takes a minimum of five days to get from Montréal to Vancouver.

The **CanRailpass** is another particularly interesting option. Besides the advantageous price, you only need to purchase one ticket for travel throughout Canada. The ticket allows 12 days of unlimited travel in a 30-day period. At press-time the CanRailpass was $572 in the high season and $390 in the low season. CanRailpass holders are also entitled to special rates for car rental.

Via Rail offers several discounts :

Reductions for certain days of the week, during the off-season and on reservations made at least five days in advance: up to 40% off depending on the destination.

Discount for students and those 24 years of age or less: 10% throughout the year or 40% if the reservation is made five days in advance, except during the holidays.

Discount for people aged 60 and over: 10% on certain days, not during peak travel times.

Special rates for children: children two to 11 travel for half-price; children under two accompanied by an adult travel free.

Finally, take note that first-class service is quite exceptional, including a meal, wine, and alcoholic beverages free of charge.

For further information:

In Canada: ☎ 1-800-561-8630
In the United States: ☎ 1-800-561-3949 or by contacting Amtrak
In Europe: in the United Kingdom contact Thomas Cooke Holidays at ☎ 733-331-777. Express Conseil in Paris ☎ 44.77.87.94 can also book Via tickets.
Internet: http://www.viarail.ca

During the summer, the **Great Canadian Railtour Company Ltd.** offers **Rocky Mountain Railtours** between Calgary and Vancouver with a stop in Banff. For more information, see p 281.

■ **By Car**

By car is the best way to see Western Canada at your own pace, especially when you consider the excellent road conditions and the price of gas, which is three times cheaper than in Europe. An extensive network of roads links the United States and Canada as well as the eastern provinces with the rest of the country. The most famous of these is by far the impressive TransCanada Highway which links Saint John's in Newfoundland with Victoria in British Columbia.

Driver's licenses from western European countries are valid in Canada and the United States. While North American travellers won't have any trouble adapting to the rules of the road in Western Canada, European travellers may need a bit more time to get used to things. Here are a few hints:

Pedestrians: Drivers in Western Canada are particulary courteous when it comes to pedestrians, and willingly

Practical Information

										Banff
									Calgary	125
								Edmonton	294	401
							Grande Prairie	447	725	682
						Hope	1163	1005	825	697
					Jasper	644	397	365	412	287
				Lethbridge	626	1034	935	509	216	347
			Medicine Hat	165	703	1099	982	526	286	411
		Penticton	955	799	670	245	1260	963	669	543
	Prince George	700	1305	1247	374	634	543	740	789	661
Vancouver	778	395	981	816	744	149	1313	1155	975	847
Victoria	69	821	433	1015	852	832	188	1503	1193	1013	885

Table of Distances (km)

stop to give them the right of way even in the big cities, so be careful when and where you step off the curb. Pedestrian crosswalks are usually indicated by a yellow sign. When driving pay special attention that there is no one about to cross near these signs.

Turning **right on a red light** when the way is clear is permitted in Western Canada.

When a **school bus** (usually yellow in colour) has stopped and has its signals flashing, you must come to a complete stop, no matter what direction you are travelling in. Failing to stop at the flashing signals is considered a serious offense, and carries a heavy penalty.

Wearing of **seatbelts** in the front and back seats is mandatory at all times.

Almost all highways in Western Canada are toll-free, and just a few bridges have tolls. The **speed limit** on highways is 100 km/h. The speed limit on secondary highways is 90 km/h, and 50 km/h in urban areas.

Gas Stations: Because Canada produces its own crude oil, gasoline prices in Western Canada are much less expensive than in Europe, and only slightly more than in the United States. Some gas stations (especially in the downtown areas) might ask for payment in advance as a security measure, especially after 11pm.

Winter driving: Though roads are generally well plowed, particular caution is recommended. Watch for violent winds and snow drifts and banks. In some regions gravel is used to increase traction, so drive carefully.

Always remember that wildlife abounds near roads and highways in Western Canada. It is not unheard of to come face to face with a deer only minutes from Calgary. Pay attention and drive slowly especially at nightfall and in the early morning. If you do hit any large animal, try to contact the Royal Canadian Mounted Police (RCMP). Dial 0 or 911 to reach the police.

Certain roads in northern British Columbia and Alberta are not paved. Make sure you rent the appropriate vehicle (4-wheel drive, high clearance) if you plan on covering any rough terrain.

Car Rentals

Packages including air travel, hotel and car rental or just hotel and car rental are often less expensive than car rental alone. It is best to shop around. Remember also that some companies offer corporate rates and discounts to auto-club members. Some travel agencies work with major car rental companies (Avis, Budget, Hertz, etc.) and offer good values; contracts often include added bonuses (reduced ticket prices for shows, etc.).

When renting a car, find out if the contract includes unlimited kilometres, and if the insurance provides full coverage (accident, property damage, hospital costs for you and passengers, theft).

Certain credit cards, gold cards for example, cover the collision and theft insurance. Check with your credit card company before renting.

To rent a car you must be at least 21 years of age and have had a driver's license for **at least** one year. If you are between 21 and 25, certain companies (for example Avis, Thrifty, Budget) will ask for a $500 deposit, and in some cases they will also charge an extra sum for each day you rent the car. These conditions do not apply for those over 25 years of age.

A credit card is extremely useful for the deposit to avoid tying up large sums of money.

Most rental cars come with an automatic transmission, however you can request a car with a manual shift.

Child safety seats cost extra.

Accidents and Emergencies

In case of serious accident, fire or other emergency dial ☎ **911** or **0**.

If you run into trouble on the highway, pull onto the shoulder of the road and turn the hazard lights on. If it is a rental car, contact the rental company as soon as possible. Always file an accident report. If a disagreement arises over who was at fault in an accident, ask for police help.

■ By Ferry

Vancouver Island and regions along British Columbia's Pacific coastline are accessible by ferry. For more information please see the appropriate chapter.

■ By Bus

Extensive and inexpensive, buses cover most of Canada. Except for public transportation, there is no government run service; several companies service the country.

Greyhound (☎ *403-256-9111)* Canada services all the lines in Western Canada in cooperation with local companies like Voyageur in Québec. For example the trip from Montréal to Vancouver costs $301.80 (one-way) and takes three days.

The major stations are as follows:

Montréal: ☎ (514) 842-2281
Québec City: ☎ (418) 525-3000
Toronto: ☎ (416) 393-7911
Calgary: ☎ (403) 256-9111
Edmonton: ☎ (403) 421-4211
Vancouver: ☎ (604) 662-7575

Smoking is forbidden on almost all lines and pets are not allowed. Generally children five years old or younger travel for free and people aged 60 or over are eligible for discounts.

Airports

■ **British Columbia**

Vancouver International Airport

Vancouver International Airport (☎ *276-6101)* receives international flights from Europe, the United States and Asia as well as several national flights from other Canadian provinces. At press-time, major renovations were underway to double the capacity of the airport. Presently 19 airline companies use the airport. The airport lies 15 km from downtown. Expect about 30 minutes by car or bus to reach downtown from the airport. Besides the many taxis and limousines that provide transportation in to the city for just over $30, the **Airport Express Bus** (☎ *604-270-4442)* provides shuttle service to the major hotels from the centre of the airport from about $9 per person.

In addition to the regular airport services (duty-free shops, cafeteria, restaurants, etc) there is also a currency exchange office and several car rental companies. These include Avis, Thrifty, Tilden, ABC Rent-A-Car and Budget (see p 56).

Victoria Airport

Victoria Airport is the second largest in the province. There is an exchange office open from 6am to 9pm. Several car rental companies also have offices at the airport. Taxis and limousines can bring you downtown for about $50. A shuttle bus goes downtown for $11.

■ **Alberta**

Calgary International Airport

Calgary International Airport is the largest airport in the province of Alberta and the fourth largest in Canada. Upon arrival you will be greeted with staff dressed in western garb who can provide you with tourist information. There is a currency exchange office open from 6am to 9pm. Taxis and limousines can take you downtown for about $25, while the **Airporter** (☎ *531-3909)* shuttle bus takes passengers downtown for $11. Several car rental companies have offices at the airport, these include Avis, Thrifty, Dollar, Economy, Hertz, Budget and Discount.

Edmonton Airport

Edmonton Airport is the second largest airport in the province. A taxi or limousine from the airport downtown is about $30, while the **Grey Goose** (☎ 463-7520) costs $11 per person. Several car rental companies have offices at the airport. These include Avis, Thrifty, Rent-A-Wreck, Budget, Discount, Dollar and Hertz.

Time Difference

Western Canada covers two different time zones: Mountain Time and Pacific Time. Alberta is therefore two hours behind Eastern Standard Time, while British Columbia is three hours behind. Continental Europe is nine hours ahead of British Columbia and eight hours ahead of Alberta. The United Kingdom, on the other hand is eight and seven hours ahead respectively. Daylight Savings Time (+ 1 hour) begins the first Sunday in April.

Business Hours and Public Holidays

■ **Business Hours**

Stores

Generally stores remain open the following hours:

Mon to Fri	10am to 6pm;
Thu and Fri	10am to 9pm;
Sat	9 am or 10am to 5pm;
Sun	noon to 5pm

Well-stocked convenience stores that sell food are found throughout Western Canada and are open later, sometimes 24 hours a day.

Banks

Banks are open Monday to Friday from 10am to 3pm. Most are open on Thursdays and Fridays, until 6pm or even 8pm. Automatic teller machines are widely available and are open night and day.

Post Offices

Large post offices are open Monday to Friday from 9am to 5pm. There are also several smaller post offices located in shopping malls, convenience stores, and even pharmacies; these post offices are open much later than the larger ones.

■ **Holidays and Public Holidays**

The following is a list of public holidays in the provinces of Alberta and British Columbia. Most administrative offices and banks are closed on these days.

January 1 and 2
Easter Monday
Victoria Day: the 3rd Monday in May
Canada Day: July 1st
Civic holiday: 1st Monday in August
Labour Day: 1st Monday in September
Thanksgiving: 2nd Monday in October
Remembrance Day: November 1 (only banks and federal government services are closed)
Christmas Day: December 25

Mail and Telecommunications

■ Mail

Canada Post provides efficient mail service across the country. At press time, it cost 45¢ to send a letter elsewhere in Canada, 50¢ to the United States and 90¢ overseas. Stamps can be purchased at post offices and in many pharmacies and convenience stores.

■ Telecommunications

The telephone area code is ☎ 403. At press time, the area code for the entire province of British Columbia was ☎ 604. BC Tel does, however, have plans to change this in the fall of 1996. The lower mainland and Vancouver and area will keep the ☎ 604 area code, while the area code for Vancouver Island, eastern, central and northern British Columbia will become ☎ 250.

Long distance charges are cheaper than in Europe, but more expensive than in the U.S.. Pay phones can be found everywhere, often in the entrance of larger department stores, and in restaurants. They are easy to use and most accept credit cards. Local calls to the surrounding areas cost $0.25 for unlimited time. Have a lot quarters on hand if you are making a long distance call. It is less expensive to call from a private residence. 1-800 numbers are toll free.

Both BC Tel (in British Columbia) and AGT (in Alberta) sell phone cards in various denominations for use in pay phones to place local and long distance calls.

Money and Banking

■ Exchange

Most banks readily exchange American and European currencies but almost all will charge **commission**. There are, however, exchange offices that do not charge commissions and have longer hours. Just remember to **ask about fees** and **to compare rates**.

Traveller's Cheques

Traveller's cheques are accepted in most large stores and hotels, however it is easier and to your advantage to change your cheques at an exchange office. For a better exchange rate buy your traveller's cheques in Canadian dollars before leaving.

Credit Cards

Most major credit cards are accepted at stores, restaurants and hotels. While the main advantage of credit cards is that they allow visitors to avoid carrying large sums of money, using a credit card also makes leaving a deposit for car rental much easier and some cards, gold cards for example, automatically insure you when you rent a car (check with your credit card company to see what coverage it provides). In addition, the exchange rate with a credit card is generally better. The most commonly accepted credit cards are Visa, MasterCard, and American Express.

CANADIAN DOLLAR EXCHANGE RATES

$1	= $0.74 US		$1 US	= $1.35
$1	= 48 p		1£	= $2.10
$1	= $0.93 Aust		$1 Aust	= $1.07
$1	= $1.05NZ		$1 NZ	= $0.95
$1	= 0.86 SF		1 SF	= $1.16
$1	= 2.17 BF		1 BF	= $0.46
$1	= 1.06 DM		1 DM	= $0.94
$1	= 88 pesetas		100 pta	= $1.12
$1	= 1123 lira		1000 lira	= $0.89

■ Banks

Banks can be found almost everywhere and most offer the standard services to tourists. Visitors who choose to stay in Canada for a long period of time should note that **non-residents** cannot open bank accounts. If this is the case, the best way to have money readily available is to use traveller's cheques. Withdrawing money from foreign accounts is expensive. However, several automatic teller machines accept foreign bank cards, so that you can withdraw directly from your account. Money orders are another means of having money sent from abroad. No commission is charged but it takes time. People who have residence status, permanent or not (such as landed-immigrants, students), can open a bank account. A passport and proof of residence status are required.

■ Currency

The monetary unit is the dollar ($), which is divided into cents (¢). One dollar = 100 cents.

Bills come in 2, 5, 10, 20, 50, 100, 500 and 1000 dollar denominations, and coins come in 1 (pennies), 5 (nickels), 10 (dimes), 25 (quarters) cent pieces, and in 1 (loonies) dollar and 2 dollar coins. The new 2 dollar coin will eventually replace the 2 dollar bill, though the bill will remain legal tender.

Climate and Clothing

■ Climate

The climate of Western Canada varies widely from on region to another. The Vancouver area benefits from a sort of micro-climate thanks to its geographic location between the Pacific and the mountains. Temperatures in Vancouver vary between 0°C and 15°C in the winter and much warmer in the summer.

The high altitudes of the Rocky Mountains and the winds of the Prairies make for a varied climate throughout the rest of the region. Winters are cold and dry and temperatures can drop to -40°C, though the average is about -15°C. Winters in southern Alberta are often marked by the phenomenal Chinook wind which can melt several feet of snow is a matter of hours (see p 297). Summers are dry, with temperatures staying steady around 25°C on the plains and lower in the mountains.

Winter

December to March is the ideal season for winter-sports enthusiasts (skiing, skating, etc.). Warm clothing is essential during this season (coat, scarf, hat, gloves, wool sweaters and boots). Vancouver on the other hand, has a particulary wet winter so don't forget your raincoat. In southern British Columbia the mercury rarely falls below 0.

Spring and Fall

Spring is short (end of March to end of May) and is characterized by a general thaw leading to wet and muddy conditions. Fall is often cool. A sweater, scarf, gloves, windbreaker and umbrella will therefore come in handy.

Summer

Summer lasts from the end of May to the end of August. Bring along t-shirts, lightweight shirts and pants, shorts and sunglasses; a sweater or light jacket is a good idea for evenings. If you plan on doing any hiking, remember that temperatures are cooler at higher altitudes.

Health

■ **General Information**

Vaccinations are not necessary for people coming from Europe, the United States, Australia and New Zealand. On the other hand, it is strongly suggested, particularly for medium or long-term stays, that visitors take out health and accident insurance. There are different types so it is best to shop around. Bring along all medication, especially prescription medicine. Unless otherwise stated, the water is drinkable throughout Western Canada.

In the winter, moisturizing lotion and lip balm are useful for people with sensitive skin, since the air in many buildings is very dry.

During the summer, always protect yourself against sunburn. It is often hard to feel your skin getting burned by the sun on windy days. Do not forget to bring sun screen!

■ **Emergencies**

For all emergencies dial ☎ **911** in both Alberta and British Columbia.

Shopping

■ **What to Buy**

Salmon: you'll find this fish on sale, fresh from the sea, throughout the coastal areas of British Columbia.

Western wear: Alberta is the place for cowboy boots and hats and other western leather gear.

Local crafts: paintings, sculptures, woodworking items, ceramics, copper-based enamels, weaving, etc.

Native Arts & Crafts: beautiful native sculptures made from different types of stone, wood and even animal bone are available, though they are generally quite expensive. Make sure the sculpture is authentic by asking for a certificate of authenticity issued by the Canadian government.

Accommodations

A wide choice of types of accommodation to fit every budget is available in most regions of Western Canada. Most places are very comfortable and offer a number of extra services. Prices vary according to the type of accommodation and the quality/price ratio is generally good, but remember to add the 7% G.S.T (federal Goods and Services Tax) and the provincial sales tax of 7% in British Columbia. Alberta has no provincial sales tax, though there is a 5% tax on lodging. The Goods and Services Tax is refundable for non-residents in certain cases (see p 40). A credit card will make reserving a room much easier, since in many cases payment for the first night is required.

■ Hotels

Hotels rooms abound, and range from modest to luxurious. Most hotel rooms come equipped with a private bathroom. There are several internationally reputed hotels in Western Canada, including several beauties in the Canadian Pacific chain.

■ Inns

Often set up in beautiful historic houses, inns offer quality lodging. There are a lot of these establishments which are more charming and usually more picturesque than hotels. Many are furnished with beautiful period pieces. Breakfast is often included.

■ Bed and Breakfasts

Unlike hotels or inns, rooms in private homes are not always equipped with a bathroom. Bed and breakfasts are well distributed throughout Western Canada, in the country as well as the city. Besides the obvious price advantage, is the unique family atmosphere. Credit cards are not always accepted in bed and breakfasts.

■ Motels

There are many motels throughout the province, and though they tend to be cheaper they often lack atmosphere. These are particularly useful when pressed for time.

■ Youth Hostels

Youth hostel addresses are listed in the "Accommodations" section for the cities in which they are located.

■ University Residences

Due to certain restrictions, this can be a complicated alternative. Residences are generally only available during the summer (mid-May to mid-August); reservations must be made several months in advance, usually by paying the first night with a credit card.

This type of accommodation, however, is less costly than the "traditional" alternatives, and making the effort to reserve early can be worthwhile. Visitors with valid student cards can expect to pay approximately $25 plus tax. Bedding is included in the price, and there is usually a cafeteria in the building (meals are not included in the price).

■ Camping

Next to being put up by friends, camping is the most inexpensive form of accommodation. Unfortunately, unless you have winter-camping gear, camping is limited to a short period of the year, from June to August. Services provided as well as prices vary considerably, from $8 to $20 or more per night, depending on whether the site is private or public.

Taxes and Tipping

■ Taxes

The ticket price on items usually **does not include tax**. There are two taxes, the G.S.T. or federal Goods and Services Tax, of 7% applicable in both Alberta and British Columbia, and the P.S.T. or Provincial Sales Tax (British Columbia 7%, Alberta has no provincial tax). They are cumulative and must be added to the price of most items and to restaurant and hotel bills.

There are some exceptions to this taxation system, such as books, which are only taxed with the G.S.T. and food (except for ready made meals), which is not taxed at all.

Tax Refunds for Non-Residents

Non-residents can obtain refunds for the G.S.T. paid on purchases. To obtain a refund, it is important to keep your receipts. Refunds are made at the border or by returning a special filled-out form.

For information, call:
☎ 1-800-991-3346

■ Tipping

In general, tipping applies to all table service: restaurants, bars and nightclubs (therefore no tipping in fast-food restaurants). Tips are also given in taxis and in hair salons.

The tip is usually about 15 % of the bill before taxes, but varies of course depending on the quality of service.

Restaurants and Bars

■ Restaurants

There are several excellent restaurants throughout western Canada. The local specialties are without a doubt Pacific salmon and Alberta beef. Every city has a wide range of choices for all budgets, from fast food to fine dining.

Bars and Discos

In most cases there is no cover charge, aside from the occasional mandatory coat-check. However, expect to pay a few dollars to get into discos on weekends. The legal drinking age is 19; if you're close to that age, expect to be asked for proof.

Wine, Beer and Alcohol

The legal drinking age is 19. Beer, wine and alcohol can only be purchased in liquor stores run by the provincial governments.

Advice for Smokers

As in the United States, cigarette smoking is considered taboo, and it is being prohibited in more and more public places:

in most shopping centres;
in buses;
in government offices.

Most public places (restaurants, cafés) have smoking and non-smoking sections. However, the city of Vancouver has recently passed a by-law prohibiting smoking in all restaurants. Cigarettes are sold in bars, grocery stores, newspaper and magazine shops.

Safety

By taking the normal precautions, there is no need to worry about your personal security. If trouble should arise, remember to dial the emergency telephone number ☎ 911.

Children

As in the rest of Canada, facilities exist in Western Canada that make travelling with children quite easy, whether it be for getting around or when enjoying the sights. Generally children under five travel for free, and those under 12 are eligible for fare reductions. The same applies for various leisure activities and shows. Find out before you purchase tickets. High chairs and children's menus are available in most restaurants, while a few of the larger stores provide a babysitting service while parents shop.

Calgary is the only "Child-Friendly" city in North America. Essentially every restaurant, museum and attraction is rated by children.

Weights and Measures

Although the metric system has been in use in Canada for several years, some people continue to use the Imperial system in casual conversation. Here a some equivalents:

1 pound (lb) = 454 grams
1 kilogram (kg) = 2.2 pounds (lbs)
1 foot (ft) = 30 centimetres (cm)
1 centimetre (cm) = 0.4 inch
1 metre (m) = 40 inches
1 inch = 2.5 centimetres (cm)
1 mile = 1.6 kilometres (km)
1 kilometres (km) = 0.63 miles

General Information

Illegal Drugs: are against the law and not tolerated (even "soft" drugs). Anyone caught with drugs in their possession risk severe consequences.

Electricity: Voltage is 110 volts throughout Canada, the same as in the United States. Electricity plugs have two parallel, flat pins, and adaptors are available here.

Laundromats: are found almost everywhere in urban areas. In most cases, detergent is sold on site. Although change machines are sometimes provided, it is best to bring plenty of quarters (25¢) with you.

Movie Theatres: There are no ushers and therefore no tips.

Museums: Most museums charge admission. Reduced prices are available for people over 60, for children, and for students. Call the museum for further details.

Newspapers: Each big city has its own major newspaper:

Vancouver	*Vancouver Sun*
	Vancouver Province
Calgary	*Calgary Sun*
	Calgary Herald
Edmonton	*Edmonton Journal*

The larger newspapers, for example *The Globe and Mail*, are widely available, as are many international newspapers.

Pharmacies: In addition to the smaller drug stores, there are large pharmacy chains which sell everything from chocolate to laundry detergent, as well as the more traditional items such as cough drops and headache medications.

Religion: Almost all religions are represented.

Restrooms: Public restrooms can be found in most shopping centres. If you cannot find one, it usually is not a problem to use one in a bar or restaurant.

OUTDOORS

British Columbia and Alberta both boast vast, untouched stretches of wilderness protected by national and provincial parks, which visitors can explore on foot, by bicycle or by car. You'll discover coasts washed by the waters of the Pacific Ocean (Pacific Rim and Gwaii Haanaf National Parks), vast rain forest harbouring centuries-old trees (Vancouver Island), majestic mountains that form the spine of the American continent (Banff, Jasper, Kootenay and Yoho National Parks) and some of the world's richest dinosaur fossil beds in the badlands of the Red Deer River Valley (Dinosaur Provincial Park). The following pages contain a description of the various outdoor activities that can be enjoyed in these unspoiled areas.

Parks

In Western Canada, there are eleven national parks, run by the federal government, and more than 400 provincial parks, each administered by the government of the province in question. Most national parks offer facilities and services such as information centres, park maps, nature interpretation programmes, guides, accommodation (B&Bs, inns, equipped and primitive camping sites) and restaurants. Not all of these services are available in every park (and some vary depending on the season), so it is best to contact park authorities before setting off on a trip. Provincial parks are usually smaller, with fewer services, but are still attractively located.

Outdoor Activities

A number of parks are crisscrossed by marked trails stretching several kilometres, perfect for hiking, cycling, cross-country skiing and snowmobiling. Primitive camping sites or shelters can be found along some of these paths. Some of the camping sites are very rudimentary, and a few don't even have water; it is therefore essential to be well equipped. Take note, however, that in the national parks in the Rocky Mountains, wilderness camping is strictly forbidden due to the presence of bears and other large animals. Since some of the trails lead deep into the forest, far from all human habitation, visitors are strongly advised to heed all signs. This will also help protect the fragile plant-life. Useful maps showing trails, camping sites and shelters are available for most parks.

It is important to be well aware of the potential dangers before heading off into the wild of the provincial and national parks. Do not forget that each individual is ultimately responsible for his or her own safety. Dangers to watch out for include avalanches and rock slides, risks of hypothermia or sunstroke, rapid changes in temperature (especially in mountainous regions), non-potable water, glacier crevasses concealed by a thin layer of snow, strong waves or tides on the Pacific coast and wild animals like bears and rattlesnakes.

Never stop in an avalanche or rock slide area. Cross-country skiers and hikers must take particular care when passing through these areas. It is always best to check with park staff about the stability of the snow before heading out.

Hypothermia begins when the internal body temperature falls below 36°C, at which point the body loses heat faster than it can produce it. Shivering is the first sign that your body is not able to warm itself. It is easy to discount the cold when hiking in the summer. However, in the mountains, rain and wind can lower the temperature considerably. Imagine sitting above the tree line in a downpour, with the wind blowing at 50 km/h. Then imagine that you are tired and have no raincoat. In such conditions your body temperature drops rapidly and you run the risk of hypothermia. It is therefore important to carry a change of warm clothes and a good wind-breaker with you at all times. When hiking, it is preferable to wear several layers instead of a big jacket that will prove too warm once you start exercising intensely, but too light when you stop to rest. Avoid wet clothes at all costs.

Water can be found in most Canadian parks, but it is not always clean enough to drink. For this reason, be sure to bring along enough water for the duration of your hike, or boil any water you find for about 10 minutes.

Visitors who enter the national and provincial parks run the risk of encountering wild, unpredictable and dangerous animals. It is irresponsible and illegal to feed, trap or bother wild animals in a national park. Large mammals like bears, elk, moose, deer and buffalo may feel threatened and become dangerous if you try to approach them. It is even dangerous to approach animals in towns like Banff and Jasper, where wild animals roam about in an urban setting. Stay at least 30 m from large mammals and at least 50 m from bears and buffalo. Prairie rattlesnakes are common in arid southern Alberta; however, these snakes are much more afraid of us than we are of them, and will only attack if provoked.

The Pacific Ocean is often presented as a surfer's paradise. It is true that the surf in some places is exceptional, but wave-seekers should bear in mind factors such as strong tides, large waves and cold water temperatures when visiting the Pacific beaches.

■ **National Parks**

There are eleven national parks in Western Canada: Glacier National Park (British Columbia), Yoho National Park and Kootenay National Park (in the Rockies, in British Columbia), Mount Revelstoke National Park (in the Columbia River Valley in British Columbia), Pacific Rim National Park (on Vancouver Island), Gwaii Haanas (in the Queen Charlotte Islands), Waterton Lakes National Park (on the American border in Alberta), Banff National Park and Jasper National Park (in the Rockies), Elk Island National Park (east of Edmonton) and finally Wood Buffalo National Park (in Northern Alberta, on the border with the Northwest Territories). In addition to these parks, the Canadian Park Service also oversees a number of national historic sites, which are described in the "Exploring" section of the appropriate chapters.

For more information on national parks, you can call ☎ 1-800-651-7959 (toll-free from Alberta and British Columbia), or contact the regional offices by mail.

Parks Canada Western Region
Room 250
Box 2989, Station M
220 4th Avenue SE
Calgary, AB
T2P 3H8
☎ (403) 292-4401
⇌ (403) 292-4242

Parks Canada Prairie and Northern Region (for Wood Buffalo National Park)
457 Main Street
Winnipeg, Manitoba
R3B 3E8

■ **Provincial Parks**

Each of the two provinces manages a wide variety of parks; there are more than 400 in all. Some of these are small, day-use areas, while the larger ones offer a broader scope of activities. These parks provide visitors with access to beaches, campsites, golf courses, hiking trails and archaeological preserves. Throughout this guide, the most important parks are described in the "Parks and Beaches" section of each relevant chapter. For more information on provincial parks, contact:

British Columbia

Ministry of Environment Lands and Parks
2nd Floor
800 Johnston Street
Victoria, BC
V8V 1X4
☎ (604) 582-5200

BC Parks
Parliament Buildings
Victoria, BC
V8V 1X5

Alberta

Environmental Protection and Natural Resources administer the provincial parks, but travellers are better off contacting Tourism Alberta at ☎ 1-800-661-8888 for information.

Summer Activities

When the weather is mild, visitors can enjoy the activities listed below. Anyone intending to spend more than a day in the park should remember that the nights are cool (even in July and August) and that long-sleeved shirts or sweaters will be very practical in some regions. In June, and throughout the summer in northern regions, an effective insect repellent is almost indispensable for an outing in the forest.

Hiking

Hiking is an activity open to everyone, and it can be enjoyed in all national and most provincial parks. Before setting out, plan your excursion well by checking the length and level of difficulty of each trail. Some parks have long trails that require more than a day of hiking and lead deep into the wild. When taking one of these trails, which can stretch tens of kilometres, it is crucial to respect all signs.

To make the most of an excursion, it is important to bring along the right equipment. You'll need a good pair of walking shoes, appropriate maps, sufficient food and water and a small first-aid kit containing a pocket knife and bandages.

Bicycling

Visitors can go bicycling and mountain biking all over Western Canada, along the usually quiet secondary roads or the trails crisscrossing the parks. The roads offer prudent cyclists one of the most enjoyable means possible of touring these picturesque regions. Keep in mind, however, that distances in these two vast provinces can be very long.

If you are travelling with your own bicycle, you are allowed to bring it on any bus; just be sure it is properly protected in an appropriate box. Another option is to rent one on site. For bike rental locations, look under the heading **"Bicycling"** in the "Outdoor Activities" section of the chapters on each province, contact a tourist information centre or check under the "Bicycles-Rentals" heading in the *Yellow Pages*. Adequate insurance is a good idea when renting a bicycle. Some places include insurance against theft in the cost of the rental. Inquire before renting.

Canoeing

Many parks are strewn with lakes and rivers which canoe-trippers can spend a day or more exploring. Primitive camping sites have been laid out to accommodate canoers during long excursions. Canoe rentals and maps of possible routes are usually available at the park's information centre. It is always best to have a map that indicates the length of the portages in order to determine how physically demanding the trip will be. Carrying a canoe, baggage and food on your back is not always a pleasant experience. A 1 km portage is generally considered long, and wil be more or less difficult depending on the terrain.

Beaches

Whether you decide to stretch out on the white sand of Long Beach on Vancouver Island, or prefer the more family-oriented atmosphere of Qualicum Beach, with its calm waters, or Wreck Beach, the driftwood-carvers' rendez-vous, you'll discover one of Western Canada's most precious natural attractions, British Columbia's Pacific Coast. Swimming is not always possible, however, because of the heavy surf and cold water temperatures. Alberta even has some lovely beaches lining crystal-clear fresh-water lakes.

Fishing

In British Columbia and Alberta, anglers can cast their line in the ocean or in one of the many rivers and lakes. Don't forget, however, that fishing is a regulated activity. Fishing laws are complicated, so it is wise to request information from the Ministry of Natural Resources of the two provinces and obtain the brochure stating key fishing regulations. Furthermore, keep in mind that there are different permits for fresh-water and ocean fishing.

For ocean fishing, contact:

Federal Department of Fisheries and Oceans
555 West Hastings Street
Vancouver, BC
V6B 5G2
☎ (604) 666-3545

For fresh-water fishing, contact:

B.C. Ministry of Environment Lands and Parks
2nd Floor
800 Johnston Street
Victoria, BC
V8V 1X4
☎ (604) 582-5200

Alberta Fish and Wildlife Services
Main Floor,
North Tower, Petroleum Plaza
9945 108th Street
Edmonton, AB
T5K 2G6

As a general rule, however, keep in mind that: it is necessary to obtain a permit from the provincial government before going fishing; a special permit is usually required for salmon fishing; fishing seasons are established by the ministry and must be respected at all times; the seasons vary depending on the species; fishing is permitted in national parks, but you must obtain a permit from park officials beforehand (see regional office addresses in this chapter, or in the parks section of the chapter on the provinces); for more information, look under the "Fishing" heading in the "Outdoor Activities" section of the relevant chapter.

Bird-watching

The wilds of Western Canada attract all sorts of birds, which can easily be observed with the help of binoculars. Some of the more noteworthy species that you might spot are hummingbirds, golden eagles, bald eagles, peregrine falcons, double-crested cormorants, pelicans, grouse, ptarmigans, countless varieties of waterfowl, including the mallards, barnacle geese, wild geese, trumpeter swans (which migrate from the Arctic to Mexico) and finally the grey jay, a little bird who will gladly help himself to your picnic lunch if you aren't careful. For help identifying them, purchase a copy of *Peterson's Field Guide: All the Birds of Eastern and Central North America*, published by Houghton Mifflin. Although parks are often the best places to observe certain species, bird-watching is an activity that can be enjoyed throughout Alberta and British Columbia.

Whale-watching

Whales are common along the coasts of British Columbia. Visitors wishing to catch a closer view of these impressive but harmless sea mammals can take part in a whale-watching cruise or go sea-kayaking. The most commonly sighted species are orcas (also known as killer whales), humpbacks and grey whales. These excursions usually start from the northeastern end of Vancouver Island, in the Johnstone Strait, or from Long Beach.

Seal-watching

Seals are also found along British Columbia's coasts, and anyone wishing to observe them from close up can take part in an excursion designed for that purpose. Occasionally, attracted by the boat, these curious mammals will pop their heads out of the water right nearby, gazing at the passengers with their big black eyes.

Golf

Magnificent golf courses, renowned for their remarkable natural settings, can be found throughout British Columbia and Alberta. Stretching along the ocean, or through narrow mountain valleys, these courses boast exceptional views and challenging holes. A few courses have been laid out in provincial parks (in Kananaskis Country) and near the parks of the Rockies (in the valley of the Columbia River), where peace and quiet reign supreme and luxurious hotels are just a short distance away.

Winter Activities

In winter, most of Western Canada is covered with a blanket of snow creating ideal conditions for a slew of outdoor activities. Most parks with summer hiking trails adapt to the climate, welcoming cross-country skiers. This largely mountainous region boasts world-class resorts that will satisfy even the most demanding skiers.

Cross-country Skiing

Some parks, like those in Kananaskis Country and in the Rocky Mountains, are renowned for their long cross-country ski trails. The cross-country skiing events of the 1988 Winter Olympics were held in the small town of Canmore, Alberta. Daily ski rentals are available at most ski centres.

Downhill Skiing

Known the world over for its downhill skiing, the Rockies attract millions of downhill skiers every year, including countless fans of powder skiing, who are whisked to the highest summits by helicopter, and deposited there to enjoy the ski of their lives.

Snowmobiling

This winter activity has many fans in British Columbia and Alberta. Each province is crisscrossed by trails.

Visitors can explore the west by snowmobile, but should take care to heed all regulations. Don't forget, furthermore, that a permit is required. It is also advisable to take out liability insurance.

The following rules should respected at all times: stay on the snowmobile trails; always drive on the right side of the trail; wear a helmet; all snowmobiles must have headlights.

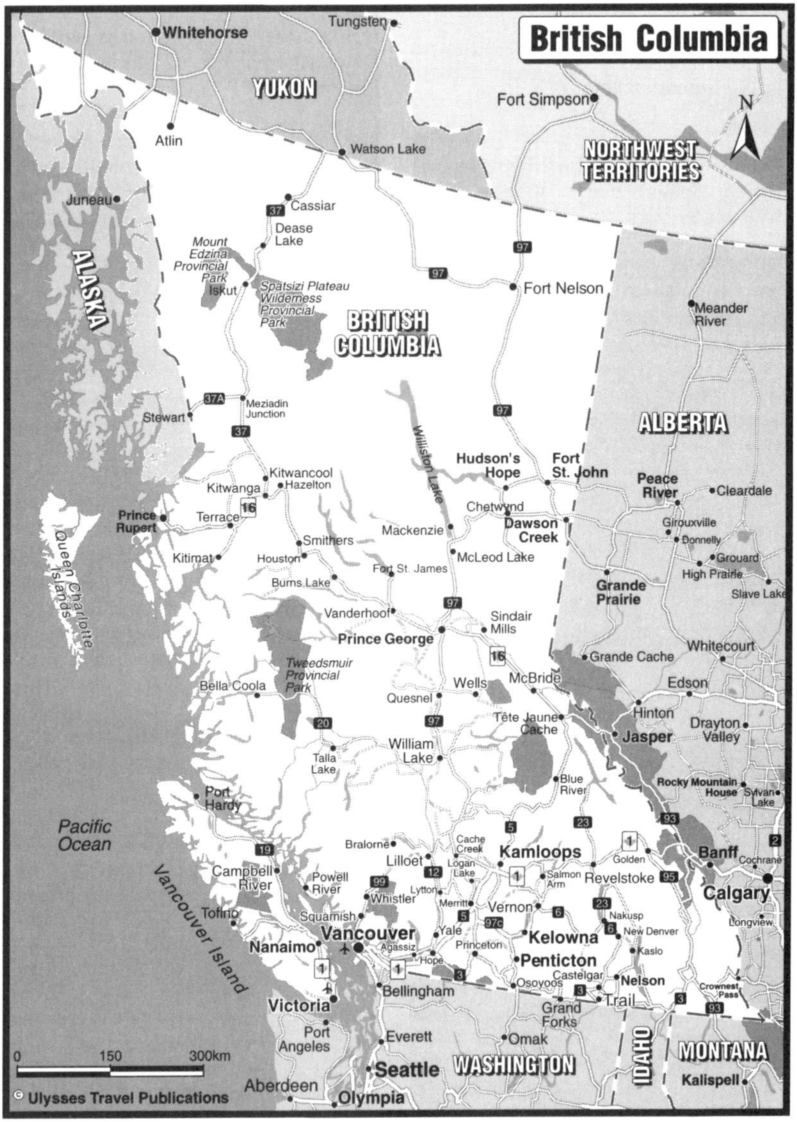
British Columbia
Whitehorse
Tungsten
YUKON
Fort Simpson
NORTHWEST TERRITORIES
Atlin
Watson Lake
Juneau
Cassiar
Dease Lake
Mount Edzina Provincial Park
Iskut
Spatsizi Plateau Wilderness Provincial Park
ALASKA
BRITISH COLUMBIA
Fort Nelson
Meander River
Stewart
Meziadin Junction
ALBERTA
Williston Lake
Hudson's Hope
Fort St. John
Peace River
Cleardale
Kitwancool
Hazelton
Kitwanga
Prince Rupert
Terrace
Chetwynd
Dawson Creek
Girouxville
Donnelly
Mackenzie
Smithers
Queen Charlotte Islands
Kitimat
Houston
McLeod Lake
Grouard
High Prairie
Fort St. James
Grande Prairie
Slave Lake
Burns Lake
Vanderhoof
Sinclair Mills
Prince George
Whitecourt
Grande Cache
Tweedsmuir Provincial Park
McBride
Bella Coola
Wells
Edson
Quesnel
Hinton
Tête Jaune Cache
Drayton Valley
Jasper
William Lake
Talla Lake
Blue River
Rocky Mountain House
Sylvan Lake
Port Hardy
Pacific Ocean
Bralorne
Cache Creek
Kamloops
Golden
Banff
Cochrane
Lillooet
Logan Lake
Salmon Arm
Revelstoke
Calgary
Campbell River
Powell River
Lytton
Whistler
Merritt
Vernon
Nakusp
Vancouver Island
Tofino
Squamish
Longview
Vancouver
Yale
Kelowna
New Denver
Nanaimo
Agassiz
Princeton
Kaslo
Hope
Penticton
Castelgar
Nelson
Osoyoos
Crownest Pass
Bellingham
Trail
Victoria
Grand Forks
Port Angeles
Everett
Omak
MONTANA
IDAHO
0
150
300km
Seattle
WASHINGTON
Kalispell
Aberdeen
Olympia
© Ulysses Travel Publications
N
37
37A
16
97
20
19
99
12
5
23
1
6
97c
3
93
95
2

VANCOUVER

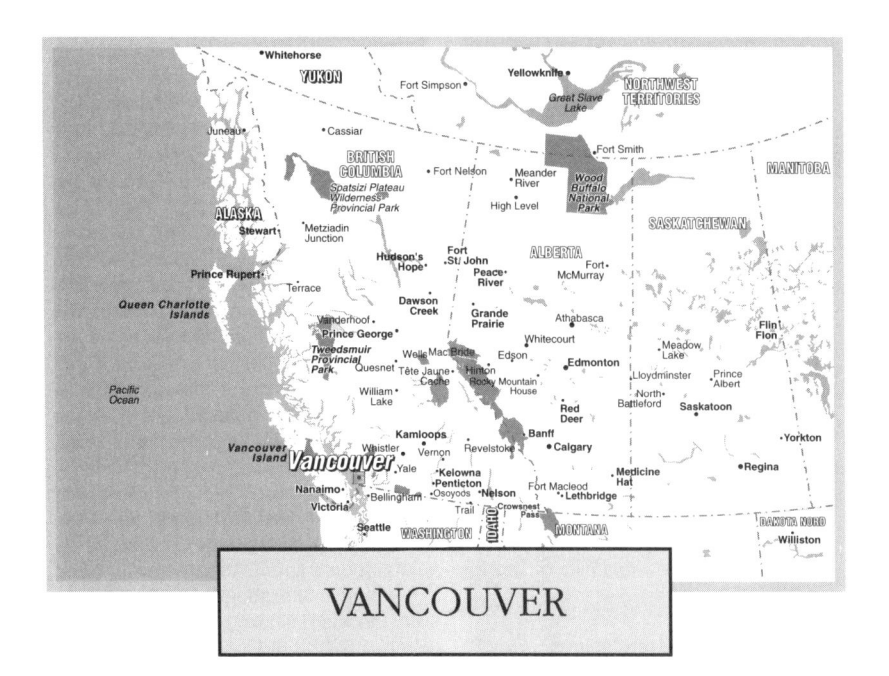

Vancouver enjoys a spectacular geographic location. No matter where you are in this city, the views are eye-catching. Flanked by mountains to the north, beaches to the south and English Bay to the west, Vancouver lies ensconced in elements of nature. The downtown area is squeezed onto a peninsula that encloses English Bay and creates two inlets, Burrard Inlet and False Creek, around which are spread most of the city's neighbourhoods and the surrounding suburbs. Just south of the peninsula, an immense public market on Granville Island attracts both the curious and the regulars who come to do their shopping amidst the joyful mood that fills the air. At the northern extremity of this same peninsula is one of Canada's biggest urban parks, Stanley Park, where 400 hectares (1,000 acres) of forest and wildlife skirt the concrete of the downtown towers.

Vancouver faces the sea. The port is busy; cargo vessels drop anchor in English Bay while sailboats, sailboards and fishing vessels cross each other's paths. The periphery of the bay consists of a series of beaches that are accessible 12 months a year. The third biggest city in Canada, with 1.6 million inhabitants, Vancouver is the metropolis of the Western Canada. It disabuses anyone of the notion that all of Canada is blanketed by snow during the winter season. Umbrellas replace snowsuits here. And as the month of March arrives, blossoming Japanese cherry trees push aside memories of a rainy winter.

Vancouver today

Vancouver's ethnic and architectural wealth is easy to appreciate as you walk throughout the city's neighbourhoods. Starting out, Gastown harkens back to the city's early years, as do the red brick and stone buildings of Cordova and Water streets. West End represents the other extreme, the Vancouver of the past 30 years. This neighbourhood is one of the most densely populated in North America and has the advantage of being situated right next to Stanley Park. The contrast is striking: a myriad of apartment towers border a forest of century-old trees, and less than five minutes' walk from these towers, you can find yourself with your feet in the sand contemplating a sunset over English Bay. The many residential neighbourhoods that lie along these beaches make it easy to forget the proximity of the big city.

You have to penetrate neighbourhoods like Chinatown and East Vancouver to discover and taste Vancouver's multi-ethnic life. East Vancouver is home to Chinese, Japanese, Italian, Portuguese and East Indian immigrants. Enlivened by Chinese and Italian markets, Commercial Drive is the backbone of the city's many ethnic neighbourhoods. Late in the day, cafés, restaurants and nightclubs along the street keep things hopping. The southern part of English Bay embraces some of the more stylish neighbourhoods. In contrast to the densely populated West End, Kitsilano and Point Grey give way to comfortable single-family abodes occupied by Vancouver's wealthy families earlier in the century. Many of these wooden houses have now been divided into smaller dwellings in response to the needs of a new occupants. Some of the wealthier families now live on the hills overlooking English Bay.

The University of British Columbia is situated on Vancouver's western point.

The campus offers unmatched views of Strait of Georgia, the Gulf Islands and the mountains of Vancouver Island. A visit to the campus is worth a detour as much for its architecture as for the museums to be found there (see page 68).

Vancouver continues today to incite plenty of interest among both the Canadian and international communities. The city scarcely suffered from the recession of the early 1990s, in large part because of the massive infusion of Asian capital from Hong Kong and the abundance of nearby natural resources. A huge variety of international cuisines is just one of the delightful particularities of the city's cosmopolitan population. Museums and shopping malls abound in Vancouver, but the main activity remains walking. Each street, boulevard, bus stop and piece of sidewalk offers views of a natural spectacle, making a visit to this city a definite must!

A brief history

By land and sea we prosper

Vancouver marked its centennial in 1986, but it was in 1792 that the English sea captain George Vancouver discovered the site. He called it lotus land, or paradise on earth. Indigenous peoples had been living in this paradise since about 500 B.C., on the shores of Burrard Inlet and along the Fraser River, where fish, especially salmon, abounded. Lumberman's Arch village was founded on what is now Stanley Park. The Musqueam Indian reserve, south of Vancouver, on the north shore of the Fraser River, is one of the few nearby Amerindian communities. Most of the beaches in the area, among them Point Grey, Kitsilano and Locarno, used to border native villages. Rather than banding together, these communities lived autonomously, each with its own territory. Today there are many reserves close to Vancouver, but you have to head as far as the Queen Charlotte Islands to find traditional Amerindian villages.

Europeans

The Spanish and the English were the first to explore the region, in their search for a Northwest Passage leading to India. Mandated in 1791 by the king of Spain to explore the northwestern coast of the American continent, José María Navírez landed at Point Grey, at the entrance to English Bay. In the summer of 1792, an English vessel entered the same waters. It was the *Discovery*, commanded by Captain George Vancouver. He was the first European to cross English Bay and to navigate the interior waters of Burrard Inlet. Vancouver continued his voyages along the coast during the two following summers. He died in Britain in 1798.

Meanwhile, across the Rocky Mountains, the Hudson's Bay Company and other companies were extending the fur trade by exploring the new western territories. In 1793, Alexander Mackenzie managed to cross the Rockies and to reach the sea by an overland route. In 1808, Simon Fraser, an employee of the North West Company, followed the river that was to bear his name right to its mouth, where the Musqueam Indian reserve is now situated. The fur trade was to remain the economic mainstay of the entire province for another half-century. Furs were carried east to Montréal, forming a link across what would become the Dominion of Canada.

Natural resources

In 1858, gold was found in the Fraser River. This discovery drew new adventurers, most of whom would establish themselves along the river deep in the interior. That same year, London made British Columbia a new colony. After furs and gold, forestry gave new life to the region. Timber played a determining role in the economic development of Vancouver and, eventually, of the whole province. By the 1860s, timber was already being exported to Australia, South America and South Africa. Even today, forestry is one of the province's main economic sectors.

Amerindians

Early in 1870, a committee laid out the Musqueam and Kitsilano Indian reserves, confining Amerindians, or First Nation peoples, within the limits of these lands. Although they lived on the margins of white society, natives played a role in the development of the city. They were involved in the fish trade and worked in the sawmill.

Canada

In 1871, Canada as we now know it was four years old. The federal government wanted to expand the territory of the young Dominion and promised British Columbia the construction of a railway linking it to the east if it would agree to join the Canadian confederation. The years of inaction that followed lead to political disenchantment.

In the late 1870s, a team undertook the first moves to establish the route for a railway. In 1884, William Van Horne, vice-president of the Canadian Pacific Railway, travelled to the west coast to select a terminal for the transcontinental railway. He chose the territory of Granville (now Vancouver). Van Horne predicted that a great city would emerge at this site. He went as far as suggesting strongly that the place be called Vancouver. On November 7, 1885, the last rail was laid at Port Moody, at the eastern edge of Burrard Inlet. Canada, once again, was linked from sea to sea, this time by the railway.

The choice of Vancouver as terminal of the transcontinental railway would transform the city, which had received little attention from investors and newcomers. The Canadian Pacific later set up a shipping line linking Britain's Asian colonies with Britain itself which carried merchandise such as tea. The tea route was thus established by sea and rail, passing through Vancouver. On May 23, 1887, the first passenger train arrived from Montreal.

Vancouver's first steps

Early in 1886, Granville residents asked their government to incorporate their community as a city. There was some debate concerning the choice of the city's name. Some opposed Vancouver as a name because of possible confusion with the island of the same name, but Vancouver it was, and the city was officially founded on April 6, 1886. Things got off to a difficult start. Fire ravaged most of the city's buildings in its early months, and few traces are left of this first townsite. The ashes were still warm when residents set out to reconstruct their city.

Transpacific boats came to port, passing their cargoes on to transcontinental trains. The timber trade flourished; the port was very busy. In five years, the population rose from 1,000 to more than 13,000. The great majority of citizens were of English descent. Other European immigrants and French Canadians from the east came to Vancouver and blended into a homogeneous society.

Chinese immigrants began grafting themselves on to this society as early as the 1850s and 1860s, but they did not begin arriving in large numbers until the construction of the Canadian Pacific Railway starting in 1880. In the spring of 1887, race riots between whites and Chinese led the authorities to bring in policemen from Victoria to re-establish order. White workers sought to denounce the presence of Chinese, who often worked for very low wages. Ottawa had just imposed a head tax on Chinese immigrants seeking to enter Canada, while the provincial government controlled all their economic activities. Despite this, Chinese continued to immigrate to the west coast, and at the turn of the century there were more than 3,000 Chinese living in Vancouver.

1900

Vancouver had slightly more than 20,000 inhabitants at the beginning of the 20th century, growing to 122,000 by 1912. The city prospered and expanded southward. At the end of the 19th century, the arrival of gold-seekers bound for the Klondike spurred economic activity in the region. Hotels and rooming houses took in these adventurers. Vancouver merchants made fortunes furnishing essential goods to the Yukon. Boats linked

Vancouver with various points along the northern shore. Moreover, salmon and timber from the interior were in great demand across Canada and elsewhere in the world. "By land and sea we prosper" became Vancouver's slogan.

Growing quickly, Vancouver welcomed thousands of immigrants each year. In 1911, just under 44% of the population was born in Canada. Italians, concentrated in the east end of the city, built their own churches and community centres. The Japanese community was established in Vancouver at the end of the 19th century; its members worked mostly in fish plants and sawmills. Asian immigrants also clustered in the eastern part of the city. The white population, fearing assimilation at the hands of Asian immigrants who made up one-sixth of the city's inhabitants, set up groups to denounce their presence.

If the turn of the century was marked by ease and prosperity, the years preceding the two world wars were more difficult for resident. Nonetheless, the wars gave new hope to workers, with boat-building, overseas demand for forest products, and so on. Vancouver became a major port for the shipment of grain from the Canadian prairies. Shipping became more and more important, with wood able to transit by the Panamá canal, which had opened in 1914. Timber exports rose 93% between 1920 and 1928.

Even if war meant work, many workers were unhappy with their wages when set against high living costs. The trade union movement grew in importance. Meetings were held to denounce the living conditions of workers and the compulsory conscription instituted by Ottawa in 1917. Social tensions grew, especially toward Asian immigrants.

The period between the two wars saw the port of Vancouver expand, with the construction of new piers and grain silos. The business district also grew, with the erection of banks, the stock exchange, hotels, and the Marine Building, an art deco masterpiece (see p 68). The Great Depression of the 1930s brought a momentary halt to the construction of big buildings in Vancouver. The year 1939 marked the beginning of a long period of economic growth that continued until 1970. The city expanded, and its centre was redeveloped. The building of the Lion's Gate bridge, undertaken by the Guinness family to serve the British Pacific Properties, marked a turning point in the development of the north shore of English Bay.

Because of its geographic location and the province's abundance of natural resources, Vancouver is a major hub for maritime and overland trade. An important financial centre with growing links to Asia and the world, Vancouver is also the gateway to immense resort areas concealing many treasures. A voyage of discovery awaits visitors to this fascinating city, this great 21st-century metropolis of Western Canada, with its cosmopolitan face and natural setting.

To simplify your visit of Vancouver, we have outlined seven tours: **Tour A: Old Vancouver** ★; **Tour B: Chinatown** ★★ **and Commercial Drive** ★; **Tour C: The Seawall** ★★★; **Tour D: Robson Street** ★★; **Tour E: The West Side** ★★; **Tour F: The Port of Vancouver and North Vancouver** ★; and **Tour G: South of Vancouver** ★.

Finding Your Way Around

■ **By Car**

You can reach Vancouver by the Trans Canada Highway, Highway 1, which follows an east-west course. This highway crosses Canada from sea to sea, passing through most of the major cities. There are no tolls, and the highway provides some spectacular scenery. Coming from Alberta, you cross the Rockies, as well as desert regions and a breath-taking canyon. From Calgary to Vancouver is 975 km.

Most people will enter Vancouver from the east off of the Trans Canada Highway at the Downtown exit. The signs are clear and easy to read. Governments decisions prevented the building of expressways across the downtown area, which is a little unusual for a city of more than a million-and-a-half people. This means, however, that rush hours can seem longer and more congested.

Travellers arriving from northern British Columbia will come in on the Squamish Highway.

If you arrive from the United States or from Victoria by ferry, you will reach Vancouver by northbound Highway 99; expect it to take a little over 30 minutes to reach the downtown area.

Car rental companies

You can rent a car at the airport or downtown.

Downtown:
Tilden: 1440 Alberni Street (☎ 685-6111).

Budget: 450 West Georgia (☎ 668-7000).
ABC Rent-A-Car: 1133 West Hastings (☎ 681-8555 or 1-800-464-6422).
Avis: (☎ 689-2847).

■ **By air**

Vancouver International Airport is served by flights from across Canada, the United States, Europe and Asia. It takes about 30 minutes to get downtown by car or bus. For more information, please consult the General Information section (see p 34).

Vancouver International Airport

Take note: even if you have already paid various taxes included in the purchase price of your ticket, Vancouver International Airport charges every passenger an Airport Improvement Fee (AIF). The fee is $5 for flights within B.C., $10 for flights elsewhere in North America, and $15 for overseas flights; credit cards are accepted, and most in-transit passengers are exempted.

Airport information: ☎ 276-6101
Air Canada: ☎ 688-5515 or 1-800-663-9826
Air Transat: ☎ 268-9302
Canada 3000: ☎ 273-4845 or 273-4834
Canadian Airlines International:
☎ 279-6611

■ **By boat**

British Columbia Ferry Corporation (☎ 277-0277 or 669-1211). Two ferry ports serve the Greater Vancouver area for travellers from other parts of the province. Horseshoe Bay, to the west,

Finding Your Way Around 57

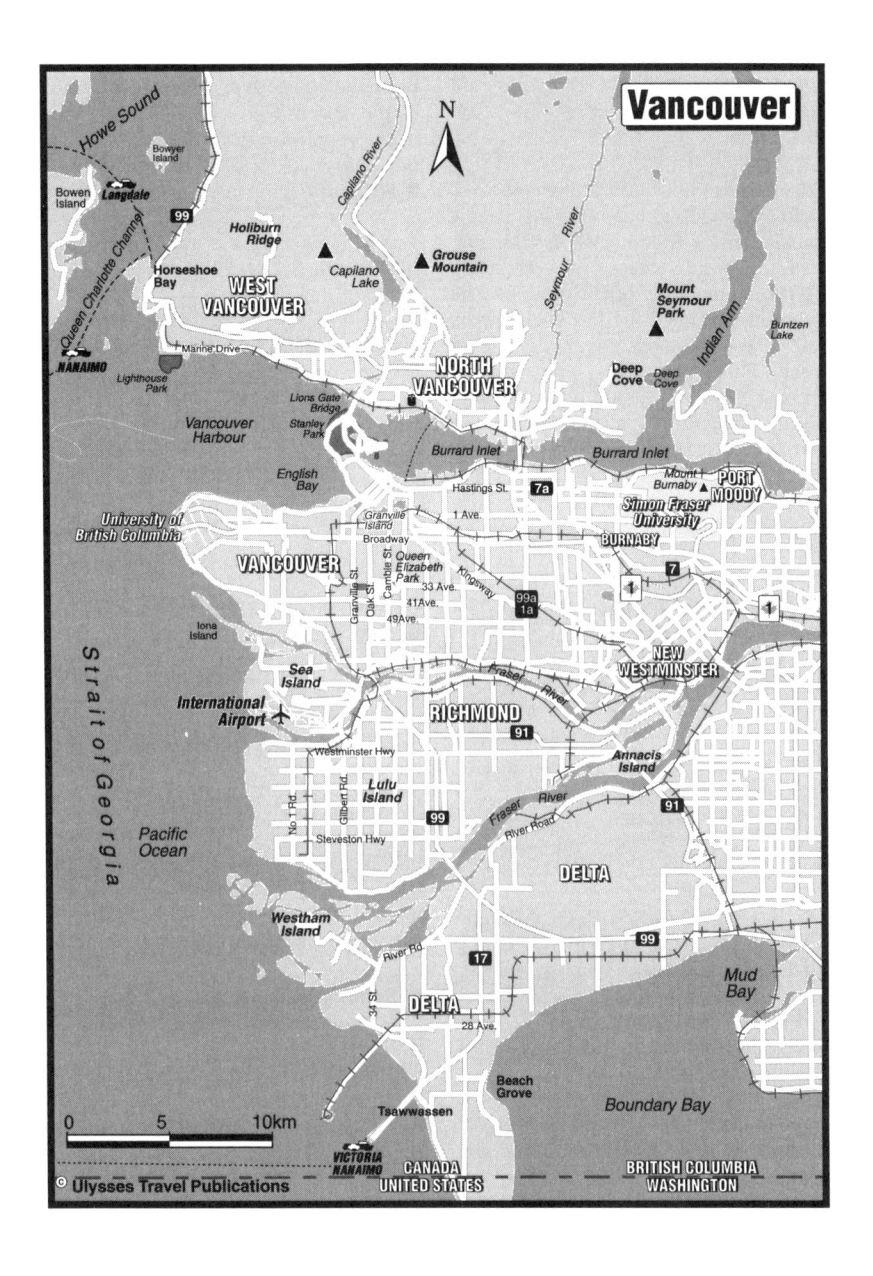

By train

Trains from the United States and from eastern Canada arrive at the intermodal **Pacific Central Station** (*Via Rail Canada*, *1150 Station Street,* ☎ *1-800-561-8630*), served by buses and by the Skytrain surface transport system. Via Rail's *The Canadian* runs to Vancouver three times a week from eastern Canada. The Edmonton-Vancouver portion constitutes a spectacular trip across the Rocky Mountains and along rivers and valleys. It is not for those in a hurry, since it takes 24 hours; it is more a tourist trip than a connection for business people. The one-way fare is less than $200; it is best to contact Via Rail for information on seasonal fares.

BC Rail (*1311 West First Street, North Vancouver,* ☎ *984-5246*). This station serves trains bound for Lillooet and Prince George. Service varies depending on the season.

By bus

The intermodal **Pacific Central Station** was inaugurated in 1993 in the existing Via Rail station, allowing passengers to connect between trains, intercity buses and local transit in one spot. There are many bus services to cities across the province and beyond.

Greyhound Lines of Canada *(Pacific Central Station, 1150 Station Street,* ☎ *662-3222 or 1-800-661-8747).*

Public transit

BC Transit bus route maps are available from the Vancouver Travel InfoCentre *(summer, every day 8am to 6pm; rest of the year, Mon to Fri 8:30am to 5pm, Sat 9am to 5pm; 200 Burrard Street,* ☎ *683-2000).*

Tickets and passes are available from BC Transit, ☎ 261-5100.

Vancouver has a rail transit system called the **Skytrain**, running east from the downtown area to Burnaby, New Westminster and Surrey. These automatic trains run from 5am to 1am all week, except Sundays when they start at 9am. The **Seabus**, a marine bus in the form of a catamaran, shuttles frequently between Burrard Inlet and North Vancouver.

Taxi

Taxis are easy to find most of the time, especially near the entrances of the big downtown hotels and along main arteries such as Robson Street and Georgia Street. The main taxi companies are:

Yellow Cabs (☎ 681-1111)
McLure's (☎ 731-9211)
Black Top (☎ 731-1111)

Specialized transport for persons with reduced mobility

A special transit service is available for persons who require wheelchairs. Reservations are required. Check with **Handydart** *(300-322 East 54th Street,* ☎ *430-2692).*

Vancouver Taxis *(2205 Main Street, ☎ 255-5111 or 874-5111)* provides transport for handicapped persons.

❓ Practical Information

■ Area code: 604

■ Tourist information

The **Vancouver TouristInfo Centre** *(May to Sep every day 8am to 6pm; Sep to May Mon to Fri 8:30am to 5pm, Sat 9am to 5pm; Plaza Level, Waterfront Centre, 200 Burrard Street, ☎ 682-2222, 683-2000 or 1-800-888-8835)*.

■ Emergencies

Emergency
☎ 911

Police station
☎ 665-3321

Vancouver General Hospital, 855 West 12th Avenue
☎ 875-4111

Downtown: Saint Paul Hospital, 1081 Burrard Street
☎ 682-2344

S.O.S. Doctors, Vancouver Hospital
☎ 875-4995

S.O.S. Dentists, Dr. Nick N. Kahwaji
☎ 469-1861; non-emergency calls, 876-5678

Ambulances
☎ 911; non-emergency calls, 872-5151

Children's emergency: British Columbia Children's Hospital, 4480 Oak Street
☎ 875-2345

24-hour pharmacy: Shoppers Drug Mart, 1125 Davie Street
☎ 669-2424 or 685-6445

Lost and found:
Public transit, ☎ 682-7887 or 985-7777
Public areas, ☎ 665-2232

Roadside Assistance:
South View Auto Towing, ☎ 435-7211
Low Cost Towing, ☎ 520-6562
CAA ☎ 268-5650

■ Banks

Most banks are closed weekends. The Bank of Montreal branch at 958 Denman in the West End area is open Saturday from 8:30am to 5:30pm. All the big Canadian banks have automatic teller machines.

■ Post offices

The main Vancouver post office is located at 349 West Georgia Street.

■ Municipal administration

Vancouver City Hall, 453 West 12th Avenue
☎ 873-7011
Persons with hearing or speech impairments can call ☎ 873-7193 Mon to Fri 8:30am to 5:30pm.

Exploring

You will need at least two days to visit Vancouver and to appreciate its people, its neighbourhoods and its green spaces. To begin your visit, take the time to head up to the deck atop **Harbour Centre** *(555 West Hastings Street, near Gastown, ☎ 689-0421)* to admire the city's beautiful setting. You will immediately understand the vision of the city's founders.

■ Tour A: Old Vancouver ★

Just a few steps from downtown, Old Vancouver is best discovered on foot. The area goes back to 1867, when John Deighton, known as Gassy Jack, opened a saloon for the employees of a neighbouring sawmill. Gastown was destroyed by fire in 1886. However, this catastrophe did not deter the city's pioneers, who rebuilt from the ashes and started anew in the development of their city, which was incorporated several months later. This area would become a major centre for the distribution of freight arriving by train or boat.

Vancouver has several buildings that reflect the great architectural movements. To learn more about this, the **Architectural Institute of British Columbia ★ (1)** *(103-131 Water Street, Gastown; ☎ 683-8588 for hours and programs)* offers free guided tours during the summer months. Visitors who prefer to discover these masterpieces themselves will find helpful information in *Exploring Vancouver: The Essential Architectural Guide*, published by UBC Press.

Start by visiting the western edge of Gastown, at the corner of Water and Cordova streets. This area lies near the Waterfront station of the Skytrain.

The railways and the Gold Rush lay at the centre of Gastown's economic development, but a westward shift in economic activity left a void in this area for nearly half a century. In the 1960s, new owners took over the development of Gastown and found new uses for the buildings. Several of these buildings have been renovated in keeping with their original structure and ornamentation, while some of the newer buildings clash with the old-fashioned cityscape.

The **Landing (2)** *(375 Water Street)*, with its brick and stone façade, was a commercial warehouse at the time of its construction in 1905; today it is a fine example of restoration. Since the late 1980s, it has housed offices, shops and restaurants. Walk east along Water Street until you reach Cambie; there you will discover the world's first steam clock. Along the way, you will notice interesting decorative elements in this collection of buildings, including coloured brick and cornices. Most of these buildings now house restaurants and souvenir shops. Farther east is the former **Hotel Europe (3)** *(4 Powell Street)*, a triangular building erected in 1908 by a Canadian hotel-keeper of Italian descent.

Return to Carrall Street and follow it to Cordova Street, the next street along, which was beautifully transformed a few years ago with the arrival of merchants and restaurateurs who set up trendy boutiques and cafés. Long the abode of artists, Gastown is now a tourist zone with trendy and often expensive boutiques here and there.

Exploring 61

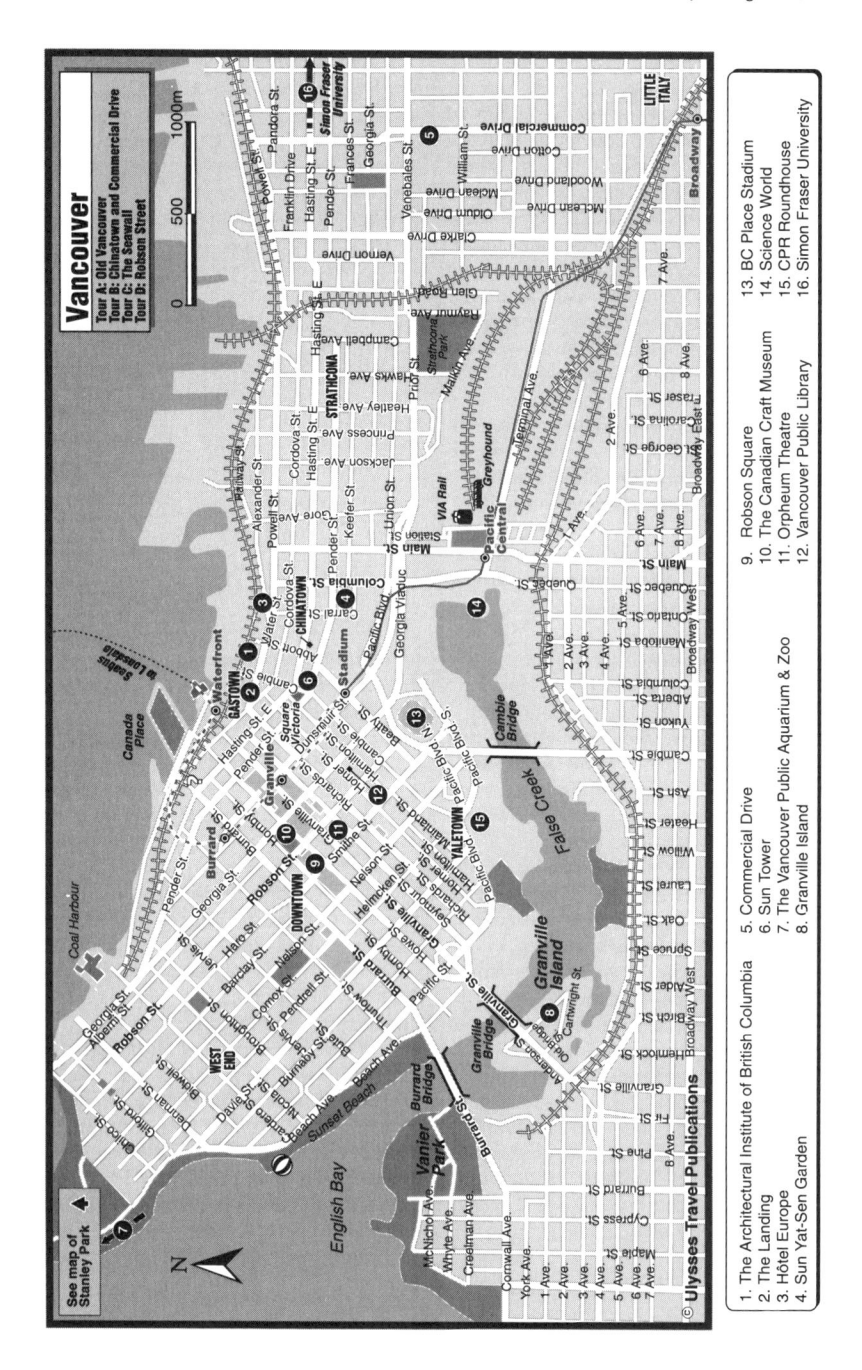

Vancouver

Tour A: Old Vancouver
Tour B: Chinatown and Commercial Drive
Tour C: The Seawall
Tour D: Robson Street

© Ulysses Travel Publications

1. The Architectural Institute of British Columbia
2. The Landing
3. Hôtel Europe
4. Sun Yat-Sen Garden
5. Commercial Drive
6. Sun Tower
7. The Vancouver Public Aquarium & Zoo
8. Granville Island
9. Robson Square
10. The Canadian Craft Museum
11. Orpheum Theatre
12. Vancouver Public Library
13. BC Place Stadium
14. Science World
15. CPR Roundhouse
16. Simon Fraser University

Continue along Carrall Street and head up to Pender Street. You will be going through Downtown East, a part of Vancouver which lay at the centre of the city's economic activity early in the 20th century. Banks, hotels, office buildings and retail outlets sprang up along Carrall, Hastings and Pender streets. Economic development just to the west affected the area's social and economic life, and its inhabitants now include many poor people. Organizations such as the Downtown Eastside Residents' Association have defended groups of people uprooted by change by persuading public authorities to refurbish abandoned buildings to house some of the poor and avoid their expulsion to other parts of the city.

■ **Tour B: Chinatown ★★ and Commercial Drive ★**

On East Pender Street, the scene changes radically. The colour and atmosphere of public markets, plus a strong Chinese presence, bring this street to life. The 1858 Gold Rush drew Chinese from San Francisco and Hong Kong; in 1878, railway construction brought thousands more Chinese to British Columbia. This community resisted many hard blows that might have ended its presence in the province. At the beginning of the 20th century, the Canadian government imposed a heavy tax on the arrival of Chinese immigrants, but this did not prevent them from fleeing Asia. Later on, Ottawa actually halted Chinese immigration, but since 1947 Chinese have again been able to immigrate to Canada. Today, Penner Street bustles with activity. Chinatown has established itself as an economically and socially dynamic community.

It is well worth stopping in at the **Sun Yat-Sen Garden ★ (4)** *($4.50; Oct to Apr every day 10am to 4:30pm; May to Sep every day 10am to 8pm; 578 Carrall Street, ☎ 689-7133)*, behind the traditional portal of the Chinese cultural centre at 50 East Pender Street. Built in 1986 by Chinese artists from Suzhou, this garden is the only example outside China of landscape architecture from the Ming dynasty (1368-1644). Back on Pender Street, go up as far as Gore Street and turn right, heading back down Keefer Street to savour the lively Chinese presence.

Turn left on Main Street, lined with hotels and former banks, to reach the Pacific Central Station. Take the Skytrain eastbound (in the same direction as Surrey) and get off at the next stop, Broadway. If you are going by car, take Georgia Street east from downtown; after reaching the viaduct, follow Prior Street and turn right on Commercial Drive.

Upon leaving the Skytrain, turn north on **Commercial Drive (5)**, a street running through the Little Italy district, which is also home to Portuguese, Spanish, Jamaicans and South Americans. Early in the 20th century, the eastern part of Vancouver became the first suburban area developed along Commercial Drive. The middle class built small single-family houses, and the neighbourhood grew. After the First World War, the arrival of European and Chinese immigrants gave the area a distinctive ethnic atmosphere. The end of the Second World War brought a fresh wave of immigrants, mostly Italians, and even today you can enjoy the special atmosphere of their cafés and restaurants. A few establishments are suggested below in the Restaurants section.

On Hastings Street, take the bus toward downtown. The route passes through the Strathcona area, where Scandinavians, Germans, Ukrainians, Jews, Portuguese and Italians lived early in the century; although these groups retain a certain presence, they are now outnumbered by Chinese, Vietnamese and Latin Americans. Ask the driver to let you off at Abbott Street, and head toward West Pender Street (you are now back downtown). This section of the city is being developed at a hectic pace; the new buildings are part of a big project called International Village, which will bring in new residents.

Continue walking west. The **Sun Tower (6)** *(100 West Pender Street)*, built in 1912, was for a time the highest building in the British Empire. Louis D. Taylor, a prominent publisher, wanted to show off his power by having this tower built. After reaching Cambie Street, discover **Victory Square**; facing it is the **Dominion Building** *(207 West Hastings Street)*, which was also at one time the highest building in the British Empire. Its mansard roof recalls the Parisian roofs along the boulevards laid out by Baron Haussmann.

■ Tour C: The Seawall ★★

The Seawall runs along the edge of Stanley Park, starting at Coal Harbour, passing beneath the Lion's Gate Bridge and hugging English Bay. It continues as far as False Creek. This pleasant promenade, more than 10 km long, can take several hours on foot, and the distance is easier to cover by bicycle.

Stanley Park ★★★, named in honour of Lord Stanley the Governor General of Canada from 1888 to 1893, is a 400-hectare (1,000-acre) forest adjacent to downtown. A road skirts the park, and several rest areas have been set up along the way. A series of trails running across the park will take you through a forest where the city seems many miles away. The park conceals beautiful gardens of flowers and plants, and a team of gardeners works year-round to maintain this magical place. Monsieur Gérard, a gardener from France who has worked their for a number of years will help you discover "his" Stanley Park. Begin your walk at the corner of Chilco and Georgia streets, where it is also possible to rent bicycles *(☎ 681-5581)*.

Three-quarters of this tour lie far from shops and restaurants. Views of the nearby mountains and of English Bay are dazzling. Along the way you will discover several sculptures, including *Girl in Wetsuit*, as well as a group of totem poles, an ornithological reserve at Lost Lagoon, and the Nine O'Clock Cannon, fired every evening at 9pm (it is better not to be close by at the moment of detonation). At one time, the firing of the cannon told fishermen it was time to pull up their nets.

The **Vancouver Public Aquarium and Zoo ★★ (7)** *($9.50, children $6.25; Jul to Sep every day 9:30am to 8pm Sep to Jun every day 10am to 5:30pm; ☎ 682-1118)*. This aquarium, situated within the park, is home to wonderful orca and beluga whales, dolphins, seals and exotic fish.

Leaving Stanley Park, this tour continues along Beach Avenue, with its towering apartment blocks filled with local young professionals. Stay along the seashore; near Burrard Bridge, take the little ferry that goes to Granville Island. If you prefer to follow a route away from the seashore, go along Denman Street or Davie Street, both

> **Gay life**
>
> Like any North American metropolis, Vancouver has attracted a substantial gay population. As the only sizable gay community west of Toronto, it is worth particular mention.
>
> It can be said that gay life here is centred more around cafés than bars. Vancouver is recognized as a tolerant place; fashionable young people and the gay community blend together so well that there are few exclusively gay establishments.
>
> Two gay monthly papers are published here, *Extra West* and *Angles*, distributed free of charge in many establishments, including the cafés along Davie Street between Jervis and Burrard streets.

frequented mostly by local people, unlike the more touristy Robson Street. Vancouver's gay community has established itself here.

Granville Island ★★ (8), located beneath Granville Bridge, was once used for industrial purposes but has seen its warehouses and factories transformed into a major recreational and commercial centre. After a few years of abandonment, the area came to life thanks to a revitalization project. A public market, many shops and all sorts of restaurants, plus theatres and artists' studios, are all part of Granville Island. Musicians and street entertainers enliven the area on weekends which is popular with Vancouverites, especially on Sundays. Not to be missed is the microbrewery tour offered by the **Granville Island Brewing Company** *(Mon to Thu 9am to 7pm, Fri and Sat 9am to 9pm; guided tours every day at 1pm and 3pm; 1441 Cartwright Street, ☎ 688-9927)*. Avoid taking your car onto the island; traffic jams are common, and parking is hard to find. Bus number 50 will take you there from Howe Street downtown. Renovations are ongoing until the summer of 1996.

■ **Tour D: Robson Street ★★**

Robson Street crosses the Vancouver peninsula in an east-west axis. It is a street of cafés, of restaurants infused by influences from all over, of shops flaunting the latest styles and, above all, of people out for a stroll. It also crosses **West End ★★**, the neighbourhood with Canada's highest population density per square kilometre. West End is inhabited by professionals and students; the gay community also has an important presence. Fashion boutiques and all sorts of restaurants sit cheek by jowl from Jervis Street to Burrard Street.

Wanderers relax at the corner cafés, enjoying the fine weather and admiring the passing scene. It is not unusual to see more than one café at a given street corner. For fans of strolling, sidewalk cafés and good coffee, this place has become a passion. The crowds walk past, ride past by bicycle, or glide past on in-line skates, often taking the time to savour a coffee. An American film star visiting Vancouver expressed astonishment at the number of cafés in this city, remarking that Vancouverites seemed hooked on caffeine though this had not changed their pace of life, recognized as rather slow.

Robson Square (9) *(on the 800 block of Robson Street)*, by Canadian architect Arthur Erickson, is an urban park where concrete and greenery are blended in cascades. Shops, restaurants and a skating rink welcome passers-by. The **Provincial Law Courts** ★ *(800 Smithe Street)*, by the same architect, enclose the British Columbia Courthouse. You can visit the vast lobby to appreciate fully the grandeur of this spot and the genius of the architect.

On the north side of Robson Street, the **Vancouver Art Gallery** *($6; May 3 to Oct 9, Mon to Wed 10am to 6pm, Thu 10am to 9pm, Fri 10am to 6pm, Sat 10am to 5pm, Sun and holidays noon to 5pm; rest of the year, closed Mon and Tue, same hours other days; 750 Hornby Street, ☎ 682-5621 or 682-4668)*. This former courthouse now houses Vancouver's art museum. It is worth visiting for the works of **Emily Carr** ★ (1871-1945) of Victoria, an important Canadian painter inspired by native peoples and west coast landscapes (see p 23).

The **Canadian Craft Museum (10)** *($4; Mon to Sat 9:30am to 5:30pm, Sun and holidays noon to 5pm; 639 Hornby Street, ☎ 687-8266)*. This small, recently built spot houses a sampling of Canadian handicrafts production and a few decorative elements that were part of the art deco Georgia Medical-Dental Building, demolished to make way for a big office tower at the corner of West Georgia and Hornby streets.

Back on Robson Street, turn east toward **Granville Street**. Granville is the street of cinemas (half-price on Tuesdays), theatres, nightclubs and retail stores. The street is busy 24 hours a day with passers-by. The concert halls of the **Orpheum Theatre (11)** *(884 Granville Street; free tours by calling ahead at ☎ 665-3050)*, the **Commodore** *(870 Granville Street, ☎681-7838)*, and the **Vogue Theatre** *(924 Granville Street)* provide venues for the greats of classical, contemporary and popular music; they also offer fine examples of European art deco and beaux-arts architecture.

Continuing east along Robson Street, at the corner of Homer Street, is the new **Vancouver Public Library** ★ **(12)** *(free admission; year-round Mon to Wed 10am to 9pm, Thu to Sat 10am to 6pm; Oct to Apr, Sun 1pm to 5pm, closed Sun in the summer; free guided tours Mon to Wed 12:30pm, 2pm and 7pm, Thu to Sat 12:30pm and 2pm; 350 West Georgia Street, ☎ 331-3600)*. This brand new building, which imitates the shape of the Roman Coliseum, is the work of Montréal architect Moshe Safdie. The project stirred lively reactions both from local people and from architecture critics. It was chosen after finally being put to a referendum. This place is grandiose, and comfortable; take the time to look around.

Located in the southeast of the downtown area, **Yaletown** was an industrial area when the railways were still king. The growth of the trucking industry shifted business away from Yaletown's big warehouses and the loading docks of Hamilton and Mainland streets have since been transformed into outdoor cafés and restaurants. A new group of tenants now occupies the old brick warehouses; designers, architects, film production companies and business people in general have brought this area back to life; trendy cafés and restaurants have followed suit.

At the eastern edge, **BC Place Stadium (13)** *(777 Pacific Boulevard)* is a football stadium which also accommodates trade shows and rock concerts. Next door, **GM Place** is Vancouver's newest venue. It is home to the National Hockey League team the Vancouver Canucks and the National Basketball Association team the Vancouver Grizzlies. Behind the stadium, the grounds of **Expo 86** were the site of a big international exhibition where transport was the central theme. The Plaza of Nations and Science World, at the eastern edge of False Creek, are all that remain. **Science World (14)** *($9, or $12 with a film showing; 1455 Quebec Street, ☎ 443-7440)* explores the secrets of science from various angles. An Omnimax cinema presents films on a giant cupola-shaped screen. All of these places are accessible by Skytrain.

South of Yaletown, a significant building from the era of steam trains, the **CPR Roundhouse (15)** *(corner Davie Street and Pacific Boulevard)* was part of a big marshalling yard that remained in use until the 1970s. The land has been bought by a real estate promoter, and a sizable development is under way in an attempt to recreate West End farther east.

The downtown campus of Simon Fraser University is close by. East of here, about a half-hour from downtown, is the campus of **Simon Fraser University ★ (16)** *(Gagliardi Way via Hastings Street, Burnaby)*, perched along the slopes of Mount Burnaby like an immense spaceship newly arrived from a distant galaxy. It is worth seeing these concrete buildings, which are both imposing and pleasant to look at. Several architects contributed to the creation of this seat of higher learning, among them Arthur Erickson, who has contributed to local architecture in a number of ways.

■ **Tour E: West Side ★★**

A look at a map of Vancouver reveals a large point jutting out into the Strait of Georgia. There you will find gorgeous residential neighbourhoods as well as several beaches and a university campus with many points of interest. If you come by car, leave the downtown area by Burrard Bridge and keep right to get onto Cornwall Street; this is the starting-point of a pleasant drive that will introduce you to this district of beaches, mountains, fine views and architectural riches. Soon you will be at Kitsilano Park and its beach, followed by a series of homes perched on a mountain slope facing the bay, and then by Jericho, Locarno and Spanish Banks beaches. North West Marine Drive will take you to UBC (the campus of the University of British Columbia), where on a clear day you can admire Vancouver Island, the Gulf Islands, the Strait of Georgia and, of course, the mountains.

Vancouver Museum (17) *($5; every day 10am to 5pm; 1100 Chestnut Street, in Vanier Park, ☎ 736-4431)*. This museum, whose dome resembles the head-dress worn by Coast Salish Indians, presents exhibitions on the history of the different peoples who have inhabited the region. At the entrance, an immense six-metre-high steel crab stands guard over the port of Vancouver, according to Indian legend. At the same spot is the **Pacific Space Centre** *($6.50; presentations Tue to Sun 2:30pm and 8pm, extra shows Sat and Sun 1pm and 4pm; ☎ 738-7827)*, a planetarium narrating the creation of our universe; it has a telescope through which you can admire the stars.

Exploring 67

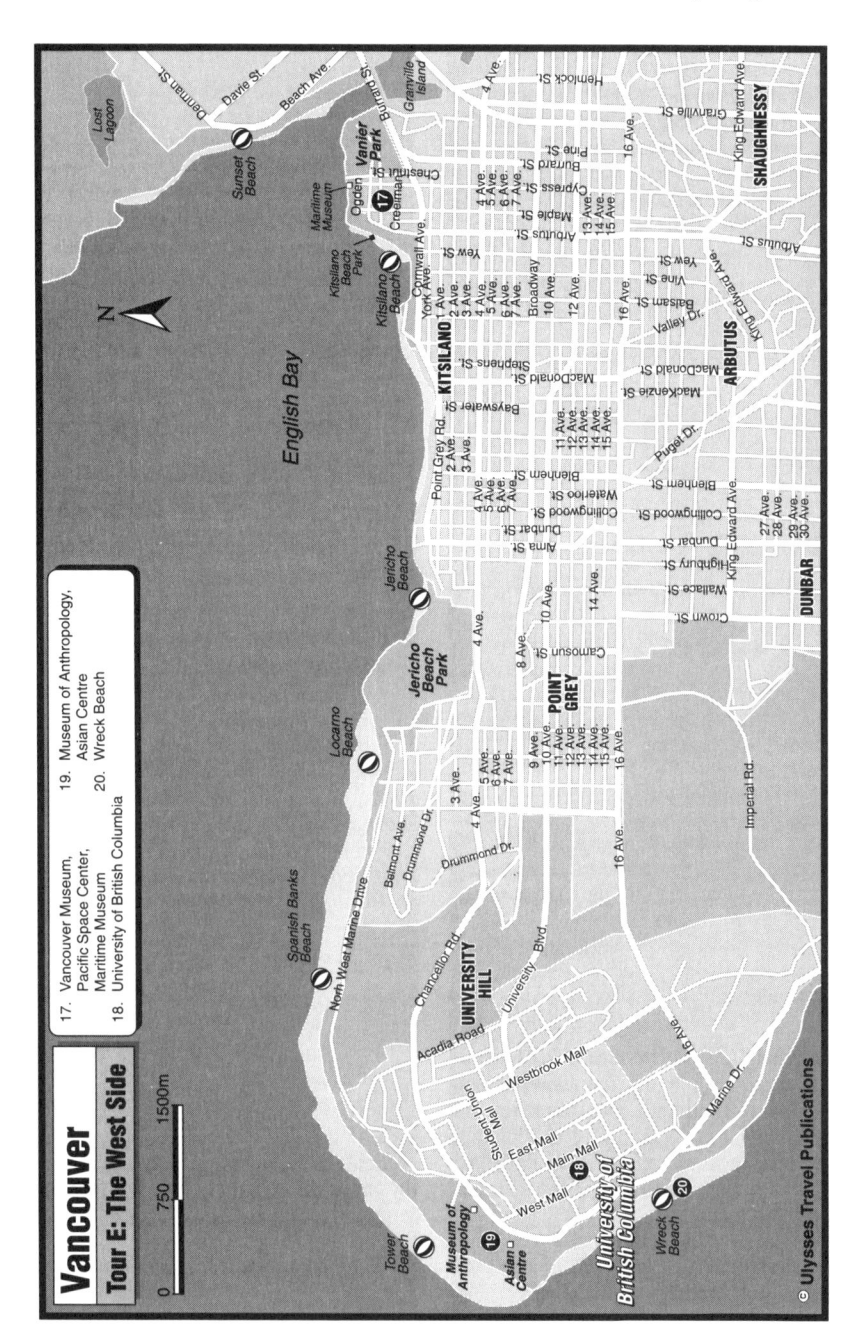

Vancouver
Tour E: The West Side

17. Vancouver Museum, Pacific Space Center, Maritime Museum
18. University of British Columbia
19. Museum of Anthropology, Asian Centre
20. Wreck Beach

© Ulysses Travel Publications

Maritime Museum (17) *($5; May to Oct, every day 10am to 5pm, Nov to Apr closed Mon; 1905 Ogden Avenue, ☎ 257-8300)*. Being a major seaport, it is only natural that Vancouver should have its own, and here it is, right near Vanier Park. The key attraction is the *Saint-Roch*, the first boat to circle North America by navigating the Panamá Canal and the Northwest Passage.

The **University of British Columbia** ★★ **(18)**, or UBC ,was created by the provincial government in 1908, but it was not until 1925 that the campus opened its doors on the current site. An architectural contest had been organized for the site layout, but the First World War halted construction work, and it took a student demonstration denouncing government inaction in this matter to get the buildings completed. Only the library and the science building were executed according to the original plans. **Set Foot for UBC** *(May to Aug, free tours organized by students, ☎ 822-3777)*.

The **Museum of Anthropology** ★★★ **(19)** *($6, free admission Tue 5pm to 9pm; in the summer, every day 11am to 5pm, in the winter closed Mon and on Dec 25 and 26; 6393 North West Marine Drive; from downtown, take bus number 4 UBC or bus number 10 UBC; ☎ 822-3825)*, is not to be missed both for the quality of native artwork displayed here, including totem poles, and for the architecture of Arthur Erickson. Big concrete beams and columns imitate the shapes of traditional native houses, beneath which have been erected immense totem poles gathered from former native villages along the coast and on the islands. Wooden sculptures and various works of art form part of the permanent exhibition.

The **Asian Centre (19)** *(1871 West Mall)* is capped with a big pyramid-shaped metal roof, beneath which are the department of Asian studies and an exhibition centre. Behind the building are the magnificent Nitobe Memorial Gardens.

The western edge of the campus harbours a spot unlike anything else, **Wreck Beach** ★ **(20)** *(North West Marine Drive at University Street)*, where students come to enjoy some of life's pleasures. Nudists have made this their refuge, as have sculptors, who exhibit their talents on large pieces of driftwood. Vendors hawk all sorts of items next to improvised fast-food stands. A long stairway, that is quite steep in places, leads down to the beach.

■ **Tour F: The Port of Vancouver and North Vancouver** ★

The Seabus is the marine bus that provides public transit between Vancouver and North Vancouver. It offers a spectacular ride, crossing Burrard Inlet and enabling you to contemplate the mountains of the north shore, which harbours the municipality of North Vancouver. The trip back allows you to admire equally lovely views of the city of Vancouver.

Before crossing Burrard Inlet, start with a visit to the **Marine Building** ★ **(21)** *(355 Burrard Street, at the corner of West Hastings)*, built during the economic crisis of 1929. This art deco building proudly exhibits its decorative elements, especially at the main entrance, where you can admire the detailed ornamentation. You can take an elevator to the mezzanine, which provides an interesting view of the

Exploring 69

Vancouver
Tour F: The Port of Vancouver and North Vancouver

Legend:
- —··—··— Baden Powell Trail
- ---- Other Trails

21. Marine Building
22. Canada Place
23. Lonsdale Quay Market
24. Capilano Suspension Bridge and Park
25. Capilano Fish Hatchery
26. Grouse Mountain
27. Mount Seymour Provincial Park
28. Deep Cove
29. Lighthouse Park
30. Cypress Provincial Park

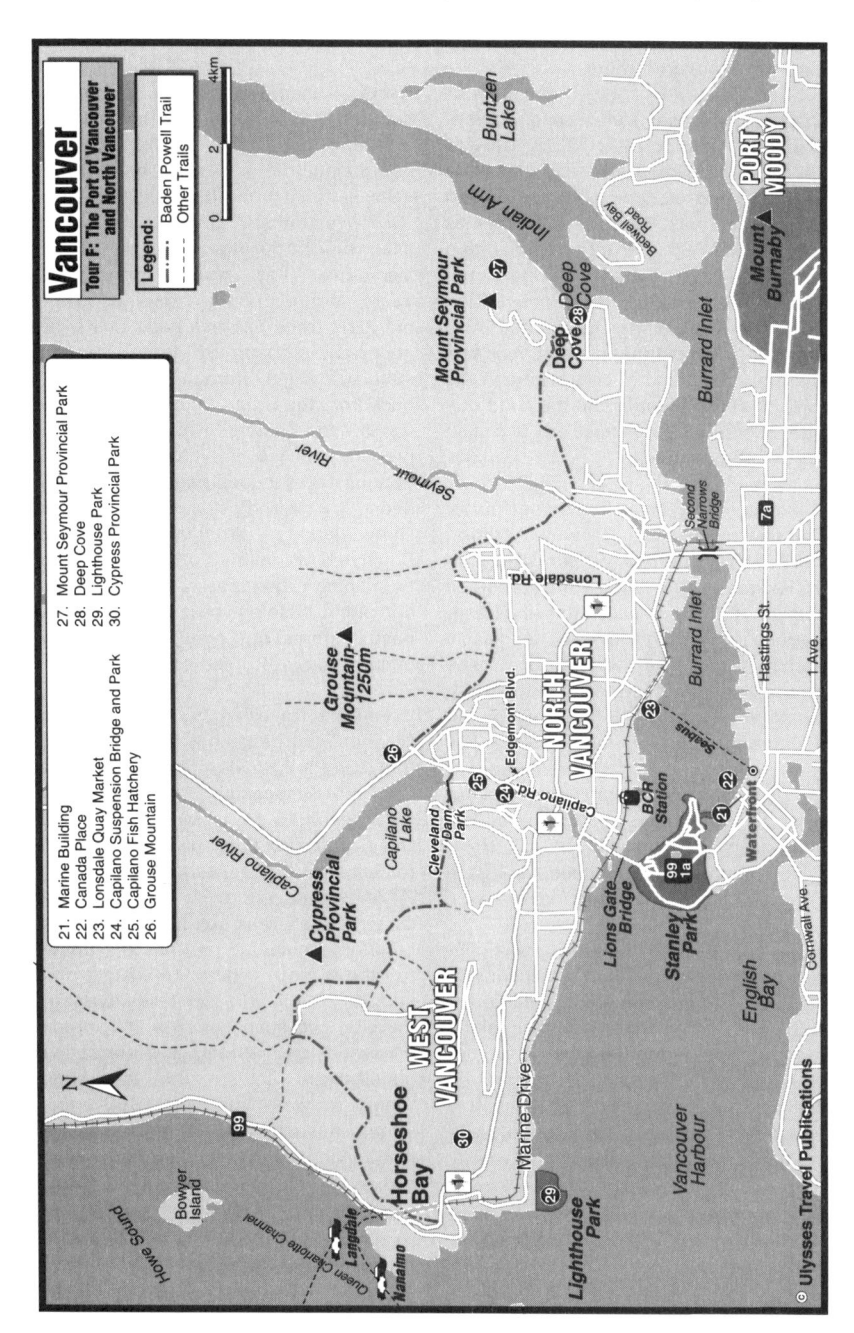

© Ulysses Travel Publications

lobby; other decorative elements can also be discovered there.

Back at the seafront, head toward **Canada Place ★ (22)** *(999 Canada Place)*, the building with the big white sails located at the end of Burrard Street. This vast complex was built as part of the 1986 international exhibition to house the Canada Pavilion and serves today mostly as a convention centre. A walk along the "bridge" will steer you toward magnificent views of the mountains and of boat traffic in the inlet. An Imax cinema and the luxurious Pan Pacific Hotel (see p 76) are also part of the complex.

Heading east, you will see the **former Canadian Pacific Railway station** *(601 West Cordova Street)*, built in 1912; today the Waterfront station of the Skytrain occupies this building, thereby preserving a jewel of neoclassic architecture. The arrival of trains downtown had given a second wind to Gastown merchants, hard hit by an economic crisis in the 1890s. The former station marks the boundary between the eastern part of downtown and the beginning of Gastown. The Waterfront station of the Skytrain, which leads to the Seabus, is just a few steps east of Canada Place.

Take the Seabus for the short 15-minute crossing to North Vancouver, arriving at **Lonsdale Quay Market ★ (23)**. Similar to the Granville Island market, this industrial-style structure was converted to a public market in 1986. The easy access and the fine views from this spot draw tourists and residents throughout the year.

North Vancouver ★

North Vancouver is an immediate suburb of Vancouver. Built on a mountain slope, this municipality came into being in the second half of the 19th century when businessmen from New Westminster decided to exploit the neighbouring forest. North Vancouver has known prosperous years and economic crisis as well; maritime trade has been and still is an important source of jobs. In this suburb, virgin forest provide the backdrop for urban living. The Lion's Gate and Second Narrows bridges provide access for motorists; the Seabus takes pedestrians right to the heart of town. Besides the Lonsdale Quay Market, a stroll along Lonsdale Boulevard will allow you to discover a flourishing urban area where old banks and public buildings bear witness to the past. Interesting retail shops now occupy some of these buildings.

If you are travelling by car, return to Marine Drive heading west and go up Capilano Park Road until you reach the **Capilano Suspension Bridge and Park (24)** *(adults $5.50, children $4; May to Oct 8:30am to 8pm; Nov to Apr 9am to 5pm; 3735 Capilano Road, ☎ 985-7474)*. If you are on foot at Lonsdale Quay Market, take bus number 236 to Edgmont Boulevard and ask the driver to show you where to catch the number 232. A little too flashy even for tourists, the suspension bridge, made of wood and metal, is interesting nonetheless, as are the footpaths. When it was built in 1899, this structure, suspended 70 metres above the Capilano River, was made of rope and wood.

Exploring 71

The **Capilano Fish Hatchery** ★ **(25)** *(free entry; 4500 Capilano Road, ☎ 666-1790)* is the first fish-rearing farm in British Columbia. This well laid out spot provides visitors with an introduction to the life cycle of the salmon.

Farther north, on Capilano Road, is the lovely **Cleveland Dam Park**, with spectacular views of the neighbouring mountains, which feed Lake Capilano with fresh water. Continuing north along Capilano Road, an **aerial tramway** *($14.95; summer Mon to Fri 9am to 10pm, Sat to Sun 8am to 10pm; ☎ 984-0661)* ferries passengers to the top of **Grouse Mountain (26)**, 1,250 metres up, where skiers or hikers can admire Vancouver by sunlight or moonlight.

To the northeast, **Mount Seymour Provincial Park (27)** encompasses part of the mountain it is named for, one of three near Vancouver with both day and night skiing.

Deep Cove (28), at the eastern edge, on the shore of Indian Arm, is a fine spot for canoeing or kayaking, or for a hike along the Baden Powell Trail, which runs 42 km farther west all the way to Horseshoe Bay.

West Vancouver ★

West Vancouver, on the north shore of English Bay, is a wealthy mountainside suburb. Besides its attractive parks, West Vancouver has three beautiful Westcoast-style properties. A ride along Marine Drive will give you an idea of what lies hidden across English Bay. Take the Lion's Gate Bridge and follow the signs west. **Lighthouse Park (29)**, the parkway running along Burrard Inlet, along with **Cypress Provincial Park (30)**, are the main points of interest here. See the Parks and Beaches section below to learn more about this region.

■ **Tour G: South of Vancouver** ★

Queen Elizabeth Park (31) *(33rd Street at Cambie Street)*. This park is noted for its beautiful gardens. The Bloedel Floral Conservatory, within the park, displays exotic plants and flowers. But the main attraction is the panoramic view of the city, the mountains and English Bay.

Shaughnessy, a neighbourhood located south of the downtown peninsula in an area looking over the city, was developed early in the 20th century by the Canadian Pacific Railway as an area reserved for the elite. Immense Tudor-style homes were built on an enchanting site, but the economic crisis of the 1930s was disastrous for many families who could no longer afford their castles. At the start of the Second World War, abandoned residences were used to house several families. A ride along The Crescent, south of 16th Street and east of Granville Street, will give you a good idea of the opulence of some families.

Van Dusen Botanical Garden (32) *($2.50; summer, every day 10am to 9pm, winter, every day 10am to 4pm, closed at Christmas; guided tours Sun at 2pm; 5251 Oak Street, ☎ 878-9274)*. Farther north in Shaughnessy, this magnificent 22-hectare (55-acre) garden was laid out with different types of vegetation from around the world.

Upon leaving the garden, take Oak Street south toward Route 99, which leads to the ferry pier for Victoria, and take the Steveston Highway West exit.

72 *Vancouver*

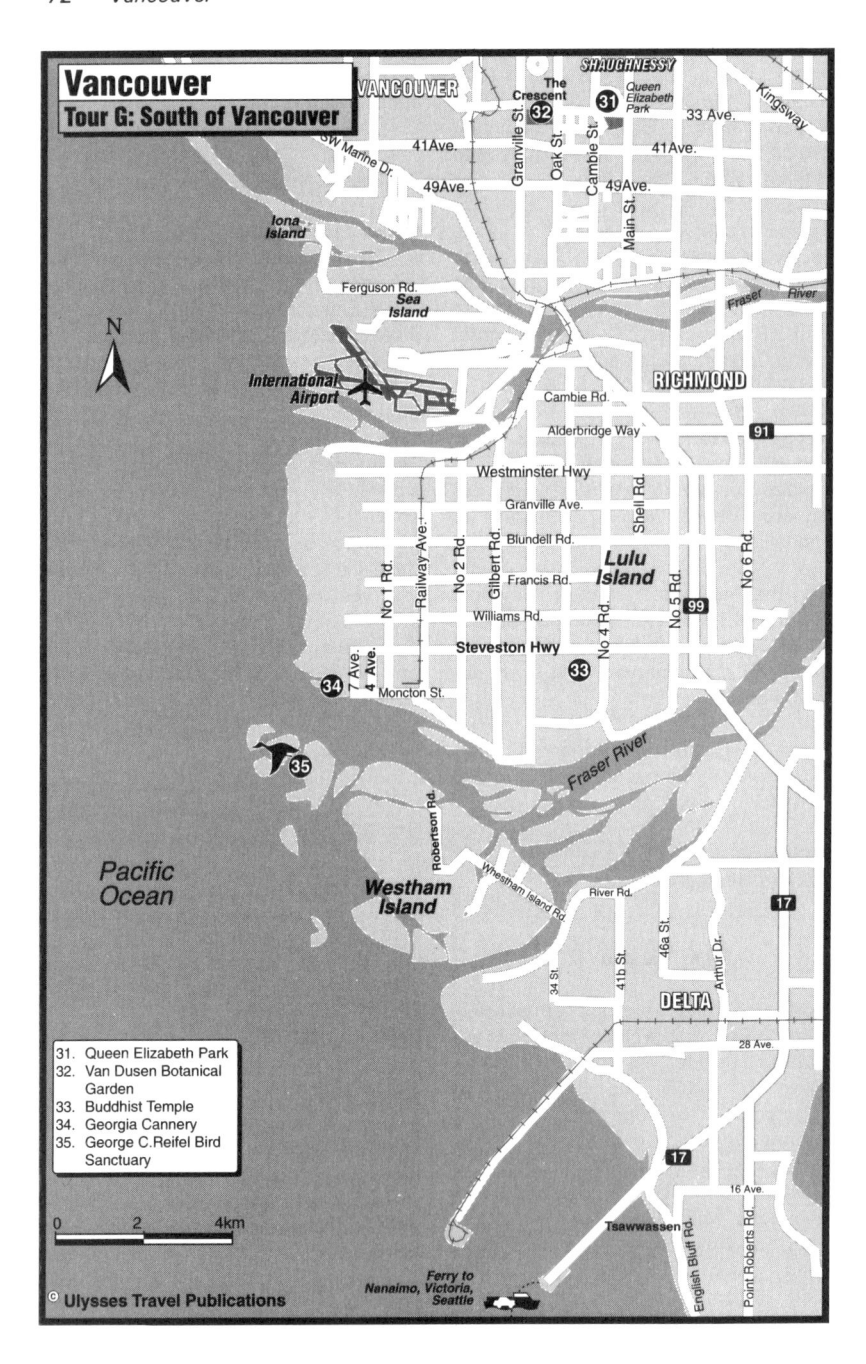

Vancouver
Tour G: South of Vancouver

31. Queen Elizabeth Park
32. Van Dusen Botanical Garden
33. Buddhist Temple
34. Georgia Cannery
35. George C. Reifel Bird Sanctuary

© Ulysses Travel Publications

Between the third and fourth streets on your left, you will see the second biggest **Buddhist temple (33)** in North America *(every day 10am to 5pm; 9160 Steveston Highway, Richmond, ☎ 274-2822)*, a place of worship with free entry.

Get back on the Steveston Highway heading west, turn left on 4th Avenue, and continue to the end of this avenue. The **Georgia Cannery ★ (34)** *(12138 4th Avenue, ☎ 664-9009)*, restored by Parks Canada, retraces the history of the fishing industry in Steveston. This historical spot explains the steps involved in conserving fish, especially salmon, and also shows how cod is transformed into pet food and oil. Very interesting. Leaving this establishment, stay along the seashore by way of the wooden walkway near the fishing boats. Fishing remains an important economic activity in this region. A commercial area with restaurants and shops invites you to relax. The day's catch is served in the restaurants.

Turn back along the Steveston Highway, this time heading east, and take Route 99 toward the ferry pier for Victoria; take the Ladner exit after the tunnel. Go along this road and follow the signs to the **George C. Reifel Bird Sanctuary ★★ (35)** *(adults $3.25; 5191 Robertson Road, Delta, ☎ 946-6980)*. Each year more than 350 species of birds visit this magical spot in the marshlands at the mouth of the Fraser River.

Parks and Beaches

The Vancouver shoreline is made up in large part of easily accessible sandy beaches. All these beaches lie along English Bay, where it is possible to walk, cycle, play volleyball and, of course, take a dip in the sea to fully enjoy this environment. Stanley Park is fringed by **Third Beach** and **Second Beach**, and then, farther east, along Beach Avenue, by **First Beach** where, on January 1, hundreds of bathers brave the icy water to celebrate the new year. A little farther east, **Sunset Beach** celebrates the day's end with gorgeous sunsets. At the southern edge of English Bay are **Kitsilano Beach**, **Jericho Beach**, **Locarno Beach**, **Spanish Banks Beach**, **Tower Beach** and, finally, **Wreck Beach** at the western edge of the University of British Columbia campus.

Kitsilano Beach is enlivened by beach volleyball tournaments and by an assortment of sports facilities, including a basketball court. Each year, contestants in a motorized bathtub race set out from Nanaimo on Vancouver Island, crossing the Strait of Georgia and ending at Kitsilano Beach. Locarno, Jericho and Spanish Banks beaches are quieter spots for family relaxation where walking and reading are key activities.

Sailing, canoeing and kayaking are practised year-round in the Vancouver area. A kayak excursion can provide a good glimpse of the city as well as offering unusual views. It is preferable to have some practice at this sport before venturing into the water. Kayaks are available from **Ecomarine Ocean Kayak Centre** *(1668 Duranleau Street, Granville Island, ☎ 689-7575)*.

74 Vancouver

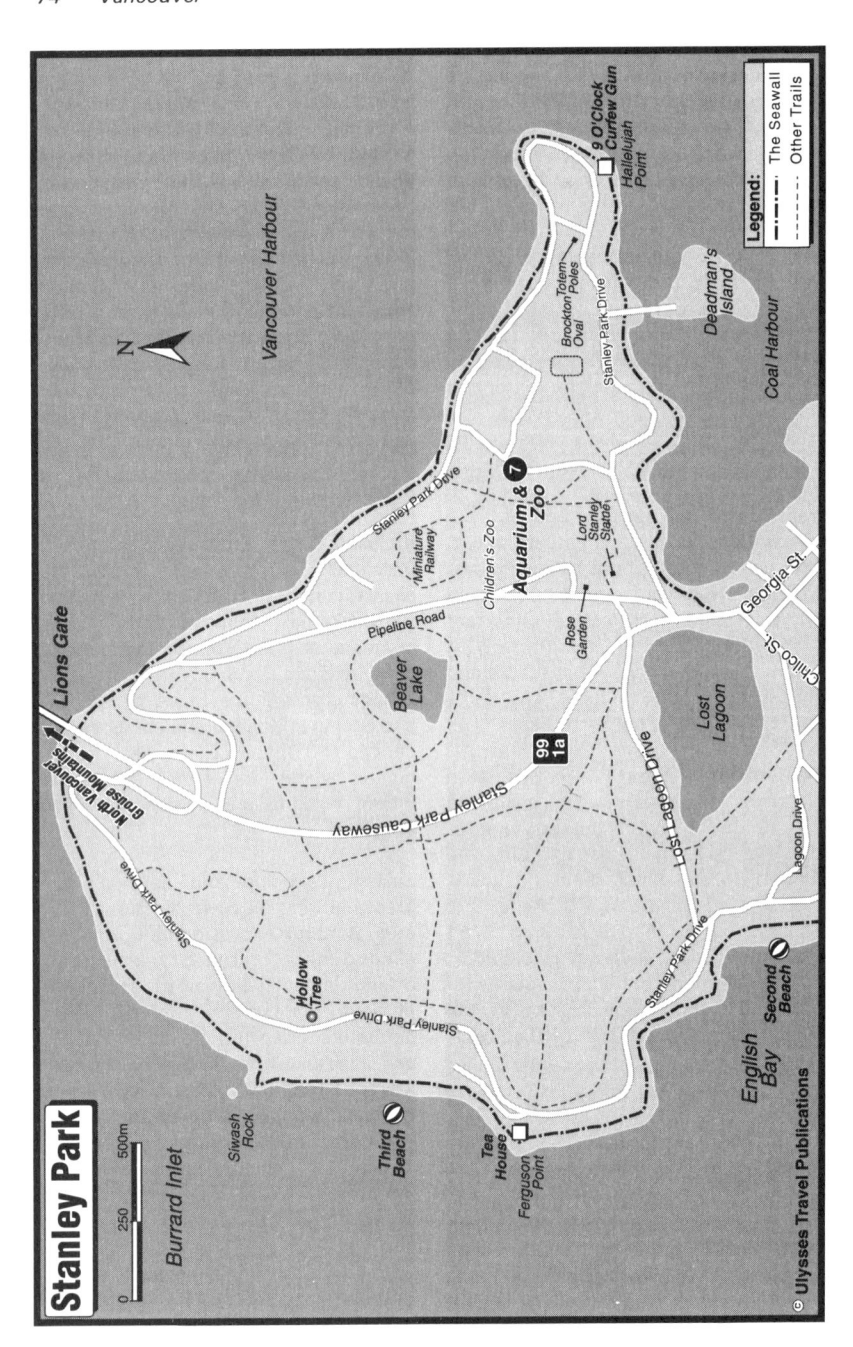

Outdoor Activities

The wide range of outdoor pursuits is endless in Vancouver, whether walking along the beach, hiking in the mountains, or strolling through the city. Believe it or not, you can ski in the morning and end your day sailing in English Bay. Vancouver is a good example of what British Columbia really is: a vast leisure park.

Hiking

Mountain hiking can be done of one of the peaks near the city centre. **Cypress Provincial Park** (☎ *926-5612*), north of the municipality of West Vancouver, has several hiking trails, among them the Howe Sound Crest Trail, which leads to different mountains including The Lions and Mount Brunswick. The views over the west shore of Howe Sound are really quite spectacular. You must wear good shoes and bring food for these hikes. To get to Cypress Park by the Lion's Gate Bridge, follow the signs west along the TransCanada Highway and take the Cypress Bowl Road exit. Take the time to stop at the lookout to contemplate Vancouver, the Strait of Georgia and, on a clear day, Mount Baker in the United States.

To the northeast, **Grouse Mountain** (☎ *984-0661*) is the highest mountain near the city centre; however, **Mount Seymour Provincial Park** (☎ *986-2261*) and **Cypress Bowl Provincial Park** are also good for hiking. The vistas are also quite different: to the east you can see Indian Arm, a large inlet of the sea that reaches into the valley.

Lighthouse Park, in West Vancouver, is well suited to hiking on flatter terrain. From this site, you will be facing the University of British Columbia, the entrance to English Bay, and the Strait of Georgia. Take the Lion's Gate Bridge and follow Marine Drive West, crossing the city of West Vancouver and hugging the seashore until you reach the western edge of English Bay. Turn left at Beacon Lane toward Lighthouse Park.

Cycling

The region has a multitude of trails for mountain biking. Just head to one of the mountains north of the city. A pleasant 8-km ride runs along the Seawall in Stanley Park. Bicycle rentals are available at Stanley Park Rentals *(676 Chilco Street, near Georgia Street,* ☎ *681-5581)*. Outside Vancouver, you can go cycling in the Fraser Valley, near farms or along secondary roads.

Bird-watching

Birders should make a trip to the **George C. Reifel Bird Sanctuary** ★★ *(5191 Robertson Road, Delta,* ☎ *946-6980)* on Westham and Reifel islands (see p 73). Dozens of species of migratory and non-migratory birds draw bird-watching enthusiasts year-round to see aquatic birds, birds of prey, and much more. Farther south, several species can also be observed at Boundary Bay and Mud Bay, as well as on Iona Island closer to Vancouver, next to the airport.

■ Winter sports

Less than a half-hour from Vancouver, three ski resorts welcome snow-lovers from morning to evening. In Cypress Provincial Park (☎ 926-5612), **Hollyburn Ridge** ★ offers 25 km of mechanically maintained trails suitable for all categories of skiers. These trails are frequented day and evening by cross-country skiers. Off-trail skiers can also venture here, as well as at **Grouse Mountain** (☎ 984-0661) and **Mount Seymour Provincial Park** (☎ 986-2261).

Accommodations

Vancouver is a big city with lodgings for all tastes and budgets. All accommodations shown here are well located, within walking distance of bus stops and, in most cases, in or near the downtown area. **Discover British Columbia** (☎ 1-800-663-6000) can make reservations for you.

■ Tour A: Old Vancouver

Canadian Pacific Waterfront Centre Hotel ($120-$295; tv, ≈, parking, ℜ; 900 Canada Place, ☎ 691-1991, ⇄ 691-1999) is a Canadian Pacific luxury hotel located just a few steps from Old Vancouver. It has 489 rooms.

Pan Pacific Hotel Vancouver ($199-$310; tv, ≈, △, parking, ℜ; 300-999 Canada Place, ☎ 662-8111 or 1-800-663-1515, ⇄ 685-8690) is a very luxurious hotel located in Canada Place on the shore of Burrard Inlet facing North Vancouver, with a good view of port activities. During their visit to Vancouver in 1993, Russian President Boris Yeltsin and all his entourage stayed at this hotel. It has 506 rooms.

■ Tour C: The Seawall

Sylvia Hotel ($55-100; pb, tv, ℜ, parking; 1154 Gilford Street, ☎ 681-9321, ⇄ 681-9321 reserved for management). Located just a few steps from English Bay, this charming old hotel, built in the early 1900s, offers unspoiled views and has 118 simple rooms. People come for the atmosphere, but also to eat or for a drink at the end of the day. For those on lower budgets, rooms without views are offered at lower rates. The manager of this ivy-covered hotel is a Frenchman who is fully and justifiably dedicated to his establishment.

Coast Plaza at Stanley Park ($119-210; ≈, △, tv, ℜ, C, ℝ, parking; 1733 Comox Street, ☎ 688-7711 or 1-800-663-1144, ⇄ 688-0885). If you are looking for a big, modern, American-style hotel close to the beach, this 267-room establishment is a good choice. The restaurant serves everything, and the food is good.

■ Tour D: Robson Street and Downtown

Simon Fraser University ($30; sb, C, ℝ, parking, no pets; Room 212, McTaggart-Cowan Hall, Burnaby, ☎ 291-4201, ⇄ 291-5903). This student residence is available from April to October and is located atop a mountain. If you bring a sleeping bag, a room for two costs about $30, saving you about $10. SFU is 20 km east of downtown Vancouver.

YWCA ($48-73; sb or pb, tv, C, ≈, no pets; 733 Beatty Street, ☎ 662-8188 or 1-800-663-1424, ⇄ 681-2550).

This establishment is not restricted to women, and families are welcome. The building in brand new and offers rooms accommodating one to five persons.

Buchan Hotel *($50-85, children under 12 free; no smoking, bicycle and ski racks, tv, sb or pb, no pets; 1906 Haro Street, ☎ 685-5354, ⇌ 685-5367)* is located in the West End residential area near Stanley Park beneath the trees. At the end of Haro Street, on Lagoon Drive, three municipal tennis courts are accessible to guests. Other tennis courts, a golf course and hiking trails can be found near this 61-room, three-story hotel.

West End Guest House Bed & Breakfast *($84-190 bkfst incl.; pb, parking, no pets, ⊗, no smoking, no children under 12; 1362 Haro Street, ☎ 681-2889, ⇌ 688-8812)*. This magnificent inn set in a turn-of-the-century Victorian house is well situated near a park and near Robson Street. Minimum stay is two days. Evan Penner will be your host. Do not hesitate: the West End Guest House has a good reputation. (Nearby, at 1415 Barclay Street, is Roedde House, built in Victorian-Edwardian style in 1893 and designed by none other than the architect Francis Rattenbury, who also created the Vancouver Art Gallery, the legislature building in Victoria, and the Empress Hotel.)

Pacific Palisades Hotel *($175-250; tv, ≈, parking, ℜ, ℝ, ℂ, no pets, ☺; 1277 Robson Street, ☎ 688-0461, ⇌ 688-4374)* is part of the Shangri-La hotel chain. Its two towers, totalling 233 rooms, offer superb views of the sea and the mountains. Rooms facing north on the upper floors provide especially fine mountain views. A big pool and a well equipped gymnasium are available to guests. All services for tourists or business travellers are looked after with professionalism. The staff are friendly and efficient.

Hotel Vancouver *($160-295; ≈, ⊛, △, ℜ, parking; 900 West Georgia Street, ☎ 684-3131 or 1-800-441-1414, ⇌ 662-1929)* belongs to the Canadian Pacific Hotel chain and was built in the 1930s in the *château* style characteristic of Canadian railway hotels, of which the Château Frontenac in Québec City was a precursor. In 1939 it hosted George VI, the first British monarch to visit Canada. You will find tranquillity and luxury in the heart of downtown near Robson Street and Burrard Street. The hotel has 508 rooms.

Sutton Place Hotel *($215-295; ≈, △, ℜ, no pets, ☺; 845 Burrard Street, ☎ 682-5511 or 1-800-543-4300, ⇌ 682-5513)*, formerly the Méridien, offers 397 rooms and the full range of five-star services normally provided by the top hotel chains. The European decor has been maintained. If you are a chocolate lover, don't miss the chocolate buffet served on Friday.

■ **Tour E: West Side**

Vancouver International Hostel *($15-19; dormitories for men and women, sb, cafeteria from Mar to Oct, tv, no smoking; 1515 Discovery Street, ☎ 224-3208, ⇌ 224-4852)*. Situated in Jericho Park, this youth hostel is open day and night; you can take bus number 4 UBC from downtown. Next to Locarno and Jericho beaches, this spot is well suited to travellers on tight budgets.

UBC Housing and Conference Centre *($20-95; sb or pb, ℂ, ℝ, parking, no pets; 5961 Student Union Boulevard,*

☎ 822-1010, ⇄ 822-1001). These campus apartments are available from May to August. Inexpensive and well located, near museums, beaches and hiking trails, this spot also provides tranquillity.

Penny Farthing Inn Bed & Breakfast ($65-155 bkfst incl.; sb or pb, no smoking; 2855 West 6th Avenue, Kitsilano district, ☎ 739-9002, ⇄ 739-9004). Lyn Hairstock receives you warmly in her home built in 1912. Wood and stained glass give the four rooms plenty of charm.

John House Bed & Breakfast ($70-$140 bkfst incl.; sb or pb, no pets, Nov-Feb by request only; 2278 West 34th Avenue, Kerrisdale district, ☎ 266-4175) occupies a magnificent, fully renovated house from the 1920s, with an extra floor added. The owners, Sandy and Ron Johnson, carried out the work; they also acquired several antiques that form part of the decor.

■ **Tour G: South of Vancouver**

Radisson Hotel (145 $; ≈, ℝ, ℜ, ⊛; 8181 Cambie Rd; ☎ 276-8181, ⇄ 279-8381) is located near the airport and offers a high level of comfort. Rooms have coffee-makers and refrigerators, as well as work desks. Decor in the guest rooms, meeting rooms and restaurants is modern and classic, providing a relaxing atmosphere. A physical fitness centre and pool are well appreciated by some, especially during the rainy season. Next to the hotel is a very impressive Chinese supermarket; the hotel is located in Richmond, a suburb with a high percentage of Chinese residents. Upstairs from the supermarket is a Buddhist temple where visitors are received gracefully and can have the various aspects of Buddhism explained to them.

Restaurants

■ **Tour A: Old Vancouver**

Water Street Café ($; closes at 9pm; 300 Water Street, ☎ 689-2832). A handsome bistro with big windows facing Gastown. Tables are decorated with pretty lanterns, and service is friendly. The menu centres around pastas prepared in creative ways.

Top of Vancouver ($$$; Sunday brunch for $21.50; every day 11:30am to 2:30pm and 5pm to 10pm, until 11pm Fri to Sat; 555 West Hastings Street). This restaurant, located atop the Observatory Deck, revolves once an hour, giving diners a city tour from high in the air while they eat. Classic West Coast cuisine is served here.

■ **Tour B: Chinatown and Commercial Drive**

Joe's Cafe ($; 1150 Commercial Drive). This spot is frequented by a regular clientele of intellectuals, Sunday philosophers and feminists, among others. What brings them together, most of all, is Joe's coffee.

Nick's Spaghetti House ($-$$; 631 Commercial Drive, ☎ 254-5633). Copious meals are served on red-and-white-checked tablecloths, amidst landscape paintings of Capri and Sorrento. People are friendly here and patrons enter the restaurant through the kitchen, a reassuring element.

Santos Tapas Restaurant *($$; 1191 Commercial Drive, ☎ 253-0444)*. Latins seem to have a gift for calming the atmosphere with the aromas of their spices and with their music. This is certainly the case here where groups of musicians perform at your table. This restaurant is frequented mostly by Vancouverites.

■ **Tour C: The Seawall**

La Baguette et L'Échalotte *($; 1680 Johnson Street, ☎ 684-1351)*. If you expect to be picnicking during your visit to Granville Island, here is where you will find French bread, pastries, croissants and take-out dishes. Arlène and Mario take good care of this little shop, located in the heart of busy Granville Island.

■ **Tour D: Robson Street and Downtown**

Flying Wedge Pizza Co. *($; 1175 Robson Street, ☎ 681-1233; 1205 Davie Street, West End, ☎ 689-2850; 3499 Cambie Street, ☎ 874-8284; 1937 Cornwall, Kitsilano, ☎ 732-8840)*. Pizza lovers, these are addresses to jot down if you're looking for pizza that doesn't remind you of something you ate last week. Try the classic Beauty and the Beef pizza, with marinated beef, onions, bean sprouts, red bell pepper and cheese: a true delight! You'll get a discount if you bring your own plate, showing that you're ecologically correct.

Ciao Espresso Bar *($; 1074 Denman Street, ☎ 682-0112)*. At a time when governments are talking of prohibiting smoking in restaurants, cafés and bars, this little West End establishment is a veritable smoking room where folks come for the strong, dark brew and a good smoke. Neighbourhood atmosphere.

Starbucks *($; 1099 Robson Street, ☎ 685-1099)*. A green logo proclaims the spot. Capuccino, espresso, big, small, medium, strong, weak, decaf, with milk, cold with chocolate or nutmeg: the choice is yours. Charming terrace. Several other branches of this Seattle-based chain are scattered around Vancouver and surrounding areas.

Bread Garden *($; open 24 hours a day; 821 Bute Street; 1040 Denman Street; 1800 West 1st Avenue; 2996 Granville Street at 14th Avenue)*. Appealing cafeterias with warm decor where everything is excellent, from the coffee to the bread, without forgetting the cheesecake and the salads. These are pleasant spots where you can eat well.

Benny's *($; open 24 hours a day; 2503 West Broadway, and on Hamilton Street, ☎ 738-7151)*. Stunning decor in a Yaletown loft. The furniture seems like something straight out of an artist's imagination: wooden tables with a giant screw as the central leg, chairs formed of a metal leaf with antennas sprouting, agave-shaped lamps, immense wooden tables seating a young but varied clientele. Elaborate lighting brings out the characteristics of this old building, in particular, its enormous wooden columns. Unfortunately, service is slow. Salads, bagels and desserts are served here. Strangely, there is no alcohol, though the place seems like a bar. Your server will find you by shouting your name when your meal is ready.

Da Pasta Bar *($; 1232 Robson Street, ☎ 688-1288)*. This Italian restaurant, located in the most refined part of

Robson Street, offer original items such as pasta with curry. Full lunches for $7.95. Pleasant decor.

India Gate *($; 616 Robson Street, ☎ 684-4617)*. You can get a curry dish for as little as $5.95 at lunchtime. In the evening, this restaurant is rather deserted. The decor is not at all exotic.

Luxy Bistro *($; 1235 Davie Street, ☎ 681-9976)*. The menu of this little black-walled restaurant offers a list of hamburgers garnished with all sorts of ingredients and pasta dishes prepared with just as much imagination. Good quality and reasonable prices. People come for the atmosphere more than anything, especially on weekend evenings.

Kamei Sushi *($-$$; 811 Thurlow Street, ☎ 684-4823; 1414 West Broadway, ☎ 732-0112)*. This chain of Japanese restaurants offers excellent dishes at reasonable prices. Service is efficient and pleasant. A fine Asian experience.

Sakae Japanese Restaurant *($-$$ for lunch; 745 Thurlow Street, ☎ 669-0067)*. It is easy to walk right past this restaurant, situated in the basement of a commercial building, but the welcoming smiles and the quality of the food compensate for its location. The sushi and sashimi will literally melt in your mouth.

Raku *($$; north of Robson, on Thurlow Street)*. A wealthy young Japanese clientele meets here and fits right in. It has the atmosphere of a noisy bar, but it is an ideal spot to begin a promising evening. The sushi and grilled meats are recommended.

Gyoza King *($$; 1508 Robson Street, ☎ 669-8278)*. The items served here range from teriyaki dishes to sashimi and include the chef's specialties such as anchovies marinated in alcohol and mustard. Warm atmosphere.

Le Crocodile *($$$-$$$$; 909 Burrard Street, entry by Smithe Street, ☎ 669-4298)*. This establishment is the beacon of French cuisine in Vancouver, as much for the quality of its food as for its service, its decor and its wine list. Lovers of great French cuisine will be spoiled by the choice of red meats and the delicacies from the sea. The salmon tartare is a must, you *are* on the Pacific coast after all!

■ **Tour E: West Side**

The Naam *($; 2724 West Fourth Avenue, ☎ 738-7151)* blends live music with vegetarian meals. This little restaurant has a warm atmosphere and friendly service. This spot is frequented by a young clientele.

Sophie's Cosmic Cafe *($; 2095 West Fourth Avenue, ☎ 732-6810)*. This is a weekend meeting-spot for the Kitsilano crowd, who come to stuff themselves with bacon and eggs. 1950s decor, relaxed atmosphere.

Raku Kushiyaki Restaurant *($$; 4422 West 10th Avenue, ☎ 222-8188)*. The young chefs of this little restaurant prepare local cuisine served with oriental aesthetic rules in mind; they will help you discover their art. Take a meal for two to appreciate the spirit of this *nouvelle cuisine*, which encourages the sharing of meals among guests. The portions may seem small, but you still come away satiated. Ingredients are chosen according to the seasons, for example wild mushrooms served accented with garlic, green bell peppers, butter, soya sauce and lime juice. This dish may seem simple, and it is, but the taste of the food is not masked by some mediocre sauce. The meats and fish are also treated with subtlety.

Star Anise *($$; brunch for $13.50 Sat and Sun; every day 11:30am to 2:30pm and 5:30pm to 11pm; 1485 West 12th Avenue, ☎ 737-1485)* is a very pretty and stylish restaurant frequented by the beautiful people. Big paintings adorn the yellow walls, and lanterns illuminate the tables.

Alma Street Cafe *($$; 2505 Alma Street, ☎ 222-2244)*. Lovers of jazz trios and of excellent desserts have no hesitation in coming here. Kitsilano's young professionals frequent this spot, which it is a bit expensive.

Located in Kitsilano, **Malinee's Thai Food** *($$-$$$; 2153 West Fourth Avenue, ☎ 737-0097)* presents this oriental cuisine with taste and subtlety. The coconut milk and cashew sauces hold some surprises.

■ **Tour F: The Port of Vancouver and North Vancouver**

Bean Around the World *($; 1522 Marine Drive, West Vancouver, ☎ 925-9600)*. A crowd of rather laid-back people squeezes into this warm, wood-panelled spot. Excellent coffees and sweets are served at reasonable prices.

Imperial *($$; Mon to Fri 11am to 2:30pm and 5pm to 10pm, Sat and Sun and holidays 10:30am to 2:30pm and 5pm to 10pm; 355 Burrard Street, ☎ 688-8191)*. Located in the Marine Building, an art deco architectural masterpiece (see p 68), this Chinese restaurant also has several art deco elements, but it is the big windows looking over Burrard Inlet that are especially fascinating. In this very elegant spot, boys in livery and discreet young ladies perform the *dim sum* ritual. Unlike elsewhere, there are no carts here: the various steamed dishes are brought on trays. You can also ask for a list, allowing you to choose your favourites among the 30 or so on offer. The quality of the food matches the excellent reputation this restaurant has acquired.

Entertainment

ARTS Hotline *(☎ 684-ARTS)* will inform you about all shows (dance, theatre, music, cinema and literature).

The Georgia Straight (1235 West Pender Street, ☎ 681-2000). This weekly paper is published every Thursday and distributed free at many spots in Vancouver. You will find all necessary information on coming shows and cultural events. This paper is read religiously each week by many Vancouverites and has acquired a good reputation.

■ **Tour A: Old Vancouver**

Town Pump Restaurant *(66 Water Street, ☎ 683-6695)*. New alternative-music groups give shows at this Gastown stage. The place is very big, and you can play pool.

■ **Tour D: Robson Street**

Commodore Ballroom *(870 Granville Street, ☎ 681-7838)*. This magnificent theatre has provided a stage for everyone, from pop singers to rockers. Take the time to try a few dance steps on the wooden floor resting on a cushion of tires. Weekend club nights attract a hopping crowd.

Royal Hotel *(1025 Granville Street,* ☎ *685-5335).* A gay crowd throngs to the 1950s decor here with a few '60s and '70s add-ons. Friday evenings are very popular, perhaps because of the live music, often country and western. People wait in line as early as 5:30pm, though Sunday evenings are more worth it.

Yale Hotel *(admission charged; 1300 Granville Street,* ☎ *681-9253).* Vancouver's blues temple. Each week, excellent groups appear before a varied crowd.

Railway Club *(admission charged; 579 Dunsmuir Street,* ☎ *681-1625).* Folk music or blues are presented in an oblong spot that brings to mind a railway car. A miniature electric train runs in a loop above the customers as they enjoy the musicians' performance.

Jazz Hotline *(435 West Hastings Street,* ☎ *682-0706).* Information is provided on jazz shows in Vancouver.

Automotive *(1095 Homer Street,* ☎ *682-0040).* This interesting establishment recalls architectural influences from the 1950s, with stainless steel dominating. A young clientele comes to the Automotive to play pool or to watch sports events on television.

The Denman Station *(860 Denman Street,* ☎ *669-3448).* A neighbourhood bar that draws a gay clientele. Loud, popular music is played and videos are shown. Dancing late in the evening.

The Odyssey *(1251 Howe Street,* ☎ *689-5256).* This big discotheque is very fashionable. It is much enjoyed by the gay community and is frequented by a young clientele.

Celebrities *(1022 Davie Street,* ☎ *689-3180).* This, the biggest discotheque in Vancouver, is visited by a mixed clientele.

Numbers *(1088 Davie Street,* ☎ *685-4077).* This three-story bar, with rustic decor, is exclusively gay and has a clientele in the 25-to-40 age group. Pool tables, dancing.

The **Town Pump** *(66 Water St.,* ☎ *683-6695)* has live bands just about every night presenting everything from rock to jazz and reggae.

Roxy *(932 Granville at the corner of Nelson)* is a perennial favourite for its retro take on everything. Live bands and theme nights are often featured.

$ Shopping

■ **Tour A: Old Vancouver**

Maxwell's Artists' Materials *(206 Cambie Street at Water Street).* As its name indicates, this shop specializes in artists' materials.

■ **Tour B: Chinatown and Commercial Drive**

Rasta Wares *(1505 Commercial Drive, 255-3600).* This shop offers incense and jewellery from India, Indonesia and Africa at low prices.

Highlife Records & Music *(1317 Commercial Drive, 251-6964)*. This is the spot to find new wave and other types of music at good prices.

■ **Tour D: Robson Street**

Duthie's *(919 Robson St., ☎ 684-4496)* is *the* bookstore in Vancouver. With the broadest selection of books in Western Canada and friendly attentive staff, Duthie's has built itself quite a reputation. They recently opened a branch *(☎ 602-0610)* in the impressive new Vancouver Library (see p 65). The move has been a huge success and has left people wondering why no one thought of doing it before!

Little Sisters Book and Art Emporium *(every day 10am to 11pm; 1221 Thurlow Street, ☎ 669-1753 or 1-800-567-1662)*. The only gay bookshop in Western Canada offers gay literature as well as essays on homosexuality, feminism, etc. It is also a vast bazaar, with products that include humorous greeting cards. With the support of several Canadian literary figures, this bookshop has been fighting Canada Customs, which arbitrarily blocks the import of certain publications. Books by recognized and respected authors such as Marcel Proust have been seized by Canada Customs, which has taken on the role of censor. Some of the same titles bound for regular bookshops have mysteriously escaped seizure by Canada Customs, leading to questions about discrimination.

Stéphane de Raucourt Shoes *(1067 Robson Street, 682-2280)*. If you are looking for quality shoes that stand out from the ordinary, here is a spot to keep in mind. They are expensive, but a little window-shopping never hurt anyone.

■ **Tour E: West Side**

Mountain Equipment Co-op *(130 West Broadway, ☎ 872-7858)*. This giant store offers everything you need for your outdoor activities. You must be a member to make purchases; but membership only costs $5.

VICTORIA

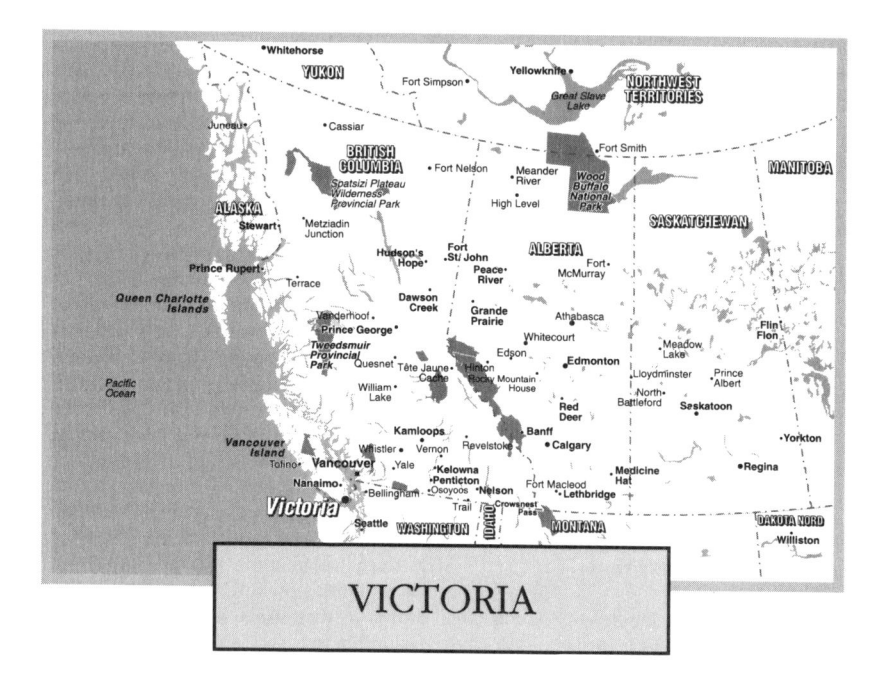

Is Victoria really more English than England, as people often say it is? When immigrants loyal to the British Crown came here to start anew, they remained true to many of their old ways. Victoria thus took on its characteristic English flavour. This is still a North American city, however. In addition to the massive influx of loyalists, it has welcomed large numbers of French Canadians, Chinese, Japanese, Scots, Irish, Germans and Americans.

Located at the southern tip of Vancouver Island, Victoria is the capital of the province and has a population of nearly 300,000 scattered across a large urban area. Its port looks out onto the Strait of Juan de Fuca, which forms a natural border with Washington State. Victoria is set against a series of small mountains no higher than 300 m in altitude, and its waterfront stretches several kilometres.

When Europeans began moving into the region in the mid-19th century, three Amerindian peoples, the Songhees, the Klallam and the Saanich, were already living here. In 1842, the Hudson's Bay Company established a fur trading post near the Victoria Harbour. One year later, aided by the Amerindians, who were given a blanket for every 40 wooden stakes they cut, the company's adventurers built Fort Victoria alongside the seaport.

The fur trade attracted new workers, and with the goldrush of 1858, Victoria developed into a large town, welcoming thousands of miners on their way inland. The city flourished, and its port bustled with activity. In 1862, Victoria was officially incorporated; shortly thereafter, the fort was demolished, making way for real-estate development. The site is now known as Bastion Square, and the former warehouses of the fort have been transformed into commercial space.

For all those years, Victoria was a colony in its own right, just like British Columbia. The two were united in 1866, and it wasn't until a couple of years later that Victoria became the capital of British Columbia. The design of the parliament buildings was chosen by way of a competition. The winner was a 25-year-old architect named Francis Mawson Rattenbury, who left his mark all over the province. One of his most noteworthy projects was the prestigious Empress Hotel.

The downtown area rises up behind the port, whose waters are shared by ships, yachts and ferries. Like a railway station surrounded by fields, the port is the focal point; the squares, hotels, museums and parliament buildings are all located nearby. Stroll along the waterfront in order to appreciate how the city has preserved a human dimension in its squares and streets.

Victoria is the seat of the provincial government. Accordingly, the civil service occupies an important place in the local economy, as does tourism. This former colony's British heritage attracts many visitors in search of traditions like afternoon tea at the Empress Hotel; quite a few people come here to purchase tartans as well.

Like the Europeans and the Amerindians, the Chinese played an important role in the city's development. They came here by the thousands to help build the railroad and settled in the northern part of town. The local Chinatown thus bears the stamp of authenticity, as it bears witness to a not so distant past. Victoria is also the home town of painter Emily Carr, who left her mark on the early 20th century with her scenes of native life on the west coast.

As the capital of a province that is currently establishing itself as an economic powerhouse, Victoria has no intention of letting itself be outranked by the federal capital, Ottawa, when it comes to national politics. British Columbia has enjoyed an economic boom since the 80s, and is no longer satisfied to be viewed merely as part of a Canadian region, but rather as an influential member of the Canadian federation. And this political powerplay is likely to become increasingly more prominent as the international economy shifts toward Asia and places British Columbia in a strategic position.

To help you make the most of your visit to Victoria, we have outlined four tours: **Tour A: The Port and Old Town**; **Tour B: The Victoria of Francis Rattenbury and Emily Carr ★★**; **Tour C: The Waterfront ★** and **Tour D: From Victoria to the West Coast Trail ★★**.

Finding Your Way Around

■ **By Plane**

Victoria International Airport (☎ 363-6600) is located north of Victoria on the Saanich Peninsula, a half-hour's drive from downtown on Highway 17.

Air Canada/Air B.C. Connector (☎ 1-800-663-3721 or 360-9074) offers 16 daily flights between Vancouver and Victoria and 11 daily

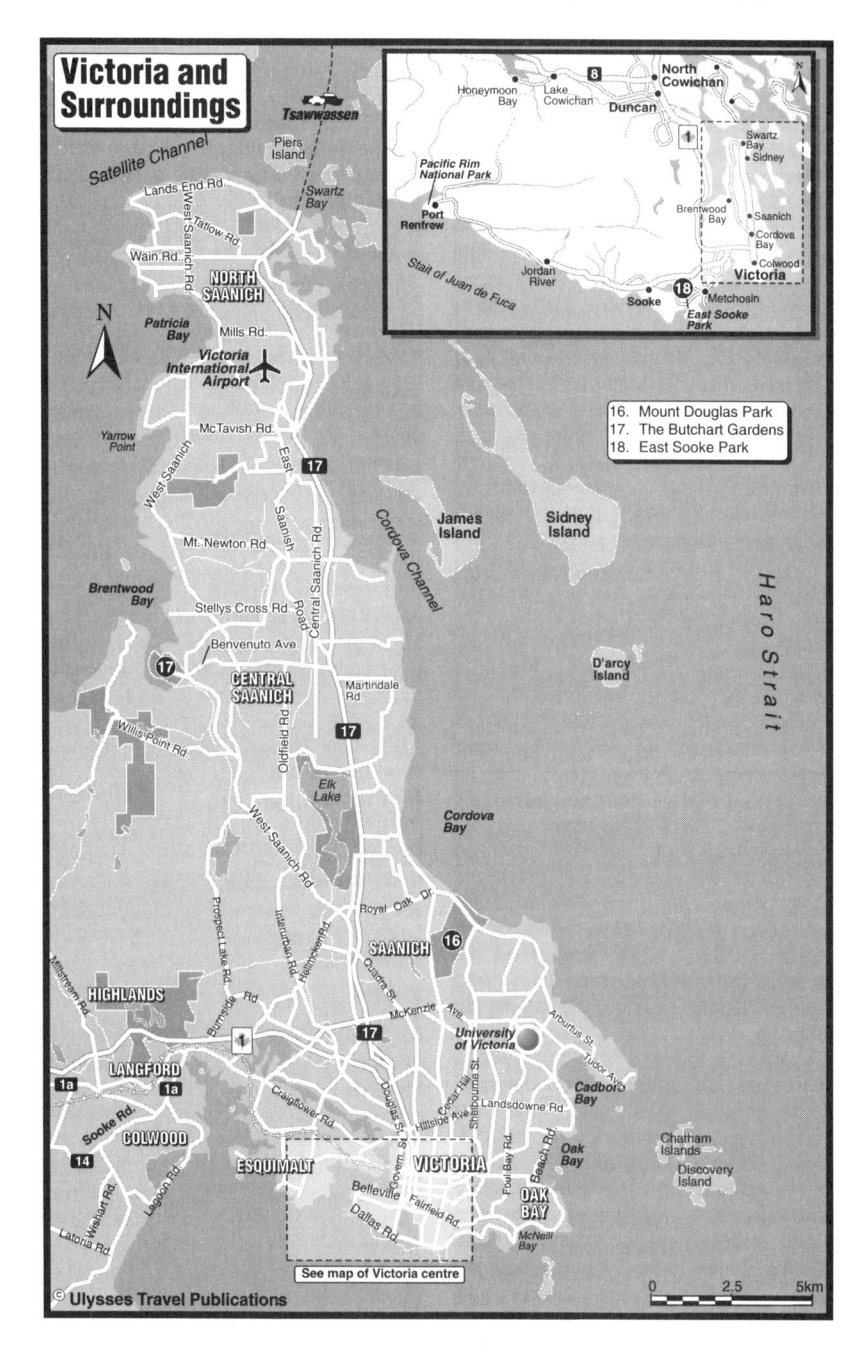

Victoria and Surroundings

16. Mount Douglas Park
17. The Butchart Gardens
18. East Sooke Park

© Ulysses Travel Publications

88 Victoria

seaplane flights between the ports of the two cities.

Canadian Airlines/Canadian Regional *(☎ 1-800-363-7530 or 382-6111)* offers 16 daily flights between Vancouver and Victoria from Monday to Friday, nine on Saturday and eleven on Sunday.

Helijet Airways *(weekdays $250 return, weekends $145 return; Victoria ☎ 382-6222, Vancouver ☎ 273-1414)* has a helicopter that shuttles back and forth between the port of Vancouver and the port of Victoria 22 times a day.

Kenmore Air *(☎ 1-800-543-9595 or Seattle, Washington ☎ 206-486-1257)* uses seaplanes, which fly back and forth between the port of Seattle, in Washington State (U.S.A.), and the port of Victoria eight times a day.

■ By Ferry

You can reach Victoria by car by taking a ferry from Tsawwassen, located south of Vancouver on the coast. This ferry *(BC Ferry Corporation; in the summer, every day on the hour from 7am to 10pm; in the winter, every day every other hour from 7am to 9pm; Victoria ☎ 386-3431, Vancouver ☎ 669-1211)* will drop you off at the Sydney terminal in Swartz Bay. From there, take Highway 17 South to Victoria.

BC Ferry also offers transportation to Victoria from the east coast of Vancouver Island *(Victoria ☎ 386-3431, Vancouver ☎ 669-1211)*. The ferry sets out from the Horseshoe Bay terminal, northwest of Vancouver, and takes passengers to Nanaimo. From there, follow the signs for the TransCanada Highway 1 South, which leads to Victoria, 113 km away.

Visitors setting out from Seattle, Washington can take the seasonal ferry operated by **Victoria Line** *(May to Sep; Victoria ☎ 480-5555, Seattle ☎ 206-625-1880 or 1-800-668-1167)*, which offers a chance to see the inland waters between Seattle and Victoria. Another option is to take the **Victoria Clipper** *(year-round; Victoria ☎ 382-8100, Seattle ☎ 206-448-5000 or 1-800-888-2535)*, a sea ferry for pedestrians only, which takes passengers directly to the port of Victoria.

Car Rentals

If you plan on renting a car, make the necessary arrangements once you arrive in Victoria; this will spare you the expense of bringing the car over on the ferry.

ABC Rent A Car: 2507 Government Street, ☎ 388-3153.
Avis Rent A Car: 843 Douglas Street, ☎ 386-8468.
Budget Rent A Car: 757 Douglas Street, ☎ 388-5525.

■ By Bus

Airporter Service *(☎ 475-2010)* transports passengers between Victoria International Airport and the downtown hotels.

Pacific Coach Lines *(☎ 385-4411 or 1-800-661-1725)* shuttles back and forth between Vancouver and Victoria eight times a day (16 times a day during summer).

■ Public Transportation

You can pick up bus schedules and a map of the public transportation system at the **Travel InfoCentre** *(812 Wharf Street, ☎ 382-2127)*.

Public transportation in the greater Victoria area is provided by **BC Transit** *(☎ 382-6161)*.

■ Taxis

Blue Bird Cabs: ☎ 382-8294 or 1-800-665-7055
Empire Taxi: ☎ 383-8888
Empress Taxi: ☎ 381-2222
Victoria Taxi: ☎ 383-7111
Watertaxi: ☎ 480-0971. This company can take you to different places in the harbour.

? Practical Information

■ **Area Code:** ☎ 604 (the area code will change to ☎ 250 in October 1996)

■ Tourist Offices

For any information regarding Victoria and its surroundings, contact the **Victoria Travel Information Centre** *(every day 9am to nightfall; tickets for guided tours and shows, hotel reservations;* ☎ *1-800-663-3883,* ☎ *382-2127; 812 Wharf Street, V8W 1T3)*.

■ Emergencies

Police
☎ 911

Victoria Police Station
625 Fisgard Street
☎ 384-4111

Victoria General Hospital
35 Helmcken Street
☎ 727-4212

Emergency Dental Service of British Columbia
☎ 911; non-urgent calls ☎ 361-8901

Children's emergencies;
Queen Alexandra Centre for Children's Health
2400 Arbutus Road
☎ 477-1826

Pharmacies:
McGill & Orme
(every day until 8pm; 649 Fort Street, ☎ *384-1195)*;
Shoppers Drug Mart, Yates & Douglas Store *(☎ 381-4321 or 384-0544)*

Roadside assistance:
Competition Towing *(day or night;* ☎ *744-2844)*
Totem Towing *(day or night;* ☎ *475-3211)*

■ Banks

American Express Canada
(1203 Douglas Street, V8W 2E6, ☎ *385-8731 or 1-800-268-9877)*
Bank of Nova Scotia
(702 Yates Street, V8W 2T2, ☎ *388-4441)*
Canadian Imperial Bank of Commerce
(1175 Douglas Street, V8W 2E1, ☎ *356-4211)*
Toronto Dominion Bank
(1080 Douglas Street, V8W 2X4, ☎ *356-4000)*
Royal Bank
(1079 Douglas Street, ☎ *356-4500)*

Currency Exchange

Currencies International *(724 Douglas Street, V8W 3M6, ☎ 384-6631)*
Custom House Currency Exchange *(815 Wharf Street, V8W 1T2, ☎ 389-6001)*
Money Mart *(1720 Douglas Street, V8W 2G7, ☎ 386-3535)*

Post Offices

Canada Post
Station B, 1625 Fort Street,
☎ 595-2552
Station E, 714 Yates Street,
☎ 953-1351 or 1-800-267-1155

★ Exploring

Downtown Victoria is cramped, which can make parking somewhat difficult. There are a number of public lots where you can pay to park your car, including a very inexpensive one on View Street, between Douglas and Blanshard, at the edge of Old Town (on weekdays and holidays, the cost is $1 a day).

Tour A: The Port and Old Town

Any tour of Victoria starts at the port, which was the main point of access into the city for decades. Back in the era of tall ships, the merchant marine operating on the Pacific Ocean used to stop here to pick up goods destined for England. Once the railway reached the coast, however, the merchandise was transported across Canada by train, thus reducing the amount of time required to reach the east side of the continent. From that point on, the merchant marine only provided a sea link to Asia.

Head to the tourist office *(812 Wharf Street, ☎ 382-2127)*, where you can take in a general view of the port and the buildings alongside it, including the **Empress Hotel ★★** (see p 92, 97) and the provincial **Parliament Buildings ★** (see p 92). Start your tour by strolling northward along Government Street. You'll pass a series of stone buildings housing bookstores, cafes, antique shops and all sorts of other businesses. At View Street, turn left and walk down the little pedestrian street to **Bastion Square ★ (1)**.

Bastion Square marks the former site of Fort Victoria, constructed by the Hudson's Bay Company in 1843, with the help of hundreds of Amerindians. Twenty years later, the fort was demolished to make way for the city. Today, the site is occupied by public buildings like the **Maritime Museum of British Columbia (2)** *(every day 9:30am to 4:30pm; 28 Bastion Square, ☎ 385-4222)*, which highlights great moments in the history of sailing, from the days when tall ships sidled up alongside one another in the harbour, up until the present time.

Walk down Bastion Square, turn right on Wharf Street, then head up the north side of Johnson Street. Go into **Market Square ★ (3)**, which is surrounded by shops facing onto the street. This place gets very lively during the jazz, blues and theatre festivals and on the Chinese New Year.

You'll soon find yourself in **Chinatown ★ (4)** *(west of Government Street, between Fisgard and Cormorant or Pandora)*, with its brightly coloured shops and its sidewalks decorated with

Exploring 91

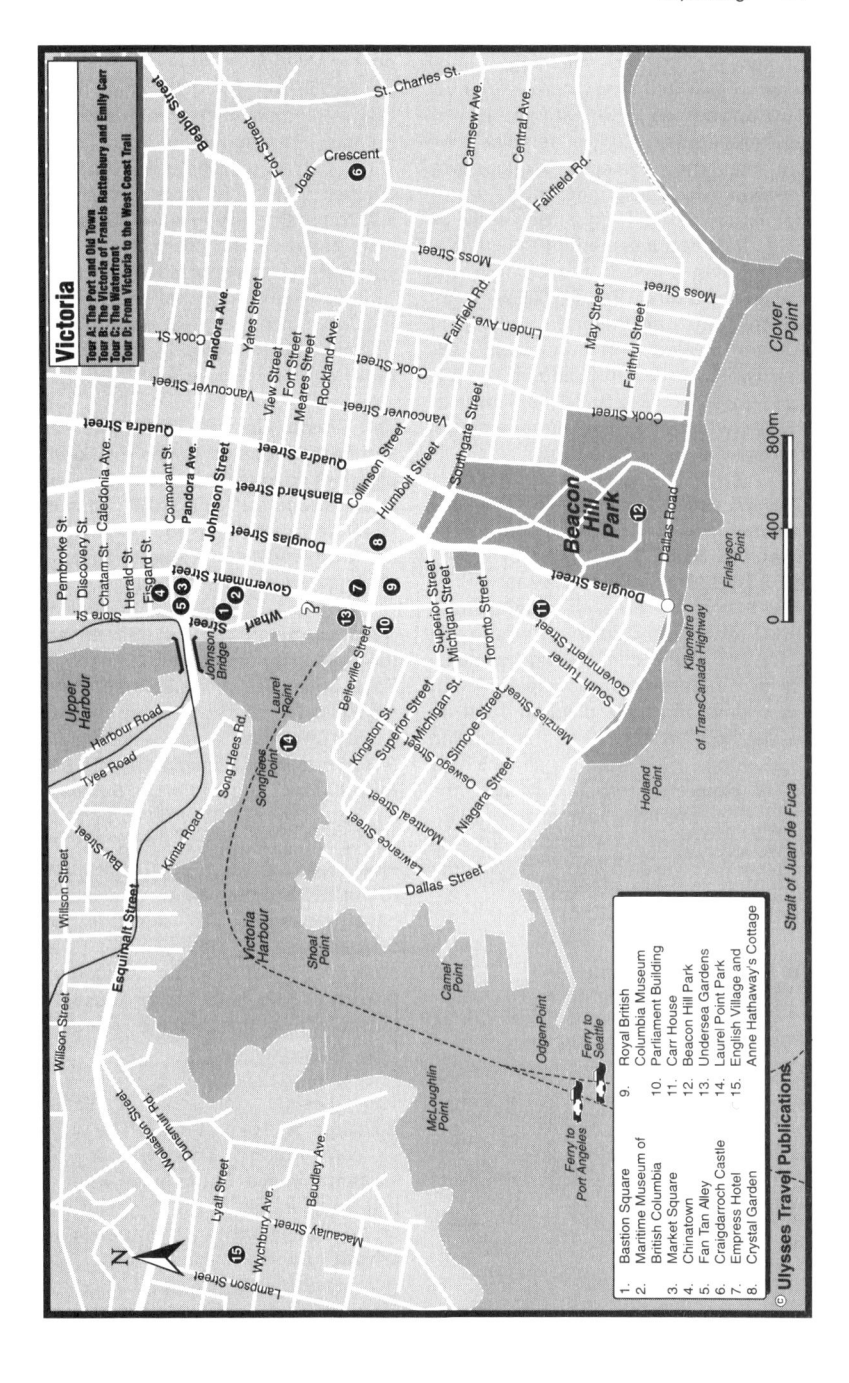

Victoria

Tour A: The Port and Old Town
Tour B: The Victoria of Francis Rattenbury and Emily Carr
Tour C: The Waterfront
Tour D: From Victoria to the West Coast Trail

1. Bastion Square
2. Maritime Museum of British Columbia
3. Market Square
4. Chinatown
5. Fan Tan Alley
6. Craigdarroch Castle
7. Empress Hotel
8. Crystal Garden
9. Royal British Columbia Museum
10. Parliament Building
11. Carr House
12. Beacon Hill Park
13. Undersea Gardens
14. Laurel Point Park
15. English Village and Anne Hathaway's Cottage

© Ulysses Travel Publications

geometric patterns, which form a Chinese character meaning "good fortune". At one time, there were over 150 businesses in Chinatown, as well as three schools, five temples two churches and a hospital. On your way through this neighbourhood, you'll come across the Tong Ji Men arch, on Fisgard Street, a symbol of the spirit of cooperation between the Chinese and Canadian cultures. **Fan Tan Alley** ★ **(5)**, which runs north-south *(south of Fisgard Street)*, is supposedly the narrowest street in Victoria. People used to come here to buy opium until 1908, when the federal government banned the sale of the drug.

Craigdarroch Castle ★ **(6)** *(in the summer, 9am to 7:30pm; in the winter, 10am to 5pm; 1050 Joan Crescent, ☎ 592-5323)* stands at the east end of the downtown area. It was built in 1890 for Robert Dunsmuir, who made a fortune in the coal mining business. He died before it was completed, but his widow and three children went on to live here. What makes this building interesting, aside from its dimensions, is its decorative woodwork and the view from the fifth floor of the tower. This residence is indicative of the opulent lifestyle enjoyed by the wealthy around the turn of the century.

■ **Tour B: The Victoria of Francis Rattenbury and Emily Carr** ★★

Architect Francis Rattenbury and painter Emily Carr both left their mark on Victoria. Rattenbury designed the buildings that now symbolize the city, while Emily Carr immortalized the wilds of British Columbia.

The **Empress Hotel** ★★ **(7)** *(behind the port of Victoria, ☎ 384-8111)* was built in 1905 for the Canadian Pacific railway company. It was designed by Francis Rattenbury in the Chateau style, just like the Chateau Frontenac in Québec City, only more modern and less romantic. As you enter through the main entrance and cross the lobby let yourself be transported back to the 1920s, when influential people found their way into the guest books. Above all, make sure to stop by the Empress for afternoon tea (see p 98).

The **Crystal Garden (8)**, by the same architect, is located behind the hotel. A big glass canopy supported by a visible metal structure, it originally housed a saltwater swimming pool and is now home to a variety of exotic birds and endangered animals.

Head south on Douglas Street, then turn right on Belleville to reach the **Royal British Columbia Museum** ★★ **(9)** *(adult $5.35, children $2.14; every day except Christmas and New Year's Day, 9:30am to 7pm during summer, 10am to 5:30pm during winter; 675 Belleville Street, ☎ 1-800-661-5411 or 387-3701, message ☎ 387-3014)*, where you can learn about the history of the city and the various peoples who have inhabited the province. The centrepieces of the collection are a reproduction of Captain Vancouver's ship and a Kwa-gulth Indian house. The museum also hosts some interesting temporary exhibitions.

The design for the **Parliament Buildings** ★ **(10)** was chosen by way of a competition. The winner was architect Francis Rattenbury, who was just 25 years old at the time and went on to design many other public and privately owned buildings.

Take Government Street south to Simcoe Street, and you will find yourself in the Carr family's neighbourhood. Built of wood, the **Carr House** ★ **(11)** *(mid-May to mid-Oct, every day 10am to 5pm; 207 Government Street, ☎ 383-5843 or 387-4697)* was erected in 1864 for the family of Richard Carr. After the American gold rush, the Carrs, who had been living in California, returned to England then came back to North America to set up residence in Victoria. Mr. Carr made a fortune in real estate and owned many pieces of land, both developed and undeveloped, in this residential area. He died in 1888, having outlived his wife by two years. Emily was only 17 at the time. Shortly after, she went first to San Francisco, then London and finally Paris to study art. She returned to British Columbia around 1910 and began teaching art to the children of Vancouver. She eventually went back to Victoria and followed in her father's footsteps, entering the real-estate business. She also began travelling more along the coast in order to paint, producing her greatest works in the 1930s. A unique painter and a reclusive woman, Emily Carr is now recognized across Canada as a great artist who left her stamp on the art world. Be sure to visit the Vancouver Art Gallery (see p 65) to learn more about her art, since the main focus here is her private life. Carr House also distributes maps of the neighbourhood, which show where the family lived at various times.

One of these places was **Beacon Hill Park** ★ **(12)** *(between Douglas and Cook Streets, facing the Juan de Fuca Strait)*, a haven of peace where Emily Carr spent many happy days drawing. A public park laid out in 1890, it features a number of trails leading through fields of wildflowers and landscaped sections. The view of the strait and the Olympic Mountains in the United States is positively magnificent from here. For a reminder of exactly where you are in relation to the rest of Canada, kilometre 0 of the TransCanada Highway lies at the south end of Douglas Street.

■ **Tour C: The Waterfront** ★

Pedestrians and motorists alike will enjoy the marvellous panoramic views around Victoria. Start off your stroll along the waterfront at the tourist office *(812 Wharf Street)*. Walk down to the piers to watch the street performers showing off their abilities. Farther along, near the Parliament Buildings, the **Pacific Undersea Gardens (13)** *(490 Belleville Street, ☎ 382-5717)* highlight marine plant-life. A little farther still lies **Laurel Point Park (14)**.

From the tourist office, head north on Wharf Street. Cross the Johnson Street Bridge, whose projecting seawall runs alongside the houses and the waterfront, offering a lovely general view of the buildings downtown. Farther along, past the Victoria Harbour, you will see the Strait of Juan de Fuca. Stop in at Spinnakers Pub and wet your whistle while taking in the panoramic view.

English Village and **Anne Hathaway's Cottage** ★ **(15)** *(entrance fee; every day 9am to 8pm during summer, 10am to 4pm during winter; 429 Lampson Street, ☎ 388-4353)* lie west of downtown Victoria. Cross the Johnson Street Bridge, and after the sixth traffic light, turn left on Lampson Street. The Munro Bus, which you can catch at the corner of Douglas and Yates Streets, stops at the entrance. This little bit of

England is a reconstruction of the birthplace of William Shakespeare and the home of Anne Hathaway, his wife. A stroll among these buildings will take you back in time. Try to make it for afternoon tea at the Old England Inn.

Back downtown, drive south on Douglas Street and turn right on Dallas Road, which follows the shore. This road runs through a number of residential neighbourhoods, offering some lovely views along the way. You'll pass alongside Oak Bay and Cadboro Bay, which are lined with Tudor style buildings and lush, well-tended vegetation. Take Tudor Avenue past Cadboro Bay and turn left on Arbutus Street, which leads to **Mount Douglas Park** ★★ **(16)**. At the entrance to the park, turn left on Cedar Hill Road, then right in order to reach the lookout, which offers a 360° view of the gulf islands, the Straits of Georgia and Juan de Fuca and the snow-capped peaks along the Canadian and American coast. The colours of the sea and the mountains are most vibrant early in the morning and at the end of the day.

Upon leaving Mount Douglas Park, turn left and follow the shoreline to Highway 17 North. The **Butchart Gardens** ★★ **(17)** *(entrance fee; every day 9am; Highway 17 North, 800 Benvenuto Avenue,* ☎ *652-4422)*, which cover 26 ha, were founded by the family of the same name in 1904. A wide array of flowers, shrubs and trees flourish in this unique space. Maps are available at the entrance. Fireworks light up the sky during July and August, and outdoor concerts are held here in the evening from June to September *(Mon to Sat)*.

■ **Tour D: From Victoria to the West Coast Trail** ★★

Head north on Government Street, which turns into Highway 1A (Old Island Highway) and follow the signs for Sooke. At Colwood, take Highway 14, which becomes Sooke Road near Port Renfrew. You'll pass through the suburbs west of town when you get to Sooke, which lies about 30 kilometres from Victoria. At the **17 Mile House** restaurant, turn left onto Gillespie Road. This will take you into **East Sooke Park** ★ **(18)**, where hiking trails lead through the wild vegetation by the sea. This is a perfect place for a family outing.

Head back to the 14, and turn left toward Port Renfrew. The highway runs alongside beaches and bays. The farther you get from Victoria, the more twists and turns there are in the road. The terrain is mountainous, and the views are spectacular. As you continue west on the 14, you'll notice a change in the landscape; forestry is still an important source of revenue for the province, and the large valleys in this region have been clear-cut.

Port Renfrew

Port Renfrew is a stopover point for people heading for the **West Coast Trail** ★★★. This 77 km trek is geared towards experienced, intrepid hikers prepared to face unstable weather conditions and widely varied terrain; in fact, it is considered one of the most difficult hiking trails in North America. You'll find more information about the West Coast Trail, which is part of Pacific Rim National Park, in the "Parks and Beaches" section of this chapter.

Parks and Beaches

Victoria is surrounded by a host of parks and beaches, which vary greatly from one to the next (city beaches, deserted beaches running alongside temperate rain forests, etc.). The west coast boasts numerous provincial parks, which all feature sandy beaches strewn with piles of driftwood. These parks offer nature lovers a breath of fresh air. Magnificent Pacific Rim National Park is located here as well, along the western shore of Vancouver Island.

■ **Tour C: The Waterfront**

There are two beaches in Victoria where families can enjoy a day of sandcastle building and swimming in calm waters. **Willows Beach** ★ *(public bathrooms, playground; in Oak Bay, at the corner of Estevan Street and Beach Drive)* lies alongside a chic residential neighbourhood near a marina and the Oak Bay Beach Hotel. **Cadboro Bay Beach** ★ *(public bathrooms, playground; at the corner of Sinclair Road and Beach Drive)*, a little farther east, is located in the University of Victoria neighbourhood and attracts a young crowd. It looks out onto a bay, with the Chatham Islands and Discovery Island in the distance. The ebb and flow of the tides has transformed the strand at **Beacon Hill Park** ★ into a pebble beach covered with pieces of driftwood.

■ **Tour D: From Victoria to the West Coast Trail**

On Highway 14, after Sooke, the waterfront is studded with beaches. **French Beach** ★, a stretch of pebbles and sand lined with logs, has picnicking facilities. It is also wheelchair accessible. A little farther west, still on the 14, lies **China Beach** ★★; to get there, you have to take a well laid-out trail down to the base of a cliff (about 15 min). The beach is absolutely magnificent. It is not uncommon to spot a seal, a sea otter or even a grey whale or a killer whale swimming offshore. Just walk a few minutes in either direction to find yourself alone in a little bay. Surfers come here for the waves. **Botanical Beach** ★★★, after Port Renfrew, is a veritable paradise for anyone interested in marine life. When the sea recedes, fish, starfish and various species of marine plant-life are left behind in little pools of water among the pebbles; if you take a walk here at low tide, you'll discover all sorts of little treasures. To make the most of your visit to the beach, however, pick up a map of the tides from **Maps B.C.** *(Canadian Tide and Current Tables; 1802 Douglas Street, Victoria, V8V 1X4,* ☎ *387-1441).*

Pacific Rim National Park *(Port Renfrew)* is a marvellous green space along the ocean front. It is divided into three sections: Long Beach, the Broken Group Islands and the West Coast Trail (see below).

Outdoor Activities

Hiking

The **West Coast Trail** ★★★ *($60 access fee; May to Sep; Pacific Rim National Park reserve; P.O. Box 280 Ucluelet, B.C., V0R 3A0)* is a 77 km hiking trail, which was cleared at the turn of the century to enable victims of shipwrecks to reach civilization, which is far removed from this harsh region on the west side of Vancouver Island. In order to protect the temperate rain forest here, the West Coast Trail has been set aside as a provincial nature reserve. The trail, which is also part of Pacific Rim National Park, is only used by hikers nowadays. In the past, Amerindians, lighthouse keepers, victims of shipwrecks and mining prospectors had to follow the shoreline and brave the wilderness to make it to civilization. Today, nature lovers come here to put their hiking skills to the test. Parks Canada has set up a reservation system called **Discover BC** *($25 for a guaranteed departure date; March every day 6am to 6pm; Vancouver* ☎ *663-6000, Canada and USA* ☎ *1-800-663-6000, elsewhere in the world* ☎ *387-1642)*, which administers the trail and monitors the number of people hiking along the coast. Groups can be no larger than ten people, and are issued a permit, which must be put in a visible place on the leader's backpack. Hikers should be experienced and equipped for rainy weather. It is strongly recommended to bring along a portable gas stove and a first-aid kit. Equally important is a good pair of hiking boots; you don't want to be wearing ill-fitting footgear on this type of expedition, when you are completely on your own. Food and water will take up a lot of space in your backpack. Anyone who dreams of hiking across this vast region abounding in plant and animal life, must prepare adequately beforehand in order to make the most of the trip once you hit the trail.

Fishing

Tour D: From Victoria to the West Coast Trail

Salmon is the big attraction here. You can catch this fish at any time of the year in the Georgia Strait. Salmon reach their maximum weight and are ready to spawn at the end of summer. At this anglers should cast their lines where rivers flow together, a favourite hang-out for the big ones. The **Sooke Charter Boat Association** *(Sooke,* ☎ *642-7783)* organizes fishing trips on the ocean and offers a hotel reservation service. The Sooke region is bounded by bays and coves where the rivers empty into the sea.

Sea Kayaking

Tour C: The Waterfront

Sea kayaking is an interesting way to take in some lovely views of Victoria. **Ocean River Sports** *(1437 Store Street,* ☎ *381-4233)* arranges personalized excursions.

Accommodations

■ **Tour A: The Port and Old Town**

The **Victoria Hostel** *($19.28; sb, C, laundry room; 516 Yates Street,* ☎ *385-4511,* ⇄ *385-3232)*, a stone and brick building with 108 beds, is located in Old Town, right near the

---

Right: Vancouver... between sea and sky (Pierre Longnus)
Totem pole: the incarnation of native culture (Pierre Longnus)

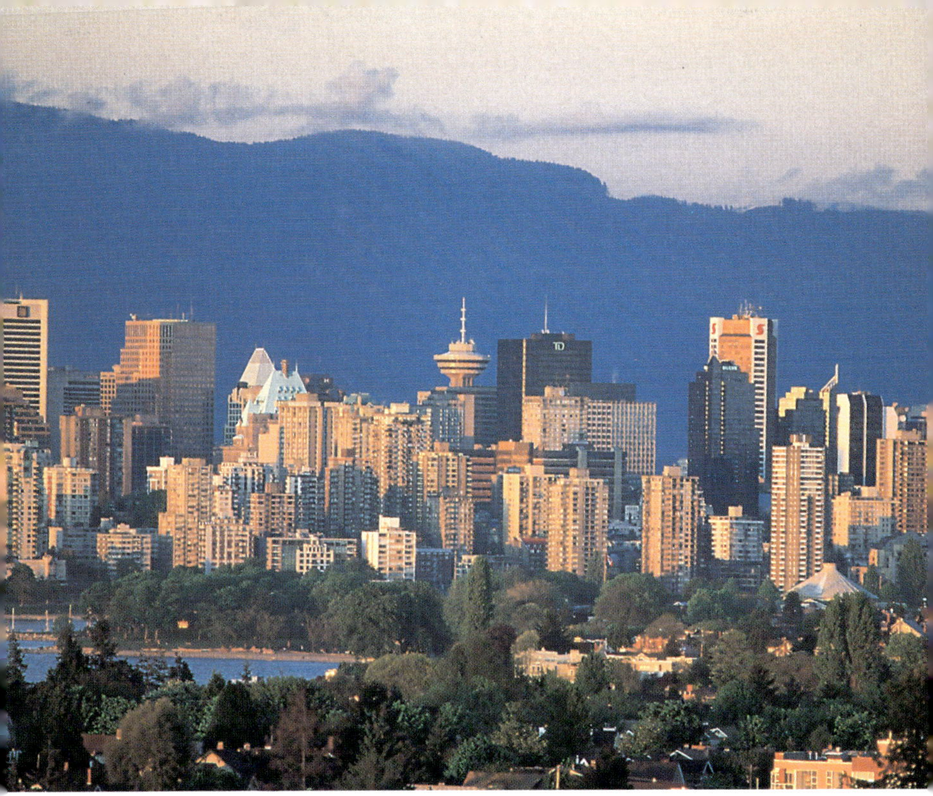

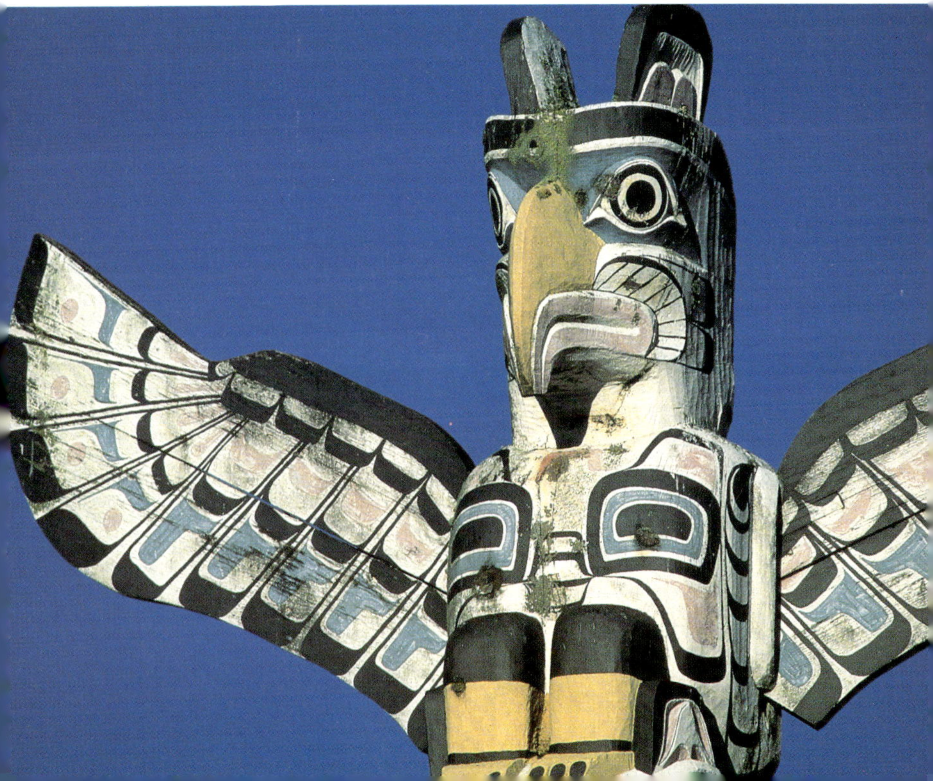

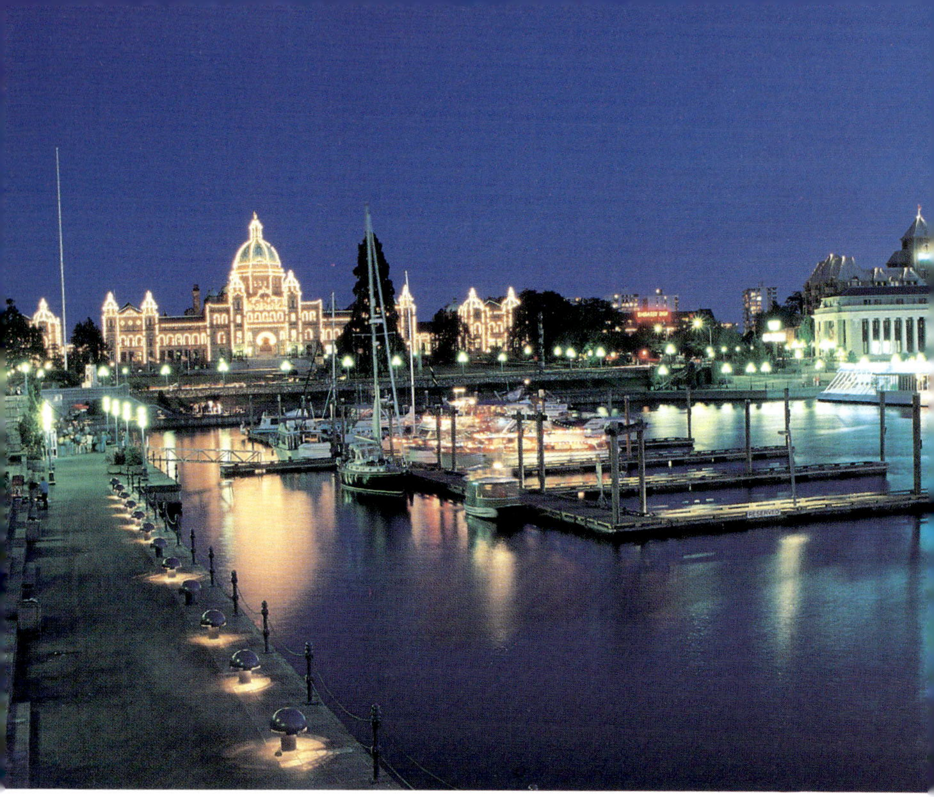

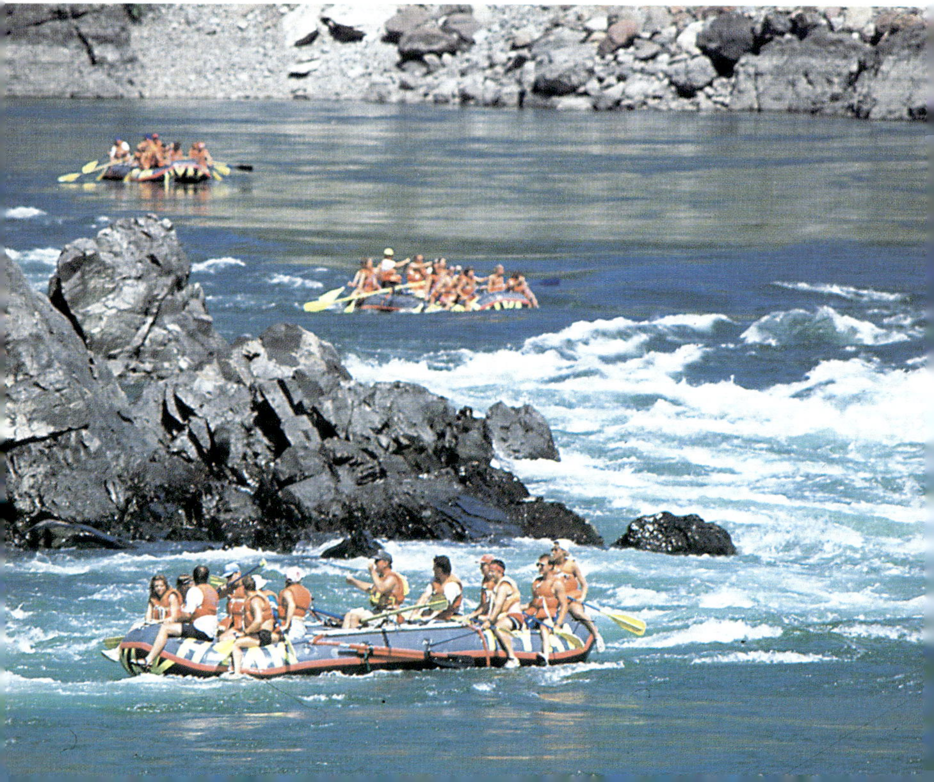

harbour. Members take precedence in youth hostels, so it can be difficult for non-members to get a bed, especially during the high season.

The **Swans Hotel** *($99-155; C, pb, tv, pub, no pets; 506 Pandora Avenue,* ☎ *361-3310 or 1-800-668-7926,* ⇄ *361-3491),* which occupies a historic building in the heart of Old Town, attracts a young, relaxed clientele. It has 29 comfortable, simply decorated rooms. A microbrewery is also located on the premises.

■ **Tour B: The Victoria
of Francis Rattenbury and Emily Carr**

The **James Bay Inn** *($72-109; sb or pb, pub,* ℜ*, no pets; 270 Government Street,* ☎ *384-7151,* ⇄ *385-2311),* a small hotel with 48 rooms, lies a few minutes' walk from the Parliament Buildings and Beacon Hill Park. It was once a retirement home called St. Mary's Priory; painter Emily Carr spent the last part of her life here. The rooms are simply furnished with a bed, a television and a small desk.

The **Empress Hotel Canadian Pacific** *($220-300;* ≈*,* ⊛*,* ◎*,* △*, tv,* ℜ*; 721 Government Street,* ☎ *384-8111 or 1-800-441-1414,* ⇄ *384-4334)* is located on the Inner Harbour, adjacent to the museums and the interesting public and commercial areas. Designed by architect Francis Rattenbury, this luxurious 483-room hotel offers a relaxing atmosphere and a Chateau style setting. A new wing has been added to the original quintessentially Victorian building without detracting from its legendary charm. Visitors stop here for tea or simply to admire the ivy-covered façade.

■ **Tour C: The Waterfront**

UVic Housing and Conference Services *($45 bkfst incl.; May 1 to Aug 31; sb, C, no pets; Sinclair and Finnerty Road,* ☎ *721-8396)* is located on the University of Victoria campus. During the summer months, 999 rooms are open to visitors. A number of these were built for the 1994 Commonwealth Games. The rates are based on triple occupancy, but single rooms are also available. The campus lies east of the downtown area on a hill, right near the Cadboro Bay Beach.

The **Oak Bay Beach Hotel** *($92-182; pb, tv, pub, no pets; 1175 Beach Drive,* ☎ *598-4556 or 1-800-668-7758,* ⇄ *598-4556),* which has 50 comfortably laid-out rooms, caters to visitors seeking English charm and a pleasant seaside atmosphere. Located on the waterfront in a residential neighbourhood, it offers an interesting view.

■ **Tour D: From Victoria
to the West Coast Trail**

The **Port Renfrew Hotel** *($25; ss, sink; at the end of Highway 14, Port Renfrew,* ☎ *647-5541)* is located on the village pier, where hikers set out for the West Coast Trail. The rustic rooms are sure to please hikers longing for a dry place to sleep. There are laundry facilities on the premises, as

---
*Left: Victoria, more English than England? (Pierre Longnus)
Rafting trip on the Thompson River (Pierre Longnus)*

well as a pub that serves hot meals (see p 99).

The soberly decorated **Traveller's Inn on Douglas Street** *($29-49 bkfst incl.; C, tv, parking, no pets; 710 Queens Avenue, ☎ 388-6641)* is a renovated building with 34 rooms. Basic services are available, but there are no telephones in the rooms.

You can enjoy a quiet, comfortable stay at the **Arundel Manor Bed & Breakfast** *($95-110 bkfst incl; pb, no smoking, no pets; 980 Arundel Drive, Victoria, ☎ 385-5442)*, a charming house built in 1912. Its three rooms are tastefully decorated, and on the side facing the water, the view is that much more striking. To get there, head north on Highway 1.

Mr. and Mrs. Philip will give you a warm welcome at the **Sooke Harbour House** *($225-295 bkfst and lunch incl.; newspapers, bathrobes, no smoking; 1528 Whiffen Spit Road, R.R. 4, Sooke, V0S 1N0, ☎ 642-3421, ⇄ 642-6988)*, their dream home. You might be taken aback when you first see the prices, but rest assured that staying here will make your trip to Vancouver Island a memorable one. The 13 rooms are all equipped with a fireplace and decorated with antiques and works of art. You will be served breakfast in your room and lunch in the dining room (see p 99).

Restaurants

■ **Tour A: The Port and Old Town**

The spacious **Java Coffeehouse** *($; every day 10am to 1pm; 537 Johnson Street, ☎ 381-2326)* has brick walls and high ceilings with exposed beams. It attracts both the young and the not so young, and has an established clientele. The coffee is excellent, the desserts (cheesecake, carrot cake, etc.) are tasty, and the lighting and paintings create a pleasant, relaxing atmosphere.

The sunny terrace at **Garrick's Head Pub** *($; Bastion Square, on View Street)*, located on a pedestrian street, is a pleasant place to get together over a local beer. The space may be limited inside, but there is a giant-screen TV for sports fans.

Il Terrazzo Ristorante *($$-$$$; 555 Johnson Street, ☎ 361-0028)* is an Italian restaurant with a menu made up mainly of pasta dishes. Creamy sauces flavoured with spices and sweet nuts make for some very interesting taste sensations. The clientele consists of young professionals and tourists. The one sour note is that the wine is kept on a mezzanine where all the heat in the room is concentrated, and is thus served at too warm a temperature.

■ **Tour B: The Victoria of Francis Rattenbury and Emily Carr**

Tea-lovers get together in the **Empress Hotel Canadian Pacific** *($-$$; behind the port, 721 Government Street, ☎ 384-8111)* for tea with scones and crumpets served with different kinds of jelly. If you've got a big appetite, stop in for High Tea, which comes complete with cucumber and cream cheese sandwiches. This tradition supposedly originated during the reign of Queen Victoria, when the Duchess of Bedford, who tended to feel faint in the late afternoon, began fortifying herself with tea and little cakes and sandwiches. The old wood floors, comfortable furniture, giant teapots and courteous service make for an altogether satisfying experience.

Recapturing the atmosphere of the British Empire of Queen Victoria, the beautiful Empress Hotel's **Bengal Lounge** *($; 721 Government Street, Victoria, ☎ 384-8111)* serves a curry buffet featuring Indian specialties. The place is tastefully decorated with Eastern furniture, and guests have lots of elbow room.

■ **Tour C: The Waterfront**

The Oak Bay Beach Hotel's pub, the **Snug** *($; 1175 Beach Drive, ☎ 598-4556)*, serves local beer and light meals. A quiet, well-kept place, it attracts a rather mature clientele.

Spinnakers Brew Pub & Restaurant *($; every day from 7am on; 308 Catherine Street, ☎ 386-2739)* serves beer and food in a laid-back setting, with the house specialties listed on big blackboards. The terrace is very well positioned, beckoning guests to kick back and relax. This place radiates a festive, convivial atmosphere.

■ **Tour D: From Victoria to the West Coast Trail**

The **Trail Cafe** *($; every day; Port Renfrew, ☎ 647-5591)*, in Port Renfrew Hotel, serves breakfast, lunch and dinner. Stop in and listen to the hikers talking about their experiences on the West Coast Trail; you might pick up some advice and ideas.

The **Old England Inn** *($; every day; 429 Lampson Street, Victoria, ☎ 388-4353)*, a restaurant adjoining the hotel of the same name, is a Tudor style building furnished with antiques. It serves tea, complete with scones, crumpets and an assortment of jellies. If you're looking for something more substantial, come for High Tea, which also includes cucumber and cream cheese sandwiches. Sit near the window facing the garden, so that you can enjoy the view of English Village; you'll think you're in England.

The **17 Mile House** *($; 5126 Sooke Road, Sooke, ☎ 642-5942)*, located right before the entrance of Sooke Harbour Park, serves light meals in a cozy setting. The thoroughly laid-back atmosphere here makes this just the place to quench your thirst after a day of walking along the waterfront in Sooke.

The **Sooke Harbour House** *($$$-$$$$; every day; 1528 Whiffen Spit Road, Sooke, ☎ 642-3421)* has been praised to the skies by people from all over the world. The Philips' gourmet cuisine has seduced thousands of palates. They settle for nothing but the best and are past masters when it comes to preparing local produce. The dining room, set up inside a country house, offers a view of Sooke Harbour. After taking your seat and looking over the menu, you will soon be swept away by the mood of the place. The dishes, prepared in the West Coast Style, reveal Japanese and French influences. See "Accommodations", p 98.

Entertainment

The **Victoria Jazz Society** *(☎ 388-4423, ⇄ 388-4407)* can provide you with information on local jazz and blues shows. The Victoria Jazz

Festival takes place from late June to mid-July.

The **Sticky Wicket Pub** *(cover charge; 919 Douglas Street, ☎ 383-7137)* is located inside the Strathcona Hotel, just behind the Empress. This place attracts people of all ages and serves good beer. In nice weather, everyone heads up to the roof for some fun in the sun and a game of volleyball.

Merlin's *(cover charge; 107-1208 Wharf Street, ☎ 381-2331)* attracts a fairly stylish crowd. People come here to party and kick up their heels on the dance floor.

Shopping

■ **Tour A: The Port and Old Town**

It is worth stopping in at **Rogers' Chocolates** *(913 Government Street, ☎ 384-7021)* to see the shop's lovely early 20th century decor and pair of Art Nouveau lamps from Italy. Victoria Creams, available in a wide variety of flavours, are the specialty of the house.

Whether you're looking for something to read in the afternoons or simply for a pleasant place to visit, head over to **Munro's Books** *(1108 Government Street, ☎ 382-2464)*, which has been set up inside an historic building. The coffered ceilings and frescoes are particularly interesting.

The **Scottish House of Tartans Ltd.** *(706 Douglas Street, ☎ 384-1322)* imports tablecloths, scarves, tea towels, sheets and clothing representative of traditional British dress.

Knives and Darts *(1306 Government Street, ☎ 383-2422)* sells an assortment of, well, knives and darts. Darts is very popular in the local pubs, and is taken quite seriously.

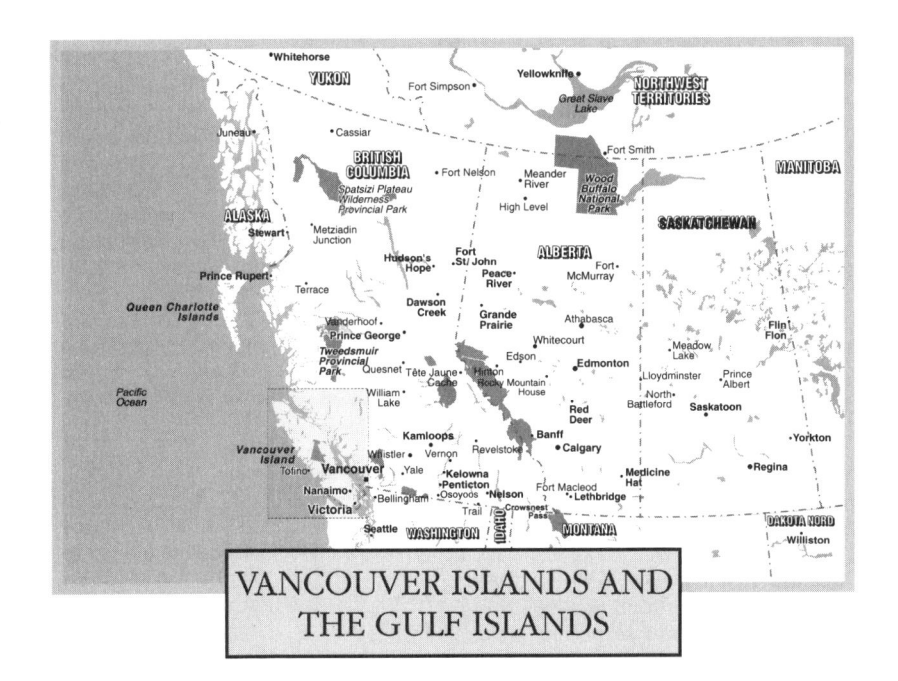

VANCOUVER ISLANDS AND THE GULF ISLANDS

Vast Vancouver Island stretches over 500 km along the west coast, with its southern tip facing the Olympic Mountains in Washington State (U.S.A.). The island is split into two distinct regions by a chain of mountains, which divide the north from the south. The sea has sculpted the west side, creating big, deep fjords; while the shoreline on the east side is much more continuous. Most of the towns and villages on the island lie either on the east coast or along the Strait of Georgia, where the Gulf Islands are located. There is another cluster of these islands in the Johnstone Strait, northeast of Vancouver Island.

The forest and fishing industries have provided several generations with a good source of income in this magnificent region. Thanks to the warm currents of the Pacific, the climate is mild all year round, enhancing the quality of life here. Isolated from the continent for years, islanders now have access to efficient, modern means of transportation. A number of ferries ply between the islands and the continent every day. This chapter offers an overview of several islands worth exploring. During your trip, you might be lucky enough to spot a whale, a seal or a sea otter. The B.C. Ferry captains have sharp eyes and will let you know if they see anything that might interest you.

To help you make the most of your visit to this part of British Columbia, we have outlined four tours: **Tour A: From Victoria to Nanaimo** ★★; **Tour B: From Nanaimo to Tofino** ★★★; **Tour C: From Qualicum Beach to Port Hardy** ★★ and **Tour D: The Gulf Islands** ★★★.

Finding Your Way Around

■ By Plane

There are regular flights from Vancouver to most towns in this region. Seaplanes transport passengers between the Gulf Islands. The majority of these islands and the municipalities on Vancouver Island are served by the following airlines:

AirBC (☎ 1-800-776-3000, Vancouver ☎ 688-5515, Victoria ☎ 360-9074). This company serves Victoria, Nanaimo, Campbell River, Comox and a number of other municipalities.

Baxter Aviation (Nanaimo ☎ 754-1066, Vancouver ☎ 683-6525 or 1-800-661-5599) has a fleet of seaplanes, which fly between Vancouver and Nanaimo.

Canadian Regional (Port Hardy, ☎ 1-800-665-1177).

Coval Air (Campbell River, ☎ 287-8371) mainly serves the northern part of Vancouver Island.

Hanna's Air Saltspring (☎ 537-9359 or 1-800-665-2359).

Harbour Air (☎ 1-800-663-4267).

■ By Boat

Visitors interested in travelling from one island to another have access to a vast network of ferries, which ply back and forth between the islands on a daily basis, as well as providing transportation to the coast.

The **BC Ferry Corporation** (1112 Fort Street, Victoria, V8V 4V2, ☎ 386-3431, ⇄ 381-5452) carries passengers back and forth between Vancouver Island and the coast. Departure times: Vancouver ☎ 277-0277, Victoria ☎ 656-0757, Nanaimo ☎ 753-6626. For all information concerning the schedules for the Gulf Islands (every day 7am to 10pm): Vancouver ☎ 277-0177, Victoria ☎ 386-3431.

If you're going from Port Hardy to the Queen Charlotte Islands or Prince Rupert, you can leave your car on the mainland.

Barkley Sound Service (P.O. Box 188, Port Alberni, V97 7M7, ☎ 723-8313 or 1-800-663-7192). This ferry crosses Barkley sound and links Port Alberni to Bamfield, north of the West Coast Trail, and Ucluelet, south of Long Beach.

BC Ferry provides service between Little River, on the coast east of Comox, and Powell River, on the Sunshine Coast.

Tri-Island Ferry (Port McNeill, ☎ 956-4533) links Port McNeill to Sointula and Alert Bay.

■ By Bus

Island Coach Lines (700 Douglas Street, Victoria, V8W 2B3, ☎ 385-4411) offer transportation from Nanaimo to Port Alberni, Ucluelet and Tofino, on the west coast of Vancouver Island.

Pacific Coach Lines (700 Douglas Street, Victoria, V8W 1B1, ☎ 385-4411) operates from downtown Vancouver to downtown Victoria in conjunction with BC Ferry. These buses also serve the Gulf Islands.

Finding Your Way Around 103

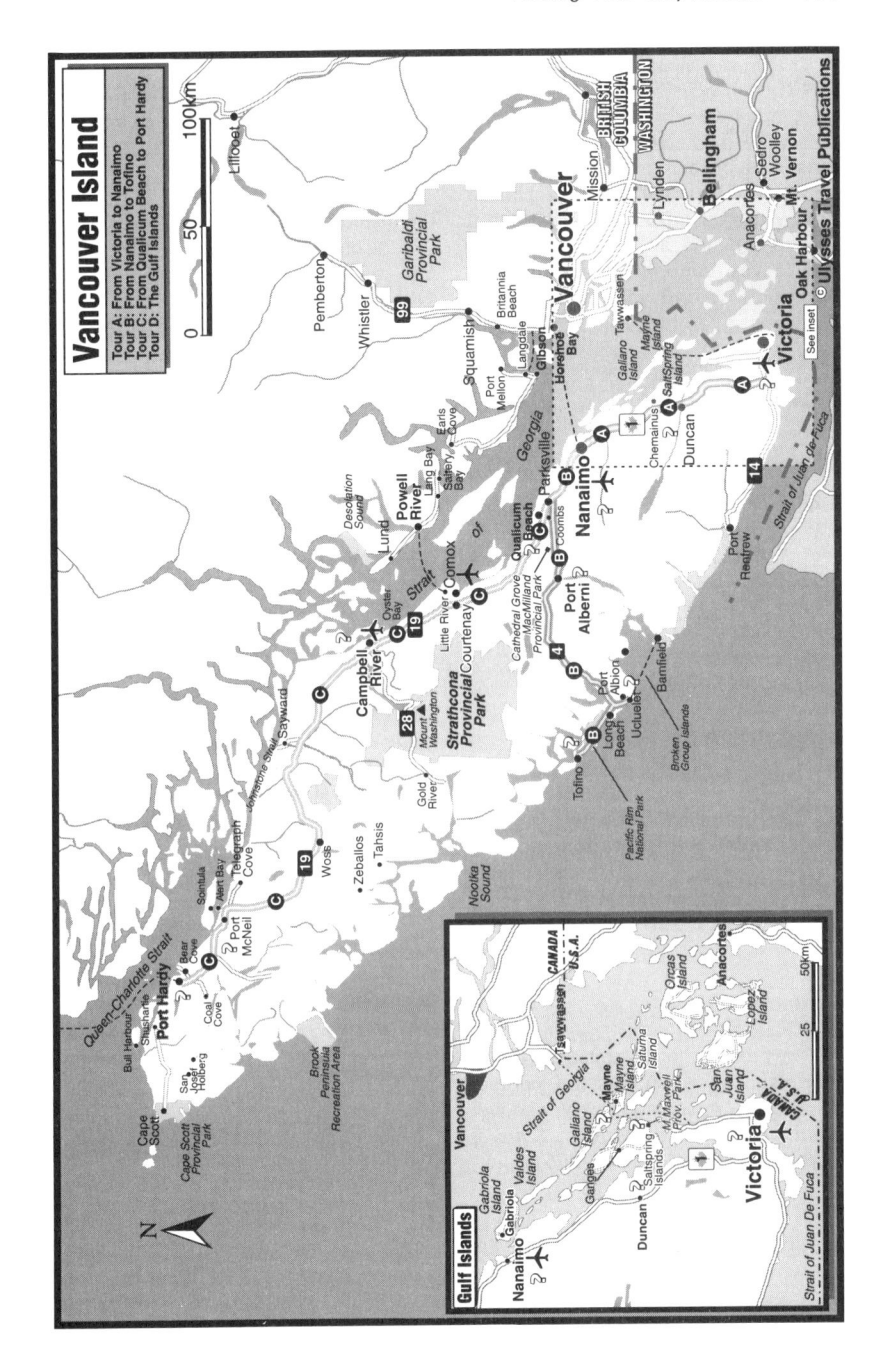

By Train

E&N (Via Rail) *(450 Pandora Avenue, Victoria, V8W 3L5, ☎ 1-800-561-8630)* provides transportation along the east coast of the island. The major stops on this line are Victoria, Duncan, Nanaimo, Qualicum Beach and Courtenay. The train leaves Victoria at 8:15am from Monday to Saturday and at noon on Sunday.

Car Rental Agencies

Nanaimo

Budget *(☎ 753-1195)* will pick you up at the ferry terminal.
Rent-A-Wreck *(111 South Terminal Avenue, ☎ 753-6461)*.
Avis *(☎ 753-1111)*.

Port Hardy

Budget Rent-A-Car *(☎ 949-6442)*.

Practical Information

Area Code: ☎ 604 (the area code will change to ☎ 250 in October 1996)

Information

To learn more about Vancouver Island before setting out on your trip, contact the Tourism Association of Vancouver Island *(302-45 Bastion Square, Victoria, V8W 1J1, ☎ 382-3551)*.

Tour A: From Victoria to Nanaimo

Duncan-Cowichan Travel InfoCentre *(year-round; 381 TransCanada Highway, Duncan, V9L 3R5, ☎ 746-4636)*.

Chemainus Travel InfoCentre *(seasonal; 9758 Chemainus Road, P.O. Box 575, Chemainus, V0R 1K0, ☎ 246-3944 or 246-4701)*.

Nanaimo Travel InfoCentre *(year-round; 266 Bryden Street, Nanaimo, V9S 1A8, ☎ 754-8474 or 1-800-663-7337)*.

Tour B: From Nanaimo to Tofino

Alberni Valley Chamber of Commerce *(year-round; 2533 Redford Street, RR2, Suite 215, Comp 10, Port Alberni V9Y 7L6, ☎ 724-6535)*.

Ucluelet Travel InfoCentre *(year-round; 227 Min Street, P.O. Box 428, Ucluelet, V0R SA0, ☎ 726-4641)*.

Tofino Travel InfoCentre *(seasonal; 380 Campbell Street, P.O. Box 476, Tofino, V0R 2Z0, ☎ 725-3414)*.

Tour C: From Qualicum Beach to Port Hardy

Qualicum Beach Travel InfoCentre *(year-round; 2711 West Island Highway, Qualicum Beach, V9K 2C4, ☎ 752-9532)*.

Campbell River Travel InfoCentre *(year-round, 1235 Shopper's Row, P.O. Box 400, Campbell River, V9W 586, ☎ 287-4636 or 1-800-463-4386)*.

Practical Information

Police: ☎ 286-0100.

Port McNeill Travel InfoCentre *(seasonal; Beach Drive, P.O. Box 129, Port McNeill, V0N 2R0, ☎ 956-3131)*.

Port Hardy Travel InfoCentre *(year-round; 7250 Market Street, P.O. Box 249, Port Hardy, V0N 2P0, ☎ 949-7622)*.

Tour D: The Gulf Islands

Salt Spring Island Travel InfoCentre *(year-round; 121 Lower Ganges Road, P.O. Box 111, Ganges, V0S 1E0, ☎ 537-5252)*.

Galiano Island Travel InfoCentre *(seasonal; Sturdies Bay, P.. Box 73, Galiano, V0N 1P0, ☎ 539-2233)*.

Doctor: Mayne Island, ☎ 539-2312

★ Exploring

■ Tour A: From Victoria to Nanaimo ★★

Head out of downtown Victoria on Douglas Street and take the TransCanada Highway 1 North toward Duncan and Nanaimo.

Duncan

Duncan is a town of indigenous art and totem poles (22 to be exact), which line the downtown streets. The **Native Heritage Centre ★★** *($6.50; May to Oct, every day 9:30am to 5pm; in winter, every day 10am to 4:30pm; 200 Cowichan Way, ☎ 746-8119)* focusses on the Cowichan people and their history, right up until the present day. For $24, you can take in a dance performance, lunch on salmon and tour the centre. Sculptors at work will explain their art to you, and singers will tell you their legends. At lunchtime, the natives use traditional methods to cook salmon over a wood fire. There is an art gallery on the premises, which sells prints, jewellery and woollen goods. Although the wood carvings and silver jewellery might seem expensive, the prices are actually more reasonable here than in the large urban areas. This place is very touristy, but nonetheless pleasant and informative.

Chemainus ★

Chemainus is a small town located about twenty kilometres north of Duncan. It owes its existence to the forest industry and probably would have sunk into oblivion had it not been for the ingenuity of its residents. The future looked bleak when the local sawmill shut down, but people here took control of the situation, reopening the facility and creating new jobs. Later, the town organized a big competition, calling upon various artists to cover the walls with murals illustrating the history of Chemainus. The thirty or so murals are worth the trip; it takes about an hour to see them all. The tourist office distributes a map containing a description of each one.

Nanaimo

Nanaimo is an important town because of its link to the coast, where ferries pick up hundreds of tourists headed for this region. It lies 35 km from Vancouver, across the Strait of Georgia, and 1 h 30 min from Victoria

106 Vancouver Island and the Gulf Islands

Nanaimo

N

- Westwood Lake
- Bowen Rd.
- Northfield Rd.
- Departure Bay Rd.
- Hammond Bay Rd.
- Boundary
- Townsite
- Departure Bay Rd.
- Terminal Ave.
- Brechin
- Stewart Ave.
- Departure Bay
- Newcastle Channel
- Strait of Georgia
- Horseshoe Bay
- Tsawwassen
- Newcastle Island ❶
- Fourth St.
- Fifth St.
- Albert St.
- Comox Rd.
- Swy-A-Lana Park
- ❹ ❸
- Protection Island ❷
- Bruce
- Victoria Rd.
- Nicol St.
- Haliburton St.
- Tenth
- Sears
- Maki
- Nanaimo Harbour
- Gabriola Island
- Northumberland Channel

1. Newcastle Island
2. Protection Island
3. Harbourside Walkway
4. The Bastion

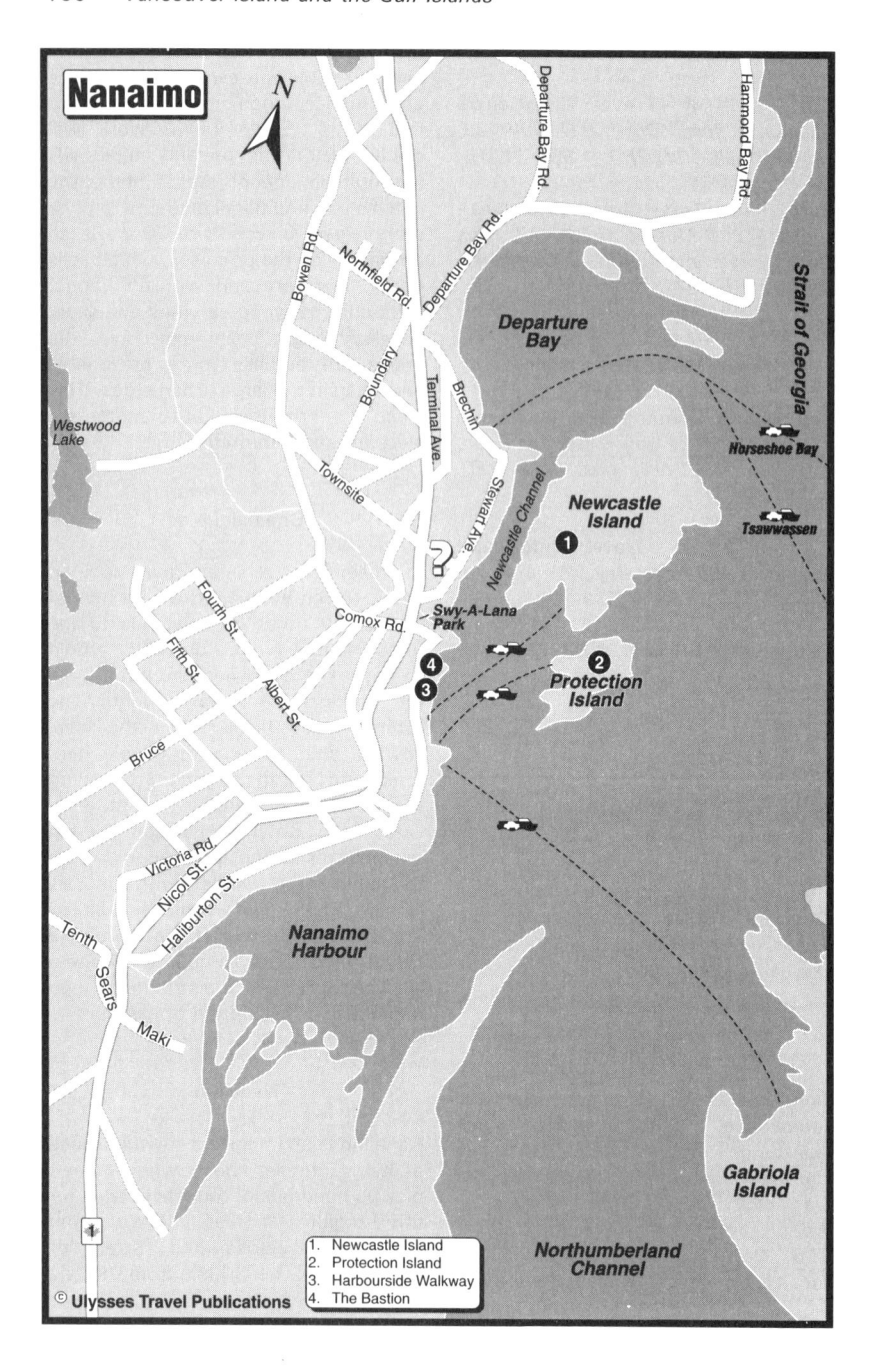

© Ulysses Travel Publications

by way of the TransCanada. Vacationers heading for the northern part of Vancouver Island or for Long Beach, to the west, pass through Nanaimo. This town is much more than just a stopover point, however; its seaport is graced with a pleasant promenade. Furthermore, visitors can easily catch a ferry to **Newcastle Island** ★ **(1)** and **Protection Island** ★ **(2)** to use the outdoor facilities and take in the view of Nanaimo. You can see all the local attractions, including old Nanaimo, on a walking tour.

Upon entering Nanaimo, Highway 1 becomes Nicol Street. Turn right on Comox Road and then immediately left on Arena Street, which will take you to Swy-A-Lana Park (you can leave your car there). Go into the park and turn right when you reach the waterfront, where you'll find **Harbourside Walkway** ★★ **(3)**, a pleasant promenade lined with parks, historic sites and shops.

The **Bastion** ★ **(4)** *(Jul and Aug 9am to 5pm)* was built by the Hudson's Bay Company in 1853 in order to protect the new trading post and the local residents. Its construction was supervised by two Quebecers, Jean-Baptiste Fortier and Leon Labine, both employees of the company. The Bastion never came under attack and was abandoned when the company left in 1862. It was later used as a prison, and has served as a gathering place and a museum since 1910.

The ferry *(every hour from 9:10am to 11:10pm;* ☎ *753-8244)* for Protection Island departs from the end of Commercial Inlet. This little island is more or less a suburb of Nanaimo, with residents commuting to their jobs in town during the week. You can enjoy a refreshing beer and some excellent fish & chips at the island's floating pub (see "Restaurants", p 118).

Nanaimo is renowned among scuba-divers. The water is at its most beautiful between November and April (see "Outdoor Activities", p 114). A lot of people come here to go bungee jumping as well.

■ **Tour B: From Nanaimo to Tofino** ★★★

Take Terminal Avenue, head toward Parksville on Highway 19, then turn off toward Port Alberni on the 4. On your way west, stop in **Coombs**, a small community of 400 inhabitants whose **Old Country Market** ★ piques the curiosity of passers-by. Built in 1975, this unusual place now lodges a family of goats!

On your way to Port Alberni, you will pass through **Cathedral Grove MacMilland Provincial Park** ★★★.

Port Alberni

Like many towns in British Columbia, Port Alberni owes its existence to the forest industry, fishing and trade. Its harbour is linked to the Pacific by a large canal, putting the town at an advantage as far as shipping is concerned. Port Alberni is also the gateway to the west coast of Vancouver Island. When you reach the top of the mountains surrounding Mount Arrowsmith, at an altitude of nearly 2,000 m, you're almost at Port Alberni.

Salmon can be found in the local waters. They are born in the rivers, and after spending a good part of their life in the sea, return there to spawn, much to the delight of both commercial and amateur fishermen.

Keep left as you enter Port Alberni. Take Port Alberni Highway to Third Avenue, turn left on Argyle Street and then right toward the harbour. The **Harbour Quay** is a pleasant place to have a cup of coffee and inquire about which boats can take you to Pacific Rim National Park for the day. In the middle of the public square, you'll see a fountain adorned with granite sculptures showing the life cycle of the salmon.

The **M.V. Lady Rose** *($12-40; year-round, Bamfield: Tue, Thu, Sat 8am, during summer; Ucluelet and Broken Group Islands: Mon, Wed, Fri 8am; Harbour Quay, ☎ 1-800-663-7192)* is a boat that offers year-round transportation between Port Alberni and Bamfield, at the north end of the West Coast Trail. During summer, it also carries passengers to and from Ucluelet and the Broken Group Islands, south of Long Beach. All sorts of discoveries await you on this trip; make sure to bring along a camera, a pair of binoculars and a raincoat.

On your way out of the port, turn left on Third Avenue and take Highway 4 in the direction of Tofino. This scenic road runs along a mountainside, passing through valleys and beside rivers. At the end, turn right toward Ucluelet.

Ucluelet ★

Located at the south end of Long Beach, Ucluelet is a charming town whose main street is lined with old wooden houses. In the past, the only way to get here was by boat. The local economy is based on fishing and tourism. Over 200 species of birds can be found around Ucluelet. Migrating grey whales swim in the coves and near the beaches here between the months of March to May, making whale-watching one of the main attractions on the west coast.

At the south end of the village, in **He Tin Kis Park ★★**, there is a wooden walkway leading through a small temperate rain forest beside Terrace Beach. This short walk will help you appreciate the beauty of this type of vegetation. The **Amphitrite Point Lighthouse ★** has stood on the shore since 1908. In those days, this area was known as the "cemetery of the Pacific" because so many ships had run up onto the reefs here. The wreckage of one tall ship still lies at the bottom of the sea near the point. The Canadian Coast Guard has a shipping checkpoint offshore *(guided tours available during summer)*.

Back on Highway 4, on your way to Tofino, stop by at the Parks Canada office *(Easter to Oct; Highway 4; ☎ 726-4212)* to pick up a map of **Long Beach ★★**.

Tofino ★

Tofino, situated at the northwest end of Long Beach, is a quiet town where visitors chat about sunsets and the outdoors. Spanish explorers Galiano and Valdes, who discovered this coast in the summer of 1792, named the place after Vincente Tofino, their hydrography professor.

Tofino has a population of just over a thousand; during summer, this number quadruples. Vacationers come here to enjoy the sun and sand at Long Beach. The water is rather cold, however.

Whale-watching and salmon fishing draw tourist as well.

This town is also an artists' colony. The local painters and sculptors draw much of their inspiration from the unspoiled landscape of the west coast. The **House of Himwitsa** ★ *(at the end of the main street, near the port)* displays works by Amerindian artists.

■ **Tour C: From Qualicum Beach to Port Hardy**

This tour starts on the waterfront, whose beaches attract walkers and sand-castle builders. You are now in the central part of Vancouver Island, on the eastern shore. Families come here to enjoy the natural setting and the relatively warm waters of the Strait of Georgia. The beaches stretch all the way to Comox Valley. Inland, there are mountains measuring over 2,000 m in altitude in Strathcona Provincial Park, which marks the division between the northern and southern parts of the island.

Qualicum Beach

Lured by the fine weather, many retirees settle in Qualicum Beach. This region gets more hours of sunshine than those farther south. Highway 19 is busy around Parksville and Qualicum Beach, whose main attraction is their series of beaches.

Campbell River

Campbell River is a choice destination for fans of salmon fishing. This sport can be enjoyed here year-round, and five varieties of salmon frequent the local waters. When you get to town, take the time to go to the **Campbell River & District Museum & Archives** ★ *($2; Jan to May, Wed to Sun noon to 4pm; May to Sep, Mon to Sat 10am to 4pm Sun noon to 4pm; Oct to Dec, Wed to Sun noon to 4pm; 470 Island Highway, opposite Sequoia Park, Fifth Avenue, ☎ 287-3103)*, a museum that is interesting not only for its elegant architecture but also for its exhibits on Amerindians and pioneers. Its collection includes a number of artifacts from Campbell River's early days. Furthermore, a significant part of the museum is devoted to Amerindian engravings, sculpture and jewellery.

On your way into the centre of town, stop for a walk along **Discovery Pier** ★ *(Government Wharf)*, from which you can admire the Strait of Georgia and the Coast Mountains. At the end, turn right and walk down Shoppers Row, where you can purchase souvenirs, food or basic necessities. The Travel InfoCentre is located on this street as well.

As you leave town, head for Gold River on Highway 28. From mid-August to mid-October, you can see the salmon swimming upriver at the **Quinsam Salmon Hatchery** ★ *(every day 8am to 4pm; Highway 28, ☎ 287-9564)* on the Campbell River.

Back on the 28, continue westward to Gold River and Nootka Sound.

Nootka Sound

The Spanish sailed these waters first, in 1774, though it was Captain James Cook who came ashore and claimed the land for England in 1778. You can explore this region, which is steeped in history, by taking a boat tour from Nootka harbour *(☎ 283-2325)*.

Backtrack to Campbell River and head toward Port Hardy on Highland Highway 19.

Sayward

When you leave the highway at Sayward Junction, stop at the **Cablehouse Restaurant** ★ (☎ 282-5532). The exterior of this building is made of cables coiled on top of one another. Lumber companies used to use these cables to transport wood to the train. More than 2 km of cables cover the walls of this restaurant. The forest industry drives the economy of the little town of Sayward. Each July, on **World Championship Logger Sports Day**, lumberjacks come here to demonstrate their skill. This region is best explored by boat. Magnificent Johnstone Strait is scattered with lovely islands and teeming with marine animal life.

Telegraph Cove ★★

This little paradise set back from the eastern shore of Vancouver Island was once the end point of a telegraph line that ran along the coast, hence the name. Later, a wealthy family set up a sawmill on land they had purchased around the little bay. From that point on, time stopped; the little houses have been preserved, and the boardwalk alongside the bay is punctuated with commemorative plaques explaining the major stages in the village's history. Today, vacationers come here to go fishing, scuba diving and whale-watching. If you're lucky, you might catch a glimpse of a seal, an otter or even a whale from the boardwalk.

Be careful along the last kilometre of the road to Telegraph Cove. A local lumber company's trucks haul huge blocks of wood along this little secondary road, which leads to Beaver Cove. According to the highway code, you are supposed to give these vehicles right of way.

Port McNeill

Farther north lies Port McNeill, a town of 2,500 inhabitants. It is the regional centre of three large lumber companies. **North Island Forest Tours** ★★ (free; 5 hour tour; Jun to Sep, Mon to Fri; North Island Forestry Centre, Port McNeill, ☎ 956-3844) will take you into the forest or along the local rivers so that you can see how trees are felled and how the men and women handle the giant trunks. You must reserve a seat and bring along a snack.

Second only to the forest industry, boat touring is very important to the local economy. Visitors to this region can also enjoy wonderful fishing trips and whale-watching excursions in the strait. Amerindian culture is well represented here, especially in Sointula and Alert Bay, on the neighbouring islands, which are served by ferries several times a day.

Alert Bay ★★

At the **U'mista Cultural Center** ★ (year-round, Mon to Fri 9am to 5pm, noon to 5pm during summer; Alert Bay, ☎ 974-5403), you can learn about the Potlatch ("to give") ceremony through the history of the U'mista Indian community. Missionaries tried to ban the ceremony; there was even a law forbidding members of the community from dancing, preparing objects for distribution or making public speeches. The ceremony was then held in secret and during bad weather, when the whites couldn't get to the island. A lovely collection of masks and jewellery adorns the walls. Don't miss the **Native Burial Grounds** and the **Memorial Totems** ★★, which testify to the richness of this art.

Port Hardy

Port Hardy, a town of fishermen and forest workers, is located at the northeast end of Vancouver Island. There is a wealth of animal life in this region, both in the water and on the land. If you aren't interested in going fishing or whale-watching, treat yourself to a walk through the forest in Cape Scott Park. Visitors en route to Prince Rupert and the Queen Charlotte Islands board the ferry in Port Hardy ($80 return).

The **Copper Maker** ★ (free admission; every day; 112 Copper Way, Fort Rupert, on the outskirts of Port Hardy, ☎ 949-8491) is an Amerindian art gallery and studio, where you'll find totem poles several metres high, some in the process of being made, others waiting to be delivered to buyers. Take the time to watch the artists at work, and ask them to tell you about the symbolism behind their drawings and sculptures.

At the end of Highway 19, you'll find the town port, the starting point of a promenade along the waterfront. You can enjoy a pleasant stroll here while taking in the scenery and watching the boats on their way in and out of the harbour.

■ Tour D: The Gulf Islands ★★★

Each of these islands is a different place to commune with nature and enjoy a little seclusion, far from traffic jams. Time is measured here according to the arrival and departure of the ferries. A convivial atmosphere prevails on these little havens of peace, especially at the end of the day, when visitors and islanders mingle at the pub. Surprises await you on each trip — an island straight out of your dreams, perhaps, or the sight of a seal swimming under your kayak — moments that will remain forever etched in your mind.

The Gulf Islands consist of some 200 islands scattered across the Strait of Georgia between the eastern shore of Vancouver Island and the west coast, near the San Juan Islands (U.S.A.).

Salt Spring ★

Salt Spring is the largest and most populous of the Gulf Islands. Amerindians used to come here during summer to catch shellfish, hunt fowl and gather plants. In 1859, the first Europeans settled on the island and began establishing farms and small businesses here. Today, many artists have chosen Salt Spring as their home and place of work. When they aren't practising their art on the street, they welcome the public into their studios. As Vancouver Island is just a short trip from Salt Spring, some residents work in Victoria. The town of Ganges is the commercial hub of the island. A promenade runs alongside its harbour, past a number of shops and through two marinas.

Galiano ★★

With just over a tenth of the population of Salt Spring, this island is a quiet, picturesque place. It was named after Dionisio Galiano, the Spanish explorer who first sailed these waters. About thirty kilometres long and over 2 km wide, Galiano faces northwest on one end and southeast on the other. Its shores afford some lovely views and are dotted with shell beaches.

Mayne Island ★

Mayne Island, Galiano's neighbour to the south, is a quiet place inhabited mainly by retirees. The limited number of tourists makes for a peaceful atmosphere, while the relatively flat terrain is a cyclist's dream. In the mid-19th century, during the gold rush, miners heading from Victoria to the Fraser River used to stop here before crossing the Strait of Georgia, hence the name Miners Bay. The first Europeans to settle on the island grew apples here, and their vast orchards have survived to this day. A few local buildings bear witness to the arrival of the pioneers. The **St. Mary Magdalene** ★ *(Georgina Point Road)* church, built entirely of wood in 1897, merits a visit. Take the opportunity to go see the stained-glass windows on Sunday, when the church is open for Mass.

The **Active Pass Lighthouse** ★ *(every day 1pm to 3pm; Georgina Point Road)* has been guiding sailors through these waters since 1885. The original structure, however, was replaced by a new tower in 1940, which was in turn replaced in 1969. The place is easy to get to and is indicated on most maps of the region.

Parks and Beaches

■ **Tour A: From Victoria to Nanaimo**

Newcastle Island Provincial Park *(picnic areas, campground, bicycle trails, swimming, hiking trail, fishing, restaurant, toilets; Comox Road, behind the Civic Arena, Nanaimo, ☎ 753-5141 or 391-2300)* is a 306 ha island in the Nanaimo harbour. Its shore is studded with beaches, caverns and escarpments. The Coast Salish Indians lived on this island before its coal-rich subsoil attracted miners here. A Japanese fishing community ran a saltery here for 30 years, up until 1941, when the Canadian government, at war with Japan at the time, placed the Japanese living and working on the coast into internment camps. The island later became a popular resort after being purchased by Canadian Pacific, which hosted big parties for its employees here. It has been public property since 1955.

■ **Tour B: From Nanaimo to Tofino**

Pacific Rim National Park, Long Beach section ★★★ *(Long Beach information centre, Highway 4, ☎ 726-4212)* This park is trimmed with kilometres of deserted beaches, running alongside temperate rain forests. The beaches, hiking trails and various facilities are clearly indicated and easy to reach. The setting is enchanting, relaxing and stimulating at once, as well as being accessible year-round. The beaches are popular with surfing buffs, and **Live to Surf** *(☎ 725-4464)* rents out surfboards and wetsuits.

Exploring the Tofino area by boat will enable you to uncover the hidden treasures of the neighbouring islands and bays. If you feel like walking about, you can check out the sulphur springs in the caves or the bears in the forest. **Explore Sea Trek** *(441B Campbell Street, Tofino, ☎ 725-4412)* can arrange an excursion for you.

■ **Tour C: From Qualicum Beach to Port Hardy**

Qualicum Beach and **Parksville** are popular for their sandy beaches just off Highway 19.

Strathcona Park ★★ *(swimming, hiking, fishing and 161 campsites; 59 km west of Campbell River on Highway 28, ☎ 755-2483)* is the oldest provincial park in British Columbia. Its 210,000 ha of forest and fresh water abound in natural treasures, including huge Douglas firs over 90 m high. The highest peak on Vancouver Island is found here, the Golden Hinde, it measures 2,220 m in altitude.

The **Haig-Brown Kingfisher Creek Heritage Property** ★ *(guided tours Jun 24 to Aug 31, 10:30am, 1:30pm and 3:30pm; 2250 Campbell River Road, Campbell River, ☎ 286-6646)*, located alongside the Campbell River, is worth a visit. It once belonged to celebrated Canadian author Roderick Haig-Brown, who fought all his life to protect wild animals and their natural surroundings.

Miracle Beach Park ★ *(28 km south of Campbell River, at the intersection of Miracle Beach Road and Highway 19)* is the perfect place for families wishing to enjoy the beach while remaining close to all conveniences.

Cape Scott Provincial Park ★★ *(67 km northwest of Port Hardy on Holberg Road; reservations ☎ 949-7622; for all other information, BC Parks District Manager, Parksville, ☎ 248-3931)* encompasses 15,070 ha of temperate rain forest. Scott was a merchant from Bombay (India) who financed all sorts of commercial expeditions. Many ships have run aground on this coast, and a lighthouse was erected in 1960 in order to guide sailors safely along their way. Sandy beaches cover two-thirds of the 64 km stretch of waterfront. On the hilly terrain farther inland, you'll find various species of giant trees, such as red cedars and pines. This remote part of Vancouver Island receives up to 500 mm of rainfall annually, and is frequently hit by storms. It is best to visit here during summertime.

■ **Tour D: The Gulf Islands** ★★

Mount Maxwell Provincial Park ★ *(from Fulford-Ganges Road, take Cranberry Road, then Mount Maxwell Road all the way to the end)* lies on a mountainside. The lookout is easily accessible, and the view of Vancouver Island and the islands to the south is worth the trip.

There are some lovely provincial parks along the shores of **Galiano Island**.

Dionisio Point Provincial Park ★★ *(from Sturdies Bay, head towards Porlier Pass, turn right on Wineyard then left on Beach Road and go all the way to the end)* lies at the northern tip of the island, opposite Porlier Pass. The view of the continental coast is quite simply breathtaking. The park is edged with beaches and rocks sculpted by the sea.

Another very interesting place is **Montague Harbour Provincial Park** ★★ *(on the west side of Galiano, 10 km from the ferry terminal, ☎ 387-4363)*, a top-notch park featuring a lagoon, a shell beach and an equipped campground. The view of the sunset from the north beach will send you off into a reverie.

Bluffs Park ★ *(take Bluff Drive from Georgeson Bay Road or Burrill Road)* offers a view from above of aptly named Active Pass, where ferries heading for Swartz Bay (Victoria) and Tsawwassen (Vancouver) cross paths.

Outdoor Activities

Hiking

Tour B: From Nanaimo to Tofino

At **Pacific Rim National Park, Long Beach** section ★★★ *(Long Beach information centre, Highway 4, ☎ 726-4212)*, you can hike the **rain forest trail** ★★★ *(6.4 km north of the information centre)*, which runs through a temperate rain forest. Panels explaining the cycles of the forest and providing information on the animal species who live here have been set up along two trails. This park is steeped in history, and a number of trails provide a chronicle of bygone days. It is wise to ask park officials about the risk of encountering animals during your hike. Trails are occasionally closed when there are bears in the vicinity.

Tour C: From Qualicum Beach to Port Hardy

Cape Scott Provincial Park ★★ *(67 km northwest of Port Hardy via Holberg Road; reservations ☎ 949-7622; for all other information, BC Parks District Manager, Parksville, ☎ 248-3931)* encompasses 15,070 ha of temperate rain forest. Hiking trails provide the only means of access to the cape, and it takes a good eight hours to get there from the parking lot at San Josef Bay. You can, however, return to Port Hardy by boat *(AK Trips & Charters; $80; Port Hardy, ☎ 949-7952)*.

Scuba Diving

Tour A: From Victoria to Nanaimo

Each year, hundreds of divers flock to the eastern shore of Vancouver Island, lured by the colourful underwater scenery and rich marine life. The Nanaimo region is a wonderful place for this type of sightseeing. **Sundown Diving Charters** *(Unit 105, 1840 Stewart Avenue, Nanaimo, V9S 4E6, ☎ 753-1880)*.

Tour C: From Qualicum Beach to Port Hardy

Campbell River Snorkel Tours *(adults $49.95; 3 hours; Jun 1 to Oct 15, ☎ 286-0030)* will take you where the salmon flock in the Campbell River. All the necessary equipment (mask, flippers and diving suit) is provided; all you have to do is let yourself be guided through the scores of salmon, some of which can measure up to 1 m long.

Sun Fun Divers *(1630 McNeill Road, Port McNeill, ☎ 965-2243)* arranges scuba diving trips in the Telegraph Cove, Alert Bay and Port McNeill regions. The water is clearest during the winter months.

Sailing

Tour D: The Gulf Islands

You can explore the shores of Galiano and the neighbouring islands aboard a superb 14 m catamaran, thanks to **Canadian Gulf Islands Catamaran Cruises** *($35; 4 hour cruise, snack included; Montague Harbour, Galiano Island, ☎ 539-2930)*. Depending on where you are — in a bay or farther offshore — you're sure to spot some land or sea creatures. Two-hour guided sea kayak tours are also available for $25.

■ Bungee Jumping

Tour A: From Victoria to Nanaimo

If you're looking for some excitement, head to the **Bungy Zone** *(15 min south of Nanaimo via Highway 1; turn right on Nanaimo River Road; P.O. Box 399, Station A, Nanaimo, V9R 5L3; Internet http://wv.com/bungy, ☎ 753-5867 or 1-800-668-7771)*. The spectacle of thrill-seekers leaping off a bridge over the Nanaimo River has become a local attraction.

Whale-watching

Tour B: From Nanaimo to Tofino

Chinook Charters *($46; 450 Campbell Street, P.O. Box 501, Tofino, V0R 2Z0, ☎ 725-3431 or 1-800-665-3646)* will take you out to sea to observe grey whales at close range. The best time to go is in March and April, when there are large numbers of these sea mammals in the area.

Tour C: From Qualicum Beach to Port Hardy

Robson Bight Charters *(adults $60; Jun to Oct 9:30am; Sayward, ☎ 282-3833, Campbell River, ☎ 286-3474)* arranges whale-watching tours in the Johnstone Strait. Each year, killer whales use this area as a sort of training ground for the new members of their families. A sight to remember.

Fishing

Tour C: From Qualicum Beach to Port Hardy

You can rent basic fishing equipment at any time, day or night, on **Discovery Pier** *($1; 24 hours a day; Government Wharf, Campbell River, ☎ 286-6199)*, which stretches 150 m. This is a popular place to go for a stroll.

Bailey's Charters *($52 an hour; north of Discovery Pier, 871-C Island Highway, Campbell River, ☎ 286-3474)* arranges guided salmon and trout fishing trips, which are a terrific way to explore the region's beautiful shoreline.

Downhill Skiing

Tour C: From Qualicum Beach to Port Hardy

At the **Mount Washington Ski Resort** *(Howard Road, ☎ 338-1386)*, skiers can enjoy a 360° view encompassing the Coast Mountains and the dozens of islands at the mouth of the Strait of Georgia. The mountain, which is 1,609 m high, receives heavy snowfall every year. The ski season starts in December.

Accommodations

■ Tour A: From Victoria to Nanaimo

Nanaimo

The **Best Western Northgate** *($69-79; ℜ, lounge, ≡, C, ⊛, ○; 6450 Metral Drive, ☎ 390-2222, ⇄ 390-2412)* has 76 simply decorated, comfortable rooms. The layout is the same at the other Best Westerns in this region. A safe bet.

The **Jingle Pot Bed & Breakfast** *($75 bkfst incl.; pb, heated bathroom floor, ○, bicycles, ≡, tv; 4321 Jingle Pot Road, V9T 5P4, ☎ 758-5149)*, run by a sailor named Captain Ivan, has one room, which has been fitted out in a luxurious fashion to ensure that guests enjoy a pleasant stay. If you're planning on going boating, the captain can give you some good advice.

As its name suggests, the **Rocky Point Ocean View Bed & Breakfast** *($75 bkfst incl.; 4903 Fillinger, ☎ 751-1949)* offers a wonderful view of the Strait of Georgia and, in clear weather, the mountains along the coast. The three rooms are a bit over-decorated, but the warm welcome more than compensates for this minor drawback.

■ Tour B: From Nanaimo to Tofino

Ucluelet

The **Ucluelet Campground** *($15-24; 100 sites, toilets, showers; 260 Seaplane Base Road, ☎ 726-4355)* is located within walking distance of Ucluelet. Reservations required.

The **Canadian Princess Resort** *($49-109; sb or pb, no pets; Peninsula Road, ☎ 726-7771 or 1-800-663-7090, ⇄ 726 7121)* is a ship that sailed the waters along the coast for nearly 40 years, and is now permanently moored at the Ucluelet pier. It has 26 rooms, which are small and don't have a lot of extras, but offer a pleasant nautical atmosphere.

Tofino

The recently built **Midori's Place Bed & Breakfast** *($69 bkfst incl.; pb; 370 Gibson Street, ☎ 725-2203)*, located in the village, has three comfortable, soberly decorated rooms. The amusing resident parrot enjoys repeating everything guests say. The house is within walking distance of restaurants, shops and the village pier.

Picture a house on a beach lined with lush vegetation with the setting sun reflecting off the water; that's what awaits you at the heavenly **Chesterman's Beach Bed & Breakfast** *($85 bkfst incl.; pb; 1345 Chesterman's Beach Road, ☎ 725-3726)*. A simple walk on the beach every day is all you need to enjoy a satisfying vacation here. Three rooms are available.

The **Tin-Wis Best Western** *($115; tv, pb, ℜ, beach, no pets; 1119 Pacific Rim Highway, ☎ 725-4445 or 1-800-528-1234, ⇄ 725-4447)* is a large hotel run by Tla-O-Qui-Aht Indians. It offers all the comforts you would expect from a Best Western. The plants and wooden decorative elements blend harmoniously with the immediate surroundings, but the place is oversized (56 rooms).

■ **Tour C: From Qualicum Beach to Port Hardy**

Qualicum Beach

The **Quatna Manor Bed & Breakfast** *($55-80 bkfst incl.; sb or pb, no smoking; 512 Quatna Manor, Qualicum Beach, ☎ 752-6685)* is definitely a place to keep in mind. The friendly reception you will receive from hosts Bill and Betty will make your stay at their Tudor style home that much more pleasant. A hearty breakfast is served in the dining room. Bill is retired from the air force. His job required a great deal of travelling, and his stories make for memorable breakfast conversation.

Campbell River

As its name suggests, the pretty little **Edgewater Motel** *($40-50; C, pb, tv; 4073 South Island Highway, near Oyster Bay, ☎ 923-5421)* is located on the waterfront. The rooms are decent for the price, and you can prepare meals in them — a real plus if you're on a tight budget.

The **Haig-Brown House** ★★ *($75-80 bkfst incl; sb; 2250 Campbell River Road, Campbell River, ☎ 286-6646, ⇄ 286-6694)* once belonged to Roderick Haig-Brown, renowned for both his writing and his efforts to protect the environment. Literary workshops are held on the estate, which is now a provincial heritage property. This spectacular place lies on the banks of the Campbell River. The rooms are simply decorated in old-fashioned style, and the walls of the reading room are lined with books. The dining room is bathed in natural light. The house and guest rooms are minded by Kevin Brown, who has a passion for both literature and the history of the Haig-Brown estate.

Telegraph Cove

The **Telegraph Cove Resorts** *($19.25 for a campsite for two adults, water, electricity; $60-135 for a cabin for 2 to 8 people, C, pb, ☎ 928-3131 or 1-800-200-3554, ⇄ 928-3105)* welcome visitors from May to October. The campground, equipped with basic facilities, is somewhat bare, but the view of the bay makes up for that. The cabins blend into the picturesque setting. The service is friendly, and you'll feel as if you're at some sort of summer camp. If you have to spend a few days in the northern part of the island, Telegraph Cove is a thoroughly pleasant place to visit.

Port Hardy

Hosts Herma and Frank will give you a warm welcome at **Mrs. P's Bed & Breakfast** *($49 bkfst incl.; sb; 8737 Telco Street, Port Hardy, ☎ 949-9526)*, which has two soberly decorated rooms in the basement. The place is located within walking distance of the harbour and a number of restaurants. Many travellers passing through town on their way to Prince Rupert arrive late and leave early, which would explain why local residents make so little fuss about renting rooms to visitors in need of a place to stay.

The **Seagate Hotel** *($74-80; tv, ℜ, pub, no pets; 8600 Granville Street, ☎ 949-6348 or 1-800-663-3676, ⇄ 949-6347)* is located a stone's throw from the town pier. All of the rooms are sparingly decorated, and the view makes those facing the port much more attractive.

■ **Tour D: The Gulf Islands**

An incredible number of **bed and breakfasts** have appeared on the Gulf Islands, offering visitors a wide range of choices. Though these places are generally quite expensive, you are unlikely to hear any complaints from the guests.

Galiano

The campground at the **Dionisio Point Provincial Park** *($6, cash only; chemical toilets, no fires; Vineyard Road and Porlier Pass,* ☎ *387-4363)* is open year-round, but is only maintained twice a month from late September on. The beaches and boulders make for an enchanting setting.

At **La Berengerie** *($60-75 bkfst incl.; sb or pb, ℜ; Montague Harbour Road, Galiano,* ☎ *539-5392)*, which has three rooms, guests enjoy a relaxing atmosphere in the woods. Huguette Benger has been running the place since 1983. Originally from the South of France, Madame Benger came to Galiano on a vacation and decided to stay. Take the time to chat with her; she'll be delighted to tell you all about the island. Breakfast is served in a large dining room. La Berengerie is closed from November to March.

The extremely inviting **Sutil Lodge Bed & Breakfast** *($65-75 bkfst incl.; sb, beach, fireplace; Montague Harbour,* ☎ *539-2930,* ⇄ *539-5390)*, located near the water, is a former fishing camp. Erected in the early 20th century, this large wooden building is surrounded by trees and faces the sea. The grounds and architecture of the lodge are reminiscent of a New England estate. Hosts Tom and Ann Hennessy arrange a number of boating trips.

Salt Spring

The **Summerhill On Salt Spring Bed & Breakfast** *($75 bkfst incl.; pb; 209 Chu-an Drive,* ☎ *537-2727)* has been completely renovated by its owners. The interesting combination of landings and terraces let in the sunlight and allow for some beautiful views of the Sansum Narrows. The breakfast is unusual and absolutely delicious. You'll feel right at home here.

Mayne Island

The **Root Seller Inn** *($70 bkfst incl.; sb, no smoking; 478 Village Bay Road,* ☎ *539-2621,* ⇄ *539-2411)* lies hidden behind the flowers and trees lovingly planted by charming Joan Drummond, who has been welcoming guests to the island for over 30 years. It all started at the Springwater Hotel in 1960, when she and her husband, having just arrived on the island, opened a hotel. Since 1983, Joan has been receiving guests in her home and showing them the island. The big wooden Cape Cod-style house, can accommodate 16 people in three large rooms. It lies near Mariners Bay, guests can thus contemplate the scenery and watch the ferries on their way through Active Pass from the blacony.

Restaurants

■ **Tour A: From Victoria to Nanaimo**

Nanaimo

Dinghy Dock Pub *($; 11am to 11pm; P.O. Box 771, Protection Island,* ☎ *753-2373)*. At this floating pub, which is attached to the Protection Island pier, you can enjoy a good local beer while observing the comings and goings in the Nanaimo harbour. The fish & chips are succulent. To get to the island, take the ferry from Commercial Inlet *(every hour from 9:10am to 11:10pm)*.

Located on the seawall, the **Javawocky Coffee House** *($; 8-90 Front Street, Pioneer Plaza,* ☎ *753-1688)* serves a wide assortment of coffee and light meals and offers a view of the Nanaimo port and the crowd strolling about there.

■ **Tour B: From Nanaimo to Tofino**

Ucluelet

People come to the **Matterson Restaurant** *($; 1682 Peninsula Road,* ☎ *726-2200)*, located on the main street, for lunch and tea. Don't hesitate to order salmon here; it's very fresh.

Long Beach

Set on a big rock overlooking the beach, the **Wickaninnish Restaurant** *($-$$; 11am to 9:30pm; Wickaninnish,* ☎ *726-7706)* offers a spectacular view of the Pacific Ocean. The menu is made up of seafood dishes. The pasta with smoked salmon is sure to please your palate. Whatever you choose, your meal will be that much better accompanied by a glass of British Columbian white wine.

Tofino

The **Schooner** *($-$$; on the main street in downtown Tofino)* is a classic. It serves seafood and British Columbian wines. An inviting place, it has been decorated to look like a ship's hold and deck. The soft lighting creates a relaxing comfortable atmosphere.

■ **Tour C: From Qualicum Beach to Port Hardy**

Campbell River

Hammond's Fish & Chips *($; Mon to Sat 11:30am to 7:30pm, Sun 4pm to 8pm; 151 G Dogwood Street,* ☎ *286-0814)* is a family-style restaurant that serves up fried cod and halibut. You won't go hungry here.

The **Seasons Bistro** *($; 6:30am to 2pm and 5:30pm to 10pm; 261 Island Highway,* ☎ *286-1131)* has an original menu featuring seafood pasta and pheasant with passionfruit. This place attracts both locals and tourists, and jazz lovers in particular.

Sayward

The **Cablehouse Restaurant** *($;* ☎ *282-5532)* offers simple, quality meals at reasonable prices. This is a fun place, with walls made of coiled cables.

Port Hardy

The **Seagate Hotel Restaurant** *($; from 6:30am on; 8600 Granville Street,* ☎ *949-6348)* has a wide-ranging menu. While enjoying a view of the harbour, you will dine alongside local residents, including fishermen fresh from a day at sea.

Tour D: The Gulf Islands

Galiano

La Berengerie *($$; open only in the evening; Montague Harbour Road,* ☎ *539-5392)* has a four-course menu with a choice of fish or meat. The dining room, located on the ground floor of a B&B, is furnished with antiques. Candlelight makes the atmosphere that much more inviting. Owner Huguette Benger prepares the delicious meals herself. During the day, her son's restaurant, **La Bohème**, serves vegetarian dishes on the terrace looking out onto the garden.

Entertainment

Tour D: The Gulf Islands

Galiano

The **Hummingbird Pub** *($; every day until 11pm; 47 Sturdies Bay Road,* ☎ *539-5472)* is a friendly place where tourists and locals mingle over a good beer and a plate of fries.

Shopping

Tour B: From Nanaimo to Tofino

Ucluelet

The **Du Quaii Gallery** *(1971 Peninsula Road,* ☎ *726-7223)* exhibits native art. It is worth the trip just to see the building, which looks like a Longhouse (a traditional Amerindian cedar building).

Tofino

The **House of Himwitsa** *(300 Main Street,* ☎ *725-2017)* is an art gallery that displays drawings, paintings, sculptures and silver and gold jewellery. Ask about the legends referred to in these pieces and the symbolism employed by the artists.

Tour C: From Qualicum Beach to Port Hardy

The **Tyee Plaza** *(behind the Travel InfoCentre,* ☎ *286-1621)* has a covered walkway and 24 stores and restaurants of all different sorts. If you are in a rush or looking for a shopping mall, this is the place to go.

Port Hardy

The **Copper Maker** *(every day; 112 Copper Way, Fort Rupert,* ☎ *949-8491)* displays the works of a number of native artists. Masks, pottery and symbolic jewellery can all be purchased here. These articles might seem expensive, but the prices are lower than in the bigger cities.

SOUTHERN BRITISH COLUMBIA

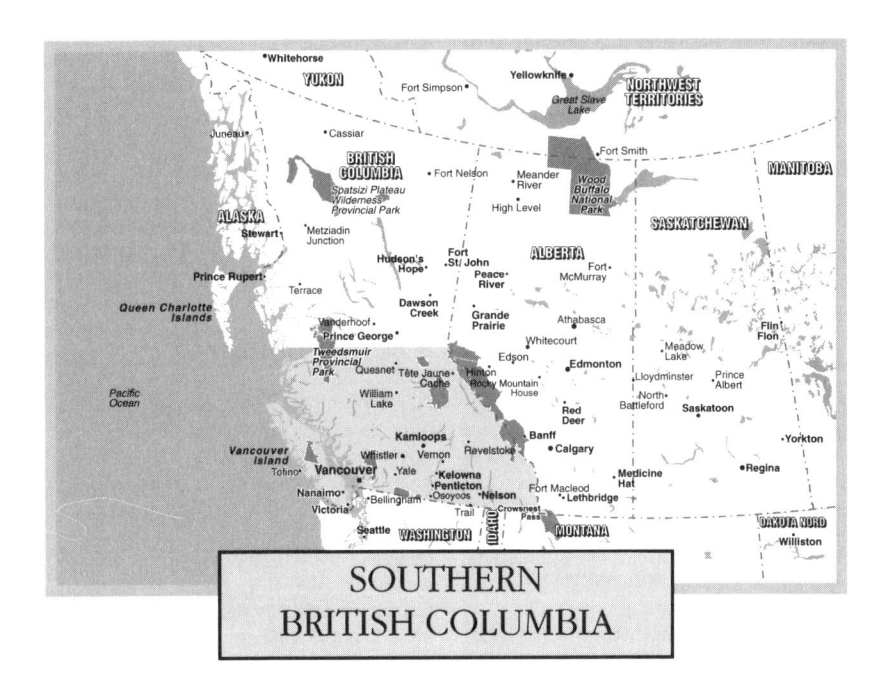

This region, which borders on the United States, is characterized by a blend of the urban and the undeveloped. The Vancouver area, for example, resembles a big American city, though it is set against a backdrop of green mountains and blue sea; here, you will find both wilderness and civilization. The Okanagan Valley is home to countless orchards and some of the best wineries in the province. As one majestic landscape succeeds the other, your eyes will be dazzled by the sea, the everlasting snows and the spring colours, which appear very early in this region.

Communing with nature is a memorable experience of any trip in southern British Columbia. The waters that wash the deserted beaches beckon you to relax and let your mind wander. Stately trees stand guard over tranquil areas untouched by the forest industry. Dotted with national and provincial parks, which lie stretched across the loveliest parts of the province, this region has an extremely varied landscape, with everything from perpetual snows to desert valleys and rivers teeming with fish.

Finding Your Way Around

A trip to southern British Columbia offers a chance to explore towns and parks set between the sea and the sky and meet people from a wide range of cultures. We have outlined five tours through four large areas whose character and appearance range from one extreme to the other: Southwestern BC, the High Country, Kootenay Country and the Okanagan-Similkameen. The tours are as follows:

Tour A: The Fraser and Thompson Rivers as Far as Revelstoke ★★; Tour B: Kootenay Country ★★; Tour C: Okanagan-Similkameen ★★★; Tour D: The Sea to Sky Highway ★★; Tour E: The Sunshine Coast ★★.

■ **By Plane**

A number of airlines serve the various parts of the province.

AirBC: Kamloops, Kelowna, Penticton, Vernon, Powell River; in Vancouver ☎ 688-5515 or 1-800-663-3721.

Canadian Regional: Kamloops, Kelowna, Penticton; in Vancouver ☎ 279-6611 or 1-800-665-1177.

Central Mountain Air: Kamloops, Kelowna, ☎ 1-800-663-3905.

■ **By Car**

Every highway in southern British Columbia is more spectacular than the last. One of these is the TransCanada Highway 1, which runs east-west, across mountains, rivers, canyons and desert valleys.

Highway 1, the TransCanada, provides an easy route eastward out of Vancouver, although the traffic is always fairly heavy. The road leads to Calgary, running along the Fraser River, the Thompson River and Lake Shuswap at different points along the way. Another option is to take Highway 7 (the continuation of Broadway Avenue) out of downtown Vancouver, along the north bank of the Fraser River. If you're pressed for time, you can take the newly opened Coquihalla Highway, which runs between Hope and Kamloops. This is a toll highway, the only one in the province; what's more, it is not as attractive as the others.

The spectacular Sea to Sky Highway 99 will take you up into northern British Columbia; simply cross Lions Gate and follow the signs for Whistler and Squamish.

■ **By Train**

Once extremely busy, railway stations only see a few regular trains nowadays. The *Canadian* still crosses the Rockies, running along mountainsides and through numerous tunnels. From North Vancouver, you can take a train that skirts northward around Howe Bay, passing through Squamish and Whistler along the way, and offering passengers a chance to contemplate the landscape.

BC Rail *(1311 West 1st Street, North Vancouver,* ☎ *984-5246)* serves the towns in the northern part of the province by way of the Whistler resort area.

Via Rail Canada *(1150 Station Street, Vancouver,* ☎ *1-800-561-8630)* serves the following towns: Port Coquitlam, Matsqui, Chilliwack, Hope, Boston Bar, Ashcroft, Kamloops North and several other communities in the northeastern part of the province.

■ **By Bus**

Fraser Valley Bus *(44580 Yale Road West, Sardis,* ☎ *795-7443, Vancouver,* ☎ *662-7953)*. Scheduled stops in major towns along the Fraser River Valley.

Greyhound Lines of Canada *(Pacific Central Station, 1150 Station Street,*

Finding Your Way Around 123

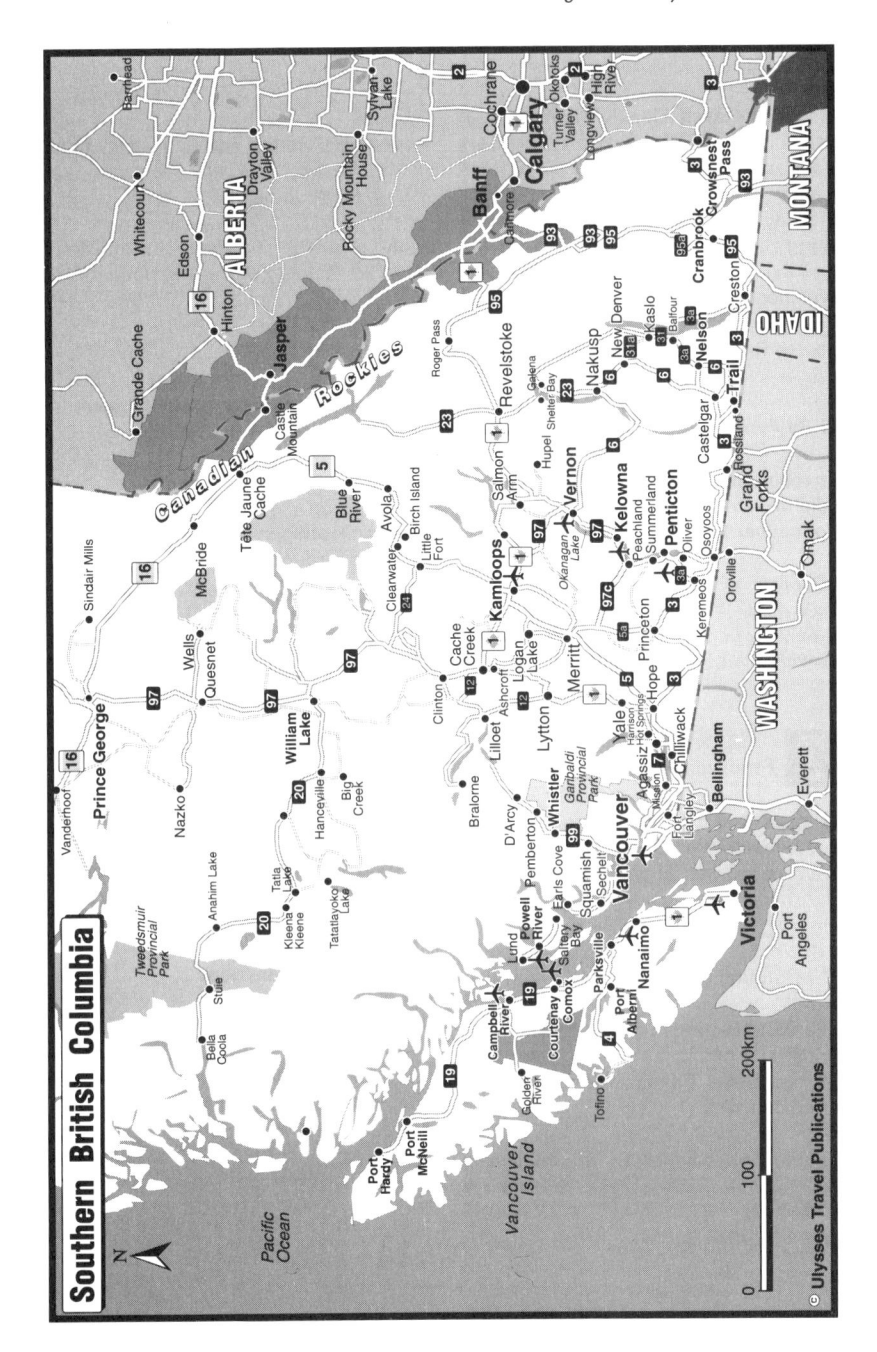

Vancouver, ☎ 662-3222 or 1-800-661-8747).

Maverick Coach Lines (Pacific Central Station, 1150 Station Street, Vancouver, ☎ 662-8051). Caters mainly to skiers going to Whistler for the day, but also serves other towns along Highway 99.

Whistler Transit System, ☎ 932-4020.

Powell River; terminus, ☎ 485-5030.

■ **By Ferry**

To reach the Sunshine Coast, you must take a ferry from the coast or from Vancouver Island.

BC Ferry (1112 Fort Street, Victoria, V8V 4V2, ☎ 386-3431, Vancouver, ☎ 669-1211, Saltery Bay, ☎ 487-9333, Powell River, ☎ 485-2943).

? Practical Information

■ **Area Code:** ☎ 604 (for areas north and west of Whistler and Hope, the area code will change to ☎ 250 in October 1996.)

■ **Information**

The various tourist offices in southern British Columbia are listed below by region. There are local offices in many towns as well.

Tourism Association of Southwestern B.C. (204-1755 West Broadway, Vancouver, BC V6J 4S5, ☎ 739-9011 or 1-800-667-3306).

Okanagan-Similkameen Tourism Association (1332 Water Street, Kelowna, BC V1Y 9P4, ☎ 860-5999).

Kootenay Country Tourist Association (610 Railway Street, Nelson, BC V1L 1H4, ☎ 352-6033).

High Country Tourism Association (1-1490 Pearson Place, Kamloops, BC V1S 1J9, ☎ 372-7770 or 1-800-567-2275).

■ **Tour A: The Fraser and Thompson Rivers as Far as Revelstoke**

Harrison Hot Springs

Harrison Hot Springs Travel InfoCentre. Open year-round (Highway 9, 499 Hot Springs Road, ☎ 796-3425).

Hope

Hope Travel InfoCentre (919 Water Avenue, ☎ 869-2021).

Lytton

Lytton Travel InfoCentre (400 Fraser Street, ☎ 455-6669).

Kamloops

Kamloops Travel InfoCentre (1290 West TransCanada Highway, ☎ 374-3377). All of the major banks are located on Victoria Street, near 3rd Avenue. The post office is at the corner of St. Paul Street and 3rd Avenue.

Revelstoke

Revelstoke Travel InfoCentre *(206 Campbell Avenue, ☏ 837-5345 or 837-3522)*.

Revelstoke City Hall, ☏ 837-2161; police, ☏ 837-5255; hospital, ☏ 837-2131.

■ **Tour B: Kootenay Country**

Nakusp

Nakusp and District Travel InfoCentre *(92 West Sixth Avenue, ☏ 265-4234)*.

Nelson

Nelson & District Chamber of Commerce *(225 Hall Street, ☏ 352-3433)*.

Emergencies: hospital, ☏ 352-3111; ambulance, ☏ 352-2112; police, ☏ 352-3511.

Rossland

Rossland Tourist Information *(Chamber of Commerce, at the corner of Columbia Avenue and St. Paul Street, ☏ 362-5666)*.

■ **Tour C: Okanagan-Similkameen**

Osoyoos

Osoyoos Travel InfoCentre *(at the intersection of Highways 3 and 97, ☏ 485-7142)*.

Penticton

Penticton Chamber of Commerce *(185 Lakeshore Drive, ☏ 493-4055)*.

Emergency: ☏ 911; police, ☏ 492-4300.

Penticton Regional Hospital *(☏ 492-4000)*.

Kelowna

Kelowna Travel InfoCentre *(544 Harvey Avenue, ☏ 861-1515)*.

Emergency: ☏ 911.

Hospital: Kelowna General Hospital *(2268 Pandosy Street, ☏ 862-4000)*.

Merritt

Merritt Travel InfoCentre *(on Highway 5, ☏ 378-2281)*.

Princeton

Princeton Travel InfoCentre *(57 Highway 3E, ☏ 295-3103)*.

■ **Tour D: The Sea to Sky Highway**

Squamish

Squamish & Howe Sound Chamber of Commerce *(37950 Cleveland Avenue, ☏ 892-9244)*.

Whistler

Whistler Travel InfoCentre *(2097 Lake Placid Road, ☏ 932-5528)*.

Ambulance, fire department and police: ☎ 911

Whistler Activity and Information Center (☎ 932-2394).

Whistler Resort Accommodations Reservations (☎ 932-4222; Vancouver, ☎ 664-5625 or 1-800-Whistler).

■ **Tour E: The Sunshine Coast**

Gibsons

Gibsons Travel InfoCentre (668 Sunnycrest Road, ☎ 886-2379).

Powell River

Powell River Travel InfoCentre (4690 Marine Avenue, ☎ 485-4701).

Exploring

British Columbia is exceptional in many respects, first of all because it has something to offer all manner of tourists, whether they're travelling by car or hiking. The southern part of the province is a large territory, which is flat in certain places and then suddenly very hilly in others. The construction of the railroad blazed a trail for the highways, each of which is more spectacular than the last.

■ **Tour A: The Fraser and Thompson Rivers as Far as Revelstoke ★★**

Fort Langley

Fort Langley National Historic Site ★ ($4; every day 10am to 4:30pm; Exit 66 North of the Trans Canada, towards Fort Langley, at the intersection of Mavis and Royal Streets; ☎ 888-4424). Fort Langley was erected in 1827, 4 km downriver from its present location, on the south bank of the Fraser. It was moved in 1839, only to be ravaged by fire the following year. The Hudson's Bay Company used the fort to store furs that were to be shipped out to Europe.

On November 19, 1858, British Columbia's status was officially proclaimed here, marking the end of the Hudson's Bay Company's control over the territory. Of the 16 buildings that once stood inside the palisade, only the warehouse remains. Erected around 1840, it is the oldest European-style structure on the west side of the Rockies. Six other buildings, as well as the palisade itself, have been reconstructed in order to acquaint the public with that era.

On your way out, take the little *Albion Ferry* to the north bank of the Fraser, then head to Mission on Highway 7 East. You'll have to slow your pace on this secondary road, which winds through fields full of berries. Most of the local farmers are of East Indian origin. This community boasts its own schools, public transport system and temples.

Mission

Xa:ytem Long House Interpretive Centre (3 km east of Mission; donations welcomed, ☎ 820-9725). This Amerindian archaeological site was discovered in 1990. Xa:ytem (pronounced HAY-tum) is a native word designating a boulder on a plateau on the Fraser River. According to geologists, the rock was deposited

Exploring

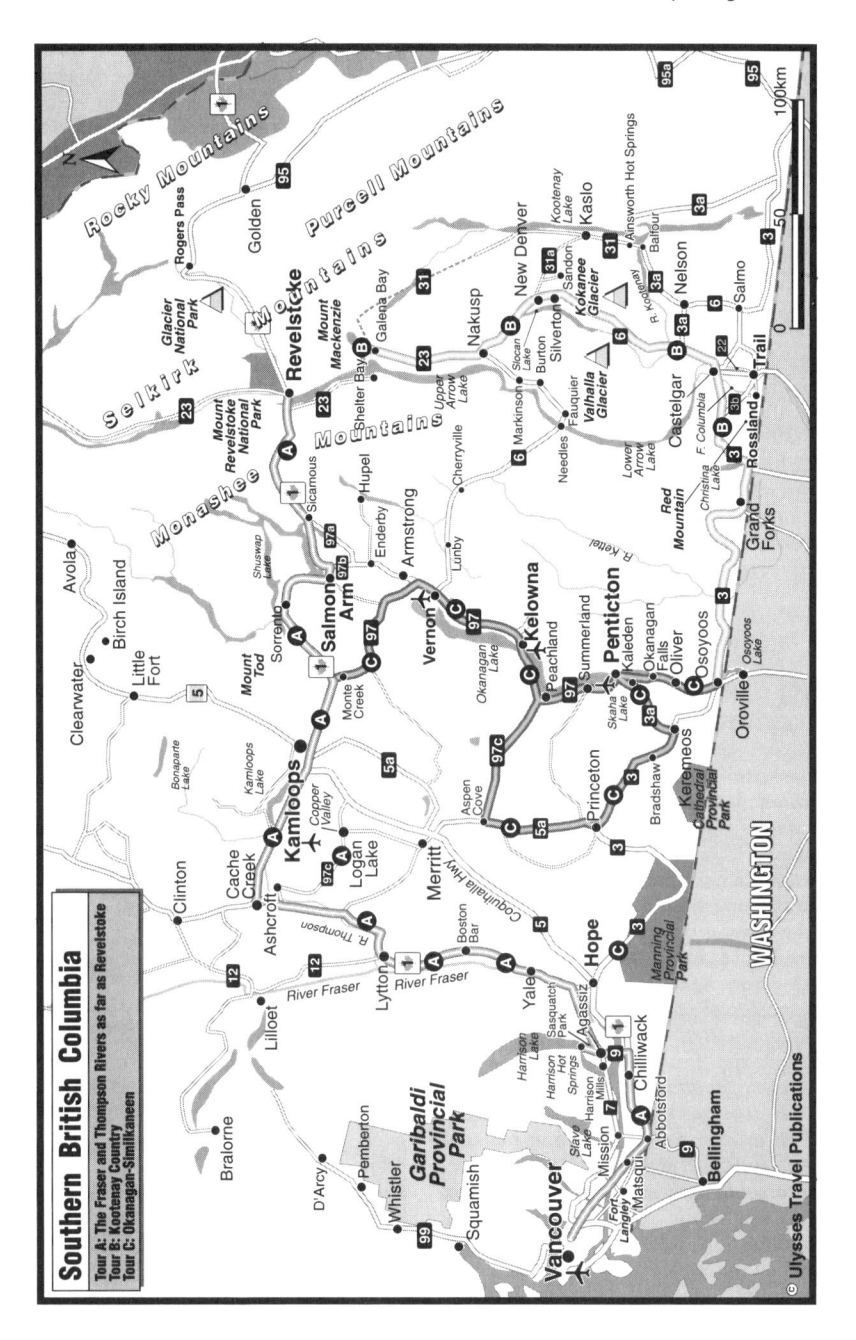

Southern British Columbia

Tour A: The Fraser and Thompson rivers as far as Revelstoke
Tour B: Kootenay Country
Tour C: Okanagan-Similkameen

© Ulysses Travel Publications

there by shifting glaciers. The Sto:lo Indians, who have inhabited this region for more than 4,000 years, explain the boulder's presence by saying that it is what became of three chiefs who had committed a sin. Hundreds of relics have been found in this area, including tools and weapons made out of stone. These articles are displayed in the centre, where the guides are Sto:lo Indians.

As you continue eastward, the landscape changes, with the mountains in the background looming larger. On your way over the Harrison Mills Bridge, take a good look at the magnificent river, where eagles compete for salmon during fall and winter. Take Highway 9 to Harrison Hot Springs.

Harrison Hot Springs ★

The **Harrison Hot Springs** are located at the southern end of Harrison Lake. The Coast Salish Indians used to come to here to soak in the warm mineral water, which supposedly has curative powers. Gold prospectors discovered the springs in 1858, when a storm on Lake Harrison forced them to return to shore and they happened to step into the warm water. The lake is surrounded by successive mountains peaks that stand out against the sky, making for a spectacular setting.

The indoor **Harrison Hot Springs Public Pool** ★ *(adults $6.50, children $4.50; May to Nov, every day 8am to 9pm; Dec to Apr, Sun to Thu 8am to 7pm, Fri and Sat 8am to 10pm; at the intersection of Hot Springs Road and Lilloet Avenue)* offers access to the springs. In addition to running the public pool, the Harrison Hotel has acquired rights to the springs. Every year in September and October, sand-castle enthusiasts flock to the beaches on Harrison Lake, with impressive results. The road, which runs alongside the lake, leads to Sasquatch Provincial Park (see p 146).

Double back and take Highway 7 toward Agassiz until you reach the TransCanada 1 East, then head for Yale and Cache Creek. The highway follows the Fraser River, plunging into an immense gorge. Clear weather is an absolute must if you want to take in the majestic spectacle unfolding before you.

Yale

Three major historical events contributed to the development of Yale: the growth of the fur trade, the gold rush and the construction of the railway. The town also marks the beginning of the Fraser Canyon, so buckle your seatbelts and keep your eyes wide open.

The **Alexandria Bridge** spans the Fraser at a striking point along the river that is only accessible by foot. The bridge is no longer part of the road system, but you can enjoy some splendid views of the Fraser from its promenade. A sign alongside the TransCanada Highway shows the way.

Hell's Gate ★ *(adults $8.50, children $6.50; ☎ 867-9279)* owes its name to Simon Fraser, the first European to navigate along this river. For a while, even the salmon had trouble making their way through this gorge, which had become narrower and narrower as a result of major landslides. The current was so strong that the fish couldn't swim upriver to spawn. To solve the problem, a pass was cleared. A cablecar will take you down to the water's edge, 152 m below.

Lytton

Lytton, the rafting centre of the province, marks the point at which the Thompson flows into the Fraser. Here again, the scenery is breathtaking. The valleys are desert-like, with low, dense vegetation. Those interested in running the rapids can rely solely on paddles or opt for a motorized canoe.

Ashcroft

Ashcroft lies a few kilometres east of Highway 1. In 1860, gold prospectors heading north set out from here. Take Highway 97C from Ashcroft to Logan Lake. As you make your way through a magnificent desert valley, you'll see the Sundance Guest Ranch (see p 152 for details on staying there), which looks out over the Thompson River. Ever since the 1950s, this ranch has been sending visitors off on horseback rides across thousands of hectares of fields. Like most ranches in the region, it was once the home of stockbreeders.

You can now get back on the TransCanada 1 East and make your way to Kamloops, passing through Cache Creek on the way in order to skirt round Kamloops Lake and see the ginseng fields (see below). We recommend taking Highway 97C to Logan Lake and the Copper Valley mine.

Copper Valley ★★ *(May to Sep, Mon to Fri 9:30am to 1pm; tours last 2 hrs 30 min;* ☎ *575-2443)*. Copper Valley is one of the largest open-cut copper mines in the world. The industrial machinery and the equipment used to transport the ore are completely outsized. Though you can't tour the mine, you'll notice its lunar landscape from the highway.

Continue driving east. When you reach the Coquihalla Highway (5), head for Kamloops.

Kamloops

Kamloops (pop. 68,500), the capital of inland British Columbia, is a major stopover point. The local economy is driven chiefly by the forest and tourist industries, with mining and stockbreeding playing a subsidiary role.

West of Kamloops, ginseng crops lie hidden in the fields beneath big pieces of black cloth. Large farms produce this root, which is highly coveted by Asians for the health benefits it is supposed to procure. The variety grown here, known as American ginseng, was discovered in eastern Canada several hundred years ago by Amerindians, who made potions with it. At the **Sunmore company** *(925 McGill Place,* ☎ *374-3017)*, you can learn about ginseng farming in North America and how local methods differ from those employed in Asia. You can also take a tour of the fields.

Another activity that underlines the importance of the rivers in British Columbia is a cruise aboard the *Wanda-Sue*, which sails along the Thompson River through bare mountains. Amerindians, trappers, gold prospectors, lumberjacks and railway workers all travelled by boat before the railway lines and roads were laid here. The *Wanda-Sue* ★ sets out from the Old Kamloops Yacht Club *(adults $10, children $6; Apr to Sep; the trip lasts* two hours; 1140 River Street, near Tenth Avenue, ☎ 374-7447).

Leave Kamloops and head towards Revelstoke on the TransCanada, which runs alongside the water, beaches, mountains and golf courses. The towns of Sorrento and Salmon Arm look out onto vast Shuswap Lake, which is popular with water sports fans, due to the pleasant temperature of its waters. One way of exploring the lake is to rent a houseboat from **Waterway Houseboat Vacations** (9am to 5pm; Sicamous, ☎ 836-2505 or 1-800-663-4022). The boats are well-equipped and as comfortable as hotel rooms. The forest industry and tourism are the mainstays of the local economy.

The TransCanada continues its route across valleys and mountains; the gorges become narrower and narrower and the heart of the Rockies appears on the horizon. The vegetation is much more luxuriant here, with small blue-grey shrubs giving way to mighty trees.

Revelstoke ★★

The history of **Revelstoke** is closely linked to the construction of the transcontinental railway. Large numbers of Italians came here to apply their expertise in building tunnels. To this day, the town's 9,000 residents rely mainly on the railroad for their income. Tourism and the production of electricity also play an important role in the economy of this magnificent town.

Revelstoke is a century-old town that has managed to retain its charm. Numerous Queen Anne, Victorian, Art Deco and neoclassical buildings here bear witness to days gone by. Pick up a copy of the **Heritage Walking & Driving Tour** ★ at the town hall, located on Mackenzie Avenue between 1st and 2nd Streets (☎ 837-2161).

The **Canadian Pacific Railway Museum** ★ (Feb to Apr, Mon to Fri 9am to 5pm; May and Jun, every day 9am to 5pm; Jul and Aug, every day 9am to 8pm; Sep to Dec, Wed to Mon 9am to 5pm; 719 Track Street, ☎ 837-6060) focuses on the construction of the railway across the Rockies and the history of Revelstoke. The exhibit features old objects, photos from the local archives and most importantly a 1940s locomotive and a company director's personal railway car, built in 1929.

At the **Revelstoke Dam** ★ (free admission; Mar to Jun, 9am to 5pm; Jun to Sep, 8am to 8pm; Sep and Oct, 9am to 5pm; closed Nov to Mar, although group visits are permitted during the low season; take Highway 23 North, ☎ 837-6211), you can learn about the production of hydro electricity and visit a number of rooms, as well as the dam itself, an impressive concrete structure.

Hiking buffs will be thrilled by all the outdoor excursions to be enjoyed in this area (see p 148).

Revelstoke is a crossroads between the Rockies and the Kootenays, to the south. If you plan on continuing east to Alberta, stay on the TransCanada (see p 122). We recommend driving down into Kootenays, which are much less well-known than the Rockies, but equally fascinating. Before heading south, however, continue until you reach **Rogers Pass** ★★, named after the engineer who discovered it in 1881. This valley was originally supposed to serve as a passage between the east and the west, but after a number of catastrophes, during which avalanches claimed the lives of hundreds of people, the Canadian Pacific railway company decided to build a tunnel instead. At the **Rogers Pass Centre** ★ (☎ *837-6274)*, located an hour from Revelstoke in Glacier National Park, visitors can learn about the epic history of the railway. A trail that runs along the former tracks will take you past the ruins of a railway station destroyed in an avalanche.

Back in Revelstoke, cross the town bridge and head toward Shelter Bay on Highway 23 South in order to take the free ferry *(every day 5pm to 12:30am)*. Get your camera ready during the trip across Upper Arrow Lake (25 min), because you're in for some splendid views of the Kootenays.

■ **Tour B: Kootenay Country** ★★

Located off the beaten tourist track, this region is a gold mine for visitors with a taste for mountains, lakes, history and chance encounters. Once again, the landscape is one of the major attractions; this is British Columbia, after all! Because this region is underappreciated, it remains virtually unspoiled, making it that much more interesting to explore.

Located in the southeast part of the province, the Kootenays are a series of mountains (the Rockies, the Purcells, the Selkirks and the Monashees) stretching from the north to the south. The great Columbia River runs through this region, creating the vast body of water known as Arrow Lake on its way. Natural resources such as forests and mines have played a major role in the region's development. A number of towns bear witness to the different stages in the Kootenays' history.

Nakusp

Before setting off across the Kootenays, you might want to stop at Nakusp's **Leland Hotel** *(Forth Avenue)*, located on the shores of Arrow Lake. You can sit on the terrace and have a bite to eat while taking in the scenery. During the mining boom, hundreds of prospectors flooded into Nakusp and other places like it throughout these mountains.

New Denver

New Denver was the gateway to silver country at the turn of the century, when there was an abundant supply of the metal in this region. The history of that era is presented at the **Silvery Slocan Museum** *(Jul to Sep; at the corner of 6th St. and Marine Drive, ☎ 358-2201)*. When Canada declared war on Japan during the Second World War, Japanese residents of British Columbia were interned in camps in a number of towns in this region, including New Denver and Sandon. To learn more about their experience, stop in at the **Nikkei Internment Memorial Centre** *(May to Oct, 9:30am to 5pm; by appointment during winter; 306 Josephine Street, ☎ 358-7288)*.

Get back on Highway 31A in the direction of Kaslo, and stop at **Sandon**, the former capital of Canada's silver mines.

Sandon ★★

At the turn of the century, 5,000 people lived and worked in **Sandon**. By 1930, the price of silver had dropped and the mine had been exhausted, prompting an exodus from the town. During World War II, Sandon became an internment centre for Japanese who had been living on the coast. Shortly after the war, it became a ghost town once again, and a number of buildings were destroyed by fire and floods. Today, visitors can admire what remains of a number of old buildings, as well as the first hydroelectric power plant constructed in the Canadian West, which still produces electricity.

A 12 km road, negotiable with an all-purpose vehicle, leads from Sandon to the Idaho Lookout, where you can take in a view of the Kokanee and Valhalla glaciers. Get back on Highway 31 and continue on to Kaslo.

Kaslo

Kaslo was built on the hills on the west shore of Kootenay Lake during the heyday of silver mining. A walk along the waterfront and a visit to the town hall will give you a glimpse of how beautiful the setting is. At the beginning of the century, people used to come here by paddle-boat. For nearly 60 years, up until 1957, the *SS Moyie* shuttled passengers back and forth across Kootenay Lake for Canadian Pacific. The boat has since been transformed into a museum.

At **Ainsworth Hot Springs** ★ *($6; swimsuit and towel rentals available;* ☎ *229-4212)*, which is located in an enchanting setting along the shore to the south, bathers can alternate between very cold and very warm water. The swimming pool overlooks Kootenay Lake and the valley which is brilliant at sunset. The U-shaped cave studded with stalactites, the humidity and the almost total absence of light will transport you to another world. The temperature rises as you near the springs at the back of the cave, reaching as high as 40°C.

Continue along Highway 31 south. At Balfour, take Highway 3A to Nelson.

Nelson ★★

Make sure to park your car as soon as possible and explore this magnificent town on foot. Located at the southern end of the West Arm of Kootenay Lake, Nelson lies on the west flank of the Selkirk Mountains. In 1887, during the silver boom, miners set up camp here, working together to build hotels, homes and public facilities. Numerous buildings now bear witness to the town's prosperous past. Nelson has managed to continue its economic growth today, thanks to light industry, tourism and the civil service.

The **Travel InfoCentre** *(225 Hall Street)* distributes two small pamphlets that will guide you through over 350 historic buildings. The town's elegant architecture makes walking about here a real pleasure. Classical, Queen Anne and Victorian buildings proudly line the streets. The stained-glass windows of the **Nelson Congregational Church** ★ *(at the corner of Stanley and Silica Streets)*, the Château-style **town hall** ★ *(502 Vernon Street)*, the group of buildings on **Baker Street** and above all the Italian-style **fire station** ★ *(919 Ward Street)* are eloquent reminders of the opulence of the silver mining era.

Its lovely architecture is not the only thing that sets Nelson apart from the other inland towns in British Columbia. You will also find a number of art galleries here, many of which are integrated into restaurants, so you can contemplate works of art while looking over the menu. This setup is known as the **Artwalk**, which enables artists to exhibit their work in participating businesses each year. For further information, contact the **West Kootenay Regional Arts Council** (☎ 354-1550).

Nelson was also chosen as the location for the American film *Roxanne*, starring Steve Martin. While strolling through town, you will come across the places where various scenes were shot, most notably the fire station overlooking town. For details, contact the **Nelson & District Chamber of Commerce** (☎ 352-6355).

The **Nelson Brewing Company** ★ *(512 Latimer Street, by appointment ☎ 352-3582)* was founded in 1893, and still produces beer for the local market. The company has occupied the same Victorian building since 1899.

Old **Streetcar no. 23** of the **Nelson Electric Tramway Company** *(May 22 to Labour Day, Sat, Sun and Easter holidays; May 22 to Labour Day, every day noon to 9pm; Labour Day to Oct Sat and Sun)* has been put back into service and carries passengers 1 km through Lakeside Park, near the town bridge.

At the intersection of Ward and Vernon Streets, head for Highway 3A, which will take you to Castlegar.

Castlegar

Castlegar, which lies at the confluence of the Columbia and Kootenay Rivers, has no downtown area. While crossing the bridge in the direction of the airport, you'll see a suspended bridge built by the Doukhobors; turn left for a closer look.

Back on the highway, go uphill, then turn right to reach the **Doukhobor Museum** ★ *(adults $4, children $2; Wed to Sun 9am to 5pm)*. Fleeing persecution in Russia, the Doukhobors emigrated to Canada in 1898. They wanted to live according to their own rules rather than those of the state; for example, they were against participation in any war. They established communities on the prairies and farmed the land, adhering to their traditional way of life and gradually developing towns and setting up industries. One group, led by Piotr Verigin, left the prairies for British Columbia and took up residence in the Castlegar area. After the economic crisis of 1929 and the death of Verigin, the community diminished, but their descendants have taken up the task of telling visitors about their ancestors.

After exiting the museum, turn right and take Highway 3 in the direction of Grand Forks, then turn onto the 3B in order to reach Rossland. You can take the 22 there as well, but the 3 and the 3B are worth the detour.

Rossland ★

Rossland is a picturesque little turn-of-the-century town that thrived during the gold rush and has managed to retain its charm. Located inside the crater of a former volcano, at an altitude of 1,023 m above sea level, it attracts skiers and people who simply enjoy being in the mountains. Nancy Greene Provincial Park, named after the 1968 Olympic champion, a native of Rossland, boasts several majestic peaks. Red Mountain, renowned for its high-quality powder, is a world-class resort. Skier Kerrin Lee-Gartner, who won the gold medal in the 1992 Olympic Games, is also from Rossland.

All of the gold was mined from this region long before these Olympic skiers arrived. In 1890, a prospector discovered a large vein of gold here. The news spread, and hundreds of adventurers came to try their luck, resulting in a gold rush. Numerous hotels, offices and theatres were built, and Rossland flourished. Then came the crash of 1929, which hit the town hard; that same year, a major fire destroyed part of the downtown area. Rossland was on the decline; the famous **Le Roi** mine closed down, and the future did not look bright. Visitors can learn about the history of the gold rush at the **Le Roi mine** ★ and the **Rossland Historical Museum** *($4; every day 9am to 5pm; at the intersection of the 3B and the 22; take Columbia Avenue east of the downtown area, ☎ 362-7722)*, which features an audiovisual presentation and a collection of objects from that era. The **Ski Hall of Fame**, located in the same building, highlights the careers of Nancy Greene and Kerrin Lee-Gartner.

Trail

The neighbouring town of **Trail** came to Rossland's rescue in a way. This large mining town has been transforming the ore from Rossland's mines since 1896. Cominco, a large metallurgical company, employs a sizeable portion of the local population to this day.

Rossland's yellow gold has been replaced by the "white gold" on the slopes, which attracts thousands of skiers here every year. See "Red Mountain" (p 150).

Get back on Highway 3 and head for Grand Forks. This pleasant road runs alongside Christina Lake on its way across the southern part of the Monashee Mountains.

Grand Forks

Grand Forks lies at the confluence of the Kettle and North Fork Rivers. Numerous artifacts have been found here, indicating that Amerindians once lived in this area. The first Europeans to come to this valley regularly were trappers working for the Hudson's Bay Company. The region later developed around the mining industry, but a drop in the price of copper in 1919 thwarted the community's growth. Thanks to farming and forestry, Grand Forks is once again a thriving town.

Keep heading west on Highway 3.

Starting in **Grand Forks**, the landscape becomes desert-like again. The road leads through some lovely valleys, but the real highlight of the trip comes when you enter the **Okanagan** valley from the east. A town and a lake are visible several hundred metres below.

■ Tour C: Okanagan-Similkameen ★★★

All sorts of natural treasures await discovery in this part of British Columbia. With its stretches of water and blanket of fruit trees, the Okanagan Valley, which runs north-south, is one of the most beautiful areas in the province. Okanagan wines have won a number of prizes; the orchards feed a good portion of the country, and the lakes and mountains are a dream come true for sporty types. The climate is conducive to a wide variety of activities; the winters, mild in town and snowy in the mountains, can be enjoyed by all. In the spring, the fruit trees are in bloom, while in summer and fall, a day of fruit-picking is often followed by a dip in one of the many lakes.

For more information on the wine route, touring the vineyards and the wine festival, contact the **Okanagan Wine Festival Office** *(185 Lakeshore Drive, Penticton,* ☎ *490-8866)* or the **Okanagan-Similkameen Tourism Association** *(1332 Water Street, Kelowna,* ☎ *860-5999)*.

Osoyoos

Osoyoos lies at the bottom of the valley, flanked on one side by Osoyoos Lake and on the other by verdant slopes decked with vineyards and orchards. It is located a few kilometres from the U.S. border, in an arid climate more reminiscent of an American desert, or even southern Italy, than a Canadian town. The main attraction here is the exceptionally warm lake, where you can enjoy a variety of water sports during summer.

Osoyoos's main street is crowded with lousy motels, which detract from the beauty of the setting. The public parks on the west side are worth visiting, however, especially at the end of the day, when the sun lights up the valley.

On your way out of town, take Highway 3 West and continue past Highway 97 to take a look at **Spotted Lake** ★. A natural phenomenon causes white rings to form on the surface of this lake, whose waters contain high levels of mineral salts. The lake is located on private property, so you can only look at it from the road.

Backtrack to Highway 97 and head toward Penticton. You'll soon enter an area covered with grape vines and peach and apple trees.

The wine route runs through the vast Okanagan region. North of Osoyoos and south of Oliver, you'll come across the **Domaine Combret** ★ *(*☎ *498-8878)*. In 1995, the *Office International de la Vigne et du Vin*, based in Burgundy, France, awarded this French-owned vineyard the highest international distinction for its Chardonnay. Its Reisling also won a prize in 1995. You must call beforehand for a tour of the premises, as the wine growers spend a good part of the day outside among the vines during the grape-picking season. Originally from the south of France, the Combrets come from a long line of wine makers. Robert Combret first visited the Okanagan Valley in the 1950s, while he was spending some time at the University of British Columbia. He returned in the early 1990s. His son Olivier runs the family business now. Stop by and enjoy a sample some of his wine.

Without irrigation, this valley would still be like a desert, and the orchards and vineyards would not have been able to thrive and bear fruit each year. The 97 North will guide you through this annual spectacle; let yourself be carried away across this colourful sea of ripe fruit.

Penticton ★

Penticton lies between Okanagan Lake, to the north, and Skaha Lake, to the south. The town has nearly 30,000 inhabitants and boasts a dry, temperate climate. Tourism is the mainspring of Penticton's economy. The Amerindians christened the site *Pen-tak-tin*, meaning "the place where you stay forever". A beach lined with trees and a pedestrian walkway run along the north end of town. The dry landscape, outlined by the curves of the sandy shoreline, contrasts with the vineyards and orchards. People come to Penticton for the outdoor activities, fine dining and local *joie de vivre*.

Take Main Street to Lakeshore Drive, turn left and stop in front of the **SS Sicamous** *($2; Mon to Sat 7am to 3pm)*, a survivor of a bygone era. This paddle-boat was once the principal means of transportation on Okanagan Lake. Built in Ontario in 1914 and assembled here, it was in service for over 20 years before being hauled up onto the beach.

Penticton hosts a major sporting event, the World Cup **Ironman** triathlon, a swimming, cycling and running race. Athletes from all over the world take part in the Ironman, and many of them live in Penticton while awaiting the next competition. They train here, and it is not uncommon to see them working in the fields. The triathlon takes place in August, at the beginning of the fruit-picking season. For further information, see Mike Barrett, the owner of the **Hog's Breath Coffee Co.** *(202 Main Street, ☎ 493-7800)*, who has competed in numerous triathlons. The athletes often congregate at this café.

A visit to an orchard is a must, especially in the heart of summer, during the fruit-picking season. Not only is the fruit plentiful, but more importantly, it's delicious. From July to late September, the region is covered with fruit trees bursting with scent and colour. The **Dickinson Family Farm** *(turn left onto Jones Flat road from Highway 97 North, then right onto Bentley Road 17208, ☎ 494-8732)* invites visitors to stroll through its rows of fruit trees. You can purchase fruit (apples, pears, etc.) and fruit-based products on the premises. For a real treat, try the peach butter and the freshly pressed apple juice. Head out of Penticton on Lakeshore Drive and take the 97 North toward Summerland.

An outing in the mountains along the former route of the **Kettle Valley Railway** ★★ offers another perspective of the Okanagan Valley. Laid at the turn of the century, these tracks connected Nelson, in the east, to Hope, in the west, thus providing a link between the hinterland, where tons of ore were being extracted, and the Pacific coast. Mother Nature was a major obstacle throughout the railway's short existence; fallen debris, avalanches and snowstorms made the tracks impossible to use, and the line was abandoned. The 20 million dollar cost of building the railway was never recovered.

You can follow the tracks on foot or by bicycle. The railway runs through Penticton on either shore of Okanagan Lake, and the terrain is relatively flat, making for a pleasant outing. The directions, however, are not very clear. Start on Main Street, in downtown Penticton, and follow the signs for Naramata Road, then turn right onto MacMillan. At this point, the signs seem to disappear. Take the main road; as soon as its name becomes Chute Lake, keep right and then turn right again on Smethurst Road and keep going until you reach the end. You can either leave your car in town or drive the first 6 km (at your own risk); pedestrians and cyclists have priority. You'll enjoy a direct view of Okanagan Lake along the way. After 4.8 km, you'll pass through a small tunnel. Make noise as you walk to drive off any rattlesnakes, black bears or cougars.

Exploring 137

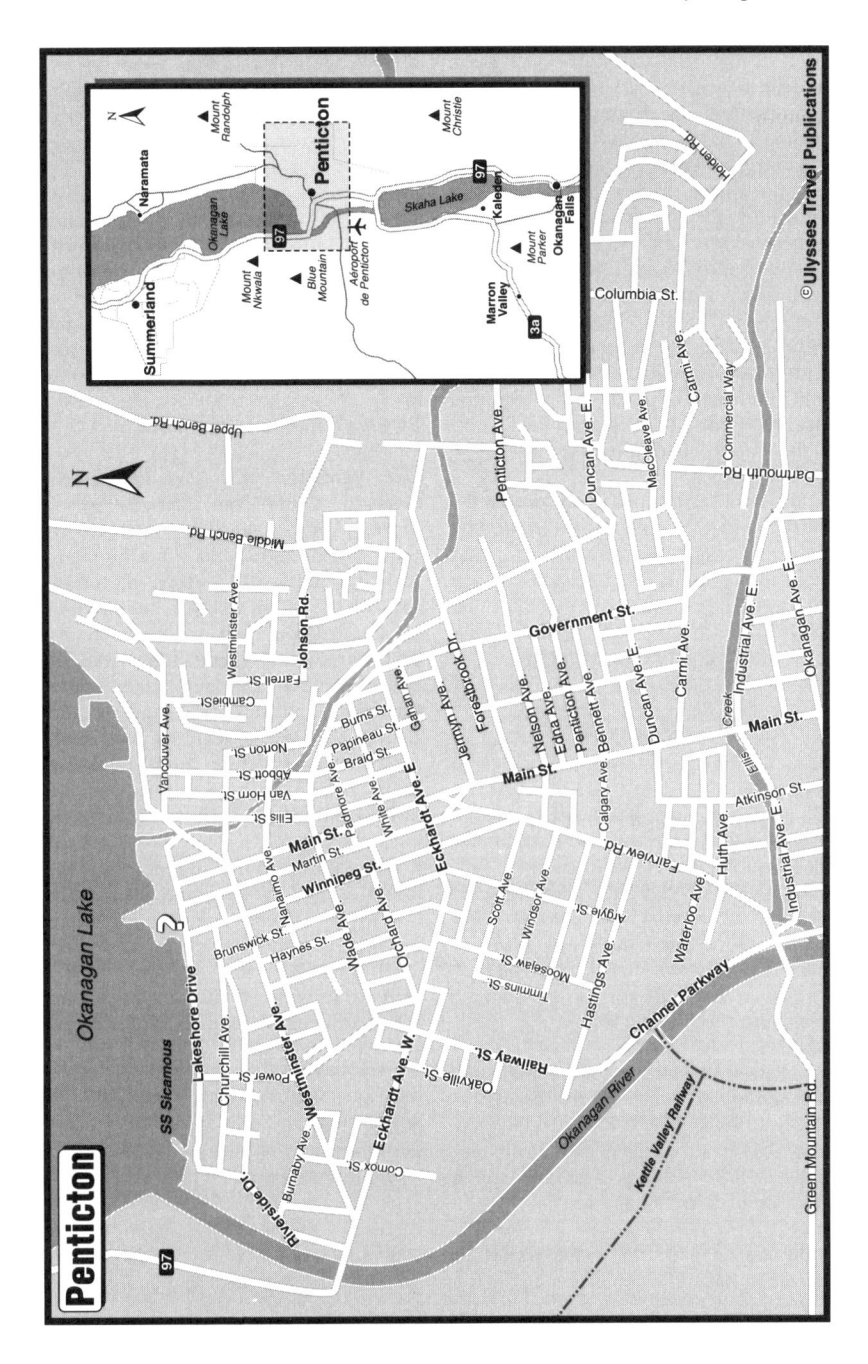

On the west shore, in Summerland, a part of the track is now used by a steam engine. Head toward Summerland on Highway 97 North, turn left on Solly Road and follow the signs for the **West Summerland Station of the Kettle Valley Steam Railway** (☎ 494-8422). Maps for both areas are available at the Penticton tourist office on Lakeshore Drive. The next stops on this itinerary are Kelowna and Hope.

After visiting the southern part of the Okanagan Valley, between Osoyoos and Penticton, you can continue heading west by taking Highway 3A, to Kaleden and beyond (see p 139).

Your other option is to stay on the 97 North, which leads through the towns of **Summerland** and **Peachland** on the way to **Kelowna**. This stretch of road runs along a mountainside, and is lined with orchards, wineries and stopping areas from one end to the other.

Kelowna ★

Kelowna is the heart and mind of the Okanagan Valley. It was here that a French Oblate by the name of Father Charles Pandosy set up the first Catholic mission in the hinterland of British Columbia in 1859. He introduced apple and grape growing into the Okanagan Valley, and was thus largely responsible for its becoming a major fruit-producing region.

The **Father Pandosy mission** (every day; on Benvoulin Road, at the corner of Casorso Road, ☎ 860-8369), which has been listed as a provincial historic site since 1983, includes a church and a number of farm buildings.

Kelowna, one of the most important towns in inland British Columbia, has a population of 80,000. Its economy is driven by fruit farming, wine-making and, as of more recently, a few light industries as well. Tourism is also important to Kelowna, and the town has a lot to offer its many visitors.

Located on the shores of Okanagan Lake, Kelowna boasts several waterfront parks. One of these is **Knox Mountain Park**, where you'll find a magnificent viewing area. You might even catch a glimpse of Ogopogo, the monster that supposedly inhabits the lake. To get to the park, take Ellis Street north out of downtown.

Like Penticton, Kelowna is located along the **Kettle Valley Railway**; again, though, you have to know where you're going, since there are no signs to follow between the downtown area and the top of the valley. After strolling along Bernard Street and the beaches on Okanagan Lake for a little while, get back in your car and take South Pandosy Street, turn left (eastward) on K.L.O. Road, which becomes McCulloch, and then right on June Springs Road. Free parking is available at the end of the road.

It takes about 20 min to reach the first metal bridge, which stretches across the **Myra Canyon ★★**. If you enjoy walking, you'll love this excursion. The local Chamber of Commerce (544 Harvey Avenue, ☎ 861-1515) or the Okanagan-Similkameen Tourism Association (1332 Water Street, ☎ 860-5999) can help you plan outings that take several days. Cyclists can pedal about to their heart's content; the more adventurous can spend a day riding to Penticton.

Almost all the wine produced in British Columbia comes from the Okanagan region. Over the past few years, local

Exploring   139

wines have won a number of international prizes. There are three vineyards along Lakeshore Road, south of Kelowna, including the **Cedar Creek Winery** *(5445 Lakeshore Road, ☎ 764-8866)*, which, like its competitors in the region, produces much more white wine than red. It is located on a pretty hill surrounded by vines and looking out onto Okanagan Lake. A free tour of the premises will give you a chance to sample some of the wines; the chardonnay is particularly noteworthy. You can also purchase a few bottles while you're there.

Vernon

Get back on the 97 North and continue on to Vernon, which is set amidst three lakes. The town started out modestly in the 1860s, when Cornelius O'Keefe established a ranch here. The northern part of Vernon is an important stockbreeding area. Stop by at the **Historic O'Keefe Ranch** *(every day May to Oct; 12 km north of Vernon on Highway 97, ☎ 542-7868)*, where you'll find the original ranch house, wooden church and ranching equipment. Forestry and agriculture play a greater economic role here than in Kelowna and Penticton, where tourism is more important.

Highway 97 North intersects with the TransCanada at Monte Creek, east of Kamloops. You can also reach the 1 from the 97A, which leads to Sicamous, west of Revelstoke. Otherwise, backtrack to Kelowna and take Highway 97C to Merritt.

Merritt

Merritt lies in a region with over 150 lakes, surrounded by mountains and pastures where tens of thousands of heads of cattle can be seen grazing. If you'd like to step back in time to the days when cowboys met here to talk and live it up, head downtown to the **Coldwater Hotel**, built in 1908, or over to the **Quilchena Hotel**, located 23 km northeast of Merritt on the 5A.

Backtrack to Penticton and pick up the 3A south of town.

Kaleden

Tucked away atop a mountain near **Kaleden** is the **Dominion Radio Astrophysical Observatory** ★ *(Jul and Aug, Sun 2pm to 5pm)*, run by the Canadian Research Council. If you're looking for a star, this place can help you find it.

Peaceful Highway 3A runs through a valley lined with lakes, affording some lovely views.

Keremeos

In **Keremeos**, history is recounted at the **Grist Mill** ★ *(May to Oct; R.R. 1, Upper Bench Road, ☎ 499-2888)*, founded in 1877 to produce flour for the local Amerindians, cowboys and miners. The water mill, equipment and original buildings have been restored and are now part of British Columbia's heritage.

Cathedral Provincial Park ★★ covers 33,000 ha of mountains, lakes, valleys, wildlife and flowers. It is crisscrossed by trails that everyone can enjoy, since most cover fairly level terrain and are suitable for a variety of fitness levels. Furthermore, almost all of the bears in this region were driven off by the cowboys decades ago. A mountaintop inn accommodates visitors wishing to stay in the park (see "Parks and Beaches" p 146 and "Hiking" p 149).

At the park exit, get back on Highway 3, which will take you to Princeton.

Princeton

American researchers come to the **Princeton Museum and Archives ★** *(Jul and Aug, every day 9am to 6pm; Sep to Jun, Mon to Fri 1pm to 5pm; Margaret Stoneberg, curator, ☎ 295-7988, home ☎ 295-3362)* to study its impressive collection of fossils. You'll get caught up in curator Margaret Stoneberg's enthusiasm as she tells you about the pieces and how they bear witness to the region's history. Due to underfunding the fossils pile up without being properly displayed, but it is nevertheless amazing to see how much the museum holds.

The **Maverick Cattle Drives Ltd.** *($100; lunch, morning and afternoon outings, cattle driving; ☎ 295-3893)* welcomes visitors who want to experience life on a ranch. You'll find yourself on the back of a horse, riding in the warm summer breeze across fields of wheat, taking in the view of the nearby glaciers. This wonderful experience also involves carrying out a number of tasks on the ranch. At the end of the day, all the cowboys get together at the saloon.

As you continue westward on Highway 3, you will be leaving the vast Okanagan-Similkameen region and heading into the southwestern part of the province, back to the confluence of the Fraser and Coquihalla Rivers.

Located 45 min from Princeton, **Manning Provincial Park ★★** attracts hundreds of visitors each season. Twice the size of Cathedral Park, it covers 60,000 ha of wilderness, where you'll find all sorts of treasures (see "Parks and Beaches" p 146 and "Hiking" p 148).

Hope

Hope, located at the confluence of the Coquihalla, Fraser and Nicolum Rivers, marks the gateway to the Fraser Canyon. The Hudson's Bay Company established a fur-trading post named Fort Hope on this site in 1848; 10 years later, prospectors lured by the discovery of gold would stock up on supplies here.

The **Kettle Valley Railway** left a significant mark on the Hope region. Five tunnels known as the **Othello Tunnels** were bored through walls of granite so that the train could cross the Coquihalla canyon. Like other sections of this railroad, fallen debris and avalanches got the better of the tracks.

A visit to this magnificent linear park will enable you to appreciate the genius of those who built the railway and admire the majestic landscape looming up in front of it. Hollywood even picked this spot as a setting for the films *First Blood* and *Shoot to Kill*. Take Wallace Street from downtown Hope, turn right on 6th Avenue, then left on Kawkawa Lake Road; after crossing a bridge and a set of railroad tracks, turn right on

Othello Road. The entrance to the parking lot will be on your right. Don't forget to bring a camera.

A local chainsaw sculptor creates impressive pieces that delight visitors and residents alike. It all started when sculptor Pete Ryan transformed the trunk of a large tree in Memorial Park into an eagle with a salmon in its claws. Ever since, a number of his works, covering a variety of themes, have come to adorn downtown Hope.

If you'd like to take in a bird's-eye view of the region, go to the Hope airport and take a ride in a glider (see "Outdoor Activities", p 151).

Pick up the TransCanada Highway 1 and head for Vancouver, 150 km to the west. Past Vancouver, the 1 runs alongside English Bay, on the west coast; at Horseshoe Bay, get on the Sea to Sky Highway (99), in the direction of Squamish-Whistler, or take a ferry to the Sunshine Coast.

■ **Tour D: The Sea to Sky Highway** ★★

Magnificent panoramic views abound all along the coast. Whether you are travelling by car, by train or aboard a ferry, a succession of fjords, mountains, forests and scenic viewpoints will unfold before you. The Sea to Sky Highway is a winding road used by many visitors who come to Whistler for sporting vacations in both winter or summer. Forestry and tourism are the two mainsprings of this vast region's economy. The first stop on the 99 is Britannia Beach.

Britannia Beach

For nearly a century, **Britannia Beach** ★ was an important mining town, where thousands of tons of copper were extracted. It has now been transformed into a giant museum, where visitors can learn how the mines operated from the turn of the century to the early 1960s, when they shut down. A walk through the tunnels will take you back to another era, while a guide explains and demonstrates the various drilling techniques that were used as the machinery became more and more advanced. The tour ends at the mill, where the ore was cleaned. The **B.C. Museum of Mining** ★ *($9, students $7; May and Jun, Wed to Sun; Jul and Aug, every day; Sep and Oct, Wed to Sun, 10am to 4:30pm;* ☎ *688-8735 or 896-2233).*

Highway 99 runs alongside Howe Sound to Squamish. For many years, the only means of getting to the town from the south was by boat; some communities still rely on ferries to reach the coast farther north.

Squamish

Located at the north end of Howe Sound, **Squamish** owes its existence to the forest industry, which still helps support the local economy. You can see the forestry workers in action in the woods, at the sawmill or in the sorting yard, where gigantic machines put the blocks of wood in place. The **Soo Coalition for Sustainable Forests** ★ *($20; 4-hour walk in the woods, reservations required; tour of Squamish facilities, $5; Mon to Fri 9am to 5pm;*

☎ *892-9766)* is an organization that works toward preserving both the forest and the jobs related to the industry. It arranges tours of the forest and the lumber yard in order to educate the public on this subject.

The historic **Royal Hudson Steam Train** *($35 round-trip; Jun to Sep, Wed to Sun; 10am departure from North Vancouver; 1311 West First Street; it is also possible to come back by boat; the fare is $59;* ☎ *688-7246 or 1-800-663-8238)* runs back and forth between North Vancouver and Squamish, following the coastline and offering unimpeded views of the island and the snow-capped peaks of the Coast Mountains.

Windsurfers come to Squamish, whose name means "mother of the wind", for the wind that sweeps down the sound and then shifts inland. Mountain-climbing is also becoming more popular in this region. The place to go is **Stawamus Chief Mountain**. The trails leading to this granite monolith will take you to places where you can watch the mountain climbers. For more information, contact the Squamish & Howe Sound District Chamber of Commerce *(*☎ *892-9244)*.

Highway 99 heads inland and runs alongside Garibaldi Park on its way through the valley that leads to Whistler.

Whistler ★★

Whistler ★★ attracts skiers, golfers, hikers, sailors and snowboarders from all over the world. An impressive hotel complex graces the little village at the foot of Blackcomb and Whistler Mountains. Other amenities at this internationally renowned resort include restaurants, shops, sports facilities and a convention centre. Whistler is popular in summer and winter alike, and each season offers its own assortment of activities.

In the early 1960s, a group of adventurers wanted this area to host the 1968 Winter Olympics, and created Garibaldi Park for that purpose. Although their hopes for the Olympics did not come through, they did not give up on the idea of turning the valley into a huge ski resort. The population of Whistler increased tenfold in 20 years, and in the year 1993 alone, over a million people enjoyed the outdoors here.

Whistler receives, on average, nearly 1,000 cm of snow each year, and the temperature hovers around -5°C during the winter months. For details about the host of activities available here, refer to the "Outdoor Activities" section (see p 147).

Whistler hosts all sorts of events throughout the year, including the men's World Cup downhill competition, World Cup acrobatic skiing, gay skiers' week and a jazz festival.

Take the time to walk through the hotel village at the foot of the mountains and soak up the festive, relaxed atmosphere. Everything has its price here, and enjoying yourself can be quite expensive.

Outside of the little village, at the edge of the Whistler area, lies Function Junction, a small-scale industrial centre (of sorts).

Exploring 143

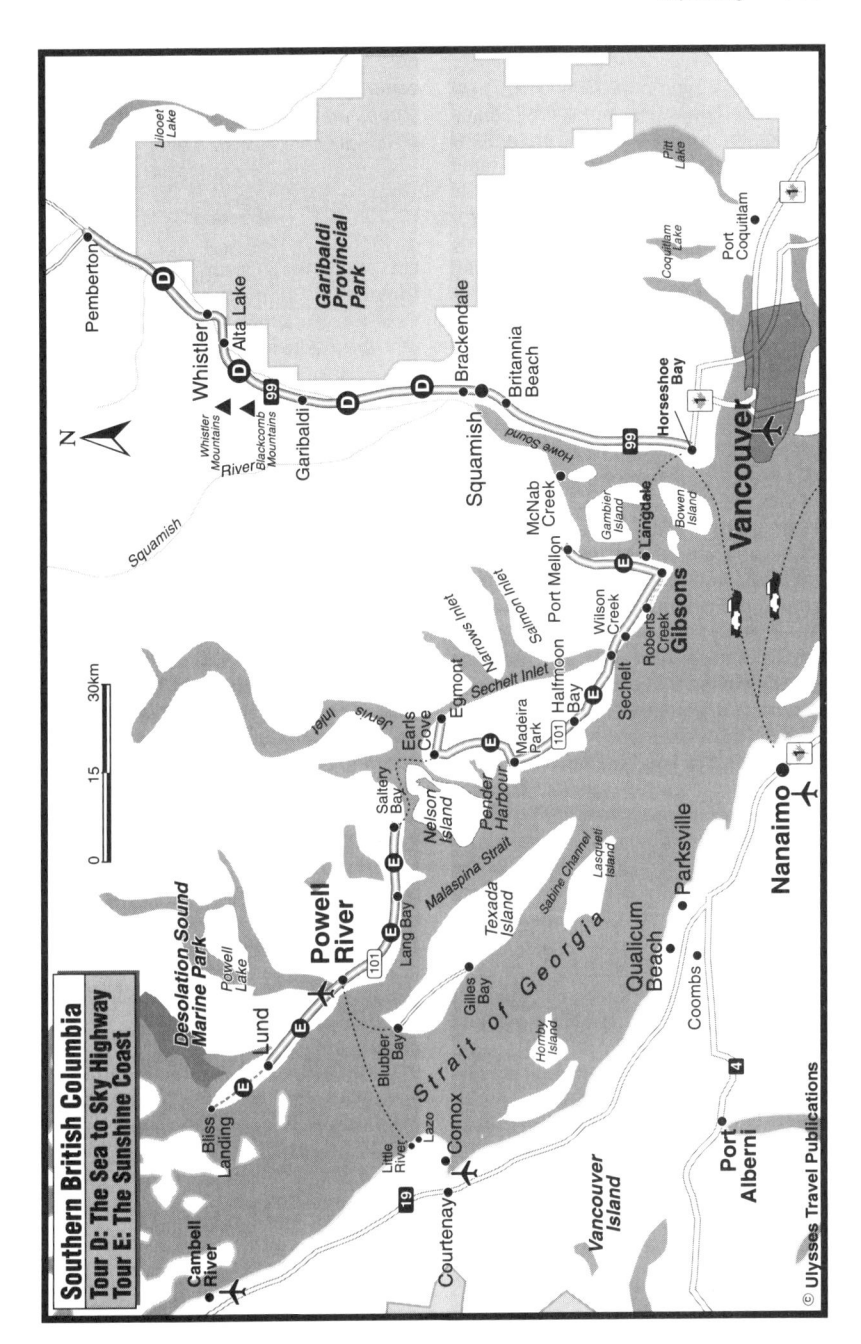

■ Tour E: The Sunshine Coast ★★

Most people get to the Sunshine Coast by boat. There are no roads linking Vancouver to these resort towns; the daily comings and goings are dictated by the ferry schedule. As a result, the mentality here is completely different. The towns that have grown up along this coast benefit from the sea and what it yields. The Sunshine Coast runs along the Strait of Georgia, and is surrounded by Desolation Sound to the north, the Coast Mountains to the east and Howe Sound farther south.

Langdale

It takes 40 min to reach **Langdale**, a small port city at the southern tip of the Sunshine Coast. The ferries shuttle back and forth several times a day, but you have to arrive at the Horseshoe Bay terminal at least an hour early for some weekend departures *(BC Ferry, information 7am to 10pm; Vancouver ☎ 669-1211, Victoria ☎ 386-3431)*. **Horseshoe Bay** lies 20 km northwest of Vancouver. You can save up to 25% on the price of your ticket if you return by way of Vancouver Island instead of opting for a round-trip. Ask for the Sunshine Coast Circlepac. You have to travel on a weekday between 10am and 4:30pm to obtain the discount.

During the ferry ride, your notion of distance will change; the time required to get from point A to point B can no longer be measured in the same way. Let yourself be carried away; just sit back and contemplate the view between the sea and the mountains.

The Coast Salish Indians were the first people to inhabit the coast. The Squamish and Sechelt tribes lived in the present-day Gibsons region. Europeans first sailed these waters in the 1790s, but it wasn't until Captain Richards came here in 1859 and 1860 that a record was made of all the bays, coves, islands and sounds.

Gibsons

On the way from **Langdale** to **Gibsons ★**, stop off at **Molly's Reach Café** to take a look at the photographs of the actors from the popular Canadian television show, *The Beachcombers* and to explore the little shops and restaurants along **Molly's Lane ★**. A visit to the **Sunshine Coast Maritime Museum ★** *(at the end of Molly's Lane, ☎ 886-4114)* is a must. You will be greeted by a charming woman, who will inspire you with her passion for the local marine life.

The Sunshine Coast has been developed in a thin strip alongside the forest. The area abounds in plant and animal life — orchids and wild roses, deer and black bears. River otters and beavers can be found near the coast, while sea-lions and seals swim about farther offshore.

Sechelt

To get to **Sechelt**, take Highway 191 northward. The landscape is rather dreary, but its beauty is soon enhanced by the sea and the islands. Sechelt is an important administrative centre for the Amerindian community. At the **House of Hewhiwus** *(5555 Highway 101, beside the tourist office)*, you'll find a theatre, an art gallery and a souvenir shop. Members of the community can tell you about Amerindian art, each piece of which is associated with a legend.

The Sunshine Coast is best explored aboard a boat on one of the neighbouring waterways. Turn right on Wharf Road and go to Government Wharf. **TZOONIE Tours** ★ *($55; Wed to Sun 9:30am to 2:30pm;* ☎ *885-0351; or Tzoonie Gift House, 5644 Cowrie Street, Sechelt,* ☎ *885-9802)* arranges outings on Sechelt Inlet, as far as the Skookumchuck Rapids, aimed at familiarizing visitors with the local marine life. A salmon barbecue is served on the shore, and a you'll enjoy a ride on the Skookumchuck ("strong waters") Rapids at high tide, when the water is over 3 m higher. If you simply want to take a look at the rapids, go to Egmont; to get there, keep right before Earls Cove on the road to Powell River. The parking lot is nearly 4 km from the viewing area.

Pender Harbour

Still heading toward Earls Cove, you will pass alongside **Pender Harbour**, whose series of little islands are a fisherman's dream come true. Easily accessible by both land and water, this place is popular with salmon fishermen. Lowe's Resort *(*☎ *883-2456)* arranges sea excursions.

The Sunshine Coast is divided in two. A ferry will take you from Earls Cove to Saltery Bay, offering yet another opportunity to take in British Columbia's splendid scenery.

Powell River ★

Powell River, an important waterfront town, boasts magnificent sunsets over Vancouver Island and the islands in the Strait of Georgia. The spotlight is on outdoor activities in this region, since the temperate climate is conducive to year-round fun and games. Forestry plays an important role in the local economy, but visitors come here for the lakes, the woods, the wildlife and the views.

After a walk in the mountains or along the waterfront, the most beautiful views of the Strait of Georgia will be forever etched in your mind. Visitors to this region enjoy a host of water sports twelve months a year. There are activities to suit every budget, and all of them are immediately accessible.

The limpid water lures scuba buffs here every year, especially during winter. In the **Saltery Bay Provincial Park** ★, a bronze statue of a mermaid lies hidden away among the ocean's treasures at a depth of 20 m.

Lund ★

Lund, located at the beginning (or the end, depending on what direction you're heading in) of Highway 101, is the gateway to marvellous **Desolation Sound** ★★, a marine life sanctuary easily accessible by canoe or kayak. The town port is magnificent, with its old hotel, its adjoining shops and its wooden promenade, which skirts round the bay. Imagine a typical fishing village and your harbour will undoubtedly be filled with the fishing boats moored here. In terms of activities, there is much to choose from here, from fishing and whale-watching trips to snorkelling and kayaking, a sport everyone can enjoy.

You can take the ferry from Powell River to Vancouver Island or backtrack to Landale and return to Vancouver by way of Horseshoe Bay.

Parks and Beaches

■ Tour A: The Fraser and Thompson Rivers as Far as Revelstoke

The **Sasquatch Provincial Park** *(beach, playground, boat-launching ramp; Cultus Lake,* ☎ *858-7161)* lies tucked away in the mountains by Harrison Lake. You can camp, and beaches have been laid out so that visitors can spend a pleasant day here enjoying one of the lakes. According to a Coast Salish Indian legend, the Sasquatch is half-man, half-beast and lives in the woods. To this day, some natives claim to have seen the creature around Harrison Lake.

Manning Provincial Park ★★ *(tourist information, summer 8am to 8pm, winter 9am to 5pm;* ☎ *840-8836)* is located on the boundary of the southwestern part of the province and the huge Okanagan-Similkameen region. It lies 225 km from Vancouver, making it a popular getaway for city-dwellers in search of vast green spaces.

You can explore the woods on scores of paths in **Revelstoke** ★★ and **Glacier** ★★ **National Parks** *(for maps, information and regulations, contact Parks Canada in Revelstoke,* ☎ *837-7500 or in Rogers Pass,* ☎ *837-6274)*. The level of difficulty varies; some trails run past centuries-old trees or lead to the tops of mountains, affording splendid panoramic views.

■ Tour B: Kootenay Country

Kokanee Glacier Provincial Park ★★ *(contact the BC Parks District Manager for maps; Nelson,* ☎ *825-4421)* has about ten hiking trails of average difficulty, which require a total of about 4 hours of walking. The park, which looks out over two lakes (Kootenay and Slocan), is accessible from a number of different places.

■ Tour C: Okanagan-Similkameen

Knox Mountain Park lies north of Kelowna and offers a beautiful view of Okanagan Lake, whose waters are supposedly inhabited by a monster named Ogopogo. To get there from downtown, head north on Ellis Street.

Cathedral Provincial Park ★★ *(For detailed maps and information, contact the* **BC Parks District Manager**; *1050 West Columbia Street, #101, B.C. V2C 1L2,* ☎ *371-6400 or Box 399, Summerland, B.C. V0H 1Z0,* ☎ *494-0321)* is located 30 km southwest of Keremeos, in the southern part of the province, right alongside the U.S. border. There are two distinct kinds of vegetation here — the temperate forest and the plant growth characteristic of the arid Okanagan region. At low altitudes, Douglas firs dominate the landscape, giving way to spruce and heather higher up. Deer, mountain goats and wild sheep sometimes venture out near the turquoise-coloured lakes.

■ Tour D: The Sea to Sky Highway

Vast **Garibaldi Provincial Park** ★★ *(information Garibaldi/Sunshine District, Brackendale; 10 km north of Squamish,* ☎ *898-3678)*, which covers 195,000 ha, is extremely popular with hikers during summertime. Highway 99 runs along the west side of the park, offering access to the various trails.

In the Whistler valley, near the village, there are five lakes where you can go swimming, windsurfing, canoeing and sailing. Here are two or them:

At little **Alpha Lake** *(at the traffic like at Whistler Creekside, turn left on Lake Placid Road and continue until you reach the beach)*, you can enjoy a picnic, rent a canoe or play tennis or volleyball.

Alta Lake *(north of Whistler Creekside on Highway 99; turn left on Alta Vista Road and right on Alpine Crescent, then keep left until the end of the road to reach Lakeside Park)* attracts windsurfers. Sailboard rentals are available here, along with canoes and kayaks (**Whistler Outdoor Experience Company**, ☎ *932-3389)*.

■ **Tour E: The Sunshine Coast**

Saltery Bay Provincial Park *(north of the Saltery Bay terminal, 42 campsites, beaches, scuba diving, wheelchair access; B.C. Parks, Garibaldi/Sunshine Coast District,* ☎ *898-3678)* is an outstanding place to go scuba diving; a bronze mermaid awaits you underwater, and you have a good chance of spotting a killer whale, a seal or a sea-lion.

Desolation Sound Marine Park ★★★ *(north of Lund, accessible by boat; campsites, hiking, kayaking, swimming, fishing, scuba diving, potable water, toilets; B.C. Parks District Manager, Garibaldi/Sunshine Coast District,* ☎ *898-3678)* is popular with ocean lovers, who come here to observe the animal life inhabiting these warm waters. More and more people are coming here to go sea kayaking *(***Eagle Kayaking Adventures** *$79; kayak ride,* guide and lunch; ☎ *483-4012)*, something even novices can enjoy.

Outdoor Activities

River Rafting

Tour A: The Fraser and Thompson Rivers as Far as Revelstoke

Hundreds of adventurers come to the gorges of the Fraser and Thompson Rivers each year to brave the tumultuous waters in small groups. A number of packages are available to visitors wishing to travel downriver on inflatable rafts, including those offered by **Kumsheen Raft Adventures** *(Lytton* ☎ *455-2296 or 1-800-663-6667)*.

Canoeing

Tour E: The Sunshine Coast

A canoe trip is a must, especially if you're dying to discover a series of lakes and are up for portaging. The **Powell Forest Canoe Route** ★, a tour of eight lakes, takes four days. For more information, contact the **Sunshine Coast Forest District Office** *(7077 Duncan Street,* ☎ *485-0700)*.

Sailing

Tour B: Kootenay Country

Lakeside Park, to the right of the bridge on the way into Nelson, offers access to Kootenay Lake. During summer, you can swim and windsurf here to your heart's content.

Tour D: The Sea to Sky Highway

Windsurfers come to **Squamish** for the constant winds that sweep down the sound then head inland. For information, contact the Squamish & Howe Sound District Chamber of Commerce (☎ 892-9244).

Alta Lake *(north of Whistler Creekside on Highway 99; turn left on Alta Vista Road and right on Alpine Crescent, then keep left until the end of the road to reach Lakeside Park)* attracts windsurfers. This little lake is located in an enchanting setting, which offers lovely panoramic views of Whistler and Blackcomb. **Whistler Outdoor Experience Company** (☎ 932-3389) rents sailboards.

Golf

Tour C: Okanagan-Similkameen

There are about thirty golf courses in the province's hinterland, most located near the towns of **Penticton**, **Kelowna** and **Vernon**. The terrain varies greatly depending on whether you're playing in the north, amidst wooded mountains, or in the desert-like south, which is scattered with little blueish shrubs.

Tour D: The Sea to Sky Highway

People come to Whistler Valley from May to October to play golf in spectacular surroundings. The greens fees vary greatly from one club to the next. At the **Whistler Golf Club** *($50-70; May to Oct; take the Village Gate Boulevard, turn right at Whistler Way and go under the 99,* ☎ *932-4544)* in Pemberton, 23 km north of Whistler, you'll discover a magnificent, winding golf course set against the steep cliffs of the mountains. The **Pemberton Valley Golf and Country Club** *($30-35; May to Oct;* ☎ *894-5122)* is just as beautiful as the clubs in Whistler, but much less expensive.

Hiking

Tour A: The Fraser and Thompson Rivers as Far as Revelstoke

Manning Provincial Park *(tourist information, summer 8am to 8pm, winter 9am to 5pm;* ☎ *840-8836)* is located on the boundary of the southwestern part of the province and the huge Okanagan-Similkameen region. It is popular with Vancouverites in search of vast green spaces. The magnificent mountains and valleys are crisscrossed by hiking trails.

There are a number of trails in **Mount Glacier National Park** *(for maps, information and regulations, contact Parks Canada in Revelstoke,* ☎ *837-7500 or in Rogers Pass,* ☎ *837-6274)*, which enable you to view the flourishing plant and animal life up close. There are varying levels of difficulty; some trails run past centuries-old trees or climb to the tops of mountains, offering views of the neighbouring peaks.

At **Mount Revelstoke National Park** ★★ *(adults $3, children $1.50; permit required for entry into the park; east of the bridge on the TransCanada Highway, InfoLine* ☎ *837-7500)*, you have to drive 24 km up to the summit of the mountain, where you'll find a trail and a number of picnic areas.

Tour B: Kootenay Country

Kokanee Glacier Provincial Park *(for maps, contact the BC Parks District Manager; Nelson,* ☎ *825-4421)* has about ten hiking trails of average difficulty, for a total of about 4 hours of walking. The Woodbury Creek Trail, which takes less than two hours to cover, leads to Sunset Lake via Ainsworth Hot Springs.

Tour C: Okanagan-Similkameen

The entrance to **Cathedral Provincial Park** *(for detailed maps and information, BC Parks District Manager; 1050 West Columbia Street, #101, B.C. V2C 1L2,* ☎ *371-6400 or Box 399, Summerland, B.C. V0H 1Z0,* ☎ *494-0321)* is located near Keremeos, on Highway 3. Some of the trails here extend more than 15 km, and require a day of hiking on average. At the summit, the trails are shorter and crisscross a hilly terrain teeming with plant and animal life. You can ride to the top in an all-purpose vehicle; to reserve a seat, call the **Cathedral Lakes Lodge** *(☎ 499-5848)*.

Tour D: The Sea to Sky Highway

Except for the built-up area around Whistler, **Garibaldi Provincial Park** *(information Garibaldi/Sunshine District, Brackendale; 10 km north of Squamish,* ☎ *898-3678)* is a huge stretch of untouched wilderness. Hiking here is a magical experience, especially when you reach Garibaldi Lake, whose turquoise waters contrast with the blue of the glacier in the background. The trails cover long distances, so you have to bring along food, as well as clothing for different temperatures.

A series of hiking trails run all the way up **Whistler Mountain** *(☎ 932-3434 or 1-800-Whistler)* and **Blackcomb Mountain** *(☎ 932-3141 or 1-800-Whistler)*. From atop Whistler, you can see Black Tusk, a black sugar-loaf 2315 m high.

Tour E: The Sunshine Coast

Inland Lake Park, located 12 km north of Powell River, has been specially designed to enable people in wheelchairs to enjoy nature. The lake is 13 km in circumference. Campsites have been laid out, and a few log houses are reserved for people with limited mobility. The picnic tables and swimming docks have been built with wheelchair-users in mind. The premier of British Columbia awarded the forest ministry a medal for the layout of this park.

Skiing

Tour A: The Fraser and Thompson Rivers as Far as Revelstoke

Albeit smaller than Whistler, the **Sun Peaks** *(45 min north of Kamloops on Mount Tod;* ☎ *578-7222 or 1-800-663-2838)* resort has recently undergone major renovations, and now offers new equipment and an accommodations.

Located 6 km south of downtown on Airport Way, **Mount Mackenzie Ski** *(Revelstoke* ☎ *837-5268)* is a family resort renowned for its high-quality powder. It is also fully equipped with ski lifts, dining facilities, a ski school and an equipment rental centre.

Mount Revelstoke National Park *(visitors must register with Parks Canada at the Revelstoke Information Office, Park Headquarters, 301 Campbell Avenue, Mon to Fri 8am to 4pm; ☎ 837-5155)* covers an immense stretch of virgin snow set against a backdrop of white peaks. This is a good place for cross-country skiing, since a number of longer trails have been laid out with shelters.

The immense skiing area at **Glacier National Park** *(go to the park's administrative office in Rogers Pass; winter: every day around the clock, summer: every day 7am to 11pm; Parks Canada, ☎ 837-7500 or ☎ 837-6867)* is perfect for those in search of adventure and quality powder. Because of the steep slopes and risk of avalanches, visitors are required to obtain a permit in order to ski here.

Heli-skiing is available in this region, attracting a large number of skiers in search of unexplored terrain, far from ski lifts and artificial snow. This region receives record snowfall; in fact, Environment Canada has set up a centre here in order to measure the levels of precipitation. A number of outfits, including **Cat Powder Skiing Inc.** *(☎ 837-9489)* and **Selkirk Tangiers Heli-Skiing Ltd.** *(☎ 1-800-663-7080 or 837-5378)*, offer package deals.

Tour B: Kootenay Country

Kokanee Glacier is a provincial park located 21 km northeast of Nelson on Highway 3A. The road is gravel for 16 of the 21 kilometres, and is not maintained in winter, when the only way to reach the park is on cross-country skis or by helicopter. Visitors are strongly advised to obtain specialized equipment for this type of excursion. The Slocan Chief Cabin can accommodate up to 12 people, but you have to make reservations through the **BC Parks District Manager** *(Nelson, ☎ 825-4421)*.

Ski Whitewater lies a few minutes south of Nelson on Highway 6. This resort is the perfect place to spend a day skiing, whether you're an expert or just starting out.

Red Mountain, located 5 min from Rossland, is one of the main centres of economic activity in this region. In the past, miners used to work the mountain; today, it is a playground for skiiers. Granite Mountain, renowned for its deep, fluffy powder, is also part of this resort. Opposite Red Mountain, **BlackJack Cross Country Trails** consists of 50 km of cross-country ski trails of all different levels of difficulty. **Red Mountain Resorts Inc.** *(☎ 362-7384, ski conditions ☎ 362-5500, reservations ☎ 1-800-663-0105)*.

Tour C: Okanagan-Similkameen

You can go downhill skiing all over this region. The major resorts are the **Apex Resort**, near Penticton, **Big White Ski Resort** and the **Silver Star Mountain Resort** near Kelowna.

Tour D: The Sea to Sky Highway

Two mountains measuring over 2,000 m in altitude, surrounded by glaciers and blanketed with powder, welcome thousands of skiers of all different levels each year to this region. Two sides of **Whistler Mountain** *($46; ☎ 932-3434 or 1-800-Whistler)* have been developed since the resort opened in 1966. Whistler Creekside was the hub of sporting activities in this region until some forward-thinking individuals came up with the idea of building Whistler Village at the foot of the two mountains. The skiable area is surprisingly large; you can literally spend days skiing the bowls, fields and variety of trails.

Blackcomb Mountain *($46; ☎ 932-3141 or 1-800-Whistler)* has been open since 1980. Like Whistler, it is a highly renowned resort. There is something for everyone here—glaciers, steep slopes, glades, moguls and family slopes. When the whole area is covered with powder, it is a veritable paradise. You can ski on both mountains for $50, but it's not worth it, since it takes too much time to get from one to the other. Those interested in skiing during the summer can hit the glacier from June 17 to August 7.

If you're looking for a thrill, you can hop aboard a helicopter and set off for vast stretches of virgin powder. Contact **Whistler Heli-Skiing Ltd.** *($390, three rides up, lunch, guide; ☎ 932-4105)*.

Flying

Gliding enthusiasts have claimed the piece of sky over Hope as their flying space. A westerly wind sweeps down the Fraser River valley and up the big mountains around Hope, enabling the aircraft to stay in the air for hours. For $60, you can accompany a pilot aboard his engineless plane. At Exit 165 on Highway 1, west of Hope, follow the sign for the airport; turn left at Old Yale, right before the viaduct, and continue until you reach the red and white building of the **Vancouver Soaring Association** *(☎ 521-5501)*.

Mountain Biking

Rossland, in Kootenay Country, is the self-proclaimed mountain bike capital of British Columbia—with good reason, it would seem. Long trails of varying levels of difficulty make this place accessible to anyone with an interest in the sport. Former railway lines, cross-country trails and wood-cutting paths all converge near the centre of town. The terrain is far from flat; this is a very mountainous region. You can pick up a map of the trails at the local Chamber of Commerce *(☎ 362-5666)* or at any of the bike rental centres.

Mountain Climbing

Tour C: Okanagan-Similkameen

The Penticton region is renowned among North American mountain climbers for its wide assortment of rock walls. Many of these surfaces measure a single rope's length, and the level of difficulty can vary greatly. For further information, contact Ray Keetch of **Ray's Sports Den** *(215 Main Street, Penticton, ☎ 493-1216)*.

Tour D: The Sea to Sky Highway

Mountain-climbing is becoming more popular in this region. The place to go is **Stawamus Chief Mountain**. The trails leading to this granite monolith also lead to spots where you can watch the mountain climbers. For more information, contact the Squamish &

Howe Sound District Chamber of Commerce (☎ 892-9244).

Accommodations

■ **Tour A: The Fraser and Thompson Rivers as Far as Revelstoke**

Harrison Hot Springs

At the **Sasquatch Provincial Park** *($9.50 for four people; 177 wooded lots, beach, sb, playground, boat-launching ramp; cash only; Cultus Lake, ☎ 858-7161)*, you choose your own campsite and a park employee passes by to collect payment. Hidden in the mountains near Harrison Lake, this park has three campgrounds, which welcome nature lovers every year. According to a Coast Salish legend, the Sasquatch is half-man, half-beast and lives in the woods. To this day, some natives claim to have seen the creature around Harrison Lake.

Harrison Heritage House and Kottage *($55-80 bkfst incl.; 2 rooms, sb, no smoking, no pets, one very large suite, pb and a small cottage, pb, ℭ also available, but they are not part of the B&B, $105-115; 312 Lilloet Avenue, ☎ 796-9552)*. Jo-Anne and Dennis Sandve will give you a warm welcome at their pretty house, located one street away from the beach and the public pool. Jo-Anne makes her own preserves.

The **Little House on the Lake** *($125 bkfst incl.; 3 rooms, pb, ⊛, no smoking, no children under 16, no pets; 6305 Rockwell Drive, ☎ 796-2186 and 1-800-939-1116)* is a superb log-house set on the east shore of the lake. This is an extremely comfortable place to relax and enjoy water sports like sailing and kayaking.

Located alongside the lake, the **Harrison Hot Springs Hotel** *($90-200; 303 rooms, pb, ≈, ℜ, △, dancing; 100 Esplanade; ☎ 796-2244 or 1-800-663-2266)* has an advantage over its competitors in that it is the only hotel with access to the mineral springs.

Hope

Manning Provincial Park *(four campsites, as well as wilderness camping, sb, tourist information, summer 8am to 8pm, winter 9am to 5pm; ☎ 840-8836)* lies on the boundary of the southwestern part of the province and the huge Okanagan-Similkameen region, 225 km from Vancouver. City-dwellers come here by the thousands to enjoy all sorts of sports, the most popular being hiking and mountain biking and cross-country skiing in the winter. During summer, you can drive up to Cascade Lookout to take in the view.

Simon's On Fraser *($65-95 bkfst incl.; 3 rooms, sb; 690 Fraser Street, ☎ 869-2562)*, a pretty little house located adjacent to Memorial Park, has simply decorated, cozy rooms. The house, which is adorned with woodwork, has been completely renovated and repainted in bright colours.

Ashcroft

Run by former clients, the **Sundance Guest Ranch** *($120, low season Mar to Apr and Oct except on holidays; $142, high season; all meals included, horseback riding twice a day (cowboy boots required, rentals available), ≈, tennis, tv; Highland Valley Road,*

☎ *453-2422)* will take you back to a bygone era when cowboys roamed freely on horseback across as yet unexplored regions. The cost covers a stay of at least one day. Guests have access to a living room, where they can bring their drinks; there is a separate living room just for children.

Kamloops

Located steps away from the centre of town, **Joyce's Bed & Breakfast** *($35-55 bkfst incl.; four rooms, ≡, sb, parking, no smoking, laundry; 49 West Nicola Street,* ☎ *374-1417)* is a turn-of-the-century house whose big balconies offer a view of the surrounding scenery. You've got to be a cat-lover to stay here, since the house has four feline residents. Although you'll find little to inspire you indoors, the armchairs on the huge balcony beckon travel-weary visitors to relax and enjoy the view of Kamloops. The four rooms are decent, and given the price, it's worth making an effort. The owner is crazy about building and renovating.

Located right near the TransCanada Highway on the way into town, the **Best Western Kamloops Towne Lodge** *($80-100; 122 rooms, ≈, ⊛, △, no pets; 1250 Rogers Way,* ☎ *828-6698 or 1-800-665-6674)* is a very comfortable, classic-style hotel that offers some splendid views of Kamloops and the Thompson River. You can also enjoy the scenery from one of the nearby motels, which vary only in price.

Revelstoke

The **Piano Keep Bed & Breakfast** *($55-85 bkfst incl.; 3 rooms, no smoking, pb, ≡; 815 MacKenzie Avenue,* ☎ *837-2120)* is an imposing Edwardian-style house set in the midst of a garden. Host Vern Enyedy welcomes his guests in a charming setting featuring pianos from different eras. Both a collector and a music lover, Vern will demonstrate his musical skill.

The **Best Western Wayside Inn** *($89-109; 88 rooms, ≡, tv, ≈, ⊛, △, ℜ; 1901 Laforme Boulevard,* ☎ *837-6161 or 1-800-528-1234)*, on the north side of the TransCanada Highway, is not only close to everything, but offers the added attraction of a pastoral setting with views of Revelstoke and the Columbia River.

■ **Tour B: Kootenay Country**

Ainsworth Hot Springs

The **Ainsworth Hot Springs Resort** *($75-95; 43 rooms, ≈, tv, ℜ, △ in the caves, naturally warm water and ice-cold ≈, ⊛, no pets; Highway 31,* ☎ *229-4212)* is part of the facilities surrounding the caves. Guests have free access to the caves, and can obtain passes for friends.

Nelson

The **City Tourist Park** *($12-14; 35 sites, sb, picnic tables, no charge for children under 14; 90 High Street,* ☎ *352-9031, off-season* ☎ *352-5511)* is a campground located in downtown Nelson, within walking distance of the major local attractions and restaurants. At the end of the day, head over to neighbouring Gyro Park to take in the view of the town and Kootenay Lake.

The **Heritage Inn** *($56-76, bkfst incl.; 36 rooms, tv, ℜ, pub, no pets; 422*

Vernon Street, ☎ 352-5331) was established in 1898, when the Hume brothers decided to build a grand hotel. Over the years, the building has been modified with each new owner. In 1980, major renovations breathed new life into the old place. The library is worth visiting; with its woodwork and fireplace, it has all the elements necessary to create a pleasant atmosphere. The walls of the rooms and corridors are covered with photographs capturing the highlights of Nelson's history.

Inn the Garden Bed & Breakfast *($65-105 bkfst incl.; 6 rooms, sb or pb, adults only, no smoking, parking, no pets; 408 Victoria Street, ☎ 352-3226)*. This charming Victorian house, renovated by owners Lynda Stevens and Jerry Van Veen, lies steps away from the main street. The couple's warm welcome will make your stay in Nelson that much more pleasant. Ask them to tell you about the town's architectural heritage; it is one of their passions.

Rossland

An inviting house owned by Tauna and Greg Butler, the **Ram's Head Inn, Bed & Breakfast** *($65-85 bkfst incl.; 12 rooms, pb, ☻, △, no smoking, no pets; at the foot of the slopes on Red Mountain Road, ☎ 362-9577)* feels like a home away from home. The fireplace, woodwork, simple decor and pleasant smells wafting out of the kitchen create a pleasant, informal atmosphere.

■ Tour C: Okanagan-Similkameen

Osoyoos

At the **Lake Osoyoos Guest House** *($50-125 bkfst incl.; 3 rooms, pb, garden and waterfront, ☻, ₡, pedalboat, cash only; 5809 Oleander Drive, ☎ 495-3297 or 1-800-671-8711)*, Sofia Grasso cooks up breakfast in her huge kitchen while guests sip freshly squeezed juice at the edge of Osoyoos Lake. Guests have use of a pedalboat to enjoy the lake and the changing colours of the valley as the day wears on.

Penticton

The **Riordan House, Bed & Breakfast** *($55-75 bkfst incl.; 3 rooms, sb or pb, children 13 and older, no pets, no smoking; 689 Winnipeg Street, ☎ 493-5997)* is an Arts & Crafts style house built in 1920. Its owners, John and Donna Ortiz, have decorated it with antiques. Their little dog, Dust, will give you a loud welcome, but his bark is bigger than his bite.

Tiki Shores Condominium Beach Resort *($74-105; 40 rooms, ☻, △, tv, pb, ℛ, no smoking, no pets; 914 Lakeshore Drive, ☎ 492-8769 or 1-800-668-6746)*. This motel is located steps away from the beach on Okanagan Lake, near the tourist office and a number of restaurants.

Summerland

The **Illahie Beach** *($16-20; 170 campsites, free showers, laundry facilities, pay phone, convenience store, beach; north of Penticton on Highway 97, Summerland, ☎ 494-0800)* campground welcomes vacationers from April to October. The beaches and views of the Okanagan Valley make for a heavenly setting.

Kelowna

The **Crawford View Bed & Breakfast** *($45-65 bkfst incl.; 3 rooms, pb; 810 Crawford Road, ☎ 764-1140)* looks out over the valley and Okanagan Lake. You will be enchanted by your hosts, Fred and Gaby Geismayr, as well as by the beautiful surroundings. The recently built wooden house is surrounded by an apple orchard, a tennis court and a swimming pool. At the end of September, the Geismayrs are busy picking apples, but all the activity simply adds to the charm of the place.

Merritt

The historic **Quilchena Hotel** *($64-74; 16 rooms, sb, ℜ, pub, lake, fishing, bike rentals, no pets, historic site; Apr to Oct, 23 km northeast of Merritt on Highway 5A, ☎ 378-2611)*, located by the shore of a lake, harkens back to the days when cowboys used to relax around the dinner table. The place is furnished with a number of antiques.

Southwest of Penticton

Olde Osprey Inn, Bed & Breakfast *($60-70 bkfst incl.; 3 rooms, sb, no smoking; Sheep Creek Road, ☎ 497-7134)*. This magnificent log house was built by Mr. Whitley, who astutely chose a site on a mountainside with an unimpeded view of Yellow Lake and the surrounding area. Mrs. Whitley, for her part, takes care of making sure your stay is as comfortable as possible. She is a painter, and some of her work is on display here. The couple's son, furthermore, is a musician. This amiable family knows how to put their guests at ease. The occasional osprey flies by, at which point everything comes to a halt as all eyes turn skyward.

Cathedral Provincial Park

Cathedral Lakes Lodge *($96-170; everything included; ten rooms, along with a dormitory and number of small cottages, sb, canoe and rowboat, fireplace, bar, transportation to and from the base of the mountain, no pets, no smoking; Jun to Sep, rates vary depending on the season, Jul and Aug high season; reservations required, ☎ 499-5848)*. The road to the top of the mountain is only open to the lodge's all-terrain vehicle, so you have to leave your car on Ashnola River Road. If you go by foot, it will take you more than six hours to reach the lodge. Do not forget to reserve your seat in the vehicle. Turn left 4.8 km past Keremeos, cross over the covered bridge and drive along Ashnola River Road for 20.8 km. If you plan on taking the bus, you have to call the lodge ahead of time to make arrangements for someone to pick you up. All this might seem complicated, but once you reach the top, you're sure to be enchanted by the mountain goats, marmots and flowers, not to mention the glaciers stretching as far as the eye can see.

■ Tour D: The Sea to Sky Highway

The village of **Whistler** is scattered with restaurants, hotels, apartments and bed & breakfasts. There is a reservation service to help you take your pick. **Whistler Resort** *(☎ 932-4222,*

Vancouver ☎ 664-5625, outside British Columbia ☎ 1-800-944-7853).

Whistler

The **Shoestring Lodge** ($55-100 for a room, depending on the season, $20 for a shared room; pb, tv, shuttle, pub, parking; 1 km north of the village, to the right on Nancy Green Drive, ☎ 932-3338) is one of the least expensive places to stay in Whistler. Its low rates make it very popular, so reservations are imperative. The rooms include a bed, a television and a small bathroom; the decor is as neutral as can be. The youthful atmosphere will make you feel as if you're at a university summer camp where the students just want to have fun, and that's pretty much what this place is. The pub is known for its excellent evening entertainment (see p 160).

The recently built **Chalet Beau Sejour** (summer $65, winter $90 bkfst incl.; 3 rooms, pb, ⊛, shuttle, no smoking; 7414 Ambassador Crescent, White Gold Estate, ☎ 938-4966, Vancouver ☎ 263-2365), run by Sue and Hal, is a big, inviting house set on a mountainside. You can take in a lovely view of the valley and the mountains while eating the copious breakfast Sue loves to prepare. A tour guide, she knows the region like the back of her hand; don't hesitate to ask her what to see and do.

The **Listel Whistler Hotel** ($69-159; 98 rooms, pb, tv, heated ≈, ⊛, △, ℜ; 4121 Village Green, ☎ 932-1133, Vancouver ☎ 688-5634 or 1-800-663-5472) is located in the heart of the village, so you don't have to look far to find some place to eat or entertain yourself. The simple layout of the rooms makes for a comfortable stay.

The luxurious **Canadian Pacific Chateau Whistler Resort** ($125-225; pb, tv, ≈, ⊛, △, ℜ; 4599 Chateau Boulevard, ☎ 938-8000 or 1-800-441-1414) lies at the foot of the slopes of Blackcomb Mountain. It resembles a smaller version of Whistler village, fully equipped to meet all your dining and entertainment needs and to ensure that your stay is a relaxing one.

■ **Tour E: The Sunshine Coast**

Gibsons

The **Maritimer Bed & Breakfast** ($75 bkfst incl.; pb, children 12 and over, no smoking, no pets; 521 South Fletcher Road, ☎ 886-0664), run by Gerry and Noreen Tretick, overlooks the town and the marina. The charming scenery, friendly hosts and cozy atmosphere are sure to please. A new room has recently been laid out in the attic. On the ground floor, there is a large room decorated with antique furniture and works of art by Noreen; a beautiful quilt graces one of the walls. Breakfast, served on the terrace, which looks right out onto the bay, includes an oyster omelette; this is the seashore, after all.

Powell River

Beacon Bed & Breakfast ($75-95 bkfst incl.; pb, wheelchair access, no smoking, ⊛, children 12 and over; 3750 Marine Avenue, ☎ 485-9450). Your hosts, Shirley and Roger Randall, will make you feel right at home. What's more, they will take great pleasure in telling you all about their part of the country. The Beacon faces west and looks out onto the sea, so you can enjoy the sunset while taking a bath, no less! The simply laid-out rooms each have a fully equipped bathroom. Breakfast includes a special treat, blueberry pancakes.

The recently built **Best Western Towne Centre Hotel** *($73-150; pb, ⊛, tv, no smoking; 4660 Joyce Avenue; 485-3000 or 1-800-528-1234)* is located in the centre of Westview, a suburb of Powell River. It is soberly decorated and offers a full range of services, from dining room to pub.

The **Beach Gardens Resort Hotel** *($59-159; pb, tv, tennis, interior ≈, △, pub, ℜ, marina, no pets; 7074 Westminster Ave., ☎ 485-6267 or 1-800-663-7070)* is a full-service resort complex with a magnificent dining room, comfortable guest-rooms, a sports centre, a marina, and a splendid view of the Georgia Strait. This is the ideal spot for those who want everything within arm's reach.

Lund

A relaxing atmosphere prevails at the century-old **Lund Hotel** *($66; pb, tv, ℜ, marina, at the end of Highway 101, ☎ 483-3187)*, which opens onto the bay. The peaceful location and view of the boats coming and going more than compensate for the motel-style rooms.

Restaurants

■ **Tour A: The Fraser and Thompson Rivers as Far as Revelstoke**

Kamloops

Located in Riverside Park, the **Grass Roots Tea House** *($$; Apr to Sep, 8am to 2pm, tea 2pm to 4pm, lunch 6:30pm to 10pm; reservations required during winter; 262 Lorne Street, ☎ 374-9890)* is a charming place surrounded by trees, where you can enjoy a cup of ginseng tea. Reservations are required for dinner, and the menu varies depending on what day of the week it is.

Déjà Vu *($$$; Tue to Sat 5pm to 10pm; 172 Battle Street, ☎ 374-3227)* serves West Coast and French cuisine featuring an imaginative blend of fruit and seafood.

Revelstoke

At the **Frontier Restaurant** *($; every day 6am to 9pm; right near the tourist office, at the intersection of the TransCanada Highway and the 23, ☎ 837-5119)*, you can put away a big breakfast in a typically western setting.

The **Black Forest** *($$-$$$; 5 min west of Revelstoke, on the TransCanada Highway, ☎ 837-3495)* is a Bavarian-style restaurant, which serves Canadian and European cuisine. Top billing on the menu goes to cheese and fish. The setting and view of Mount Albert are enchanting.

■ **Tour B: Kootenay Country**

The successful **El Zocalo Mexican Cafe** *($$; 802 Baker Street, ☎ 352-7223)* occupies a Mexican-style building and features live Mexican music. Guests enjoy delicious, traditional Mexican cuisine in a fiesta-like atmosphere.

The **All Seasons Cafe** *($$-$$$; every day, lunch 11am, dinner 5pm; 620 Herridge Lane, behind Baker Street, ☎ 352-0101)* is not to be missed. It lies hidden beneath the trees, so its terrace is bathed in shade. The soups might surprise you a bit — apple and broccoli (in season) is one example. The menu is determined by the season and what's available in the area, with lots of space accorded to the fine wines of British Columbia. The friendly, efficient service, elegant decor and quality cuisine make for an altogether satisfying meal. The walls are adorned with works of art.

Rossland

Elmer's Corner Café *($; every day; at the corner of Elmer and Washington Streets)* is a little place that serves excellent thin-crust pizza. Vegetarian and meat dishes are also available, along with home-made Montreal-style bagels and bread. During summer, you can eat on the terrace.

■ **Tour C: Okanagan-Similkameen**

Penticton

The **Hog's Breath Coffee Co.** *($; every day; 202 Main Street, ☎ 493-7800)* is the perfect place to start off your day with a good cup of coffee, and even more importantly, some peach muffins (in season); you'll love them! If you're looking for somewhere to go outdoors, the owner, Mike Barrett, will gladly offer some suggestions.

Seafood fans will find their favourite foods at **Salty's Beach House** *($-$$; 1000 Lakeshore Drive, ☎ 493-5001)*. Make sure to come here at lunchtime so you can enjoy the view of Okanagan Lake from the terrace. The pirate ship decor gives the place a festive atmosphere.

Theo's Restaurant *($$-$$$; 687 Main Street, ☎ 492-4019)*. Fine Greek cuisine and a relaxed atmosphere make for a pleasant meal at this extremely popular spot.

Granny Bogners Restaurant *($$$; 302 Eckhardt Avenue West, ☎ 493-2711)*. This magnificent Tudor house was built in 1912 for a local doctor. In 1976, Hans and Angela Strobel converted it into a restaurant, where they serve fine French cuisine made with local produce.

Kelowna

Joey Tomato's Kitchen *($-$$; every day; 300-2475 Highway 97 North, at the intersection of Highway 33, ☎ 860-8999)* is located near a large boulevard in a neighbourhood of shopping malls. The people who run this place have successfully created a pleasant atmosphere. The terrace, with its plants, parasols and little Italian car will keep your attention. The dining room is also extremely attractive — a large space brightened up by cans of food and bottles of oil, making you feel as if you're, well, in Joey's kitchen. And the pasta! Make sure to try the fettucine with salmon and tomatoes; it's a real treat.

If you're looking for a place to enjoy a relaxing meal, head to the **Suisse Marmite** *($$$; every day, 11am to 1am; 262 Bernard Avenue, ☎ 860-4344)*, where you can sit on a terrace near the lake and savour a good fondue and fine local white wine.

Merritt

Both the restaurant and the saloon in the **Coldwater Hotel** *($-$$; restaurant Sun to Thu 7:30am to 8:30pm, Fri and Sat 7:30am to 9:30pm; saloon

11:30am to 2am; at the corner of Quilchena and Voght, ☎ 378-5711) have always been popular with the local cowboys. The food is somewhat heavy, but the prices are right. The rooms can be rented by the month or by the year.

■ Tour D: The Sea to Sky Highway

Whistler

If you want to be among the first to ski the slopes in the morning, head to **Pika's** ($; from 7:30am on in Dec, at the top of the Whistler Village Gondola ski lift, ☎ 932-3434) for breakfast; it is worth getting up early the day after a storm.

Located in the heart of the village, **Città Bistro** ($; every day 11am to 1am; Whistler Village Square, ☎ 932-4117) has an elaborate menu with selections ranging from salads to pita pizzas and pasta. This is the perfect place to sample one of the local beers. In both winter and summer, a pleasant mix of locals and tourists makes for an extremely inviting atmosphere.

The **Hard Rock Cafe** ($-$$; every day 11:30am to 11pm; in the village of Whistler, near Blackcomb Way, ☎ 938-9922) has a lively clientele and a menu featuring salads and hamburgers.

As may be gathered by its name, **Thai One On** ($$; every day lunch and dinner; in the Le Chamois hotel, at the foot of the Blackcomb Mountain slopes, ☎ 932-4822) serves Thai food, with its wonderful blend of coconut milk and hot peppers.

At the **Trattoria di Umberto** ($$-$$$; near Blackcomb Way, on the ground floor of the Mountainside Lodge, ☎ 932-5858), you'll find pasta dishes, red and white checked tablecloths and a homey atmosphere.

Les Deux Gros ($$$-$$$$; 2 km south of Whistler Creekside, to the right on Alta Lake Road, ☎ 932-2112) serves traditional French cuisine featuring products from the Kootenay region, including red meat and fish. Reservations recommended.

■ Tour E: The Sunshine Coast

Powell River

Sam Okamoto, the owner of the **Jitterbug Café** ($$-$$$; closed Sun; 4643 Marine Avenue, ☎ 485-7797), is a virtuoso chef who worked in Tokyo, Montreal and Vancouver before coming to the Sunshine Coast; he has also written a great deal about culinary art. He uses traditional Japanese cooking techniques adapted to suit British Columbian foodstuffs.

The dining room of the **Beach Gardens Resort Hotel** ($$-$$$; 7074 Westminster Avenue, ☎ 485-6267 or 1-800-663-7070) looks out onto the Malaspina Strait. The menu lists divine seafood dishes flavoured with Okanagan wines. The bouillabaisse is a testimony to the quality of the ingredients.

Lund

Strategically located **Carver's Café** ($; at the south end of the bay, ☎ 483-3412) offers a view of the bay, the islands, the comings and goings of the boats, and the hotel, and is a delightful place to relax and sip a cappuccino.

Entertainment

■ **Tour D: The Sea to Sky Highway**

Whistler

At the **Boot Pub** *(1 km north of the village on the right, on Nancy Greene Drive, ☎ 932-3338)*, located in the Shoestring Lodge hotel, live musicians play R&B to an enthusiastic clientele.

Young reggae fans get together at **Tommy Africa's** *(on Gateway Drive, in the village of Whistler, ☎ 932-6090)*. The popularity of the spot means that line-ups are common.

The relaxed atmosphere at **Cinnamon Bear Bar** *(in the Delta Hotel, 4050 Whistler Way, ☎ 932-1982)* attracts sporty types of all ages.

Shopping

■ **Tour D: The Sea to Sky Highway**

Whistler

Outside the little village, at the edge of the Whistler region, lies Function Junction, a small industrial area of sorts. You won't find just any industries here, however!

Schöni Breads *(to the right on Alpha Lake Road)* is a small bakery whose delicious, top-quality breads, made with plums, nuts, vegetables, herbs and multigrains are sure to please.

Whistler Brewery *(free admission; Alpha Lake Road, Function Junction, south of Whistler Creekside, ☎ 932-6185)*. This microbrewery distributes its products locally, and they are extremely popular. You just might learn the recipe for their beer while touring the facilities.

Right: Calm over Kathlyn Lake, Smithers B.C. (Pierre Longnus)

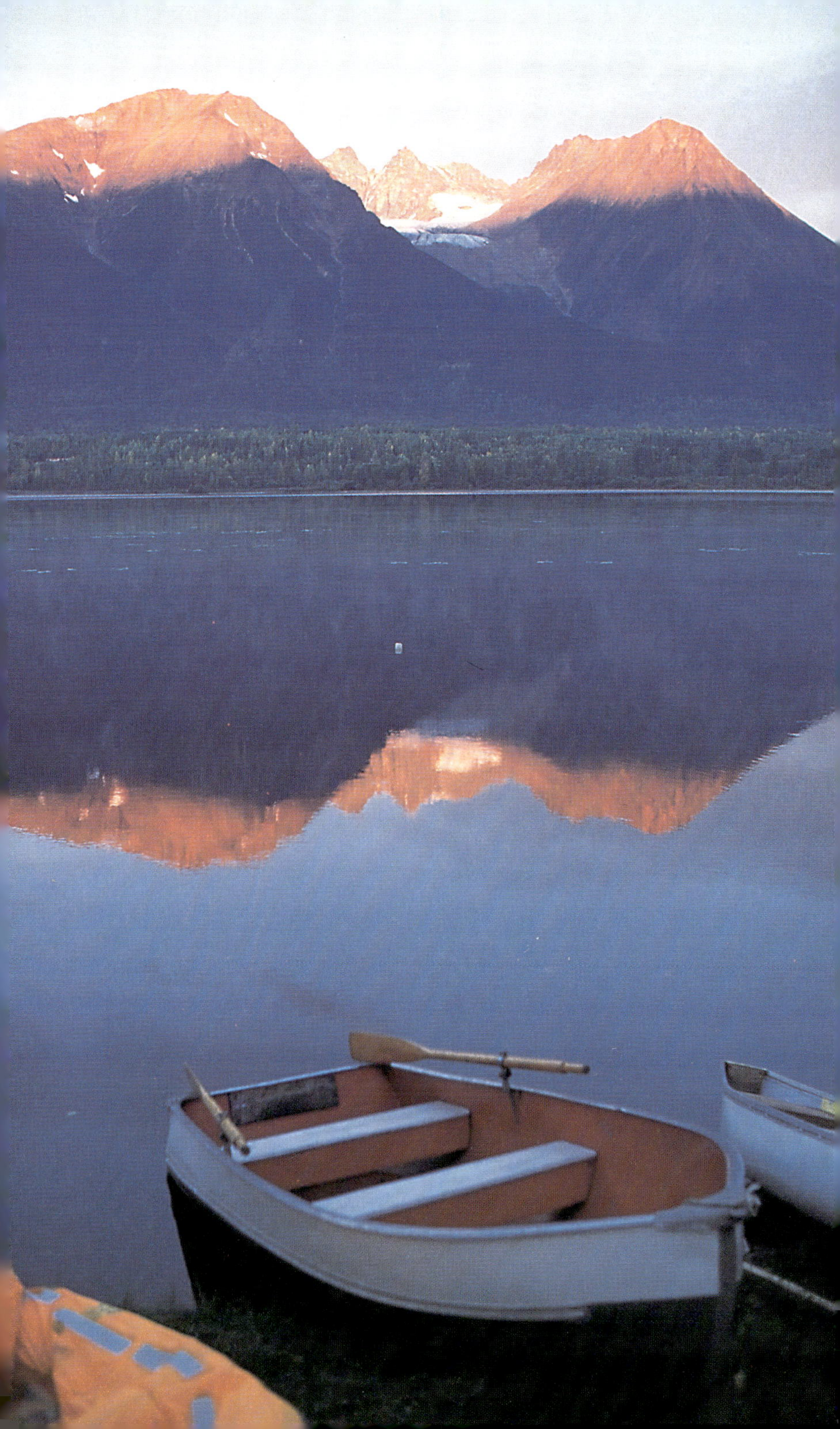

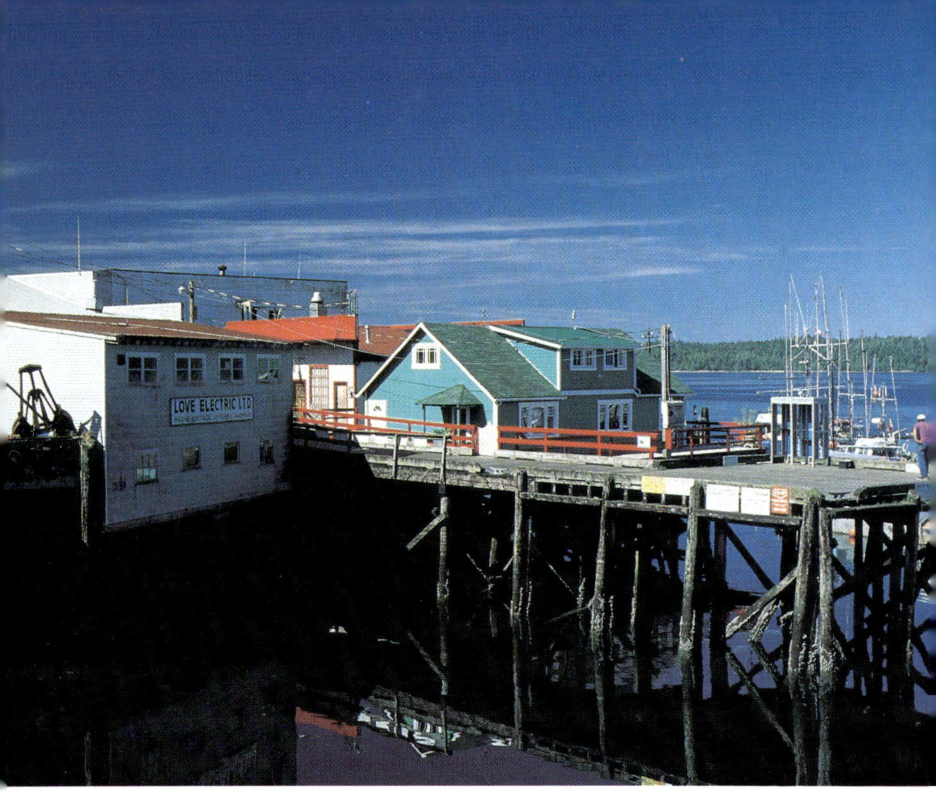
LOVE ELECTRIC LTD

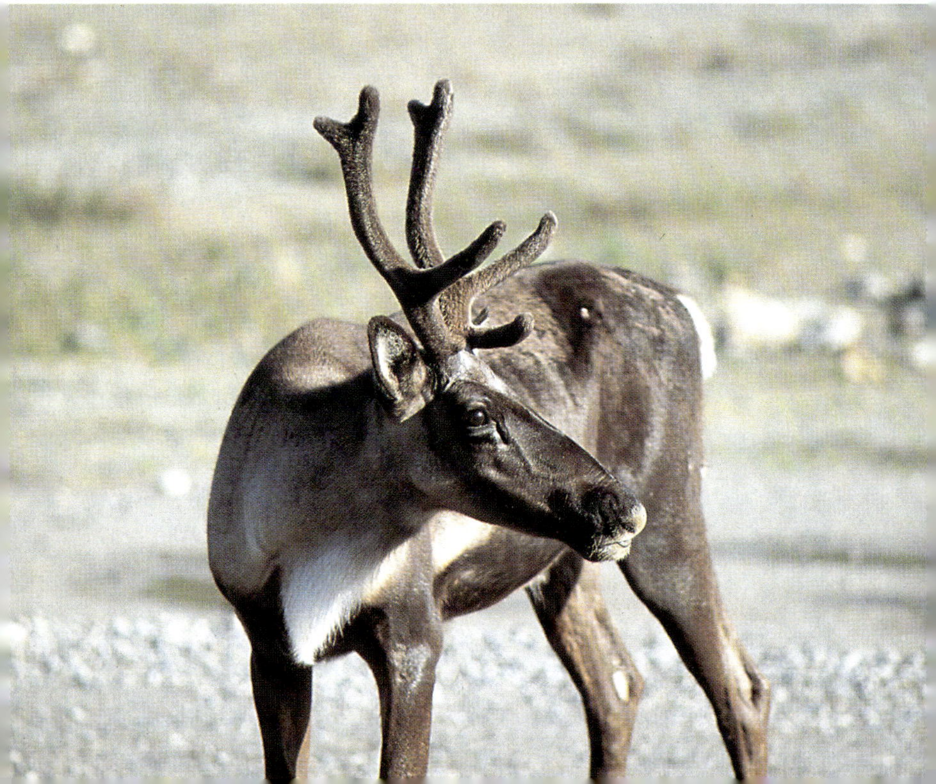

NORTHERN BRITISH COLUMBIA

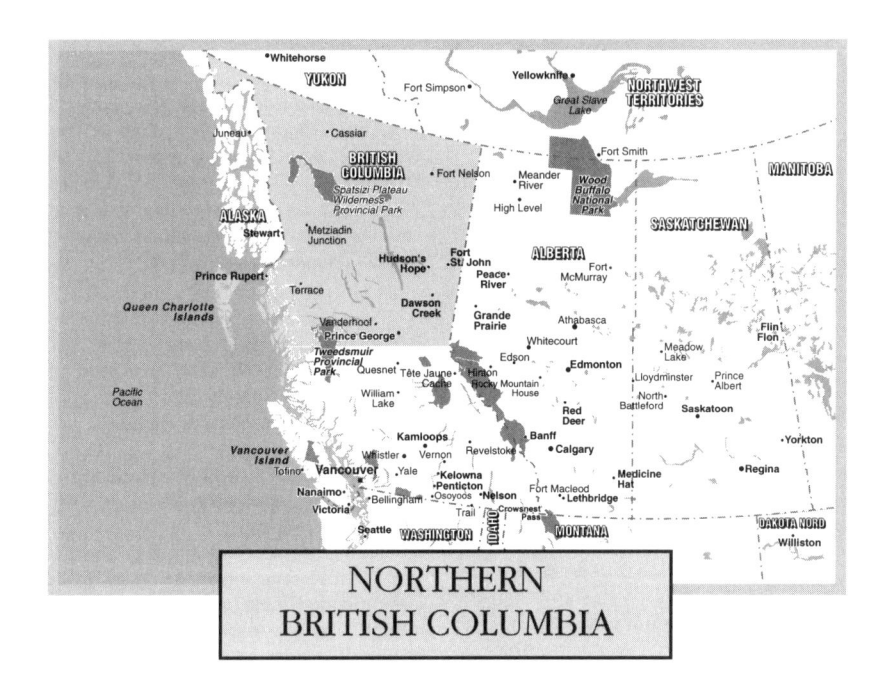

British Columbia has long been renowned for its exceptional and varied range of outdoor activities. If you have a taste for adventure and exploring, or if you simply love nature, you will be repeatedly delighted and surprised by the unspoiled, little known northern part of the province.

Eighty percent of this territory is studded with mountains, many of which are perpetually covered with snow or glaciers. The lakes, which collect the run-off from the glaciers, shimmer with iridescent colours, while the forests are among the most renowned in the world. These enchanting surroundings offer endless possibilities for outdoor activities — just let your imagination run wild.

Two distinct regions make up northern British Columbia, the North by Northwest and Peace River Alaska Highway regions; together, they account for 50% of the province's total area. Despite their isolated location, a number of towns are fully equipped to welcome tourists with campgrounds, hotels and restaurants that offer amenities comparable to those found in big cities.

Only three major roads lead through these vast northern spaces. The Stewart-Cassiar Highway (Highway 37), to the west, passes through the heart of the North by Northwest region. The Alaska Highway, in the east, starts at Dawson Creek. And finally, the Yellowhead Highway (Highway 16) runs along the southern partof these

---

Left: *Cow Bay in Prince Rupert (Pierre Longnus)*
Caribou (Pierre Longnus)

Northern British Columbia

two regions, all the way to the shores of the Pacific, where visitors can set out for the Queen Charlotte Islands.

The starting point of any visit to northern British Columbia is the city of Prince George. From there north, the days grow noticeably longer. This phenomenon becomes more and more evident the farther north you go. The summertime sky never darkens completely, and depending on where you find yourself, you might even see the midnight sun. Near the province's border with the Yukon, along the 60th parallel, the sky never gets very dark during summer, and the northern lights, or aurora borealis, are a common sight during the long winter months. The summertime climate is characterized by long sunny days with temperatures often higher than in the south. The winters are long. In the northwest, where the snowfall is very heavy, the weather is relatively mild, despite sub-zero temperatures (in Celsius). In the northeast, the climate is continental, with less snow and severe, dry cold.

Contrary to popular belief, the cost of living in the country is by no means less expensive than in big cities. Farming and stockbreeding are not carried out on a major scale in northern British Columbia, nor are any raw materials processed here; as a result, food, fuel, hotels, etc. are all 50 to 100% more expensive, depending on where you are. As far as telephone calls are concerned, keep in mind that phone booths are quite rare, and can only be found near parks and in towns and villages.

A trip to northern British Columbia offers a chance to take in some of the most beautiful scenery in Canada. To help you make the most of your trip, we have outlined seven tours: **Tour A:** **To the Alaska Highway** ★★; **Tour B: The Hudson's Hope Route** ★★; **Tour C: The Alaska Highway** ★★★; **Tour D: The Stewart-Cassiar Highway** ★★★; **Tour E: To Stewart, BC and Hyder, AK** ★★★; **Tour F: The Yellowhead Highway** ★★★ and **Tour G: The Queen Charlotte Islands (Haida Gwaii)** ★★★.

Finding Your Way Around

■ **Tour A: To the Alaska Highway**

Highway 97 leads from Prince George to Dawson Creek, kilometre/mile 0 of the Alaska Highway. The region has developed mostly around the lumber and hydroelectric industries. It is quite common to come across bears and moose here, particularly in the provincial parks, which have well laid-out campsites. Halfway through the tour, you will reach the turn-off for Highway 39, which leads to Mackenzie, another 29 km away. Since the 39 is a dead-end, you'll have to backtrack to pick up the 97 again. Crossing Pine Pass, you'll see the first foothills of the Rockies and discover how truly immense the forest is. About 100 km past Powder King, the ski resort, lies the town of Chetwynd. From there, you can reach Tumbler Ridge, but you will have to double back to the 97 again to complete the tour.

Prince George

Bus station: Greyhound, at the corner of 12th and Victoria Streets (☎ 564-5454).

Airport: A few kilometres east of downtown; accessible by way of the Yellowhead Bridge to the north and the Simon Fraser Bridge to the south

Finding Your Way Around 163

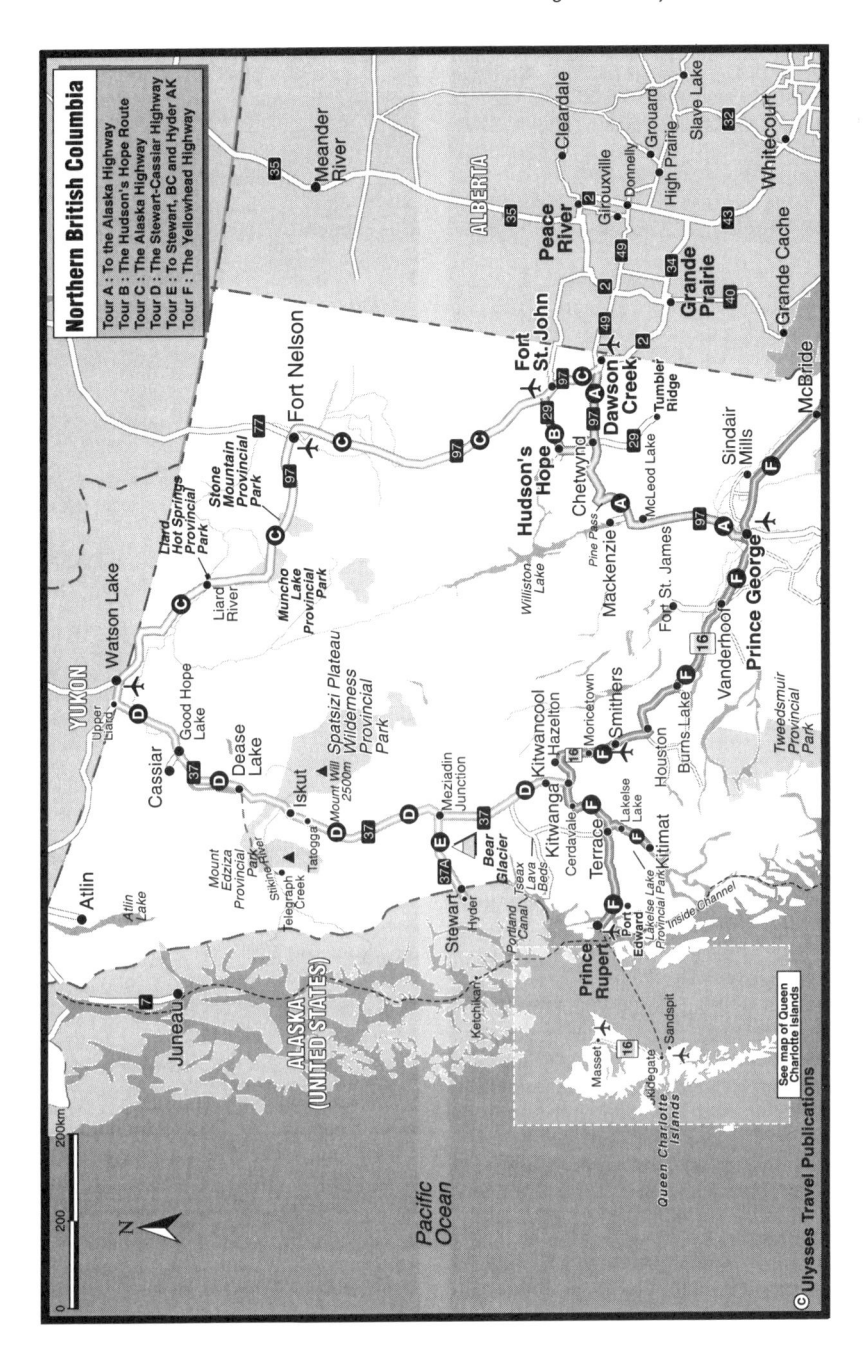

Northern British Columbia

- Tour A: To the Alaska Highway
- Tour B: The Hudson's Hope Route
- Tour C: The Alaska Highway
- Tour D: The Stewart-Cassiar Highway
- Tour E: To Stewart, BC and Hyder AK
- Tour F: The Yellowhead Highway

164 Northern British Columbia

(☎ 963-2400). The airport is served by Air B.C. (☎ 561-2905), Canadian International (☎ 563-0521), Central Mountain (☎ 963-9022) and N.T. Air (☎ 963-9611).

■ Tour B: The Hudson's Hope Route

Another way of getting to the Alaska Highway from Prince George is to take the 29 North, which leads to the village of Hudson's Hope and intersects with the Alaska Highway at kilometre 86.

■ Tour C: The Alaska Highway

This tour covers the part of the Alaska Highway that runs through British Columbia. It starts at kilometre/mile 0, in Dawson Creek, and leads to the town of Watson Lake, a little over a thousand kilometres away, just over the province's border with the Yukon. The first town you will pass through is Fort St. John, followed by Fort Nelson and the Stone Mountain, Muncho Lake and Liard Hot Springs Provincial Parks.

When the Alaska Highway was first being laid, distances were gauged in miles. Since Canada adopted the metric system in the 1970's, the Canadian portion of this legendary highway has been officially measured in terms of kilometres as well. Even today, however, it is not uncommon to come across road maps and government brochures with distances still labelled in miles. Furthermore, in deference to tradition (and American influence), the entire road is studded with commemorative milestones showing no metric equivalents.

Visitors can combine Tours C and D into a single big loop, since the Stewart-Cassiar Highway and the Alaska Highway intersect at Junction 37, at mile 649 of the Alaska Highway, not far from Watson Lake.

Dawson Creek

Bus station: Greyhound, 1201 Alaska Avenue (☎ 782-3131).

Airport: Dawson Creek Municipal Airport, south of town, accessible by way of Highway 2. It is served daily by Air B.C. (☎ 782-1661); regional flights are offered by Kenn Borek Air (☎ 782-5561).

Fort St. John

Bus station: Greyhound, 101st Avenue (☎ 785-6695).

Airport: 10 km from town, on the road to Cecil Lake, along 100th Avenue. It is served by Canadian Regional (☎ 787-7781).

Fort Nelson

Bus station: Greyhound, at the corner of West 51st and Liard Streets (☎ 774-6322).

Airport: 10 km from downtown via Airport Road (☎ 774-3111). Served by Canadian Regional (☎ 774-3111).

Watson Lake (Yukon)

Area code: 403

Bus station: Greyhound, at the corner of the Campbell and Alaska Highways (☎ 536-2606).

Finding Your Way Around 165

Airport: 13 km from downtown; take the Campbell Highway north (☎ 993-5440). It is served by Alkan Air, the Yukon's main airline (☎ 993-5440), as well as a number of other companies.

■ **Tour D: The Stewart-Cassiar Highway**

Visitors usually take this tour from south to north, starting at Kitwanga. On the left, 169 km from Kitwanga, Highway 37 A branches off toward Stewart and Hyder, Alaska (see Tour E below). You will head north on Highway 37 for the entire tour, which covers a little under 600 km. The road passes numerous little towns along the way, including Tatoffa, Iskut, Dease Lake, Good Hope Lake and Upper Liard (Yukon). Once you've arrived at Dease Lake, it is worth taking the time to visit Telegraph Creek, 129 km away; a well-marked and well-maintained dirt road leads there. Like Tour C, Tour D ends at Watson Lake, in the Yukon. You can combine Tours C and D into one big loop, since the Stewart-Cassiar and Alaska Highways intersect at Junction 37, at mile 649 of the Alaska Highway, near Watson Lake.

Watson Lake (Yukon)

Bus station: Greyhound, at the corner of the Campbell and Alaska Highways, ☎ 536-2606.

Airport: 13 km from downtown; take the Campbell Highway north (☎ 993-5440). It is served by Alkan Air, the Yukon's main airline (☎ 993-5440), as well as a number of other companies.

Stewart

Bus station: Seaport Limousine, 516 Railway Street (☎ 636-2622).

■ **Tour E: To Stewart, BC and Hyder, AK**

This tour starts at Meziadin Junction, along the Stewart-Cassiar Highway; turn right onto Highway 37 A, commonly known as Glacier Highway. The town of Stewart lies 65 km away, while the village of Hyder, Alaska lies 2 km farther, on the road that runs alongside the Portland Canal.

■ **Tour F: The Yellowhead Highway**

This tour will take you from the town of McBride, in eastern British Columbia, to Prince Rupert, on the coast, about 1,000 km away. The Yellowhead Highway runs through an impressive variety of landscapes (mountains, plains and plateaus), as well as several sizeable towns, including Prince George, Smithers, Terrace and Prince Rupert.

Prince George

Bus station: Greyhound, at the corner of 12th and Victoria Streets (☎ 564-5454).

Airport: A few kilometres east of downtown, by way of the Yellowhead Bridge to the north or the Simon Fraser bridge to the south. It is served by Air B.C. (☎ 561-2905), Canadian Regional (☎ 563-0521), Central Mountain (☎ 963-9022) and N.T. Air (☎ 963-9611).

Smithers

Bus station: Greyhound, on Highway 16, right near the Travel InfoCentre (☎ 847-2204).

Train station: On Railway Avenue, not far from downtown (☎ 1-800-561-8630).

Airport: On Highway 16, 10 km west of Smithers (☎ 847-3664). It is served by Central Mountain Air (☎ 847-5000) and Canadian Regional (☎ 1-800-665-1177).

Prince Rupert

Bus station: Greyhound, at the corner of 3rd Avenue and 6th Street (☎ 624-5090).

Train station: Via Rail, on Waterfront Avenue (☎ 627-7589).

Airport: On Digby Island; transportation there provided by a small municipal ferry ($11 one-way) at the end of Highway 16, at the southwest end of Prince Rupert. The airport is served by Air B.C. (☎ 624-4554) and Canadian Regional (☎ 624-9181).

B.C. Ferry terminal: At the west end of 2nd Avenue (Highway 16) in Fairview (☎ 624-9627 or 1-800-663-7600 throughout British Columbia).

■ **Tour G: The Queen Charlotte Islands (Haida Gwaii)**

To get to this archipelago, you must take either a plane or a ferry to Graham Island, the largest and most populous of the 150 islands. The one driveable road there runs the length of the east coast. A small ferry shuttles back and forth between Skidegate Landing, on Graham Island, and Alliford Bay, on Moresby Island, the second largest of the Queen Charlotte Islands.

B.C. Ferry terminal: In Skidegate (☎ 624-9627), in Vancouver (☎ 669-1211) and throughout British Columbia (☎ 1-800-663-7600). Reservations are strongly recommended, especially during summer.

Airports: There is one in Masset, on the northern part of Graham Island, and another in Sandspit, on Moresby Island. Both are clearly indicated. These airports are served by Thunderbird Air (☎ 231-8933 or 1-800-898-0177) and Canadian Regional (☎ 1-800-665-1177).

Practical Information

■ **Area Code:** The area code for the entire territory is ☎ 604; the only exception is Watson Lake, in the Yukon, where it is ☎ 403. The area code for the British Columbian territory covered in this chapter will change to ☎ 250 in October 1996.

■ **Tourist Information**

British Columbia tourist information
☎ 1-800-663-6000

■ **Tour A: To the Alaska Highway**

Prince George

Tourist information: 1198 Victoria Street, Prince George, ☎ 562-3700.

Mackenzie

Tourist information: *(at the intersection of Highways 39 and 97, 29 km from downtown,* ☎ *750-4497)* only open in the summer; during the rest of the year, you can obtain information from the **Chamber of Commerce** *(86 Centennial Street,* ☎ *997-5459)*.

Dawson Creek

Tourist information: *(in summer, every day 8am to 8pm; in winter, Tue to Sat 9am to 5pm)* ☎ 782-9595

■ Tour B: The Hudson's Hope Route

Hudson's Hope

Tourist information: *(mid-May to mid-Sep)* Opposite the museum and the church, ☎ 783-9901.

■ Tour C: The Alaska Highway

Dawson Creek

Tourist information: 900 Alaska Avenue, Dawson Creek, ☎ 782-9595.

Road conditions: ☎ 1-800-663-4997, or 774-7447 in Fort Nelson.

Fort St. John

Tourist information: In keeping with this oil community's industrial character, the tourist office *(9323 100th Street,* ☎ *785-3033)* is located at the foot of a 50 m derrick, just steps away from the centre of town.

Fort Nelson

Tourist information: *(8am to 8pm)* at the west end of the downtown area, inside the Omnisport Centre, ☎ 774-2541.

Watson Lake (Yukon)

Tourist information: *(every day, mid-May to mid-Sep)* at the junction of the Alaska and Campbell Highways, ☎ 403-536-7469.

■ Tour D: The Stewart-Cassiar Highway

Dease Lake

Tourist information: In Dease Lake, on Highway 37 (☎ 771-3900).

Kitwanga

Tourist information: *(every day June to Sep)* on Valley Road, ☎ 849-5760.

Telegraph Creek

Tourist information: ☎ 235-3196.

■ Tour E: To Stewart, BC and Hyder, AK

Stewart

Tourist information: On the left as you enter downtown Stewart, ☎ 636-2111.

On the Way to Stewart

Tourist information: in the round wooden house at the corner of 5th and Columbia Streets, ☎ 636-2251.

Hyder, Alaska

Tourist information: The tourist office is located inside the **museum ★★**, which houses the town archives, on Premier Street, ☎ 636-2637.

■ Tour F: The Yellowhead Highway

Prince Rupert

Tourist information: On 1st Avenue, adjoining the Museum of Northern British Columbia (☎ 1-800-667-1994 or 624-5637). Yellowhead Highway Association (☎ 1-800-661-8888).

McBride

Tourist information: *(every day 9am to 5pm)* in a railway car; the sculpture of a family of grizzlies at the entrance makes it easy to spot.

Vanderhoof

Tourist information: downtown on Burrard Street *(☎ 564-2124)*, you can find out where the best fishing spots are.

Fort St. James

Tourist information: In the Chamber of Commerce, ☎ 996-7023.

Houston

Tourist information: Along the highway; you'll spot the fishing pole from far away, ☎ 845-7640.

Smithers

Tourist information: In a railway car at the intersection of Highway 16 and Main Street ☎ 847-5072.

Kitimat

Tourist information: ☎ 632-6294 or 1-800-664-6554

■ Tour G: The Queen Charlotte Islands (Haida Gwaii)

Queen Charlotte City

Tourist information: Travel InfoCentre, a few hundred metres before the village of Queen Charlotte City, ☎ 559-4742; Queen Charlotte Islands Chamber of Commerce, in Masset, ☎ 626-3300.

Masset

Tourist information: In a small trailer on the south edge of the village; open in summer only ☎ 626-3300.

★ Exploring

■ Tour A: To the Alaska Highway ★★

This tour starts in the town of Prince George. You can reach kilometre/mile 0 of the Alaska Highway, in Dawson Creek, by taking Highway 97, which crosses the Rocky Mountains. The itinerary suggested below leads through pleasant wooded areas strewn with lakes.

Prince George ★★

Prince George (pop. 70,000) considers itself the capital of northern British Columbia. As any map will tell you, however, it actually lies in the centre of the province. Its geographic location has enabled it to become a hub not only for the railway, but also for road transport, since it lies at the intersection of Highway 16, which runs the width of the province, and Highway 97, which runs the length.

Prince George lies 800 km north of Vancouver, about an hour's flight or ten hours' drive along the TransCanada and Highway 97 North. The town's history is linked to two rivers, the Nechako and the Fraser. By the beginning of 19th century, trappers and *coureurs des bois* were using these waterways to reach the vast territories of the north. Before long, they saw that the region was abounding in wolves, minks, muskrats, foxes, etc. Fur-trading posts thus began to spring up along the banks of the two rivers.

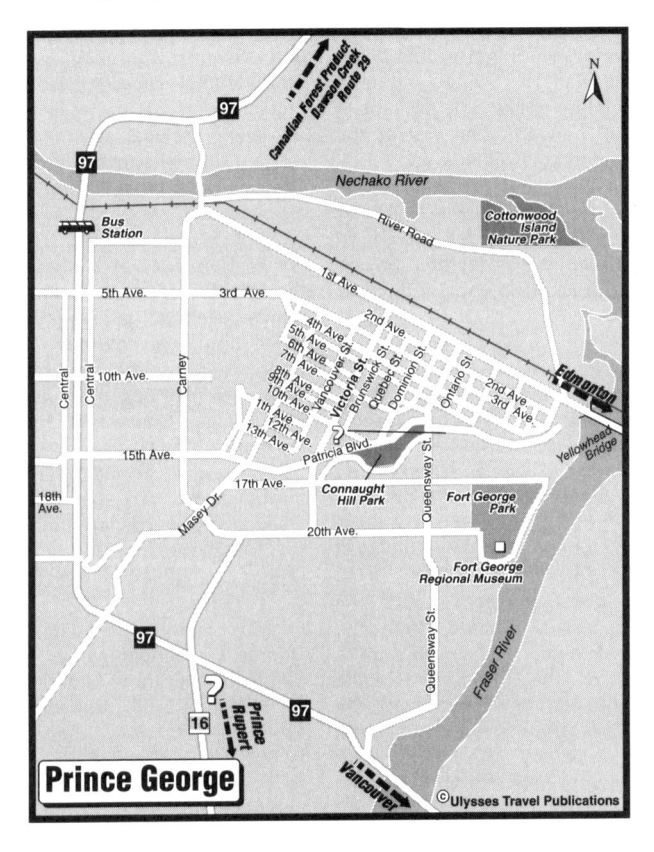

In 1807, the first building, Fort George, was erected. In 1821, it was taken over by the Hudson's Bay Company. In 1908, when the Grand Trunk Pacific Railway (GTR) was constructed, Fort George was slated to become an important distribution centre for the transcontinental railroad. All of these major changes led to a considerable growth in population, and it became necessary to develop a second living area, known as South Fort George.

The GTR finally began operating in the region in 1914. A second area, Prince George, had to be developed to accommodate the flood of new arrivals. Now the third largest city in British Columbia, Prince George derives most of its income from forestry. It is home to no fewer than 15 sawmills and three pulp and paper mills. The climate is continental — warm and dry in the summer and cold in the winter.

The numerous brochures available at the **tourist office** *(every day, Mon to Fri 8am to 5pm; 1198 Victoria Street,* ☎ *562-3700)* can help you get to know the region.

The **Fraser Fort George Regional Museum** ★★ *(mid-May to mid-Sep, Mon, Wed and Sat 10am to 5pm and Tue 10am to 8pm; mid-Sep to mid-May, Tue noon to 8pm and Wed to Sun noon to 5pm; at the end of 20th Avenue,* ☎ *562-1612)* stands on the very site where Fort George was erected in 1807. The museum is an excellent place to learn about the history of Prince George, from the arrival of Alexander Mackenzie and the beginning of the fur trade to the introduction and development of the forest industry. The museum's Northwood Gallery, a sure hit with young children, presents an exhibit on the region's flora and fauna. Not far from the Fort George Regional Museum lies the **Railway & Forest Industry Museum** ★★ *(mid-May to mid-Sep, every day 10am to 5pm;* ☎ *565-7351)*, which will take you back in time to the days when the railroad was new and modern woodcutting techniques had yet to be developed.

If you enjoy and appreciate Amerindian art, make sure to stop at the **Prince George Native Art Gallery** *(Tue to Sat 9am to 5pm; 144 George St.,* ☎ *562-7385)*. This private gallery displays a wide array of tribal art, including sculptures, prints and jewellery.

The **Prince George Art Gallery** *(Mon to Sat 10am to 5pm and Sun 1pm to 5pm; 15th Avenue,* ☎ *563-6447)* is a municipal art gallery, which presents the work of local artists with styles ranging from abstract to impressionist. This is a good place to find local crafts at reasonable prices.

For a short walk or a picnic, head to the **Cottonwood Island Nature Park** ★★, which covers 33 ha along the Nechako River, right near downtown. It has an interesting animal-watching area, where you can observe foxes, beavers and eagles. **Connaught Hill Park** ★, located in the centre of town, offers a 360° view of Prince George and its surroundings. To get there, take Queensway southward, then turn right on Connaught Drive and right again on Caine.

Forestry is the mainspring of Prince George's economy, so it is not surprising that three factories are open to the public. **Canadian Forest Products** ★★ *(PG Pulpmill Road,* ☎ *563-0161)* offers free tours of its facilities. A bus takes visitors to cutting and replanting areas. At the **Northwood**

Exploring 171

Pulp & Timber and North Central Plywoods ★★★ *(mid-May to Sep; reservations recommended, ☎ 562-3700)*, everything is very modern, from the greenhouse where the next generation of trees is nurtured to the sawmill where the trunks are cut up. The third factory, owned by Northwood, is supposedly the "greenest" in Canada. It produces pulp and paper, as well as construction materials. Visitors will learn how paper, chipboard and plywood are made. As the tour involves a long walk, partly on uneven terrain, it is recommended to wear closed, flat shoes and pants.

Mackenzie

A small, ultra-modern community, Mackenzie is a typical boom town. It was built in 1966, following the construction of the Peace River dam. Less than a year after the first stone was laid, hundreds of workers arrived in the area, which was completely undeveloped at the time. Today, with a population of 5,700, Mackenzie has become a village of superlatives, boasting the largest artificial lake on the continent, **Williston Lake**, a byproduct of the dam, as well as the world's biggest **tree-chipper**, which was used to clear a passage through the forest back when the town was founded.

Chetwynd

This little town was once known as Little Prairie, but its name was changed in honour of Railway Minister Ralph Chetwynd, who pioneered rail transport in northern British Columbia. Today, Chetwynd is a prosperous working-class town. It was constructed to the north of one of the largest coal deposits in the world. Natural gas and the forest industry have further strengthened the local economy. A simple walk down the street reveals how important forestry is here; Chetwynd is the self-proclaimed **world capital of chainsaw sculpture**, and carved animals adorn the tops of buildings all over town. To find out where they all are, stop at the **tourist office** *(in a log cabin in the upper part of town, ☎ 788-3345)*.

Dawson Creek ★

Dawson Creek was named after Dr. George Dawson, a geologist who, in 1879, discovered that the surrounding plains were ideal for agriculture. He might have thought that Dawson Creek would become a farming capital, but he probably never suspected that oil and natural gas would be discovered here.

The other major turning-point in Dawson Creek's history took place in 1942, when the town became kilometre/mile 0 of the Alaska Highway. Today, nearly 30,000 tourists from all over the world come to Dawson Creek to start their journey northward.

The **tourist office** *(in summer, every day 8am to 8pm; in winter, Tue to Sat 9am to 5pm; ☎ 782-9595)* is open year-round. Like the **Station Museum ★** and the **Dawson Creek Art Gallery ★**, it is part of the **Northern Alberta Railway Park (NAR) ★★**. You can't miss the NAR, with its immense grain elevator, which was renovated in 1931 and stands at the corner of Alaska Avenue and 8th Street.

The **Station Museum ★** *(Jun to Sep, every day 8am to 8pm)* traces the history of the Alaska Highway, as well as that of the area's first inhabitants.

Northern British Columbia

Dawson Creek

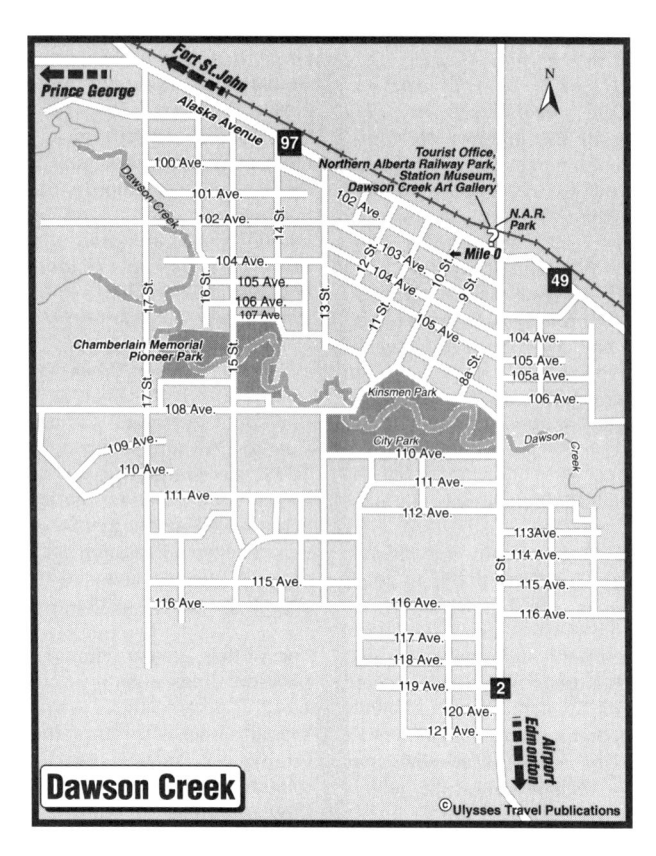

The collection on display includes the largest mammoth tusk ever found in the Canadian West, as well as a number of dinosaur bones.

Inside the grain elevator, the **Dawson Creek Art Gallery** *(in winter, Tue to Sat 10am to noon and 1pm to 5pm; rest of the year, every day 9am to 6pm)* displays handicrafts and works by local artists, as well as hosting travelling exhibitions.

Right beside the NAR Park, you'll spot a sign — surely the most photographed one in the province — indicating the starting point of the Alaska Highway.

The legendary **Mile 0 Post**, also worth a picture, is located downtown.

If you'd like to sample the local produce, stop at the **Dawson Creek Farmer's Market** *(Sat 8am to 3pm)*, which is held near the NAR Park, just behind the sign for the Alaska Highway.

■ **Tour B: The Hudson's Hope Route** ★★

This tour is an alternate route from Prince George to Dawson Creek.

Simply take Highway 29 from Chetwynd.

Hudson's Hope

This area was first explored in 1793 by Alexander Mackenzie. In 1805, a fur-trading post was set up here. Nowadays, Hudson's Hope is known mainly for its hydroelectric complexes, one of which was built in the 1960s (WAC Bennett), the other slightly more recently (Peace Canyon).

The **tourist office** *(in a log cabin in the centre of the village,* ☎ *783-9901)* is located right near **St. Peter's United Church ★**, a charming old wooden building. Also nearby is the **Hudson's Hope Museum**, which displays fossils, some of dinosaurs, and various artifacts from the area.

Of course, the major points of interest in Hudson's Hope are the **WAC Bennett ★★★** *(about 20 km west of Hudson's Hope,* ☎ *783-5211)* and **Peace Canyon ★★** *(7 km south of Hudson's Hope,* ☎ *783-9943)* hydroelectric facilities. Free tours are available at both. The WAC Bennett dam is the largest structure in the world, a hodgepodge of stone and concrete that fills in a natural valley. Its reservoir, Williston Lake, is the largest artificial lake on the planet!

■ **Tour C: The Alaska Highway ★★★**

This tour starts at kilometre/mile 0 of the highway, in Dawson Creek, and ends at kilometre 1011/mile 632, in Watson Lake, in the Yukon. The entire road is paved and well-maintained. Before setting out, though, make sure that your car's engine and tires are in good condition, since there aren't very many repair shops along the way. A lot of roadwork is carried out during summer, and the resulting dust makes driving conditions more difficult. You are therefore better off leaving your lights on at all times. In summer as in winter, it is always wise to check the **road conditions** before setting out by calling ☎ **1-800-663-4997**.

The Alaska Highway started out as a war measure. The Americans, who initiated the project, wanted to create a communication route that would make it possible to transport military equipment, provisions and troops by land to Alaska. Construction started in March 1942, in the village of Dawson Creek, which had only 600 inhabitants at the time. Within a few weeks, over 10,000 people, mostly military workers, had flooded into the area.

Over 11,000 American soldiers and engineers, 6,000 civilian workers and 7,000 machines and tractors of all manner were required to accomplish the formidable task of clearing a passage through thousands of kilometres of wilderness. The cost of this gargantuan project, which stretched 2,436 km and inclued 133 bridges, came to 140 million Canadian dollars. Even today, the building of the Alaska Highway is viewed as a feat of engineering on a par with the Panamá Canal. The Canadian section was given to Canada by the United States in 1946 and remained under military supervision until 1964.

Today, this extraordinary highway is a vital social and economic link for all northern towns. It also offers tourists from all over the world unhoped-for access to the majestic landscapes of this region.

Fort St. John ★
kilometre 75.6/mile 47

Fort St. John is the largest community on the British-Columbian section of the Alaska Highway. A prosperous, modern little town of about 14,000, it has a highly diversified economy. Agriculture plays a significant role here, as there are 800 farms in the area, but petroleum and natural gas are the main sources of income. It is not without good reason that Fort St. John calls itself the energy capital of British Columbia.

In keeping with this oil community's industrial calling, the **tourist office** *(9323 100th Street,* ☎ *785-3033)* is located at the foot of a 50 m-high derrick, just steps away from the downtown area. In the same building, the **North Peace Museum** ★ *(at the corner of 93rd Avenue and 100th Street,* ☎ *787-0430)* deals with the prehistoric past of the Fort St. John region, with a collection of nearly 6,000 objects, including fossils and bones. The **Peace Gallery North** *(in the cultural centre,* ☎ *787-0993)* exhibits a large number of works by local artists. **The Honey Place** ★ *(kilometre 67.2/mile 42 of the Alaska Highway,* ☎ *785-4808)* arranges guided tours of the world's largest glassed-in hive, offering visitors a chance to observe firsthand the marvellous spectacle of bees making honey.

Fort Nelson
kilometre 454.3/mile 283

This small industrial town has fewer than 4,000 inhabitants. Its history has been linked to the fur trade since 1805. In 1922, the town was connected to Fort St. John by the Godsell Trail, thus ending its isolation. In those years, Fort Nelson was home to only 200 Amerindians and a handful of whites. Later, after the Alaska Highway was constructed, the town grew considerably when service stations, hotels and restaurants set up business here. It officially became a municipality in 1987.

The **tourist office** *(8am to 8pm; at the west end of the downtown area,* ☎ *774-2541)* is located inside the Omnisport Centre. History lovers will enjoy a visit to the **Fort Nelson Heritage Museum** ★ *(opposite the tourist office, downtown,* ☎ *774-3536)*.

Stone Mountain Provincial Park ★★★
kilometre 627/mile 392

The entrance to Stone Mountain Provincial Park *(BC Parks,* ☎ *787-3407)* is located at the highest point on the Alaska Highway, at an altitude of 1,267 m. It covers 25,691 ha of rocky peaks, geological formations and lakes, and is home to the largest variety of animal life in northern British Columbia. There are large numbers of moose here, as well as deer, beavers, black bears, grizzlies and wolves, not to mention the hundreds of caribou, which can often be seen near the road. Visitors unaccustomed to walking in the mountains in northern latitudes are advised not to venture too high. The climatic conditions can change rapidly, and the temperature can drop more than 10 degrees in a few hours. It snows quite often on these peaks, even in the middle of summer.

Wokkpash Recreation Area ★★★

The Wokkpash Recreation Area is a provincial park connected to Stone Mountain *(BC Parks,* ☎ *787-3407)*.

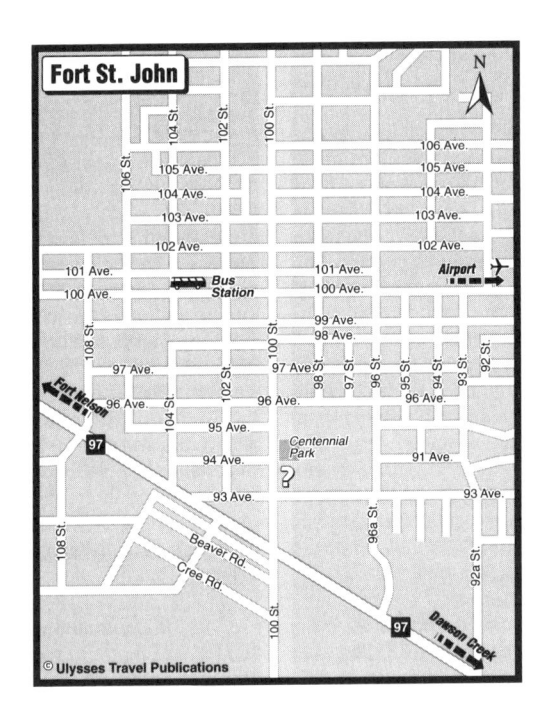

Only accessible by foot or on horseback, this 37,800 ha stretch of wilderness is not a place for inexperienced hikers. Simply getting there is an expedition. The most well-known trail leads from MacDonald Creek to Wokkpash Valley, covering a distance of 70 km, with a 1,200 m change in altitude. It requires at least seven days of walking. Beware of flash floods on rainy days.

Muncho Lake Provincial Park ★★★
kilometre 729/mile 456

Muncho Lake *(BC Parks,* ☎ *787-3407)* is one of the loveliest provincial parks in Canada and definitely one of the highlights on the British-Columbian portion of the Alaska Highway. It encompasses 88,416 ha of bare, jagged mountains around magnificent Muncho Lake, which stretches 12 km. Like all parks in the region, it owes its existence to the Alaska Highway. Large numbers of beavers, black bears, grizzlies, wolves and mountain goats make their home here, while the magnificent plant-life includes a variety of orchids.

Liard Hot Springs Provincial Park ★★★
kilometre 764.7/mile 477.7

Liard Hot Springs Provincial Park *(BC Parks, ☎ 787-3407)* is the most popular place for travellers to stop. Here, you can relax in natural pools fed by 49° hot springs. The microclimate created by the high temperature of the water, which remains constant in summer and winter alike, has enabled a unique assortment of plants to thrive here. Giant ferns and a profusion of carnivorous plants give the area a slightly tropical look.

Watson Lake (Yukon) ★★
kilometre 1021/mile 612.9

The Alaska Highway tour comes to an end at Watson Lake, in the Yukon. The first stop here is the **tourist office** *(mid-May to mid-Sep, every day; at the intersection of the Alaska and Campbell Highways, ☎ 403-536-7469)*.

Around 1897, an Englishman by the name of Frank Watson set out from Edmonton to lead the adventurous life of a gold-digger in Dawson City. After passing through regions that hadn't even been mapped yet, he ended up on the banks of the Liard River. He decided to stop his travels there and take up residence on the shores of the lake that now bears his name. The construction of a military airport in 1941 and the laying of the Alaska Highway the following year enabled Watson Lake to develop into a real town. It is now a transportation, communication and supply hub for the neighbouring communities, as well as for the mining and forest industries.

A visit to the **Alaska Highway Interpretive Centre ★★** *(the building adjoining the tourist office; mid-May to mid-Sep, every day 8am to 8pm; ☎ 536-7469)* is a must for anyone interested in the history of the Alaska Highway. The epic story of the famous highway comes to life through slide shows and photographs. The **Alaska Highway Signpost Forest ★★★** is far and away the main attraction in Watson Lake. It is a collection of over 20,000 signs from the world over, placed on the posts by the tourists themselves. Some of them are highly original. You can create your own sign when planning your trip, or have one made for you on the spot for a few dollars.

The **1940's Canteen Show ★★** *(Jun to Aug, every night at 8pm; behind the Signpost Forest, ☎ 403-536-7781)* is a musical that will take you back to the 1940's, when the Alaska Highway was under construction.

■ Tour D: The Stewart-Cassiar Highway ★★★

This tour usually starts in Kitwanga, but travellers who have taken the Alaska Highway can set out from Watson Lake instead. You can actually combine Tours C and D into one big loop, as the two highways intersect at **Junction 37**, at kilometre 1038/mile 649 of the Alaska Highway, a few kilometres from Watson Lake.

Completed in 1972, the Stewart-Cassiar Highway (37) meets all highway standards and can thus be used at any time of the year. Three large sections of the road are unpaved, however, and get dusty in dry, hot weather and muddy in the rain, making driving conditions difficult from time to time. For this reason, the Ministry of Transportation recommends keeping your lights on at all times. Although you are better off driving this road with a car with high ground clearance or with an all-terrain 4-wheel drive vehicle, you can get by with a conventional automobile.

The Stewart-Cassiar Highway is the trucking route used to bring supplies to communities in the northern part of the province and beyond. While the trip is a bit shorter than the Alaska Highway, the scenery is equally magnificent.

Kitwanga ★

Kitwanga, which has just under 1,500 inhabitants, is the first community you'll come across on your way south. Known mainly for its historic past, it is home to **Battle Hill ★**, where Amerindians fought one another 200 years ago. Now a national park, the site is open year-round and is located near the video club that doubles as the local **tourist office** *(Jun to Sep, every day, on Valley Rd, ☎ 849-5760)*.

If you'd like to see some beautiful **totem poles ★**, make a quick stop at the **Gitwangak Indian Reserve** *(shortly before the village of Kitwanga, just after the intersection of Highways 16 and 37)*; a whole series of them is lined up opposite **St. Paul's Anglican Church ★**, built in 1893.

Kitwancool ★

This little Amerindian village is known chiefly for its **antique totem poles ★**. The oldest one, *Hole-in-the-Ice*, dates back nearly 140 years.

Meziadin Junction

Meziadin Junction, located 170 km from Kitwanga, is the starting point for the excursion to **Stewart, BC and Hyder, AK ★★★**. See Tour E, p 179.

Spatsizi Plateau Wilderness Park ★★★

The Spatsizi Plateau Wilderness Park is only for real adventurers *(On Tattoga Lake, not far from Iskut, on Highway 37, 361 km north of the intersection of Highways 16 and 37, in Kitwanga. Take Ealue Lake Road for 22 km. Cross the Klappan River to the BC Rail dirt road, which leads 114 km to the southwest end of the park. **Never set out on an excursion here without calling BC Parks beforehand**, ☎ 847-7320)*. The plateau stretches across 656,785 ha of wilderness, and is accessible by foot, by boat or by hydroplane.

Spatsizi means "red goat" in the language of the Tahltan Indians. The name was inspired by the scarlet-coloured mountains, whose soil is rich in iron oxide. The park is in fact located on a plateau, at a nearly steady altitude of about 1,800 m. The highest peak in the park is Mount Will (2,500 m), in the Skeena Mountain chain.

This region's dry, continental climate is characterized by cold winters with only light snowfall and summers with an average temperature of 20°C and little rainfall. These weather conditions have enabled a large number of animals, including caribou, grizzlies, beavers, and nearly 140 bird species, to make their home here.

Iskut

Iskut is a small community of 300 people, mostly Amerindians. In the heart of the reserve, you will find a service centre — that is, a gas station, a post office and a grocery store *(Iskut Lake Co-op, ☎ 234-3241)*. Iskut's most distinguishing feature is its surrounding **countryside ★★★**, which is positively magnificent, especially when it is decked out in autumn colours. In the fall, it is not uncommon to see wolves crossing the highway at nightfall.

Mount Edziza Provincial Park ★★★

Mount Edziza Provincial Park covers 230,000 ha in the northwest part of the province, west of the Iskut River and south of the Stikine River. It is most notable for its volcanic sites, the most spectacular in all of Canada.

Mount Edziza (2,787 m), the highest peak in the park, is a perfect example of a volcanic formation. The eruption that created this impressive basalt cone occurred nearly four million years ago. The lava from Mount Edziza flowed almost 65 km. Afterward, numerous little eruptions took place, creating about thirty more cones, including the perfectly symmetrical Eve cone.

Like many parks in northern British Columbia, Mount Edziza Provincial Park is very hard to reach and offers no services. Only experienced, well-equipped hikers can get there safely. Although the temperature can climb as high as 30° during summer, it can snow at any time of the year here. *(To plan a trip, call BC Parks, ☎ 771-4591, at Dease Lake)*.

Dease Lake

With 750 inhabitants, Dease Lake is the largest community on the Stewart-Cassiar Highway (Highway 37). It is the self-proclaimed jade capital of the world, due to the large number of quarries around the village. Lovely handcrafted sculptures are available in the many shops along the highway. Dease Lake is also an important industrial centre and a hub for government services.

Above all, this is a place to enjoy outdoor activities. Vast **Dease Lake ★★★**, which stretches 47 km, is ideal for trout and pike fishing, as well as being the point of departure for plane and horseback rides in **Mount Edziza Provincial Park ★★★** and the **Spatsizi Plateau Wilderness Park ★★★**. The **tourist office** *(Chamber of Commerce, at the southwest edge of town, along Highway 37, ☎ 771-3900)* can provide you with information on available activities.

Telegraph Creek ★★★

It is worth going to Telegraph Creek, if only for the pleasure of driving there. Laid in 1922, the winding road leads through some splendid scenery. The village at the end beckons visitors back in time to the pioneer era.

To get there, go to the end of Boulder Street, Dease Lake's main street. The road that leads to Telegraph Creek, 119 km away, is well-maintained but rather narrow, making it extremely ill-suited to large vehicles and trailers. All along the way, you'll enjoy unforgettable **views** ★★★ of **Tuya River**, the **Grand Canyon of the Stikine**, the **Tahltan-Stikine lava beds**, etc. The village itself, a small community of 450 people, makes a striking first impression. While its **period buildings** ★★★ give it a quaint look, it is fully equipped to accommodate the needs of tourists (gas station, repair shop, restaurant, hotel, etc.). For information about tourist activities in the area, head to the **Stikine RiverSong** *(café, inn, grocery store and information office;* ☎ *235-3196)*.

Good Hope Lake

This little Amerindian village (pop. 100) is of interest mainly for its magnificent crystal-clear **lake** ★★★.

■ Tour E: To Stewart, BC and Hyder, AK ★★★

The Trip to Stewart ★★★

This tour starts at Meziadin Junction, along the Stewart-Cassiar Highway. Head west on Highway 37A, aptly nicknamed Glacier Highway. You will notice a major change in the scenery along the way. The mountains, with their snow- and glacier-capped peaks, look more and more imposing the closer you get.

Exactly 23 km from Meziadin Junction, around a bend in the road, you will be greeted by the spectacular sight of **Bear Glacier** ★★★, which rises in all its azure-coloured splendour out of the milky waters of **Strohn Lake** at the same level as the road! Nineteen kilometres farther, you'll reach Stewart, a frontier town located just 2 km from the little village of Hyder, Alaska. Both communities lie at the end of the 145 km-long **Portland Canal** ★★★, the fourth deepest fjord in the world. In addition to forming a natural border between Canada and the United States, this narrow stretch of water gives Stewart direct access to the sea, making this little town of 1000 people the most northerly ice-free port in Canada.

The **setting** ★★★ is simply magnificent. The town is surrounded on all sides by towering, glacier-studded mountains. In the summer, the mild temperature is governed by the occasionally damp Pacific climate, while heavy snowfall is common in the winter (over 20 m total). The **tourist office** should be your first stop *(in a log house at the corner of 5th and Columbia Streets,* ☎ *636-2251)*.

Stewart boasts a large number of period buildings, such as the **Fire Hall** (1910), located on 4th Street, and the **Stone Storehouse**, on the Canadian-U.S. border. The latter was erected by the American army in 1896 and originally served as a prison.

Hyder, Alaska ★★

Hyder (pop. 70) considers itself the most friendly ghost town in Alaska. This little community is known mainly for its three pubs, open 23 hours a day, and its duty-free shops. Keep in mind that although there is no customs office between the two countries here, the border still exists, and ignorance of the law is no excuse. It is best to respect all regulations concerning limits on tax-free merchandise. The **tourist office** is located inside the **museum** ★★, which exhibits documents related to

Hyder's history (Premier Street, ☎ 636-2637).

Fifteen minutes past Hyder lies **Fish Creek ★★★**, the most important spawning area for **pink salmon** in all of Alaska (Jul to Sep). Dozens of **black bears** and **grizzlies** come here to feast on the fish, which are easy to catch after their long, exhausting journey. A **platform** has been set up so that tourists can observe this gripping spectacle. Caution: Keep a good distance from the bears. Don't be fooled by their friendly, clumsy appearance; they are unpredictable by nature, and can run as fast as 55 km/h!

The same road leads to **Salmon Glacier ★★★**, the world's fifth largest glacier. The road is very narrow in places, making it unsuitable for large vehicles. Watch out for ruts and large rocks. The road is closed from November to June. For a worry-free trip, call **Seaport Limousine** (guided minibus tours; ☎ 636-2622). In clear weather, the view of the glacier is breathtaking.

■ **Tour F: The Yellowhead Highway ★★★**

The Yellowhead is an impressive highway that starts in Winnipeg, Manitoba, runs through Saskatchewan and Alberta, and ends at Prince Rupert. This tour covers the part between McBride, in eastern British Columbia and Prince Rupert, about 1000 km away in the westernmost part of the province. The incredibly varied scenery along the way includes high mountains, canyons, valleys and dense forests. This tour provides an excellent overview of the geology and topography of British Columbia.

McBride

This little working-class community of 620 people is sustained by the forest industry. It lies in a pleasant setting at the foot of the Rockies, on the banks of the Fraser River. Information about the area is available at the **tourist office** (in a railway car, easily recognizable by the sculpture of a family of grizzlies at the entrance; every day 9am to 5pm). We recommend walking up to the **Tear Mountain overlook ★★★**, which offers an unimpeded view of the region.

Prince George ★★

See Tour A: To the Alaska Highway, p 169.

Vanderhoof

Vanderhoof is a small farming community with a population of just over 4,000. Its main attraction is the **Vanderhoof International Airshow ★★★**, the second largest such event in British Columbia, which generally takes place during the third weekend of July (Vanderhoof International Airshow, P.O. Box 1248, Vanderhoof BC, V0J 3A0, ☎ 567-3144). The town is surrounded by lakes renowned for trout fishing. You can find out where the best spots are at the **tourist office** (in the centre of town on Burrard Street, ☎ 564-2124).

Fort St. James

Fort St. James, a little town of 2,000 inhabitants, lies about 60 km from Vanderhoof via Highway 27. Its main claim to fame is **Fort St. James National Historic Park ★★** (every day mid-May to mid-Sep, 9:30am to 5pm;

☎ 996-7191), an authentic trading post established by the Hudson's Bay Company in 1896. Actors in period dress recreate the atmosphere of bygone days. The **tourist office** is in the Chamber of Commerce (☎ 996-7023).

Burns Lake

There's no doubt that Burns Lake is a perfect place for **fishing**. The carved wooden fish at the entrance to town is a clear indication of what kind of atmosphere you'll find here. The local mottos are "3,000 Miles of Fishing" and "The Land of a Thousand Lakes". Fishermen flock here for the lake trout, salmon and pike. However, knowing where exactly to cast your line can prove quite difficult if you're not familiar with the region, given the maze of dirt roads. Your best bet is to stop at the **Chamber of Commerce** before setting out (☎ 692-3773).

Houston

Houston, like Burns Lake, has clearly identified its summertime vocation: **fishing**. Not just any fishing, though; Houston is the self-proclaimed world steelhead capital. This famous sea trout is among the noblest of fish. Fishing buffs will be encouraged by the sight of the world's largest fly rod (20 m) at the entrance of the **tourist office** *(set up alongside the road, the rod is visible from far away;* ☎ *845-7640)*, which also distributes a guide to the good fishing spots.

Smithers ★★

Smithers is a pretty, pleasant town with unusual **architecture** ★★. The mountain setting ★★★, dominated by glacier-capped **Hudson Bay Mountain**, is splendid. Since being reconstructed in 1979, the town has taken on the look of a Tyrolean village. For this reason, many Europeans, lured by the local atmosphere and way of life, have taken up residence here. The **Hudson Bay Mountain** ★★★ (153 m vertical drop, 18 runs) ski area, which looks out over the valley, has powdery conditions from November on. Start your tour of this little town of 5,000 at the **tourist office** *(in a railway car at the intersection of Highway 16 and Main Street,* ☎ *847-5072)*. A few metres away, the **Bulkley Valley Art Gallery and Museum** ★★ *(every day 10am to 5pm during summer and 1pm to 5pm during winter;* ☎ *847-5322)* exhibits objects used by the pioneers and photographs from the local archives. Another interesting place to visit is **Driftwood Canyon Provincial Park** ★★, a major fossil site in this region. The tourist office can provide you with a map so you don't lose your way. On the last weekend in August, Smithers hosts the **Bulkley Valley Fall Fair** ★★★, one of the largest agricultural fairs in British Columbia.

Moricetown Canyon and Falls ★★★

Along the Bulkley River, 40 km west of Smithers on Amerindian land, there is a fishing area known as **Moricetown Canyon**, which has been frequented by natives for centuries. Today, the natives still use the same fishing methods as their ancestors. Using long poles with hooks on them, they catch onto the **salmon**, then trap them in nets as they swim upstream. This is a very popular place to take pictures.

Hazelton ★★

Hazelton is the largest of three villages, the other two being South Hazelton and New Hazelton. Inhabited mainly by Amerindians (pop. 8,000), these three communities date back to the late 19th century, when the Hudson's Bay Company established a fur-trading post in the area (1868). The main attraction here is the **Ksan Indian Village ★★★** *(7 km from Highway 16, shortly after Hazelton, ☎ 842-5544)*, a replica of a Gitksan Indian village, where visitors can watch sculptors at work and learn about age-old canoe-building techniques. The **tourist office** is located at the intersection of Highways 16 and 62 *(May to Sep, every day; ☎ 842-6071; Sep to Apr, ☎ 842-6571)*.

Terrace

Terrace is one of the larger towns on the Yellowhead Highway (Highway 16). It lies on the banks of the magnificent **Skeena River**, the second largest river in the province after the Fraser, and is surrounded by the Coast Mountains. Terrace is a typical example of a community dedicated to work, in that little effort has been put into making the town pretty and inviting. The surrounding **scenery ★★★**, on the other hand, is splendid. Arriving from the east on Highway 16, you will see the **tourist office**, housed in the log building that serves as the Chamber of Commerce *(every day 9am to 8pm during summer, Mon to Fri 9am to 5pm during winter; ☎ 635-2063 or 685-4689)*.

You can start your tour of the town at the **Heritage Park Museum ★★** *(every day 10am to 6pm during summer; on Kerby Street, ☎ 567-2991)*, which deals with the history of the pioneers. There are a number of period buildings here, including a hotel, a barn, a theatre and six log cabins. Most date from 1910.

Also of interest in this area is the **Northern Light Studio & Gardens ★★** *(Mon to Sat 9:30am to 5:30pm; 4820 Halliwell Avenue, ☎ 638-1403)*, an art gallery located in a pretty little residential neighbourhood. Articles on display include jewellery, Amerindian handicrafts and works by local artists. In the magnificent Japanese garden adjoining the gallery, a number of rare plants, many of them exotic, bloom in the sunshine.

Tseax Lava Beds ★★★

If you get off Highway 16 and head northward out of Terrace on Kalum Lake Drive, you'll reach the Tseax Lava Beds, the only natural site of its kind in Canada. Here, you'll find a number of **volcanic craters** and a stretch of lava 3 km wide and 18 km long. According to experts, the last eruptions took place about 350 years ago, which, on a geological scale, equates to a few minutes. Turquoise-coloured water has reappeared on the surface, adding a bit of colour to this lunar landscape. Right beside the lava beds is the Nisga'a Memorial Lava Bed Park, founded in memory of the 2,000 Nisga'a Indians who perished during the last eruption. With a little luck, you'll spot a Kermodei bear. The sight of one of these creatures, which belong to the same family as the black bear, but have a pure white coat, can make for a truly unforgettable visit.

Lakelse Lake Provincial Park ★★

Located on Highway 37 halfway between Terrace and Kitimat, Lakelse Lake Provincial Park is the perfect spot for those looking to relax. On the shores of the magnificent lake for which the park is named, you'll find a splendid **sandy beach** ★★★. A number of picnic areas have been laid out here, along with hiking trails and a campground.

Kitimat

Visitors interested in both industry and nature will find a combination of the two in the little town of Kitimat (pop. 11,300), less than an hour from Terrace. You can start your tour at the **tourist office** (☎ *632-6294* or *1-800-664-6554*), located at the edge of town. Kitimat is an industrial town in the true sense of the term. It was established in the mid-1950's to accommodate workers from the **Alcan** (☎ *639-8259*) aluminum factory, the **Eurocan Pulp** (☎ *632-6111*) paper mill and the **Methanex** (☎ *639-9292*) petrochemical plant, which together employed over two thirds of the population. All three companies offer free guided tours of their facilities, but reservations are required. Those interested in local history can stop at the **Centennial Museum** *(May to Sep, Tue to Sat 10am to 5pm, Fri until 10pm; rest of the year, open at 11am; 293 City Centre,* ☎ *632-7022)*, which exhibits Amerindian artifacts found in the area. Although the surrounding mountains make Kitimat seem landlocked, the town is actually a port with direct access to the Pacific by way of the **Douglas Channel** ★★★. **Salmon** pass through this natural fjord on their way to the ocean's tributaries, making Kitimat a popular place for fishing. You can find out where the best spots are at the tourist office.

From Terrace to Prince Rupert ★★★

The 132 km stretch of highway between Terrace and Prince Rupert is undoubtedly one of the loveliest in Canada. The road follows the magnificent **Skeena River** ★★★ almost curve for curve as it peacefully weaves its way between the **Coast Mountains** ★★★. On fine days, the scenery ★★★ is extraordinary. Rest and picnic areas have been laid out all along the way.

Prince Rupert ★★★

The landscape changes radically near Prince Rupert. Huge hills covered with vegetation typical of the Pacific coast (large cedars, spruce trees) stretch as far as the eye can see. There is water everywhere, and although you will feel as if you are surrounded by lakes, what you are actually looking at is the ocean creeping inland. If you take a look at a map, you'll see that there are thousands of islands and fjords in this region. In fact, the town of Prince Rupert itself is located on an island, Kaien Island, 140 km south of Ketchikan (Alaska). Prince Rupert is the most northerly point serviced by BC Ferry, as well as being an important terminal for ferries from Alaska (Alaska Marine Highway).

The **scenery** ★★★ is quite simply superb; mountains blanketed by a dense forest encircle the town, and a splendid **natural harbour** ★★★, the second largest in the Canadian West, will remind you that you have reached the coast. The history of Prince Rupert dates back to 1905, when engineers from the Grand Trunk Pacific Railway (GTPR), the transcontinental railroad, came here to look into the possibility of ending the line where the town is now located. Over 19,000 km of possible routes were studied before it was decided that the railroad would in fact run alongside the Skeena River. Charles Hays, president of the GTPR, held a contest to christen the new terminus. The name Prince Rupert was chosen from nearly 12,000 entries, in honour of the explorer and first head of the Hudson's Bay Company, a cousin of Charles II of England.

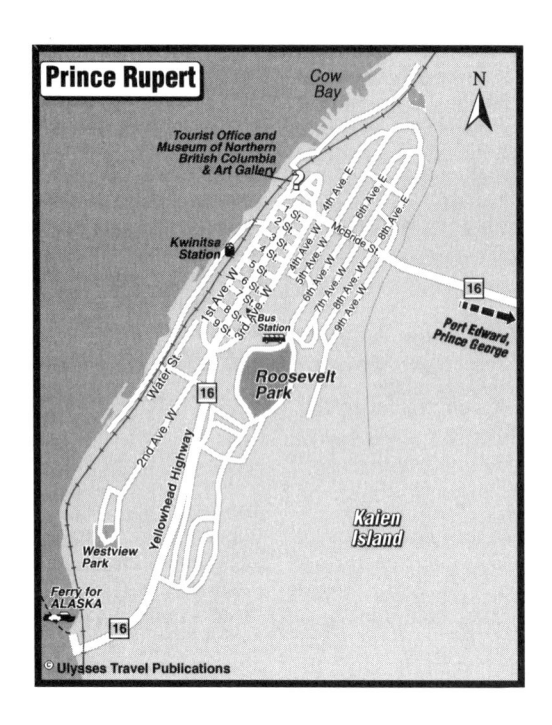

Today, Prince Rupert (pop. 20,000) is a
lovely, prosperous community unlike any other town in northern British Columbia. You won't find any concrete or garish neon signs here; instead, you will be greeted by opulent-looking Victorian **architecture** ★★, large, pleasant streets, lovely shops and numerous restaurants reflecting a cosmopolitan atmosphere.

Start off your tour of Prince Rupert at the **tourist office** *(mid-May to Sep, Mon to Sat 9am to 9pm and Sun 9am to 5pm; rest of the year, Mon to Fri 10am to 5pm; at the corner of McBride Street* and 1st Avenue, on the way into town, ☎ 624-5637), which offers direct access into the interesting **Museum of Northern British Columbia & Art Gallery** ★★ *(in the summer, Mon to Sat 9am to 9pm, Sun 9am to 5pm; rest of the year, Mon to Sat 10am to 5pm;* ☎ *624-3207)*. This museum displays various artifacts, as well as magnificent works of art and jewellery, which serve as proof that Amerindians have been living in this region for over 5,000 years. The art gallery, located inside the museum, features a vast selection of books on indigenous art, as well as displaying handicrafts and paintings.

Boat trips ★★★ to **archeological sites** can be arranged at the tourist office. Space is limited and reservations are required.

Little **Kwinitsa station** *(this station-museum is only open during summer)*, built in 1911, is located alongside the sea. It is one of 400 identical stations along the Grand Trunk Pacific Railway, the transcontinental line from Winnipeg to Prince Rupert. If you head north on 6th Avenue, you will see signs for the **Seaplane Base** ★★, one of the largest of its kind in Canada. The continuous spectacle of the aircraft taking off and landing has something hypnotic about it, and makes for lovely photographs.

The picturesque neighbourhood of **Cow Bay** ★★★, built on piles and overlooking a pretty sailing harbour, is a must-see. All sorts of shops, cafes and restaurants are clustered together in a colourful seaside setting. The **Seafest** takes place on the first weekend in June. Paraders march through the streets at 11am on Saturday, and sporting activities are held all weekend.

About 15 km from Prince Rupert, in the little village of Port Edward, you will find the **North Pacific Cannery Village Museum** ★★ *(May to Sep, every day 10am to 7pm; Oct to Apr, Wed to Sun 10am to 4pm; 1889 Skeena Drive,* ☎ *628-3538)*, a former salmon canning factory built over 106 years ago. During summer, actor David Boyce puts on a show that traces the history of the Skeena River and salmon fishing, which has been the mainspring of the regional economy for over a century now.

■ **Tour G: The Queen Charlotte Islands (Haida Gwaii)** ★★★

However you choose to get to the islands, upon arriving you'll discover an atmosphere and landscape that are truly beyond compare. Though the 5,000 islanders seem to be very modest about their little piece of paradise, they actually do everything in their power to attract visitors from all over the world and show them a warm welcome. The archipelago consists of 150 islands of various sizes. Almost all of the urban areas are located on the largest one, **Graham Island**, to the north. **Moresby Island** is the second most populous. Here, you'll find two villages, Sandspit and Alliford Bay, as well as the amazing **Gwaii Haanas National Park**.

The Queen Charlotte Islands lie about 770 km, as the crow flies, from Vancouver. Because they are located so far west, the sun rises and sets at different times here than on the mainland. Although the islands are known for their wet climate, the more populated eastern coasts receive only slightly more rainfall than Vancouver (1,250 mm). The precipitation on the western coasts, however, reaches record levels (4,500 mm). The jagged relief of the **Queen Charlotte and San**

Christoval Mountains has always protected the east coast from the westerly storms. Despite these weather conditions, 10,000 years ago, the **Haidas**, who already inhabited the archipelago, established living areas on the west coast. The Haidas are known to this day for their high-quality handicrafts and beautiful works of art.

Because the islands are so isolated, services are limited here. There are only two **automated-teller machines** on the archipelago, one in Masset and the other in Queen Charlotte City.

The islands are accessible by **plane** *(Thunderbird Air, ☎ 1-800-898-0177, Canadian Airlines, ☎ 1-800-663-3502)* or by **ferry** *(BC Ferry, ☎ 1-800-663-7300)*. All the local villages are linked by a single 120 km road, Highway 16.

When planning a trip to the Queen Charlotte Islands (*Haida Gwaii*, or "Haida Land" in the language of the natives), it is wise to contact the local **tourist office** *(2 km north of Queen Charlotte City, ☎ 559-4742)*.

Skidegate

This is the first place you'll see if you take the ferry to the Queen Charlotte Islands, since the landing stage is located at the edge of the village. Skidegate is a small native community of 470 inhabitants, located on the beach in the heart of **Roonay Bay ★★★**. While you're here, make sure to visit the internationally renowned **Queen Charlotte Islands Museum ★★★** *(Tue to Fri 10am to 5pm, Sat and Sun 1pm to 5pm, closed Mon; ☎ 559-4643)*, devoted exclusively to articles made by the Haidas over the ages, up until the present day. All modes of expression are represented here; you'll find everything from totem poles, sculptures and drawings to fabrics and basketry, not to mention jewellery made with precious metals. The shop boasts an impressive selection of books and quality souvenirs, but the prices are prohibitive.

Balance Rock, the area's most unusual sight, lies a kilometre away in the opposite direction (northward). As its name indicates, it is a boulder balanced on a pretty pebbly **beach ★★**. You can't miss it.

Queen Charlotte City ★★

Located 4 km south of Skidegate, Queen Charlotte City is a pleasant coastal village with 1,100 inhabitants. The atmosphere is very relaxed here, and the streets are filled with young people during the summer season. This is the rallying point for sea kayak expeditions.

Right before Queen Charlotte City, on your way from Skidegate, you'll see **Joy's Island Jewellers**, a souvenir shop that doubles as the archipelago's official **tourist office** *(2 km north of Queen Charlotte City, ☎ 559-4742)*. There is not much to do in town. The islands' greatest attractions are the sea, the forest, the fauna (there are eagles everywhere) and the coasts, where you will discover traces of the Haida civilization.

As far as organized tours are concerned, the best-known company is definitely **Queen Charlotte Adventures** *(on the way into town, ☎ 559-8990 or 1-800-668-4288, ⇄ 559-8983)*, which will take you to the **Gwaii Haanas National Park ★★★** *(☎ 559-8818 or 637-5362)* by motorboat, sailboat or

Exploring 187

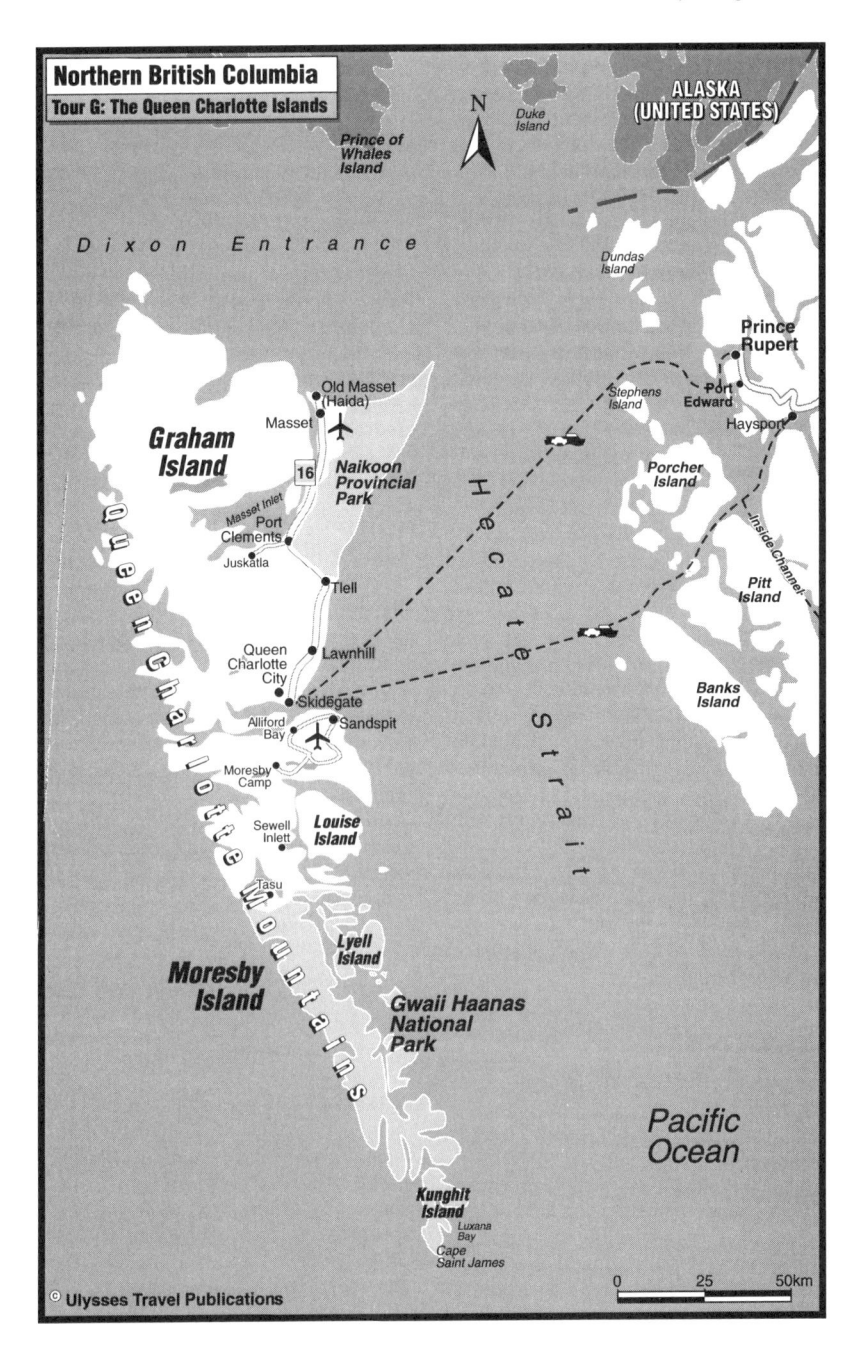

Northern British Columbia
Tour G: The Queen Charlotte Islands

seaplane, since the area cannot be reached by land. This park, located at the southern tip of the archipelago, is home to many unusual sights, each more remarkable than the last. First, there is **Hot Springs Island** ★★★, a paradise for anyone who enjoys a good soak. Then there's **Laskeek Bay** ★★★, frequented by dolphins and whales. Another major attraction is **Ninstints** ★★★, a former Haida village on the tip of the island of Sgan Gwaii. Here, you will find the largest collection of totem poles and Amerindian-built structures in the Queen Charlotte Islands. There is something unreal and mystical about the location itself. Ninstints has been declared a UNESCO World Heritage Site.

Sandspit

A village of lumberjacks, Sandspit (pop. 740), like Gwaii Haanas National Park, is located on Moresby Island. It has the second largest **airport** on the archipelago, after Masset's. Canadian Airlines *(☎ 1-800-663-3502 and 637-5388)* offers twice-daily service between Sandspit and Vancouver and Prince Rupert. The ferry shuttles back and forth between Queen Charlotte City and Moresby Island several times a day. The fare is inexpensive, and the crossing only takes a few minutes.

Tlell

This pretty little rural village (pop. 150) lies 43 km north of Skidegate along the lovely **Tlell River**, which is popular with fishing buffs.

Port Clements

Port Clements is a community of 450 people, most of whom derive their income from fishing or the forest industry. The big draw here is the incredible **Golden Spruce** ★★★, which stands 6 km from the centre of the village *(a well-marked dirt road leads to it; watch out for trucks!)*. Fifty metres high and three centuries old, this impressive tree actually has gold-coloured branches. This unusual genetic mutation remains a mystery to scientists. Under sunny blue skies, the effect is striking.

Masset

Masset is the most important town on the Queen Charlotte Islands, with a population of 1,400 people. Since 1971, life here has been shaped to some extent by the local Canadian Forces base. Along with Queen Charlotte City and Sandspit, Masset is one of the few towns on the archipelago with a **tourist office** *(in a small trailer at the south edge of town, open during summer only; ☎ 626-3300)*. It has all of the services one would expect to find in a large town, including an airport *(daily flights to Vancouver; Thunderbird Air, ☎ 1-800-898-0177)*, restaurants, an auto-repair shop, a hospital, etc.

Old Masset

Old Masset, also known as Haida, is an Amerindian village of 630 inhabitants, which faces onto peaceful **Masset Sound**. It is best to go straight to the local **tourist office** *(Mon to Fri 8:30am to noon and 1pm to 4:30pm; ☎ 626-3337)*, where you can learn the addresses of the resident **artists**. You'll find many works of art at **Haida Arts and Jewellery**, a shop with traditional architecture *(every day 11am to 5pm during summer)*. The two totem poles at its entrance make it easy to spot.

Naikoon Provincial Park

Naikoon is one of the islands' treasures. You can get there from the highway in Masset, or through Tlell, where the park headquarters are located *(BC Parks, ☎ 557-4390)*. The former option, through McIntyre Bay, is the most spectacular. The road runs along **South Beach ★★★**, an extraordinary 15 km stretch of sand, through a dense, damp and mossy forest **★★★**. It ends at **Agate Beach ★★★**, where the park campground is located. Agate Beach lies at the foot of **Tow Hill ★★★**, a 109 m-high rock that is home to a number of bald eagles. The **view ★★★** from the top is phenomenal (30 min by foot). After Tow Hill, the beach continues, becoming **North Beach ★★★** for 10 km. The park is also known for its lengthy hiking trails, which can be a real adventure. A good example is the one at **East Beach ★★★**, which covers 89 km along an endless beach, through forests and across tidewaters.

Parks and Beaches

About a hundred provincial and national parks lie scattered across the vast territory of northern British Columbia. Inland, hikers can enjoy provincial parks like Stone Mountain and Mount Edziza, while Gwaii Haanas National Park, on the Queen Charlotte Islands, is sure to delight fans of sea kayaking. Finally, there are scores of little roadside parks, offering vacationers access to all sorts of lovely campsites and picnic areas.

■ Parks

Cottonwood Island Nature Park ★★ *(Tourism Prince George, 1198 Victoria Street, ☎ 562-3700)* covers 33 ha along the Nechako River in downtown Prince George. You'll find an interesting animal-viewing area here.

Connaught Hill Park ★, also located in downtown Prince George, offers a 360° view of the region.

The entrance to **Stone Mountain Provincial Park ★★★** *(kilometre 627/mile 392 of the Alaska Highway; BC Parks, ☎ 787-3407)* lies at the end of the Alaska Highway, at an altitude of 1,267 m. The park, which covers 25,291 ha, is suitable only for experienced, well-equipped hikers. The climatic conditions change very quickly in this northerly region at such a high altitude. In fact, snowfall on the peaks is not uncommon, even in the middle of summer.

The **Wokkpash Recreation Area ★★★** *(BC Parks, ☎ 787-3407)* encompasses an area of 27,800 ha alongside Stone Mountain, and is only accessible by foot or on horseback. Getting there is a real expedition. The best-known trail is the one between MacDonald Creek and Wokkpash Valley, which covers 50 km, with a 1,200 m change in altitude. It requires at least a week of hiking.

Muncho Lake Provincial Park ★★★ *(kilometre 729/mile 456 of the Alaska Highway; BC Parks, ☎ 787-3407)* is one of the loveliest parks in Canada. It covers 88,416 ha of bare, jagged mountains around magnificent Muncho Lake, which stretches 12 km. Like the other parks in the region, it owes its existence to the Alaska Highway. There are almost no trails in the park, so the best way to explore it is by driving along the Alaska Highway.

Liard Hot Springs Provincial Park ★★★ *(kilometre 764.7/mile 477.7 of the Alaska Highway, BC Parks,* ☎ *787-3407)* is a perfect place to stop for a rest after hours of driving. Here, you can relax in natural pools fed by hot springs (49 °C). Giant ferns and a profusion of carnivorous plants give the area a tropical look.

The **Spatsizi Plateau Wilderness Park** ★★★ *(On Tattoga Lake, not far from Iskut, on Highway 37, 361 km north of the intersection of Highways 16 and 37, in Kitwanga. Take Ealue Lake Road for 22 km. Cross the Klappan River to the BC Rail dirt road, which leads 114 km to the southwest end of the park.* **Never set out on an excursion here without calling BC Parks beforehand,** ☎ *847-7320)* stretches across 656,785 ha of untouched land, and is only suitable for real adventurers. Since there are no roads leading into the park, you must go there by foot, by boat or by hydroplane. The park is located on a plateau at an altitude of about 1,800 m. The dry, continental climate in this region is characterized by cold winters with only light snowfall and summers with little rain. Caribou, grizzlies, beavers, and nearly 140 bird species make their home here.

Mount Edziza Provincial Park ★★★ *(to plan an outing, contact BC Parks in Dease Lake,* ☎ *771-4591)* covers 230,000 ha in the northwest part of the province, west of the Iskut River and south of the Stikine River. It has the distinction of including the most spectacular volcanic sites in all of Canada. Like most parks in northern British Columbia, Mount Edziza is very difficult to reach; only experienced, well-equipped hikers can get there safely.

From July to September, **Fish Creek** ★★★ *(15 min from the village of Hyder, in Alaska)* is the most important spawning area for **pink salmon** in all of Alaska. Dozens of black bears and grizzlies gather alongside the water to devour the fish. A platform has been set up so that visitors can safely observe the animals.

The **Tseax Lava Beds** ★★★ *(take Kalum Lake Drive north off of Highway 16 in Terrace)* are unique in Canada. The site consists of a number of **volcanic craters** and a stretch of lava 3 km wide and 18 km long. The last eruptions supposedly took place about 350 years ago.

Gwaii Haanas National Park ★★★ *(Parks Canada,* ☎ *559-8818 or 637-5362)*, at the southern tip of the Queen Charlotte archipelago, is one of the loveliest marine parks in the world. It can only be reached by motorboat, sailboat or seaplane. Located within the park, on the island of Sgan Gwaii, is the former Haida village of Ninstints ★★★, a UNESCO World Heritage Site.

Located on Highway 37, halfway between Terrace and Kitimat, **Lakelse Lake Provincial Park** ★★ is a perfect place for visitors looking to relax. On the shores of the magnificent lake for which the park is named, you'll find a splendid **sandy beach** ★★★. A number of picnic areas have been laid out here, along with hiking trails and a campground.

Naikoon Provincial Park ★★★ *(BC Parks,* ☎ *557-4390)* is one of the islands' treasures. You can get there from the highway in Masset, or through Tlell, where the park headquarters are located. The former option, through McIntyre Bay, is the most spectacular. The road runs along **South Beach** ★★★, an extraordinary 15 km stretch of sand, through a dense, damp and mossy forest ★★★. It ends at **Agate Beach** ★★★, where the park campground is located. Agate Beach lies at the foot of **Tow Hill** ★★★, a 109 m-high rock that is home to a number of bald eagles. The **view** ★★★ from the top is phenomenal (30 min by foot). After Tow Hill, the beach continues, becoming **North Beach** ★★★ for 10 km. The park is also known for its lengthy hiking trails, which can be a real adventure. A good example is the one at **East Beach** ★★★, which covers 89 km along an endless beach, through forests and across tidewaters.

■ Beaches

Lakelse Lake Provincial Park ★★ *(on Highway 37, between Terrace and Kitimat)* is a lovely green space, which boasts a splendid fine sand beach looking out onto a magnificent lake. Visitors have access to picnic areas, campsites and a number of hiking trails.

Naikoon Provincial Park ★★★ *(BC Parks, ☎ 557-4390)*, at the northeast tip of the Queen Charlotte archipelago, boasts some of the most spectacular beaches in Canada. South Beach is an extraordinary 15 km stretch of sand. It stops at the foot of Tow Hill, a rock that towers 109 m, then continues shortly after, under the name of North Beach, for another 10 km. The East Beach trail, on the east side of the park, extends 89 km along an seemingly endless beach.

Outdoor Activities

Hiking

Hiking is far and away the top activity in northern British Columbia. It enables visitors to appreciate the region's enchanting, unspoiled wilderness at close range. There are so many provincial and national parks here that even the most demanding outdoor enthusiast will have a hard time choosing between them. Those not to be missed include Stone Mountain, Wokkpash Recreation Area, Muncho Lake, Liard Hot Springs, the Spatsizi Plateau Wilderness Park, Mount Edziza and the Tseax Lava Beds.

Fishing

Northern British Columbia is a fishing paradise, for trout as well as the king of fish, salmon. The latter can be caught either in the region's rivers or in the sea. Don't forget to obtain a permit beforehand.

There are a number of well-known spots, like **Burns Lake**, whose town slogans say it all: "3,000 Miles of Fishing" and "The Land of a Thousand Lakes". The **Chamber of Commerce** *(☎ 692-3773)* is a mine of information for fishing buffs. As in Burns Lake, life in **Houston** centres around fishing during the summer—and not just any kind of fishing; the town is the self-proclaimed steelhead capital of the world. The **tourist office** *(☎ 845-7640)* can show you where you have the best chances of catching this famous sea trout. Around **Smithers**, the Bulkhead River is teeming with steelhead and salmon. **Kitimat** is also renowned for fishing, for it is here that salmon swim up the Douglas Channel, a natural fjord, to the ocean's tributaries. A wealth of information is available at the **tourist office** (☎ 632-6294 or 1-800-664-6554). The Queen Charlotte archipelago is ideal for deep-sea fishing, for it is home to the Chinook salmon, aptly nicknamed the "King" because of its size (up to 40 kg). For further information, contact **Queen Charlotte Adventures** (☎ 559-8990 or 1-800-668-4288).

Bird-watching

These vast northern spaces are abounding with birds. Most notably, the Queen Charlotte Islands are home to the largest concentration of peregrine falcons in North America. Egrets and bald eagles, furthermore, are as common a sight around local villages as pigeons are in the big cities to the south.

■ **Winter Activities**

During winter, snow takes over the landscape. Cross-country skiing and snowshoeing can be enjoyed just about everywhere. As for downhill skiing, **Hudson Bay Mountain** (☎ 847-5072) in Smithers, with a 533 m vertical drop and 18 runs, offers powdery conditions beginning in November. It is the largest ski area in the northern part of the province. **Powder King**, a smaller resort located between Prince George and Dawson Creek, boasts excellent snow coverage.

Accommodations

■ **Tour A: To the Alaska Highway**

Prince George

South of Prince George, you will find a heavenly place called the **Westhaven Cottage by-the-Lake** ($60; 23357 Fyfe Road, ☎ 984-0181). Set in the heart of nature, this charming cottage offers a splendid view of the lake. Guests have access to a private beach and hiking and cross-country ski trails.

The **Buckhorn Bed & Breakfast** ($50; 14900 Buckhorn Place, ☎ 963-8884) is located at the southern edge of Prince George, 1 km east of Highway 97 and 13 km south of the Fraser Bridge. A charming Victorian house, it has two bedrooms, each with a double bed and an adjoining bathroom.

"Elegant" is the word that best describes the **Manor House** ($95; ⊛, ℂ, pb; 8384 Toombs Dr, ☎ 562-9255), located northwest of town on the banks of the Nechako River. This immense place lives up to its name. The luxurious rooms are equipped with a gas fireplace, a bathroom, a kitchenette, a private entrance (in some cases) and an outdoor whirlpool bath.

The more rustic **Vivian Lake Resort** ($50 for 4 people; RR3, Site 31, alongside Highway 97, 40 km northwest of Prince George) has cabins that can accommodate up to four people each, as well as 90 campsites. A large number of picnic areas have been laid out on the shores of Vivian Lake. Guests can also rent motorboats and go trout fishing.

The **Connaught Motor Inn** *($60; ≈, R, tv; 1550 Victoria, ☎ 562-4441)* is located downtown, right near all sorts of shops and services. It is a large, comfortable motel with a swimming pool and 98 rooms, each equipped with cable television and a refrigerator. Pets welcome.

If you like urban comfort, try the **Coast Inn of the North** *($100; ≈, ⊙, △; 770 Brunswick, ☎ 563-0121)*, also located downtown. A modern, 150-room hotel, it boasts a swimming pool, sauna, workout room, nightclub, pub, shop, etc. Pets welcome.

Mackenzie

As far as accommodations in Mackenzie are concerned, the 99-room **Alexander Mackenzie Hotel** *($70; C, 403 Mackenzie boulevard, ☎ 997-3266)* is hard to beat. This modern, luxurious place is like an oasis in the midst of the region's vast stretches of wilderness. It is located right in the centre of town, just a few steps away from Williston Lake, and includes a shopping centre with 37 stores. The rooms are spacious, and some have a kitchenette.

Chetwynd

Chetwynd's main street is studded with quality motels. The **Stagecoach Inn** *($60; △, C, R, ℜ, tv; 5413 South Access, ☎ 788-9666)* is situated in the heart of the village, close to all the local services. It has a restaurant, a sauna and 55 rooms, some with a kitchen. The modern, spacious rooms are equipped with a television with a movie channel.

Similar to the Stagecoach in style, the **Country Squire Inn** *($65; △, R, tv; 5317 South Access Road, ☎ 788-2276)* is a full-comfort modern hotel, complete with refrigerators in every room, satellite television, a laundry, an ice machine, a sauna and a whirlpool.

■ **Tour B: The Hudson's Hope Route**

Hudson's Hope

The **Sportsman's Inn** *($50; △, ℜ, C, 10501 Cartier Avenue, ☎ 783-5523)* is well-suited to long stays, as 37 of its 50 rooms are equipped with a kitchenette. The hotel also includes a sauna, a bar and a restaurant. All sorts of information of interest to fishing buffs is provided free of charge.

■ **Tour C: The Alaska Highway**

Dawson Creek

The **Alaska Hotel** *($50; sb; 10209 10th Street, ☎ 782-7998)* is the symbol of Dawson Creek just as the Eiffel Tower is that of Paris. It would be hard to miss this green building, built in 1928, with "Alaska" written in capital letters on its façade. The rooms have not lost their old-fashioned charm, and the bathrooms for some are on the landing. On the ground floor, the best pub in town features live rock and blues music every weekend.

Somewhat different in style, the **George Dawson Inn** *($70; tv, ℜ; 11705 8th Street, ☎ 782-9151)* is a large modern hotel with 80 spacious, well-equipped rooms, some with a big-screen tv. Luxury suites are also available. The inn has a tavern and a restaurant as well.

Fort St. John

Set on 2 ha of land, the **Alaska Highway Bed & Breakfast** *($50; SS#2, Site 7, ☎ 785-3532)* offers a real taste of rural life. The country-style house, with its panoramic view and comfortable, rustically decorated rooms, is typical of the region.

The **Pioneer Inn** *($90; ≈, ⊛, △, ℜ, tv; 9830 100th Avenue, ☎ 787-0521)*, located in the centre of town, just 8 km from the airport, is the last luxury hotel on the British-Columbian portion of the Alaska Highway. It contains a bar, a restaurant, an indoor pool, a sauna and a whirlpool. The large, well-equipped rooms have cable television with sports and movie channels.

Fort Nelson

With its almost "city-style" level of comfort, the **Coach House Inn** *($70; ≡, ≈, △, ℜ; 4711 50th Avenue South, ☎ 774-3911)* is far and away the best hotel in Fort Nelson. It is located in the centre of town, on the west service road of the Alaska Highway, and offers 72 spacious, air-conditioned rooms, some of which are reserved for non-smokers. Guests enjoy the use of a swimming pool, a sauna, a bar and two restaurants. Special rates are available for seniors, members of the military and business travellers.

Muncho Lake Provincial Park

The **Highland Glen Lodge** *($70; mile 462 of the Alaska Highway, ☎ 776-3481)* is becoming better known in Europe than in Canada. The owners, a brush pilot named Urs and his wife Marianne, attract many visitors from Germany, their native country. It is not uncommon to find charter buses parked in front of this 19-unit hotel, located just a stone's throw from the lake. Some of the rooms are motel-style, others cottage-style.

The **J & H Wilderness Resort** *($50; mile 463 of the Alaska Highway; ☎ 776-3453)* is the ultimate northern mo☎ Its eight little rustic-style wood cabins lie just steps away from magnificent Muncho Lake. The rooms have no telephone or television, but nothing beats the feeling of spending the night in a cabin in such heavenly surroundings.

Liard Hot Springs Provincial Park

Located at kilometre 801/mile 497 of the Alaska Highway, just opposite the entrance to Liard Hot Springs Provincial Park, the **Trapper Ray** *($70; ℜ; kilometre 801/mile 497 of the Alaska Highway, ☎ 776-7349)* is a brand new establishment built in the purest northern style. An immense, two-story log "cabin", it has 12 rooms, a restaurant, a souvenir shop and a gas station.

Watson Lake (Yukon)

The **Watson Lake Hotel** *($110; ℜ; downtown, right near the Signpost Forest, on the east side of the Alaska Highway, ☎ 403-536-2724)* is the most well-known place to stay in town. Watson Lake's oldest hotel, it has typical Yukon architecture, with massive beams and log walls. The 48 rooms are extremely comfortable. Senior and group discounts are available in the coffee shop, restaurant and bar.

With its trailer-style architecture, the **Big Horn Hotel & Tavern** *($100; ☒, C; on the west side of the Alaska Highway, downtown, ☎ 403-536-2020)* is not exactly attractive from the outside. Nevertheless, the place has 29 spacious, luxurious and comfortable rooms (some equipped with a kitchenette and a whirlpool), whose elaborate decor is worth a look. The rates, moreover, are reasonable for the area.

The **Belvedere Motor Hotel** *($100; on the west side of the Alaska Highway, downtown, ☎ 403-536-7712)* is located right near the Big Horn Hotel & Tavern, to which it bears certain similarities. Unlike its competitor, however, it also offers rooms with a waterbed, and houses a travel agency, a magazine and souvenir shop and a hairdressing salon.

■ **Tour D: The Stewart-Cassiar Highway**

Iskut

The **Red Goat Lodge** *($70; May to Sep; near the centre of the village, ☎ 234-3261)* looks out onto pretty Eddontenajon Lake. It lies adjacent to a campground, which is truly first-rate, considering its isolated location here in the wild. Only four rooms are available. This is a popular place, so it is wise to make reservations. Guests have use of laundry machines, as well as canoes.

Trappers Souvenirs *($28; 7 km north of Iskut; radiomobile 2M3 520 Mehaus Channel)* is a souvenir shop that rents out a log cabin at a modest price.

Dease Lake

The **Northway Motor Inn** *($70; C, ℜ; downtown on Boulder Avenue, ☎ 771-5341)* has 44 spacious, comfortable units, most of which have a kitchen equipped with a dishwasher. Monthly rates are available as well. A restaurant and a coffee shop lie a short walk away.

Telegraph Creek

Set up inside an historic building, the **Stikine Riversong** *($50; on Stikine Avenue, ☎ 235-3196)* is a cafe, an eight-room inn and a grocery store rolled into one. The rooms are somewhat basic but nonetheless very pleasant. This is the only place of its kind in Telegraph Creek, so it is wise to make reservations in order to avoid any unpleasant surprises.

■ **Tour E: To Stewart, BC and Hyder, AK ★★★**

Stewart

The **King Edward Hotel & Motel** *($70; C, right in the centre of the village, at the corner of 5th and Columbia Streets; ☎ 636-2244)* is the best hotel in Stewart. It has a total of 90 comfortable, well-equipped units, some with a complete kitchen for long stays. There is also a cafeteria on the premises.

Hyder, Alaska

The **Sealaska Inn** *($70 US; on Premier Avenue, ☎ 604-636-2486)* is a pleasant place located over a pub. The atmosphere is lively, and can get noisy, especially on weekends, so you might

Tour F: The Yellowhead Highway

Prince George

See Tour A: To the Alaska Highway, p 192.

Vanderhoof

The **Vanderhoof Hotel** *($50; ℜ, C; 2351 Church Street, ☎ 567-3188)* lies in the centre of town, one block north of Highway 16. It is one of the larger hotels in Vanderhoof, with 32 units, some of which include a kitchen. The rooms are simple but comfortable. A hairdressing salon, a pub and a restaurant are all located on the premises.

Fort St. James

The **Stuart Lodge** *($55; tv; Stone Bay Rd, ☎ 996-7917)* is set on 24 ha of land on the shores of Stuart Lake, 5 km north of Fort St. James. In addition to offering a view of the lake, its six charming little cottages are fully equipped, complete with a barbecue and a television. Small motorboats are also available for rent.

Smithers

In Smithers, make sure to stop at the **Lakeside Gallery Bed & Breakfast** *($60; less than 1 km west of Smithers, along Highway 16, ☎ 847-9174)*. This big white house on the shores of Kathlyn Lake offers an almost unreal view of glacier-capped Hudson Bay Mountain. The place has four rooms, all decorated in an elegant manner. Small boats and canoes are available so that visitors can enjoy an outing on the lake. The friendly owner, Charlie, can show you where the good salmon fishing spots are. This is probably the best place to stay on the Yellowhead Highway.

Berg's Valley Tours Bed & Breakfast *($50; 3924 13th Avenue, ☎ 847-5925)* is perfect for active types, as the owners, David and Beverley, offer guided hikes in the mountains, including a trip in an all-terrain vehicle and a snack, as well as skiing packages and guided driving tours of the region.

Terrace

A big hotel for a big town, the **Coast Inn of the West** *($140; 4620 Lakelse Avenue, ☎ 638-8141)* is impeccable but expensive. It has 55 luxurious rooms with nothing lacking. A number of floors are reserved for non-smokers.

With its water slides and swimming pools filled by natural hot springs, the **Mount Layton Hotsprings Resort** *($70; 15 min south of Terrace via Highway 37, ☎ 798-2214)*, located just 22 km from Terrace, is a fantastic place to stay during summertime. Its 22 rooms are comfortable and well-equipped.

Lakelse Lake Lodge *(on Highway 37, halfway between Terrace and Kitimat, ☎ 798-9541)* resembles a European-style boarding-house. The friendly owner, Emmanuel, a Frenchman from the Basque Country, serves good light dishes. He enjoys chatting with his guests, and can tell you where to go for some "miraculous" trout fishing.

Kitimat

The **City Centre Motel** *($45; C; 480 City Centre, ☎ 632-4848)* is right in the centre of town, near all the local services. The comfortable, spacious rooms are equipped with a kitchenette. This is definitely one of the best deals in town.

The **Aluminium Motel** *($60; C, R; 633 Dadook Crescent, ☎ 639-9323)* is located just a few minutes' walk from the salmon river, making it the perfect place for fishing buffs. Its parking lot was designed to accommodate pickup trucks pulling boat trailers. All 50 units are equipped with a refrigerator, and some have a kitchenette as well. Special rates are available for families who plan on spending an extended period of time here.

Prince Rupert

The **Crest Motor Hotel** *($120; R; 222 1st Avenue, ☎ 624-6771)* boasts the best view in town, since it is located alongside a cliff overlooking the port. The rooms are worthy of the finest luxury hotel, and the service is impeccable. You really get your money's worth here. The Crest also has two excellent restaurants. All of these things combined make it one of the finest hotels in the North by Northwest region.

■ **Tour G: The Queen Charlotte Islands (Haida Gwaii)**

Queen Charlotte City

The **Sea Raven** *($70; tv, R, R; 3301 3rd Avenue, ☎ 559-4423)* is a comfortable modern hotel. All of the rooms are equipped with a refrigerator and a big-screen television, and some offer a view of the sea. Maureen, the owner, is originally from Great Britain. The restaurant adjoining the hotel is excellent.

The pretty **Spruce Point Lodge** *($65; pb, tv; 609 6th Avenue, tel. 559-6234)* has very simple yet very comfortable rooms, each with a bathroom, a television, and its own private entrance. There is a common terrace with a view of magnificent Hecate Strait. Mary, the owner, keeps up to date on everything that's going on in the region, and knows a lot about the various companies that organize outdoor activities and adventures.

Tlell

The **Tl'ell River House** *($70; R; Beltush Road, ☎ 557-4211)* is an inn hidden away in the woods, in a pleasant setting alongside the Tlell River and Hecate Strait. The rooms are simple and comfortable, and the restaurant serves quality food. Boat rentals are available on site.

Port Clements

The **Golden Spruce Motel** *($50; C; 2 Grouse Street, ☎ 557-4325)* is one of the few hotels in the Port Clements area. It has 12 very simple units, some of which are equipped with a kitchenette. There is also a coin laundry on the premises.

Masset

Located on the way into town, the **Singing Surf Inn** *($75; tv, R; 1504 Old Beach Road, ☎ 626-3318)* is a veritable institution in Masset. The comfortable rooms are equipped with satellite television, and some offer a view of the port. The hotel also has a souvenir shop, a bar and a restaurant.

The **Alaska View Lodge** *($65; at the entrance of Naikoon Provincial Park, midway between Masset and Tow Hill,* ☎ *626-3333)* boasts a privileged site at the edge of the renowned Pacific forest, alongside South Beach, a magnificent 10 km stretch of sand. The owners, Eliane, from Paris, and her husband Charlie, from Bern (Switzerland), have created an "Old World" atmosphere for their guests. The Alaska View Lodge is an excellent choice for visitors looking to step out of their element into truly heavenly surroundings.

Sandspit

Just a stone's throw away from the airport, the **Seaport Bed & Breakfast** *($35; C, 371 Alford Bay Road,* ☎ *637-5698)* has three cottages, which are actually trailers with a view of the bay. Each one is equipped with a kitchenette. Smoking is not permitted in the rooms, and credit cards are not accepted, but you won't find better value for your money on Moresby Island.

Restaurants

■ **Tour A: To the Alaska Highway**

Prince George

Niner's Diner *($$; 508 George Street,* ☎ *562-1299)*, one of Prince George's trendiest spots, has a 1950's decor and serves very generous portions. The menu includes gigantic salads, delicious burgers and gargantuan pasta dishes. Line-ups are common at lunchtime.

If you're tired of gobbling down hamburgers, try the **Cariboo Steak & Seafood** *($$; 1155 5th Avenue,* ☎ *564-1220)*, which serves very good steak and has a large all-you-can-eat buffet at lunchtime.

Another excellent place for steak is **The Keg** *($$; 582 George Street,* ☎ *563-1768)*, one of the chain of restaurants of the same name. In fact, steak is the specialty of the house, and is prepared in a number of ways. You can have yours served with seafood if you like.

Mackenzie

The **Alexander Mackenzie Hotel** *($$; 403 Mackenzie Boulevard,* ☎ *997-3266)* is *the* place to eat in town. The menu lists a variety of hamburgers, as well as chicken and a good choice of salads.

Chetwynd

The **Stagecoach Inn** *($; 5413 South Access,* ☎ *788-9666)*, in the heart of the village, is a small family-style restaurant. You won't find gourmet cuisine here, but the food is of good quality.

The **Swiss Inn Restaurant** *($$; downtown on Highway 97, 800 m east of the traffic light,* ☎ *788-2566)* serves Swiss German-style cuisine. The menu lists dishes like schnitzel, as well as typical North American fare, such as pizza, steak and seafood. The all-you-can-eat lunchtime buffet is worth checking out.

Tour B: The Hudson's Hope Route

Hudson's Hope

The restaurant of the **Sportsman's Inn** ($; 10501 Cartier Avenue, ☎ 783-5523) is without a doubt the best place to eat in Hudson's Hope. This is a family-style place with a traditional menu.

Tour C: The Alaska Highway

Dawson Creek

The all-you-can-eat lunch buffet at the **Dynasty** ($; 1009 102nd Street, ☎ 782-3138) features good Chinese food, as well as traditional meat and seafood dishes. The atmosphere is very homey.

The **Alaska Restaurant** ($$; 10209 10th Street, ☎ 782-7040), a green building dating back to 1928, with the word "Alaska" written in orange letters on its façade, is easy to spot from a distance. The "gold rush" decor is pleasant, and the food, high-quality. The impressive wine list is especially noteworthy.

The lively atmosphere at **Uncle Buck's Sports Bar & Grill** (1725 Alaska Avenue, ☎ 782-2829) will appeal to sports buffs, who can watch hockey on television while enjoying a big, juicy hamburger.

Fort St. John

As indicated by its name, **Boston Pizza** ($; 9824 100th Street, ☎ 787-0455) serves a wide selection of pizza. The menu also lists spicy ribs, pasta dishes, steaks and sandwiches.

The restaurant of the **Pioneer Inn** ($$; 9830 100th Avenue, ☎ 787-0521), located downtown, has a varied menu and serves generous portions.

Fort Nelson

Mister Milkshake ($; one block west of Town Square, ☎ 774-2526), serves about twenty different flavours of milkshakes, as well as pizza, fried chicken, hamburgers and home-made pie.

The restaurant at the **Coach House Inn** ($$; 4711 50th Avenue South, ☎ 774-3911), a traditional stopping place for travellers on the Alaska Highway, is always very busy during summer. It serves a variety of dishes and even has a special menu for children. An all-you-can-eat buffet is sometimes served at dinnertime.

Muncho Lake Provincial Park

At the restaurant of the **J & H Wilderness Resort** ($; mile 463 of the Alaska Highway, ☎ 776-3453), the Clubhouse steak is so thick that only those with hearty appetites will be able to finish it.

The **Highland Glen Lodge** ($$; mile 462 of the Alaska Highway, ☎ 776-3481) serves hamburgers, as well as German dishes. You won't go wrong ordering the sausages and sauerkraut. Close your eyes and let your imagination transport you to Alsace or Germany. German beer is available on tap here—of course!

Liard Hot Springs Provincial Park

The **Trapper Ray** *($; kilometre 801/mile 497 of the Alaska Highway,* ☎ *776-7349)*, just opposite the entrance to the park, serves tasty, copious breakfasts.

Watson Lake (Yukon)

Junction 37 Service *($$; kilometre 1043/mile 649 of the Alaska Highway)* is a service station with a decent restaurant. This is hardly gourmet cuisine, but a meal here is sure to satisfy even the heartiest appetite.

The **Watson Lake Hotel** *($$$; kilometre 1021/mile 635 of the Alaska Highway, downtown on the east side of the highway, right near the Signpost Forest,* ☎ *403-536-2724)* has two restaurants. One serves relatively standard fare, like sandwiches, and occasionally has a salad bar, while the other offers a fixed-price menu featuring more elaborate cuisine. In both cases, there's something for everyone. The prices are rather high, though.

■ **Tour D: The Stewart-Cassiar Highway**

Iskut

The restaurant of the **Black Sheep Motel** *($; in the centre of the village, along Highway 37,* ☎ *234-3141)* sometimes serves unexpected dishes at dinnertime, depending on the choice of ingredients delivered that week.

Dease Lake

With its big green roof, the brand new **Northway** *($; on Boulder Avenue, downtown,* ☎ *771-5341)* is the easiest restaurant to find in town. The menu lists soups and sandwiches.

Telegraph Creek

The **Stikine Riversong** *($$; on Stikine Avenue,* ☎ *235-3196)*, located in an historic building, is a small bistro (as well as an inn and a grocery store) open only during summer. It has a good reputation, and is the one place in Telegraph Creek where you can enjoy a good meal.

■ **Tour E: To Stewart, BC and Hyder, AK**

Stewart

The **King Edward Restaurant** *($; at the corner of 5th and Columbia Streets, in the heart of the village,* ☎ *636-2244)* is a perpetually busy cafeteria, where truckers, miners and tourists start arriving in the morning for breakfast.

Hyder, Alaska

The restaurant of the **Sealaska Inn** *($$; on Premier Avenue,* ☎ *604-636-2486)* is proud of its fish and chips, which are actually pretty good. The hamburgers are also worth a try.

■ **Tour F: The Yellowhead Highway**

Prince George

See Tour A: To the Alaska Highway, p 198.

Smithers

The **Aspen** (*$$$; west of town on Highway 16, inside the Aspen Motor Inn,* ☎ *847-4551*), which serves good, fresh seafood, is highly reputed in Smithers.

Smitty's Family Restaurant (*$$; downtown on Highway 16,* ☎ *847-3357*) has special menus for children and seniors. The sandwiches are very thick, and the desserts will satisfy even the biggest appetites.

Cedarvale

The **Cedarvale Cafe** (*$; along Highway 16, halfway between Hazelton and Terrace,* ☎ *849-5539*) serves the best club sandwich in the region.

Terrace

The **White Spot** (*4620 Lakelse Avenue,* ☎ *638-7977*) is located in the same building as the Coast Inn of the West. It is one of a chain of restaurants in the province, known for their sandwiches, salads and burgers.

The **Lakelse Lake Lodge** (*$$$; on Highway 37, halfway between Terrace and Kitimat,* ☎ *798-9541*) resembles a European boarding-house. The owner, Emmanuel, a Frenchman from the Basque Country, prepares light dishes using local game, trout and salmon. The atmosphere is pleasant and convivial.

Kitimat

The **Chalet Restaurant** (*$$; 852 Tsimshian,* ☎ *632-2662*) offers a varied menu, in keeping with Kitimat's cosmopolitan character. It serves generous breakfasts in the morning.

Prince Rupert

The **Breakers Pub** (*$$; Cow Bay Road,* ☎ *624-5990*), located in the pretty neighbourhood of Cow Bay, serves excellent fish and chips, well-prepared fish dishes and a good crab salad on a lovely terrace with a view of the port. This is a very pleasant place to spend the afternoon. A wide choice of draft beer is also available.

Smile's Seafood Café (*$$; in the heart of the Cow Bay area,* ☎ *624-3072*) is the most highly reputed place in town for seafood and fish, with good reason. The portions are generous, and the prices relatively modest.

The **Crest Motor Hotel** (*$$$; 222 1st Avenue,* ☎ *624-6771*) has two good restaurants. The first, something like a snack-bar, serves tasty sandwiches, while the other, more classic in style, prepares delicious and very elaborate dishes.

■ Tour G: The Queen Charlotte Islands (Haida Gwaii)

Queen Charlotte City

The **Sea Raven Restaurant** (*$$; 3301 3rd Avenue,* ☎ *559-4423*) is a very good seafood restaurant with a varied menu. The daily special is always well-prepared.

The **Oceana** (*$$$; 3rd Avenue,* ☎ *559-8683*) is a top-notch Chinese restaurant with a pretty view of the strait. The dishes are well-prepared and served in generous portions.

Tlell

The **Tl'ell River House** *($$$; Beltush Road,* ☎ *557-4211)* serves gourmet dishes in the purest country-style European tradition. It is one of the finest restaurants on the island. Watch out, though: the prices add up quickly!

Masset

The **Singing Surf Inn Restaurant** *($; 1504 Old Beach Road,* ☎ *626-3318)* is an institution in Masset. You won't find gourmet cuisine here, but the setting and the view are pleasant.

At the **Cafe Gallery** *($$; Collison Avenue,* ☎ *626-3672)*, located downtown, you can admire paintings by native artists while eating. There's nothing too exciting on the menu, with the exception, perhaps, of the Reuben sandwich. It's best with strong mustard.

Shopping

■ Tour A: To the Alaska Highway

Dawson Creek

Make sure to stop at the **Dawson Creek Farmer's Market** *(Sat 8am to 3pm)* to sample the local produce. It is located near the NAR Park, right behind the sign for the Alaska Highway.

THE ROCKY MOUNTAINS

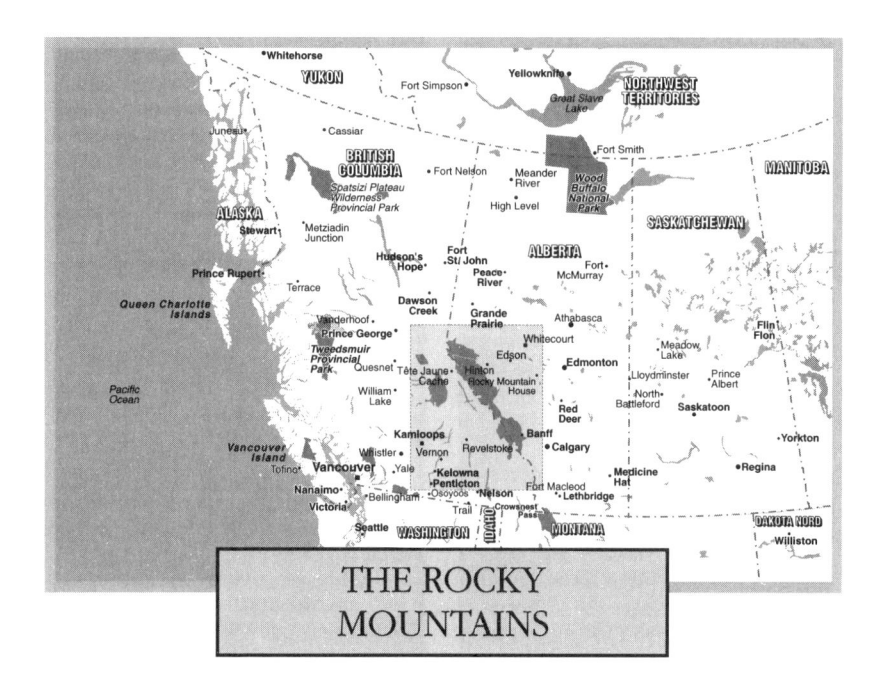

In Canada, the term "Rockies" designates a chain of high Pacific mountains reaching elevations of between 3,000 and 4,000 m. These mountains consist of crystalline and metamorphic rock that has been thrust upwards, crushed and then carved out by glaciers. The mountain chain runs east-west along the border between Alberta and British Columbia, and covers the Yukon territory. This vast region, which stretches more than 22,000 km², is known the world over for its natural beauty and welcomes some six million visitors each year. Exceptional mountain scenery, wild rivers sure to thrill white-water rafting enthusiasts, still lakes whose waters vary from emerald green to turquoise blue, parks abounding in all sorts of wildlife, world-renowned ski centres and quality resort hotels all come together to make for an unforgettable vacation.

Geography

The history of the Rockies begins about 600 million years ago, when a deep sea covered the area where the mountains now stand. Bit by bit, layers of sediment, including clay shale, silt-laden rocks, sand and conglomerates from the erosion of the Canadian Shield to the east, accumulated at the bottom of this sea. These sedimentary layers were up to 20 km deep in some places, and under the pressure of their own weight they crystallized to form a rocky platform. This explains the presence of marine fossils like shells and seaweed in many cliff faces; the Burgess Shale in Yoho National Park, declared a UNESCO World Heritage Site in 1981, is one of the most important fossil sites in the world with the fossilized remains of some 140 species. About 160 million years ago, following a shift of the tectonic plates, the earth's forces began to exert a tremendous amount of pressure on the sedimentary rock, compressing, folding and pushing it upward until it finally broke apart. The western chains emerged first (Yoho and Kootenay National Parks) and then the principal chains (the highest including the immense ice fields and Mount Robson, the highest point in the Rockies at 3,954 m) straddling the continental divide, the line that separates the drainage basins of North America. A few million years later, the chains next to the prairies emerged, and then, after a final terrestrial upheaval, the rolling foothills of the Rockies. The effect of the earth's forces on this ancient platform of sedimentary rock are evident everywhere. The rippling of the rock can be seen on mountain faces; when the movement has resulted in the rock forming an "A" geologists refer to them as "anticlinal", and when it forms a "U", as "synclinal".

Of course, the Rocky Mountains were further shaped by other forces, the next step was the extreme erosion caused by constant battering by wind, rain, snow, ice, freezing and thawing.

Initially, water was the most important factor in the transformation of the Rockies' strata. One need only consider the fact that 7,500 km^3 of water falls on Earth each year, to imagine the enormous destructive potential of the waterways that would result from that much rain. A constant flow of water can erode even the hardest rock, acting just like sandpaper. The grains of sand broken loose from the rock and transported by the torrential waters of mountain streams scrape the rocky bottom; gradually polishing the surface and infiltrating crevices. These slowly get bigger and bigger until huge pieces of rock break off or enormous cavities are hollowed out like those in the Maligne River Canyon, which are called "potholes". When the rock is of a more crumbly variety, or even water soluble like limestone, the rain and snow easily carve out deep fissures. The mountains finally lost their primitive look thanks to this slow but unrelenting erosion, as the water eventually worked its way through several layers of rock, forming deep V-shaped valleys.

■ Glaciers

About two million years ago, during the first ice age, a huge, moving ice field covered more than one-fifth of the surface of the earth, through which only the highest summits of the Rockies emerged. The ice receded and advanced over this region a total of three times.

The glaciers and their runoff radically changed the landscape of the Rockies, breaking off the upper portions of the rock along the edges, and reshaping the rock over which they advanced. Contrary to the water, that bored deep into the earth, the glaciers altered the mountains in depth and width, creating huge U-shaped valleys known as glacial troughs. The icefields region is an excellent example, with its wide, steep-sided valleys. The bigger the glacier the more destructive it was to the mountain and the deeper and wider the valley it created. In the icefield region, visitors will see what are termed suspended valleys which result from the erosion caused by a small glacier that attached itself to a larger mass of ice. The valley left behind by the smaller glacier is not nealry as deep as the one left by the larger glacier, and appears to be suspended once the ice has melted; an example is the Maligne

Valley, which is suspended 120 m above the Athabasca Valley.

■ **Flora**

The forests of the Rocky Mountains are essentially made up of **lodgepole pine**. The Amerindians used these trees to build their teepees because they grow very straight, are fairly tall and have little foliage. Ironically, forest fires are what guarantee the trees' survival. The heat causes the resin in the pine cones to melt slowly, releasing the seeds that are held within. The seeds are then dispersed by the wind, and the forest essentially rises from its own ashes. If such fires were completely eliminated, the lodgepole pines would get old and the forest would be taken over by other vegetation and die, which would in turn force out the moose. From time to time, therefore, Parks Canada sets controlled fires, and the burnt-out trunks of lodgepole pine are a common sight along the roads.

The **aspen** is the most common broad-leaved tree in the forests of the Rocky Mountains. Its trunk is white and its leaves round. The slightest breeze makes the leaves tremble, and for this is it often called a trembling aspen.

The **Englemann spruce** is found at high altitudes, near the tree line. It is the first tree to grow at these altitudes on the gravel of ancient moraines. This tree has a long lifespan; some near the Athabasca glacier are more than 700 years old. It generally has a twisted trunk due to strong winds that sweep across the mountainsides. In the valleys, the spruce can measure up to 20 m.

The **Douglas fir**, found north of Jasper, grows in forests at the bottom of the valleys of the Rockies.

The wildflower season does not last very long in alpine regions. The flowering time, production of seeds and reproduction are a veritable race against the clock during the few short weeks of summer. Their perennial nature, however, helps them to survive. In fact, perennial plants store everything they need for new shoots, leaves and flowers in their roots and rhizomes or in the previous year's bulb. Before the snow has even melted, they are ready to emerge from the earth. The secret of alpine zone flowers lie in the fact that they lie dormant all winter, and then take full advantage of the humidity and strong sunshine in the summer.

The **western anemone** is a common sight in mountainous zones. Though it is not common to see it in bloom, it is easy to spot in summer, when its stem has a downy covering. Towards the end of summer, the seeds, with their long feather-like appendage, are carried off by the wind, assuring the reproduction of the flower.

Heather has also adapted well to the rigours of the alpine zone. Its hardy leaves help it to store energy, and spare it from having to produce new leaves every year. Among the many types of heather you'll likely encounter are **pink heather**, which has little red flowers, **yellow heather** with white flowers and yellow sepals, and **purple heather** with white, bell-shaped flowers and reddish-brown sepals. The purple heather resembles a cushiony sponge and grows at the treeline on mountain slopes long ago abandoned by glaciers.

Grizzly Bear

Black Bear

The **Indian paintbrush** varies from pale yellow to vibrant red. The flower is easy to spot since it is actually its leaves that are coloured, while the flower lies tucked among the upper folds of the stem.

The **bluebell** is a tiny blue flower that grows close to the ground in the gravel or sand at water's edge.

■ Fauna

The **black bear** is the smallest bear in North America. As its name suggests, it is usually black, although there are some with dark brown fur. The head is quite high and the line between the shoulders and the hindquarters is much straighter than on the grizzly. The male weighs between 170 and 350 kg and can grow to up to 168 cm long and 97 cm at the withers. The female is one-third smaller. These bears are found in dense forests at lower altitudes and in clearings. They are mammals and feed on roots, wild berries and leaves.

The **grizzly**'s colouring varies between black, brown and blond and its fur often appears to be greying, hence its name. Larger and heavier than its cousin the black bear, the grizzly measures 110 cm at the withers, and up to 2 m when standing on its hind legs. Its average weight is about 200 kg, though some have been known to weigh up to 450 kg. The grizzly can be distinguished from the black bear by the large hump at its shoulders. This hump is actually the muscle mass of its imposing front paws. Its hindquarters are also lower than its shoulders, and it carries its head fairly low. Despite these differences, it is often difficult to tell a young grizzly from a black bear. Take extreme caution if you encounter a bear, as these animals are unpredictable and can be very dangerous.

Cougars (also called pumas and mountains lions) are the largest of the Felidae, or cat family, that you are likely to encounter in the Rockies and Kananaskis Country, where about one

Bighorn sheep

Mountain goat

hundred have been counted. These large cats weigh from 72 to 103 kg (45 kg for females), and when hungry can attack pet dogs and even humans. Unfortunately, these nocturnal felines can rarely be spotted.

Lynxes are also members of the cat family, but are much smaller than pumas, weighing about 11 kg. Their bob tail and pointed ears, topped with a little tuft of longer fur make them easy to identify. Also nocturnal, they are hard to spot.

Cervidae: The Rockies are a veritable paradise for these animals, which can be seen in great numbers. It is not uncommon to spot **moose**, those huge mammals that can weigh up to 500 kg and whose characteristic antlers are large and impressive-looking. **Mule-deer, white-tailed deer, mountain caribou** and **moose** can often be spotted along the highways.

Bighorn sheep are not cervidae, but rather horned ungulates, or hoofed animals. The difference between these two families is that ungulates do not lose their horns every year, but rather keep them for their whole life. Bighorn sheep are easy to spot thanks to their curved horns. They are a common sight along the road. They are quite tame and will readily approach people in the hopes of being fed. Under no circumstances should you give them any food since they will quickly develop the bad habit of approaching people and thus run the risk of being killed by the many cars that travel park roads.

Mountain goats also belong to the horned ungulate family. Their numbers are low, and they are rarely spotted, except in alpine areas. They are recognizable by their long white fur and two small, black pointed horns. They are very timid and will not tolerate being approached.

Wolves, coyotes and foxes can also be seen in the parks, especially in the forests of Kananaskis Country.

Birds: The **bald eagle, golden eagle, great-horned owl** and several **falcon** species are among the birds of prey found in the Rockies.

Ptarmigans resemble chickens. Their colouring changes with seasons, varying between a white-speckled brown in the summer to snowy white in the winter. **Grouse** are also common.

Two other noteworthy, though sometimes annoying, birds are the **grey jay** and the **Clark's nutcracker**, who won't hesitate to swipe the food right off your plate the minute you decide to have a picnic in the forest. The Clark's nutcracker has grey breast plumage, black and white wings and a relatively long beak. The grey jay's plumage is dark and its beak much shorter.

Lastly, two types of pesky insects abound during certain seasons in the Rockies. First the **mosquito**, of which there are no less than 28 different species, all equally exasperating to human beings. Arm yourself for an encounter with these critters, either with insect repellent or mosquito netting. Between the months of April and June, another insect, the **Anderson tick**, makes life in the Rockies more of an adventure. These should be avoided but not to the point of panic (on the rare occasions when it is carrying Rocky Mountain fever it can cause death). The tick is found in the dry grassy parts of the Rockies. Regularly check your clothes and yourself if you are walking in these areas in the spring. If you find one, slowly remove it (burning it does not work) and see a doctor at the first sign of headache, numbness or pain.

History

The presence of human beings in this area goes back some 11,000 years, but the arrival of the first whites dates from the era of the fur trade, towards the middle of the 18th century. The Stoney Indians, who knew the region well, served as guides to these new arrivals, showing them mountain passes that would play an important role in the fur trade.

No less than 80° of longitude separate the most easterly point of Newfoundland and the Queen Charlotte Islands in the west. This immense territory, however, had only about four million inhabitants by 1850. To overcome the threat posed by the American giant to the south, which was richer and more populous, and following political and economic crises in 1837 under the government of William Mackenzie, a desire emerged to establish a more efficient organization in the form of Canadian Confederation, eventually leading to the 1867 vote on the British North America Act. This new Canadian state, which went from colony to British Dominion, consisted originally of four provinces, Ontario, Québec, Nova Scotia and New Brunswick, all located in the east. Therefore, when the United States purchased Alaska from Russia for seven million dollars in March of 1867, British Columbia found itself in a precarious position, hemmed in on two sides by the United States. Furthermore, British Columbia was cut off geographically from Canadian Confederation, such that when delegates from this province wanted to get to Ottawa they first had to get to San Francisco by boat and then take the new transcontinental train line through Chicago to Toronto. Before Canada could be united, therefore, British Columbia demanded an end to this isolation and the construction of a road connecting the province with the rest of Confederation. To its great surprise, the Macdonald government offered even more, the construction of a railway! Linking the Maritime provinces in the east to Victoria was indeed a prodigious feat and certainly an unprecedented technological and financial challenge for such a young and sparsely populated country. Transportation creates commerce, and such a vast nation clearly could not grow and prosper without relying on modern modes of communication. It had to establish commercial stability despite the harsh realities of winter, which slowed down and occasionally immobilized ground and maritime transportation, thereby isolating entire regions of this huge country.

The economy of the Rocky Mountains took off following the construction of the railway, as prospectors, alpinists, geologists and all sorts of visitors joined the railway agents, participating in some of the most memorable moments in the region's history.

Economy

"If we can't export the scenery, we'll import the tourists!" This statement by William C. Van Horne, vice-president of the Canadian Pacific Railway, pretty well sums up the situation. The economy of the Canadian Rockies, in the five national parks of Alberta and British Columbia, relies almost solely on tourism. The preservation of these areas is assured by their status as national parks, which also guarantees the complete absence of any type of development be it mining or forestry related. In fact, coal, copper, lead and silver mines (see Silver City, p 221) as well as ochre deposits (see paint pots, p 233) were abandoned, and the villages moved in order to return the mountains to their original state, and to stop human industry from marring all this natural beauty.

Finding Your Way Around

■ Access to the Rockies

Very reasonable fees are charged to gain access to the national parks of the Canadian Rockies, and must be paid at the entrance gates of each park *($8 for one day, $16 for up three days)*.

Up until recently, the fees only applied to cars entering the parks, but from now on every person must pay an individual fee. This allows Parks Canada to earn extra revenue from travellers arriving by foot, bike, train or bus, which goes to maintaining park facilities.

Parks Canada also charges travellers wishing to practise certain activities (excursions of more than one day, rock-climbing, interpretive activities...) and for the use of certain facilities, like hot springs.

A complete list of the fees for each year is available at the entrance gate, at the parks' information centres (see addresses and telephone numbers below) or by calling 1-800-651-7959.

Parks Canada Offices

Banff
Box 1298
Banff, Alberta
T0L 0C0
☎ (403) 762-8421
⇄ (403) 762-8163

Jasper
500 Connaught Drive
Jasper, Alberta
T0E 1E0
☎ (403) 852-6171

Radium Hot Springs
Kootenay National Park
Box 220
Radium Hot Springs, BC
V0A 1M0
☎ (604) 347-9615

■ By plane

Most people fly into the airports in Calgary, Edmonton or Vancouver and then drive to the national and provincial parks.

■ By car

Because of the hemmed-in location of the Rockies, driving is the most practical means of transportation here. The roads throughout this mountainous region are generally in good condition considering the winds, snow and ice that quickly deteriorate the infrastructure. Driving along these winding roads does, however, require extra attention and caution, especially in winter. Be sure to stop regularly to rest and, of course, to admire the spectacular scenery.

It is important to check road conditions before heading off in the winter, as heavy snowfalls often lead to road closures. Furthermore, your car should also be equipped with snow tires, studded tires or in some cases chains. Generally, however, the major arteries are open year-round, while secondary roads are often used as cross-country skiing trails in the winter.

For information on road conditions, you can call **Environment Canada** in Banff (☎ 403-762-2088), the weather service in Jasper (☎ 403-852-3185) or the **Alberta Motor Association** (☎ 403-852-4444 or 1-800-642-3810). For Yoho National Park, call the tourist office (☎ 604-343-6324) and for Kootenay National Park, the park office (☎ 604-347-9615).

This kind of information is also available at the entrance gates of the national parks and in all local offices of Parks Canada.

This chapter is divided into five tours: **Tour A: Banff National Park** ★★★; **Tour B: The Icefields Parkway** ★★★; **Tour C: Jasper National Park** ★★★, **Tour D: Yoho and Kootenay National Parks** ★★ and finally **Tour E: Kananaskis Country** ★★.

Tour A: Banff National Park

Banff National Park is the most well-known and visited of Canadian parks. It is incredibly beautiful, but its renown also makes it one of the busiest parks, overrun with visitors from all over the world. Its main town, Banff, has grown as a result of tourism and is home to a large number of shops, hotels and restaurants of all different types.

This tour starts in the small town of Canmore, located only about 20 km from the entrance to the park, then

Finding Your Way Around 211

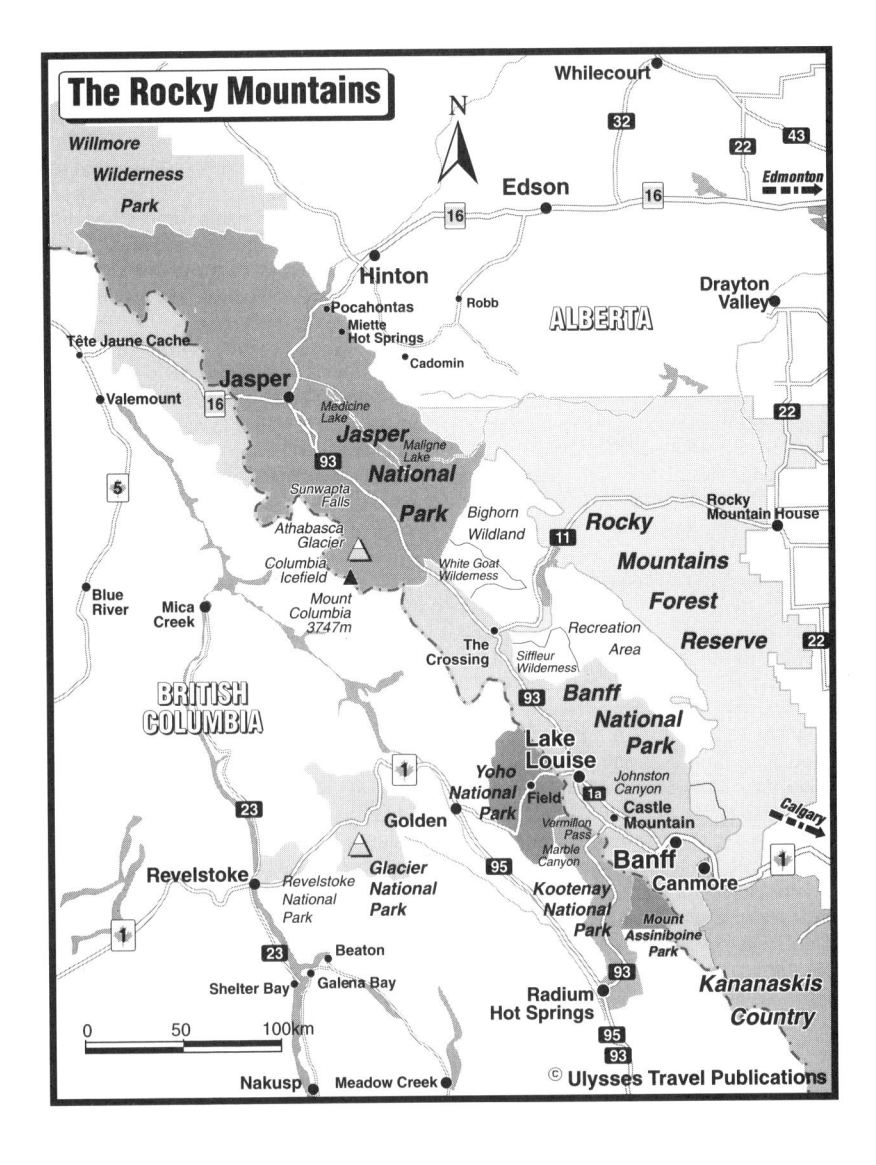

The Rocky Mountains

leads to Banff on the TransCanada Highway or on the Bow Valley Parkway, Hwy 1A, which runs parallel to the former. The tour weaves its way around Banff townsite and ends up in the village of Lake Louise, known the world over for its exquisite, shimmering emerald-green lake.

The **Greyhound Bus Station** (☎ *403-522-2121 or 1-800-661-8747)* is located on the way into town on Mount Norquay Road, at the corner of Gopher Road. The offices of **Brewster Transportation and Tours** (☎ *403-762-6700)* are in the same building. This company takes care of local transportation and organizes trips to the icefields and Jasper. The **CP Train Station** is right next to the bus station on Railway Drive. Taxis are available for the trip downtown (☎ *403-762-3353 or 762-3351)*.

Tour B: The Icefields Parkway

This tour starts in the village of Lake Louise and snakes its way through Banff National Park on Hwy 93. It allows you to discover some of the highest summits of the Canadian Rockies before ending up in the immense Columbia icefield. Stunning landscapes line the whole route, and by stopping at the various lookout points along the way you'll find yourself journeying through the geological history of these mountains and valleys and reliving the experiences of the adventurers who discovered this region. The focal point of this tour is the Athabasca Glacier, at the entrance to Jasper National Park. With the proper equipment and an understanding of safety techniques for hiking on ice, adventurers can set off from the Columbia Icefields information centre to conquer the Athabasca, Dome and Stutfield glaciers. If you have never been on this type of excursion before, **Brewster Transportation and Tours** will take you out in the fields in specially-designed buses.

Tour C: Jasper National Park

This tour explores the surroundings of Jasper, the central point of the national park of the same name, before heading northeast on Hwy 16 to the small town of Hinton, located about 30 km from the entrance to Jasper National Park.

The **Greyhound Bus Station** (☎ *403-852-3926)* and the **Via** (☎ *1-800-561-8630)* train station are located right in the middle of the town of Jasper on Connaught Drive. **Heritage Cabs** (☎ *403-852-5558)* serves the area.

Tour D: Kootenay and Yoho National Parks

Sometimes referred to as the golden triangle, this tour starts out from Castle Mountain in Banff National Park, then heads down Hwy 93, which passes through Kootenay National Park to Radium Hot Springs. The tour then heads back up the valley of the Columbia River towards Golden and then on to Lake Louise through Yoho National Park.

Tour E: Kananaskis Country

Due to its extensive facilities for travellers, Canmore is the obvious focal point of this tour. It is therefore from this little town that you will discover Kananaskis Country. Though its mountainous scenery is slightly less spectacular than that of the Rocky

Mountain national parks, this region nevertheless offers nature lovers beautiful hiking trails without as many hordes of tourists as in Banff and Jasper.

On your way in from Hwy 1A, you'll pass the **Alberta Visitor Information Centre** (☎ *403-678-1935)* at the western edge of Canmore, at Dead Mans Flats.

Practical Information

The parks in the Rocky Mountains straddle two Canadian provinces, Alberta and British Columbia, which have two different area codes. To avoid confusion, we will mention the area code in each telephone number throughout this chapter. The area code is ☎ **403** for Alberta, and ☎ **604** for British Columbia. (Take note that as of October 1996, the area code for eastern British Columbia will change to ☎ **250**.)

Information about the different parks and regions is available through the offices of Parks Canada and the tourist information offices.

■ **Tours A and B: Banff National Park and the Icefields Parkway**

Banff Visitor Centre
224 Banff Avenue
Box 900
Banff, AB
T0L 0C0
☎ (403) 762-1550
⇄ (403) 762-8163

Lake Louise Visitor Information Centre
☎ (403) 522-3833

Banff National Park
Box 900
Banff, AB
T0L 0C0
☎ (403) 762-1551
⇄ (403) 762-7834

■ **Tour C: Jasper National Park**

Jasper Tourism and Chamber of Commerce
Box 98
632 Connaught Drive
Jasper, AB
T0E 1E0
☎ (403) 852-3858
⇄ (403) 852-4932

Same address and phone number for the offices of Parks Canada.

■ **Tour D: Kootenay and Yoho National Parks**

Kootenay National Park
Box 220
Radium Hot Springs, BC
V0A 1M0
☎ (604) 347-9615

The **Golden and District Chamber of Commerce and Travel Information Centre** (☎ *604-344-7125)* is located in the centre of town.

■ **Tour E: Kananaskis Country**

Kananaskis Country Head Office
Suite 100, 1011 Glenmore Tr. SW
Calgary, AB
T2V 4R6
☎ (403) 297-3362

Bow Valley Provincial Park Office
Located near the town of Seeby
☎ (403) 673-3663

Peter Lougheed Provincial Park Visitor Information Centre
Located 3.6 km from Kananaskis Trail (Hwy 40)
☎ (403) 591-6344

Alberta Environmental Protection Kananaskis Country
Box 100
Kananaskis Village, AB
T0L 2H0
☎ (403) 591-7555

Exploring and Parks

Tour A: Banff National Park ★★★

The history of the **Canadian Pacific** railway is inextricably linked to that of the national parks of the Rocky Mountains. In November of 1883, three workmen abandoned the railway construction site in the Bow Valley and headed towards Banff in search of gold. When they reached Sulphur Mountain, however, brothers William and Tom McCardell and Frank McCabe discovered sulphur hot springs instead. They took a concession in order to turn a profit with the springs, but were unable to counter the various land rights disputes that followed. The series of events drew the attention of the federal government, which sent out an agent to control the concession. The renown of these hot springs had already spread from railway workers to the vice-president of Canadian Pacific, who came here in 1885 and declared that the springs were certainly worth a million dollars. Realizing the enormous economic potential of the Sulphur Mountain hot springs, which were already known as **Cave and Basin**, the federal government quickly purchased the rights to the concession from the three workers and consolidated its property rights on the site by creating a natural reserve the same year. Two years later, in 1887, the reserve became the first national park in Canada and was called Rockies Park, and then Banff National Park. In those days there was no need to protect the still abundant wildlife, and the mindset of government was not yet preoccupied with the preservation of natural areas. On the contrary, the government's main concern was to find an economically exploitable site with which to replenish the state coffers, in need of a boost after the construction of the railroad. To complement the springs which were already in vogue with wealthy tourists in search of spa treatments, tourist facilities and luxury hotels were built. Thus was born the town of Banff, today a world-class tourist mecca.

At first glance, Banff looks like a small town made up essentially of hotels, motels, souvenir shops and restaurants all lined up along Banff Avenue. The town has much more to offer, however.

The best spot to start your visit of Banff is at the **Banff Visitor Centre** *(downtown, at the corner of Banff Ave. and Wolf St., next to the Presbyterian Church, ☎ 403-762-8421, 762-0270).* If you are visiting Banff in the summer, you can pick up a calendar of events for the Banff Arts Festival. The offices of Parks Canada are located in the same building.

A bit farther along Banff Avenue, stop in at the **Natural History Museum ★ (1)** *(adults $3, free for children under 10; Sep to Jun 10am to 8pm, Jul and Aug 10am to 10pm; 112 Banff Ave., ☎ 403-762-1558).* This museum retraces the history of the Rockies and

Exploring and Parks 215

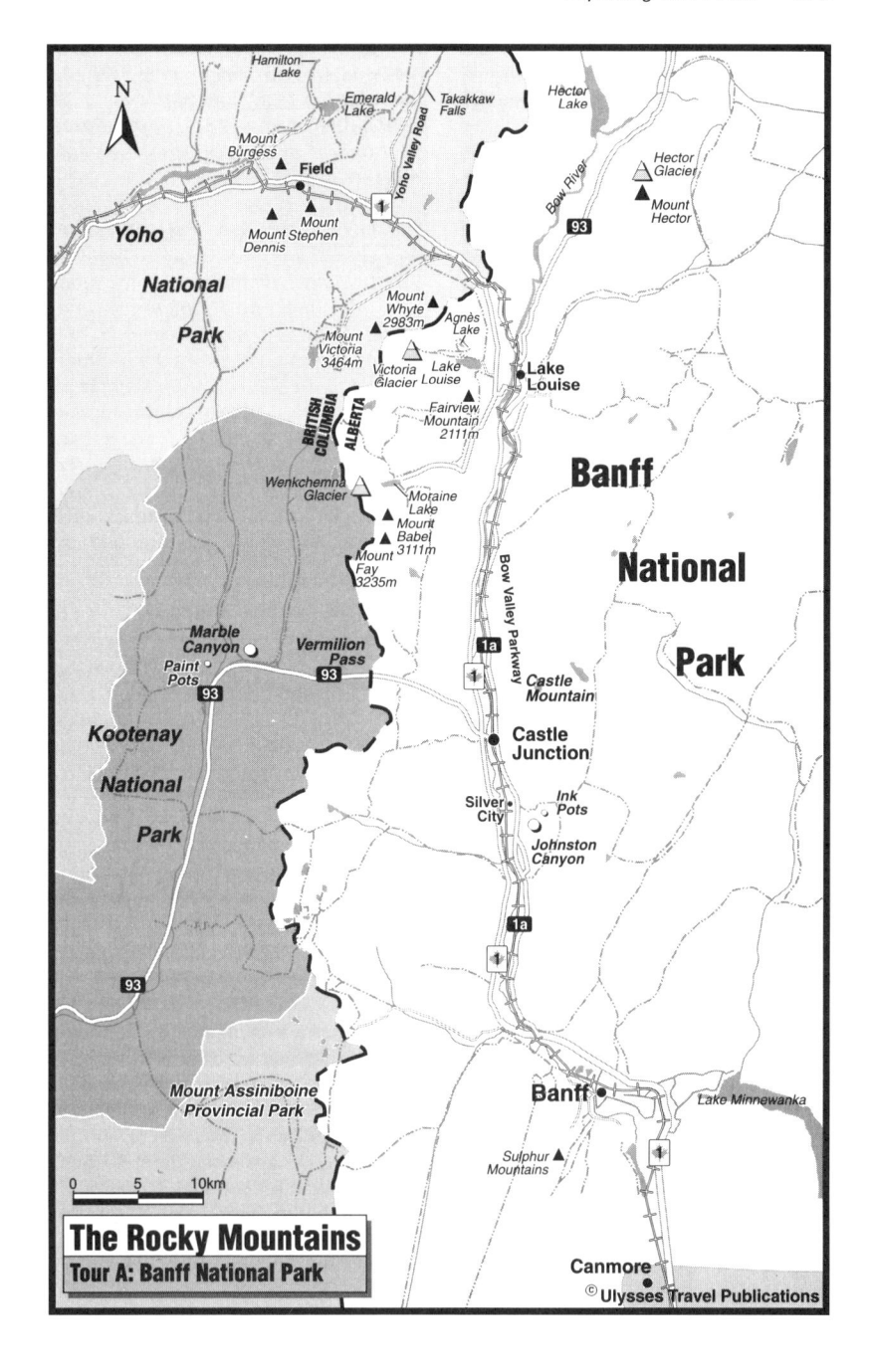

The Rocky Mountains
Tour A: Banff National Park

displays various rocks, fossils and dinosaur tracks, as well as several plant species that you're likely to encounter while hiking.

Located just before the bridge over the Bow River, the **Banff Park Museum** ★★ **(2)** *(adults $2.25, children $1.25; Jun to Aug, every day 10am to 6pm; Sep to May 1pm to 5pm; 93 Banff Ave., ☎ 403-762-1558)* is the oldest natural history museum in Western Canada. Guided tours are given regularly at 3pm, but if you get a group together, you can call the museum to organize a special guided tour. The interior of the building is in pure Victorian style, with lovely wood mouldings. There is a collection of stuffed mounted animals, some of which date from 1860. The museum has been declared a national historic site.

The view down Banff Avenue ends on the other side of the bridge, at the famous **Cascade Gardens (3)** and the administrative offices of the park. The park itself offers a wonderful view of Cascade Mountain.

The **Whyte Museum of the Canadian Rockies** ★★★ **(4)** *(adults $3; Jul and Aug 10am to 9pm; Sep to Jun 10am to 6pm; 111 Bear St., ☎ 403-762-2291)* relates the history of the Canadian Rockies. You'll discover archaeological findings from ancient Kootenay and Stoney Indian encampments, including clothing, tools and jewellery. Museum-goers will also learn the history of certain local heros and famous explorers like Bill Peyto as well as that of the history of the railway and the town of Banff. Personal objects and clothing that once belonged to notable local figures are exhibited. The museum also houses a painting gallery and extensive archives, in case you want to know more about the region. Right next to the Whyte Museum is the **Banff Public Library (5)** *(Mon, Wed, Fri and Sat 11am to 6pm, Tue and Thu 11am to 9pm, Sun 1pm to 5pm; at the corner of Bear and Buffalo Streets, ☎ 403-762-2661)*.

The **Luxton Museum** ★★ **(6)** *(adults $4.50, children $2; Jun to mid-Oct 9am to 9pm; 1 Birch Ave., on the other side of the Bow River Bridge, ☎ 403-762-2388)* is dedicated to the lives of the Amerindians of the northern plains and the Canadian Rockies. Their way of life, rituals and hunting techniques are explained, and various tools they used are displayed. The museum is accessible to handicapped individuals and guided tours are available, but must be arranged by calling the museum ahead of time.

Cave and Basin ★★★ **(7)** *(adults $2.25, children $1.25; Jun to Aug, every day 9am to 6pm; Sep to may 9:30am to 5pm; at the end of Cave Ave., ☎ 403-762-1557)* is now a national historic site. The springs are at the origin of the vast network of Canadian national parks (see p 214). However, despite extremely costly renovations to the basins in 1984, the pool has been closed for security reasons since 1992. The sulphurous content of the waters actually deteriorates the cement, and the pool's paving is badly damaged in some places. You can still visit the cave into which the three Canadian Pacific workers descended in search of the springs, and smell the distinctive odour of the sulphurous gas caused by the bacteria that oxydize the sulphates in the water before it spurts out of the earth. The original basin is still there, but swimming is no longer permitted. If you watch the water, you'll see the sulphur gas bubbling to the surface, while at the bottom of the basin you can see depressions appearing in the

Exploring and Parks 217

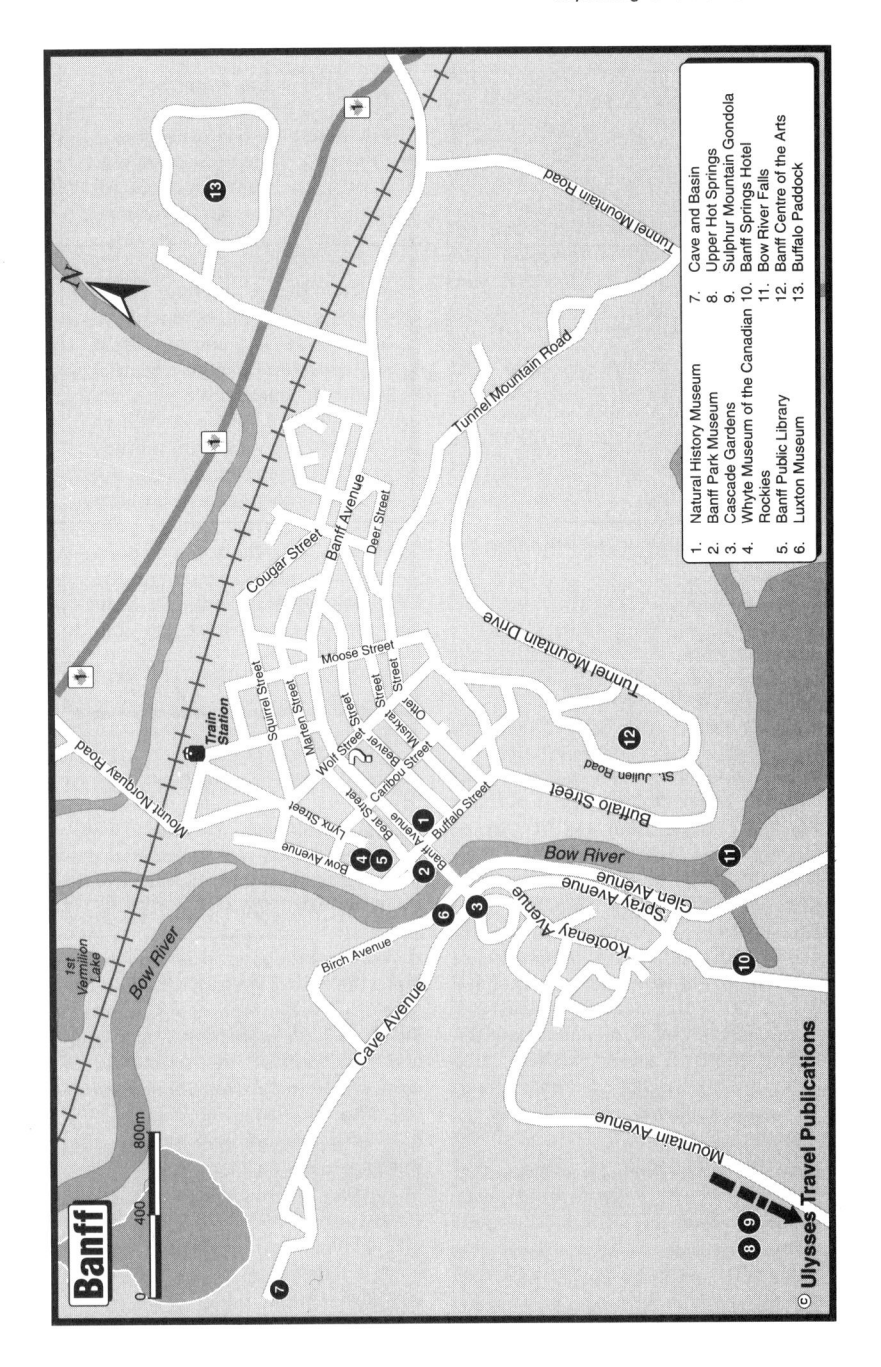

Banff

1. Natural History Museum
2. Banff Park Museum
3. Cascade Gardens
4. Whyte Museum of the Canadian Rockies
5. Banff Public Library
6. Luxton Museum
7. Cave and Basin
8. Upper Hot Springs
9. Sulphur Mountain Gondola
10. Banff Springs Hotel
11. Bow River Falls
12. Banff Centre of the Arts
13. Buffalo Paddock

© Ulysses Travel Publications

sand caused by this same gas (this is most obvious in the centre of the basin). In the theatre you can take in a short film on Banff National Park and the history of the hot springs and their purchase by the government for only $900. You'll learn that the McCardell brothers and Frank McCabe were not actually the first to discover the springs, as Assiniboine Indians were already familiar with their therapeutic powers. European explorers had also already spoken of them. However, the three Canadian Pacific workers, knowing a good thing when they saw it, were the first to try to gain exclusive rights over the springs and the government simply followed suit.

If you want to experience the sensation of Sulphur Mountain's waters (and how rapturous it is to lounge about after a long day of hiking), head up Mountain Avenue, at the foot of the mountain, to the hot spring facilities of **Upper Hot Spring** ★★★ **(8)** *(adults $5, children 3-16 $3.50 for access to the pool; $20 for the whirlpool thermal baths and basins; bathing suit and towel rentals available; every day May 20 to Jun 22, 10am to 9pm; Jun 23 to Sep 4, 8:30am to 10:30am; Sep 5 to Oct 9, 11am to 7:30pm; up from Mountain Ave., ☎ 403-866-3939)*. The establishment includes a hot water (40°C) bath for soaking and a warm pool (27°C) for swimming. If you have at least an hour and are at least 17 years old, then by all means try out the thermal baths. This is a turkish style bath which consists of immersion in hot water followed by aromatherapy treatment. You then lay out on a bed and are ensconced in sheets and blankets. The soothing effect is truly divine.

Amerindians and early visitors alike believed in the curative powers of sulphurous waters, which were thought to improve one's health, and even to cure skin problems. Though the water's curative powers are contested these days, there is no denying their calming effect on body and soul.

If you haven't got the energy to hike up to the top of the mountain, you can take the **Sulphur Mountain Gondola (9)** *(adults $9, children 5 to 11 $4; at the end of Mountain Ave., at the far end edge of the Upper Hot Springs parking lot)*. The panoramic view of the town of Banff, Mount Rundle, the Bow Valley, and Aylmer and Cascade Mountains is superb. The gondola starts out at an altitude of 1,583 m and climbs to 2,281 m. Be sure to bring along warm clothes, as it can be cold at the summit.

Why is the water hot?

By penetrating into fissures in the rock, water makes its way under the western slope of Sulphur Mountain, absorbing calcium, sulphur and other minerals along the way. At a certain depth, the heat of the earth's centre warms the water as it is being forced up by pressure through a fault in the northeastern slope of the mountain. As the water flows outside, the calcium settles around the source in pale-coloured layers that eventually harden into rock, called **tufa**. These formations can be seen on the mountainside, at the small exterior spring 20 m from the entrance to the facilities.

The **Banff Springs Hotel** ★★★ **(10)** is also worth a look. After visiting the springs at Cave and Basin, William Cornelius Van Horne, vice-president of the Canadian Pacific railway company, decided to have a sumptuous hotel built to accommodate the tourists who would soon be flocking to the hot springs. Construction began in 1887, and the hotel opened its doors in June 1888. Although the cost of the project had already reached $250,000, the railway company launched a promotional campaign in order to attract wealthy visitors from all over the world. By the beginning of the century, Banff had become so well known that the Banff Springs Hotel was one of the busiest hotels in North America. More space was needed, so a new wing was built in 1903. It was separated from the original building by a small wooden bridge in case of fire. A year later a tower was built at the end of each wing. Even though this immense hotel welcomed 22,000 guests in 1911, the facilities again proved too small for the forever increasing demand. Construction was thus begun on a central tower. The building was finally completed as it stands today in 1928. The Tudor style interior layout, as well as the tapestries, paintings and furniture in the common rooms, are all original. If you decide to stay at the Banff Springs Hotel (see p 254) you may run into the ghost of Sam McAuley, the bellboy who helps guests who have lost their keys, or that of the unlucky young bride who died the day of her wedding when she fell down the stairs and supposedly haunts the corridors of the hotel.

Heading downhill from the Banff Springs Hotel, you can stop a while at a pretty lookout point over **Bow River Falls (11)**.

The **Banff Centre of the Arts (12)** *(between St. Julien Rd. and Tunnel Mountain Dr., ☎ 403-762-6100)* was created in 1933. More commonly known as the Banff Centre since 1978, this renowned cultural centre hosts the **Banff Festival of the Arts** in the month of August. The festival attracts numerous artists, and involves presentations of dance, opera, jazz and theatre. The centre also offers courses in classical and jazz ballet, theatre, music, photography and pottery. Finally, each year the centre organizes an international mountain film festival. There is a sports centre inside the complex as well.

Around Banff

The **Buffalo Paddock** ★★ **(13)** *(free admission; to get there, head towards Lake Minnewanka, then take the TransCanada towards Lake Louise, the entrance lies 1 km farther on the right)* provides an interesting opportunity, if you're lucky, to admire these majestic creatures up close. It is important, however, to stay in your car, even if you want to take photographs, as these animals can be very unpredictable and the slightest provocation may cause them to charge. This paddock was originally built by a group of wealthy Banff residents, who were planning to make it into a zoo. Since the whole idea of a zoo is not in keeping with the spirit of national parks, the plains bison were sent off by train to be liberated in Wood Buffalo National Park, in northern Alberta and the southwest part of the Northwest Territories. They were replaced by wood buffalo who had migrated into the area and had to protected from diseases that were killing off their species.

The **Mount Norquay Ski Centre** was the first one created in Banff National Park. This 2,522 m mountain was named in honour of John Norquay, Premier of Manitoba. In the winter, a cablecar carries passengers to the summit to admire the magnificent scenery of the Bow River Valley, as well as the town of Banff.

By following the Lake Minnewanka road, you'll soon come upon the vestiges of the former mining town of **Bankhead** ★. The disappearance of this small town is linked to the creation of Banff National Park. In fact, Bankhead, a by-product of the coal mining activity in the area, had to be completely dismantled because all forms of mining and forestry development are prohibited in natural parks. Today a trail leads around the few remaining foundations and slag heaps, visible in the distance. Back on the road, 200 m higher up on the right, you'll see the remains of the church steps. The pleasant **Upper Bankhead** site, a bit farther along on the left, has been equipped with picnic tables and small firepits.

Twenty-two kilometres long and two kilometres wide, **Lake Minnewanka** ★★ is now the biggest lake in Banff National Park, but this expanse of water is not completely natural. Its name means "lake of the water spirit". These days it is one of the few lakes in the park where motor boats are permitted. Originally, the area was occupied by Stoney Indian encampments. Because of the difficulties involved with diving in alpine waters, and the scattering of vestiges that can be seen here, this lake popular with scuba diving enthisuasts. Guided walks are given Tuesdays, Thursdays and Saturdays at 2pm. Besides taking a guided boat-tour with **Cruise and Tour Devil's Gap** *(adults $20, children under 11 $10; Lake Minnewanka Boat Tours, Box 2189, Dept B, Banff, ☎ 403-762-3473)*, you can fish on the lake if you first obtain the appropriate permit from Parks Canada. Canoeing is another possibility *(canoe rentals $20 for an hour, $70 for the day)* in the summer, skating in the winter. A 16 km hiking trail leads to the far end of the lake. At the **Aylmer Lookout Viewpoint** you will probably spot some of the mountain goats who frequent the area.

Bow Valley Parkway ★★

To get from Banff to Lake Louise, take the Bow Valley Parkway (Hwy 1A), which is a much more picturesque route than the TransCanada. About 140 million years ago, the mountains emerged from an ancient sea as a result of pressure from the earth's strata. Flowing from the mountains, the Bow River was born, littering the plains to the east with sediment. Forty million years later, the foothills rose from the plains and threatened to prevent the river from following its course. However, even when rocks got in its path, the river managed to continue its route, sweeping away the rocky debris. This continual erosion resulted in the formation of a steep-sided V-shaped valley.

At the beginning of the ice age, about a million years ago, the riverbed of the Bow was taken over by moving ice. The glacier transformed the steep sides of the valley, which took on the shape of a U. As the last glacier receded, it left behind the debris it had been carrying, and the meltwater formed a torrential river which tumbled down the valley. Meltwater no longer feeds the Bow, which can barely make it through the debris left behind by the glaciers.

Weaving its way along the mountains, the Bow Valley Parkway affords some exquisite views of the Bow River. It is important to heed the drive slowly warning as animals often approach the road at sunrise and sunset.

A stop at beautiful **Johnston Canyon** ★★★, located on the right-hand side about 20 km beyond Banff, is a must. A small dirt trail has been cleared through the canyon, where you can behold the devastating effect even a small torrent of water can have on all kinds of rock. The first waterfalls, called the "upper falls", are only 1.1 km along the trail, and the path there is easy, though a bit slippery in spots. The second, called the "lower falls" lie another 1.6 km farther. This canyon is a veritable bird sanctuary, you might spot some dippers, who live in the canyon year-round and like to dive into the icy waters in search of insect larvae. Black swifts build their nests in the shady hollows of the canyon. They arrive in mid-June and stay until the beginning of fall, long enough to raise their young before heading back south to the warmth of the tropics. Beyond both these falls, you can see what are called the "shimmering walls". A sign explains the phenomenon, which results from the combination of several varieties of algae saturated with minerals. When the sun hits the wall the effect is spectacular. The second waterfalls are the highest in the canyon. The trail continues for another 3 km to the **Ink Pots**, formed by seven cold springs in different shades of blue and green. The Ink Pots trail is 5.8 km long.

The abandoned town of **Silver City** lies farther up the Bow Valley Parkway, on the left. Silver, copper and lead were discovered in the area in 1883. Prospectors arrived two years later, but the mineral deposits were quickly exhausted and ultimately the town was abandoned. In its glory days, this little city had some 175 buildings and several hotels, but just a handful of vestiges remain.

Lake Louise ★★★

Jewel of the Canadian Rockies, Lake Louise is known the world over thanks to its small, still, emerald-green lake. Few natural sites in Canada can boast as much success: this little place welcomes and average of about six million visitors a year! The public's fancy with this spot is nothing new, and visitors today owe its rediscovery (not discovery, since this area was already well known to Amerindians) to Tom Wilson, a railway surveyor for Canadian Pacific. In 1882, while working near the Pipestone River, Tom Wilson heard the rumbling of an avalanche coming from the Victoria Glacier. He proceeded to ask a Stoney Indian named Nimrod to lead him to the "Lake of the Little Fishes", which is what the local Amerindians called the lake. Struck by the colour of the water, Tom Wilson renamed the lake "Emerald Lake". Well aware of how beautiful the site was, the railway company erected a first building on the shores of the lake and at the foot of the glacier, in 1890. This construction was completely destroyed by fire and rebuilt in 1909; it could accommodate about 500 people. At the time, rooms at the Chateau Lake Louise were $4. To transport the numerous visitors already eager to view the scenery, construction of a railway line was undertaken. Up until 1926, when a road was finished, all of the tourists arrived by train at the Laggan station, located 6 km from the lake. From there, guests of the Chateau Lake

The Rocky Mountains
Lake Louise and Surroundings

Louise were brought to the hotel in a sort of horse-drawn trolley.

Today, you can reach the lake by car; finding a place to park here can be a real challenge. Stroll quietly around the lake or climb the mountain along the network of little trails radiating out from the lake's shore for a magnificent view of the Victoria Glacier, the lake and the glacial valley. Reaching **Lake Agnes** requires extra effort, but the view ★★★ of **Victoria** (3,464 m), **White** (2,983 m), **Fairview** (2,111 m), **Babel** (3,111 m) and **Fay** (3,235 m) Mountains is well worth the exertion.

If you aren't up to such a climb, you can always take the **Lake Louise Gondola**, which is open from 8am to 9pm and transports you to an altitude of 2,089 m in just 10 minutes.

Though the present-day **Chateau Lake Louise** ★★ has nothing to do with the original construction, it remains an attraction in itself. This vast Canadian Pacific Hotel can accommodate 700 visitors. Besides restaurants, the hotel houses a small shopping arcade with boutiques selling all kinds of souvenirs.

In the centre of the village of Lake Louise, the Samson Mall houses the tourist information office (☎ 403-522-3833) and the offices of Parks Canada. Souvenir shops, photo shops, bookstores and a few café-restaurants, all busy with visitors, are located next door. Be careful, as prices tend to be a bit high; you are better off bringing along lots of film so that you won't have to stock up here.

Moraine Lake ★★★

When heading to Lake Louise, you will come to a turnoff for Moraine Lake on the left. This narrow, winding road weaves its way along the mountain for about 10 km before reaching Moraine Lake, which has been immortalized on the old Canadian $20 bill. Though much smaller than Lake Louise, Moraine Lake is no less spectacular. Inaccessible in the winter, the lake often remains frozen until the month of June. Don't arrive unprepared for the cool temperatures, even in the summer. Bring a sweater and a wind-breaker if you plan to stroll along the shores. The valley of Moraine Lake, known as the "valley of the 10 peaks", was created by the **Wenkchemna** Glacier, which is still melting. The 10 summits were originally named after the Assiniboine words for the numbers 1 to 10 respectively, but many have since been rechristened, and only the name Wenkchemna remains. The Moraine Lodge, on the shore of the lake, has a restaurant and a small café (see p 267) where you can warm yourself up.

Canmore ★

The name Canmore comes from the Gaelic *Ceann mor* which means "big head". The name was given as a nickname to the Scottish king Malcolm III, son of Duncan I, who became king in 1054 and established his place in history by killing the usurper Macbeth.

After searching for the most practical route for the railway to the west, Canadian Pacific chose to go through the Bow Valley. It was decided that the supply station for the project would be placed at the entrance to the Rockies, and thus was born the town of Canmore. Mineral deposits found here later were mined until July 13th, 1979.

This quiet little town of about 6,000 experienced its finest hour during the 1988 Winter Olympics. The cross-country, nordic combined and biathlon events were held here, along with the handicapped cross-country skiing demonstration event. Since the games, the facilities at the **Canmore Nordic Centre** *(every day; from the centre of town head up Main St., turn right on 8th Ave. and right to cross the Bow River. Turn left and head up Rundle Dr., then turn left again on Sister Dr. Take Spray Lake Rd. to the right and continue straight. The parking lot of the centre is located farther up on the right, ☎ 403-678-2400)* have been used for other international events like the World Cup of Skiing in 1995. In summer the cross-country trails become walking and mountain biking trails. Domestic animals are permitted between April 11th and October 30th if they are on a leash. Bears are common in the region in the summer, so be extra careful.

By continuing beyond the Canmore Nordic Centre, you'll come upon two small lakes called **Grassi Lakes**. To reach them, head up Three Sisters Drive and turn right on Spray Lakes Road. Turn left at the turn-off near the artificial lake called the Reservoir, then left again on the first small dirt road. The starting point for a hiking trail begins a bit farther along. The lakes are named after Lawrence Grassi, an Italian immigrant who worked for the Canadian Pacific railway company and cleared the trail to the lakes. A short walk climbs quickly up to the Grassi Falls and then on to the crystal-clear lakes. A great view of Canmore and the Bow Valley can be had from this spot. Good walking shoes are necessary. The Canmore area is also well known for its dog-sled races.

Marvellously well situated at the entrance to Banff National Park and at the gateway to Kananaskis Country, Canmore welcomes many visitors each year, but it is often easier to find accommodations here than in Banff. Nevertheless, it is a good idea to reserve your room well in advance.

The main attraction of this small town, besides the Canmore Nordic Centre, is its exceptional location and the many outdoor activities possible here. Besides skiing, dog-sled races, ice-climbing, heli-skiing, snowmobile trips and ice fishing in the winter, summer activities include parasailing, hang-gliding, hiking, mountain biking, rock-climbing, canoeing, and the list goes on... All sorts of useful addresses can be found in the outdoor activities section (see p 238).

The **Canmore Centennial Museum** *(free admission; every day; 801 7th Ave., ☎ 403-678-2462)* is a tiny little museum that retraces the town's mining history. It also has a section on the 1988 Winter Olympics.

The **Canmore Recreation Centre** *(every day 8:30am to 4:30pm; 1900 8th Ave., ☎ 403-678-5597, ⇄ 678-6661)* organizes all sorts of summer activities for children. The facilities include a municipal pool, a sports centre, an exercise centre and a golf course.

Right: *Moraine Lake (Pierre Longnus)*
   Downhill skiing in Banff National Park (Calgary Convention Visitors Bureau)

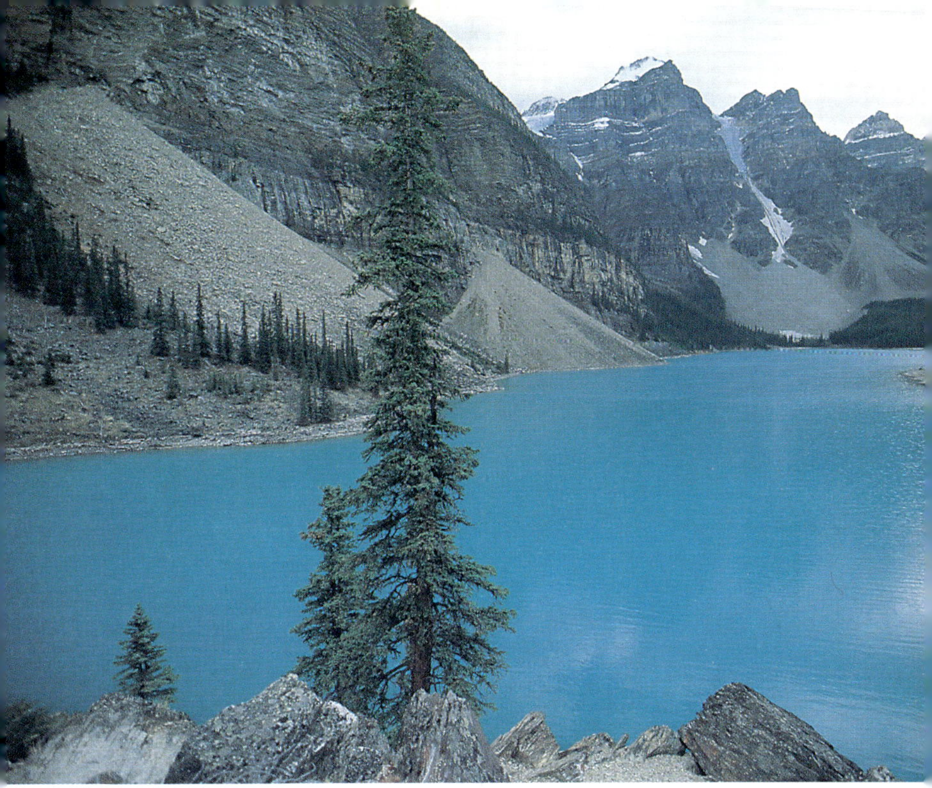

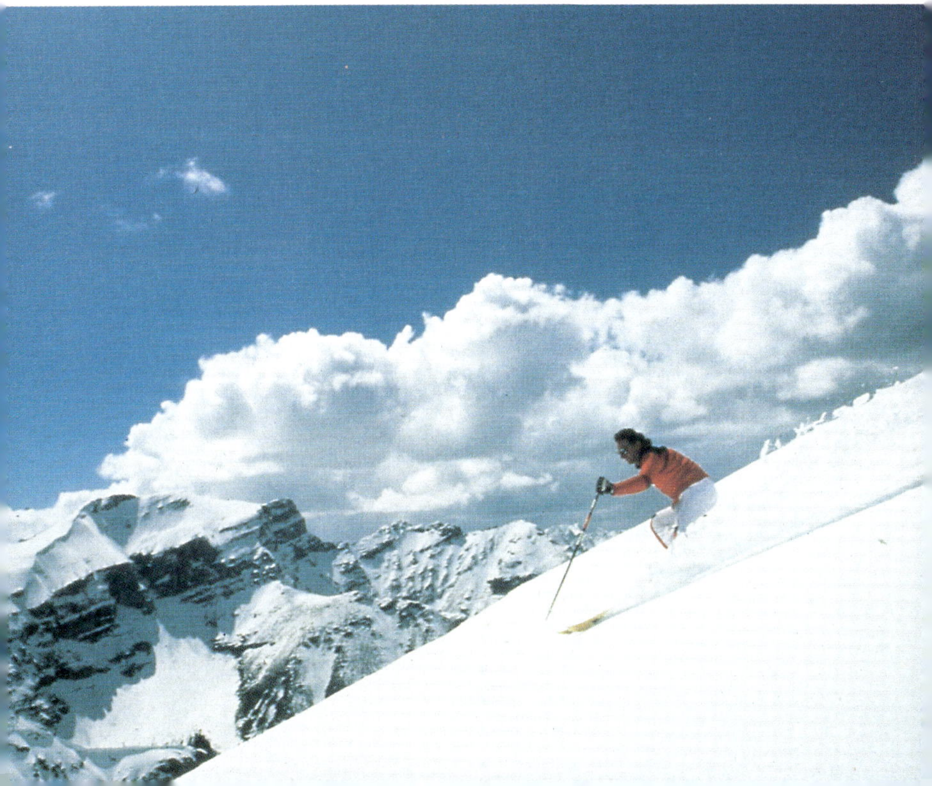

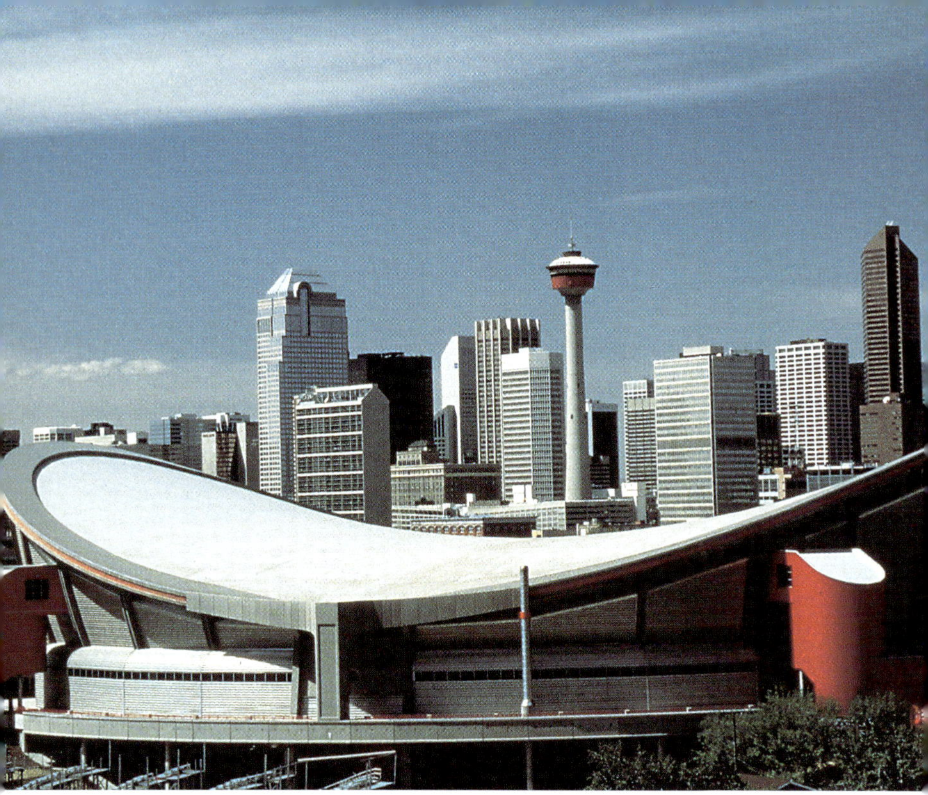

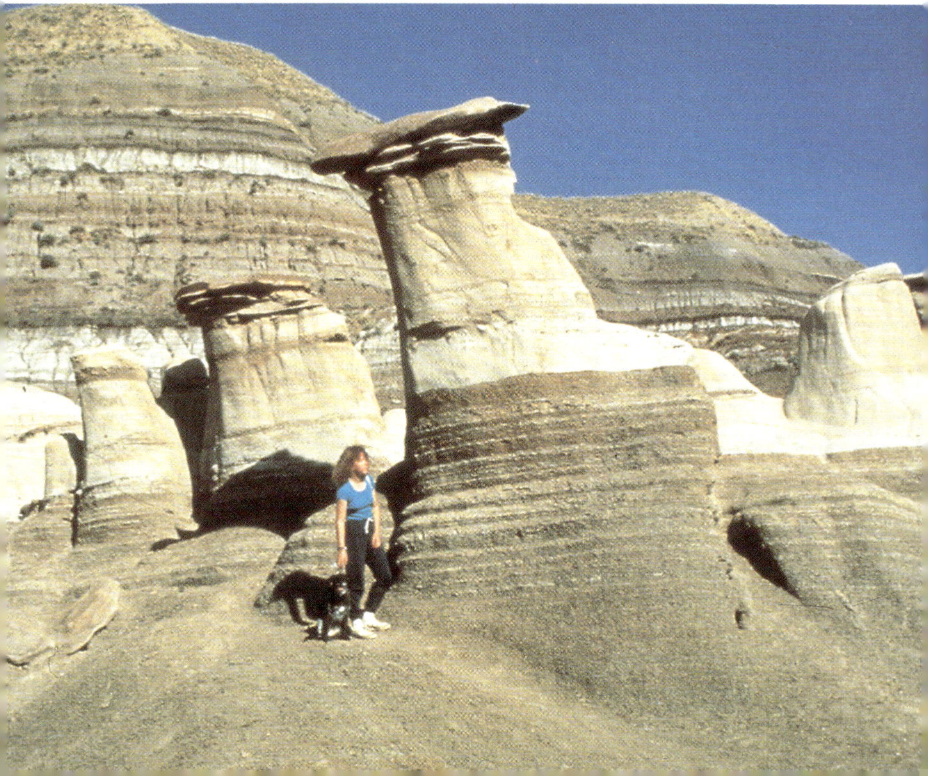

■ Tour B: The Icefields Parkway ★★★

The route through the icefields follows Hwy 93 from Lake Louise for 230 km to the Continental Divide, which is covered by glaciers, before ending up in Jasper. This wide, well paved road is one of the busiest in the Rockies during the summer, with a 90 km/h speed limit. It runs through some incredibly majestic scenery.

The **Hector Lake** ★★ lookout on the left, 17 km from Lake Louise, offers a great view of both the lake and Mount Hector. The lake is fed by meltwater from the Balfour Glacier and the Waputik Icefields.

One kilometre before **Mosquito Creek**, you can clearly see the Crowfoot Glacier from the road. Photographs reproduced on information panels by the road show just how much the glacier has melted in recent years. A bit farther along you can stop to take in the magnificent view of Bow Lake, and then visit little **Num-Ti-Jah** (an Amerindian name which means "martyr") Lodge built in 1922 by a mountain guide named Jimmy Simpson. At the time, there was no road leading this far, and all the building materials had to be hauled in on horseback. One of Simpson's descendants has since converted the place into a hotel and cleared an a road for guests. Since all the tour buses stop here, the administration of the Num-Ti-Jah Lodge (see p 259) has decided in an effort to protect the privacy of its clientele, that only people with reservations for the night should be permitted to enter the building. It is therefore preferable to limit your tour to the outside of the chalet; otherwise you may receive a rather gruff welcome.

Bow Summit ★★ (2,609 m) lies at the highest point of the Icefields Parkway and on the continental divide for the waters of the Bow and Mistayac rivers. At this point the vegetation changes drastically, giving way almost completely to sub-alpine plant-life. By the sideof the road, there is a rest area that overlooks **Peyto Lake** (pronounced Pee-Toh). You can take a hike through an area of alpine vegetation, and if the weather is right, you can admire a lovely little lake. Western anemones (*Anemone Occidentalis)* line the trail, as do various types of heather and the very pretty Indian paintbrush. Bring a good sweater and a jacket for this walk to protect yourself from the wind and the cool temperatures at this altitude. Originally from the region of Kent in England, Bill Peyto is one of the most well known local characters. During your trip through Banff National Park, you will certainly encounter his image complete with cocked hat, pipe and piercing gaze. Peyto arrived in Canada at the age of 18, and settled in the Rockies where he became one of the most celebrated trappers, prospectors and mountain guides. He enjoyed stopping off at Bow Summit to admire the little lake down below, which was named in his memory. Curiously, the colour of this lake varies considerably depending on the season. With the first signs of spring it brightens to a marvellous metallic blue, which becomes paler and pale as more and more sediment mixes with the water.

Left: Calgary skyline and the Saddledome (Gerald Vader Pyl)
Hoodoos in Drumheller (Calgary Convention Visitors Bureau)

226   *The Rocky Mountains*

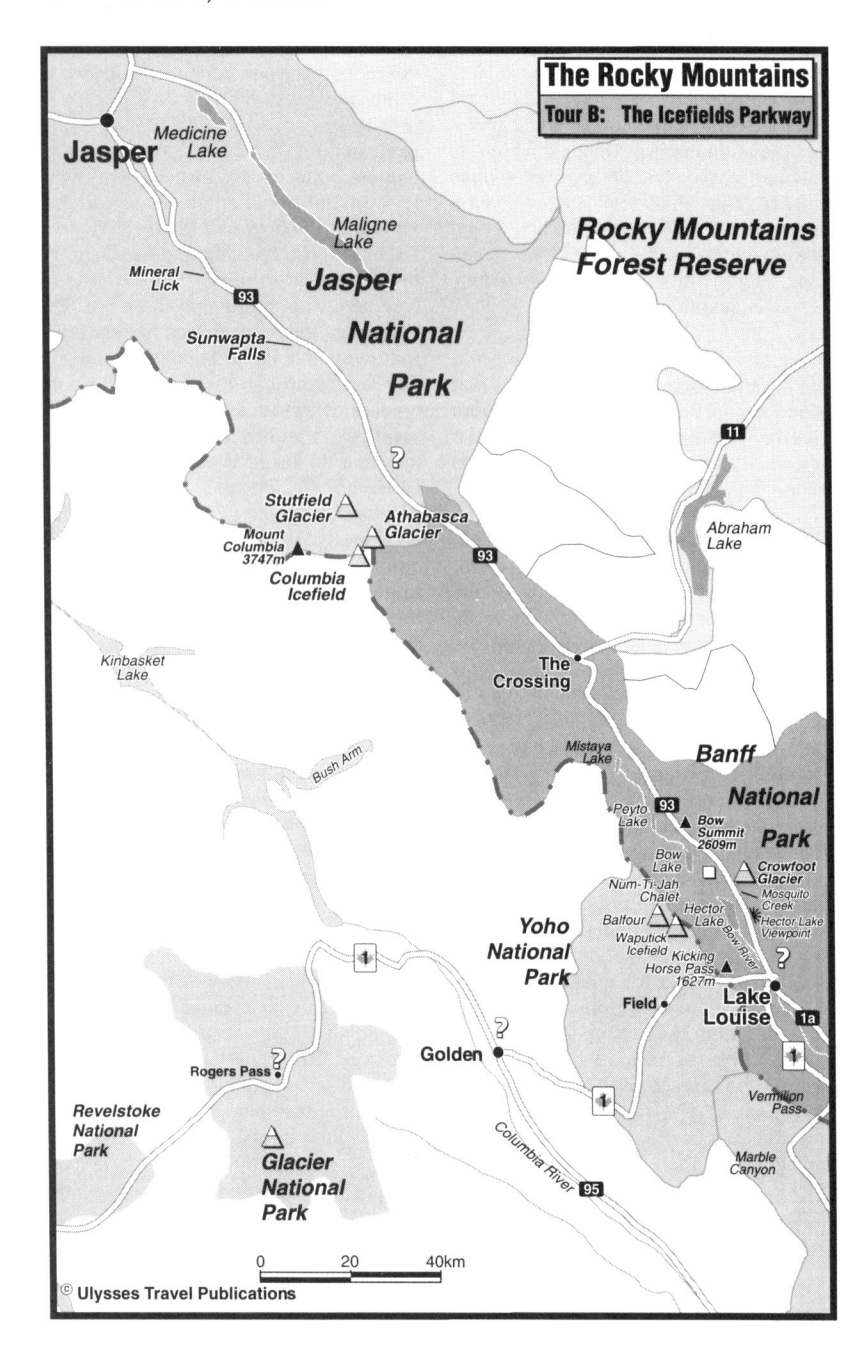

The Rocky Mountains
Tour B: The Icefields Parkway

Jasper

Medicine Lake

Maligne Lake

Mineral Lick

93

Sunwapta Falls

Jasper National Park

Rocky Mountains Forest Reserve

Stutfield Glacier

Mount Columbia 3747m

Athabasca Glacier

Columbia Icefield

93

11

Abraham Lake

Kinbasket Lake

The Crossing

Bush Arm

Mistaya Lake

Banff National Park

Peyto Lake

Bow Summit 2609m

Bow Lake

Num-Ti-Jah Chalet

Crowfoot Glacier

Mosquito Creek

Balfour

Hector Lake

Hector Lake Viewpoint

Waputick Icefield

Kicking Horse Pass 1627m

93

Yoho National Park

1

Field

Bow River

Lake Louise

1a

1

Rogers Pass

Golden

95

Columbia River

1

Vermilion Pass

Revelstoke National Park

Glacier National Park

Marble Canyon

0   20   40km

© Ulysses Travel Publications

At the intersection of Hwys 93 and 11, called **The Crossing**, you'll find a few souvenir shops, a hotel and some restaurants. Make sure your gas tank is full since there are no gas stations before Jasper. This region was once nhabited by Kootenay Indians, who were forced to the western slopes by Peigan Indians, armed with guns thanks to white merchants from the southeastern Rockies. Fearing that the Kootenay would eventually arm themselves thanks to the whites as well, the Peigans blocked the way of white explorers who were attempting to cross the pass, and thus kept their enemies completely isolated.

About 30 km farther along, at the **Weeping Wall** lookout, you can see several waterfalls cascading over the cliffs of **Mount Cirrus** as the ice melts. In the winter, the falls freeze, forming a spectacular wall of ice, to the delight of ice-climbers.

The **Castleguard Cave** is located 117 km from Jasper. A network of underwater caves, the longest in Canada, extends over 20 km under the Columbia Icefield. Because of frequent flooding and the inherent dangers of spelunking, you must have authorization from Parks Canada to enter the caves.

The **Parker Ridge** ★★ trail, just 3 km farther, makes for a wonderful outing. About 2.5 km long, it leads up to the ridge, where, if you're lucky, you may spot some mountain goats. It also offers a great view of the Saskatchewan Glacier. Both the vegetation and the temperature change as you pass from the subalpine to the alpine zone. Warm clothing and a pair of gloves are a good idea.

At the **Sunwapta Pass** you can admire the grandiose scenery which marks the dividing line between Banff and Jasper National Parks. At 2,035 m, this is the highest pass along the Icefields Parkway, after Bow Summit.

The **Athabasca Glacier** ★★★ and the **Columbia Icefield** are the focal point of the icefields tour. At the Athabasca Glacier, information panels show the impressive retreat of the glacier over the years. Those who wish to explore the ice on foot should beware of crevasses, which can be up to 40 m deep. There are 30,000 on the Athabasca Glacier, some hidden under a thin layer of snow or ice. Those without sufficient experience climbing on glaciers or the proper equipment are better off with a ticket aboard the **Snow Coach** *($20; May to mid-Oct, every day; tickets sold at the Brewster counter, near the tourist information centre)*. These specially equipped buses take you out onto the glacier. Once there, passengers can get off the bus to explore a specific area, determined to be safe by the staff of **Brewster Transportation**. The Brewster Transportation company was created in 1900 by two Banff businessmen, brothers Jim and Bill Brewster. The company has continuously contributed to the expansion of tourism in the Banff National Park area, even building a few hotels. Today the prosperous enterprise offers millions of travellers the opportunity to get around the national parks and more importantly, to explore the magnificent Athabasca Glacier up close.

The **Stutfield Glacier** ★★ lookout provides a view of one of the six huge glaciers fed by the Columbia Icefield, which continues 1 km into the valley.

About 3 km farther, on the west side, are several avalanche corridors, some of which come right up to the road. Generally, however, park rangers trigger avalanches before the thick layers of snow become dangerous.

Fifty-five kilometres before Jasper, the **Sunwapta Falls** ★★★ and canyon are a good example of how water can work away at limestone. The countryside offers some typical examples of suspended valleys, which result when a smaller glacier attaches itself to a larger one. The valley left by the larger glacier is much deeper, and the shallower, smaller one appears suspended. Several hiking trails have been cleared, one of which leads to the base of the Sunwapta Falls. Be careful while hiking as this is one of the prime habitats of bears and moose in the park.

Seventeen kilometres farther, heading to Jasper, you'll come to an area called the **Mineral Lick**, where mountain goats often come to lick the mineral-rich soil.

The trail leading to the 25 m-high **Athabasca Falls** ★★, located seven kilometres farther along, takes about an hour to hike. The concrete structure built there is an unfortunate addition to the natural surroundings, but heavy traffic in the area would have otherwise destroyed the fragile vegetation. Furthermore, some careless types have suffered accidents becuase they got too close to the edge of the canyon. Travellers are therefore reminded not to go beyond the barriers; doing so could cost you your life.

■ **Tour C: Jasper National Park** ★★★

Jasper and Surroundings ★★

The town of Jasper takes its name from an old fur-trading post, founded in 1811 by William Henry of the Northwest Company. Jasper is a small town of just 4,000 residents, which owes its tourist development to its geographic location and the train station built here in 1911. When the Icefields Parkway was opened in 1940, the numbers of visitors who wanted to discover the region's majestic scenery just kept growing. Although this area is a major tourist draw, Jasper remains a decidedly more tranquil and less commercial spot than Banff. This doesn't prevent hotel prices from being just as exorbitant as elsewhere in the Rockies, however.

A good place to start your visit of Jasper and its surroundings is at the tourist office *(every day 8am to 7pm; 500 Connaught Dr.,* ☎ *403-852-3858)*, where you can pick up maps of the region. The offices of Parks Canada are in the same building *(*☎ *403-852-6176)*.

The **Jasper-Yellowhead Museum and Archives** ★ **(1)** *(free admission; every day 9am to 5pm; 400 Pyramid Lake Rd., facing the Aquatic Centre,* ☎ *403-852-3013)* tells the story of the region's earliest Amerindian inhabitants, as well as mountain guides and other legendary characters from this area. Works by local artists are exhibited on the second floor.

Exploring and Parks 229

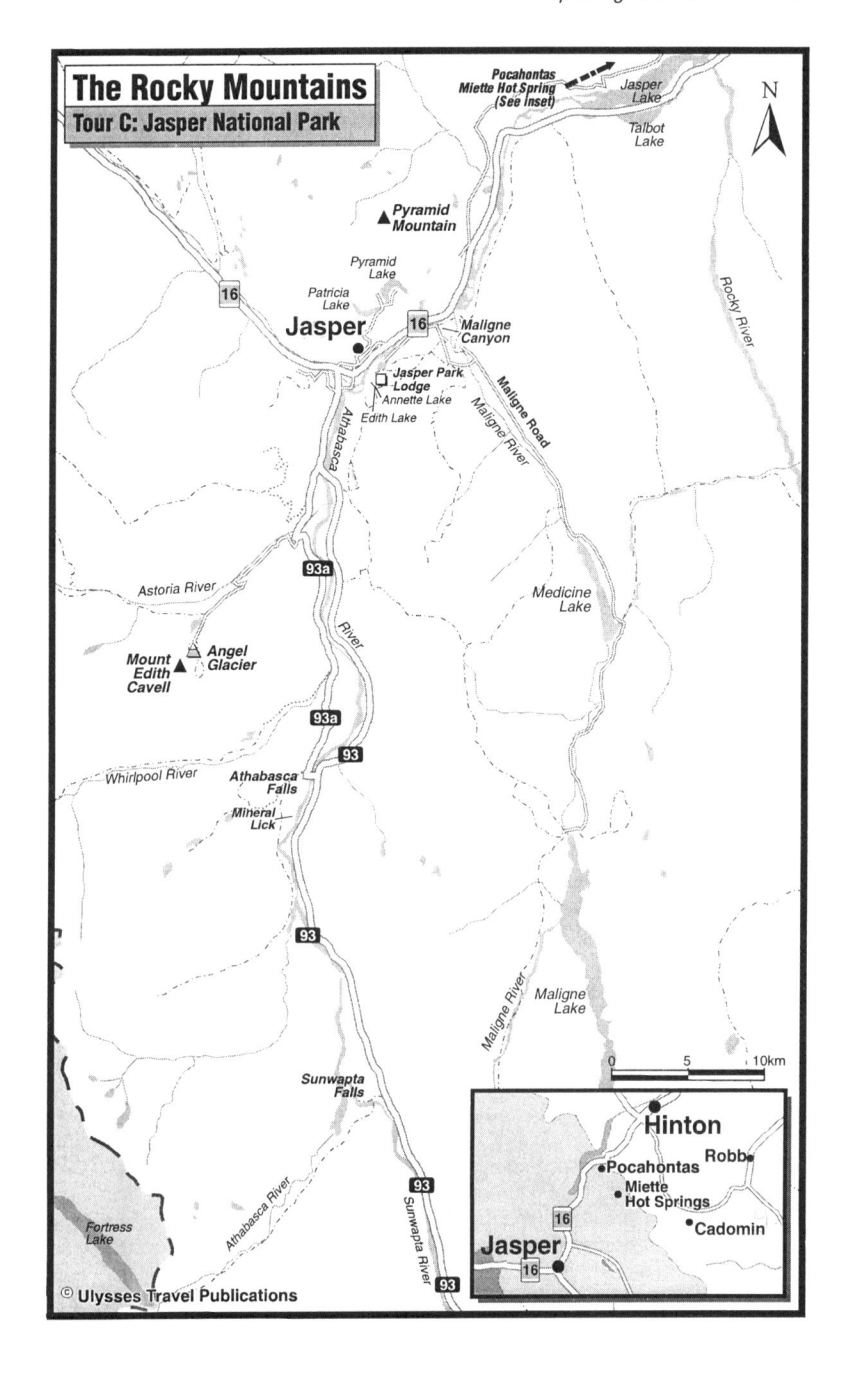

The **Den Wildlife Museum** ★ (2) *($3; every day until 6pm; at the corner of Connaught Dr. and Miette St., inside the Whistler Hotel, ☎ 403-852-3361)* exhibits a collection of stuffed and mounted animals from the region.

The **Jasper Aquatic Centre (3)** *(adults $4, seniors $3, children $2; 401 Pyramid Lake Rd., ☎ 403-852-3381)* and the **Jasper Activity Centre** *(on Pyramid Ave., near the Aquatic Centre, ☎ 403-852-3381)* are both open to visitors who want to go for a swim, take a sauna or shower, or play tennis or racquetball. During the month of August, a rodeo contest is organized inside the Jasper Activity Centre (ask at the tourist information office for the dates).

Mount Edith Cavell ★★★ is 3,363 m high. To get there, take the southern exit for Jasper and follow the signs for the Marmot ski hill. Turn right, then left, and you'll come to a narrow road, which leads to one of the most lofty summits in the area. The road snakes through the forest for about 20 km before coming to a parking lot. Several hiking trails have been cleared to allow visitors to enjoy a better view of this majestic mountain, as well as its suspended glacier, the **Angel Glacier**. The mountain is named after Edith Louisa Cavell, a British nurse who became known in World War I for her refusal to leave her post near Brussels in Belgium so that she could continue caring for the wounded in two camps. Arrested for spying by the Germans and accused of having assisted Allied prisoners escape, she was shot on October 12th, 1915. To commemorate this woman's exceptional courage, the government of Canada decided to name the most impressive mountain in the Athabasca Valley after the martyred nurse. Previous to this, Mount Edith Cavell had been known by many other names. The Amerindians called it "the white ghost", while travellers who used it as a reference point called it "the mountain of the Great Crossing", then "the Duke", "Mount Fitzhugh" and finally "Mount Geikie". No name had stuck, however, until the government decided to call the mountain Mount Edith Cavell.

In just a few minutes, the **Jasper Tramway** ★★ *($10; take the southern exit for Jasper and follow the signs for Mount Whistler, ☎ 403-852-3093)* whisks you up some 2,277 m and deposits you on the northern face of **Mount Whistler**. You'll find a restaurant and souvenir shop at the arrival point, while a small trail covers the last few metres up to the summit (2,470 m). The view is outstanding.

The road to Maligne Lake follows the valley of the river of the same name for 46 km. Because of the tight curves of this winding road and the many animals which cross it, the speed limit is 60 km/h. Before reaching the lake, the road passes by one of the most beautiful resorts in Canada, the **Jasper Park Lodge**, run by Canadian Pacific. You can have a picnic, go boating or take a swim in one of the two pretty little lakes, **Agnes** and **Edith** right next to this facility. Ten thousand years ago, as the glacier was retreating out of this valley, two immense blocks of ice broke free and remained in place amidst the moraines and other debris left by the glaciers. As they melted they formed these two small lakes. Lake Agnes has a beach.

Maligne Canyon ★★★ lies at the beginning of the Maligne Road. Hiking trails have been cleared so that visitors can admire this spectacular narrow gorge abounding with cascades, fossils

Exploring and Parks 231

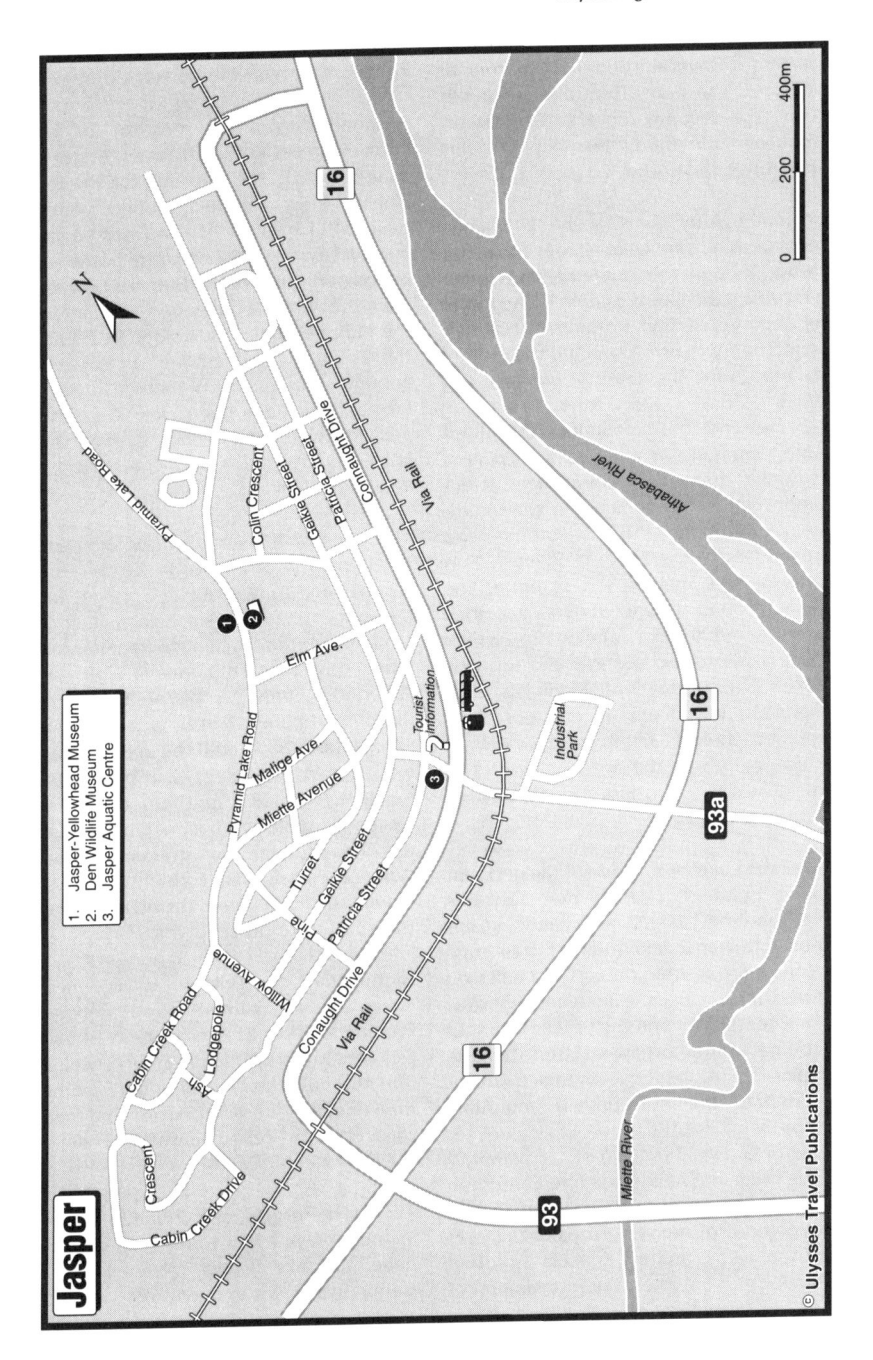

Jasper

1. Jasper-Yellowhead Museum
2. Den Wildlife Museum
3. Jasper Aquatic Centre

and potholes sculpted by the turbulent waters. Several bridges span the canyon. The first offers a view of the falls; the second, the effect of ice on rock and the third, the deepest point (51 m) of the gorge.

Dominated by the Maligne and Colin chains, **Medicine Lake** ★ looks like any other lake in the summer, but come October it disappears completely. In the spring, you'll find nothing but a tiny stream flowing slowly along the muddy lake-bottom. The depth of this lake can vary 20 m over one year, a phenomenon the Amerindians attributed to a reprimand by a medicine man. It is actually due to the presence of an underwater river which has worked its way through the limestone and reappears in the Maligne River. When the glaciers melt in the summer, the underground network of rivers becomes insufficient to drain the water, which thus rises to the surface and forms a lake. The bottom of Medicine Lake consists of dolines (shallow, funnel-shaped holes) filled with gravel, through which the water flows. The short lower trail offers a good view of some of these.

Maligne Lake ★★ is one of the prettiest lakes in the Rockies. Water activities like boating, fishing and canoeing are possible here, and a short trail runs along part of the shore. The chalet on the shore houses a souvenir shop, a café-restaurant and the offices of a tour company that organizes trips to little **Spirit Island**, the ideal vantage point for admiring the surrounding mountain tops.

The road that heads north to Edmonton crosses the entire Athabasca Valley. A large herd of moose grazes in this part of the valley, and the animals can often be spotted between the intersection of the Maligne Road and the old town of Pocahontas, near Miette Hot Springs.

By continuing on the road to Hinton, you'll soon reach the hottest springs in all the parks in the Rockies, the **Miette Hot Springs**. The sulphurous water gushes forth at 57°C, and has to be cooled down to 39°C for the baths. A paved path follows the Sulphur Stream past the water purification station to the old pool, built out of logs in 1938; the trail finally ends at one of three hot springs beside the stream. Several hiking trails have been cleared in the area for those who wish to explore the back-country and admire the splendid scenery.

The ruins of the town of **Pocahontas**, abandoned in 1921, lie at the turn-off for the road to Miette Hot Springs. Bit by bit, nature has reclaimed the remains of the buildings. Pocahontas was originally the name of an Amerindian princess. When coal was discovered here in 1908, a concession was established, and the region was exploited extensively. Full of hope, The residents named the town after the famous Virginia coal basin, Pocahontas, the headquarters of the company. When the mines shut down in 1921, many buildings were dismantled and transported to other towns.

Highway 16, the Yellowhead Highway, links Jasper with Mount Robson Provincial Park, 26 km away in British Columbia. It traverses the main chains of the Rockies, affording some magnificent panoramic vistas. The road runs through Yellowhead Pass, along the Continental Divide.

To reach **Patricia** and **Pyramid** lakes, located only 7 km from Jasper, you have to take Cedar Avenue from Connaught Drive in downtown Jasper.

This road becomes Pyramid Avenue and leads to Pyramid Lake. This is an ideal spot for a walk or a picnic. You can go swimming or canoeing in the lake; motorized canoes are permitted here as well.

■ **Tour D: Kootenay and Yoho National Parks** ★★

Kootenay National Park ★★

Although less popular with the public than Banff and Jasper, Kootenay National Park nevertheless boasts beautiful, majestic landscapes, and is just as interesting to visit as its more touristy neighbours. It contains two large valleys, the humid Vermillion River Valley and the drier Kootenay River Valley; the contrast is striking. The park owes its existence to a bold attempt to lay a road between the Windermere region and the province of Alberta. In 1905, Randolphe Bruce, a businessman from the town of Invermere who became lieutenant governor of British Columbia, decided to turn a profit with the local orchards. To accomplish this end, he had to be able to transport produce to other parts of the country, hence the necessity of laying a road between isolated Windermere and the cities to the east. Bruce was so influential that construction began in 1911. A number of obstacles presented themselves, and the audacious project soon proved too costly for the province to finance alone. The 22 kilometres of road, born of a bitter struggle between man and nature, ended up leading nowhere, and the enterprise was abandoned. Refusing to admit defeat, Bruce turned to the federal government, which agreed to help in return for the property alongside the road; thus was born Kootenay National Park in 1922.

To reach Kootenay National Park from Banff, take the TransCanada to Castle Mountain Junction. Highway 93, on the left, runs the entire length of the park.

Vermillion Pass, at the entrance of Kootenay Park, marks the continental divide; from this point on, rivers in Banff Park and points east flow to the east, while those in Kootenay Park flow west and empty into the Pacific.

A few kilometres farther lies **Marble Canyon** ★★, along with a tourist office where visitors can see a short film on the history of the park. Marble Canyon is very narrow, but you'll find a lovely waterfall at the end of the trail there. Several bridges span the gorge, and the erosion caused by the torrential waters makes for some amazing scenery. Five hundred metres to the right, after the canyon, you'll find a trail leading to the famous **Paint Pots** ★★. These ochre deposits are created by subterranian springs, which cause iron oxide to rise to the surface. The Amerindians supposedly used this substance as paint. They would clean the ochre, mix it with water, and mould it into little loaves, which they would bake in the fire. They would then ground it into a fine powder and mix it with fish oil. They could use the final product to paint their bodies or decorate their teepees and clothing. According to the Amerindians, a great animal spirit and a thunder spirit lived in the streams. Sometimes they would hear a melody coming from here, other times battle songs; in their minds, this meant that the spirits were speaking to them. For these natives, the ochre was the symbol of spirits, legends and important customs, while the first whites to come here saw it as an opportunity to make money. At the beginning of the century, the ochre

234 The Rocky Mountains

Moose

Radium Hot Springs

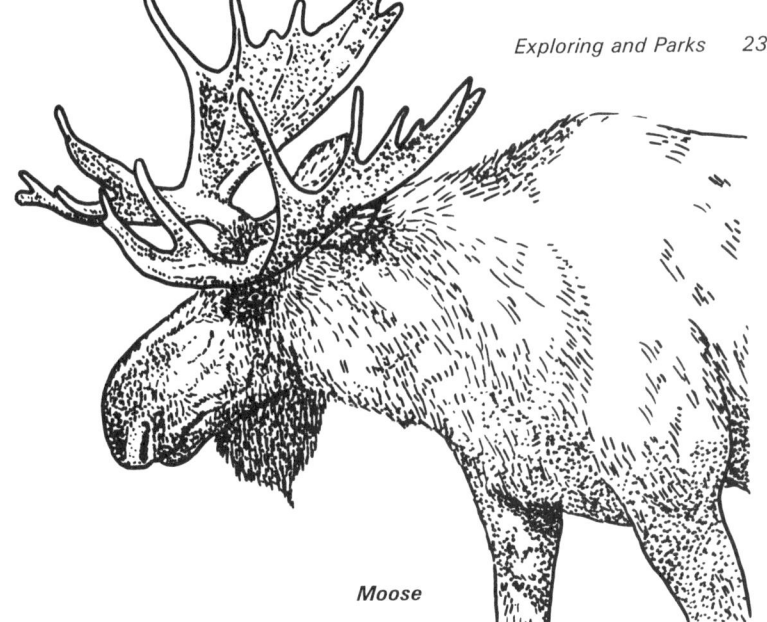

was extracted by hand and then sent to Calgary to be used as a coloring for paint. You can still see a few remnants of this era, including machines, tools and even a few piles of ochre, which were left behind when the area was made into a national park and all work here came to a halt.

One of the best places in the park for elk- and moose-watching is the **Animal Lick**, a mineral-rich salt marsh. The best time to go is early in the morning or at dusk. Viewing areas have been laid out along the road so that you can admire the scenery. The view is particularly lovely from the **Kootenay Valley Viewpoint** ★★, located at the park exit.

Upon arriving at Radium Hot Springs, right after the tunnel, you will see a parking lot on your left. You can get out of your car and take a look at the limestone cliffs, which have been stained red by iron oxide.

This little town, located at the entrance to the park, is surprisingly nondescript. You can, however, take a dip in the pool at the **Aquacourt** ★★ *(adults $3, children $2; at the entrance of Kootenay Park)*, whose warm waters are apparently renowned for their therapeutic virtues. Whether or not you believe these claims, which have yet to be backed by any medical evidence, a soak in these 45°C non-sulphurous waters is definitely very relaxing.

To continue your tour from Radium Hot Springs, head up Highway 95, which runs along the bottom of the Columbia River Valley, to the little town of Golden. The scenery along this road is quite pretty, with the foothills of the Rockies on one side and the Purcell Mountains on the other.

Yoho National Park ★★

As in all the other parks in the Rockies, you must pay an entrance fee *($8 for one day, $16 for three, $50 a year)* if you wish to stay here. This fee does not apply if you are simply passing through the park.

About 5 km from the park entrance, on the right, you'll find a trail leading to **Wapta Falls**, on the **Kicking Horse River**, thus named when adventurer James Hector suffered the painful misfortune of being kicked in the chest by his horse here in 1858. The river is a very popular place to go rafting. The falls are 30 m high, and the trail leading to them is fairly short and easy.

A little farther along, you'll find another trail leading to the **Hoodoos**, natural rock formations created by erosion. The trail, which starts at the Hoodoo Creek campground, is very steep but only 3.2 km long and offers an excellent view of the Hoodoos.

A small road offers access to the **Natural Bridge**, sculpted by the torrential waters of Kicking Horse River. There were falls here before, but the water, full of sand and gravel, acted like sandpaper, gradually wearing its way into the rock and creating the formation we see now. This spot also offers a splendid view of **Mount Stephen** (3,199 m) and **Mount Dennis** (2,541).

Hiking to **Emerald Lake** ★★ has become a tradition here in Yoho National Park. A short trail (5.2 km) takes you around the lake. You can then visit the **Hamilton Falls**. Picnic areas have been laid out near the lake. Thanks to a small canoe-rental outfit, you can also enjoy some time on the water. There is a small souvenir shop beside the boat-launching ramp.

The park's tourist office is located in Field, 33 km east of the park entrance. During summer, visitors can learn more about the Yoho Valley by taking part in any number of interpretive activities. There are 400 km of hiking trails leading through the valley deep into the heart of the region. Maps of these trails, as well as those reserved for mountain bikes, are available at the **tourist office** *(every day 9am to 6pm; on the way into town,* ☎ *604-343-5324)* in **Field**. You can also purchase a topographical map of the park for $14.79. If you plan on staying more than a day here, you must register at the Parks Canada office, located in the same place. You can climb some of the mountains, but a special permit is required to scale Mount Stephen, because fossils have been discovered in the area you must pass through to reach the top.

You can buy some provisions at the little **Siding General Store** *(every day 8am to 8pm; on Stephen Avenue, opposite the post office)* in Field.

You must be accompanied by a guide to visit the **Burgess Shale** ★★★. In 1886, a paleontologist discovered several large trilobite beds on Mount Stephen, near Field. Since the Rockies were once covered by an ocean, all of these fossils were beautifully preserved by a thick layer of marine sediment. The invaluable fossil beds on Mount Burgess, beside Mount Stephen, were pushed to the surface by the geological upheavals that led to the emergence of the Rockies. You'll need to set aside an entire day to visit the Burgess Shale, since the trip there and back is a 20 km hike. To enlist the services of a guide, contact the park offices

(☎ 604-343-6524) or **Canadian Wilderness Tours** (☎ 604-343-6470) several days in advance.

A few kilometres past Field, **Yoho Valley Road** branches off to the left, toward **Takakaw Falls**. On the way, you can stop at the **Upper Spiral Tunnel Viewpoint** ★★ to admire the advanced technology the engineers working for the railway company had to employ in order to lay a dependable line across this hilly terrain. The small road twists and turns for 13 km, leading to a wonderful scenic viewpoint, from which you can contemplate the Yoho and Kicking Horse Rivers. It comes to a dead end at the **Takakaw Falls** ★★ (254 m), which are among the highest falls in Canada.

■ **Tour E: Kananaskis Country** ★★

When Captain John Palliser led a British scientific expedition here from 1857 and 1860, the numerous lakes and rivers he found led him to christen the region Kananaskis, which means "gathering of the waters". Located 90 km from Calgary, this region covers more than 4,000 km², including the **Bow Valley**, **Bragg Creek** and **Peter Lougheed** provincial parks. Because of the its proximity to Calgary, its beautiful scenery and the huge variety of outdoor activities that can be enjoyed here, it soon became one of the most popular destinations in the province, first with Albertans and then with visitors from all over the world.

No matter what season it is, Kananaskis Country has a great deal to offer. During summer, it is a veritable paradise for outdoor enthusiasts, who can play both golf and tennis here, or go horseback riding, mountain biking, kayaking, river rafting, fishing or hiking.

Exploring and Parks 237

With its 250 km of paved roads and 460 km of marked trails, this region is easier to explore than any other in Alberta. In winter, the trails are used for cross-country skiing and snowmobiling. Visitors can also go downhill skiing at Fortress Mountain or Nakiska, speed down the toboggan runs, go skating on one of the region's many lakes or try dogsledding. Maps pertaining to these activities are available at the **Park Ranger Service** *(every day 9am to 6pm, except Fri 9am to 7pm; near Barrier Lake,* ☎ *403-673-3663)*, where you'll also find the torch from the Calgary Olympics. It was carried all over Canada for three months, and then used to light the Olympic flame in Calgary on February 13, 1988. Eight events (downhill, slalom and giant slalom) were held in the Kananaskis region, on Mount Allan, in Nakiska.

The **Nakiska ski resort** *(near Kananaskis Village,* ☎ *403-591-7777)* was designed specifically for the Olympic Games, at the same time as the Kananaskis Village hotel complex. It boasts top-notch, modern facilities and excellent runs.

Kananaskis Village consists mainly of a central square surrounded by three luxurious hotels. It was designed to be the leading resort in this region. Its construction was funded by the Alberta Heritage Savings Trust and a number of private investors. The village was officially opened on December 20, 1987. It has a post office, located beside the tourist information centre *(Mon and Tue 9am to 4pm, Wed Thu and Fri 9am to 5pm, Sat 9am to 3pm, closed Sun)*, as well as a sauna and a whirlpool *(free admission, every day 9am to 8pm)*, both of which are open to the general public. The Kananaskis Hotel houses a shopping arcade complete with souvenir and clothing shops, cafes and restaurants.

The **Kananaskis Golf Club** leaves absolutely nothing to be desired. Its fabulous 36-hole course stretches along the narrow Kananaskis River valley at the foot of **Mount Lorette** and **Mount Kidd**.

The **Fortress Mountain ski resort** (turn right at Fortress Junction, ☎ 403-229-3637 or 591-7108) is less popular than Nakiska, but nevertheless has some good runs. Furthermore, snowfall is heavy here on the continental divide, at the edge of the Peter Lougheed Provincial Park.

The tourist office in the **Peter Lougheed Provincial Park** (near the two Kananaskis Lakes) features an interactive presentation, which provides all sorts of information on local flora, fauna, geography, geology and climatic phenomena. Mount Lougheed and the park were named after two well-known members of the Lougheed family. Born in Ontario, the honorable Sir James Lougheed (1854-1925) became a very prominent lawyer in both his home province and Alberta, particularly in Calgary, where he was Canadian Pacific's legal advisor. He was named senator in 1889, led the Conservative Party from 1906 to 1921 and finally became a minister. The park owes its existence to his grandson, the honorable Peter Lougheed (1928-), who was voted Premier of Alberta on August 30, 1971. You can pick up a listing of the numerous interpretive programs offered here at the tourist office.

Right near the tourist office, you'll find the **William Watson Lodge**, a centre for the handicapped and the elderly, which offers a view of **Lower Kananaskis Lake**. At the end of the road leading to **Upper Kananaskis Lake**, turn left and drive a few kilometres farther to **Interlakes**, where you can take in a magnificent view. The **Smithdorien Trail**, a gravel road stretching 64 km, leads back to Canmore. Although parts of it have been deeply rutted by the rain and snow, the road is wide and you'll have it almost all to yourself. There are no service stations along the way. This is a beautiful area, which seems completely cut off from the rest of the world. The road comes to an end at the Grassi Falls in Canmore.

Outdoor Activities

The Canadian Rockies, which cover an area of over 22,000 km^2, are a paradise for anyone who appreciates mountain landscapes and clean air, enjoys having lots of space to roam about and takes pleasure in outdoor activities like hiking, mountain climbing, horseback riding, canoeing, river rafting, golf and cross-country or downhill skiing. Because this region has been set aside as a series of national parks, it has not been marred by the unbridled construction of ski resorts and chalets, which do not always blend harmoniously with the landscape. Consequently, although the Rockies welcome six million visitors annually, you don't have to go far off the beaten track to enjoy some quiet moments that will remain with you forever.

Hiking

Hiking is probably the most popular outdoor activity in the region's national parks, which are crisscrossed by trails

A few geological terms used to describe mountain terrain

Suspended valley: A valley whose floor is higher than that of the valley towards which it leads.

Glacial cirque: a crescent-shaped basin formed in a mountainous region by the erosive action of ice. When two cirques meet they form a ridge.

Crevasse: a deep crack or fissure in the top layer of ice of a glacier. "Transversal crevasses" fracture the ice from one side to the other and are commonly seen when the glacier covers a steep uphill section of the mountain, "marginal crevasses" are found on the edge of glaciers and result from friction with the mountainside, and finally "longitudinal crevasses" which are found at the extremities of the glacier.

Sérac: serie of crevasses where the glacier overhangs a cliff or on a steep slope. As the glacier continues to advance, the crevasses at the base of the cliff will close up while others will open farther up.

Ogive: You'll notice on a glacier that the clolour is not uniform, but actually contains stripes of white and grey. The lighter and paler areas are called ogives and result from the crevasses of a sérac which when they open in summer gather dust and silt, and when they open in winter collect snow and air pockets.

Moraine: glacial deposits (mix of silt, sand, gravel and rock debris carried by a glacier). As the glacier and retreats it deposits this mass of rocky debris at its sides, called "lateral moraines" when it comes from the neighbouring faces or a "frontal moraine" at the end of the glaicer.

Névé or firn: mass of hardened, porous snow that attaches to the glacier.

Glacial trough: A U-shaped valley carved out by a glacier.

Icecap: A convex-shaped thick mass of ice that covers an area of land. Several glaciers can branch off from one icecap, as is the case in the Columbia icefields.

Alpine glacier: smaller glaciers located in high-altitude valleys that resemble long tongues of ice and do not originate from an icecap. The Angel Glacier on Mount Edith Cavell is a good example.

Glacial nest: smaller glaciers that form on rocky cliffs and appear suspended.

suitable for everyone from novices to experts. Environment Canada's park service puts out free brochures on some of the wonderful hiking trips to be enjoyed in the Rockies; these are available at the tourist information offices in Banff, Lake Louise and Jasper. You can pick up a map of the hiking trails in Kootenay National Park for $1 at the Parks Canada offices located at each entrance of the park. Keep in mind that if you plan on spending several days in the heart of one of these parks, you must register with Parks Canada, specifying your itinerary and the length of your stay.

■ Respect the mountain!

As a hiker, it is important to realize your role in preserving and respecting the fragility of the ecosystem, and to comprehend your impact on your surroundings. Here are a few guidelines:

First of all, stay on the trails even if they are covered in snow or mud in order to protect the ground vegetation and avoid the widening of the trail.

Unless you're heading off on a long trek, wear lightweight hiking boots, they do less damage to the vegetation.

When in a group in alpine regions, spread out and walk on rocks as much as possible to avoid damaging the vegetation.

It is just as important to protect waterways, bodies of water and the ground water when in mountainous regions. When digging backcountry latrines, place them at least 30 m from all water sources, and cover everything (paper included) with earth.

Never clean yourself in lakes or streams.

At campsites dispose of waste water only in designated areas.

The water in mountain regions is not always potable and therefore should be boiled for at least 10 min before drinking it.

Never leave any garbage behind. Bags for this are provided at Parks Canada offices.

Certain types of flowers are endangered, so do not pick anything.

Leave everything as you find it, that way those that follow can enjoy the beauties of nature as you did.

For safety reasons, always keep your dog on a leash, or leave it at home. Dogs that roam free have a tendency to wander off and chase after wild animals. They have even been known to chase down a bear and then take refuge with their master.

Finally if you are exploring the Rockies on horseback, remember that only trails set aside for these animals can be followed.

■ Climate

The sun in the mountains

The cool winds that characterize the Rockies might make you forget the dangers of the sun, which in mountain regions are very real. Be sure to prepare yourself with a good sunscreen, a hat and sunglasses. When hiking in the mountains the combination of the physical exertion, the sun and the changing weather conditions can often lead to hypothermia, which can ultimately lead to death. The best way to avoid these problems is to dress properly.

Clothing

An excursion in the mountains requires careful planning. Whether you plan on visiting the Rockies in winter or summer, it is important to always bring along warm and comfortable clothing.

During the winter, do not forget to bring along warm long underwear that allows your skin to breathe, natural wool or synchilla sweaters, a few good pairs of socks, a jacket and pants that break the wind, gloves, a scarf and a hat.

If you plan on doing any cross-country skiing, remember that it is always better to wear layers instead of one heavy jacket which will prove too warm when you make the least exertion, but not warm enough when you stop to rest. A small backpack is a good idea to carry some food, an extra sweater and a pair of socks in case your feet get wet. Never stop to rest in wet clothes, bring along a change of clothes instead.

The same precautions should be taken in the summer. Temperatures are much lower at higher altitudes, and the smallest wind can significantly lower temperatures. Furthermore, climactic changes occur quickly in the mountains. Be sure to dress properly when heading out on an excursion, a good sweater and windbreaker are a good idea, even in summer. An ear warmer and gloves might also come in handy. Rain is common, so bring along a water resistant jacket. Finally, with proper footwear including a good pair of socks and a solid pair of hiking boots, you'll be ready to tackle the most spectacular trails of the region.

■ Tour A: Banff National Park

Banff

The relatively easy **Cave and Basin Trail** (6.8 km) leads to the historic site of the same name, offering some lovely views of the Bow River along the way. It starts at the Banff Centre, on St. Julian Road. Follow the Bow River trail to the falls and walk alongside the water. Go over the Banff Avenue bridge and turn right on Cave Avenue. The trail leads to the parking lot of the Cave and Basin hot springs. Return the way you came.

The continuation of the Cave and Basin trail, the **Sundance Canyon Trail** (13.6 km), is even easier. Go past the Cave and Basin building and head back down toward the Bow River. The well-marked trail runs alongside Sundance Creek, climbing up to the canyon and then making a loop, giving you a chance to see a little more of the landscape.

The **Sulphur Mountain Trail** is a little more difficult than the two mentioned above because it involves a significant change in altitude. It starts near the base station of the Sulphur Mountain Gondola, then winds its way up the mountain, offering a magnificent panoramic view of the Bow River valley.

The trail leading to the **Vermilion Lakes** starts at the Banff Centre, although there are all sorts of other ways to get there. Follow the Tunnel Mountain Trail, which leads to the Bow River falls. Take Buffalo Street, then, a little farther along on the left, the trail that runs along the river. Cross the Banff Avenue bridge, then walk along the banks of the Bow River. You will come to the canoe rental service on Bow Avenue. The first of the three Vermilion Lakes lies just over the railroad tracks. Continue your tour along Vermilion Lakes Drive. The area around these swampy lakes is wonderful for bird-watching. This hike is a bit long, but very easy. You can also reach the Vermilion Lakes by canoe, starting from the Bow River.

If you would like to take part in a longer excursion organized by professionals, you can contact one of the following outfits: **White Mountain Adventures** *(P.O. Box 2294, Canmore, Alberta, TOL 0M0, ☎ 403-678-4099)* and **Time Travel's Nature Photography & Hiking Excursions** *(☎ 403-678-3336)*. Reservations required.

Lake Louise

To reach **Lake Agnes and the Big Beehives**, start out at the Chateau Lake Louise and walk along the lakeside promenade. On the right, you will see a little trail leading up the mountain through the forest. This will take you to Mirror Lake (2.7 km) and Agnes Lake (3.6 km). When you get to Agnes Lake, which lies 365 m higher than Lake Louise, you will find a small cafe set up inside a cabin, where you can regain your strength over a cup of tea or hot chocolate before continuing your ascent to the Big Beehives. The trail runs alongside little Agnes Lake then climbs steeply for 140 m, to the Little Beehives. The Big Beehives lie another 30 m uphill. Your efforts will be richly rewarded by a superb view of Lake Louise and its valley.

You can also set out on an excursion to the **Plain of the Six Glaciers** from the Chateau Lake Louise. Walk along the lakeside promenade, and instead of taking the trail that branches off toward Agnes Lake, keep following the waterfront. The trail runs near some moraines (masses of rocks deposited by glaciers), then comes to an end 5.5 km from the starting point near a small cabin, where you can have a light meal or a hot drink. From there, you can climb 1.3 km farther to the magnificent viewpoint at Abbot Pass and Death Trap.

Immediately to the left after the parking lot at Moraine Lake, is a trail leading to the **Consolation Lakes**. This trail, which is only 3 km long and requires little effort, affords some magnificent panoramic views of the Temple Mountains and the Ten Peaks. Visitors are advised to wear a good pair of walking shoes for this outing, since the trail is scattered with moraines and large rocks.

For a view of Moraine Lake and the Ten Peaks, which are depicted on the old Canadian $20 bill, take the **Moraine Lakeshore Trail**, a short path leading all the way to the far end of the lake.

■ Tour C: Jasper National Park

Mount Edith Cavell

The **Path of the Glacier Trail** (1.5 km) starts near the parking lot at Mount Edith Cavell and leads to a small lake formed by the run-off from the glacier. You can admire the glacier suspended above you and ponder on the dramatic impact the glaciers have had on the vegetation and topography of these mountain valleys.

To reach the **Cavell Meadow Trail and Peak** from the parking lot at Mount Edith Cavell, walk up the trail on the left, which will take you opposite the Angel Glacier. You won't have to look hard to spot some marmots and pikas along the way. Upon reaching the forest, the trail climbs steeply up to a clear-cut zone. You can already see the Angel Glacier from here; in fact, it appears to be very close. You can keep going to Cavell Meadow Park, since the trail winds its way farther and farther up. The last 500 m are the most demanding, but your efforts will be richly rewarded by a magnificent view.

Maligne Lake

The **Maligne Lake Trail** is a short lakeside trail, which starts at the second parking lot near the chalet, where you can purchase drinks and souvenirs. Only 3.2 km long and easy enough to be enjoyed by the most inexperienced hiker, it leads to the Schäffer Viewpoint, which was named after Mary Schäffer, the first woman to explore the valley. After the viewpoint, the trail leads into the forest, where you'll find "potholes" created by the glaciers, then heads back to the chalet.

The trail to **Mona and Lorraine Lakes** is also short, relatively easy and extremely pleasant. It leads through a forest of lodgepole pines to the two charming little lakes.

Patricia Lake

To reach the trail that skirts round **Patricia Lake**, take the road to Pyramid Lake as far as the parking lot for the stables. This short (4.8 km), easy hike makes for a charming excursion. The trail starts out by climbing gently through the forest, then heads back down to the south shore of the lake. It then winds its way down to a small valley frequented by deer, moose and beavers, as well as a large number of birds. It is best to come here in the early morning or late afternoon, when the temperature is cool and the animals come out of the forest to feed in the fields and quench their thirst at the watering holes. Trivia buffs might be interested to know that Patricia Lake was named after the daughter of the Duke of Connaught, Canada's Governor General from 1911 to 1914.

Mountain Biking

Mountain bikes are permitted on certain trails. Always keep in mind that there might be people or bears around each bend. We also recommend limiting your speed on the downhill portions of each trail.

■ **Tour A: Banff National Park**

You won't have any trouble renting a bicycle in Banff, since you can do so at a number of hotels. Just the same, here are a few places you can try: **Mountain Bike Rental** *(from $4 an hour or $16 a day; every day 8am to 8pm; Ptarmigan Inn, 339 Banff Avenue,* ☎ *403-762-8177)*; **Rocky Mountain Worldwide Cycle Tour** *($50;* ☎ *403-678-6770)*, which organizes mountain bike trips in the Banff area (each package includes a bicycle, a helmet, transportation to the point of departure, refreshments and the services of a guide); and **Rocky Mountain Scuba** *(inns of Banff, 600 Banff Avenue,* ☎ *403-762-5326)*, which rents out bicycles and diving gear.

Tour C: Jasper National Park

The Jasper area is crisscrossed by bike trails.

A 9 km trail leads from the parking lot opposite the Jasper Aquatic Centre to **Mina Lake and Riley Lake**. The pitch is fairly steep until you reach the firebreak road leading to Cabin Lake. Cross this road and continue to Mina Lake. Three and a half kilometres farther along, another trail branches off toward Riley Lake. To return to Jasper, take Pyramid Lake Road.

The **Saturday Night Lake Loop** starts at the Cabin Creek West parking lot and climbs gently for 24.6 km, offering a view of the Miette and Athabasca Valleys. After Caledonia Lake, it winds through the forest to the High Lakes, where the pitch becomes steeper. It then leads to Saturday Night Lake and Cabin Lake. From there, follow the firebreak road to Pyramid Lake Road, which will take you back to Jasper.

The **Athabasca River Trail** (25 km) starts at the Old Fort Point parking lot, near the Jasper Park Lodge. For the first 10 km of the trail, after the lodge's golf course, you will have to climb some fairly steep slopes, especially as you approach the Maligne Canyon. Bicycles are forbidden between the first and fifth bridges of the canyon trail, so you have to take Maligne Road for this part of the trip. After the fifth bridge, turn left and ride alongside the Athabasca River on trail no.7. If you don't want to go back the way you came, take Highway 16.

Like the Athabasca River Trail, the **Valley of the Five Lakes Trail** and the **Wabasso Lake Trail** both start at the Old Fort Point parking lot. Trails no. 1, 1A and 9 begin here. The trip, which covers 11.2 km, is quite easy up until the first lake in the valley, although a few spots are a bit rocky. At the first lake, the trail splits in two; take the path on the left, since it offers the best view of the lakes. The two trails merge into one again near a pond at the turn-off for Wabasso Lake. Pick up Highway 93, unless you want to go to Wabasso Lake, in which case you have to take trail no. 9 (19.3 km), to the left of the pond. Head back to Jasper on the Icefields Parkway.

You have to drive to the parking lot at Celestine Lake, which marks the beginning of the trail (48 km). A gravel road leads to the **Snake Indian Falls**, 22 km away. About 1 km farther, the

---

Mountain Bike Rentals

Freewheel Cycle *(611 Patricia Street, Jasper, ☎ 403-852-3898)* rents out good mountain bikes. You can also have repairs done here.

At **On-Line Sport & Tackle** *($14 per day; 600 Patricia Street, Jasper, ☎ 403-852-3630)*, you'll find bikes, helmets and maps of bike paths.

To get to **Beyond Bikes** *(4 Cedar Avenue, Jasper, ☎ 403-852-5982)*, continue past the Jasper tourist office on Connaught Drive. Right after the Astoria Hotel, turn left on Cedar Avenue. The bike rental shop will be on your left.

road turns into a small trail, which will take you to Rock Lake.

Motorcycling

■ **Tour C: Jasper National Park**

Some people dream about touring the Rockies by motorcycle. **SMV Motorcycle Tours & Rentals** *(site 53, Industrial Park, P.O. Box 2404, Jasper, TOE 1E0,* ☎ *403-852-5752)* rents out a variety of bikes, ranging from small-engined vehicles (50 ccs) to the powerful Suzuki GS 750EZ and BMW K 75 S. Rates range from $10 to $50 an hour.

Fishing

Fishing permits are required in all Canadian national parks. You can obtain one at any of the parks' administrative or tourist information offices, from park rangers and at some boat rental outfits. Visitors under the age of 16 do not need a permit if they are accompanied by a permit-holder. The waters are teeming with rainbow and brown trout, char and pike. There are a number of rules to follow. You can obtain a copy of the regulations concerning sports fishing in the region's national parks through any Parks Canada office. Fishing is permitted year-round in the Bow River, but is only legal during very specific periods on some lakes. For more information on these dates, contact Parks Canada.

■ **Tour A: Banff National Park**

Banff Fishing Unlimited *(P.O. Box 216, Canmore, TOL 0M0,* ☎ *403-762-4936,* ⇄ *678-8895)* rents out equipment and provides professional guides, who can direct you to the best spots. **Monod Sports** *(P.O. Box 310, Banff, TOL 0C0,* ☎ *403-762-4571,* ⇄ *762-3565)*, which also rents out equipment and provides guides, specializes in fly fishing. **Minnewanka Tour** *(every day 9am to 9pm; on the landing stage at the entrance to Minewanka Lake; P.O. Box 2189, Banff, TOL 0C0,* ☎ *403-762-3473)*. **Mountain Fly Fishers** *(P.O. Box 2414, Canmore, TOL 0M0,* ☎ *403-678-9522 or 1-800-450-9664,* ⇄ *678-2183)* arranges fly fishing trips that last several days. The prices vary according to the length of the trip.

■ **Tour C: Jasper National Park**

Maligne Tours *(from $135 per person; 626 Connaught Drive, Jasper,* ☎ *403-852-3370)* offers guided fishing trips, with meals and equipment included. Reservations required.

On-Line Sport & Tackle *($99 for half a day, $129 for a full day; 600 Patricia Street, Jasper,* ☎ *403-852-3630,* ⇄ *852-4245)* also arranges guided fishing trips.

Scuba Diving

Extra caution is required when scuba diving in the Rockies, since the decompression scales are different at high altitudes. For this reason, don't venture into the lakes here unless you are accompanied by a professional or have taken the time to learn about diving under these conditions.

Tour A: Banff National Park

Rocky Mountain Scuba *(Inns of Banff, 600 Banff Avenue,* ☎ *403-762-5326)* can provide you with information and advice on diving at high altitudes and arranges group dives. Reservations required.

River Rafting

The rivers running through the Rockies have a lot to offer thrill-seekers. Whether it's your first time out or you already have some rafting experience, you'll find all sorts of interesting challenges here.

The most popular places to go rafting in the Banff area are **Kicking Horse River** and **Lower Canyon**. A few words of advice: wear a bathing suit and closed running shoes that you don't mind getting wet, dress very warmly (heavy wool and a windbreaker) and bring along a towel and a change of clothes for the end of the day.

Tours A and D: Banff, Kootenay and Yoho National Parks

Hydra River Guides has two branches in Banff, **Peak Experience** *(209 Bear Street, Banff,* ☎ *403-762-4554)* and **Shades on Caribou** *(Sundance Mall, Banff,* ☎ *403-762-8991)*, and another in Canmore, **Spoke Nedge** *(801 8th Street, Canmore,* ☎ *403-678-2838)*. The prices vary according to the level of difficulty of the trip. For example, the cost of a day of rafting is $65 (taxes and insurance included) on Kicking Horse River and only $45 in Lower Canyon. The latter option is only open to people with experience running rapids.

Wild Water Adventures *(Lake Louise and Banff,* ☎ *403-522-2211)* offers full- and half-day packages at a cost of $89 and $59 respectively (taxes not included).

Rocky Mountain Raft Tours *(P.O. Box 1771, Banff,* ☎ *403-762-3632)* offers tours of the major waterways in the region.

The **Glacier Raft Company** *($79 per day, $49 for half a day; Banff, Alberta,* ☎ *403-762-4347 and Golden, BC,* ☎ *604-344-6521)* organizes trips down Kicking Horse River. There is a special rate *($99, tax included)* for the **Kicking Horse Challenge**, which is slightly wilder ride than the others.

Wet'n'Wild Adventure *($45 and up; Golden, BC,* ☎ *604-344-6546, ⇄ 344-7650)* offers trips from Golden, Radium Hot Springs, Lake Louise and Banff. A half-day on Kicking Horse River will cost you about $45. Those wishing to spend several days on the water can take advantage of some interesting package deals ranging in price from $125 to $150 per person. A minimum number of passengers is required, however.

The **Alpine Rafting Company** *($120-155 plus tax; P.O. Box 1409, Golden, BC, V0A 1H0,* ☎ *604-344-5016 or 1-800-663-7080)* has a variety of packages for novice and experienced rafters. One thing that sets this company apart is that it offers trips down the Illecillewaet, in Mount Revelstoke Park, as well as down Kicking Horse River. The Alpine Rafting Company also has a counter in the lobby of the Chateau Lake Louise.

The **Kootenay River Runners** *($49-289; P.O. Box 81, Edgewater, BC, V0A 1E0,* ☎ *604-347-9210 or 1-800-599-4399)* also have a branch in Banff (☎ 403-762-5385O), at the corner of Caribou and Bear Streets.

Rocky Mountain Rafting *($49 and up; P.O. Box 1767, Golden, BC, V0A 1H0, ☎ 604-344-6979 or 1-800-808-RAFT)*, located right beside the Shell station, arranges trips down Kicking Horse River.

■ **Tour C: Jasper National Park**

Whitewater Rafting *(P.O. Box 362, Jasper, T0E 1E0, ☎ 403-852-RAFT or 1-800-557-RAFT)* has a counter in the **Jasper Park Lodge** *(☎ 403-852-3301)*, and another at the **Avalanche Esso** *(702 Connaught Drive, ☎ 403-852-4FUN)* gas station. This company can organizes trips down the Athabasca, Maligne and Sunwapta Rivers.

Maligne River Adventures *($50 and up; 626 Connaught Drive, P.O. Box 280, Jasper, T0E 1E0, ☎ 403-852-3370, ⇄ 852-3405)* will take you on an interesting three-day excursion down the Kakwa River for $450. Some experience is required, since these are class IV rapids, and are thus rather difficult to negotiate.

Two outfits offer trips for novices and children who would like to try rafting on less swift-moving rapids: **Jasper Raft Tours** *(children $15.50, adults $31; P.O. Box 398, Jasper, T0E 1E0, ☎ 403-852-3613, ⇄ 852-5949)* and **Mount Robson Adventure Holidays** *($15 and up for children, $35 and up for adults; P.O. Box 687, Valemount, BC, Mount Robson Provincial Park, V0E 2Z0, ☎ 604-566-4268, ⇄ 566-4351)*, which also has a branch in Jasper *(604 Connaught Drive)*.

Horseback Riding

Horseback riding is a pleasant way to explore the more remote parts of the parks in the Rockies. A number of trails have been set aside for riders and their mounts. If you would like to ride your own horse, you must inform the agents at one of the Parks Canada offices and obtain a map of the bridle paths.

■ **Tour A: Banff National Park**

Warner Guiding and Outfitting *(P.O. Box 2280, Banff, T0L 0C0, ☎ 403-762-4551, ⇄ 762-8130)* offers short, easy rides of one, two or four hours, as well as real expeditions. Three days of riding in Mystic Valley will cost you about $360; a six-day wildlife interpretation trip, $840; and six days in Mount Assiniboine Park, $1,040. In all, there are over fifteen excursions to choose from, with something for everyone, whether you're a camping buff or prefer staying in lodges. All of these outings, of course, are led by professional guides, who can tell you anything you might like to know about the flora, fauna and geological characteristics of the areas you will be riding through. Warner Guiding and Outfitting also organizes expeditions in collaboration with Parks Canada.

The **Brewster Lake Louise Stables** *($20 an hour, $80 per day; P.O. Box 964, Department L, Banff, T0L 0C0, ☎ 403-762-5454 or 522-3511, ⇄ 762-3953)* are located right beside the Chateau Lake Louise.

Tour C: Jasper National Park

Maligne Tours *($55 per person; 626 Connaught Drive, Jasper, T0E 1E0, ☎ 403-852-3370, or Jasper Park Lodge, ☎ 403-852-4779)* organizes short rides to the top of the Bald Hills every morning and afternoon (10am and 2pm). These outings give visitors a chance to admire a variety of magnificent landscapes and take in a splendid view of the glaciers.

Pyramid Stables *(near Patricia Lake, about 6 km from Pyramid Lake, ☎ 403-852-3562)* arranges short pony rides for little children and longer outings for adults.

Sunrider Stables *(from $20; Jasper Park Lodge, Jasper, T0E 1E0, ☎ 403-852-4215 or 852-3301 ext. 6189)*.

Tour D: Kootenay and Yoho National Parks

Longhorn Stables *($18 an hour, $34 for two hours, $95 per day; P.O. Box 387, Radium Hot Springs, BC, V0A 1M0, ☎ 604-347-9755 or 347-6453)* is located right at the edge of Radium, on the way to Golden.

Skydiving

This activity is forbidden in some of the national parks in the Rockies. The Parks Canada offices in each park can provide you with more information on this sport. Skydiving is permitted in Kananaskis Country. For further details, contact **Glenn Derouin** *(P.O. Box 2662, Canmore, AB, T0L 0M0, ☎ 403-678-4973, ⇄ 678-4973)*.

Golf

Tour A: Banff National Park

Canmore Golf & Curling Club *($21.50 for 9 holes, $34 for 18; ☎ 403-678-5959)*. Equipment can be rented on the premises.

The **Banff Springs Hotel** *(☎ 403-762-2211)* has a magnificent 18-hole course set in enchantingly beautiful surroundings.

Tour C: Jasper National Park

There is a lovely golf course near the **Jasper Park Lodge**. Reservations can be made at the front desk of the lodge or through the **Sawridge Hotel** *(☎ 403-422-7547 or 1-800-661-6427)*.

Tour D: Kootenay and Yoho National Parks

The Columbia River Valley is a veritable paradise for golfers, with more courses than you can count. We have only indicated a few below; for a more exhaustive list, pick up the golfing brochure at the tourist office in Radium Hot Springs.

The magnificent golf course at the **Golden Golf & Country Club** *(from $19 for 9 holes, $32 for 18 holes; P.O. Box 1615, Golden, BC, V0A 1H0, ☎ 604-344-2700, ⇄ 344-2922)* is surrounded by grandiose landscapes. It lies alongside the TransCanada Highway, near the Columbia River, between the Rockies and Purcell Mountains.

The nine-hole **Way-Lyn Ranch Golf Course** *(Highway 95A, S.S.3, site 19-4, Cranbrook, BC, V1C 6H3, ☎ 604-*

427-2825) is located between the towns of Cranrook and Kimberley.

Trickle Creek *($26 for 9 holes, $37 for 18; P.O. Box 190, Kimberley, BC, V1A 2Y6, ☎ 604-427-5171)* is an 18-hole golf course. Reservations recommended.

The golf course at the **Radium Hot Springs Resort** *(P.O. Box 310, Radium Hot Springs, BC, V0A 1M0, ☎ 604-347-9311, ⇄ 347-9588)* is only open to guests of the hotel.

The **Springs at Radium** *(P.O. Box 430, Radium Hot Springs, BC, V0A 1M0, ☎ 604-347-6444 or 1-800-667-6444, ⇄ 347-9707)* is one of the loveliest golf courses in British Columbia.

■ **Downhill Skiing**

It is impossible to look at the Rockies without imagining the hours of pleasure you'll have tearing down the endless slopes. Able to satisfy the most demanding skiers, the resorts here offer a variety of beautifully maintained trails covering all levels of difficulty and excellent skiing conditions. The ski season generally starts around October and can continue into May.

■ **Tour A: Banff National Park**

Mystic Ridge and Mount Norquay *(adults $30 per day, children $13; on Norquay Road, P.O. Box 1258, Banff, AB, T0L 0C0, ☎ 403-762-4421)* was one of the first ski resorts in North America. It takes just 10 minutes to drive here from downtown Banff. For skiing conditions, call ☎ 403-221-8259. The resort has both a ski school and a rental shop.

Sunshine Village *(adults $38 per day, students $33, children $10; 16 km west of Banff, P.O. Box 1510, Banff, AB, T0L C0, ☎ 403-762-6500)* is a beautiful ski resort located at an altitude of 2,700 m on the continental divide between the provinces of Alberta and British Columbia. This resort has the advantage of being located higher than the tree line and thus gets lots of sun. For skiing conditions, dial ☎ 403-227-SNOW). Ski rentals available.

Lake Louise *(adults $39.50 per day, students $35, children $10; P.O. Box 5, Lake Louise, AB, T0L 1E0, ☎ 403-522-3555)* has the largest ski resort in Canada, covering four mountainsides and offering skiers over 50 different runs. Both downhill and cross-country equipment are available for rent here. For skiing conditions, call ☎ 403-256-8473.

■ **Tour C: Jasper National Park**

Marmot Basin *(adults $32 plus tax per day, students $26, children $13; take Highway 93 toward Banff, then turn right to get to the resort; P.O. Box 1300, Jasper, AB, T0E 1E0, ☎ 403-852-3816, or ☎ 488-5909 for skiing conditions)* is located about 20 min by car from downtown Jasper. Ski rentals available.

■ **Tour D: Kootenay and Yoho National Parks**

The **Kimberley Ski Resort** *(adults $33 per day, students $26, children $15; P.O. Box 40, Kimberley, BC, V1A 2Y5, ☎ 604-427-4881 or 1-800-667-0871)* is the only real attraction in Kimberley, an amazing little Bavarian village. It has some decent trails that are perfect for family skiing.

Whitetooth *(adults $25 per day, children under 12 $11; P.O. Box 1925, Golden, BC, V0A 1H0,* ☎ *604-344-6114)* is relatively small, but getting bigger every year. It has a few good, well-maintained runs.

■ **Tour E: Kananaskis Country**

Nakiska *(adults $33 plus tax per day, students $27, children $12; P.O. Box 1988, Kananaskis Village, AB, T0L 2H0,* ☎ *403-591-7777, or* ☎ *235-9191 for skiing conditions)* hosted the men's and women's downhill, slalom and combination events during the 1988 Winter Olympics. Built specifically for that purpose, along with Kananaskis Village, this resort boasts an excellent modern infrastructure and top-notch trails. Downhill and cross-country equipment are both available for rent here.

Fortress Mountain *(adults $29 plus tax per day, students $22; children $12; take Highway 40 past Kananaskis Village and turn right at Fortress Junction; suite 505, 1550 8th Street S.W., Calgary, AB, T2R 1K1,* ☎ *403-229-3637 or 591-7108;* ☎ *245-4909 for skiing conditions)*, located on the continental divide, at the edge of **Peter Lougheed Provincial Park**, is less popular than Nakiska but nevertheless has some very interesting runs.

Cross-country Skiing

There are countless cross-country trails in the parks of the Rockies, whose tourist information offices distribute maps of the major trails around the cities of Banff and Jasper and the village of Lake Louise. The **Canmore Nordic Centre** *(P.O. Box 1979, Canmore, AB, T0L 0M0;* ☎ *403-678-5508)*, which hosted the cross-country events of the 1988 Winter Olympics, deserves a special mention for its magnificent network of trails.

■ **Heliskiing**

Heliskiing is an extraordinary experience for top-notch skiers longing for untouched stretches of powder snow. You'll be stricken by the calmness and immensity of your surroundings as you take in panoramic views that could once be enjoyed only by mountainclimbers. Prices for this type of excursion vary greatly, depending on where the helicopter takes you. We therefore recommend shopping around a bit.

Assiniboine Heli Tours *(P.O. Box 2430, Canmore, AB, T0L 0M0,* ☎ *403-678-5459,* ⇄ *678-5600)* organizes group outings to the peaks around Banff, Lake Louise and Whistler, as well as the Purcell, Selkirk and Chilcotin Mountains.

Canadian Helicopters *(P.O. Box 2309, Canmore, AB, T0L 0M0,* ☎ *403-678-2207)* offers heliskiing excursions in a variety of price ranges, as well as helicopter tours for visitors who simply want to take in the view.

Canmore Helicopters *(from $75; P.O. Box 2069, Canmore, AB, T0L 0M0,* ☎ *403-678-4802,* ⇄ *678-2176)* offers tours year-round for visitors wishing to explore the highest peaks in the national parks in the Rockies. During winter, experienced guides will help you discover the beauties of the most majestic snowy peaks in the Rockies.

Canadian Mountain Holidays *(P.O. Box 1660, Banff, AB, T0L 0C0,* ☎ *1-800-*

661-0252) has been in operation for 30 years, and the quality of the service leaves nothing to be desired. You can choose from a wide variety of excursions ranging from one to several days in length. Professional guides escort visitors to Mount Revelstoke, Valemount, the Monashees and the Cariboos.

Selkirk Tangiers Helicopter Skiing *(Jan to mid-Apr; P.O. Box 1409, Golden, BC, V0A 1H0,* ☎ *1-800-663-7080, or 403-762-5627 for Alberta, or 604-344-5016 for British Columbia)* offers day- and week-long excursions in the Selkirk and Monashee Mountains.

R.K. Heli-ski Panorama *(Dec to Apr; reservation counters in the Banff Spring Hotel and the Chateau Lake Louise;* ☎ *604-342-3889 or 1-800-661-6060, ⇄ 604-342-3466)* arranges guided excursions for intermediate and advanced skiers on the Purcell Mountains in British Columbia.

Mountain Climbing

■ **Tour A: Banff National Park**

Professional guides from the **Canadian School of Mountaineering (CSM)** *(629 10th Street, P.O. Box 723, Canmore, AB, T0L 0M0,* ☎ *403-678-4134)* can give you lessons in mountain and glacier climbing, as well as telemark skiing.

■ **Tour C: Jasper National Park**

Peter Amann of the **Mountain Guiding and Schools** *(from $120 for 2 days; P.O. Box 1495, Jasper, AB, T0E 1E0,* ☎ *403-852-3237)* offers mountaineering lessons for novices and experienced climbers alike.

Dogsledding

■ **Tour A: Banff National Park**

Kingmik Expeditions Dog Sled Tours *(P.O. Box 1679, Canmore, AB, T0L 0M0,* ☎ *403-678-4080 or 678-2880)* has a variety of packages ranging from half-hour lessons to five-day expeditions.

Snowy Owl Sled Dog Kennel & Tours *(P.O. Box 1232, Canmore, AB, T0L 0M0,* ☎ *403-678-4369, ⇄ 678-6702)* specializes in dogsledding and ice-fishing trips.

Snowmobiling

■ **Tour A: Banff National Park**

The guides at **Challenge Enterprises Snowmobile Tours** *(P.O. Box 2008, Canmore, AB, T0L 0M0,* ☎ *403-678-2628, ⇄ 679-2183)* are all instructors. Some tours last several days and offer a chance to explore some of the region's back country. The nights are spent in mountain lodges.

■ **Tour D: Kootenay and Yoho National Parks**

The **Golden Snowmobile Club** *(P.O. Box 167, Golden, BC, V0A 1H0; Chamber of Commerce,* ☎ *604-344-7125)* arranges outings in the Golden area. You will be supplied with a map of the various trails.

Accommodations

■ Tour A: Banff National Park

Banff

A list of private homes that receive paying guests is provided at the tourist information office located at 224 Banff Avenue. You may obtain this list by writing to the following address:

Banff-Lake Louise Tourist Office
P.O. Box 1298
Banff, AB
T0L 0C0
☎ (403) 762-8421 or 762-0270
⇄ (403) 762-8163

It is impossible to reserve a campsite in advance in the park, which has a policy of first come, first served, unless you are leading a fairly large group, in which case, you should contact the Parks Canada offices in Banff.

Campsites generally cost between $13 and $16, according to the location and the facilities at the site. We advise you to arrive early to choose your spot. In the high season, the Banff campgrounds are literally overrun with hordes of tourists. It is forbidden to pitch your tent outside the area set aside for this purpose. Camping at unauthorized sites is strictly prohibited, for reasons of safety and also to preserve the natural environment of the park.

Tunnel Mountain Trailer Campground *(electricity, showers, toilets, ☎; on Tunnel Mountain Road, near the Banff Youth Hostel)* has more than 300 spaces set up exclusively for trailers.

Tunnel Mountain 1 and 2 *(toilets, showers, ☎; on Tunnel Mountain Road near the Banff Youth Hostel)* has about 840 spaces for trailers and for tents.

The two **Two Jack Lake Campgrounds** *(toilets, ☎; take the road going to Lake Minnewanka, then head toward Two Jack Lake)* are located on either side of the road that runs alongside Two Jack Lake. There are showers at the campground near the water. The other campground, deeper in the forest, offers a more basic level of comfort. It is easier to find spaces at these two campgrounds than at those in Banff.

Set in the forest, the **Johnston Canyon Campground** *(toilets, showers, ☎; on Highway 1A, toward Lake Louise, a little before the Castle Mountain crossroads)* is much less busy than the other campgrounds. Set up for trailers and tents, it offers about 100 places.

Banff International Youth Hostel *($17 per person; on Tunnel Mountain Road, Box 1358, Banff, AB, T0L 0C0, ☎ 403-762-4122 or 1-800-363-0096, in Calgary ☎ 237-8282)* remains the cheapest solution, but it is often full. It is essential to reserve well in advance or else to arrive early. This friendly youth hostel is only about 20 minutes' walk from the centre of town. It offers a warm welcome, and the desk staff will be pleased to help you organize river rafting and other outdoor activities.

YWCA *($19-50 per person; 102 Spray Avenue, ☎ 403-762-3560)* offers a very basic level of comfort. You must bring your own sleeping-bag if you want to sleep in a dormitory. Otherwise, for about $50, you can rent a private room with a bathroom. Very near the centre of town.

Holiday Lodge *($40-75 bkfst incl.; 311 Marten Street, Box 904, Banff, AB, T0L 0C0, ☎ 403-762-3648, ⇄ 762-8813)* has seven clean and relatively comfortable rooms. This old restored house, located in the centre of town, offers good and copious breakfasts.

Park Avenue Bed & Breakfast *($50 bkfst incl., no credit cards; 1358 Park Avenue, Box 783, Banff, AB, T0L 0C0, ☎ 403-762-2025)* rents two rooms exclusively to non-smokers.

Tannanhof Pension *($55-120 bkfst incl.; 121 Cave Avenue, Box 1914, Banff, AB, T0L 0C0, ☎ 403-762-4636, ⇄ 762-5660)* has 10 rooms and two suites located in a lovely big house. Some rooms have cable television and private bath, while others must share a bathroom. Each of the two suites has a bathroom with tub and shower, a fireplace and a sofa-bed for two extra persons. Breakfast is German-style with a choice of four dishes. Pets are allowed.

Spruce Grove Motel *($65; pb, tv; Banff Avenue, Box 471, Banff, AB, T0L 0C0, ☎ 403-762-2112, ⇄ 760-5043)* is a small and very ugly motel whose only advantage, in our opinion, is the relatively low price, in case the youth hostel or private homes are full.

Banff Voyager Inn *($95-$150; pb, tv, △, ≈, ℜ; 555 Banff Avenue, P.O. Box 1540, Banff, AB, T0L 0C0, ☎ 403-762-3301 or 1-800-879-1991, ⇄ 762-4131)* has comfortable rooms, some with mountain views.

The **Bow View Motor Lodge** *($105-$120; pb, tv, ≈, ℜ; 228 Bow Avenue, P.O. Box 339, Banff, AB, T0L 0C0, ☎ 403-762-2261 or 1-800-661-1565, ⇄ 762-8093)* has the immense advantage of being located next to the Bow River and far from noisy Banff Avenue. Only a five minute walk from the centre of town, this charming hotel provides comfortable rooms; those facing the river have balconies. The restaurant, pretty and peaceful, welcomes you for breakfast.

High Country Inn *($105-180; tv, pb, ≈, ⊛, heated underground parking; 419 Banff Avenue, Box 700, Banff, AB, T0L 0C0, ☎ 403-762-2236 or 1-800-661-1244, ⇄ 762-5084)*. Located on Banff's main drag, this inn has big, comfortable, spacious rooms with balconies. Furnishings are very ordinary, however, and detract from the beauty of the setting.

Inns of Banff, Swiss Village and **Rundle Manor** *($110-270; pb, tv; 600 Banff Avenue, Box 1077, Banff, AB, T0L 0C0, ☎ 403-762-4581 or 1-800-661-1272, ⇄ 762-2434)*. These three hotels are really one big hotel, with a common reservations service. Depending on your budget, you have the choice of three distinct buildings. Inns of Banff, the most luxurious, has 180 very spacious rooms, each facing a small terrace. The Swiss Village's cabins have a little more character and fit the setting much better, the rooms, however are a bit expensive at $120 and are less comfortable. Finally, the Rundle Manor is the most rustic of the three but lacks charm. The Rundle's units have small kitchens, living rooms and one or two separate bedrooms. This is a safe bet for family travellers. Guests at the Rundle Manor and Swiss Village have access to the facilities of the Inns of Banff.

Timberline Lodge *($120-175 for rooms, $250 for cabins; a little before the entrance to Banff, north of the TransCanada Highway and near Mount Norquay, Box 69, Banff, AB, T0L 0C0,*

☎ 403-762-2281, ⇄ 762-8331) offers views of Mount Norquay from its lower-priced rooms, and views of the valley and city of Banff from the others. Though the higher-priced rooms have a prettier view, they do unfortunately also overlook the TransCanada. There are two very peaceful cabins available on the Mount Norquay side in the middle of the forest, one for six persons and the other for eight.

Traveller's Inn *($135-155; pb, tv, △, ⊛; 401 Banff Avenue, Box 1017, Banff, AB, TOL 0C0, ☎ 403-762-4401 or 1-800-661-0227, ⇄ 762-5905)*. Most rooms at the hotel have small balconies that offer fine mountain views. Rooms are simply decorated, big and cosy. The hotel has a small restaurant that serves breakfast, as well as heated underground parking, an advantage in the winter. During the ski season, guests have the use lockers for skis and boots, as well as a small store for the rental and repair of winter sports equipment.

Banff Rocky Mountain Resort *($150-235, $325 for the presidential suite; pb, tv, ⊛, ≈, ☉, squash courts, massage room, tennis courts; at the entrance to the city along Banff Avenue, Box 100, Banff, AB, TOL 0C0, ☎ 1-800-661-9563, ⇄ 403-762-5166)* is an ideal spot if you are travelling as a family in Banff National Park. The delightful little cabins are warm and very well equipped. On the ground floor is a bathroom with shower, a very functional kitchen facing a living-room and dining-room with a fireplace while upstairs are two bedrooms and another bathroom. These apartments also have small private terraces. Near the main building are picnic and barbecue areas as well as lounge chairs where you can lie in the sun.

Rundle Stone Lodge *($155-220; pb, tv, ≈, ⊛; 537 Banff Avenue, Box 489, Banff, AB, TOL 0C0, ☎ 403-762-2201 or 1-800-661-8630, ⇄ 762-4501)*. Occupying a handsome building along Banff's main street, this hotel has two wings, one more recent than the other. In the old part of the building, the hotel offers rather ordinary motel-style rooms, while in the part of the building located along Banff Avenue, the rooms are attractive and spacious, each with a balcony. Some also have whirlpool baths. The hotel offers its guests a covered, heated parking area in the winter. Rooms for handicapped persons are available on the ground floor.

Caribou Lodge *($155-260; pb, tv, ℜ, ≈, △, ☉; 521 Banff Avenue, Box 279, Banff, AB, TOL 0C0, ☎ 403-762-5887 or 1-800-563-8764, ⇄ 762-5918)* is another Banff Avenue hotel offering comfortable, spacious rooms. A rustic western decor of unvarnished wood characterizes the reception area and guest rooms.

Mount Royal Hotel *($159-249; pb, tv, bar, ⊛, ☉, ℜ, billiards room; 138 Banff Avenue, Box 550, Banff, AB, TOL 0C0, ☎ 403-762-3331 or 1-800-267-3035, ⇄ 762-8938)* is right in the centre of town, not far from the tourist information centre. Rooms are freshly renovated and comfortable.

Banff Springs Hotel *($180-375; pb, tv, ℜ, ≈, bar; Spray Avenue, Box 960, Banff, AB, TOL 0C0, ☎ 403-762-2211 or 1-800-441-1414, ⇄ 762-5755)* is the biggest hotel in Banff. Overlooking the town, this five-star hotel, part of the Canadian Pacific chain, offers 828 luxury rooms in an atmosphere reminiscent of an old Scottish castle. The hotel was designed by architect Price, to whom we also owe Windsor Station in Montréal and the Château

Frontenac in Quebec City. Besides the typical turn-of-the-century chateau syle, the old-fashioned furnishings and the superb views from every window, the hotel offers its guests bowling, minigolf, tennis courts, a pool, a sauna, a large whirlpool bath, and a massage room. You can also stroll and shop in the more than 50 shops in the hotel. Golfers will be delighted to find a superb 27-hole course, designed by architect Stanley Thompson, on the grounds.

Between Banff and Lake Louise

Johnston Canyon Resort *($55-136; tv, pb; from Banff, take the TransCanada Highway to the Bow Valley exit, then take Highway 1A, the Bow Valley Parkway, Box 875, Banff, AB, TOL OCO, ☎ and ⇄ 403-762-2971)* constitutes a group of small log cabins right in the middle of the forest. The absolute calm is suitable for retreats. Some cabins offer a basic level of comfort, while others are fully equipped and have kitchens, sitting rooms and fireplaces. The biggest cabin can accommodate four people comfortably. A small grocery store, offering a basic range of products, is part of this tourism complex.

Near Silver City

Castle Mountain Youth Hostel *($11 for members, $16 for non-members; 27 km from Banff on Highway 1A, at the Castle Junction crossroads, across from Castle Mountain Village; for reservations, call the Calgary reservations office ☎ 403-283-55512, ⇄ 283-6503)* occupies a small building with two dormitories and a common room set around a big fireplace. The atmosphere is very pleasant, and the owner, who is from Québec, will be happy to advise you on hikes in the area.

Castle Mountain Campground *($12-15; on your right, just after Silver City)*. No reservation is required to spend the night here. You have to register yourself at the campground entrance, by placing your payment in the envelopes provided and dropping it into the payment box.

Castle Mountain Village *($90-125 per cabin; pb, tv, ℂ; Box 178, Lake Louise, AB, TOL 1E0, ☎ 403-522-2783 or 762-3868)* is a superb collection of 21 small log cabins located at Castle Junction on Highway 1A. Each cabin can accommodate two to six people. A small grocery store provides everyday products. The interiors of the cabins are very comfortable and seem intended to make you feel at ease. Kitchens are fully equipped and include microwave ovens and dishwashers. The main bathrooms have whirlpool baths. A roaring fire in the fireplace and the VCR provided in the newer cabins constitute the perfect remedy for those cold mountain evenings. A very good choice.

Lake Louise

Lake Louise Campground *($15; showers; leaving the TransCanada Highway, turn left at the main Lake Louise crossroads and continue straight, then cross the railroad and turn left on Fairview; the campground is at the end of the road)*. As everywhere in Lake Louise, there are few places available, making it important to arrive early. The Bow River traverses the campground.

The Canadian Alpine Centre *($18.50-22.50 for youth hostel members, $25-$29 for non-members; △, sb; on Village Road, Box 115, Lake Louise, AB, T0L 1E0, ☎ 403-522-2200, ⇌ 522-2253)* is a youth hostel offering rooms with two, four or six beds. Although fairly expensive, it is much more comfortable than the other youth hostels. Guests have access to a laundromat, a common kitchen, a library, and the little **Bill Peyto's Café**. The hostel is equipped to receive handicapped persons. A piece of advice: reserve well in advance.

Skoki Lodge *($99 per person with full board; open mid-Dec to Apr and Jun to Sep; △, tv, pb; reached by an 11-km road from the Lake Louise ski slopes, Box 5, Lake Louise, AB, T0L 1E0, ☎ 403-522-3555)*. All meals are included in the price of the room.

Deer Lodge *($110-160; pb, ℜ, ⊛, tv; near the lake, on the right before reaching the Chateau Lake Louise, P.O. Box 1598, Lake Louise, AB, T0L 1E0, ☎ 403-522-3747, ⇌ 522-3883)* is a very handsome and comfortable hotel. Rooms are spacious and tastefully decorated. The atmosphere is very pleasant.

Paradise Lodge & Bungalows *($110-215; pb, tv, ℝ; on your right, just after the Lake Moraine cutoff, Box 7, Lake Louise, AB, T0L 1E0, ☎ 403-522-3595, ⇌ 522-3987)* is a complex with 21 small log bungalows and 24 luxury suites. It should be noted that rooms do not have telephones. Pets are not admitted.

Lake Louise Inn *($120-195; pb, tv, ≈, ℜ; 210 Village Road, Lake Louise, AB, T0L 1E0, ☎ 403-522-3791, ⇌ 522-2018)* is located in the village of Lake Louise. The hotel offers very comfortable, warmly decorated rooms.

Mountaineer Lodge *($120-200, tv, pb, ⊛; Box 150, Lake Louise, AB, T0L 1E0, ☎ 403-522-3844, ⇌ 522-3902)*. Located in the village of Lake Louise, the Mountaineer Lodge has 80 rather simply furnished rooms.

The magnificent **Post Hotel** *($145-375; tv, ≈, pb, ℜ; Box 69, Lake Louise, AB, T0L 1E0, ☎ 403-522-3989 or 1-800-661-1568, ⇌ 522-3966)* is part of the Relais et Châteaux chain. Everything at this elegant establishment, from the rooms to the grounds is tastefully and carefully laid out. The restaurant is exquisite and the staff, friendly. If you can afford the extra cost and are looking to treat yourself, then this is the best place in Lake Louise. Pets are not allowed.

Moraine Lake Lodge *($210-245; pb, ℜ; Box 70, Lake Louise, AB, T0L 1E0, ☎ 403-522-3733 Jun to Sep or 604-985-7456 Oct to May, ⇌ 604-985-7479)* is located at the edge of Lake Moraine. Rooms do not have phones or televisions. The setting is magnificent but packed with tourists at all times, detracting from the tranquillity.

Chateau Lake Louise *($179-459; pb, tv, ≈, ℜ, △; Lake Louise, AB, T0L 1E0, ☎ 403-522-3511, ⇌ 522-3834)* is one of the best known hotels in the region. Built originally in 1890, the hotel burned to the ground in 1892 and was rebuilt the following year. Another fire devastated parts of it in 1924. Since then, it has been expanded and embellished almost continuously. Today, this vast hotel, which belongs to the Canadian Pacific chain, has 511 rooms with space for more than 1,300 guests, and a staff of nearly 725 to look after your every need. Perched by the turquoise waters of Lake Louise, facing the Victoria Glacier, the hotel boasts a divine setting.

Canmore

Restwell Trailer Park *($15; across Highway 1A and the railway line, near Policeman Creek,* ☎ *403-678-5111)* has 275 spaces for trailers and tents. Electricity, toilets, showers and water are available.

Two other campgrounds have also been set up for trailers and tents less than 10 km from Canmore on the way from Calgary. The **Bow River Campground** and the **Three Sisters Campground** each charge about $10 per site.

Rundle Mountain Motel & Gasthaus *($48-125; pb, tv, ≈; Mountain Avenue, Box 147, Canmore, AB, T0L 0M0,* ☎ *403-678-5222 or 1-800-661-1610,* ⇄ *678-5813)* is a motel modelled on Savoy-style chalets. It has 51 rooms that are in keeping with this type of establishment. Pets are not allowed.

Ambleside Lodge *($55-85; non-smokers only; 123 Rundle Crescent, Box 3479, Canmore, AB, T0L 0M0,* ☎ *403-678-3976)* welcomes you to a large and handsome residence in the style of a Savoyard chalet just a few minutes from the centre of town. The big and friendly common room is graced with a beautiful fireplace. Some rooms have private bath.

Cougar Canyon *($60-80; 3 Canyon Road, Box 3515, Canmore, AB, T0L 0M0,* ☎ *403-678-6636,* ⇄ *250-3293)* offers three ground floor rooms sharing a bathroom and two upstairs rooms each with private bath. When the weather is good, you can relax on the terrace. The owners also speak German.

Canyon Place *($65-85; non-smokers only; 3 Canyon Place, P.O. Box 2215, Canmore, AB, T0L 0M0,* ☎ *403-678-5471)*. Lodgings at this private home are provided by friendly hosts in a lovely big, bright house. Three rooms have been set up to receive guests. Two of them share a bathroom, while the third, which can accommodate three people, has its own bathroom. A very good choice!

Lady MacDonald Country Inn *($90-150; pb, tv; Bow Valley Trail, Box 2128, Canmore, AB, T0L 0M0,* ☎ *403-678-3665 or 1-800-567-3919,* ⇄ *678-7201)* is a magnificent little inn established in a very pretty house. Nine elegantly decorated rooms are placed at your disposal. Some rooms have been specially equipped to receive handicapped persons; others are spread over two floors to welcome families of four. The superb "Three Sisters Room" offers a magnificent view of the Rundle Range and Three Sisters mountains, as well as a fireplace and a whirlpool bath.

Rocky Mountain Ski Lodge *($90-220; pb, C, tv; 1711 Mountain Avenue, Box 3000, Canmore, AB, T0L 0M0,* ☎ *403-678-5445 or 1-800-665-6111,* ⇄ *678-6484)* faces a pleasant little garden. Rooms are clean and spacious. Units with living-rooms, fireplaces, and fully-equipped kitchens start at $120.

Georgetown Inn *($95 bkfst incl.; pb, tv, ℜ; 1101 Bow Valley Trail, Box 3327, Canmore, AB, T0L 0M0,* ☎ *403-678-3439,* ⇄ *678-3630)* has resolutely gone for an old-fashioned British ambiance. Rooms are comfortable, and some are equipped with whirlpool baths. Breakfast, which you can take in the Three Sisters dining room, is included in the price of your room. The fireplace, the old books and the reproductions hung on the walls give this place a warm atmosphere.

To reach the **Best Western Green Gables Inn** *($115-135; pb, ≈, ℜ, tv, ☺, ☺; Bow Valley Trail, Box 520, Canmore, AB, T0L 0M0, ☎ 403-678-5488 or 1-800-661-2133, ⇄ 678-2670)* take the Canmore exit from the highway and follow Highway 1A. This Best Western hotel has plenty of charm, and the rooms are particularly spacious and tastefully decorated in very warm tones.

■ **Tour B: The Icefields Parkway**

Between Lake Louise and the Icefields Parkway

Waterfall Lake Campground *($12; $3 extra to make a wood fire; above Lake Mistaya, just after the Mount Chephren lookout)*. As everywhere in the parks, it is first come, first served. Reservations are not possible unless you are a group. If that is the case, call the Parks Canada offices in Banff.

Rampart Creek Campground *($10; $3 extra to make a wood fire; a few kilometres from the intersection of Highways 11 and 93)*. The entrance to the campground is unguarded. You must register yourself, and leave the payment for your stay in an envelope.

Wilcox Creek Campground and **Columbia Icefield Campground** *($10; $3 extra to make a wood fire; a few kilometres from the Columbia icefield)*. These two campgrounds are equipped with the basics. You have to register yourself.

Jonas Creek Campground *($10; $3 extra to make a wood fire; 77 km south of Jasper and 9 km north of the Beauty Creek Youth Hostel)*.

Honeymoon Lake Campground *($10; $3 extra to make a wood fire; 51 km south of Jasper and 52 km north of the Columbia icefield interpretation centre)*. With the Sunwapta falls close by, this campground promises you a fine view of the Athabasca Valley.

Mount Kerkeslin Campground *($10; $3 extra to make a wood fire)* is located 35 km south of Jasper.

Mosquito Creek Youth Hostel *($10 per person for members, $14 per person for non-members; △; on Highway 93, a few kilometres after Lake Hector; to reserve, call the Banff Youth Hostel, ☎ 403-237-8282 or 762-4122)* offers a very basic level of comfort, with no running water or electricity. There is however a wood-fired sauna. Lodging is in mixed dormitories.

Rampart Creek Youth Hostel *($9 per person for members; near the campground of the same name on Highway 93, ☎ 403-762-4122 or the Calgary reservations centre, ☎ 403-237-8282)* comes off as a little rustic, but it is very well situated for hikers and cyclists visiting the glaciers.

Hilda Creek Youth Hostel *($9 per person for members; a little before the entrance to Jasper National Park, ☎ 403-762-4122 or the Calgary reservations centre, ☎ 403-237-8282)*. This is a genuine mountain refuge, with no running water or electricity. This spot is heartily recommended for hikers, because of its proximity to the finest hiking areas around the Athabasca Glacier. Information is available here, and the staff will be happy to indicate the must-sees. The welcome is friendly, and the scenery will take your breath away.

Beauty Creek Youth Hostel *($9 per person for members; 87 km from Jasper and 17 km north of the Columbia Icefield interpretation centre, ☎ 403-439-3139).* A day's pedalling from Jasper, this is a good spot for cyclists. The level of comfort is basic, but the atmosphere is pleasant. Moreover, you can take a side trip to the beautiful Stanley Falls, located close by.

Athabasca Falls Youth Hostel *($9 per person for members; 32 km south of Jasper, ☎ 403-439-3139).* In keeping with the rustic decor, this hostel has gas lighting. It is situated next to Athabasca Falls. Cyclists and hikers will appreciate this hostel's great location.

At press time, a 32-room hotel was under construction near the Columbia icefield, just in front of the glacier. Besides the hotel, the building will also house a tourist office and offices for the Brewster tour company. The hotel will be open from May 1 to Oct. 15, which coincides with the season for guided tours on the Columbia glacier. For information and reservations, call **Brewster Transportation & Tours** *(☎ 403-852-7031, ⇌ 762-6750).*

The Crossing *($68-73; ℜ, pb, tv, ⊛, cafeteria, pub; at the crossroads of Highways 93 and 11, 80 km from Lake Louise, Box 333, Lake Louise, AB, T0L 1E0, ☎ 403-761-7000, ⇌ 761-7006)* is a good place to stop along the Icefields Parkway.

Num-Ti-Jah Lodge *($81-142; pb, on the shore of Bow Lake, about 20 km from Lake Louise, ☎ 403-522-2167, ⇌ 522-2425)* was built by Jimmy Simpson, a famous mountain guide and trapper from the region. Jimmy Simpson's two daughters also have a place in the history of the Rockies. Peg and Mary became world-class figure skaters in their time and made numerous tours of Canada and the United States. The name Num-Ti-Jah comes from a Stoney Indian word meaning hammer. The spot is popular with tourists, for Bow Lake is one of the most beautiful in the region.

■ **Tour C: Jasper National Park**

Jasper

Athabasca Hotel *($49-101; ℜ, bar, tv; Box 1420, Jasper, AB, T0E 1E0, ☎ 403-852-3386, ⇌ 852-4955)* is located right in the centre of Jasper, facing the Via Rail station and the Brewster and Greyhound bus terminal. Decorated in old English style, the rooms are not very big, while they are appealing. The least expensive are near a central bathroom, but the others have their own facilities. Neither flashy nor luxurious, this hotel is quite adequate, and the rooms are pleasant. This is the cheapest place to stay in Jasper, so you'll have to reserve in advance. The hotel does not have an elevator.

Skyline Accommodation *($50-60; sb; 726 Patricia Street, Box 2616, Jasper, AB, T0E 1E0, ☎ 403-852-5035).* Roger and Judy Smolnicky have renovated their big house to create two spacious guest rooms. The shared bath is very clean.

Private Accommodation at the Knauers' *($50-60 bkfst incl.; sb/pb, tv; 708 Patricia Street, Box 4, Jasper, AB, T0E 1E0, ☎ 403-852-4916)* has three failrly large rooms that have the advantage of having their own private entrance. Two of the rooms, with rates set at $50, are next to a big and attractive bathroom, while the other has its own facilities. There is a refrigerator at the entrance for guests. This spot is for non-smokers, and pets are not admitted. Continental breakfast is served in the rooms.

Whistler Inn *($99; tv, pb, ℜ, △; Box 250, Jasper, AB, T0E 1E0, ☎ 403-852-3361 or 1-800-282-9919, ⇄ 852-4993)* is certainly not the most beautiful hotel in Jasper. The rooms are rather dingy, but the rates are reasonable for Jasper.

Marmot Lodge *($123-168; tv, ≈, ℜ, ℂ, ⊛; on Connaught Drive, at the Jasper exit, toward Edmonton; Box 687, Jasper, AB, T0E 1E0, ☎ 403-852-4471 or 1-800-661-6521, ⇄ 852-3280)* offers very attractive rooms at what are considered reasonable prices in Jasper. The rooms are fully renovated and decorated in bright colours. Old photographs of Amerindians hang on the walls, for a change from the normal decor. The bathrooms have also been redone and are modern. A terrace with tables has been set up in front of the pool, and this is a good spot for sunbathing. The decor, the friendly staff and the scenery all contribute to making this hotel a very pleasant place. It provides the best quality-to-price ratio in town.

Tonquin Inn *($139-179; tv, ≈, △, ℂ, ℜ; on Connaught Drive, at the entrance to Jasper coming from Icefields Parkway, Box 658, Jasper, AB, T0E 1E0, ☎ 403-852-4987 or 1-800-661-1315, ⇄ 852-4413)*. A new wing has recently been added around the pool, providing all rooms direct access to it. The rooms in the old wing are less attractive and resemble motel rooms, though they do provide an adequate level of comfort. We suggest, nevertheless, that you request a room in the new wing when reserving your room.

Maligne Lodge *($150-180; tv, pb, ≈, ℜ, △, ⊛, laundromat; on Connaught Drive, leaving Jasper toward Edmonton, Box 757, Jasper, AB, T0E 1E0, ☎ 403-852-3143 or 1-800-661-1315, ⇄ 852-4789)* offers 98 very comfortable rooms and suites, some of them with fireplaces and whirlpool baths. Some rooms have also been equipped to receive handicapped persons.

Sawridge Hotel *($160-220; tv, pb, ≈, ℜ, ⊛, △, laundromat, discotheque; 82 Connaught Drive, Box 2080, Jasper, AB, T0E 1E0, ☎ 403-852-5111 or 1-800-661-6427, ⇄ 852-5942)* offers big, warmly decorated rooms.

Jasper Inn *($170-295; tv, ℜ, ≈, ⊛, ℝ; 98 Geikie Street, Box 879, Jasper, AB, T0E 1E0, ☎ 403-852-4461 or 1-800-661-1933, ⇄ 852-5916)* offers spacious, attractive, comfortable rooms, some of them equipped with kitchenettes.

Chateau Jasper *($205-320; ≈, ℜ, heated parking; Box 1418, Jasper, AB, T0E 1E0, ☎ 403-852-5644 or 1-800-661-9323, ⇄ 852-4860)* offers comfortable, very attractive rooms.

Jasper Park Lodge *($276-$490; ≈, ℜ, ℝ, tv, ☺, ⊛, △; P.O. Box 40, Jasper, AB, T0E 1E0, ☎ 403-852-3001 or 1-800-441-1414, ⇄ 852-5107)* constitutes beyond a doubt the most beautiful hotel complex in the whole Jasper area. Now part of the Canadian Pacific chain, the Jasper Park Lodge has attractive, spacious, comfortable rooms. It was built in 1921 by the Grand Trunk Railway Company to compete with Canadian Pacific's Banff Springs Hotel. The staff are very professional, attentive and friendly. A whole range of activities are organized for guests. These include horseback riding and river rafting. You will also find one of the finest golf courses in Canada, several tennis courts, a big pool, a sports centre, and canoes, sailboards and bicycles for rent in the summer, plus ski equipment in the winter. Several hiking trails criss-cross the site, among them a very pleasant 3.8-km trail alongside Lake Beauvert. Whether you're staying in a room in the main building or perhaps you prefer a small cabin, you are assured of comfort and tranquillity. Each year Jasper Park Lodge organizes theme events, and hotel guests are invited to participate. Some weekends may be dedicated to the mountains and relaxation, with yoga and aerobics classes as well as water gymnastics and visits to the sauna; while another weekend may be set aside for the wine tastings of Beaujolais Nouveau; other activities are organized for New Year's. Ask for the activities leaflet for more information.

Outside Jasper

Whistler Campground *($13-19; open May 5 to Oct 10; 2.5 km south of Jasper; take Highway 93, then turn on the road leading to the Whistler Mountain ski lift, taking the first left for the campground)*, with its 781 sites, has facilities for both trailers and tents. Water, showers and electricity are available. You can also find firewood on the site. The maximum stay at the campsite is 15 days. To reserve, call the Parks Canada office in Jasper (see p 210).

Wapiti Campground *($14-15.50; open Jun 9 to Sep 11; 4 km from Jasper)*, with its 366 sites welcomes trailers and tents. Water, electricity and toilets are available.

Jasper's three youth hostels are located outside the town.

Mount Whistler Youth Hostel *($14 per person for members, $17 per person for non-members; 7 km west of Jasper taking the Skytram road toward the ski lift, ☎ 403-852-3215)* is quite a comfortable establishment. It is a few minutes' walk from the ski lift that goes to the top of Whistler Mountain, from where there is a superb vista over the Athabasca Valley. Reserve well in advance.

Mount Edith Cavell Youth Hostel *($9 per person for members, $14 per person for non-members; 26 km south of Jasper; take highway 93A and then go 13 km up the curvy road leading to Mount Edith Cavell, ☎ 403-439-3139)* constitutes a genuine high mountain refuge, without water or electricity. It is built on one of the most beautiful mountains in the area, Mount Edith Cavell. Take warm clothing and a good sleeping bag, for you are in a high mountain area, and the temperatures are unpredictable. If you enjoy tranquillity and beautiful walks, you are in paradise here.

Maligne Canyon Youth Hostel *($9 per person for members, $14 per person for non-members; 11 km east of Jasper, on the Maligne Lake road, ☎ 403-439-3139)* also comes across as the ideal spot for anyone who likes hiking and other outdoor activities. The Skyline hiking trail begins right near the hostel, leading experienced hikers through Alpine scenery. The hike takes two or three days, but the superb view over the Jasper valley is a good reward for your efforts. Also located near the hostel, the Maligne River canyon offers some fine rapids and waterfalls photo opportunities. Do not hesitate to talk with the owner of the hostel: he is an expert on local fauna and conducts research for Jasper National Park.

Pine Bungalow Cabins *($65-90; C; on Highway 16, near the Jasper golf course, Box 7, Jasper, AB, T0E 1E0,* ☎ *403-852-3491)* fit the category of a motel. The cabins are fully equipped, and some even have a fireplace, but furnishings are very modest and in rather poor taste. All the same, it is one of Jasper's cheapest places to stay.

Becker's Chalets *($90-135 per cabin; pb, tv, C, ℜ; on Icefields Parkway 5 km south of Jasper, Box 579, Jasper, AB, T0E 1E0,* ☎ *403-852-3779,* ⇄ *852-7202)*, also located along the Athabasca River, are comfortable and well equipped. You will also find a laundromat.

Alpine Village *($90-180 per cabin; pb, tv, C, R, ⊛; 2 km south of Jasper, near the cutoff for Mount Whistler, Box 610, Jasper, AB, T0E 1E0,* ☎ *403-852-3285)* is an attractive group of comfortable little wood cabins. Facing the Athabasca River, the spot is calm and peaceful. If possible, ask for one of the cabins facing the river directly: these are the most pleasant. Pets are not accepted. Reserve far in advance, as early as January for the summer.

Jasper House *($98-148; tv, pb, C, ℜ; a few kilometres south of Jasper on Icefields Parkway, at the foot of Mount Whistler, Box 817, Jasper, AB, T0E 1E0,* ☎ *403-852-4535,* ⇄ *852-5335)* consists of a group of little chalet-style log houses built along the Athabasca River. Comfortable and quiet, the rooms are big and well equipped.

Pyramid Lake Resort *($115-172; tv, pb, ℜ; on the shore of Pyramid Lake, 5 km from Jasper; take Pyramid Lake Road to Jasper and follow the signs to Lake Patricia and Pyramid Lake, Box 388, Jasper, AB, T0E 1E0,* ☎ *403-852-4900,* ⇄ *852-7007)* offers simple but comfortable rooms facing Pyramid Lake, where you can enjoy of your favourite nautical activities. Rentals of motorboats, canoes, sailboards and water skis are available at the rental counter located right next to the hotel *(same address as the hotel,* ☎ *403-852-3536)*.

Miette Hot Springs

Pocahontas Bungalows *($65-90 per cabin; C; on Highway 69, near Punchbowl Falls, Box 820, Jasper, AB, T0E 1E0,* ☎ *403-866-3732 or 1-800-843-3372,* ⇄ *866-3777)* is a small group of cabins located at the entrance to Jasper National Park, on the road leading to Miette Hot Springs. The least expensive cabins do not have kitchenettes.

Miette Hot Spring Bungalows *($65-110; tv, pb, ℜ; next to the Miette Hot Springs, Jasper East, Box 907, Jasper, AB, T0E 1E0,* ☎ *403-866-3750 or 866-3760, in the off-season* ☎ *852-4039,* ⇄ *866-2214)* offers accommodations in bungalows and a motel. The motel rooms are rather ordinary, but those in the bungalows are of good quality.

Outside Hinton

The **Overlander Mountain Lodge** *($70-140; pb, ⊛, ℜ; 2 km to the left after leaving Jasper National Park toward Hinton; 553 Gregg Avenue, Hinton, AB, T7V 1N2,* ☎ *403-866-2330,*

⇄ 866-2332) has several charming cabins. This establishment is rendered more pleasant by the fact that it is set in a much calmer area than the outskirts of Jasper, and the surrounding scenery is truly exquisite. This place stands out from the majority of motel-style establishments in this town. Reservations should be made far in advance, as Hinton is a common alternative to lodging in Jasper.

■ **Tour D: Kootenay and Yoho National Parks**

From Castle Junction to Radium Hot Springs

Kootenay Park Lodge *($68-86 per cabin; pb, ℜ, ℝ; on Highway 93 heading south, 42 km from Castle Junction, Box 1390, Banff, AB, T0L 0C0, ☎ 403-762-9196)* rents 10 small log cabins clinging to the steep slopes of the mountains of Kootenay National Park. On site you will find a small store offering sandwiches and everyday items. The restaurant is open only from 8am to 10am, 12 to 2pm and 6pm to 8:30pm.

Storm Mountain Lodge *($125 per cabin; pb, ℜ; after Castle Mountain Junction, go toward Radium Hot Springs, at your right from the Continental Divide between Alberta and British Columbia, Box 670, Banff, AB, T0L 0C0, ☎ 403-762-4155)* is comprised of 12 small cabins at the eastern entrance of Kootenay National Park. The level of comfort is basic, but the setting is enchanting. The small restaurant closes very early.

Radium Hot Springs

Surprisingly accommodations in Radium Hot Springs consist essentially of very ordinary motel rooms. All along the town's main drag you will find motel fronts that rival each other in ugliness. The region is popular with visitors, however, so here are a few suggestions.

Canyon Camp *($15-20; toilets, showers, ☎; Box 279, Radium Springs, BC, V0A 1M0, ☎ 604-347-9564, ⇄ 347-9501)* is an attractive campground with many spaces for trailers and tents along Sinclair Creek. The spots shaded by numerous trees confer a pleasing atmosphere on this campground.

Misty River Lodge *($55-75; pb, tv, C; 5036 Highway 93, Box 363, Radium Hot Springs, BC, V0A 1M0, ☎ 604-347-9912, ⇄ 347-9397)* is the only exception to the "ugly-motel" rule in Radium Hot Springs. The rooms were renovated recently to offer a decent level of comfort. The bathrooms are spacious and very clean. Without a doubt, the best motel in town.

Both the **Crystal Springs Motel** *($55-60; pb, tv, ❀; Box 218, Radium Springs, BC, V0A 1M0, ☎ 604-347-9759, ⇄ 347-9736)* and the **Crescent Motel** *($65-70; pb, tv; Box 116, Radium Hot Springs, BC, V0A 1M0, ☎ 604-347-9570)* have typical motel-style rooms.

Motel Tyrol *($60-70; pb, ≈, ❀; Box 312, Radium Hot Springs, BC, V0A 1M0, ☎ 604-347-9402)* offers adequate, modestly furnished rooms. The terrace by the pool is pleasant.

The Chalet *($65-85; pb, tv, ❀; Box 456, Radium Hot Springs, BC,*

VOA 1M0, ☎ 604-347-9305) offers several rooms with balconies, modestly furnished but comfortable. Perched above the little town of Radium Hot Springs, this big Savoy chalet-style house offers an interesting view of the valley below.

Radium Hot Springs Lodge *($70-165; pb, tv, ℜ, ≈, △; facing the Radium Hot Springs thermal pool, Box 70, Radium Hot Springs, BC, VOA 1M0, ☎ 604-347-9341, ⇄ 347-9342)* has large, extremely ordinary, though modestly furnished, rooms. It's restaurant tries to be chic but serves over-priced food of average quality. All the same, the hotel does have the advantage of being well located and can be considered among the few good spots in Radium Hot Springs.

Fairmont Hot Springs Resort *($139; pb, ≈, ℜ, tv, ℝ; on Highway 93-95, near the Fairmont ski hills, Box 10, Fairmont Hot Springs, BC, VOB 1L0, ☎ 604-345-6311, ⇄ 345-6616)* is a magnificent hotel complex, wonderfully laid out, offering special spa packages. Hotel guests can also take advantage of tennis courts and a superb golf course. This establishment also has a vast adjacent campground.

Golden and surroundings

Whispering Spruce Campground and R.V. Park *($12-14; open Apr 15 to Oct 15; laundromat, showers, ☎; 1422 Golden View Road, Box 233, Golden, BC, VOA 1H0, ☎ 604-344-6680)* has 45 spaces for tents and trailers. Arrive early to reserve your place.

Golden Municipal Campground *($8-10; showers, toilets; 1407 South 9th Street, Box 350, Golden, BC, VOA 1H0, ☎ 604-344-5412)* has 67 spaces for tents and trailers. The campground is situated next to tennis courts and a pool.

Columbia Valley Lodge *($40-68 bkfst incl.; on Highway 95 a few kilometres south of Golden, Box 2669A, Golden, BC, VOA 1H0, ☎ 604-348-2508)* has 12 rustic rooms. It resembles a mountain refuge with a basic level of comfort, but it is nonetheless completely adequate. This is a good stopping point for cyclists travelling around the area.

McLaren Lodge *($50-60 bkfst incl.; above Highway 95 leaving Golden toward Yoho National Park, Box 2586, Golden, BC, VOA 1H0, ☎ 604-344-6133, ⇄ 344-7650)* is an interesting spot in Golden for nature-lovers. The owners of this little hotel organize river rafting excursions. Rooms are rather small and have a pleasant old-fashioned air. This spot has the best quality-to-price ratio in Golden.

Golden Village Motor Inn *($79; pb, ℜ, tv; Box 371, Golden, BC, VOA 1H0, ☎ 604-344-5996)* has ordinary motel-style rooms.

Prestige Inn *($70-130; pb, ℂ, ⊛, tv, ≈, ℜ, ⊘; 1049 TransCanada Highway, Box 9, Golden, BC, VOA 1H0, ☎ 604-344-7990)* is Golden's best hotel. Rooms are quite spacious, and bathrooms, well equipped.

■ Tour E: Kananaskis Country

Eau Claire Campground *($11; just north of Fortress Junction, near the Fortress Mountain)* is a small campground situated right in the forest. Dress warmly, for the nights are cool in this spot.

Accommodations

Kananaskis Lake Campgrounds *($11; leaving Upper Kananaskis Lake, go left and follow the road a few kilometres until Interlakes)* offers you a superb vista over the lakes and forest. There is a no-reservations, first-come first-served policy here.

Mount Kidd RV Park *($14-24; toilets, showers, laundromat, △, ≈; on Highway 40, a few kilometres south than Kananaskis Village, ☎ 403-591-7700)* has a surprising set-up. Located at the edge of the river in a forested area, it is definitely the most pleasant campground in the region. Guests also have the use of tennis courts or can head off on any of the many hiking trails in the area. Be sure to reserve ahead (groups especially) at this popular spot.

Kananaskis Village

Ribbon Creek Youth Hostel *($12 per person for members, $17 per person for non-members; along the road leading to the central square of Kananaskis village, TOL 2H0, ☎ 403-722-4122)* is a pleasant little hostel and nearly always crowded. Do not wait to the last minute to reserve, or you will be disappointed. The common room, in front of the fireplace, is a pleasant spot to recover from the day's activities.

Kananaskis Inn Best Western *($120-170; pb, tv, ℂ, △, ⊛, ≈, ℜ; on the central square of Kananaskis Village, TOL 2H0, ☎ 403-591-7500 or 1-800-528-1234, ⇄ 591-7633)* has 95 comfortable, pleasantly furnished rooms. The atmosphere at this hotel is quite agreeable, and the staff are friendly. However, the lobby is often besieged by visitors searching for souvenir shops or tea rooms.

Hotel Kananaskis *($150-220; pb, tv, ℜ, ≈, △, ⊛, ❂; on the central square of Kananaskis Village, TOL 2H0, ☎ 403-591-7711 or 1-800-441-1414, ⇄ 591-7770)* has 70 big and very comfortable rooms. The friendly staff make this hotel very pleasant.

The Lodge at Kananaskis *($150-220; pb, tv, ℜ, ≈, △, ⊛, ❂; on the central square of Kananaskis Village, TOL 2H0, ☎ 403-591-7711 or 1-800-441-1414, ⇄ 591-7770)*, along with the Hotel Kananaskis, are part of the Canadian Pacific hotel chain. The lodge has 250 very comfortable, spacious and warmly decorated rooms. An excellent establishment, though advance reservations are recommended year-round.

Restaurants

■ **Tour A: Banff National Park**

Banff

The restaurant of the Caribou Lodge (see p 254), **The Keg**, serves American breakfasts and buffet-style food.

Joe BTFSPLK's (pronounced bi-tif'-spliks) *($; 221 Banff Avenue, facing the tourism information centre, ☎ 403-762-5529)* is a small restaurant with 1950s decor and good hamburgers. You'll learn that Joe BTFSPLK was a strange comic book character who walked around with a cloud above his head causing disasters wherever he went. It seems the only way today to avoid annoyances (such as spending too much money) may be to come to this little restaurant, very popular with locals for the burgers, fries, salads, chicken nuggets and milkshakes. The restaurant also serves breakfasts for under $6.

Rose and Crown *($; every day 11am to 2am; upstairs at 202 Banff Avenue, ☎ 403-762-2121)* prepares light meals consisting essentially of hamburgers, chicken wings and *nachos*. In the evening, the spot becomes a bar with musicians.

The Cake Company *($; every day; 218 Bear Street)* is a little tea room that is ideal for a hot drink and a delicious slice of home-made cake.

Silver Dragon Restaurant *($; every day 11:30am to 10pm; 211 Banff Avenue, ☎ 403-762-3939)* offers adequate Chinese cuisine. They also deliver.

Ticino *($$; 415 Banff Avenue, ☎ 403-762-3848)* serves pretty good Italian cuisine as well as fondues. The decor is very ordinary, and the music tends to be too loud.

Sukiyaki House *($$; every day; upstairs at 211 Banff Avenue, ☎ 403-762-2002)* offers excellent Japanese cuisine at affordable prices. The sushis are perfect, and the staff are very courteous. The impersonal decor, however, leaves a bit to be desired.

Balkan Restaurant *($$; every day 11am to 10pm; 120 Banff Avenue, ☎ 403-762-3454)* is Banff's Greek restaurant. The blue and white decor with fake vines and grape clusters, recalls the Mediterranean. The main dishes are good, although unimaginative and often showing North American influences. The staff seem overworked and are not always very pleasant.

Grizzly House *($$; every day 11:30am to midnight; 207 Banff Avenue, ☎ 403-762-4055)* specializes in big, tender, juicy steaks. The western decor is a bit corny, but your attention will quickly be taken over by your delicious meal.

Korean Restaurant *($$; every day from 11am; upstairs at Cascade Plaza, 317 Banff Avenue, ☎ 403-762-8862)*. For anyone who has never tried Korean cuisine, here is a good chance to discover fine, deliciously prepared food. The staff will be happy to advise you in your selections.

Caboose *($$$; every day from 5pm; corner of Elk Street and Lynx Street, ☎ 403-762-3622 or 762-2102)* is one of Banff's better eating spots. The fish dishes, trout or salmon, are excellent, or you may prefer the lobster with steak, American style, or perhaps the crab. This is a favourite with regular visitors.

Le Beaujolais *($$$; every day; 212 Buffalo Street, ☎ 403-762-2712)* prepares excellent French cuisine. The dining room is very elegant and the staff are highly attentive. British Columbia salmon, baked with Pernod, is a true delicacy, as are the chicken breasts with sesame oil and cognac. The best food in Banff.

Lake Louise

Gondola Chinese Food Express *($; Tue to Sat 6pm to midnight; delivery only; ☎ 403-522-3942)* offers inexpensive Chinese food.

Lake Louise Grill & Bar *($; every day; in Samson Mall, in the centre of Lake Louise village, ☎ 403-522-3879)* serves Chinese food and traditional American cuisine in lacklustre fashion.

Beeline Chicken & Pizza *($; every day; in Samson Mall, in the centre of Lake

Louise village, ☎ 403-522-2006) prepares good hamburgers as well as pizzas, nachos and burritos.

The **Moraine Lake Lodge** *($$; every day; at the edge of Morraine Lake,* ☎ *403-522-3733)* has a restaurant where you can enjoy good meals while contemplating the superb vista over the lake and the Ten Peaks which stretch before your eyes.

The Edelweiss Dining Room *($$$; every day; Chateau Lake Louise,* ☎ *403-522-3511)* offers delicious French cuisine in very elegant surroundings with a view over the lake. Reservations are recommended.

Deer Lodge Restaurant *($$$; every day; near the lake on the right before reaching the Chateau Lake Louise,* ☎ *403-522-3747)* is an attractive restaurant with somewhat rustic decor. The food is excellent.

Post Hotel *($$$; at the edge of the Pipestone River, near the youth hostel,* ☎ *403-522-3989)* houses an excellent restaurant recognized by the Relais et Châteaux association. Reservations are necessary, for this is one of the best eating spots in Lake Louise. The setting of the hotel is enchanting.

Canmore

Boston Pizza *($; every day from 11am; 1704 Bow Valley Trail,* ☎ *403-678-3300)* falls into the fast-food category. This restaurant serves a big variety of pizzas, *nachos* and big sandwiches.

Located right next to the Georgetown Inn (see p 257), the **Miner's Lamp Pub** *($; to 10pm,* ☎ *403-678-3439)* can serve you simple meals. This is a very attractive English pub.

Nutter's *($; every day; 900 Railway Avenue,* ☎ *403-678-3335)* is the best spot to find the fixings for sandwiches or other snacks for your back-country hikes. You will find a big choice of energizing or natural foods to take out, or you can eat in at the small tables near the windows.

Santa Lucia *($; every day; 714 - 8th Street,* ☎ *403-678-3414)* is a small Italian restaurant with a family atmosphere. The *gnocchis* are excellent. They also deliver.

The Kabin *($; every day; 1702 Highway 1A,* ☎ *403-678-4878)* offers copious breakfasts, as well as lunches and suppers, in a restored old wooden house. In warm weather, you can eat on the terrace.

Sinclairs *($$; every day; 637 8th Street,* ☎ *403-678-5370)* offers good food in a warm ambiance enhanced by a fireplace. Reservations are recommended in high season, for the restaurant is often full. The restaurant also offers an excellent selection of teas, a rarity around here.

Peppermill *($$; 726 9th Street,* ☎ *403-678-2292)* is a good little 12-table restaurant with a traditional menu. The house specialty is pepper steak. The Swiss chef will happily serve you a delicious *fendant du Valais*. Reservations are recommended.

Chez François *($$; adjacent to the Best Western Green Gables Inn, Highway 1A,* ☎ *403-678-6111)* is probably the best eating spot in Canmore. The chef, who comes from Quebec, offers you excellent French cuisine and a warm atmosphere in his restaurant.

■ Tour B: The Icefields Parkway

This tour crosses a sparsely populated area, and eating spots are few and far between. There are nonetheless a few little cafés that serve light meals.

The café of the **Num-Ti-Jah Lodge** *($; every day; at the edge of Bow Lake, about 20 km from Lake Louise, ☎ 403-522-2167)* serves sandwiches, muffins and cakes. You can warm up in this little café with tea or other hot beverage. This spot is popular with tourists and is often crowded.

The Crossing *($; every day; at the junction of Highways 93 and 11, 80 km from Lake Louise, ☎ 403-761-7000)* houses a fairly large cafeteria with light meals where just about every traveller seems to stop. As a result, it is very crowded, with long line-ups.

A new hotel in the Columbia Icefields, under construction at press time, will also house a restaurant. For more information, call **Brewster Transportation & Tours** *(☎ 403-852-7031)*, which will be operating this new complex.

■ Tour C: Jasper National Park

Jasper

Coco's Café *($; every day; 608 Patricia Street, ☎ 403-852-4550)* is a little spot with bagels, sandwiches and cheesecake.

If you get hit by a hamburger craving, **A&W** *($; every day; 624 Connaught Drive, ☎ 403-852-4930)* is the local answer.

Light meals and freshly-squeezed juices are served at **Spooner's Coffee Bar** *($;* *every day; 610 Patricia Street, ☎ 403-852-4046)*. The café has a good selection of teas. The view over the nearby mountains and the young atmosphere combine to make this a very pleasant spot.

Miss Italia Ristorante *($; every day; 610 Patricia Street, upstairs at the Center Mall, ☎ 403-852-4002)* offers decent Italian cooking. The staff are friendly and attentive.

Smitty's Restaurant *($; near the tourism information centre, ☎ 403-852-3111)* is a rather ugly family restaurant, but they serve good pancake breakfasts as well as simple meals throughout the day.

Soft Rock Café *($; every day; in the Connaught Square Mall, 622 Connaught Drive, ☎ 403-852-5850)* offers excellent breakfasts and sandwiches. Cake and ice-cream are the specialty for lazy afternoons.

Cantonese Restaurant *($$; every day; across from the bus terminal on Connaught Drive, ☎ 403-852-3559)* serves Sichuan and Cantonese dishes with typically Chinese decor.

The **Amethyst Dining Room** *($$; every day; in the Amethyst Lodge, 200 Connaught Drive, ☎ 403-852-3394)* has been fully renovated and now offers its traditional menu in a pleasant atmosphere.

Jasper Inn Restaurant *($$; every day; Jasper Inn, 98 Geikie Street, ☎ 403-852-3232)* serves up excellent fish and seafood. This is a very popular spot in Jasper.

Tokyo Tom's Restaurant *($$; every day; 410 Connaught Drive, ☎ 403-852-3780)* serves good Japanese food. The *sukiyaki* is excellent, but the gloomy decor is not.

Beauvallon Dining Room *($$$; every day; Charlton's Chateau Jasper, 96 Geikie Street,* ☎ *403-852-5644)* prepares excellent French cuisine and is one of Jasper's finest dining establishments.

Beauvert Dining Room *($$$; every day; in Jasper Park Lodge, at the northern approach to Jasper,* ☎ *403-852-3301)* is a rather fancy restaurant. The French cuisine on offer is excellent. One of the best in Jasper.

Outside Jasper

The restaurant of the **Pyramid Lake Resort** *($; every day; at the edge of Pyramid Lake, 5 km from Jasper; take Pyramid Lake Road to Jasper and follow the signs to Lake Patricia and Pyramid Lake,* ☎ *403-852-4900)* serves simple meals. The cuisine is good and unpretentious.

The restaurant of the **Alpine Village** *($$; every day; 2 km south of Jasper, near the Mount Whistler cutoff,* ☎ *403-852-3285)* does not have particularly pleasant decor, but the food is acceptable nonetheless.

Becker's Chalet Restaurant *($$; every day; on Icefield Parkway, 5 km south of Jasper,* ☎ *403-852-3779)*, located at the edge of the Athabasca River, serves perfectly decent traditional cooking. Unfortunately, the decor is rather impersonal.

Hinton and surroundings

Cafe Fortune *($; every day; corner of highway 16 and Mountain Street,* ☎ *403-865-7222)* is a good spot for a simple meal.

Athens Corner Restaurant *($; every day; in the Hill Shopping Centre,* ☎ *403-865-3956)* offers tried-and-true Canadian dishes as well as Greek and Italian items, all at reasonable prices.

Mama's Pizza *($; every day; in the Hill Shopping Centre,* ☎ *403-865-4116)* obviously prepares all sorts of pizzas. This spot is generally quite busy.

The **Pizza Hut** chain *($; every day; Carmichael Lane,* ☎ *403-865-8455)* is well known. The variety of pizzas is extensive and reasonably priced.

Greentree Cafe *($; every day; in the Greentree Motor Lodge,* ☎ *403-865-4074)* prepares delicious and copious breakfasts at unbeatable prices.

Rose's Place *($$; every day; in the Valley Shopping Centre,* ☎ *403-865-2175)* prepares good traditional cuisine. The dining room is a bit drab and could use some sprucing up.

Fireside Dining Room *($$; every day; in the Greentree Motor Lodge,* ☎ *403-865-4074)* is the best and most attractive restaurant in Hinton.

The **Overlander Mountain Lodge**'s *($$$; every day; in the Overlander Mountain Lodge, 2 km after the toll booths leaving Jasper National Park heading toward Hinton, go left toward the hotel,* ☎ *403-866-2330)* attractive restaurant serves excellent food. Give into temptation and savour the rainbow trout stuffed with crab and shrimps and covered with a *béarnaise* sauce.

■ **Tour D: Kootenay and Yoho National Parks**

Kootenay Park Lodge Restaurant *($; every day 8am to 10am and 6pm to 8:30pm; on Highway 93 heading south, 42 km from Castle Junction, ☎ 403-762-9196)* offers light meals in simple surroundings. Isolated amidst grandiose scenery, you may want to finish your meal with a stroll through the surrounding countryside.

Storm Mountain Lodge Restaurant *($$; every day 7am to 10:30am, 12 to 2pm and 5:30pm to 7:30pm; after Castle Mountain Junction, head toward Radium Hot Springs, watching for the restaurant on your right, ☎ 403-762-4155)* closes very early. The braised salmon and the clams are excellent.

Radium Hot Springs and surroundings

Husky House Restaurant *($; every day 6am to 10:30pm; next to the gas station, at the junction with Highway 93, ☎ 604-347-9811)* offers simple meals at affordable prices.

Silver Garden Restaurant *($; every day; 4935 Highway 93, ☎ 604-347-9848)* offers excellent Chinese food.

For a copious breakfast, head to **Munchkins** *($; on Highway 93-95, ☎ 604-347-9811)*, is a good way to start the day with a bang.

Radium Hot Springs Lodge *($$; every day; across from the Radium Hot Springs thermal ≈, ☎ 604-347-9342)* houses, it is said, the best eating spot in Radium Hot Springs. This restaurant, however, seems a tad put-on and serves food that unfortunately is not worth what they charge for it and the staff are not very courteous.

The restaurant of the **Fairmont Hot Springs Resort** *($$; every day; on Highway 93-95, near the Fairmont ski hills, ☎ 604-345-6311)* will satisfy the most demanding customers. Its healthy food is excellent, and the decor is pleasant.

Golden

As you cross the city, you will pass several fast-food restaurants.

Golden Rim Motor Inn *($; every day; 1416 Golden View Road, ☎ 604-344-2216)* houses a gloomy little restaurant which prepares simple traditional items.

Smitty's *($; every day; on Highway 16, next to the Tara Vista Motel, ☎ 604-865-6151)* is a family restaurant where simple meals are served, including hamburger and steak.

Apple Valley Restaurant *($; every day; Valley Shopping Centre, 150 Athabasca Avenue, ☎ 604-865-2999)* offers American-style Chinese food.

There is a restaurant in the **Golden Village Inn** *($$; every day; on the TransCanada Highway, at the entrance to Golden, ☎ 604-344-5996)*. The building, perched on a hill, is relatively uncrowded, and the food is adequate.

The restaurant of the **Prestige Inn** *($$; every day; 1049 TransCanada Highway, ☎ 604-344-7990)* encompasses the best of traditional cuisine in Golden.

■ **Tour E: Kananaskis Country**

Chief Chiniki *($; every day; on Highway 21, at Morley,* ☎ *403-881-3748)* offers typical North American dishes at reasonable prices. The staff are very friendly and attentive. A great brunch is served every Sunday.

Obsessions *($; every day; in Kananaskis Village)* is a little bar reserved for non-smokers where light meals are served.

The **Kananaskis Inn Restaurant** *($$; in the Kananaskis Inn, in the centre of the village,* ☎ *403-591-7500)* has a simple but warm decor. The menu is interesting, and the food is quite good.

Mount Engadine Lodge *($$; Spray Lakes Road,* ☎ *403-678-2880)* offers an interesting *table d'hôte*. The European-style cuisine is delicious.

L'Escapade *($$$; in the Hotel Kananaskis,* ☎ *403-591-7711)* is the hotel's French restaurant. Prettily decorated with red carpeting, comfortable armchairs and bay windows, this spot exudes warmth, all the better to linger over the excellent cuisine.

Entertainment

■ **Tour A: Banff National Park**

Banff

The primarily tourist existence of the small town of Banff has lead to the opening of several establishments aimed at entertaining visitors. There is something for everyone.

The **Banff Springs Hotel** *(Spray Avenue,* ☎ *403-762-6860)* has a number of different dance floors, depending on what kind of music you're looking for. The Whiskey Creek Saloon plays contemporary music, shows music videos on a big screen and attracts a young crowd. Dancing is also possible in the Alhambra dining rooms or in the Rob Roy room. Those in search of something more soothing can spend the evening in the Rundle Lounge where classical music played on harp and piano is presented.

Eddy's Back Alley *(137 Banff Avenue,* ☎ *403-762-8434)* is a hopping night club that occasionally showcases live bands.

The **Rose and Crown** *(206 Banff Avenue,* ☎ *403-762-2121)* combines the western motif with classic English pub decor. There is a dance floor, and live bands often play here. You can also try your hand at a game of darts or billiards.

Silver City *(110 Banff Avenue,* ☎ *403-762-3337)* is *the* big club in Banff; you can get down to the latest chart-topping hits.

If you prefer kicking up your heels in a real "western" setting, pull on your jeans and cowboy boots, grab your Stetson and saddle up for **Wild Bill's Legendary Saloon** *(upstairs at 201 Banff Avenue,* ☎ *403-762-0333)*. With a bit of luck, a friendly cowboy may just show you how to dance the two-step.

The **Barbary Coast** *(upstairs at 119 Banff Avenue,* ☎ *403-762-4616)* presents rock and blues bands just about every night. This is a pleasant, friendly spot.

Pool fans hang out at **King Eddy's Billiards** *(upstairs at 137 Banff Avenue, ☎ 403-762-4629)*.

The **Buffalo Paddock Lounge and Pub** *(124 Banff Avenue, ☎ 403-762-3331)* is a huge, slightly noisy bar in the basement of the Mount Royal Hotel.

Bumper's Loft Lounge *(603 Banff Avenue, ☎ 403-762-2622)* often shows short skiing films and plays traditional and folk music.

Lake Louise

Nights out are considerable more laid back in the town of Lake Louise. There are however two favourites that are sure to please some night owls.

The charming little **Charlie II's Pub** is located in the **Lake Louise Inn** *(Village Road, ☎ 403-522-3791)*. This is a pleasant spot for a drink and listening to some music. Bands are occasionally presented on weekends. Simple dishes are also served.

The **Glacier Saloon** *(Chateau Lake Louise, ☎ 403-522-3511)* generally attracts a young, dancing crowd.

■ **Tour C: Jasper National Park**

Jasper

There are three good spots for those in search of the latest tunes. They are **Tent City** *(in the basement of the Jasper Park Lodge, ☎ 403-852-3301)*, **Pete's on Patricia** *(upstairs at 614 Patricia Street, ☎ 403-852-6262)* and finally the **Night Club** *(Athabasca Hotel, 510 Patricia Street, ☎ 403-852-3386)*. These three places all offer dance floors, the latest dance music and a bar.

Nick's Bar *(Juniper Street between Connaught Drive and Geikie Street, ☎ 403-852-4966)* shows acrobatic skiing movies on a large screen. The stuff of dreams for those who wish they could tear down the slopes on two skis. A few light dishes are also served here. A pianist provides the musical entertainment some evenings.

Those in search of an English-style pub have two choices: the **Wistler Inn** *(105 Miette Avenue, ☎ 403-852-3361)* si great for a pint and a game of darts or pool (a warm fireplace makes for a cost atmosphere), while **Champs Walter's** *(Sawridge Hotel, 82 Connaught Drive, ☎ 403-852-5111)* offers a similar type of diversion with dart boards and pool tables.

Country music fans can do some two-stepping at **Buckles Saloon** *(at the west end of Connaught Drive, ☎ 403-852-7074)*. The decor is in keeping with Canada's wild west. You can dine on beer, hamburgers and sandwiches.

For a more relaxing ambience, you may prefer a fine liqueur and the classical harp music at the **Bonhomme Lounge** *(Chateau Jasper, 96 Geikie Street, ☎ 403-852-5644)*.

Shopping

■ **Tour A: Banff National Park**

Banff

Banff's main drag is lines with souvenir shops, sports stores and clothing

Shopping 273

stores of all kinds. When it comes to shopping the landscape is dotted with jewellery, souvenirs, essentials, sporting goods and t-shirts.

The **Hudson's Bay Company** *(125 Banff Avenue,* ☎ *403-762-5525)* is owned by the oldest clothing manufacturing company in Canada, established in 1670, and still sells clothes, along with souvenirs, cosmetics and much more.

The Shirt Company *(200 Banff Avenue,* ☎ *403-762-2624)*, as its name suggest, sells t-shirts for all tastes and sizes.

Monod Sports *(111 Banff Avenue,* ☎ *403-762-3725)* is the place for all of your outdoor needs. You'll find a good selection of hiking boots, all sorts of camping accessories as well as clothing.

Known throughout Canada for their quality leather goods, **Roots Canada** *(124 Banff Avenue,* ☎ *403-762-3260)* sells shoes, purses, handbags and beautiful leather jackets, as well as comfortable clothing.

Orca Canada *(121 Banff Avenue,* ☎ *403-762-2888)* jewellers is good place for gift ideas. Many pieces found here, and in other jewellers in the region, contain "ammolite", a fossilized rock found in Alberta. Though it can be expensive, it does make a typically Albertan gift.

A Bit of Banff *(120 Banff Avenue,* ☎ *403-762-4996)* sells every kind of souvenir imaginable from postcards to posters, picture books on the Rockies, moccasins and Amerindian masks, as well as native soapstone carvings. Be careful, however, as these carvings tend to be overpriced here.

The **Luxton Museum Shop** *(Luxton Museum, 1 Birch Avenue,* ☎ *403-762-2388)* is a small souvenir shop that sells native artwork as well as books on the subject.

The **Chocolaterie Bernard Callebaut** *(Charles Reid Mall, 127 Banff Avenue and in the Banff Springs Hotel,* ☎ *403-760-2418)* is a favourite of Belgian chocolate lovers. The truffles are excellent.

Godiva *(Cascade Plaza, 131 Banff Avenue,* ☎ *403-762-2035)* chocolates hardly need any introduction. Their reputation for fine chocolates is known the world over.

The **Wine Store** *(in the basement of 302 Caribou Street,* ☎ *403-762-3528)* is the place *par excellence* for a good bottle of wine.

Lake Louise and Surroundings

Canadian Traditions in Art, Clothing and Souvenirs *(Moraine Lake Lodge,* ☎ *403-522-3733)* is a small boutique where you'll find pieces of native artwork.

Woodruff and Blum Booksellers *(Samson Mall, Lake Louise,* ☎ *403-522-3842,* ⇄ *522-2536)* have an excellent selection of both souvenir photo books and practical books on hiking trail in the region, rock-climbing, fishing and canoeing. They also sell postcards, compact discs, posters and topographical maps.

Pipestone Photo *(Samson Mall, Lake Louise,* ☎ *403-522-5617)* offers a one-hour photo developing service.

Tour C: Jasper National Park

Jasper

Maligne Lake Books *(Beauvert Promenade, Jasper Park Lodge, ☎ 403-852-4779)* sells beautiful books of photography, newspapers and novels.

Exposures Keith Allen Photography *(612 Connaught Drive, ☎ 403-852-5325)* not only develops your film but can also show you a photo album containing unedited photographs of Marilyn Monroe during the shooting of the film *River of No Return*, filmed in Jasper. You can also buy a video of the Glacier parkway.

Besides photo-developing services, **Film Lab** *(Beauvert Promenade, Jasper Park Lodge, ☎ 403-852-4099)* also offers professional photographer services.

The **Pinnacle Sports with Fashion** *(621 Patricia Street, ☎ 403-852-5151)* boutique sells all sorts of sportswear for adults and children.

Jasper Originals *(Beauvert Promenade, Jasper Park Lodge, ☎ 403-852-5378)* sells interesting pieces of art in the form of paintings, sculptures, pottery and jewellery that make lovely souvenirs.

Jasper Camera and Gifts *(412 Connaught Drive, ☎ 403-852-3165)* has a good selection of books on the Rockies. You will also find Crabtree & Evelyn products. The shop rents out video cameras and sells binoculars so that you can observe the wildlife up-close when adventuring in the mountains.

The Liquor Hut *(Patricia Street and Hazel Avenue, ☎ 403-852-3152)* stocks a fine selection of wines and spirits.

Surroundings of Jasper

The **Sunwapta Falls Resort Gift Shop** *(53 km south of Jasper, on the Icefields Parkway, ☎ 403-852-4852)* sells native artwork like blankets, moccasins and soapstone carvings. The jewellery section of the boutique includes jade, lapis-lazuli and "ammolite" pieces.

ALBERTA

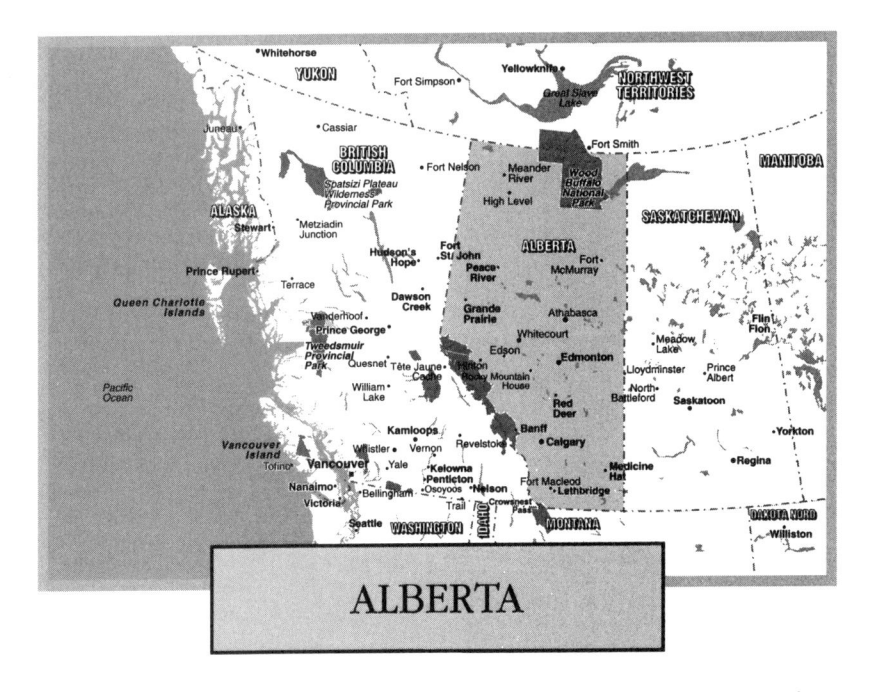

Alberta is a land that greets visitors with a multitude of landscapes, from the never-ending and flat fields of the prairies in the east, to the arid southern river valleys, to the dense hinterland of the north; from the ranchmen turned businessmen of Calgary and the oilmen of Edmonton to those majestic, unforgettable Rocky Mountains to the west. Originally inhabited by Amerindians with definitive territories, the province of Alberta is no longer a vast expanse of buffalo grazing grounds. The province, as it was established in 1905, is now peopled by newcomers and descendants of the original homesteaders. They have filled a vacuum created by the destruction of the buffalo herds and the natives who depended on them for a living. And the optimistic energy of the province's 2.6 million residents has grown out of the fact that from the beginning they have seen themselves as its creators, rather than its inheritors.

The fur-trading companies, present in the area as of the end of the 18th century, were only interested in fur and offered nothing in the way of law enforcement. American whisky traders were thus drawn north to this lawless land. With dwindling buffalo herds, natives were exploited and generally taken advantage of by the Americans, not to mention the deleterious effect the whisky trade had on them. Uprisings, including the Cypress Hills Massacre (see p 335), prompted the formation of the North West Mounted Police and the "March West" began. Starting from Fort Garry in Winnipeg, the Mounties crossed the plains lead by James Macleod. Their presence ridded Fort Whoop-Up of whisky traders in 1874; they then set about establishing four forts in southern Alberta including Fort Macleod and Fort Calgary.

Settlers began arriving in the Northwest Territories, of which Alberta was a district, in the 1880s. With the inclusion of these territories in Canadian Confederation, Amerindians had little choice but to negociate treaties and move onto the reserves.

Most settlers arrived when the Canadian Pacific Railway reached Fort Calgary in 1883, and eight years later in 1891, when the Grand Trunk Railway's northern route reached Edmonton. Ranchers from the United States and Canada initially grabbed up huge tracts of land with grazing leases, that in the case of the Cochrane Ranche, west of Calgary, occupied 100,000 acres. Much of this open range land was eventually granted to homesteaders.

To Easterners, the West was ranches, rodeos and cheap land, but the reality was more often a sod hut and loneliness. Though a homestead could be registered for $10, a homesteader first had to cultivate the land and own so many head of cattle. But the endless potential for a better future kept people coming from far and wide. Alberta's population rose from 73,000 in 1901 to 375,000 in 1911.

The district of Alberta, Northwest Territories had been a part of Canada Confederation in 1867. In 1905, Alberta became a province in the Canadian Confederation and Edmonton was named the capital.

Despite the fact that Alberta was the country's agricultural leader in the early 20th century, these were hard economic times. In 1923, the Alberta Wheat Pool was established to ensure farmers received a fair price for their exported grain. But even this could not curb the disastrous effects of the dirty thirties, when the west was hit particularly hard by drought and the depression.

The 1935 election of evangelical revivalist William Aberhart of the Social Credit party as provincial Premier proved a decisive moment in the province's history. Known as Bible Bill, Aberhart promised redemption for the lone brave man who would dare to stand up against the Eastern financiers. Though he remained Premier until his death in 1943, he never actually succeeded in implanting his proposed reforms to Alberta's monetary policy and economic structure because of federal constitutional restrictions. His successor, Ernest Charles Manning, did however succeed in bringing Social Credit from mere prairie radicalism to a reactionary force of Western politics.

Small oil discoveries had been made in Turner Valley in 1914 and elsewhere following this, but the most significant discovery, without a doubt, was made at Leduc in 1947. Foreign investment and the sale of oil and gas leases more than doubled the government's income and solved all of its financial problems. Foreign companies set up their headquarters in Calgary, where all the deals were made, while Edmonton found itself in the midst of an oil boom and became a technological and supply centre. In 1964 construction began on a plant to develop the Athabasca oil sands, they have since proven to contain the world's largest single oil deposit.

The formation of the Organization of Petroleum Exporting Countries (OPEC) in the seventies and the huge rise in foreign oil prices was the break Alberta had been waiting for. The value of the province's natural resources increased more than a 1000%. Meanwhile, the elcetion of Peter Lougheed and a Conservative provincial government brought an end to the reign of the Social Credit Party, which had been in power since the forties. The oil boom was the perfect vehicle for Lougheed's vision of a powerful and prosperous West. He diversified the economy, enriching the government's coffers and sparing no expense to ensure the prosperity of the cities of Edmonton and Calgary and the quality of life for Albertans throughout the province.

All of this spending did have its downside, however. In 1993, Ralph Klein was elected by a population fed up with debt. Klein proceeded to make cuts in government spending. The hardest hit areas were education and health care. Presently, issues like users fees for medical services and private clinics, both of which are forbidden under Canada's Medicare system, are under debate. Despite all his cuts, Klein remains well supported, although less so in the public sector.

The petroleum industry is still the leader in Alberta's economy even though the boom is over. Tourism is the second most important industry. Natural gas, coal, minerals, forestry and agriculture complete Alberta's economic pie. Major crops include, wheat, followed by barley, canola, oats, rye and flax. Some 4 million head of cattle represent the largest portion of Alberta's agricultural output.

The largest ethnic group is represented by descendants of homesteaders from the British Isles lured to the province at the turn of the century. The second largest group consists of Germans who migrated over a longer period. German Hutterites today live in closed communities throughout central and southern Alberta. They are recognizable by their particular, traditional dress. Ukrainians are the third largest group. They left their homeland, attracted by the promise of free land. The fourth largest ethnic group is French. Early French fur traders and missionaries were actually the first permanent settlers in the province. Other large ethnic groups include Chinese, Scandinavian and Dutch.

Alberta was settled in a few short years by people from a variety of ethnic backgrounds. With no forerunners to either absorb or alienate them, these newcomers found that geography and history had created a Western Canadian subculture. As a people, Albertans have always been inspired by their common future, rather than by their disparate pasts. Alberta's future has always seemed bright, after all it isn't just the 2,000 hours of sunshine a year that have earned it the nickname "sunny Alberta".

Wildlife abounds throughout the province and travellers with cars should keep their eyes open when driving in open areas for mule-deer and white-tailed deer. Even just outside the city of Calgary these animals can often be seen. Pronghorns scampering across grasslands are a common sight, and coyotes and occasionally wolves can also be spotted near northern highways. Black bears are found in forested areas throughout the province, while grizzly bears inhabit Waterton Lakes National Park, also home to cougars and bighorn sheep.

Finding Your Way Around

This chapter divides Alberta into five areas and outlines a tour of each below: **Tour A: Calgary** ★★; **Tour B: Southern Alberta** ★★★, **Tour C: Central Alberta** ★, **Tour D: Edmonton** ★★, **Tour E: Northern Alberta** ★. The Rocky Mountains are covered in a separate chapter, see p 203.

By car

The Alberta Motoring Association, the AMA can provide up-to-date information on road conditions to its members. Non-Albertans who are members of similar organizations like CAA or AAA can also benefit from this service; call ☎ 1-800-642-3810. Otherwise call the talking Yellow Pages in Edmonton at ☎ 493-9000, code 3000, or in Calgary at ☎ 521-5222, code 3000.

Calgary

The majority of Calgary's streets are numbered, and the city is divided into four quadrants, NE, NW, SE and SW. This may seem extremely unimaginative on the part of city-planners, but it makes it easy for just about anyone to find their way around. Avenues run east-west and streets run north-south. **Centre Street** divides the city between east and west, while the Bow River is the dividing line between north and south. The TransCanada Highway runs through the city, where it is known as 16th Ave. N. Many of the major arteries through the city have much more imaginative names, not only are they not numbered but they are called trails, an appellation that reflects their original use. These are **Macleod Trail**, which runs south from downtown (ultimately leading to Fort Macleod, hence the name); **Deerfoot Trail** which runs north-south through the city and is part of Hwy 2; and **Crowchild Trail** which heads northwest and joins **Bow Trail** before becoming Hwy 1A.

Calgary's "Motel Village" is located along 16th Ave. NW between 18th St. NW and 22nd St. NW.

Southern Alberta

The tour of southern Alberta essentially traces a triangle starting in Calgary and heading south to Waterton Lakes National Park, passing through the municipality of Crowsnest Pass on the way. The tour then heads east with stops in Lethbridge, the exceptional Head-Smashed-In Buffalo Jump and Writing-on-Stone Provincial Park before a stunning drive through the never-ending fields all the way to Medicine Hat. The tour winds up with a dinosaur odyssey of sorts with visits to Dinosaur Provincial Park and the town of Drumheller. All highways are paved, though the road from Writing-On-Stone Provincial Park to Medicine Hat could use some patchwork.

Lethbridge and Medicine Hat both have numbered street systems. Most of Lethbridge's hotels and motels are located along Mayor McGrath Dr, on your way into town on Hwy 5. Medicine Hat's motel and hotel strip is located on the TransCanada, east of downtown.

Central Alberta

The tour of Central Alberta is essentially a means of getting from

Finding Your Way Around 279

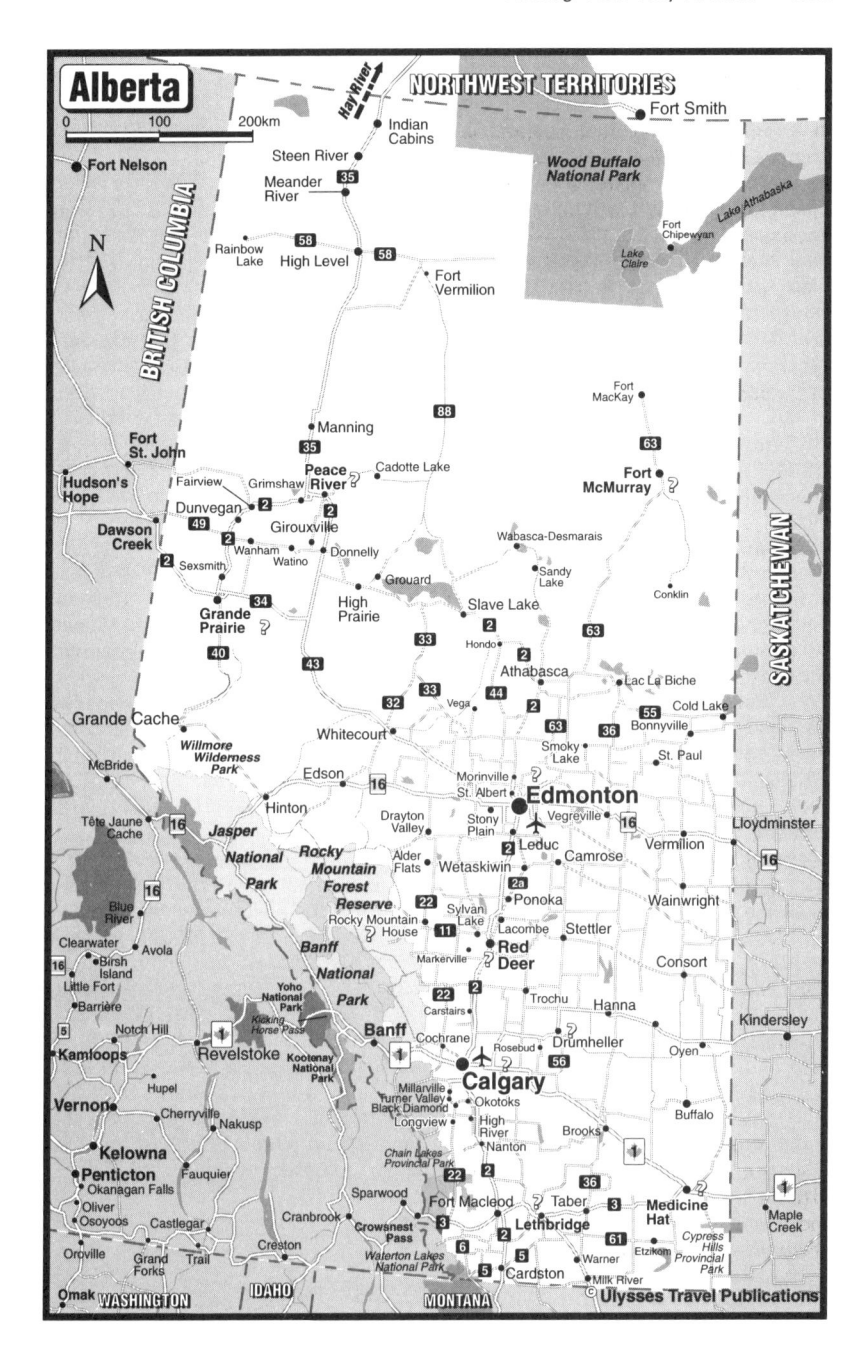

Calgary to Edmonton and back again. Some travellers may prefer to visit Drumheller at the beginning of this tour as it lies just over an hour northeast of Calgary. Otherwise the tour heads north on Hwy 2 to Red Deer before taking a jog east to Wetaskiwin and continuing up to Edmonton. On the way back to Calgary, the route heads west stopping in at Rocky Mountain House, Markerville and Cochrane before returning to Calgary.

Edmonton

Edmonton's streets are also numbered; the avenues run east-west and the streets run north-south. The major arteries include **Calgary Trail**, which runs north into the city (northbound it is also known as 103rd St. and southbound as 104th St.); **Whitemud Drive** runs east-west, it lies south of the city centre providing access to West Edmonton Mall, Fort Edmonton Park and the Valley Zoo; **Jasper Avenue** runs east-west through downtown where 101st Ave. would naturally fall; Hwy 16, the Yellowhead Highway, crosses the city north of downtown providing access to points in the tour of northern Alberta.

A collection of hotels line Calgary Trail south of downtown, and along Stony Plain Road west of the city centre.

Northern Alberta

The tour of northern Alberta is actually three routes leading to the frontiers of Alberta. The first heads east on Hwy 16, the Yellowhead Highway; the second and third head north of Edmonton on Hwy 2 to Athabasca, where the former continues northwest along Hwy 2 and the latter heads northeast up Hwy 63.

■ By Plane

Alberta has two international airports. **Calgary International Airport** is located northeast of downtown Calgary. It is Canada's fourth-largest airport and houses a whole slew of facilities and services. **Edmonton International Airport** is located south of the city centre and also offers many services and facilities. Both airports feature restaurants, an information centre, hotel courtesy phones, major car rental counters, currency exchange and a bus tour operator.

Air Canada, Canadian Airlines, American Airlines, Delta Airlines, Northwest Airlines, and United Airlines all have regular flights to both airports. K.L.M. services Calgary, while Lufthansa services Edmonton. Regional companies (Air B.C. and Canadian Regional) serve Calgary International, while in Edmonton they fly in and out of the municipal airport, located north of the city.

There is a shuttle from the Calgary airport to the major downtown hotels; the **Airporter** (☎ 531-3907) charges about $11, while a taxi will run about $25.

The **Grey Goose** (☎ 463-7520) is Edmonton's equivalent, with shuttles to the downtown hotels and to Edmonton's municipal airport. The trip ranges from $9 to $12. A taxi from the airport to downtown costs about $30.

■ By Train

Via Rail's transcontinental railway passenger service makes a stop in Edmonton three times a week, continuing west to Jasper and Vancouver or east to Saskatoon and beyond. Via does not service Calgary. Tickets on Via Rail can be booked through a travel agent or by calling Via directly at ☎ 1-800-561-8630 in Canada, or 1-800-561-3949 in the United States, or by fax at ⇄ (403) 420-6046. Americans can also book passage on a Via train through Amtrak. In the United Kingdom, contact Thomas Cooke Holidays at ☎ 733-331-777. Express Conseil in Paris ☎ 44.77.87.94 can also book Via tickets. Students and seniors benefit from reductions, and there is also a reduction for all tickets purchased at least five days in advance. The train station in Edmonton is located under the CN Tower at 10004 104th Ave.

Via's **Canrail Pass** is an interesting option for anyone who wants to see a lot of Canada. It offers unlimited travel on Via trains for 13 days in a 30-day period. At only $572 for adults and $513 for students and seniors from June to September, or $390 for adults and $352 for students and seniors the rest of the year, it is a great deal!

The only rail service from Calgary is offered by **Great Canadian Railtour Company Ltd. - Rocky Mountain Railtours**. Trains leave three times a week from May to October for Vancouver, with a stop in Banff to pick up passengers (you cannot get off in Banff). The trip takes two days and includes two breakfasts and two lunches as well as a night in a hotel in Kamloops. The train only runs during the day so you don't miss any of the spectacular scenery. It costs $620 per person, or $565 per person, double occupancy. Trains depart from the CP station in Calgary, located under the Palliser Hotel *(133 9th Ave. SW)*. For information and reservations call ☎ 1-800-665-7245 or (604) 606-7200 or send a fax to ⇄ (604) 606-7250.

■ By bus

Greyhound buses cover most of the province. Tickets can be bought on the spot; no reservations are taken but you will get a discount if you buy your ticket seven days in advance. Service is regular and relatively inexpensive, for example Calgary to Edmonton one-way is $33.17. For information call ☎ 265-9111 or 1-800-661-8747.

Calgary Greyhound Bus Depot
850 16th St. SW
☎ 265-9111
services: restaurant, lockers, tourist information board

Lethbridge Greyhound Bus Depot
411 5th St. S
☎ 327-1551
services: restaurant, lockers

Drumheller Greyhound Bus Depot
1222 Hwy 9 South (Suncity Mall)
☎ 823-7566
services: restaurant, tourist information

Edmonton Greyhound Bus Depot
10324 103rd St.
☎ 421-4211
services: restaurant, lockers

Brewster Transportation and Tours offers coach service from Calgary to Banff departing from Calgary International Airport, for information call ☎ 762-6700.

Public Transit

Calgary

Public transit in Calgary consists of an extensive bus network and a light-rail transit system known as the **C-Train**. There are three C-Trains, the Anderson C-Train which follows Macleod Trail south to Anderson Rd., the Whitehorn C-Train which heads northeast out of the city and the Brentwood C-Train which runs along 7th Ave. and then heads northwest. The Brentwood train is free along 7th Ave. You can transfer from a bus to a C-Train, tickets are $1.50 for a single trip or $4.50 for a day pass. For bus information call Calgary Transit at ☎ 262-1000; you can tell them where you are and where you want to go and they'll gladly explain how to do it.

Edmonton

Edmonton's public transit also combines buses and a light-rail transit system. The LRT runs east-west along Jasper Ave., south to the university and then north to 139th St. There are only ten stops, and in the city centre the train runs underground. The LRT is free between Churchill and Grandin stops. Fares are $1.60 at peak times and $1.35 the rest of the time, a day pass is $4.25. Route and schedule information is available by calling ☎ 421-4636.

By foot

Calgary

A system of interconnected enclosed walkways links many of Calgary's downtown sights, shops and hotels. Known as the **+15**, it is located 15 feet above the ground. The malls along 7th Ave. SW are all connected as are the Calgary Tower, Glenbow Museum and Palliser Hotel.

Edmonton

Edmonton's downtown core has its own system of walkways known as the **pedway** system. It lies below, above and at street level, and seems complicated at first, though is very well indicated and easy to negotiate once you have picked up a map at the information centre.

Practical Information

- Area code: ☎ 403.

General Information

Information on everything from road conditions to movie listings to provincial parks is available from the **Talking Yellow Pages**. In Edmonton, call ☎ 493-9000, and in Calgary call ☎ 521-5222. A series of recorded messages are accessible by dialling specific codes. The codes are listed in the front of the yellow pages phone book; there is usually a phone book in every phone booth.

Tourist Information

Knowledgeable and friendly staff answer the phone lines of Travel Alberta and can send you information brochures on accommodations, summer and winter sports, campgrounds, sights and events. Call ☎ 1-800-661-8888 in North America or

(403) 427-4321, or you can fax them at ⇄ (403) 427-0867.

Just about every city and small town throughout the province has a tourist information office. Many of the smaller ones are open only in the summer. Information on the local sights and brochures for bed and breakfasts in the area are given away. These offices are usually clearly marked from the highways.

Calgary Tower Centre Tourist Information
Centre St. and 9th Ave SW
open year-round, every day 8:30am to 5pm
☎ 263-8510 or 1-800-661-1678

Lethbridge Tourist Information Centre
2805 Scenic Dr.
☎ 320-1222

Medicine Hat Tourist Information
8 Gehring Rd. SE
☎ 527-6422

Drumheller Tourist Information
at the corner of Riverside Dr. and 2nd St. W
☎ 823-1331

Red Deer Tourist Information
Heritage Ranch on Cronquist Dr.
☎ 346-0180

Rocky Mountain House
tourist information in a trailer north of town on Hwy 11
summer only
☎ 845-2414
Chamber of Commerce in Town Hall
open year-round
☎ 845-5450

Edmonton Tourism
City Hall, 1 Sir Winston Churchill Square; also in Gateway Park, south of downtown on Calgary Trail (Hwy 2)
☎ 496-8400 or 1-800-463-4667

Peace River Tourist Information
9309 100th St
open in summer only
☎ 624-4042

Grande Prairie
Chamber of Commerce
10011 103rd Ave.
☎ 532-5340

Fort McMurray Visitors Centre
just north of Oil Sands Centre
☎ 791-4336

■ **Bed and Breakfasts**

The following organizations can reserve bed and breakfast in various regions throughout the province.

Alberta Bed & Breakfast Association
1018 4th Ave.
Wainwright, Alberta,
T9W 1H2
☎ 842-5867
regroups various regional B&B associations across the province.

Alberta's Gem B&B and Reservation Agency
11216 48th Ave.
Edmonton. Alberta
T6H 0T6
handles B&B bookings throughout the province

High Country B&B Association
Box 61
Millarville, Alberta
T0K 1K0
☎ 933-4174, ⇄ 933-2870
covers the area southwest of Calgary from Priddis to Waterton Lakes National Park.

B&B Association of Calgary
☎ 531-0065, ⇄ 531-0069

Wild Rose Country B&B Network
☎ 783-5123
covers the area between Calgary and Edmonton

Edmonton Bed & Breakfast
13824 110A Ave.
Edmonton, Alberta
T5M 2M9
☎ 455-2297

North Eastern B&B Association
☎ 639-2337

Northwestern Alberta B&B Network
☎ 532-7529

■ **Youth Hostels**

There are several youth hostels throughout Alberta and most of them are run by Hostelling International. To reserve a night in a hostel in Alberta you must contact the hostel directly (see "Accommodations" section). If you plan to take advantage of the hostel system to any degree it is a good idea to become a member, which can be done at any hostel.

■ **Telephones**

AGT, Alberta's phone company, sells the **AGT Phone Pass** which can be used to make local and long-distance cards from pay phones in Alberta. They are sold in $10, $20, $50 and $100 denominations, and are available from Phone Exchanges located in major shopping malls or from Shopper's Drug Mart pharmacies throughout the province. For information call ☎ 1-800-472-9773.

★ **Exploring**

■ **Tour A: Calgary ★★**

Calgary is a thriving metropolis of concrete and steel, and a western city through and through; it is set against the Rocky Mountains to the west and prairie ranchlands to the east. This young, prosperous city flourished during the oil booms of the forties, fifties and seventies, but its nickname, Cowtown, tells a different story. For before the oil, there were cowboys and gentlemen, and Calgary originally grew thanks to a handful of wealthy ranching families.

The area now known as Calgary first attracted the attention of hunters and traders after the disappearance of the buffalo in the 1860s. Whisky traders arrived from the United States, generally causing havoc with their illicit trade. This brought the North West Mounted Police west, and in 1875, after building Fort Macleod, they headed north and built a fort at the confluence of the Bow and Elbow Rivers. It was named Calgary, which in Gaelic means "clear, running water". The first settlers came with the railroad, though, when the Canadian Pacific Railway decided the line would cross the mountains at Kicking Horse Pass. The station was built in 1883 and the townsite laid out; just nine

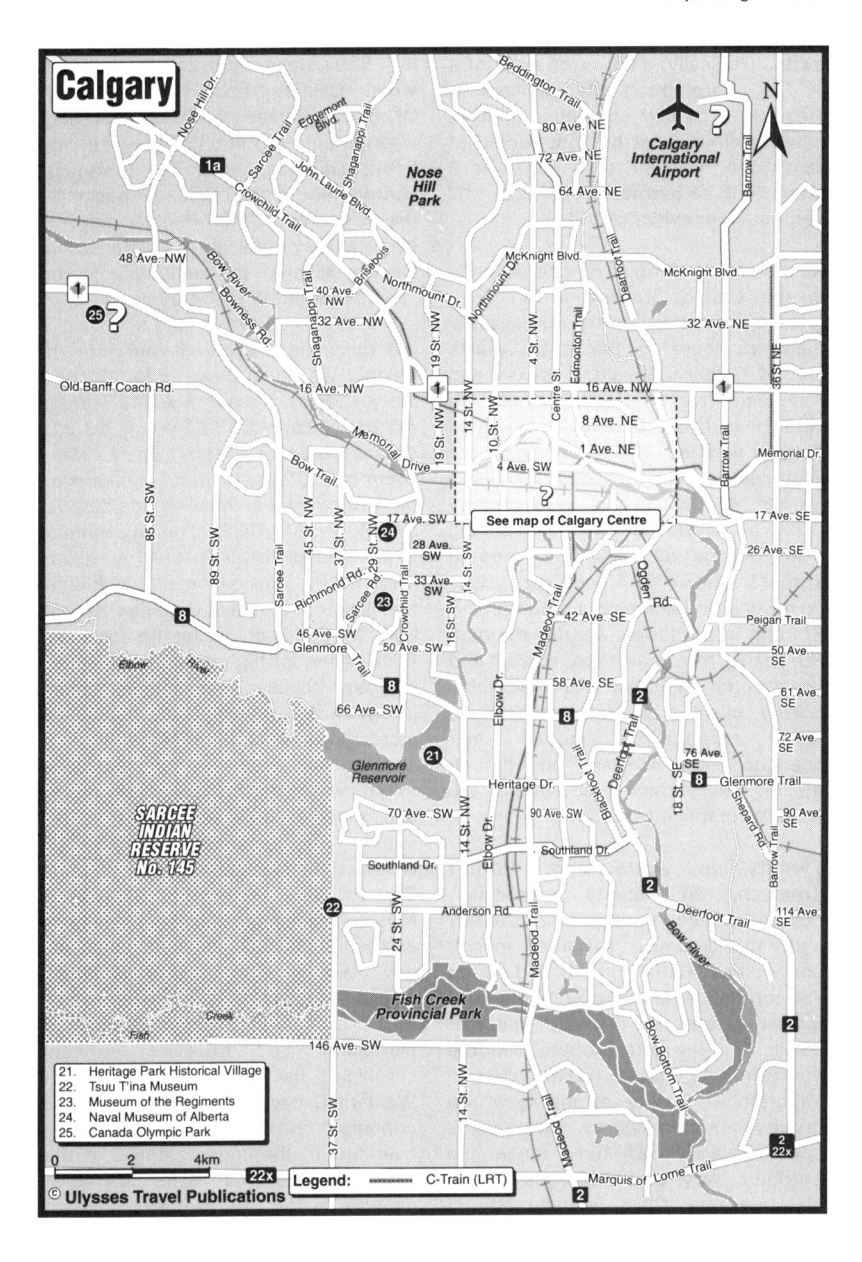

Calgary

21. Heritage Park Historical Village
22. Tsuu T'ina Museum
23. Museum of the Regiments
24. Naval Museum of Alberta
25. Canada Olympic Park

Legend: C-Train (LRT)

© Ulysses Travel Publications

years later Calgary was incorporated as a city. Tragically, a fire razed most of it in 1886, prompting city planners to draw up a by-law stipulating that all new buildings must be constructed of sandstone. Calgary thus took on a grand look of permanence that is still very much in evidence today.

Next came ranching. Over-grazed lands in the United States and an open grazing policy north of the border drew many ranchers to the fertile plains around Calgary. Wealthy English and American investors soon bought up land near Calgary, and once again Calgary boomed. The beginning of the 20th century was a time of population growth and expansion, only slightly jarred by WWI. Oil was the next big ticket. Crude oil was discovered in Turner Valley in 1914 and Calgary was on its way to becoming a modern city. Starting in the fifties, and for the next 30 years, the population soared and construction boomed. As the global energy crisis pushed oil prices up, world corporations moved their headquarters to Calgary, and though the oil was extracted elsewhere, the deals were made here.

Twenty-five years ago, Robert Kroetsch, an Alberta story-teller, novelist, poet and critic, called Calgary a city that dreams of cattle, oil, money and women. Cattle, money and oil are still top concerns of many of the local residents, and as the city matures, issues like the arts, culture and the environment have also gained importance. Quality of life is a top priority here: urban parks, cycling paths and a glacier fed river make the outdoors very accessible. Calgary is also the only Child Friendly city in North America, which means that children rate all the sights, restaurants, etc. The city gives much to its residents, and the residents give back. In 1988, they were both rewarded when Calgary hosted the Winter Olympic Games. After suffering through the drop in oil prices, the city flourished once again. The Olympics contributed something very special to the heritage of this friendly city; a heritage that is felt by Calgarians and visitors alike in the genuinely warm "howdy" attitude that prevails.

We recommend starting your tour of Calgary at the 190-m, 762-step, 55-story **Calgary Tower** ★★ (1) *(adults $4.95, children $1.95, youth $3.25, seniors $2.95; open every day, summer 7:30am to midnight, winter 8am to midnight; 9th Ave and Centre St SW, ☎ 266-7171)*. The city's most famous landmark not only offers a breathtaking view of the city, including the ski-jump towers at Canada Olympic Park, the Saddledome and the Canadian Rockies through high-power telescopes, but also houses the city's tourist information centre, a revolving restaurant and a bar. Photographers should take note that the specially tinted windows on the observation deck make for great photos.

Across the street at the corner of 1 St. SE is the stunning **Glenbow Museum** ★★★(2) *(adults $5, students and seniors $3.50, children free; every day 9am to 5pm during summer, closed Mon rest of year; 130 9th Ave. SE, ☎ 268-4100)*. Three floors of permanent and travelling exhibits chronicle the exciting history of Western Canada. The displays include contemporary and native art, and an overview of the various stages of the settling of the West, from the native peoples to the first pioneers, the fur trade, the North West Mounted Police, ranching, oil and agriculture. Photographs, costumes and everyday

Exploring 287

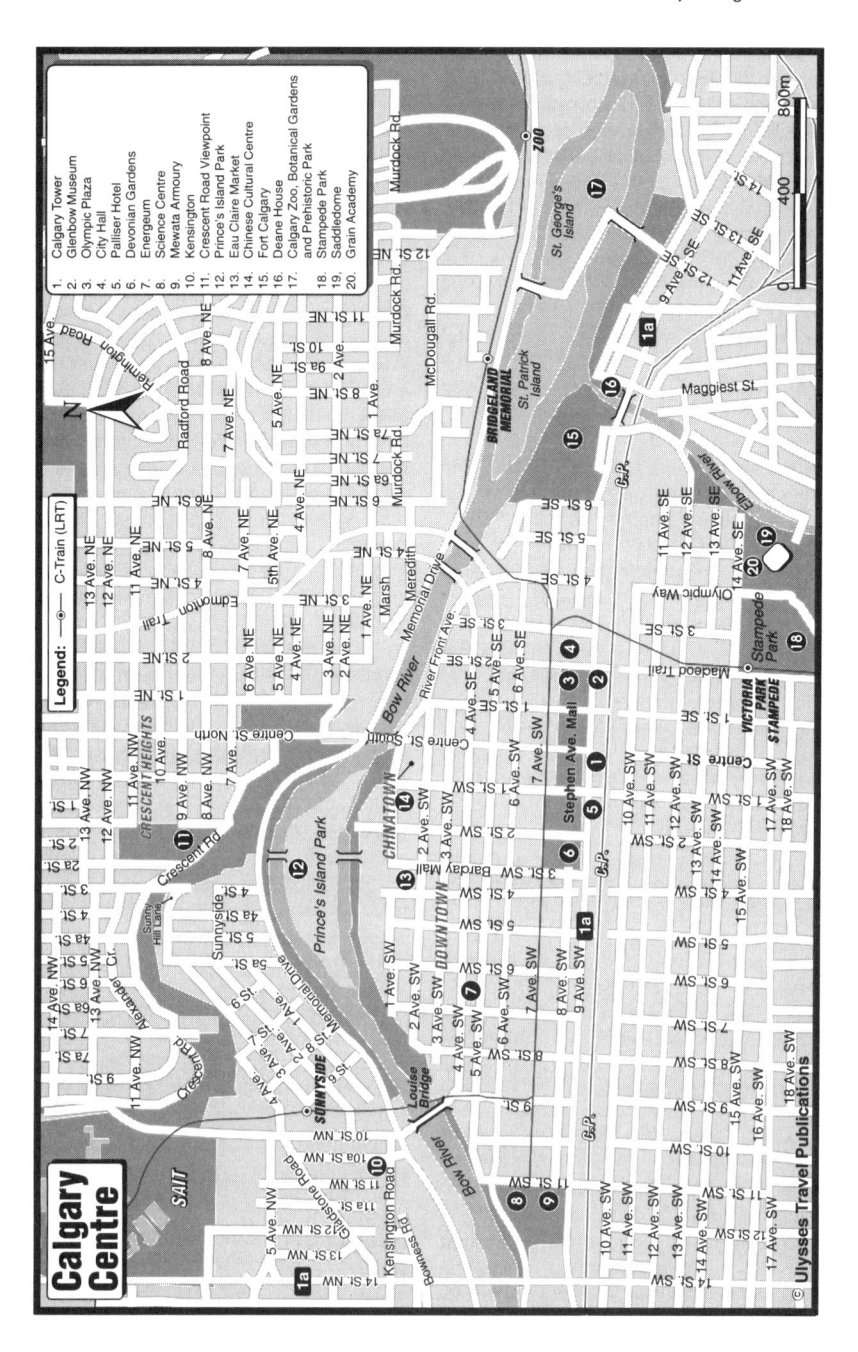

Calgary Centre

Legend: ⊙— C-Train (LRT)

1. Calgary Tower
2. Glenbow Museum
3. Olympic Plaza
4. City Hall
5. Palliser Hotel
6. Devonian Gardens
7. Energeum
8. Science Centre
9. Mewata Armoury
10. Kensington
11. Crescent Road Viewpoint
12. Prince's Island Park
13. Eau Claire Market
14. Chinese Cultural Centre
15. Fort Calgary
16. Deane House
17. Calgary Zoo, Botanical Gardens and Prehistoric Park
18. Stampede Park
19. Saddledome
20. Grain Academy

© Ulysses Travel Publications

items bring to life the hardships and extraordinary obstacles faced by settlers. There is also an extensive exhibit on the indigenous peoples of the whole country. Check out the life-sized teepee and the sparkling minerals, both a part of the province's diverse history. A great new permanent exhibit documents the stories of warriors throughout the ages. The museum also hosts travelling exhibits. Free gallery tours are offered once or twice weekly.

Head north on 2nd St. SE to the Olympic Plaza and City Hall.

Built for the medal presentation ceremonies of the '88 Winter Olympics, the **Olympic Plaza ★★★ (3)** is a fine example of Calgary's potential realized. This lovely square features a large wading pool (used as a skating rink in winter) surrounded by pillars and columns in an arrangement reminiscent of a Greek temple. The park is now the site of concerts and special events, and is frequented by street performers throughout the year; it is also a popular lunch spot with office workers. Each pillar in the Legacy Wall commemorates a medal winner, and the paving bricks are inscribed with the names of people who supported the Olympics by purchasing a brick for $19.88!

Across from the Olympic Plaza is **City Hall (4)** *(2nd St. SE)*, one of few surviving examples of the monumental civic halls that went up during the Prairies boom. It was built in 1911 and still houses a few offices.

At this point head west along Stephen Ave.

The **Stephen Avenue Mall** *(8th Ave between 2nd St. SE and 3rd St. SW)* is an excellent example not only of Calgary's potential, but also of the contrasts that characterize this cowtown metropolis — the mall is part vibrant pedestrian meeting place, part wasteland and unsavoury hangout. It has fountains, benches, cobblestone, restaurants and shops, but also more than its share of boarded-up storefronts and cheap souvenir and t-shirt shops. The beautiful sandstone buildings that line the Avenue are certainly a testament to better and different times, as are the businesses they house, including an old-fashioned shoe hospital and several western outfitters. One of these buildings is the **Alberta Hotel**, a busy place in the pre-prohibition days. Other buildings house trendy cafés and art galleries, and it is only a matter of time before the street once again becomes a meeting place for lawyers, doctors and the who's who of Calgary, just as it was at the beginning of the century.

West of 1st St SW, you might opt for the +15 walkway system, which provides an aseptic alternative to the street below. Purists may scoff at the city's system of interconnected walkways that can take you just about anywhere you want to go, but it is a wonderful alternative to the underground passages found in many large cities. And you certainly won't scoff on cold winter days, when the +15 provides a warm, bright and welcome relief!

Interconnected malls line the street west of 1st St. SW, including the Scotia Centre, TD Square, Bankers Hall and the Eaton Centre. Though this type of commercialism might not appeal to everyone, hidden within TD Square is a unique attraction — Alberta's largest indoor garden, the **Devonian Gardens ★★ (6)** *(free admission, donations accepted; every day 9am to 9pm; between 2nd and 3rd Streets*

SW, level 4 TD Square, ☎ 268-5207 or 268-3888). For a tranquil break from shopping, head upstairs, where 2.5 acres of greenery and blossoms await. Stroll along garden paths and enjoy the art exhibitions and performances that are often presented here, high above the concrete and steel.

Head west on foot along 8th Ave SW. If you are tired you can take the LRT free of charge all along 7th Ave SW, although the walk is easy and more interesting.

Among the city's stately sandstone buildings along the way is the **Hudson's Bay Company** department store, The Bay, at the corner of 1st St. SW. Stop in at A+B Sound one block up at 140 8th Ave., a music store housed in the gorgeously restored former Bank of Montreal building.

Farther west you'll come upon more fancy shops and department stores.

Head up 5th St. SW to the Energeum.

At the **Energeum** ★ **(7)** *(free admission; Mon to Fri 10:30am to 4:30pm; Energy Resources Building, 640 5th Ave. SW, ☎ 297-4293)* you can learn all about Alberta's number one resource, energy. Whether it is oil, natural gas, oil sands, coal or hydroelectricity, everything from pipelines to rigs and oil sands plants is explained through hands-on exhibits and computer games. Across the street is the Renaissance Revival **McDougall Centre**, a government building that was declared a historic site in 1982.

Return to 7th Ave. SW and take the LRT to the end, then walk a block to the Science Centre.

The peculiar looking concrete building on 11th St. SW is **The Science Centre** ★★★ **(8)** *(adults $7, children and seniors $5, families $26; every day 10am to 8pm; 701 11 St. SW, ☎ 221-3700)*, a wonderful museum that children will love. Hands-on displays and multi-media machines cover interesting subjects like dinosaurs and astronomy. The museum boasts a planetarium, an observatory, a science hall and two theatres, which showcase mystery plays and special-effects shows. In addition, a 220-seat domed theatre and a dynamic motion simulator are soon to be completed.

South on 11th St. SW is the **Mewata Armoury (9)**, an historic site that is now home of the King's Own Calgary Regiment and Calgary Highlanders. For more information on Calgary's international military history, visit the Museum of the Regiments (see p 292).

Make your way towards the Eau Claire Market by following the Bow River on the north or south side. The quicker way, which leads directly to the market, is on the south side along Bow Trail, or by taking the LRT back to 3rd St. SW, and then walking up Barclay Mall until you reach the market. A more scenic route is on the north side of the river, with a detour to the Kensington area. To do this cross the Louise Bridge at the end of 9th St. SW.

Kensington ★★ **(10)** is one of the city's trendy neighbourhoods north of the Bow. Stroll about along Kensington Road NW and 10th St. NW and enjoy the specialty shops, and cafés (see p 352, 365).

From Kensington, walk along Memorial Dr NW and turn left on 4A St. NW, right on Sunny Hill Lane, left on 4th St NW and right on Crescent Road.

This area is known as Sunnyside and Crescent Heights and has some pretty houses. A lookout on Crescent Rd called the **Crescent Road Viewpoint** ★★ **(11)** provides a great view of the city and river. A bridge at the end of 3rd St. NW leads to **Prince's Island Park** ★ **(12)**, a picturesque green space with jogging paths and picnic tables. You'll also find the lovely River Café (see p 353), which serves a delicious weekend brunch.

Traverse the island and cross the bridge on the other side which deposits you right at the Eau Claire Market.

The recently built **Eau Claire Market** ★★ **(13)** *(Mon to Wed 10am to 6pm, Thu and Fri 10am to 9pm, Sat 10am to 6pm, Sun 10am to 6pm; next to the Bow River and Prince's Island Park, ☎ 264-6460)* is part of a general initiative in Calgary to keep people downtown after hours. The large warehouse-like building houses specialty food shops selling fresh fruit, vegetables, fish, meats, bagels and baked goods; neat gift shops with local and imported arts and crafts; clothing stores; a great bookstore; fast-food and fine restaurants; a movie theatre and a 300-seat **IMAX** *(☎ 974-4600)* giant-screen theatre.

The area around the market has seen a considerable amount of development recently, including the construction of the market itself and of a beautiful new YMCA, plus the renovation of several buildings into restaurants and bars. It has become quite an appealing area to explore.

Close by is Calgary's **Chinese Cultural Centre** ★★ **(14)** *(free admission; every day 9:30am to 9pm; 197 1st St. SW, ☎ 262-5071)*, the largest of its kind in Canada. Craftsmen were brought in from China to design the building, whose central dome is patterned after the Temple of Heaven in Beijing. The highlight of the intricate tile-work is a glistening golden dragon. The centre houses a gift shop, museum, gallery and restaurant.

At the end of Centre St, the Centre Street Bridge crosses the Bow River which marks the northern boundary of downtown. Stone lions guard the bridge and seem to be taking in the view. Cross the bridge and head west to find out what they are looking at.

Calgary's small **Chinatown** lies south of the Bow, around Centre Street. Although it only has about 2,000 residents, the street names written in Chinese characters and the sidewalk stands selling durian, ginseng, lychees and tangerines all help to create a wonderful feeling of stepping into another world. The markets and restaurants here are run by descendants of Chinese immigrants who came west to work on the railroads in the 1880s.

You can reach Fort Calgary by walking east along the river for 1.5 km, or by taking bus #1 or #14 from 7th Ave.

Fort Calgary ★★★ **(15)** *(adults $3, seniors $2.55, children $1.50, under 6 free; every day 9am to 5pm; 750 9th Ave. SE, ☎ 290-1875)* was built as part of the March West, which brought the North West Mounted Police to the Canadian west to stop the whisky trade. "F" Troop arrived at the confluence of the Bow and Elbow rivers in 1875, and chose to set up camp here either because it was the only spot with clean water or because it was halfway between Fort Macleod and Fort Saskatchewan. Nothing remains of the original Fort Calgary — the structures and outline of the foundations on the site today are part of an ongoing project of excavation and discovery undertaken mostly by volunteers. In fact, the fort will never be completely rebuilt as that would interfere with archaeological work underway. An excellent interpretive centre includes great hands-on displays (the signs actually say "please touch"), woodworking demonstrations and the chance to try on a famous scarlet Mounties uniform. Friendly guides in period costume provide tours.

Right on the other side of the Elbow River, across the 9th Ave. Bridge is the **Deane House (16)** *(Wed to Sun 11am to 2pm, ☎ 267-7747)*, the last remaining house from the garrison. It was built in 1906 for Richard Burton Deane, the Fort Post Commander at Fort Calgary, and later in charge of the jail in Regina during the Rebellion of 1885, where he was Louis Riel's jailor. The house originally stood next to the fort, across the river from its present location, and has been moved three times. Used in the past as a boarding house and as an artist's coop, it has been restored and is now one of the city's better teahouses (see p 353).

Take the Whitehorn C-train from downtown northeast to the Calgary Zoo north entrance, or walk across the 12th St. Bridge to St. George's Island and the south entrance.

The **Calgary Zoo, Botanical Gardens and Prehistoric Park ★★ (17)** *(adults $7.50, seniors $5.50, children $3.75; May to Sep, every day 9am to 6:30pm; Sep to May, every day 9am to 4pm; St. George's Island, 1300 Zoo Rd. NE, ☎ 232-9300 or 232-9372)* is the second largest zoo in Canada. It opened in 1920 and is known for its realistic recreations of natural habitats, now home to over 300 species of animals and 10,000 plants and trees. Exhibits are organized by continent and include tropical birds, Siberian tigers, snow leopards and polar bears, as well as animals indigenous to this area. The Prehistoric Park recreates the world of dinosaurs with 27 full-size replicas set amidst plants and rock formations from prehistoric Alberta. The Kinsmen's Childrens Zoo Contact Centre allows children to pet a number of animals.

Take the Anderson C-Train south toward Stampede Park; if another strolling, shopping and eating detour is in order, stop off at 17th Ave. SW and explore the area known as Uptown 17, a stretch of boutiques and eateries.

Unless you're in town during Stampede in July, **Stampede Park (19)** *(14th Ave and Olympic Way SE)* has a limited appeal. The park is best known as the locale of the famous Calgary Stampede, which takes place every year in July. Known simply as "The Week" by Calgarians, it is also called the "Greatest Outdoor Show on Earth." If you are around at this time of year, get out your Stetson, hitch up your horse and get ready for a rompin' good time, Ya-hoo! See "Entertainment" section, p 362.

The Stampede grounds are used year-round for a variety of activities. The aptly named **Saddledome** has the world's largest cable-suspended roof and is a giant testimony to the city's cowboy roots. Apparently, there was some controversy over its name, though it is hard to imagine what else they could have called it! It is the home of the National Hockey League team, the Calgary Flames, and is also used for concerts, conventions and sporting events. The figure skating and ice-hockey events of the '88 Olympics were held here. Tours are available (☎ 261-0400). Also on the park grounds is the **Grain Academy ★ (20)** (free admission; year-round Mon to Fri 10am to 4pm; Apr to Sep, Sat noon to 4pm; on the +15 level of the Round-Up Centre, ☎ 263-4594), which traces the history of grain farming and features a working railway and grain elevator. Finally, thoroughbred and harness racing take place on the grounds year-round and there is also a casino.

Continue south on the Anderson C-Train to the Heritage stop, then take bus 502 to Heritage Park.

Heritage Park Historical Village ★★ (21) (adults $7.50, seniors $6.50, children 2-16 $4.50, under 2 free; May to Sep every day, Sep to Oct weekends and holidays only) is a 26-hectare park on the Glenbow Reservoir. Step back in time as you stroll through a real 1910 town with historic houses decorated with period furniture, wooden sidewalks, a working blacksmith, a teepee, an old schoolhouse, a post office, a divine candy store and the Gilbert and Jay Bakery, known for its sourdough bread. Staff in period dress play piano in the houses and take on the role of suffragettes speaking out for women's equality in the Wainwright Hotel. Other areas in the park recreate an 1880's settlement, a fur trading post, a ranch, a farm and the coming of the railroad. Not only is this a magical place for children, with rides in a steam engine and a paddlewheeler on the reservoir, but it is also a relaxing place to escape the city and enjoy a picnic.

Continue south on the Anderson C-Train, then take bus 504 to the Tsuu T'ina Museum.

The **Tsuu T'ina Museum ★ (22)** (donation; Mon to Fri 8am to 4pm; 3700 Anderson Rd. SW, ☎ 238-2677) commemorates the history of the Tsuu T'ina who are Sarcee Indians. Tsuu T'ina means "great number of people" in their language and it is what they call themselves. Nearly wiped out several times in the 1800s by diseases brought by Europeans, the Tsuu T'ina were shuffled around reserves for many years, but persevered and were eventually awarded their reserve on the outskirts of Calgary in 1881. They held on to the land, spurning all pressures to sell it. Some of the pieces on display were donated by Calgary families who used to trade with the Tsuu T'ina, whose reserve lies immediately to the west of the museum. Others items, including a teepee and two headdresses from the thirties, were retrieved from the Provincial Museum in Edmonton.

Head north on 14th St SW, turn left on Glenmore Trail and then right on Crowchild Trail to visit the Museum of the Regiments.

The **Museum of the Regiments (23)** (donation; Thu to Tue 10am to 4pm; 4220 Crowchild Trail SW, ☎ 240-7674), Canada's second largest military museum, was opened by Queen Elizabeth in 1990. It honours four regiments: Lord Strathcona's Horse Regiment, Princess Patricia's Canadian Light Infantry, the King's own Calgary Regiment and the Calgary Highlanders. Uniforms, medals, photographs and maps of famous battles are displayed. Sound effects like staccato machine-gun fire and the rumble of far-off bombs create an eerie atmosphere as you tour the museum. Vintage tanks and carriers can be viewed on the spotless grounds of the impressive building that houses the museum.

Continue north on Crowchild Trail to the Naval Museum. Or take bus #20 on Richard Road.

Believe it or not, Canada's second-largest naval museum, the **Naval Museum of Alberta (24)** *(free admission; Tue to Fri 1pm to 5pm, Sat and Sun 10am to 6pm; 1820 24th St. SW,* ☎ *242-0002)* is over 1,000 km from the ocean. It salutes Canadian sailors, especially those from the prairie provinces. The story of the Royal Canadian Navy unfolds from 1910 through photographs, uniforms, and models, as well as actual fighter planes.

Take Bow Trail, Sarcee Trail and 16th Ave NW northwest to Canada Olympic Park.

Canada Olympic Park ★★★ (25) *(museum $3.25, tours $6-10.50; on 16th Ave. NW,* ☎ *286-2632)*, or C.O.P., built for the '88 Winter Olympic Games, lies on the western outskirts of Calgary. This was the site of the ski-jumping, bobsleigh, luge, freestyle skiing and disabled events during the games, and it is now a world-class facility for training and competition. Artificial snow keeps the downhill ski slopes busy in the winter, and the park also offers tours year-round and the chance to try the luge *($12 for one ride, $20 for two)* or bobsleigh, summer ski-jumping and bungee jumping *($49.50;* ☎ *286-4334)*.

Visitors to C.O.P. have the choice of seven different guided tour packages ranging from a self-guided walking booklet to the Grand Olympic Tour for $10.50, which includes a guided bus tour, chair lift ride, the Olympic Hall of Fame and the tower. It is worth taking the bus up to the observation deck of the 90-metre ski jump tower visible from all over the city. You'll learn about the refrigeration system, which can make 1,250 tonnes of snow and ice in 24 hours, the infamous Jamaican bobsleigh team, the 90- and 70-metre towers and the plastic-surface landing material used in the summer. If you do decide to take the bus, sit on the left for a better view of the towers and tracks. The **Naturbahn Teahouse** *(*☎ *247-5465)* is located in the former starthouse for the luge. Delicious treats and a scrumptious Sunday brunch are served, but be sure to make reservations. The **Olympic Hall of Fame** *($4.50; every day 10am to 5pm)* is the world's largest museum devoted to the Olympics. The whole history of the games is presented with exhibits, videos, costumes, memorabilia and a bobsleigh and ski-jump simulator. You'll find a tourist information office and a gift shop near the entrance.

■ **Tour B: Southern Alberta ★★★**

When departing Calgary it is difficult to head south and resist the pull of the Rocky Mountains looming in the distance to the west. However, southern Alberta boasts some of the best sights and scenery of the whole province, from Waterton Lakes National Park and the mining towns of Crowsnest Pass to the historic native gathering spot at Head-Smashed-In, the badlands and the Red Deer River Valley.

Although Highway 2 is the quickest route from Calgary to Fort Macleod, the superb scenery along Highway 22, referred to by some as God's country, is well worth the extra time. This quiet two-lane highway first heads southwest of Calgary through an area synonymous with Alberta's oil-and-gas economic boom, and then runs through stunning historic ranchlands, with the Rocky Mountains as a backdrop.

Millarville

South of Calgary take Highway 22 to Millarville, home of the historic **Millarville racetrack**. This town is the only one left of five that were built to accommodate transient workers of the Turner Valley oil fields. There is not much to see in this hamlet on a weekday, but if you're passing through on a Saturday, be sure to stop at the **Farmer's Market** *($1 parking; Jun to Sep, Sat 8:30am to noon; Millarville Racetrack, ☎ 931-3411)*. Vendors from throughout the area sell crafts, fresh produce, baked goods and clothing. A three-day Christmas market is also held the first weekend in November, as well as an Agricultural fair the third Sunday in August. The **races** *(adults $4, children free; first weekend in Jul, Sat and Sun 1pm)* take place at the beginning of July. These have been running for 90 years, but betting was only allowed for the first time in 1995. Games and festivities accompany the annual races.

Head south on Highway 22 to Turner Valley.

Turner Valley

The first major crude oil discovery in Alberta (and Canada), was made in Turner Valley in 1914, but it is natural gas, discovered eleven years earlier that is the claim to fame of Turner Valley. **Dingman No. 1** was Turner Valley's first producing well. It was named after a Calgary businessman who was brought, along with R. B. Bennett, future Prime Minister of Canada, to the site by William Herron in 1903. Herron lit a flame using the gas seepage from the earth and cooked the three men breakfast. Dingman and Bennett thus agreed to finance the well which lasted until 1952. An area known as **burning ground**, where gas flares still burn round the clock, is actually the site of the former Dingman No. 2 well. The seepage was lit in 1977 as a precautionary measure. This unique site is best viewed from the Hell's Half Acre Bridge, which spans the Sheep River.

Black Diamond

Just a few kilometres east of Turner Valley is the town of **Black Diamond**, another town whose claim to fame lies in its rich natural resources. The false fronts of this town's main street bear witness to prosperous times when coal was like black diamonds. The mine here was opened in 1899, and at its peak 650 tons of coal a year were extracted.

Head east along Highway 7, then north on Highway 2A to Okotoks.

Okotoks

Okotoks is the largest city between Calgary and Lethbridge. It is also home to several antique and craft shops. The **Ginger Tea Room and Gift Shop** *(43 Riverside Dr., ☎ 938-2907)* is a Victorian mansion, where High Tea is served on weekdays and two floors of collectibles and crafts can be admired or purchased (see "Restaurants" section, p 354). A walking tour map is available at the tourist

Exploring 295

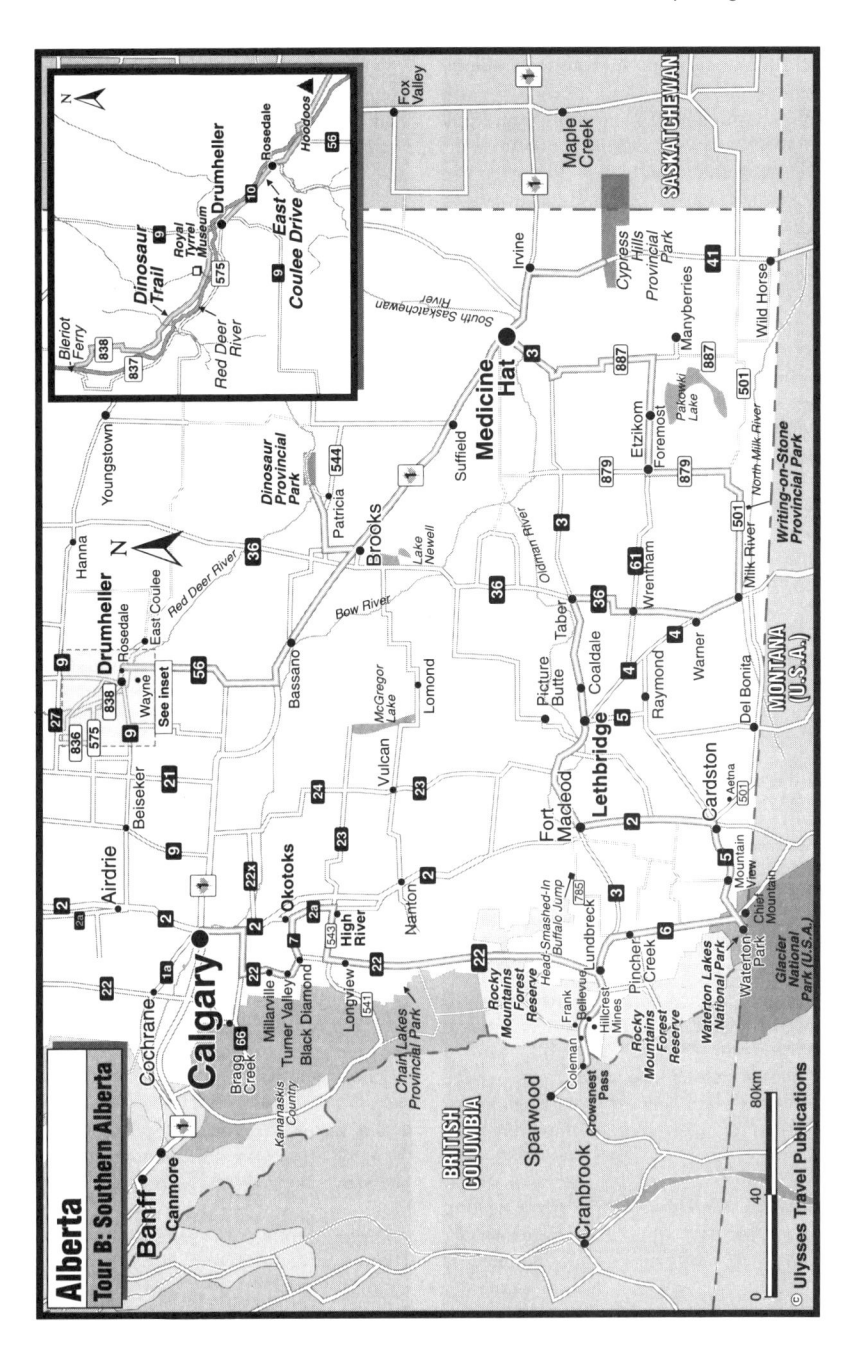

office *(53 N. Railway St., ☎ 938-2901)* and includes several historic buildings which date from when the town was a rest stop along the Macleod Trail between Fort Calgary and Fort Macleod.

The town's name comes from the Blackfoot word *okatok*, which means rock, and refers to the **Big Rock**, one of the largest glacial erratics found in North America and the town's biggest attraction. This 18,000-ton rock was deposited 7 km west of Okotoks during the Ice Age after it landed on an advancing glacier during a landslide in what is now Jasper National Park.

Okotoks is also home to the **Okotoks Bird Sanctuary**, where geese, ducks and other waterfowl can be observed from an elevated observation deck. It is an ongoing project of the Fish and Game Association.

High River

Another rest stop along the Macleod Trail, **High River**, 24 km south of Okotoks along Highway 2A, was the only place men, horses, cattle and wagons could cross the Highwood River. High River is now a small ranching community with an interesting local museum, the **Museum of the Highwood** *(adults $3, children free; May to Sep, every day 10am to 5pm; Oct to May, closed Sat and Sun; 406 1st St. West, ☎ 652-2396)*. The North American Chuckwagon Racing Championships are held here in late June. It is also the birthplace of Canada's 16th prime minister, Joe Clark.

Backtrack from High River along Highway 543 then take Highway 22 south to Longview and the Bar U Ranch.

Longview

The **Bar U Ranch National Historic Site** ★★★ *(adults $2.25, seniors $1.75, children $1.25, under 6 free; Jul 1 to Sep 4, 10am to 8pm; Sep 5 to Oct 10, 10am to 6pm; Oct 11 to May 16 phone for times; Longview, Alberta, ☎ 395-2212 or 1-800-568-4996)* opened in the summer of 1995 and commemorates the contribution of ranching to the development of Canada. It is one of four ranches that once covered almost all of Alberta, and for the moment is still a working ranch. This will change over the next five to ten years as Canadian Heritage and Parks Canada take over the site in a cooperative effort with the Friends of the Bar U Ranch Association. By 1997, people will be able to wander freely around the ranch and observe ranching operations on a scaled-down level. "Bar U" refers to the symbol branded on cattle from this ranch. A beautiful new visitors centre features an interpretive display on breeds of cattle, the roundup, branding and what exactly a quirt is. A 15-minute video on the Mighty Bar U conveys the romance of the cowboy way of life and also explains how the native grasslands and Chinook winds unique to Alberta have been a perpetual cornerstone of ranching. The Centre also houses a gift shop and a restaurant where you can savour an authentic buffalo burger.

Continue south along Highway 22 for another hundred kilometres or so to Highway 3.

Chain Lakes Provincial Park ★ is the only real attraction along this stretch of highway. It sits between the Rocky Mountains and the Porcupine Hills in a transition zone of spring-fed lakes. There is a campground, a boat launch and a beach at the southern end of the reservoir. Farther south, the splendid pale yellow grasslands, dotted occasionally by deep blue lakes, roll up into the distant rocky mountains. There is an otherworldly look about the mountains looming on the horizon.

Head west once you reach Highway 3, another stretch of scenic highway. It leads deeper into the foothills and through a series of mining towns to Crowsnest Pass and British Columbia.

Crowsnest Pass

The area along Highway 3 between Pincher Creek and the Continental Divide is known as the Municipality of Crowsnest Pass. A number of once thriving coal-mining communities along the highway are now home to a handful of sites offering an interesting historical perspective on the local mining industry. Coal was first discovered here in 1845, but it wasn't until 1898, when the CPR built a line through the pass, that towns were really settled. Coal was the only industry in the area, and when the mineral turned out to be of inferior quality and hard to get at, troubled times set in. Local coal fetched lower prices than that of British Columbia, and by 1915 the first mine had closed; the others soon followed. The municipality is Alberta's only ecomuseum and was declared a Historic District in 1988.

The first site you will come across as you head west along Highway 3 is the **Lietch Collieries** *(free admission; guided tours May to Sep, self-guided Sep to May;* ☎ *562-8635)*. This was the only Canadian-owned mine in the Pass, and the first to close in 1915. Various information panels explain the extraction process while a path leads through the mine ruins.

The Chinook Wind

A Chinook occurs when moisture-laden winds from the Pacific Ocean strike the Rocky Mountains and are forced to precipitate their moisture as rain or snow. This leaves the winds cold and dry. However, as the air descends the eastern slopes it remains dry but is condensed by the increase in atmospheric pressure and warms up. This warm dry wind brings mild conditions that can melt a foot of snow in a few hours. It is essentially because of the Chinook that Alberta's native grasses survive the winter and that cattle can graze on the prairies year-round. The warm, dry breath of the Chinook is a fabled part of Alberta history. It is the stuff of legend, with stories of farmers rushing home at the sight of the telltale Chinook arch (an arch-shaped cloud formed when the warm air pushes the cloud cover to the west), with the front legs of their horses in snow and the hind legs in mud!

Farther down Highway 3, follow the signs toward Hillcrest.

On June 19th, 1914, **Hillcrest** was the site of the worst mining disaster in Canadian history, when an explosion ripped through the tunnels of the mine trapping 235 men underground. Many that had survived the blast eventually died of asphyxiation from the afterdamp (the CO_2 and CO left over after the explosion has used all available oxygen), which along with smoke also forced back rescuers. The mine has been sealed since it shut down in 1939, and there isn't much to see except the closed-off entrance. The 189 victims of the disaster were buried in a mass grave in a cemetery located 1 km along the road from Highway 3.

Continue west through Hillcrest, and cross Highway 3 to the Bellevue Mine.

The **Bellevue Mine** opened in 1903 and had been operating for seven years without incident, when it was rocked by an underground explosion on December 9, 1910. Afterdamp poisoning lead to the death of 30 miners. The mine reopened and remained operational until 1962. Today visitors are given hard hats and miner's lamps and follow a **guided tour** ★★ *($4; Jul to early Aug, tours every half hour 10am to 5:30pm;* ☎ *564-8831)* through about 100 m of dark, cool and damp underground mine tunnels. This is the only mine in the Pass open to visitors and is a real treat for both young and old. Bring a sweater, as it can get quite cold in the mine.

Continuing along Highway 3, you'll notice a very drastic change in the landscape. Extending on both sides of the highway, covering 3 km^2, debris of the Frank Slide creates a spectacular, almost lunar landscape. Consisting mostly of limestone, these boulders are on average 14 metres deep, but exceed 30 metres in some places. The **Frank Slide Interpretive Centre** ★★ *(adults $3.25, children $1.25, under 6 free; May to Sep, every day 8am to 9pm, guided tours every 30 min; Sep to May 10am to 4pm; turn right off highway,* ☎ *562-7388)*, located north of the highway on a slight rise, presents an audiovisual account of the growth of the town and the slide itself. It explains the various theories about what caused the slide on April 29, 1903 that sent 82 million tons of limestone crashing from the summit of Turtle Mountain on top of the town of Frank, which at the time lay south of the highway at the foot of the mountain. All that remains of the town is an old fire hydrant. The mountain's unstable structure, mining, water and severe weather are believed to have contributed to the disaster. A self-guided trail through the slide area provides an interesting perspective of the scope of the slide. Sixty-eight of the town's residents were buried, but the disaster might have been worse if it hadn't been for a CPR brakeman who amazingly raced across the rocks to stop an approaching passenger train. Those who dare can climb Turtle Mountain to examine fissures and cracks near the summit that still pose a threat. The trail is not too difficult and takes between two and three hours each way.

The town of Coleman lies farther north. The Coleman Colliery closed in 1983, and the town's main street is a testament to the hard times that set in afterward. The **Crowsnest Museum** ★ *(free admission; May to Sep, every day 10am to noon and 1pm to 4pm; Sep to May, Mon to Fri 10am to noon and 1pm to 4pm; 7701 18th Ave., Coleman,* ☎ *563-5434)* recounts the history of the Pass from 1899 to 1950. There are models of coal mining rescues, coal cars from the Greenhill Mine plus a diorama of the fish and wildlife of Crowsnest Pass.

From Coleman, backtrack east along Highway 3 to Pincher Creek. Take Highway 6 south toward Waterton Lakes National Park.

Pincher Creek is reputed to be the windiest spot in Alberta, which explains all the windmills in the vicinity. This town is a gateway to Waterton Lakes National Park.

Waterton Lakes National Park

Waterton Lakes National Park ★★★ is part of the world's first International Peace Park along with Glacier National Park in Montana. With stunning scenery, an exceptional choice of outdoor activities and varied wildlife, Waterton is not to be missed. The main attraction, however, of Waterton Lakes National Park is its ambience. Many say it is like Banff and Jasper 20 years ago; before the crowds and the mass commercialism. For more information see "Parks" section, p 331.

From Waterton Lakes National Park take Highway 5 east to Cardston.

Cardston

Cardston is a prosperous-looking town nestled in the rolling foothills where the grasslands begin to give way to fields of wheat and the yellow glow of canola. The town was established by Mormon pioneers fleeing religious persecution in Utah. Their move here marked one of the last great covered wagon migrations of the 19th century. Cardston might not seem like much of a tourist town, but it is home to one of the most impressive monuments and one of the most unique museums in Alberta. The monument is the **Mormon Temple** *(free admission; May and Jun, every day 10am to 6pm; Jul and Aug, every day 9am to 8pm; 348 3rd St. W., ☎ 653-3552)*, which seems a tad out of place rising from the prairie. This truly majestic edifice took ten years to construct and was the first temple built by the church outside the United States. The marble comes from Italy and the granite was quarried in Nelson B.C. When it came time to do renovations recently, a problem arose because there was no granite left in Nelson; several blocks were fortuitously found in a farmer's field nearby, having been left there in storage when the temple was built. Only Mormons in good standing may enter the temple itself, but the photographs and video presented at the visitors centre should satisfy your curiosity.

The unique museum is the **Remington-Alberta Carriage Centre** ★★★ *(adults $5.50, children $2.25, family $13; May to Sep, every day 9am to 8pm; Sep to May, every day 9am to 5pm; 623 Main St., ☎ 653-5139)*, opened in 1993. "A museum on carriages?", you may ask yourself. The subject matter may seem narrow, but this museum is definitely worth a visit. Forty-nine of the approximately 260 carriages were donated by Mr. Don Remington of Cardston on the condition that the Alberta government build an interpretive centre to display them. The wonderfully restored carriages and enthusiastic, dedicated staff at this magnificent facility make this exhibit first-rate. Take a guided tour through the 1,675 m^2 display gallery, where town mock-ups and animated street scenes provide the backdrop for the collection, one of the best in the world among elite carriage facilities. The interesting "Wheels of Change" film tells the story of this once huge industry, which was all but dead by 1922. Visitors can also learn how to drive a carriage, watch the restoration work in progress, take a carriage ride and have an old-fashioned picture taken.

South of Cardston, just off Highway 2, is the once-thriving town of **Aetna**. **Jensen's Trading Post** has an interesting collection of antiques. Highway 2 continues to the American border and **Police Outpost Provincial Park**, named after a police outpost set up in 1891 to control smuggling. There is a campground in the park.

Head north of Cardston on Highway 2 to Fort Macleod and Head-Smashed-In Buffalo Jump. If it's getting late in the day, you may consider heading north on Highway 5, in order to spend the night in Lethbridge. Fort Macleod and Head-Smashed-In are both easily accessible from Lethbridge.

Fort Macleod

The town of Fort Macleod centres around the fort of the same name, first set up by the North West Mounted Police in an effort to stop the whisky trade. Troops were sent to raid Fort Whoop-Up (see p 302) in 1874, but got lost along the way, and by the time they got to Whoop-Up the traders had fled. They continued west to this spot by the Oldman River and established a permanent outpost. The original settlement was on an island two miles east of the present town, but persistent flooding forced a relocation in 1882. The fort as it stands now was reconstructed in 1956-1957 as a museum. The **Fort Museum** ★ *(adults $3.50, seniors $3, students $2, children $1.25; May and Jun, every day 9am to 5pm; Jul to Sep 9am to 8:30pm; Sep to mid-Oct, every day 9am to 5pm; mid-Oct to Apr, closed Sat and Sun; 25th St. and 3rd Ave., ☎ 553-4703)* houses pioneer exhibits of life at the time of the settlement, dioramas of the fort, tombstones from the cemetery and an interesting section of artifacts and photographs of the plains Blood and Peigan tribes. A Mounted Patrol performs a musical ride four times a day in July and August.

The downtown area is very representative of a significant period in history. Most of the buildings were erected between 1897 and 1914, except the Kanouse cabin which lies inside the fort walls and dates from much earlier. Walking tour pamphlets are available at the tourist office. The tour includes such notable edifices as the **Empress Theatre**, which retains its original pressed metal ceiling panels, stage and dressing rooms (complete with graffiti from 1913). Movies are still shown here, despite a ghost who occasionally gets upset with the way things are run. The **Silver Grill**, an old saloon across the street, has its original bar and bullet-pierced mirror, while the sandstone **Queen's Hotel** still rents rooms (see "Accommodations" p 344).

Drive northwest of Fort Macleod on Highway 785 to Head-Smashed-In Buffalo Jump.

The arrival of the horse in the mid-1700s signalled the end of a traditional way of hunting for buffalo among Plains Indians. For 5,700 years before this, the Plains Indians had depended on **Head-Smashed-In Buffalo Jump** ★★★ *(adults $5.50, children $2.25, family $13; May to Sep, every day 9am to 8pm; Sep to May, every day 9am to 5pm; 15 km northwest of Fort Macleod on Hwy 785, ☎ 553-2731 or 265-0048)* for meat: fresh and dried for pemmican; hides for teepees, clothing and moccasins; and bones and horns for tools and decorations. Head-Smashed-In was an ideal spot for a jump, with a vast grazing area to the west. The Indians would construct drive lines with stone cairns leading to the cliff. Some 500 people participated in the yearly hunt; men dressed in buffalo calf robes and wolf skins lured the herd towards the precipice. Upon reaching the cliff, the leading buffalo were forced over the edge by the momentum of the stampeding herd behind them. The herd was not actually chased over the cliff, but rather the natives caused fear in the herd, thus leading to a stampede. The area remains much as it did thousands of years ago, though the distance from the cliff to the ground drastically changed as the bones of butchered bison piled up, 10-metres deep in some places.

Today, the jump is the best preserved buffalo jump in North America and a UNESCO World Heritage Site. Many assume that the name comes from the crushed skulls of the buffalo, but it actually refers to a Peigan legend of a young brave who went under the jump to watch the buffalo topple in front of him. The kill was exceptionally good this particular day, and the brave was crushed by the animals. When his people were butchering the buffalos after the kill, they discovered the brave with his head smashed in — hence the name.

As you approach the jump, the cliff appears as a small ridge on a vast plain. Signs of civilization are few; in fact the interpretive centre blends so well into the landscape that it is hardly noticeable at all. You almost expect to see a herd of buffalo just beyond the rise, and can envision what the natural plain must have been like before the white man arrived. There is something truly mythical about the place.

The Interpretive Centre, built into the cliff, comprises five levels and is visited from the top down. Start off by following the trail along the cliff to the kill site, for a spectacular view of the plain and the Calderwood Jump to the left. Marmots can be seen sunning themselves on the rocks below and generally contemplating the scene. Continuing through the centre you'll learn about Napi, the mythical creator of people according to the Blackfoot. The centre leads through Napi's world, the people and their routines, the buffalo, the hunt, the contact of cultures and European settlement. An excellent film entitled "In Search of the Buffalo" is presented every 30 minutes. The tour ends with an archaeological exhibit of the excavation work at the site. Back outside the centre you can follow a trail to the butchering site. Ongoing excavation work can occasionally be observed at the dig site below the cliff. The annual Buffalo Days celebrations take place here in July. The centre has a great gift shop and a small cafeteria that serves buffalo burgers.

Lethbridge

Lethbridge, known affectionately by locals as "downtown L.A.", is Alberta's third largest city, and a pleasant urban oasis on the prairies. Steeped in history, the city boasts an extensive park system, pretty tree-lined streets, interesting sights and a diverse cultural community. You're as likely to see ranchers as business people and Hutterite people. It is definitely worth whooping-it-up a bit in Lethbridge!

Indian Battle Park ★★, in the Oldman River valley in the heart of town, is where Lethbridge's history comes alive as the setting for Fort Whopp-Up and the site of one of the worst Indian battles. On October 25, 1870, Cree Indians, displaced by European settlers into Blackfoot territory, attacked a band of Blood Blackfoot camped on the banks of the Oldman River. In the ensuing battle, the Blood were aided by a group of Peigan Blackfoot nearby; by the end some 300 Cree and 50 Blackfoot were dead.

A year earlier, American whisky traders had moved into Southern Alberta from Fort Benton in Montana. It was illegal to sell alcohol to natives in the United States, so the traders headed north into Canada, where there was no law enforcement. They set up Fort Hamilton nearby at the confluence of the St. Mary's and Oldman rivers and it became the headquarters of American activity in southern Alberta and Saskatchewan. This activity involved the trading of a particularly lethal brew which was passed off as whisky to the natives; besides whisky, this fire water might also contain fortified grain alcohol, red pepper, chewing tobacco, Jamaican ginger and black molasses. Fire destroyed the original fort, but a second, called **Fort Whoop-Up** ★★, was built and whisky and guns continued to be traded for buffalo hides and robes. Fort Whoop-Up was the first and most notorious of 44 whisky trading posts. The American encroachment on Canadian territory, the illicit trading which had a demoralizing effect on the natives, along with news of the Cypress Hills massacre (see p 335), prompted the formation of the North West Mounted Police by the Canadian government. Lead by scout Jerry Potts, the Mounties, under the command of Colonel Macleod, arrived at Fort Whoop-Up in October of 1874. Word of their arrival preceded them, however, and the place was empty when they got there. A cairn marks the site of this fort. The present fort is a reconstruction, and houses an interesting **interpretive centre** *(free admission, donation; May to Sep, Mon to Sat 10am to 6pm, Sun noon to 8pm; Indian Battle Park, ☎ 329-0444)*, where visitors can experience the exciting days of the whisky trade. You can also taste fresh bannock, a round, flat Scottish cake made from barley and oatmeal and cooked on a griddle. Guides in period costume offer tours.

After peace was restored (so to speak), by the Mounties, attention turned to an exposed coal seam along the east bank of the Oldman River. The first mine was called Coalbanks, and so was the town that eventually sprung up at the opening to the mine. The **Coalbanks Interpretive Site** now stands at the original mine entrance in Indian Battle Park. With financing from his father (Sir Alexander Galt), Elliot Galt, set up a major drift mine. It soon became clear that a railway was needed to haul the coal, and eventually the town of Lethbridge was settled on the benchlands above the river. The town was named after a man who had never even been to Alberta, but was a friend of Galt's, and a major financial contributor to the whole operation.

With 62 km of walking, biking and horseback riding trails, the recreation possibilities are endless in Indian Battle Park. There are also picnic shelters and playgrounds.

The **Lethbridge Nature Reserve** is also located in Indian Battle Park. This 82-hectare protected area preserves much of the Oldman River Valley and contains the **Helen Schuler Coulee Centre** ★ *(summer, Sun to Thu 10am to 8pm, Fri and Sat 10am to 6pm; spring/fall, Tue to Sat 1pm to 4pm, Sun 1pm to 6pm; winter, Tue to Sun 1pm to 4pm; Indian Battle Park, ☎ 320-3064)*, which features hands-on interactive displays and fact sheets on local animals and plant species that are great for kids of all ages — find out if you are a grassland guru or a prairie peewee. Three self-guided trails start from here. The reserve is also home to Alberta's provincial bird, the great horned owl, as well as porcupines, white-tailed deer and prairie rattlesnakes.

The volatile water levels of the Oldman River still wreak havoc on Lethbridge every so often. In the spring of 1995, water levels were so high that the Helen Schuler centre was half-submerged. The CPR High Level Bridge spans the Oldman River. When it was built in 1907-09, it was the longest and highest steel aqueduct in the world.

The **Sir Alexander Galt Museum** *(donation; Jul and Aug, Mon to Thu 9am to 8pm, Fri 9am to 4pm, Sat and Sun 1 to 8pm; Sep to Jun, Mon to Fri 10am to 4pm, Wed until 8pm, Sat and Sun 1pm to 4pm; just off Scenic Dr. at 5th Ave. S, ☎ 320-3898)*, overlooking Indian Battle Park, was originally built as a hospital in 1910. Since then it has been expanded to accommodate five galleries that offer an excellent perspective on the human history of the city of Lethbridge. A particularly impressive glazed viewing gallery looks out onto the river valley. The museum outlines the city's development from the discovery of coal to the waves of immigration from many different parts of the world. There are permanent and travelling exhibits, as well as extensive archives.

Paths weave their way through five traditional Japanese gardens at the **Nikka Yuko Japanese Garden** ★★ *(adults $3, seniors and children $2, children under 12 free; mid-May to mid-Jun, every day 9am to 5pm; mid-Jun to Aug every day 9am to 8pm; Sep to early Oct, every day 9am to 5pm;* *8th Ave. S and Mayor McGrath Drive, ☎ 328-3511).* These aren't bright, flowery gardens, but simple arrangements of green shrubs, sand and rocks in the style of a true Japanese garden — perfect for quiet contemplation. Created by renowned Japanese garden designer Dr. Tadashi Kudo of the Osaka Prefecture

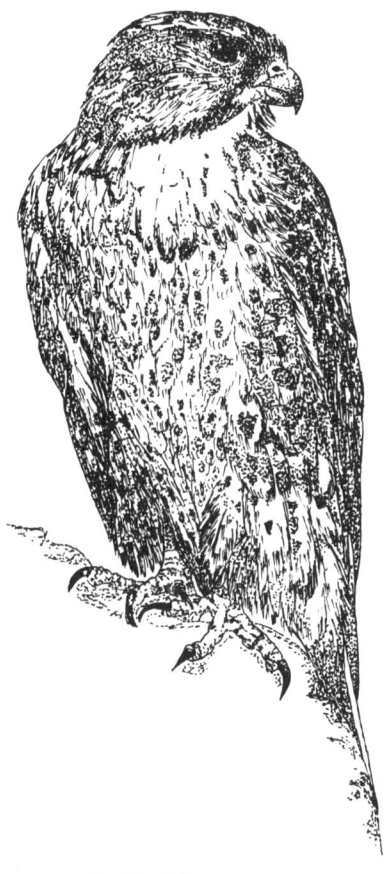

Prairie Falcon

University in Japan, Nikka Yuko was built in 1967 as a centennial project and a symbol of Japanese and Canadian friendship (*Nikka Yuko* actually means friendship). The bell at the gardens symbolizes this friendship, and when it is rung good things are supposed to happen simultaneously in both countries.

Head east on Highway 3 to Coaldale and then on to Taber.

Lethbridge to Writing-on-Stone Provincial Park

The **Birds of Prey Centre** *(adults $4, children and seniors $3, children under 5 free; May to Oct, every day 10:30am to 5pm; north of Hwy 3 in Coaldale, ☎ 345-4262)* in **Coaldale** is a living museum populated with birds from Alberta and around the world. The centre is dedicated to the survival of birds of prey like hawks, falcons, eagles and great horned owls. Many of the birds in the centre were brought here injured or as young chicks. Once they are strong enough they are released into the wild.

Taber is famous for its sweet corn, that is sold all over the province. The city is also a base for the food-processing industry. Corn season is in August, when the town holds its **Cornfest** celebrations. There is a pancake breakfast, hot-air balloons and all sorts of activities.

Backtrack on Highway 3 and head south on Highway 36 towards Milk River.

The town of **Warner** lies at the intersection of Highways 4 and 36. In 1987, an amateur paleontologist discovered a clutch of **dinosaur eggs** containing perfectly formed embryonic hadrosaur bones. There are bus tours to this significant fossil site, and the eggs can also be viewed at the Royal Tyrell Museum in Drumheller (see p 307).

In Milk River take Highway 501, and watch for signs for Writing-on-Stone Provincial Park.

The Milk River is the only river in Western Canada on the east side of the continental divide that does not eventually empty into Hudson Bay, but flows south into the Missouri River and on into the Mississippi River and the Gulf of Mexico. As a result the area has been claimed by eight different governments and countries. When France claimed all lands that drained into the Mississippi, this part of Alberta was under French jurisdiction. The Spanish, British, Americans the Hudson's Bay Company have all staked their claim at one point in history.

Writing-on-Stone Provincial Park ★★ protects fascinating examples of petroglyphs, some of which are believed to date back some 1,800 years. A wealth of animals and plant species call this arid parcel of land home. The province's hottest temperatures are recorded here in this almost desert-like setting. Great hiking is possible, but the best rock drawings lie within a restricted area, that is only accessible through guided hikes. To avoid disappointment, call ahead to find out when the hikes are heading out (see p 334).

Continue east on Highway 501, then go north on Highway 879. When you reach Highway 61, head east.

Across the prairie to Medicine Hat ★★

The prairies roll on and on as far as the eye can see along this stretch of highway surrounded by golden fields that are empty but for the occasional abandoned farmhouse. The Canadian Pacific Railway laid a track through this region, building a grain elevator and an adjoining town approximately every 16 km. Farmers were therefore never more than a day's haul from an elevator. As you drive this road, you will come upon what was once the town of Nemiskam about 16 km out of Foremost. Another 16 km down the road is Etzikom. With fewer than 100 inhabitants these days, the elimination of the Western Grain Transportation Act and the appeal of the big city, Etzikom's days may be numbered. For a look at the way things used to be, stop in at the **Etzikom Museum** ★ *(donation; May to Sep, Mon to Sat 10am to 5pm, Sun noon to 6pm; Etzikom, ☎ 666-3737 or 666-3915).* Local museums like this can be found throughout Alberta, but this is one of the best of its kind, and makes for a pleasant stop off the highway. The museum is located in the Etzikom School, and houses a wonderful recreation of the Main Street of a typical town, complete with barber shop, general store and hotel. Outside is the Windpower Interpretive Centre, with a collection of windmills, including one from Martha's Vineyard, Massachusetts, U.S.A.

Continue east along Highway 61, then head north on Highway 887, and east on Highway 3 into Medicine Hat.

Medicine Hat

Rudyard Kipling once called Medicine Hat "a city with all hell for a basement", in reference to the fact that Medicine Hat lies above some of Western Canada's largest natural gas fields. The town prospered because of this natural resource, which now supplies a thriving petro-chemical industry. Clay deposits nearby also left their mark on the city, contributing to the city's once thriving pottery industry. Medicine Hat, like many towns in Alberta, boasts several parks. As for its name, legend has it that a great battle between the Cree and Blackfoot took place here. During the battle the Cree medicine man deserted his people, and while fleeing across the river he lost his headdress in midstream. Believing this to be a bad omen, the Cree abandoned the fight, and were massacred by the Blackfoot. The battle site was called Saamis, which means medicine man's hat. When the Mounties arrived years later, the name was translated and shortened to Medicine Hat.

The **Medicine Hat Museum and Art Gallery** *(donation; summer, Mon to Fri 9am to 5pm, Sat and Sun 1pm to 5pm; winter, Mon to Fri 10:30am to noon and 1pm to 5pm, Sat and Sun 1pm to 5pm; 1302 Bromford Crescent SW, ☎ 527-6266)* is a National Exhibition Centre with first-rate local, national and international exhibits. The museum has a permanent collection depicting the history of Medicine Hat, the Plains Indians, the NWMP, ranching, farming and the railway.

Continue along Highway 1 to the Saamis Tepee and Information Office.

The **Saamis Tepee** is the world's tallest tepee. It was constructed for the 1988 Calgary Winter Olympics, and then purchased by a Medicine Hat businessman following the Games. The tepee symbolizes the Amerindian way of life, based on spirituality, the circle of life, family and the sacred home. It certainly is an architectural wonder, though its steel structure and sheer size do seem a bit inconsistent with Amerindian traditions. Below the Saamis Tepee is the **Saamis Archaeological Site**. Over eighty million artifacts are believed to be buried at the site. A self-guided walking tour leads through the site of a late winter and early spring buffalo camp and a meat-processing site.

Follow the signs to the Clay Industry Interpretive Centre.

You'll probably have seen the pamphlets for the **Great Wall of China**; this is not a replica of the real thing, but quite literally a wall of china, produced by the potteries of Medicine Hat from 1912 to 1988. Though many of the pieces on display are priceless collector's items, the best part of the **Clay Interpretive Centre** ★★ is the tour of the old Medalta plant and kilns. Medalta once supplied the fine china for all Canadian Pacific hotels. Today, workers' clothes and personal effects remain in the plant, which closed down unexpectedly in 1989. Medalta Potteries, Medicine Hat Potteries, Alberta Potteries and Hycroft China established Medicine Hat's reputation as an important pottery centre. Tour guides lead visitors through the plant and explain the intricate and labour-intensive work that went into each piece. The tour ends with a fascinating visit inside one of the six beehive kilns outside.

Historic Walking Tour Pamphlets are available at the information office for those interested in exploring the turn-of-the-century architecture of Medicine Hat's centre.

Cypress Hills

Cypress Hills Provincial Park ★ lies 65 km southeast of Medicine Hat, near the Saskatchewan border. These hills were not covered by glaciers during the last ice age, and with a maximum elevation of 1,466 m above sea level, they are the highest point in Canada between Banff and Labrador. This was the site of the Cypress Hills massacre in the winter of 1872-3, the result of which contributed to the formation of the North West Mounted Police. Animal and plant species found nowhere else in southern Alberta are the treasures of this park (see p 335).

From Medicine Hat, head northwest on Highway 1, the TransCanada, to Brooks.

Brooks

Brooks began as a railway stop in the 1880s, and soon developed a major irrigation system. The **Brooks Aqueduct** *(mid-May to Sep, every day 10am to 8pm; 3km southeast of Brooks,* ☎ *362-4451)* began operating in the spring of 1915; at the time it was the longest concrete structure (3.2 km) of its kind in the world. It was a vital part of the irrigation of southeastern Alberta for 65 years. The aqueduct is now a National Historic Site.

The town of Brooks is also a great jumping-off point for **Dinosaur Provincial Park** ★★★, declared a United Nations World Heritage Site in 1979. The landscape of this park consists of badlands, called *mauvaises terres* by French voyageurs because there was no food or beavers there. These eerie badlands contain fossil beds of international significance, where over 300 complete skeletons have been found. Glacial melt water carved out the badlands from the soft bedrock, revealing hills laden with dinosaur bones. The erosion by wind and rain continues today, providing a glimpse of how this landscape of hoodoos, mesas and gorges was formed.

There is a loop road and two self-guided trails, but the best way to see the park is to follow a guided-tour into the restricted natural preserve, though this requires a bit of planning. Unless you plan to arrive early, it is extremely important to call ahead for the times of the tours, to make sure you are there in time to reserve yourself a spot (see "Parks" section p 335). Visitors can tour the **Field Station of the Tyrell Museum** ★ *(May to Sep, everyday 9am to 9pm; Sep to May, Sat and Sun 9am to 4pm;* ☎ *378-4342)* for an introduction to the excavation of dinosaur bones, and then head off on their own adventure.

The dinosaur odyssey continues in Drumheller. From Dinosaur Provincial Park return to the TransCanada, and head north on Highway 56.

Drumheller ★★★

The main attractions in Drumheller are located along the Dinosaur Trail and East Coulee Drive; they include the Royal Tyrell Museum of Palaeontology, the Bleriot Ferry, the Rosedale Suspension Bridge, the Hoodoos, East Coulee, the Atlas Coal Mine and the Last Chance Saloon. Where the town of Drumheller now lies was once the coastal region of a vast inland sea; the climate probably resembled that of the Florida everglades and was an ideal habitat for dinosaurs. After the extinction of the dinosaurs, ice covered the land. As the ice retreated 10,000 years ago, it carved out deep trenches in the prairie; this and subsequent erosion have uncovered dinosaur bones and shaped the fabulously interesting landscape of hoodoos and coulees found in Drumheller. Besides the bones, early settlers discovered coal. Agriculture and the oil and gas industries now drive the local economy.

The most important stop along the **Dinosaur Trail ★★★** which heads northwest along the Red Deer River from Drumheller is the **Royal Tyrell Museum of Palaeontology ★★★** *(adults $5.50, children $2.25; mid-May to Sep every day 9am to 9pm; Oct to mid-May, Tue to Sun 10am to 5pm; 6 km west of Drumheller on Hwy 838,* ☎ *823-7707)*. This mammoth museum contains over 80,000 specimens, including 50 full-size dinosaur skeletons. There are hands-on exhibits and computers, fibre-optics and audio-visual presentations. The Royal Tyrell is also a major research centre, and visitors can watch scientists cleaning bones and preparing specimens for display. There is certainly a lot to thrill younger travellers here, however, the wealth of information to absorb can be a bit overwhelming. You can participate in the **Day Dig**, which offers an opportunity to visit a dinosaur quarry and excavate fossils yourself, or the **Dig Watch**, a 90-minute guided tour to an actual working excavation site, where you'll see a dig in progress. Call ahead for tour times.

Continue along the Dinosaur Trail for breathtaking views over the Red Deer River at the **Horsethief Canyon Lookout**. Turn right onto Hwy 838 to the **Bleriot Ferry**, one of the last cable-operated ferries in Alberta. The ferry was named after the famous French pilot and balloonist Louis Bleriot. The trail continues along the southern shore of the river with another great lookout, the **Orkney Hill Lookout**.

Once back in Drumheller, get on **East Coulee Drive ★★★**, which heads southeast along the Red Deer River. The town of **Rosedale** originally stood on the other side of the river next to the Star Mine. The suspension bridge across the Red Deer looks flimsy, but is said to be safe for those who want to venture across. Take a detour to cross the 11 bridges to get to **Wayne**. The bridges are perhaps the best part, as the main attraction in town, the Rosedeer Hotel with its Last Chance Saloon, leaves a bit to be desired. Rooms are available for rent, but settle for a beer and some nostalgia instead. About halfway between Rosedale and East Coulee you'll see some of the most spectacular **hoodoos ★★★** in southern Alberta. These strange mushroom-shaped formation result when the softer underlying sandstone erodes. **East Coulee**, the town that almost disappeared, was once home to 3,000 people but only 200 residents remain. Although the Atlas Coal Mine ceased operations in 1955, the **Atlas Coal Mine Museum** *(adults $3, family $8; May to Oct, every day 10am to 6pm;* ☎ *822-2220)* keeps the place alive to this day. The last standing tipple (a device for emptying coal from mine cars) in Canada stands among the mine buildings, which you can explore on your own or as part of a guided tour.

■ **Tour C: Central Alberta ★**

Visitors travelling between Calgary and Edmonton have several options. One of these, though rather roundabout, is through the spectacular Rockies mountains along the Icefields Parkway, Highway 93. You might take this route in one direction, and a more easterly route on your return. The following tour of central Alberta in effect outlines two such easterly possibilities for getting between Calgary and Edmonton.

Those travellers who have toured southern Alberta may pick up the central Alberta tour in Drumheller. Travellers heading north from Calgary can detour off Highway 2 through Rosebud, for the famous dinner theatre (see p 356), to Drumheller (see p 307), before continuing north. To reach Trochu from Drumheller, take Hwy 9 north, Hwy 27 west and Hwy 21 north. To reach Trochu from Calgary take Hwy 2 north, Hwy 27 east and Hwy 21 north.

Trochu

The **St. Ann Ranch and Trading Company** *(donation; May to Sep, Tue to Sat 2pm to 5pm; on the southeast edge of Trochu,* ☎ *442-3924)* was originally established in 1903 as part of a French-speaking settlement. The community thrived and grew to include a school, church and post office, but the onset of WWI prompted many settlers to return to their homeland of France. The ranch has been restored and is run by a descendent of one of the original settlers. A small museum displays historic pieces, while an adjoining tea-room and *gîte* (bed and breakfast, see p 346) provide an opportunity for an experience *à la française*. Ninetieth anniversary celebrations for the ranch will take place in 1996.

Thirty kilometres northeast of Trochu on Hwy 21 you'll find **Dry Island Buffalo Jump Provincial Park** a day-use park that highlights the dramatic

Exploring 309

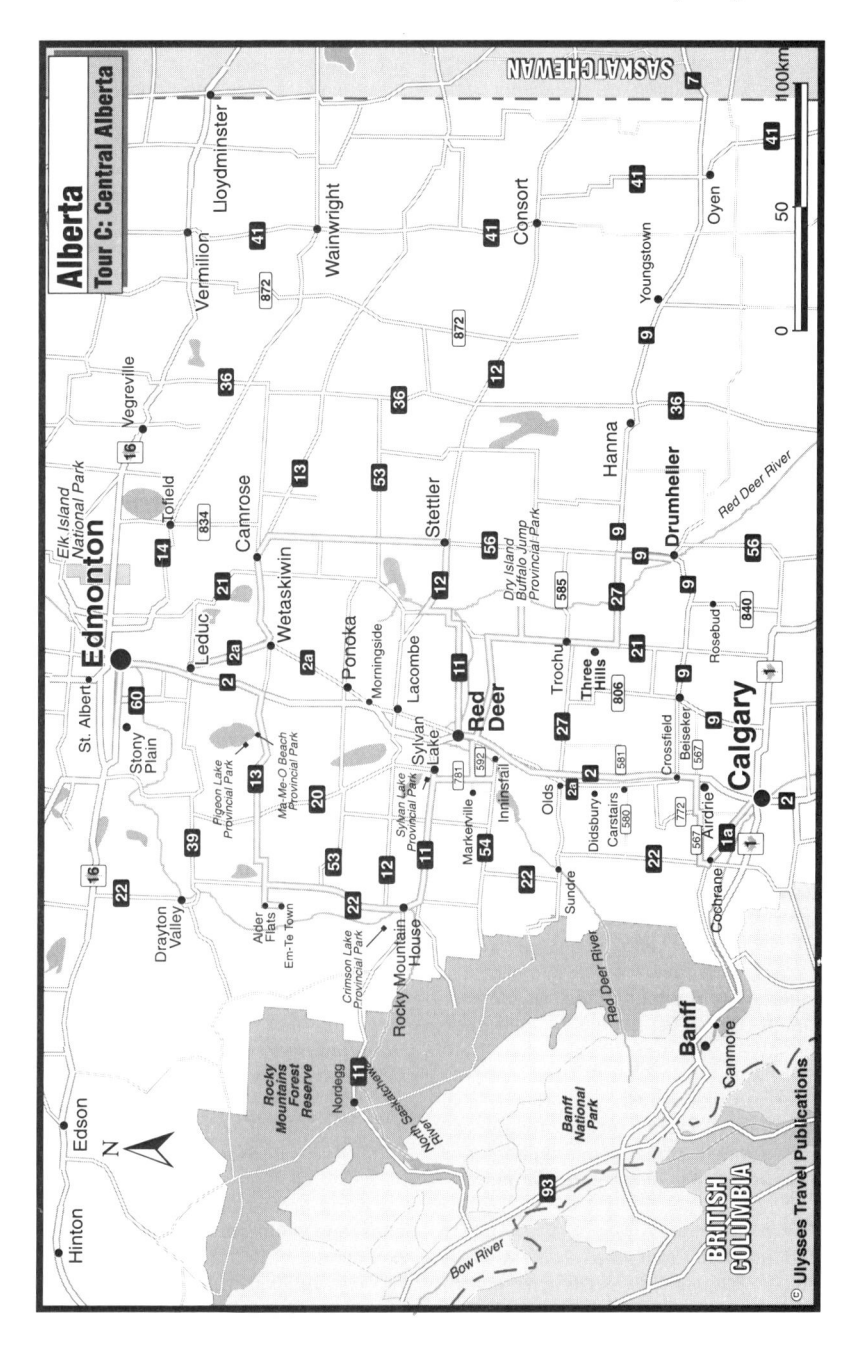

contrast between the Red Deer River Valley Floor and the surrounding farmland. The jump, once used by Cree Indians, is higher than most in Alberta; the buffalo herded over its cliffs fell about 50 metres, and were then butchered by the natives for their meat and hides.

Red Deer

Red Deer, a city of 60,000 people, began as a stopover for early commercial travellers along the Calgary Edmonton Trail. Red Deer is an erroneous translation of *Waskasoo*, which means elk in Cree. The shores of the river were frequented by elk, and Scottish settlers thought the animals resembled red deer found in Scotland. During the Riel Rebellion of 1885, the Canadian militia built Fort Normandeau at this site. The post was later occupied by the North West Mounted Police. The railway, agriculture, oil and gas all contributed to the growth of Red Deer, at one point the fastest growing city in Canada.

Red Deer is another Alberta city whose extensive park system is one of its greatest attractions. The **Waskasoo Park System** weaves its way throughout the city and through the Red Deer River valley with walking and cycling trails. The information centre is located at **Heritage Ranch** *(Cronquist Dr., ☎ 346-0180)* on the western edge of town; take the 32nd St. Exit from Hwy 2, left on 60th St. and right on Cronquist Drive. Heritage Ranch also features, among other things an equestrian centre, picnic shelters and access to trails in the park system.

Fort Normandeau *(May to Sep, Mon to Sat noon to 8pm, Sun 1pm to 4pm; ☎ 347-2010 or 347-7550)* is located west of Highway 2, along 32nd St. The fort as it stands today is a replica of the original. A stopping house next to the river was fortified and enclosed in palisade walls by the *Carabiniers de Mont Royal* under Lieutenant J.E. Bédard Normandeau in anticipation of an attack by Cree Indians during the Louis Riel Rebellion of 1885. The fort was never attacked. An interpretive centre next to the fort describes Indian, Metis and European settlement of the area. Visitors can see wool being spun, and rope, soap, candles and ice cream being made.

In downtown Red Deer, the **Red Deer and District Museum** *(donation; Jul to Sep, every day 10am to 9pm; Sep to Jun, Mon to Thu noon to 5pm and 7pm to 9pm, Fri noon to 5pm, Sat and Sun 1pm to 5pm; 4525 47A Ave., ☎ 342-6644 or 342-6844)* boasts different galleries featuring international and Canadian art, plus permanent exhibits dealing with the history of the area from prehistoric times. Walking tours of historic Red Deer depart from the museum.

Heritage Square, next to the museum, encloses a collection of historic buildings, including the unique Aspelund Laft Juc, a replica of a 17th century sod-roofed Norwegian home. Northwest of Heritage Square is **City Hall Park ★**, a lovely garden filled with 45,000 blossoming annuals.

From Red Deer, head east on Hwys 11 and 12 to Stettler.

Stettler

For a trip across the wonderful prairie landscape **Alberta Prairie Railway Excursions** *(☎ 742-2811 for schedule and reservations)* organizes trips aboard vintage coaches from the early 1900s which depart from Stettler for small towns like Rowley, Donalda and Consort (hometown of k.d. lang). Full and half-day excursions include one or two meals, and special trips include murder mystery trains and casino trains.

Take Hwy 56 north, then Hwy 26 west to Wetaskiwin.

Wetaskiwin

The city of Wetaskiwin is home to one of the finest museums in the province. Like the Remington-Alberta Carriage Centre in Cardston, the Reynolds-Alberta Museum proves again that there is more to Alberta than Calgary, Edmonton and the Rockies. Though there isn't much to see in Wetaskiwin besides the Reynolds-Alberta and the Aviation Hall of Fame, this pleasant city has an interesting main street, and respectable restaurants and hotels.

The **Reynolds-Alberta Museum** ★★★ *(adults $5.50, children $2.25, family $13 one ticket for Reynolds-Alberta and Aviation Hall of Fame; May to Sep, every day 9am to 9pm; Sep to May, every day 9am to 5pm; west of Wetaskiwin on Hwy 13, ☎ 352-5855)* celebrates the "spirit of the machine" and is a wonderful place to explore. Interactive programs for children bring everything alive. A top-notch collection of restored automobiles, trucks, bicycles, tractors and related machinery is on display. Among the vintage cars is one of about 470 Model J Duesenberg Phaeton Royales. This one-of-a-kind automobile cost $20,000 when it was purchased in 1929. Visitors to the museum will also learn how a grain elevator works, and can observe the goings-on in the restoration workshop through a large picture window. Tours of the warehouse, where over 800 pieces are waiting to be restored, are offered twice daily *($1, call ahead for times, sign up at front desk)*; pre-booked one-hour guided tours are also available.

Canada's Aviation Hall of Fame *(same hours as above)* located on the site of the Reynolds-Alberta, pays tribute to the pioneers of Canadian aviation. Photographs, artifacts, personal memorabilia and the favourite aircraft of the over 140 members of the Hall of Fame are displayed. These people include military and civilian pilots, doctors, scientists, inventors, aeronautical engineers and administrators.

Continue north on Highway 2A to Leduc, site of the biggest oil discovered in the world.

Leduc

Alberta came into its own when crude oil was discovered south of Edmonton. The **Leduc Oil Well #1** *(donation; open year-round; 2 km south of Devon on Hwy 60, ☎ 987-3435)* blew in on February 13, 1947, signalling the start of the oil boom. The oil was actually discovered on a farm northwest of Leduc in what was to become the town of Devon. A replica of the original 174-ft conventional derrick now stands on the site. Visitors get a first-hand look at equipment by climbing down to the drilling floor.

From Leduc continue north to Edmonton (see p 316).

The second option for touring central Alberta between Edmonton and Calgary is presented below. This option, like the first one, can be followed in either direction.

From Edmonton head west to Stony Plain then south on Hwy 2 to Hwy 13, head west to Ma-Me-O Beach then Alder Flats, or if you are arriving from northern Alberta, head south on Hwy 22 reaching Alder Flats first then heading east of Hwy 13 to Ma-Me-O Beach.

Stony Plain

The **Andrew Wolf Wine Cellar** *(May to Oct, Mon to Fri 10am to 8pm, Sat 10am to 6pm, Sun noon to 5pm; Stony Plain, ☎ 963-7717)* is Alberta's only winery, and the wine actually comes from California. The final aging is done here in oak vats. Wine-tastings are possible, and you can also purchase fine bottles for very reasonable prices at the gift boutique.

Ma-Me-O Beach Provincial Park is a day-use area (see p 336). **Pigeon Lake Provincial Park** located northwest of the latter has a good campground and a reputation for good fishing (see p 336).

Alder Flats

At the western end of Hwy 13 lies the town of Alder Flats, which in itself is of little interest to visitors. A few kilometres south, however, is another town that is full of attractions, a place ironically called **Em-Te Town**. Here you'll find a saloon, jailhouse, harness shop, schoolhouse, church and emporium, located in a pretty setting at the end of a gravel road. Built from scratch in 1978, this is a neat place to experience life the way it was in the old west, with trail rides and home-cooked meals at the Lost Woman Hotel. Some may find the whole experience a bit contrived. In addition to the attractions, there are campsites and cabins for rent, as well as a restaurant.

Head south of Hwy 22 to Rocky Mountain House.

The **drive** ★★★ to Rocky Mountain House runs along the edge of the Rocky Mountain Forest Reserve. Stunning views of the Rocky Mountains line the horizon on the approach into town. Highway 11, the David Thompson Highway continues west from Rocky Mountain House up into the Aspen Parkland and on into Banff National Park (see p 214). The town of **Nordegg** lies at the halfway point of the highway. In addition to an interesting museum, the Nordegg Museum, the town offers access to great fishing, the Forestry Trunk Road and camping, and is also home to the Shunda Creek Hostel (see p 347). The only services available west of Nordegg before the Hwy 93 are at the David Thompson Resort.

Rocky Mountain House

Despite its evocative name, Rocky Mountain House is not a picturesque log cabin in the woods, but rather an interesting gateway town into the majestic Rocky Mountains. The town, known locally as Rocky, is home to just under 6,000 people and represents a transition zone between the aspen parkland and the mountains. The exceptional setting is certainly one of the town's major attractions, which otherwise offers the gamut of services — hotels, gas stations and restaurants. Just on the outskirts of Rocky, however, lie the town's namesake, the Rocky Mountain House National Historic Site, and a wealth of outdoor possibilities, including river trips in voyageur canoes, golf as well as fishing, hiking and cross-country skiing at Crimson Lake Provincial Park (see p 336).

The **Rocky Mountain House National Historic Park** ★★ *(adults $2.25, seniors $1.75, children $1.25, under 6 free; May to Sep, every day 10am to 6pm, call for winter hours; 4.8 km southwest of Rocky on Hwy 11A,* ☎ *845-2412)* is Alberta's only National Historic Park and the site of four known historic sites. Rocky Mountain House is particularly interesting because it exemplifies, perhaps better than any other trading post, the inextricable link between the fur trade and the discovery and exploration of Canada. Two rival forts were set up here in 1799, Rocky Mountain House by the Northwest Company and Acton House by the Hudson's Bay Company. Both companies were lured by the possibility of establishing lucrative trade with Kootenai Indians west of the Rockies. It was after the merging of the Hudson's Bay Company and the Northwest Company in 1821, that the area was called Rocky Mountain House. Trade with the Kootenai never did materialize; in fact, except for a brief period of successful trade with Blackfoot tribes in the 1820s, the fort never prospered, and actually closed down and was then rebuilt on several occasions. It closed for good in 1875,

---

David Thompson

David Thompson began at the Hudson's Bay Company in 1784 as a clerk stationed at several posts on Hudson Bay and the Saskatchewan River. While laid up with a broken leg, he took an interest in surveying and practical astronomy. After years of exploring and surveying much of present-day northern Manitoba and Saskatchewan, he decided to switch camps and go to work for the Northwest Company in 1797. The company enlisted his services in the "Columbia Enterprise", the search for a route through the Rockies. In 1806-07, Thompson made preparations to cross the Rockies at Rocky Mountain House. However, the Peigan Indians who frequented the post opposed the project; if trade extended west of the Rockies, their enemies, the Kootenai and Flathead, would acquire guns. Thompson thus moved up-river from Rocky Mountain House to the Howse Pass in 1807. In 1810, the race to the mouth of the Columbia came to a head when news of an American expedition reached Thompson. He immediately headed west but was blocked by Peigan Indians. He headed north again, skirting Peigan territory. In 1811, he crossed the Athabasca Pass and reached the Pacific and the mouth of the Columbia River four months after the Americans had set up their post there. Thompson later settled in Terrebonne, near Montreal, and worked on the establishment of the boundary between Upper and Lower Canada. He was unsuccessful in business and died in 1857, in poverty and virtual obscurity.

rebuilt on several occasions. It closed for good in 1875, after the Northwest Mounted Police made the area to the south safe for trading. The Hudson's Bay Company thus set up a post in the vicinity of Calgary. An interesting aside, the Hudson's Bay Company, today the cross-Canada department store The Bay, makes more money on its real estate holdings than on its retail operations.

The visitors centre presents a most informative exhibit on the fur-trading days at Rocky Mountain House, including a look at the clothing of the Plains Indians and how it changed with the arrival of fur traders as well as artifacts and testimonies of early explorers. Visitors can also choose to view one of several excellent National Film Board documentaries. Two interpretive trails lead through the site to listening posts (in English and French) along the swift-flowing North Saskatchewan River. Stops include a buffalo paddock and demonstration sites where tea is brewed and York Boats, once used by Hudson's Bay Company traders, are built (the Northwest Company traders preferred the birchbark canoe, even though it was much slower). All that remains of the last fort are two chimneys.

Rocky Mountain House was also a base for exploration. David Thompson an explorer, surveyor and geographer for the Northwest Company, who played an integral role in the Northwest Company's search for a route through the Rockies to the Pacific, was based at Rocky Mountain House for a time. Ultimately beaten by the Americans in his pursuit, he travelled 88,000 km during his years in the fur trade, filling in the map of Western Canada along his way.

Head east on Hwy 11 to Sylvan Lake.

Sylvan Lake

This lakeside town, with its marina, beach, souvenir shops, hotels, waterslide and shingled buildings, looks almost like an Atlantic coast beach resort. **Sylvan Lake Provincial Park ★ (☎ 887-5575)** is a day-use area for sunbathing, swimming and picnicking. **Jarvis Bay Provincial Park** *(park office ☎ 887-5575, camping reservations ☎ 887-5522)* is also located on Sylvan Lake, and like the latter park is popular on weekends. Hiking trails lead through the aspen parkland, and provide some good bird-watching.

Head south on Hwy 781, then west on Hwy 592 to Markerville.

Markerville

The town of Markerville began as an Icelandic settlement called Tindastoll in 1888. The settlers arrived from Dakota. A year later another group of Icelanders arrived, including poet Stephan G. Stephansson (see below), and settled in a district they called Hola. The area was chosen partly because of its isolation, for the settlers wished to preserve their language and customs. In 1899, the federal government built the Markerville Creamery, and the village that grew up around it became something of an economic hub, attracting various groups of settlers including Danes, Swedes and Americans. The Icelandic culture nevertheless thrived into the 1920s. Eventually, however, intermarriage and migration changed things. Today less than 10% of the region's population is of Icelandic descent.

Once a leader in Alberta's dairy industry, the **Markerville Creamery** ★★ *(donation; May to Sep, Mon to Sat 10am to 5:30pm, Sun noon to 5:30pm; on Hwy 364A, Markerville, ☎ 728-3006)* is the only restored creamery in the province. It was opened in 1899 by the federal Department of Agriculture. An association of local Icelandic farmers maintained the building, and the government kept the books and hired a buttermaker. The buttermaker paid farmers depending on the butterfat of their cream. The creamery was the mainstay of the local economy until it closed in 1972, producing 194,870 pounds of butter at its peak. It is now a Provincial Historic Resource and has been restored to circa 1934. Visitors can take a guided tour to learn about the operation of the creamery and its equipment, which includes old pasteurizers. Adjoining the building are two neat gift shops, as well as the "Kaffistofa", where you can sample *vinarterta*, (Icelandic layer cake).

To reach the Stephansson House, continue west on the 364A across the Medicine River; shortly after the river turn right on an unnamed road. Follow this road to the 371, turn right, cross the river again, and you'll soon see the entrance to the house on your left.

The **Stephansson House** ★ *(donation; May to Sep, every day 10am to 6pm)*. Stephan G. Stephansson was among the second group of Icelandic settlers who came to the area now known as Markerville from Dakota in 1889. Few people have heard of Stephansson, perhaps one of Canada's most prolific poets, because he wrote in his native Icelandic. His original log house quickly proved too small, so a study, front room, upstairs, kitchen and front bedroom were gradually added. The house, with its newspaper insulation and attempts to copy the picturesque style, is representative of a typical struggling Canadian farm family. Stephansson, like the other Icelandic settlers, was particularly concerned with preserving his native culture and he perpetuated it with his strong views and mastery of the language. The most famous of his works to have been translated is *Androkur* or *Wakeful Nights*, (Stephansson was an insomniac). Guides give tours of the house and light the stove every day to bake delicious Icelandic cookies called *astarbollur*, or "love buns".

Take Hwy 592 east to Hwy 2. Head south to Carstairs, a few kilometres west of the highway for a bit of shopping.

Carstairs

Two of Carstairs' most interesting attractions, which are essentially great shopping opportunities, lie on the outskirts of this town, whose streets are lined with grand old houses. The **Pa-Su Farm** lies 9 km west of town on Hwy 580, while the **Custom Woolen Mills** are about 20 km east on Hwy 581 and then 4.5 km north on Hwy 791. See the "Shopping" section p 366.

Instead of heading straight back to Calgary on boring old Hwy 2, let the mountains pull you back west one last time. Head west on Hwy 567 at Airdrie, south on the 772, west on the 567 and finally get back on that old favourite, Hwy 22; continue south to Cochrane. From Cochrane take Hwy 1A or 1 back to Calgary.

Cochrane

This friendly town lies on the northern edge of Alberta's ranchlands and was the site of the first big leasehold ranch in the province. Ranching is still a part of the local economy, but more and more residents are commuting into nearby Calgary, just 20 minutes away.

The **Cochrane Ranche Historic Site** ★★ *($1 donation; visitors centre: May to Sep, every day 10am to 6pm; ranche site: open year-round; 1/2 km west of Cochrane on Hwy 1A, ☎ 932-3242 in summer, ☎ 553-2731 in winter)* commemorates the establishment in 1881 of the Cochrane Ranche Company by Québec businessman, Senator Matthew Cochrane, and the initiation of Alberta's cattle beef industry. The company controlled 189,000 hectares of sweeping grasslands, which along with three other ranches, including the Bar U (see p 296), covered most of Alberta. Though the ranch failed after two years, its legacy lives on. Travellers can relive those romantic days through interpretive programs at the visitors centre. The **Western Heritage Centre** is set to open on the site and will provide an overview of the cowboy way of life in the Canadian West, from the days of the frontier and the chuck wagon to rodeos, lariats and livestock auctions. It promises to be a world-class facility.

The **Studio West Art Foundry** *(every day 9am to 5pm; 205 2nd Ave., SE, ☎ 932-2611)*, in Cochrane's industrial park, is Western Canada's largest sculpture foundry. Artisans practise the age-old "lost wax" method of bronze casting. Wildlife and western bronze sculptures as well as woodcarvings and paintings are for sale.

Don't miss the opportunity while in Cochrane to savour some ice-cream from **McKay's Ice Cream** ★, rated one of the best in Canada. You may even want to take a day-trip from Calgary just for a cone, or stop in on your way to Banff.

■ Tour D: Edmonton ★★

Edmonton seems to suffer from an image problem, and undeservedly so. People have trouble getting past the boomtown atmosphere and the huge mall! Admittedly it is a boomtown: a city that grew out of the wealth of the natural resources that surround it. But this city of new money has more than made good with an attractive downtown core, a park system and some of Canada's best cultural facilities including theatres and many festivals (see p 364). With all this going for it, though, the city's biggest attraction still seems to be a gargantuan shopping mall. You be the judge!

Edmonton has actually experienced three booms: the first in fur, the second in gold and the third in oil. The area had long been frequented by natives who searched for quartzite to make tools and trapped the abundant beaver and muskrat. It was the supply of fur that attracted fur traders to the area in the late 18th century. The Hudson's Bay Company established Fort Edmonton in 1795 next to the Northwest Company's Fort Augustus overlooking the North Saskatchewan River where the Legislative Building now stands. Trading at the fort involved Cree and Assiniboine from the north as well as Blackfoot from the south. These normally warring peoples could trade in safety essentially because the fierce Blackfoot were more

Exploring 317

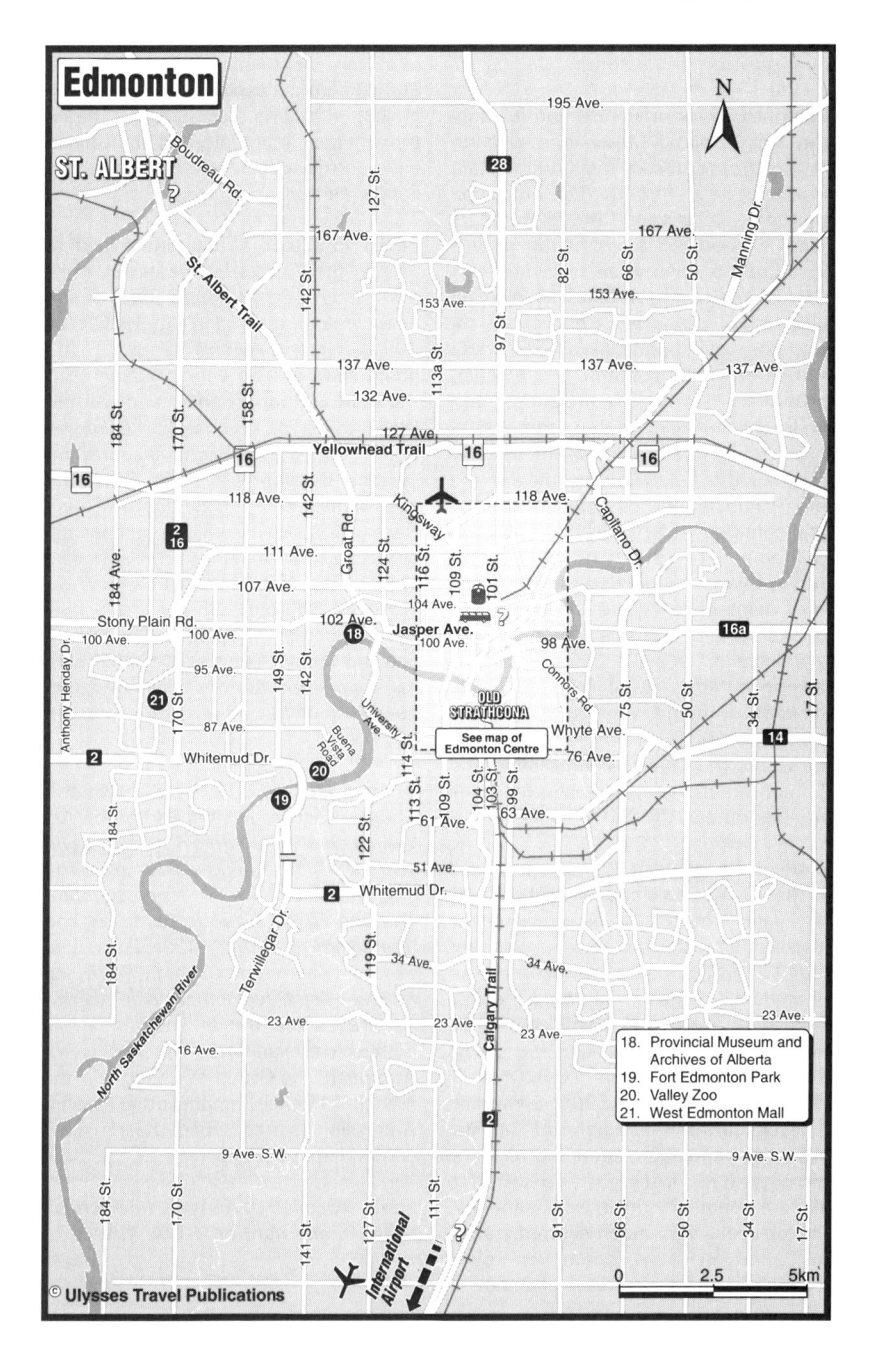

18. Provincial Museum and Archives of Alberta
19. Fort Edmonton Park
20. Valley Zoo
21. West Edmonton Mall

peaceable when they were outside their own territory to the south.

Edmonton's fortunes rose and fell until the next boom. Merchants tried to attract prospectors of the Klondike Gold Rush to pass through Edmonton on their way to Dawson City. Prospectors were encouraged to outfit themselves in Edmonton and then use this "All-Canadian Route" which was also an alternative to the Chilkoot Trail, therefore avoiding Alaska. The route turned out to be something of a scam, however, proving arduous and impractical. None of the some 1,600 prospectors lured to Edmonton actually reached the goldfields in time for the big rush in 1899. Some perished trying and some never left. Six years later, on September 1, 1905, the province of Alberta was founded and Edmonton was named the capital. Citizens of cities like Calgary, Cochrane, Wetaskiwin, Athabasca and Banff, among others, all claimed that this distinction should have been bestowed on their cities, but Edmonton persisted. In 1912, the cities of Strathcona and Edmonton merged, pushing the total population over 50,000.

Agriculture remained the bread and butter of Alberta's capital until the well at Leduc (see p 311) blew in and the third boom, the oil boom, was on. Since then Edmonton has been one of Canada's fastest growing cities. Pipelines, refineries, derricks and oil tanks sprang up all around the city in farmer's fields. Some 10,000 wells were drilled and by 1965, Edmonton had become the oil capital of Canada. As the population grew so did the downtown core in order to accommodate the business community, which is still very much centred around oil, though the boom is over. Fortunately the city took care not to overdevelop, and today this boomtown has an unusually sophisticated atmosphere (despite the shopping mall), with fine restaurants and a thriving arts community. Edmonton has become the technological, service and supply centre of Alberta.

Begin your tour of Edmonton with a visit to the **Tourist Information Centre** *(Mon to Fri 10am to 4pm, Sat and Sun noon to 4pm)* located in **City Hall (1)** *(1 Sir Winston Churchill Square)*, the hours may not be very practical, but the staff are very friendly and helpful. While there, pick up a *Ride Guide* to figure out the public transportation system. The impressive City Hall is the centrepiece of the Edmonton Civic Centre, a complex which occupies six city blocks and includes the Centennial Library, the Edmonton Art Gallery, Sir Winston Churchill Square, the Law Courts Building, the Convention Centre and the Citadel Theatre. City Hall with its impressive 8-story glass pyramid opened in 1992, on the site of the old city hall.

On the eastern side of Sir Winston Churchill Square lies the **Edmonton Art Gallery ★★(2)** *(adults $3, students and seniors $1.50, children free, free Thu pm; Mon to Wed 10:30am to 5pm, Thu and Fri 10:30am to 8pm, Sat and Sun 11am to 5pm; ☎ 422-6223)*. The excellent, permanent exhibit *From Sea to Sea - The Development of Canadian Art* traces the trends and influences with a clear explanation of the Western Approach, the Group of Seven and the French influence, among other things. Admission is free when the museum can find sponsorship.

Head east on 102A Ave., turn left on 97th St. and right on 103A Ave.

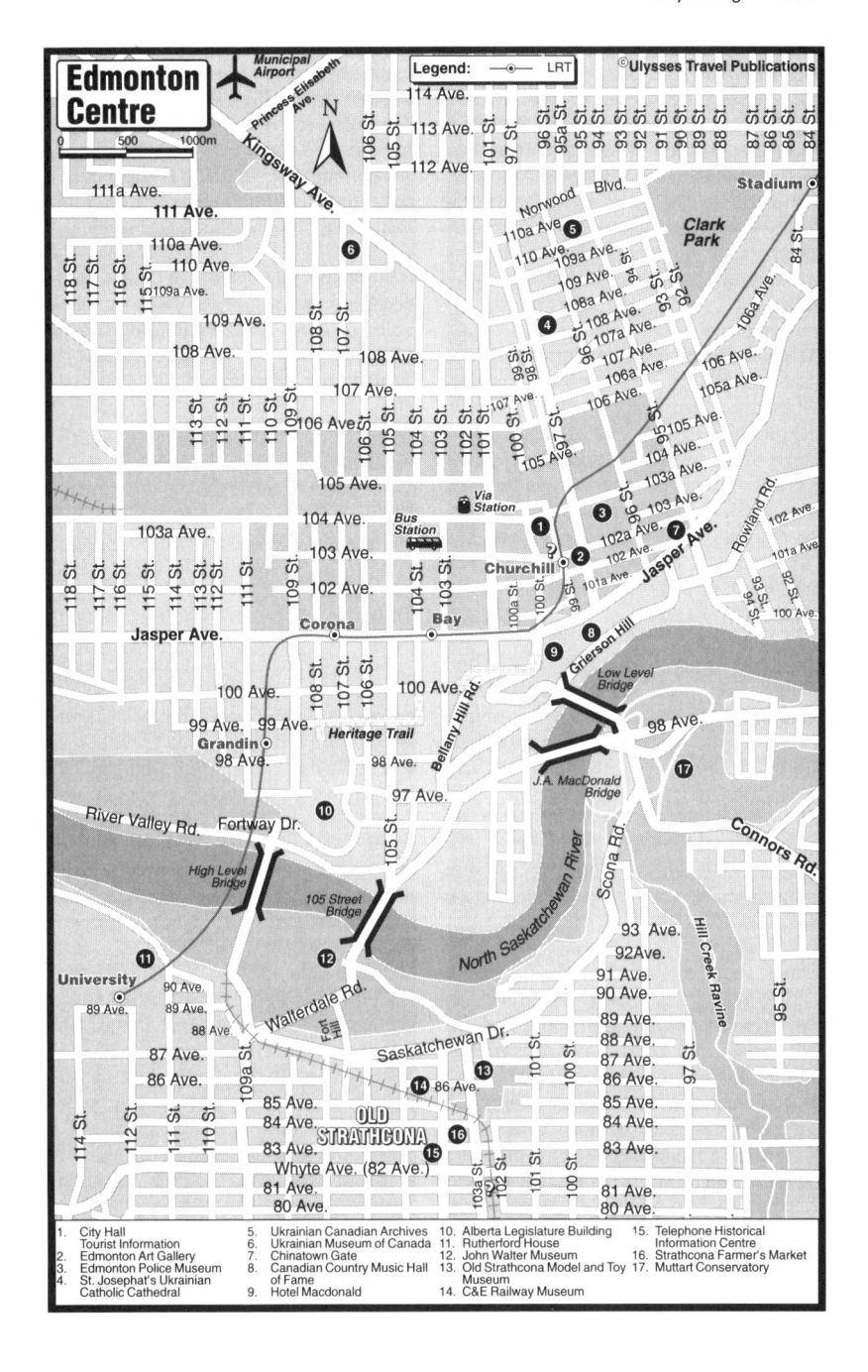

Edmonton Centre

Legend: LRT
©Ulysses Travel Publications

1. City Hall / Tourist Information
2. Edmonton Art Gallery
3. Edmonton Police Museum
4. St. Josephat's Ukrainian Catholic Cathedral
5. Ukrainian Canadian Archives
6. Ukrainian Museum of Canada
7. Chinatown Gate
8. Canadian Country Music Hall of Fame
9. Hotel Macdonald
10. Alberta Legislature Building
11. Rutherford House
12. John Walter Museum
13. Old Strathcona Model and Toy Museum
14. C&E Railway Museum
15. Telephone Historical Information Centre
16. Strathcona Farmer's Market
17. Muttart Conservatory

The **Edmonton Police Museum** ★ (3) *(free admission; Mon to Sat 9am to 3pm; 9620 103A Ave., ☎ 421-2274)* is a bit of a change from your typical museum excursion as it traces law enforcement in Alberta's history. Located on the second floor of the Police Service Headquarters it houses displays of uniforms, handcuffs, jail cells and the force's former furry mascot!

The stretch of 97th St. from 105th to 108th Ave. is Edmonton's original Chinatown with plenty of shops and restaurants. Along 107th Ave., from 95th St. to 116th St. is an area known as the Avenue of Nations with shops and restaurants representing a variety of cultures from Asia, Europe and the Americas. Rickshaws provide transportation during the summer months.

At the corner of 97th St. and 108th Ave. is **St. Josephat's Ukrainian Catholic Cathedral** ★ (4). Among Edmonton's several Ukrainian churches, this is the most elaborate and is worth a stop for its lovely decor and artwork. One block to the east, 96th St. is recognized in *Ripley's Believe It or Not* as the street with the most churches in such a short distance, 16. It is known as Church Street.

Head east to 96th St. then north to 110th Ave. to the **Ukrainian Canadian Archives and Museum of Alberta** ★ (5) *(donation; Tue to Fri 10am to 5pm, Sat noon to 5pm; 9543 110th Ave., ☎ 424-7580)* which houses one of the largest displays of Ukrainian archives in Canada. The lives of Ukrainian pioneers around the turn of the century are chronicled through artifacts, and photographs. About ten blocks to the west, the smaller **Ukrainian Museum of Canada** ★ (6) *(free admission; Jun to Aug, Mon to Fri 9am to 4pm, Sun 2pm to 5pm, winter by appt; 10611 110th Ave., ☎ 483-5932)* displays a collection of Ukrainian costumes, Easter eggs, and household items.

Head south on 95th St. to 102 Ave. to Edmonton's new Chinatown, the focal point of which is the **Chinatown Gate** (7) at 97th St. The gate is also a symbol of the friendship between Edmonton and its sister city Harbin in China. Roll the ball in the lion's mouth for good luck.

Head south to the Edmonton Convention Centre for a great view of the North Saskatchewan River Valley and a visit to the **Canadian Country Music Hall of Fame (8)** *(free admission; pedway level, 9797 Jasper Ave.)* which is actually a wall with plaques and photographs commemorating such greats as Hank Snow and Wilf Carter. After a trip through Alberta you may well have developed an appreciation for country music and want to know more.

In true Canadian Pacific tradition, the Chateau-style **Hotel Macdonald** ★★ (9) is Edmonton's ritziest place to stay, and was the place to see and be seen in Edmonton for many years. Completed in 1915 by the Grand Trunk Railway, it was designed by Montréal architects Ross and MacFarlane. The wrecker's ball came close to falling in 1983 when the hotel closed, but a $28 million dollar restoration brought the Macdonald back in all its splendour. If you aren't staying here, at least pop in to use the facilities, or better yet, enjoy a drink overlooking the river from the

---

Right: The native presence: rich, colourful and fascinating (Mike Ridewood)

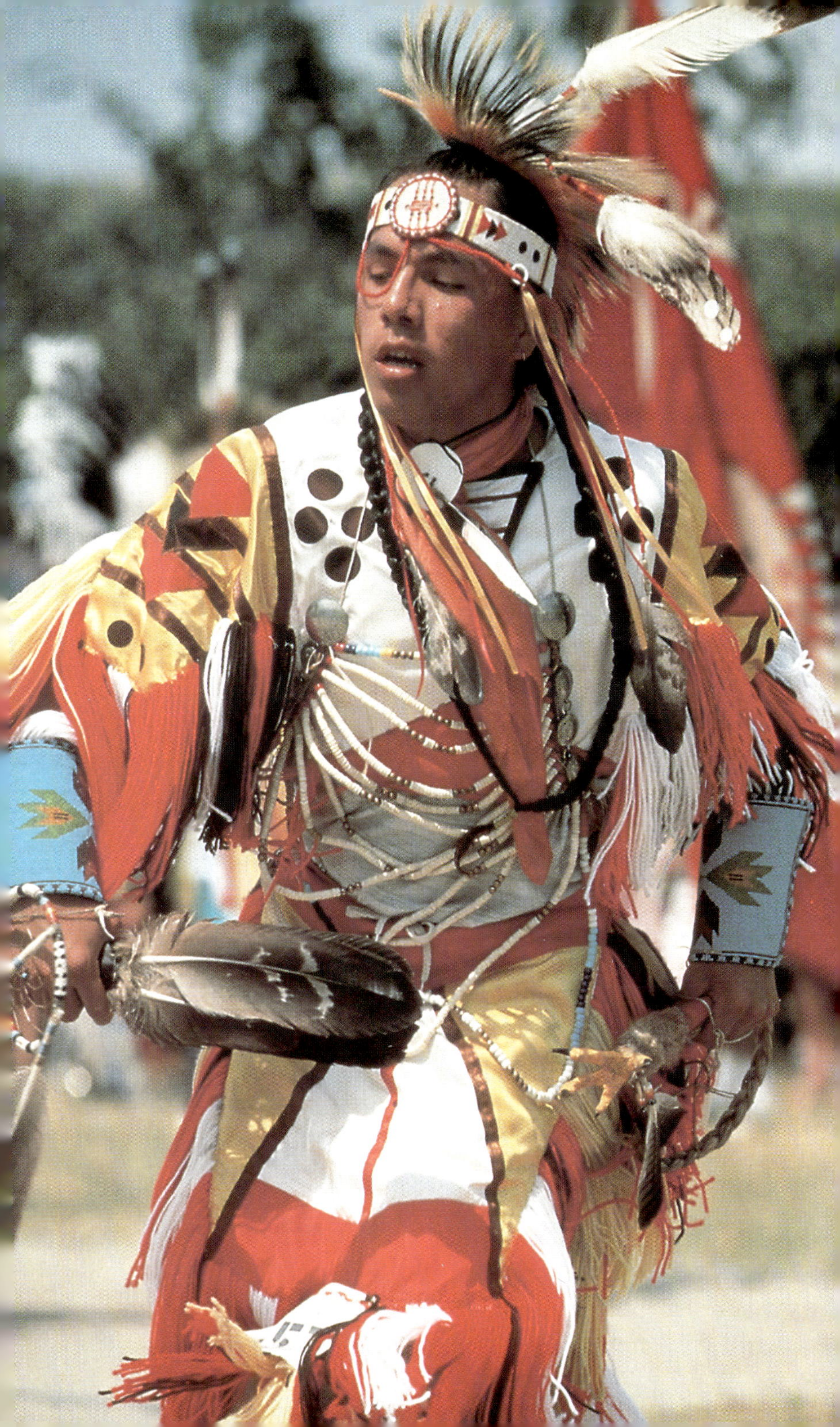

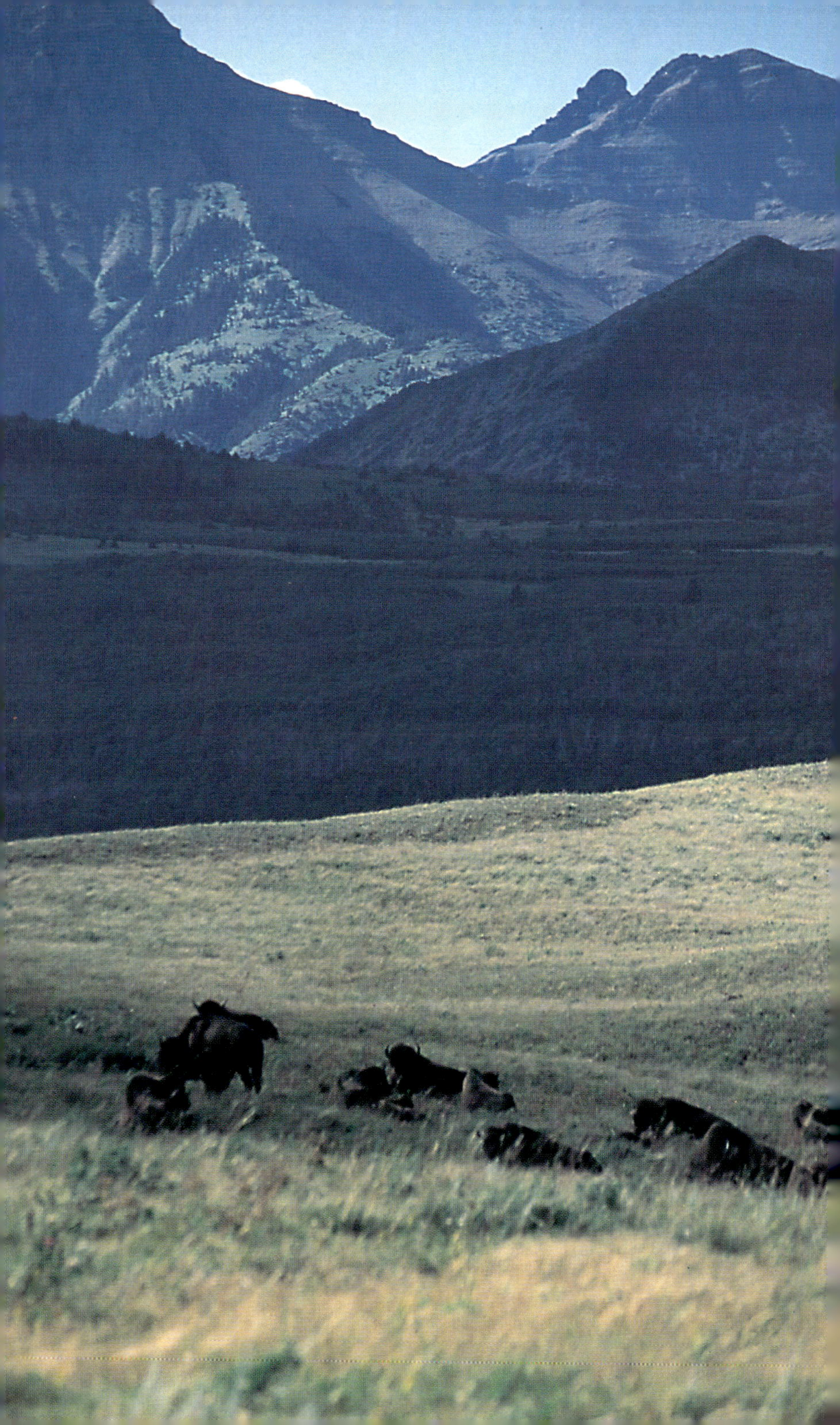

hotel's suave bar, The Library (see "Accommodations" section, p 348).

The next stop on the tour is the Alberta Legislature Building. It is a fair walk to get there from the Hotel Macdonald, but nevertheless a pleasant one along the tree-lined **Heritage Trail** ★★★. This historic fur-traders' route from the Old Town to the site of Old Fort Edmonton is a 30-min walk that follows the river bank for most of its length. A red brick sidewalk, antique light standards and street signs will keep you on the right track. The river views along Macdonald Drive are remarkable, especially at sunset.

The 16-story vaulted dome of the Edwardian **Alberta Legislature Building** ★★ **(10)** *(9am to 4pm, tours available, call ahead for times; 107th St. at 97th Ave., ☎ 427-7362)* is a landmark in Edmonton's skyline. Sandstone from Calgary, marble from Québec, Pennsylvania and Italy, and mahogany from Belize were used to build this, the seat of Alberta government, in 1912. At the time the Legislature stood next to the original Fort Edmonton. Today it is surrounded by gardens and fountains; be sure to visit the government greenhouses on the south grounds. Tours begin at the Interpretive Centre where Alberta's and Canada's parliamentary tradition is explained.

Cross the High Level Bridge, continue along 109th St., turn right on 88th Ave., turn right again on 110th St., and then left on Saskatchewan Drive to Rutherford House.

Rutherford House ★ **(11)** *(donation; May to Sep, every day 10am to 6pm;*

Sep to May, every day noon to 5pm; 11153 Saskatchewan Dr., ☎ 427-3995) is the classic Edwardian former home of Alberta's first premier, Dr. A.C. Rutherford. Guides in period costume bake scones in a wood stove, offer craft demonstrations, lead visitors through the elegantly restored mansion and operate a tea room in the summer*(☎ 422-2697)*.

If it is a Sunday, return to 88th Ave. and head east. It becomes Walterdale Road, follow it to Queen Elizabeth Park Road and turn left into the parking lot of the John Walter Museum.

The **John Walter Museum (12)** *(free admission; Sun 1pm to 4pm, until 5pm in summer; 10627 93rd Ave., ☎ 496-4852)* is in fact three houses, each built by John Walter between 1874 and 1900. Walter manned a ferry across the North Saskatchewan River, and his first house was used as a rest spot for travellers. Exhibits outline the growth of Edmonton over this period.

Continue your tour by heading to **Old Strathcona** ★★★. Once a city independent of Edmonton, Strathcona was founded when the Calgary and Edmonton Railway Company's rail line ended here in 1891. Brick buildings from that era still remain in this historic district, that is the best-preserved in Edmonton. While the area north of the North Saskatchewan River is clean, crisp and new with the unfinished feel of a boom town, south of the river, in Old Strathcona, a sense of character is much more tangible. Here an artistic, cosmopolitan and historic atmosphere prevails.

Left: Buffalo once roamed free throughout Alberta (Jennifer McMorran)

On your way to the commercial centre of Old Strathcona, Whyte Ave. (82nd Ave.) stop in at the **Old Strathcona Model and Toy Museum** ★★ **(13)** *(free admission; May to Sep, Sun to Tue 1pm to 5pm, Wed to Fri noon to 8pm, Sat 10am to 6pm; Sep to May, Wed to Fri noon to 5pm, Sat 10am to 6pm, Sun 1pm to 5pm; 8603 104 St., ☎ 433-4512)*, housed in the Mackenzie Residence, one of the best preserved buildings in Old Strathcona. This fascinating spot exhibits only models and toys made of paper or cardboard. These childhood treasures from the past will delight both young and old.

Three other interesting stops along the way are the **C&E Railway Museum (14)** *(donations; May to Aug, Tue to Sat 10am to 4pm; 10447 86th Ave., ☎ 433-9739)*, housed in a replica of the original railway station; the **Telephone Historical Information Centre** ★ **(15)** *(adults $2, children and seniors $1, family $3; Mon to Fri 10am to 4pm, Sat noon to 4pm; 10437 83rd Ave., ☎ 441-2077)*, housed in the original telephone exchange, where you'll get the real story behind switchboards and manholes; and finally the **Strathcona Farmer's Market** ★ **(16)** *(year-round, Sat 8am to 3pm; in the summer Tue 1pm to 6pm as well)* on 83rd Ave. between 104th St. and 103rd St., where fresh produce, crafts and plenty of little treasures can be bought. On the corner of Whyte Ave. and 103rd St. is the Caboose Tourist Information Centre where you can pick up brochures for walking tours of historic Old Strathcona.

Next take a stroll along **Whyte Avenue** (82nd Ave.) to explore the shops and cafés and soak up the atmosphere.

The city has a handful of other sights that merit a visit and are best reached by public transit or car.

The four glass pyramid greenhouses of the **Muttart Conservatory** ★★★ **(17)** *(adults $4.25, seniors $3.25, children $2-3.25, family $12.50; Sun to Wed 11am to 9pm, Thu to Sat 11am to 6pm; off 98 Ave. and 96A St., ☎ 496-8755)* are another of the landmarks of Edmonton's skyline. Flourishing beneath three of these pyramids are floral displays of arid, temperate and tropical climates, respectively. Every month a new vivid floral display is put together under the fourth pyramid. The conservatory is accessible from bus #51 south on 100th St.

About 6 km west as the crow flies and north of the river, is the **Provincial Museum and Archives of Alberta** ★★ **(18)** *(adults $5.50, children $2.25, family $13, ½-price Tue in winter; May to Sep, every day 9am to 8pm; Sep to May, Tue to Sun 9am to 5pm; 12845 102 Ave, ☎ 453-9100)*. The natural and human history of Alberta is traced from the Cretaceous period, through the Ice Age to the pictographs of the province's earliest indigenous peoples. The merging of their cultures and those of the early explorers and pioneers is explained in the native display. The habitat gallery reproduces Alberta's four natural regions, while the Bug Room is a-buzz with exotic live insects. Travelling exhibits complement the permanent collection. The displays are a bit dated, but nonetheless provide an interesting overview of the world of contrasts that is Alberta. Take bus #1 along Jasper Ave., or bus #116 along 102 Ave.

In the North Saskatchewan River Valley, off Whitemud and Fox Drives, lies **Fort Edmonton Park** ★★ **(19)** *($3-8;*

May and Jun, Mon to Fri 10am to 4pm, Sat and Sun 10am to 6pm; Jul to Sep, every day 10am to 6pm; over Christmas for sleigh rides; ☎ 496-8787), Canada's largest historic park and home to an authentic reconstruction of Fort Edmonton as it stood in 1846. Four historic villages recreate different periods at the fort: the fur-trading era at the fort itself; the settlement era on 1885 Street; the municipal era on 1905 Street and the metropolitan era on 1920 Street. Period buildings, period dress, period automobiles and period shops, including a bazaar, a general store, a saloon and bakery bring you back in time. Reed's Bazaar and Tea Room serves a proper English tea with scones from 12:30pm to 5pm. Theme programs for children are put on on Saturday afternoons. Admission is free after 4:30pm, but don't arrive any later in order to catch the last train to the fort, and take note that you'll be tight for time if you choose this frugal option, so it depends how much you want to see.

For a lovely walk through the North Saskatchewan River Valley, follow the 4-km long self-guided interpretive trail that starts at the **John Janzen Nature Centre** (free admission; Sep to Jun, Mon to Fri 9am to 4pm, Sat and Sun 11am to 6pm; Jul to Sep, Mon to Fri 9am to 6pm, Sat and Sun 11am to 6pm; next to Fort Edmonton Park, ☎ 496-2939). Hands-on displays and live animals, including a working beehive, are found in the centre.

The Fort Edmonton Valley Zoo Shuttle operates from the University Transit Centre and between these two sights on Sundays and holidays between Victoria Day (3rd Sunday in May) and Labour Day (early Sep). Fares are (one-way) adults $1.60, seniors and children 6-15 $0.80, and children under 5 free.

Alternately, bus #12 drops you at Buena Vista and 102nd Ave., from where you must walk 1.5 km to the zoo.

Across the river is the **Valley Zoo ★ (20)** (adults $4.95, seniors and students $3.50, children $2.50, family $14.95, cheaper in winter; May to Jun, every day 10am to 6pm; Jul and Aug, until 9pm; Sep and Nov, Mon to Fri noon to 4pm, Sat and Sun 10am to 6pm; Nov to May, every day noon to 4pm; at the end of Buena Vista Rd., ☎ 496-6911), a great place for kids. It apparently began with a story-book theme but has since grown to include an African veldt and winter quarters which permit it to stay open in the winter. The residents include Siberian tigers and white-handed gibbons along with more indigenous species. Kids enjoy run-of-the-mill pony rides and more exotic camel rides.

Last, but certainly not least, is Edmonton's pride and joy the **West Edmonton Mall ★★★ (21)** (87th Ave. between 170th St. and 178th St.). You may scoff to hear that some visitors come to Edmonton and never leave the West Edmonton Mall, and then you may swear that you won't give in to the hype and visit it, but these reasons alone are reason enough to go, if only to say you've been. There are real submarines at the Deep-Sea Adventure; dolphin shows; underwater caverns and barrier reefs; the largest indoor amusement park; an National Hockey League-size rink, where you can watch the Edmonton Oilers practise; an 18-hole golf course; a waterpark complete with wave pool, waterslides, rapids, bungee jumping and whirlpools; a casino, bingo room and North America's largest billiard hall; fine dining on Bourbon Street; a life-sized, hand-carved, hand-painted replica of

Columbus' flagship, the Santa Maria; replicas of England's crown jewels; a solid ivory pagoda; bronze sculptures; fabulous fountains including one fashioned after a fountain at the Palace of Versailles and finally, the Fantasyland Hotel (see p 349): lodging that truly lives up to its name... and oh yeah, we almost forgot, there are also some 800 shops and services, this is a mall after all. It seems it is possible to come and never leave! Even though it is a shopping mall, the West Edmonton Mall simply has to be seen and therefore merits its three stars!

If you can't afford the extra money to stay in an igloo or a horse-drawn coach, at least take a tour of the theme rooms at the **Fantasyland Hotel** *(free tour; every day 2pm; reserve ahead ☎ 444-3000)* (see p 349).

■ **Tour E: Northern Alberta**

Northern Alberta, as described in this tour covers more than half the province. This vast hinterland offers excellent opportunities for outdoor pursuits as well as the chance to discover some of Alberta's cultural communities. Distances are so great, however, that it is inconceivable to imagine touring the whole region unless you have all sorts of time. The following tour is thus presented as three routes leading to the frontiers of Alberta, passing major attractions of northern Alberta along the way. They are: east to the Saskatchewan border; northeast to Fort McMurray and Wood Buffalo National Park; and northwest, heading either farther north up the Mackenzie Highway or west into northern British Columbia (see p 161).

East to the Saskatchewan Border

Heading east from Edmonton on Hwy 16, the Yellowhead Highway, travellers will soon arrive at **Elk Island National Park** ★★. This island wilderness in a sea of grass preserves two herds of buffalo, plains bison and the rare wood bison. It is also home to a multitude of animals species. There are campgrounds, while trails and a lake offer the possibility of all sorts of outdoor activities (see "Parks" p 336).

Continuing east on Hwy 16, you will soon come upon the **Ukrainian Cultural Heritage Village** ★ *(adults $5.50, children $2.25, under 6 free, family $13; May to Sep, every day 10am to 6pm, south of Hwy 16 about 30 km east of Edmonton, ☎ 662-3640)*, where the fascinating story of the region's Ukrainian settlers is brought to life. Life at the Bloc settlement in East Central Alberta from 1892 to 1930 is recreated with staff in period costume and a whole historic townsite. Driven from their homeland, these settlers fled to the Canadian prairies, where land was practically being given away. They dressed and worked as they had in the old country thereby enriching the Canadian cultural landscape. Late August is the time for the "Harvest of the Past", featuring tsymbaly entertainment and pyroghy (potato dumpling) eating contests.

Another half hour east is the town of **Vegreville**, first settled by French farmers migrating from Kansas. These days it is better known for its Ukrainian community and its rather curious landmark, the world's largest pysanka. The traditional Ukrainian Easter egg is 8 m long.

Exploring 325

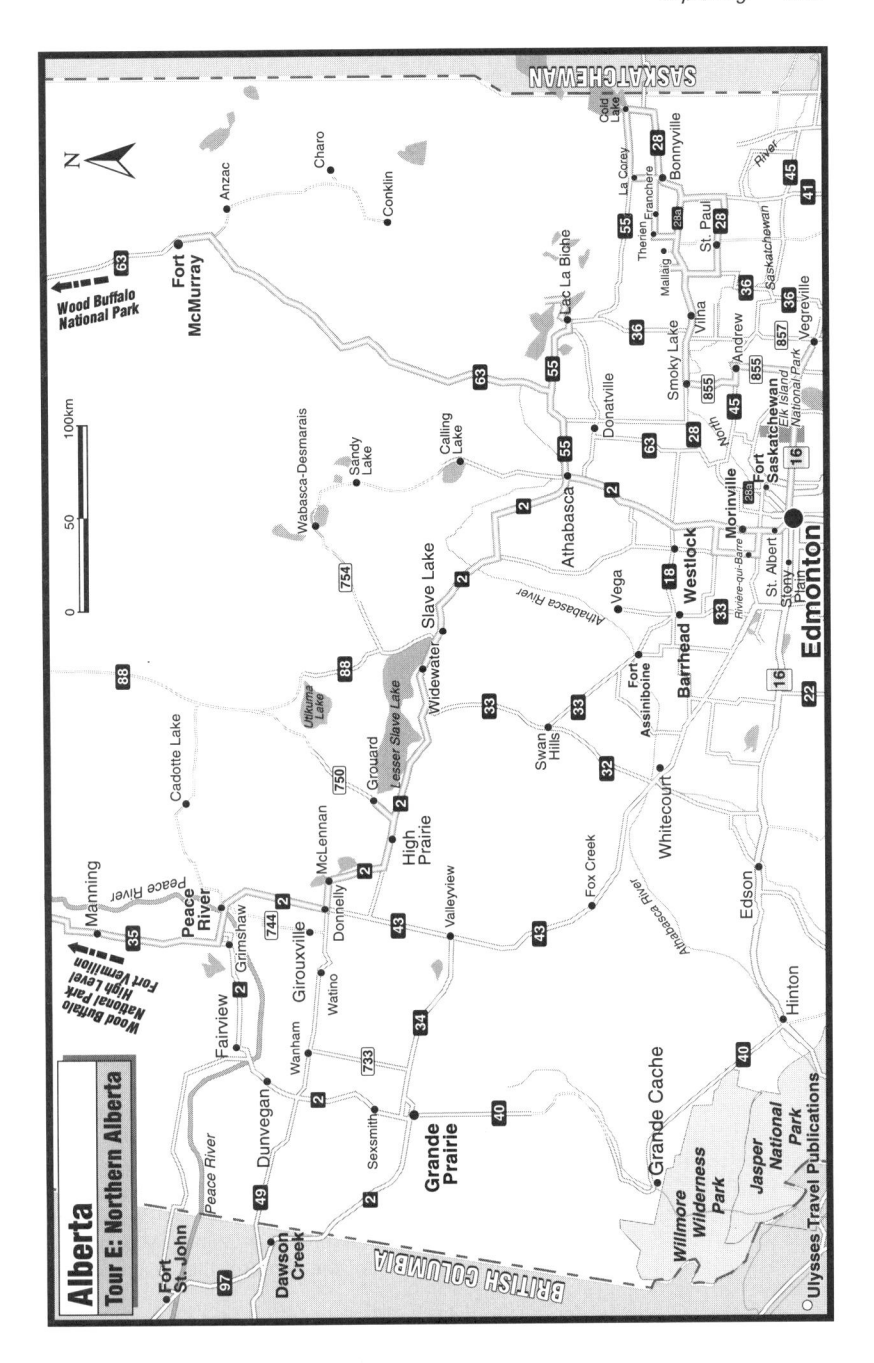

North of Vegreville on Hwy 855, just south of the town of **Smoky Lake**, lies the **Victoria Settlement** ★ *(adults $5.50, children $2.25, under 6 free, family $13; May to Sep, every day 10am to 6pm,* ☎ *645-4760).* A Methodist mission was established here in 1862, and two years later the Hudson's Bay Company set up Fort Victoria to compete with free traders at the settlement. This wonderfully peaceful spot along the Saskatchewan River, once a bustling village, was also the centre of a Metis community. The town was called Pakan, after a Cree chief who was loyal to the Riel Rebellion. When the railway moved to Smoky Lake, all the buildings were relocated; only the clerk's quarters were left behind. Exhibits and trails point out the highlights of this once thriving village that has all but disappeared. The tranquil atmosphere here makes this a nice place for a picnic.

A drive east along Hwys 28 and 28A to the Saskatchewan border leads through a region of francophone communities. These include **St. Paul**, **Mallaig**, **Therien**, **Franchère**, **La Corey** and **Bonnyville**. Bonnyville used to be known as St. Louis de Moose Lake and today houses an interesting **Historical Museum**. The town of St. Paul began in 1896 when Father Albert Lacombe (see below) established a Metis settlement here hoping to attract Metis from all over Western Canada. Only 330 of these people, who had been continuously ignored by the government, responded to his invitation. Eventually settlers from a variety of cultural backgrounds arrived. The **St. Paul Culture Centre** *(May to Sep, Mon to Fri 9am to 5pm; 4537 50th Ave.,* ☎ *645-4800)* examines the area's diverse cultural background. The old **Rectory** still stands a few blocks away *(5015 47th St.)*. The cultural make-up of St. Paul may someday be even more diversified if the **UFO Landing Pad** in town is ever put to use!

Northeast to Fort McMurray and Wood Buffalo

Just north of Edmonton lies the community of **St. Albert**, the oldest farming settlement in Alberta. It began as a small log chapel in 1861, built by the Mary Immaculate Mission and Father Albert Lacombe. Born in Québec in 1827, Albert Lacombe began his missionary work in St. Boniface near present-day Winnipeg. He convinced Bishop Alexandre Taché of the need for a mission dedicated to the Metis population, and St. Albert thus came into existence. Father Lacombe only stayed at the new mission for four years, and then continued his work throughout the prairies. Bishop Vital Grandin moved his headquarters to St. Albert in 1868 and brought a group of skilled Oblate Brothers with him, making St. Albert the centre of missionary work in Alberta. Grandin played an important role in lobbying Ottawa for fair treatment of natives, Metis and French Canadian settlers.

The **Father Lacombe Chapel** *(admission; May to Sep, every day 10am to 6pm; St. Vital Avenue, St. Albert,* ☎ *427-2022)* is the oldest known standing structure in Alberta. This humble log chapel, built in 1861, was the centre of the busy Metis settlement. It was restored in 1929 by being enclosed in a brick structure. In 1980 it was once again restored and moved to its present site on Mission Hill, where it enjoys a sweeping view out over the fields and the Sturgeon River Valley. Mission Hill is also the site of the residence of

Bishop Grandin, now known as the Vital Grandin Centre.

The **Musee Heritage Museum** ★ *(free admission; Jun to Aug, Mon to Fri 9:30am to 8pm, Sat and Sun 10am to 5pm; Sep to May, Tue to Fri 10am to 5pm, Sat and Sun noon to 5pm; 5 St. Ann St., St. Albert, ☎ 459-1528)* is located in an interesting contoured brick building called St. Ann Place. The museum houses an exceptional exhibit of artifacts and objects related to the history of the first citizens of St. Albert, including the Metis, natives, missionaries and pioneers. Tours are available in both French and English.

Continuing north on Hwy 2, you'll soon reach another area of francophone communities, some with poetic names like Rivière Qui Barre, before arriving in **Morinville**. The **St. Jean Baptiste Church** in town was erected in 1907, while the original chapel was built in 1891 under direction of Father Jean Baptiste Morin. There is a Casavant organ and large murals adorning its interior.

A little over one hundred kilometres farther north is the town of **Athabasca**, located close to the geographic centre of Alberta. The Athabasca River, which flows through the town, was the main corridor to the north, and the town of Athabasca was once a candidate for provincial capital.

The town began as Athabasca Landing, a Hudson's Bay Company trading post, and a point along one of the river trails that lead north. Traders and explorers headed west on the North Saskatchewan River to present-day Edmonton, then overland on a hazardous 80-mile portage, cut in 1823, to the Athabasca River at Fort Assiniboine, southwest of the present-day town of Athabasca. It was this pitiful trail that spelt disaster for Klondikers in 1897-8 on the "All-Canadian Route" from Edmonton (see p 318). A new trail the, Athabasca Landing Trail, was created in 1877. It soon became the major highway to the north and a transshipping point for northern posts and Peace River. Hudson's Bay Company scows built in Athabasca were manned by a group known as the Athabasca Brigade, composed mainly of Cree and Metis. This brigade handily guided the scows down the Athabasca River through rapids and shallow waters to points north. Most scows were broken up at their destination and used in building, but those that returned had to be pulled by the brigades. Paddle-wheelers eventually replaced these scows.

The town was known as a jumping-off point for traders and adventurers heading north, and to this day, it is still a good jumping-off point for outdoor adventurers as it lies right on the fringe of the northern hinterland, yet is only an hour and a half north of Edmonton. Cross-country skiing in winter, river adventures, fishing and even golf on a beautiful new 18-hole course in summer are some of the possibilities. A pamphlet featuring an historic walking tour is available at the tourist office, located in an old train car on 50th Avenue *(mid-May to mid-Sep, every day 10am to 6pm)*. Athabasca is also home to Athabasca University, Canada's most northerly university, reputed for its distance-education programs.

East on Hwy 55 lies **Lac La Biche**, located on a divide separating the Athabasca River system, which drains into the Pacific, and the Churchill River system, which drains into Hudson Bay. This portage was a vital link on the transcontinental fur-trading route and was used by voyageurs to cross the five kilometres between Beaver Lake and Lac La Biche. The Northwest Company and the Hudson's Bay Company each built trading posts here around 1800, but these were both abandoned when a shorter route was found along the North Saskatchewan River through Edmonton.

In 1853, Father René Remas organized the building of the **Lac La Biche Mission** *(May to Sep, every day 10am to 6pm,* ☎ *623-3274)*. The present restored mission lies 11 km from the original site, having been moved in 1855. The original buildings, including the oldest lumber building in Alberta, are still standing. The mission served as a supply centre for voyageurs and other missions in the area and expanded to include a sawmill, gristmill, printing-press and boat-yard. An hour-long guided tour is available.

About 250 km north on Hwy 63 lies the town of **Fort McMurray**, which grew up around the Athabasca oil sands, the largest single oil deposit in the world. The oil is actually bitumen, a much heavier type of oil whose extraction requires an expensive, lengthy process; the deposits consist of compacted sand mixed with the bitumen. The sand is brought to the surface, where the bitumen is separated and treated to produce a lighter, more useful oil. The one trillion barrels of bitumen in the sands promise to be a vital supplier of future energy needs.

The **Fort McMurray Oil Sands Interpretive Centre** ★★ *(adults $2.25, children $1.25, under six free; May to Sep, every day 10am to 6pm, Sep to May, every day 10am to 4pm; Mackenzie Boulevard, Fort McMurray,* ☎ *743-7167)* explains the extraction process, and much more, through colourful hands-on exhibits. The sheer size and potential of the operations are evident from the mining equipment and seven-story bucketwheel extractor on display. Tours of the **Suncor/Syncrude Sand Plant** are also possible *($8.50; contact Visitors Centre, 440 Saskitawaw Trail, Fort McMurray,* ☎ *791-4336)*.

The boundary of **Wood Buffalo National Park** ★★ is approximately 130 km due north as the crow flies. Though this does not seem that far, the park is difficult to access. Furthermore, only people with back-country experience should consider such a trip. Resourceful travellers who choose to venture to Wood Buffalo should mcan do so from the communities of Fort Chipewyan, Alberta or Fort Smith, Northwest Territories. See "Parks" section for more information, p 337.

North and Northwest to BC and NWT

To reach the northern and western frontiers of Alberta, continue in a northwesterly direction from Athabasca towards the town of Slave Lake.

Lesser Slave Lake is Alberta's third largest lake with an area of 1,150 ha; on its southeastern shore lies the town of **Slave Lake**, once a busy centre on the route towards the Yukon goldfields. There isn't much to see in town, except of course the spectacular scenery across the lake, which seems like a veritable inland sea in this landlocked province. Its shallow waters are teeming with huge northern pike, walleye and whitefish.

Continue west on Hwy 2 to Hwy 750 and Grouard.

Founded in 1884 as the **St. Bernard Mission** by Father Émile Grouard, the village of **Grouard**, with under 400 people, lies at the northeastern end of Lesser Slave Lake. Grouard worked in northern Alberta as a linguist, pioneer missionary and translator for 69 years. He is buried in the cemetery adjoining the mission (☎ 751-3760). A display of artifacts lies at the back of the church, which has been declared a Historic Site.

The **Grouard Native Art Museum** *(Mon to Fri 10am to 4pm; in Moosehead Lodge Building Alberta Vocational College,* ☎ *751-3915, ext. 3281)* is an interesting little museum whose aim is to promote an understanding of North America's native cultures through arts and crafts exhibits. Artifacts on display include birch bark work, decorative arts and contemporary clothing.

Continue on Hwy 2 through High Prairie, home to great walleye fishing (see p 339), and McLennan, the "bird capital of Canada" (see p 339), all the way to Donnelly.

Donnelly is home to the **Société Historique et Généalogique** *(Mon to Fri 10am to 4pm,* ☎ *925-3801)* which has traced the history of French settlement in Alberta. There isn't much to see, except perhaps an interesting map of the province that indicates the principle French settlements. Extensive archives are available for anyone who wants to trace their family tree.

Continue north on Hwy 2 to Peace River.

The mighty **Peace River** makes its way from British Columbia's interior to Lake Athabasca in northeastern Alberta. Fur trappers and traders used the river to get upstream from Fort Forks to posts at Dunvegan and Fort Vermillion. Fort Forks was established in 1792 where the town of **Peace River** now stands by Alexander Mackenzie. Mackenzie was the first person to cross what is now Canada and reach the Pacific Ocean. Exceptional scenery greets any who visits this area, and legend has it that anyone who drinks from the Peace will return.

In town, the **Peace River Centennial Museum** *(adults $2, seniors $1; May to Sep, every day noon to 5pm; Sep to May, Tue to Sun 2pm to 5pm; at the corner of 100th St. and 103rd Ave.,* ☎ *624-4261)* features an interpretive display on the natives of the area, the fur trade, early explorers and the growth of the town. All sorts of old photographs do a good job of evoking life in the frontier town.

Amerindians, explorers, shipbuilders, traders, missionaries and Klondikers all passed through what is now the town of Peace River when they took the **Shaftesbury Trail** which follows Hwy 684 on the west side of the river. Take the Shaftesbury Ferry *(in summer, every day 7am to midnight)* from Blakely's Landing to the historic Shaftesbury settlement.

Twelve Foot Davis was not a 12-foot tall man, but rather a gold-digger and free trader named Henry Fuller who made a $15,000 strike on a 12-foot claim in the Cariboo Goldfields of British Columbia. He is buried on Grouard Hill, above the town. A breathtaking view of the confluence of the Peace, Smoky and Heart Rivers can be had from the **12-Foot Davis Historical Site** accessible by continuing to the end of 100th Ave. Another lookout, called the **Sagitawa Lookout** on Judah Hill Rd. also affords an exceptional view of the surroundings.

The Mackenzie Highway starts in the town of **Grimshaw**, and continues through the larger centres of **Manning** and **High Level** where a variety of services including gas and lodging are available.

Fort Vermillion is the second oldest settlement in Alberta. It was established by the Northwest Company in 1788, the same year Fort Chipewyan was established on Lake Athabasca. Nothing remains of the original fort.

*Beyond this, the towns of **Meander River**, **Steen River** and **Indian Cabins** do not have much in the way of services besides a campground, the next big centre is **Hay River** near the shores of Great Slave Lake in the Northwest Territories.*

Heading west of Peace River, Hwy 2 leads eventually to historic Dunvegan.

With Alberta's longest suspension bridge as a backdrop, **Historic Dunvegan** ★ *(donation; mid-May to Jun, every day 10am to 6pm; Jul to Sep Mon to Fri 10am to 6pm, Sat and Sun 10am to 9pm; off Hwy 2 just north of the Peace River, ☎ 835-5244)* peacefully overlooks the Peace River. Once part of the territory of the Dunneza (Beaver) Indians, this site was chosen in 1805 for a Northwest Company fort, later a Hudsons' Bay Company fort. Dunvegan became a major trade and provisioning centre for the Upper Peace River and later the Hudson's Bay headquarters for the Athabasca district. By the 1840s Catholic missionaries were visiting Dunvegan, including a visit by the eminent Father Albert Lacombe (see p 326) in 1855. In 1867, the Catholic St. Charles Mission was established and in 1879 the Anglican St. Savior's Mission, making Dunvegan a centre for missionary activity. The missions were ultimately abandoned following the discovery of gold and the signing of Treaty No. 8 at which point the Dunneza began leaving the area. The fort operated right up until 1918 when homesteading became more important than trading, hunting and trapping. The mission church (1884), the rectory (1889) and the Hudson's Bay Company factor's house (1877) still stand on the site as well as an informative interpretive centre that is unfortunately housed in a rather ugly modern building.

Continue south to the town of Grande Prairie.

As Alberta's fastest growing city, Canada's forest capital and the Swan City, **Grande Prairie** is a major business and service centre in northern Alberta thanks to natural gas reserves in the area. The town is so named because of *la grande prairie*, highly fertile agricultural lands that are exceptional this far north. Unlike most towns in Alberta's north, Grande Prairie is not what was left behind when the trading post closed. From the start homesteaders were attracted to the area's fertile farmland.

The **Pioneer Village** *(adults $2, students and children $1; mid-Apr to mid-Oct, every day 10am to 6pm; mid-Oct to mid-Apr Sun 1pm to 5pm; corner of 102nd Ave. and 102nd St., ☎ 532-5482)* offers a glimpse of life in Peace Country at the turn of the century with historic buildings, guides in period dress, artifacts and an extensive wildlife collection.

The museum is located near **Muskoseepi Park** a 446-hectare urban park with an interpretive trail and some 40 km of walking and cycling trails.

The landmark design of **Grande Prairie Regional College** *(10726 106th Ave.)* with its curved red brick exterior is the work of architect Douglas Cardinal.

The **Prairie Gallery** ★ *(closed Mon; 10209 99th St., ☎ 532-8111)* exhibits a very respectable collection of Canadian art and international works.

Parks

■ **Tour A: Calgary**

Prince's Island Park lies across the bridge at the end of 3rd St. SW. It is a small haven of tranquility that is perfect for a picnic or morning jog.

Fish Creek Provincial Park *(from 37th St. W to the Bow River)* lies south of the city. Take Macleod Trail south and turn left on Canyon Meadows Dr. then right on Bow Bottom Tr., the information centre is located here *(☎ 297-5293)*. It is the largest urban park in Canada and boasts paved and shale trails that lead walkers, joggers and cyclists through stands of aspen and spruce, prairie grasslands and floodplains dotted by poplar and willow trees. An abundance of wildflowers can be found in the park as well as mule deer, white-tailed deer and coyotes. An interpretive trail, man-made lake and beach, playground and picnic areas are some of the facilities. Fishing is exceptional, you are virtually guaranteed to catch something. Horses can also be rented.

■ **Tour B: Southern Alberta**

Waterton Lakes National Park ★★★

Waterton Lakes National Park *(for one day: group $7, adult $4, seniors $3, children $2, under 6 free; double this fee for three days; camping from $9 to $20; for information call ☎ 859-2445 or write Waterton Lakes National Park, Waterton Park, Alberta, T0K 2M0)* is located right on the US-Canadian border and forms one half of the world's first International Peace Park (the other half is Glacier National Park, Montana). Waterton boasts some of the best scenery in the province, and is well worth the detour required to visit it. Characterized by a chain of deep glacial lakes and upside-down mountains with irregularly shaped summits, this area where the peaks meet the prairies offers wonderful hiking, cross-country skiing, camping and wildlife-viewing opportunities. The unique geology of the area is formed by 1.5 billion year old sedimentary rock from the Rockies that was dumped on the 60-million year-old shale of the prairie during the last ice age. Hardly any transition zone exists between these two regions that are home to an abundant and varied wildlife, where species from a prairie habitat mix with those of sub-alpine and alpine regions (some 800 varieties of plants and 250 species of birds). One thing to remember, and you will be reminded of it as you enter the park, is that wild animals here are just that — wild. While they may appear tame, they are unpredictable and potentially dangerous, and visitors are responsible for their own safety.

332 Alberta

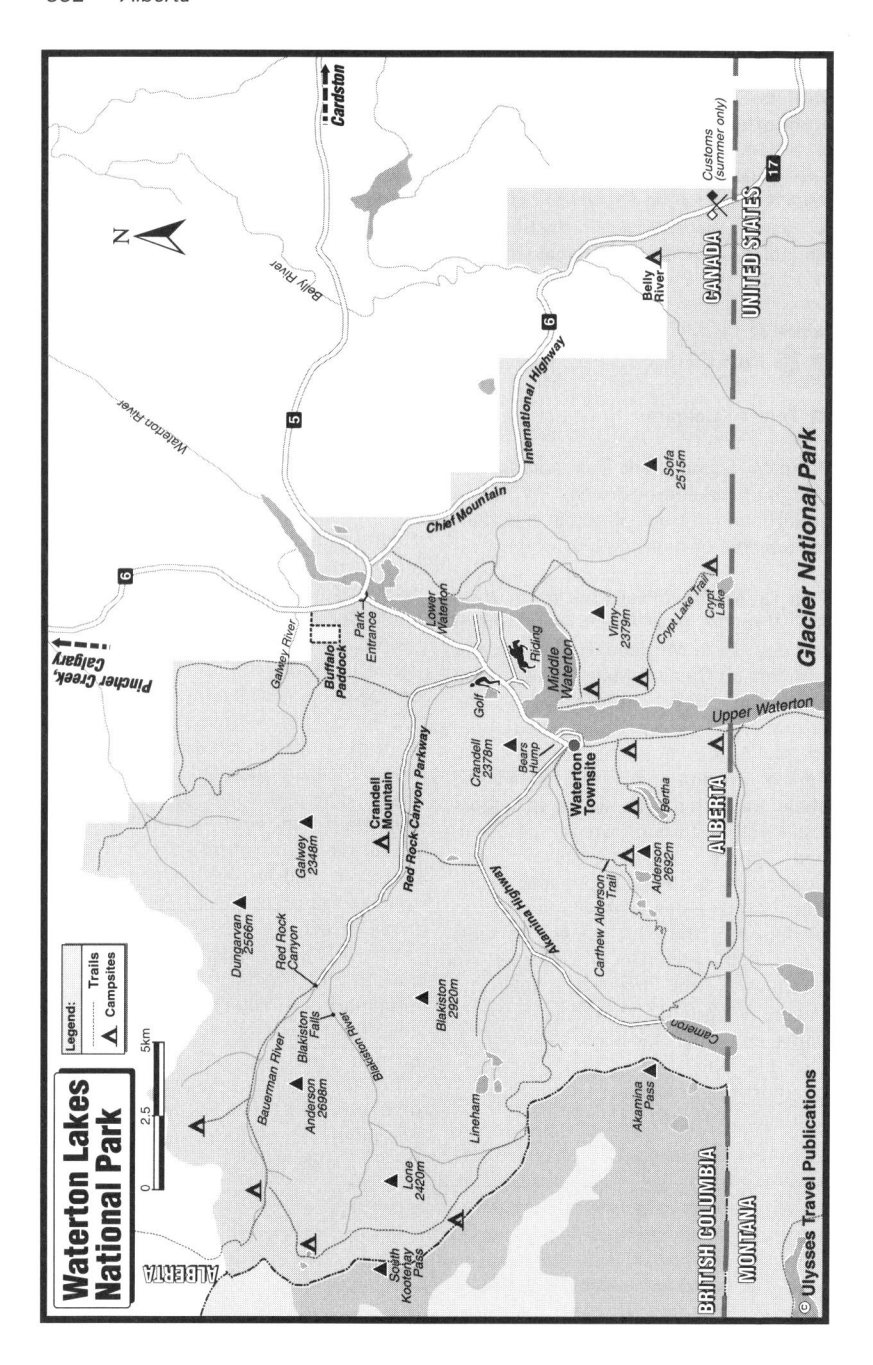

There is one park entrance accessible from Highway 6 or 5. On your way in from Highway 6, you will come upon a **buffalo paddock** shortly before the park gate. A small herd lives here and can be viewed by visitors from their cars along a loop road through the paddock. These beasts are truly magnificent, especially framed against the looming mountains of the park. Fees must be paid at the gate, and information is available at the information centre a short distance inside the park beyond the gate. Park staff can provide information on camping, wildlife-viewing and the various outdoor activities that can be enjoyed here, including hiking, cross-country skiing, golf, horseback riding, boating and swimming.

There are five scenic drives, including the **Akamina Highway** which starts near the townsite and runs for 16 km to Cameron Lake. About 1 km beyond the junction of the park road is a viewpoint over the Bear's Hump, where you have a good chance of spotting some bighorn sheep. You'll find picnic areas as well as the site of Canada's first producing oil well and the city that never was. Mount Custer and the Herbst Glacier in the United States are visible from Cameron Lake, where canoes and pedal boats can be rented. This is the starting point of several trails. The **Red Rock Canyon Parkway** is another scenic drive. It epitomizes the "prairies to peaks" region as it leads through the rolling prairie of Blakiston Valley to the rusty rocks of the water-carved gorge of Red Rock Canyon. Black bears and grizzlies can often be spotted on the slopes feeding on berries. You can also view the park's highest summit, Mount Blakiston. An interpretive trail leads into the canyon at the end of the parkway. Another drive, the **Chief Mountain International Highway** leads through the park and into Glacier National Park in Montana. Travellers crossing the border into the US must report to the Goat Haunt Ranger Station.

Waterton Lakes National Park was initially set aside as a forest reserve in 1895, with John George "Kootenai" Brown as its first warden. Brown got his nickname through his association with the Kootenai Indians. He lead an adventurous life, nearly losing it to Blackfoot Indians, and his scalp to Chief Sitting Bull before turning to more conservationist pursuits. In 1911, Waterton became a national park, and in 1932 it joined with Glacier National Park to form the first International Peace Park. The park was declared an International Biosphere Reserve in 1979. Waterton's history is also marked by a short-lived oil boom in 1901.

Unlike Banff and Jasper National Parks farther north, Waterton never had a rail link. This is still the case, with the result that Waterton remains small, pristine and unspoiled. It retains a genuine Rocky Mountain atmosphere, and so far is free of the heavy-handed touristy commercialism that can mar any adventure into the Canadian Rockies.

The park's trademark **Prince of Wales Hotel** (see p 343) was built in 1926-1927 by Louis Hill, head of the Great Northern Railway, to accommodate American tourists that the railway transported by bus from Montana to Jasper (today, the majority of visitors to the park are still American). Though the hotel has been sold twice, its ownership and operations are still based in the United States; furthermore, the view from the lobby over Upper Waterton Lake remains the same; the hotel still has 90 rooms and it is still open during the summer months only. Expansion and renovation plans for the hotel include the proposition to remain open year-round. This would certainly change things, not only at the Prince of Wales, but in Waterton National Park as well, and the prospect of a more southerly version of Banff gets very mixed reviews. The Swiss chalet-style hotel was proclaimed a National Historic Site in 1994 by the Canadian Government, and is worth a visit even if you can't afford to stay here. The Waterton Townsite is home to restaurants, bars, shops, grocery stores, laundry facilities, a post office and hotels. There is also a marina, from which lake cruises depart. Things slow down considerably in the winter, though the cross-country skiing is outstanding.

Writing-on-Stone Provincial Park ★★

As you approach **Writing-on-Stone Provincial Park** *(free admission; park office ☎ 647-2364)*, located only about 10 km from the American border, you'll notice the carved out valley of the Milk River and in the distance the Sweetgrass Hills rising up in the state of Montana. The Milk River lies in a wide green valley with strange rock formations and steep sandstone cliffs. The hoodoos, formed by iron-rich layers of sandstone that protect the softer underlying layers, appear like strange mushroom-shaped formations. These formations, along with the cliffs, were believed to house the powerful spirits of all things in the world, attracting Natives to this sacred place as many as 3,000 years ago. Writing-on-Stone Provincial Park protects more rock art — petroglyphs (rock carvings) and pictographs (rock paintings) — than any other place on the North American plains. Dating of the rock art is difficult and based solely on styles of drawing and tell-tale objects; for example, horses and guns imply that the drawings continued into the 18th and 19th centuries. Some archaeological sites date from the Late Prehistoric Period, around 1,800 years ago.

Once, buffalo, wolves and grizzly bears could be seen in the park. Though they are gone, a great variety of wildlife and plants still thrive here. Watch for pronghorn antelope, white-tailed and mule deer, yellow-bellied marmots and beavers. Catbirds, mourning doves, towhees and rock wrens also make their homes here. Finally, keep an ear out for rattlesnakes. These venomous critters are not dangerous unless provoked.

The North West Mounted Police also played a role in the history of the park, establishing a post here in 1889 to stop the whisky trade and fighting between Indian tribes. During their time here, many officers carved their names into the sandstone cliffs. The 19th century post was washed away, but a reconstruction stands on the original site. You must participate in a guided tour to view the post.

The Battle Scene, one of the most elaborate petroglyphs in the park, can be viewed along the two self-guided interpretive trails. The scene may depict an Indian battle fought in 1866, but no one is sure. One of the trails, the Hoodoo Interpretive Trail also leads through the unique natural environment of the park; a self-guiding trail brochure is available from the park office.

The majority of the rock art sites are located in the larger part of the provincial park, which is an archaeological preserve. Access is provided only through scheduled interpretive tours, and for this reason it is extremely important to call the park's **naturalist office (☎ 647-2364)** ahead of time to find out when the tours are heading out. They are given daily from mid-may to early September, and free tickets, limited in number, are required. These may be obtained from the naturalist office one hour before the tour begins. Wildlife checklists and fact sheets are also available at the naturalist office.

The park boasts an excellent camping ground. Visitors also have the opportunity to practise a whole slew of outdoor activities including hiking and canoeing — this is a convenient place to start or end a canoe trip along the Milk River.

Cypress Hills Provincial Park ★

Cypress Hills Provincial Park is a wooded oasis of lodgepole pine rising out of the prairie grassland and harbouring a varied wildlife, including deer, elk and moose and some 215 species of birds (including wild turkeys). At least eighteen species of orchid also thrive in the park. There are, however, no cypress trees in the park; the French word for lodgepole pine is *cypres*, and the name *montagnes de cyprès* was mistranslated to Cypress Hills. This was also the site of the Cypress Hill Massacre. Two American whisky trading posts had been set up in the hills in the early 1870s. During the winter of 1872-3, Assiniboine Indians were camped in the hills, close to these two posts when a party of American hunters whose horses had been stolen, and who just happened be drunk, came upon the band of Assiniboine. Believing that the natives had taken the horses the American hunters killed 20 innocent Assiniboine. The incident contributed to the establishment of the North West Mounted Police to restore order. Three-hundred Mounties arrived at Fort Walsh, in Saskatchewan and the men responsible for the massacre were arrested. Though they were not convicted because of lack of evidence, the fact that white men had been arrested gave credence in the eyes of the natives to this new police force.

The park is never busy, giving visitors the opportunity to enjoy great hiking and fishing in peace and quiet. There are 13 campgrounds here and you can rent canoes and bicycles. The visitors centre *(May to Sep, every day 9am to 5pm, information and camping reservations ☎ 893-3777)* is close to Elkwater Lake, not far from the townsite. In the off-season, visit the park office, at the eastern entrance to town, or write to Box 12, Elkwater, Alberta, T0J 1C0.

Dinosaur Provincial Park ★★★

Dinosaur Provincial Park offers amateur palaeontologists the opportunity to walk through the land of the dinosaurs. Declared a UNESCO Heritage Site in 1979, this natural preserve harbours a wealth of information on these majestic former inhabitants of the planet. Today, the park is also home to more than 35 species of animals.

The small museum at the **Field Station of the Tyrell Museum** *(adults $4.50, children $2.25, under 6 free; mid-May to Sep; ☎ 378-4342)*, the loop road and the two self-guided trails (the Cottonwood Flats Trail and the Badlands Trail), will give you a summary introduction to the park. Two exposed skeletons left where they were discovered can be viewed. The best way to see the park, however, is on one of the guided tours into the restricted natural preserve that makes up most of the park. The two-hour Badlands Bus Tour leads in to the heart of the preserve for unforgettable scenery, skeletons and wildlife; the Centrosaurus Bone Bed Hike and Fossil Safari Hike offer close-up looks at real excavation sites. Tickets for all of these tours go on sale one hour before departure time at the field station and space is limited; arrive early in July and August. To avoid missing out, visitors are strongly advised to call ahead to find out when the tours leave.

The park also features camping grounds and a Dinosaur Service Centre with laundry, showers, picnic and food. The cabin of John Ware, an important black cowboy, lies near the campground.

■ **Tour C: Central Alberta**

Crimson Lake Provincial Park *(park office ☎ 845-2340, camping reservations ☎ 845-2330)* is located just west of Rocky Mountain House and features peaceful campsites and good fishing for rainbow trout. Extensive hiking trails become cross-country trails in the winter.

Ma-Me-O Beach Provincial Park *(day use only; park office ☎ 586-2645)* and **Pigeon Lake Provincial Park** *(park office ☎ 586-2645, camping reservations ☎ 586-2644)* are for those who have had enough of the mountains and are up for a day at the beach. Both offer excellent access to the great swimming (said to be the best in Alberta) and fishing on Pigeon Lake. Boats can be rented at the Zeiner campground in the Pigeon Lake Provincial Park.

■ **Tour D: Edmonton**

The **River Valley Park System** *(Edmonton Parks and Recreation ☎ 496-4999)* lies along the North Saskatchewan River and consists of several smaller parks where you can bicycle, jog, go swimming, play golf or just generally enjoy the natural surroundings. The amount of land set aside for parks per capita is higher in Edmonton than anywhere else in the country. Bicyclists are encouraged to pick up a copy of the map *Cycle Edmonton* at one of the tourist information offices.

■ **Tour E: Northern Alberta**

Elk Island National Park

The magnificent **Elk Island National Park** ★★ *(adults $4, seniors $3, children $2; open year-round; park administration and warden Mon to Fri 8am to 4:30pm, ☎ 992-6380 or 992-6389; camping ☎ 992-2653)* preserves part of the Beaver Hills area as it was before the arrival of settlers when Sarcee and Plains Cree hunted and trapped in these lands. The arrival of settlers endangered beaver, elk and bison populations, prompting local residents and conservationists to petition the government to set aside an elk preserve in 1906. The plains bison that live in the park actually ended up there by accident, having escaped from a herd placed there temporarily while a fence at Buffalo National Park in Wainwright, Alberta was being completed. The plains bison herd that inhabits the park began with those 50 escaped bison. Elk Island is also home to a small herd of rare wood bison, North America's largest mammal. In 1940, pure wood buffalo were thought to be extinct, but by sheer luck a herd of about 200 wood buffalo were discovered in a remote part of the park in 1957. Part of that herd was sent to a fenced sanctuary in the Northwest Territories. Today the smaller plains bison, are found to the north of Hwy 16, while the wood bison live south of the highway. While touring the park, remember that you are in bison country, and that these animals are wild. Though they may look docile, they are dangerous, unpredictable and may charge without warning, so stay in your vehicle and keep a safe distance (50 to 75 metres).

Elk Island became a national park in 1930 and is now a 195 km^2 sanctuary for 44 kinds of mammals, including moose, elk, deer, lynx, beavers and coyote. The park offers some of the best wildlife viewing in the province. It is crossed by major migratory flyways; be on the look-out for trumpeter swans in the fall.

The park office at the South Gate, just north of Hwy 16, can provide information on the two campgrounds, wildlife viewing and the twelve trails that run through the park, making for great hiking and cross-country skiing. Fishing and boating can be enjoyed on Astotin Lake, and the park even boasts a nine-hole golf course.

Wood Buffalo National Park

Wood Buffalo National Park ★ is accessible from the communities of Fort Chipewyan, Alberta and Fort Smith, Northwest Territories. Fort Chipewyan can be reached by plane from Fort McMurray twice a week; in summer motorboats do travel the Athabasca and Embarras Rivers; there is a winter road open from December to March between Fort McMurray and Fort Chipewyan but this is not recommended, and finally for the really adventurous, it is possible to enter the park by canoe on the Peace and Athabasca Rivers.

The park is home to the largest, free-roaming, self-regulating herd of bison in the world; it is also the only remaining nesting ground of the whooping crane. These two facts contributed to Wood Buffalo being designated a World Heritage Site. The park was initially established to protect the last remaining herd of wood bison in northern Canada. But when plains bison were shipped to the park between 1925 and 1928 because plains in Buffalo National Park in Wainwright, Alberta were overgrazed, the plains bison interbred with the wood bison causing the extinction of pure wood bison. Or so they thought. A herd was discovered in Elk Island National Park (see below), and part of it was shipped to Mackenzie Bison Sanctuary in the Northwest Territories. As a result there are actually no pure wood buffalo in Wood Buffalo National Park.

Those who make the effort will enjoy hiking (most trails are in the vicinity of Fort Smith), excellent canoeing and camping and the chance to experience Canada's northern wilderness in the country's largest national park. Advanced planning is essential to a successful trip to this huge wilderness and a "Park Use Permit" is required for all overnight stays in the park. Also remember to bring lots of insect repellent. For more information contact the park *(Box 750, Fort Smith, NWT, XOE OPO, ☎ 872-2349, ⇄ 872-3910)*.

Beaches

Believe it or not, land-locked Alberta has a handful of beaches that are great for swimming and suntanning. In central Alberta and northern Alberta, countless lakes left behind by retreating glaciers now provide water fun for summer vacationers. **Pigeon Lake Provincial Park** has a long sandy beach with showers and picnic tables, while **Ma-Me-O Provincial Park** at the other end of Pigeon Lake, is a day-use area that's great for a picnic and catching some rays. **Sylvan Lake** is a veritable beach resort town. A beautiful beach lines one of Alberta's most spectacular lakes. Windsurfers and pedal-boats can be rented.

Lesser Slave Lake Provincial Park, next to Alberta's third largest lake, offers all sorts of opportunities for aquatic pursuits, including Devonshire Beach, a 7-km stretch of beautiful sand.

Outdoor Activities

Golf

Mapleridge Golf Course *(1240 Mapleglade Dr. SE, ☎ 974-1825)* and **Shaganappi Golf Course** *(1200 26th St. SW, ☎ 974-1810)* are two of the nicer municipal golf course in **Calgary**. Tee times for all City of Calgary courses can be booked one day in advance by calling ☎ 221-3510.

Paradise Canyon *(☎ 381-7500)* is a brand new 18-hole championship course in **Lethbridge** overlooking the Oldman River.

Waterton Lakes Golf Club *(☎ 859-2383)* was designed by Stanley Thompson and offers 18 holes of challenging and scenic golf. It is located 4 km north of town. There is a pro shop where you can rent clubs.

The **Riverside Golf Course** *(8630 Rowland Rd., ☎ 428-5330)*, overlooking the North Saskatchewan River in **Edmonton**, is one of the city's over 30 courses.

The **Athabasca Golf & Country Club** *(on the north side of the Athabasca River, ☎ 675-4599)* is a new course with beautiful scenery and 18 challenging holes.

Canoeing and Rafting

With hot summer temperatures and the possibility of spotting antelope, mule deer, white-tailed deer, coyotes, badger, beaver and cottontail rabbits, as well as several bird species, the Milk River is a great spot to explore by canoe. Set in arid southern Alberta, this river is the only one in Alberta that drains into the Gulf of Mexico. Canoes can be rented in Lethbridge.

Milk River Raft Tours *(Box 396 Milk River, Alberta, T0K 1M0, ☎ 647-3586)* organizes rafting trips along the river in the vicinity of Writing-on-Stone Provincial Park. Trips last from two to four hours, cost between $10 and $25 and can include lunch and hikes through the coulees.

Alpenglow Mountain Adventures *(Nordegg, Alberta, T0M 2H0, ☎ 721-2050)* organizes rafting, kayaking and canoeing trips along the North Saskatchewan River between Nordegg and Rocky Mountain House.

Full day trip range from $39 to $64, while overnight trips from two to three days range from $149 to $249. This outfit also organizes trips along the Athabasca River.

Also based in Rocky Mountain House, **Voyageur Adventure Tours** *(4808 63rd St., Rocky Mountain House, T0M 1T2,* ☎ *845-7878)* organizes single- and several-day trips in 10-passenger voyageur canoes. Trip cost between $45 and $180.

Bird-watching

Alberta is a veritable bird-watcher's paradise. Several species are found in **Waterton Lakes National Park** including Canada geese, mallards, sandpipers, red-tailed hawks, ospreys, grouse, kingfisher, jays, wrens, warblers and starlings, and those are just the common sightings. If you are lucky you may spot trumpeter swans, hummingbirds, golden eagles and bald eagles.

McLennan is the bird capital of Canada. Three major migratory flyways converge here, giving bird-watchers the chance to see over 200 different species. The town has an interesting interpretive centre and boardwalk that leads to a bird blind.

Fishing

Alberta's rivers and lakes are teeming with fish, offering anglers the chance to catch huge walleye, lake trout, sturgeon and pike among other species. Fishing in Alberta waters, whether in the Bow River in the middle of Calgary or Lesser Slave Lake in the north, is always productive.

Real fans may want to try their luck in the Golden Walleye Classic which takes place in **High Prairie** the third week in August. With a $100,000 prize it may just be worth your while. Anyone can join, for information call ☎ 751-2241.

Skating

Alberta's lakes freeze over in the winter for great wilderness skating, but for the chance to skate on Olympic ice head to Calgary's Olympic Oval. This world-class facility, built for the '88 Winter Olympics, is now used as a training centre. The public skating hours vary, but generally the rink is open to the public in the afternoon from noon to 1pm and in the evenings. It is a good idea to call ahead ☎ 220-7890.

Hiking and Cross-Country Skiing

Alberta cities are blessed with extensive parks and green spaces. Calgary, Lethbridge, Medicine Hat, Red Deer, Edmonton, and Grande Prairie spring to mind as places where the joys of nature are readily accessible to urban dwellers. Each of these parks is criss-crossed by trails that are ideal for walking and jogging year-round or cross-country skiing in the winter. The majority of provincial parks also maintain small trail networks.

Waterton Lakes National Park has some of the most exceptional hiking in southern Alberta. Eight trails offer hikers and cross-country skiers the opportunity to explore the far reaches of this park which lies at the meeting point between the mountains and the prairies. Complete descriptions of the trails are available at the park information centre, but take note that some of the best scenery is along the Crypt Lake Trail (8.7 km one way) and the Carthew Alderson Trail (20 km one way), there is also the shorter and very popular trail, the Bear's Hump (1.2 km one way), which offers great views. Remember, not all of these trails are maintained for cross-country skiing, and you must register at the park office for all back-country exploring in the park, winter or summer (see p 331).

Elk Island National Park offers the opportunity to view an exceptional variety of wildlife. The Shoreline Trail (3 km one way) and Lakeview Trail (3.3 km round trip) explore the area around Astotin Lake where beavers are occasionally seen. The Wood Bison Trail (18.5 km round trip) does a loop around Flying Shot Lake in the area of the park south of Hwy 16, where wood buffalo roam. These three trails are maintained as cross-country trails in the winter.

Bicycling

With its relatively flat terrain (besides, of course, in the Rocky Mountains), Alberta is an ideal place to explore by bike. The **Alberta Bicycle Association** *(11759 Groat Road, T5M 3K6, ☎ 453-8518)* can provide more information about bicycle touring in the province. The *Alberta Cycling Information Map* is available from Alberta Transportation and Utilities, Public Communications, 1st Floor, 4999 98th Ave., Edmonton, Alberta, T6B 2X3, or by calling ☎ 427-7674. There is also a map for bicycling in Edmonton called *Cycle Edmonton*, which is available at the tourist office.

Camping

Alberta Tourism publishes a repertory of campsites throughout the province that is available free of charge by calling the information line (see p 282). Besides private campgrounds, all of the national parks and a fair number of the provincial parks in this chapter have campsites. Please refer to the specific park for reservation information.

Accommodations

For hotels and motels, keep in mind that in most cases CAA, AAA and corporate discounts are available, so be sure to ask when booking your room.

■ **Tour A: Calgary**

There are often two rates for Calgary hotels and motels, a Stampede rate and a rest-of-the-year rate, and the difference between the two can be substantial in some cases.

The **Calgary International Hostel** *(members $14, non-members $19; 520 7th Ave. SE, Calgary, T2G 0J6, ☎ 269-8239, ⇌ 283-6503)* can accommodate up to 114 people in dormitory-style rooms. Two family rooms are also available in winter. Guests have access to laundry and kitchen facilities, as well as a game room and a snack bar. The hostel is advantageously located two blocks east of City Hall and Olympic Plaza. Reservations are recommended.

Another inexpensive accommodation option, only available in summer, is to stay at the residences at the **University of Calgary** *(single $27, double $36; 3330 24th Ave. NW, Calgary, ☎ 220-3203)*.

The **Bed and Breakfast Association of Calgary** *(☎ 531-0065, ⇄ 531-0069)* can arrange accommodations in nearly 40 bed and breakfasts throughout the city.

One of the many charming choices is **Inglewood Bed & Breakfast** *($65; 1006 8th Ave. SE, Calgary, T2G 0M4, ☎ and ⇄ 262-6570)*. Not far from downtown, this lovely Victorian-style house is also close to the Bow River's pathway system. Breakfast is prepared by Chef Valinda.

Downtown

The **Lord Nelson Inn** *($65; ℜ, ≡, ⊛, tv; 1020 8th Ave. SW, Calgary, T2P 1J2, ☎ 269-8262, ⇄ 269-4868)* offers reasonably-priced hotel accommodation close to downtown and the C-Train.

The **Royal Pacific Hotel** *($69; ℜ, ≡, tv, ℂ; 1330 8th St. SW, Calgary, T2R 1B3, ☎ 228-6900, ⇄ 228-5535)* is perhaps one of the best values near the downtown area. All the rooms are suites with one or two bedrooms and a kitchenette.

Travellers in search of a hotel with facilities and quality rooms should check out the **Sandman Hotel** *($89; ℜ, ≡, ≈, ⊛, tv, ☺; 888 7th Ave. SW, T2P 3J3, Calgary, ☎ 237-8626 or 1-800-736-3626, ⇄ 290-1238)*. The heated parking and 24-hour food services can come in handy.

The weekly, corporate and group rates of the all-suite **Prince Royal Inn** *($120; ℜ, △, ☺, tv, ℂ; 618 5th Ave. SW, Calgary, T2P 0M7, ☎ 263-0520 or 1-800-661-1592, ⇄ 262-9991)* make this perhaps the least expensive hotel accommodation right downtown. The fully equipped kitchens also help keep costs down.

The Palliser *($200-245; ℜ, ≡, ⊛, △, ☺, tv; 133 9th Ave. SW, Calgary, T2P 2M3, ☎ 262-1234 or 1-800-441-1414, ⇄ 260-1260)* offers distinguished, classic accommodations in true Canadian Pacific style. The hotel was built in 1914, and the lofty lobby retains its original marble staircase, solid-brass doors and superb chandelier of old. The rooms are a bit small but have high ceilings and are magnificently decorated in classic styles.

Across the street is the business-class **Radisson Plaza Hotel** *($149; ℜ, ≈, ≡, ⊛, △, ☺, tv; 110 9th Ave. SE, Calgary, T2G 5A6, ☎ 266-7331 or 1-800-333-3333, ⇄ 262-8442)*, the biggest of the downtown hotels. The spacious rooms are decorated with warm colours and comfortable furnishings.

Northeast (near the airport)

Travellers just passing through or who have early or late flight connections to make should consider the convenience and reasonable prices of the **Pointe Inn** *($45; ℜ, ≡, tv; 1808 19th St. NE, Calgary, T2E 4Y3, ☎ 291-4681 or 1-800-661-8164, ⇄ 291-4576)*. The rooms are clean but very ordinary. Laundry facilities.

The **Best Western Airport** *($59; ℜ, ≡, ≈, ☺, tv; 1947 18th Ave. NE, Calgary,*

T2E 7T8, ☎ 250-5015 or 1-800-528-1234, ⇄ 250-5019) offers similar accommodations, plus an outdoor pool.

Best Western Port O' Call Inn ($99-125; ℜ, ≡, ≈, ⊛, ☾, tv; 1935 McKnight Blvd NE, Calgary, ☎ 291-4600 or 1-800-661-1161, ⇄ 250-6827) is a full-service hotel with 24-hour shuttle service to the airport, located close by. Facilities include an indoor pool and a racquetball court.

Northwest (Motel Village)

Calgary's Motel Village is quite something: car rental offices, countless chain motels and hotels, fast-food and family-style restaurants and the Banff Trail C-Train stop. The majority of the hotels and motels look the same, but the more expensive ones are usually newer and offer more facilities. Most places charge considerably higher rates during Stampede Week.

The **Red Carpet Motor Hotel** ($39-49; ≡, ℜ, tv; 4635 16th Ave. NW, Calgary, T3B 0M7, ☎ 286-5111, ⇄ 247-9239) is one of the best values in Motel Village. Rates include breakfast, and some suites have a small refrigerator.

Econo Lodge ($58; ≡, △, ☾, tv; 2440 16th Ave. NW, Calgary, T2M 0M5, ☎ 289-2561, ⇄ 282-9713) offers clean, typical motel rooms with queen-size beds. There is no charge for local calls.

The **Avondale Motor Inn** ($59-88; ℜ, ≡, ≈, ₡, tv; 2231 Banff Tr. NW, Calgary, T2M 4L2, ☎ 289-1921, ⇄ 282-2149) is a good place for families. Children will enjoy the outdoor pool and playground, while the laundry facilities and large units with kitchenettes are very practical. The Louisiana family restaurant serves inexpensive ($) Cajun and Creole food.

Rates at the **Comfort Inn** ($59-99; ≡, ≈, △, ☾, tv; 2363 Banff Tr. NW, Calgary, T2M 4L2, ☎ 289-2581 or 1-800-325-2525, ⇄ 284-3897) include a continental breakfast. Regular rooms are spacious and comfortable; suites are also available.

The newly built **Holiday Inn Express** ($63; ≡, ≈, ⊛, △, ☾, tv; 2227 Banff Tr. NW, Calgary, T2M 4L2, ☎ 289-6600, or 1-800-HOLIDAY, ⇄ 289-6767) offers quality accommodations at an affordable price. Rooms are furnished with king- and queen-sized beds, and a complimentary continental breakfast is served.

The Scottish decor of the **Highlander Hotel** ($75, ℜ, ≡, ≈, tv; 1818 16th Ave., Calgary, T2M 0L8, ☎ 289-1961 or 1-800-661-9564, ⇄ 289-3901) is a nice change from the typically drab motel experience. Close to services and a shopping mall. Airport shuttle service available.

The **Days Inn** ($88; ₡, △, ⊛, tv; 2369 Banff Tr. NW, Calgary, T2M 4L2, ☎ 289-5571 or 1-800-325-2525, ⇄ 282-9305) offers free breakfast and movies. The rooms are nicely decorated in soft pastel colours, and the staff is friendly.

Quality Inn Motel Village ($89; ℜ, ≈, ≡, ⊛, △, ☾, tv; 2359 Banff Tr. NW, Calgary, T2M 4L2, ☎ 289-1973, 1-800-221-2222 or 1-800-661-4667, ⇄ 282-1241) has a nice lobby and an atrium restaurant and lounge. Both rooms and suites are available. Good value for the price.

The **Best Western Village Park Inn** *($99; ℜ, ≡, ≈, ⊛, tv; 1804 Crowchild Tr. NW, Calgary, T2M 3Y7, ☎ 289-0241 or 1-800-528-1234, ⇄ 289-4645)* is another member of this well-known chain. Guests enjoy many services, including Budget car rental offices. Rooms are nicely furnished with up-to-date colour schemes.

■ **Tour B: Southern Alberta**

Crowsnest Pass

The **Grand Union International Hostel** *($12.50 members, $15 non-members; 7719 17th Ave., Coleman, TOK 0M0, ☎ 563-3433)* is located in Coleman's original Grand Union Hotel, built in 1926. The interior was renovated by the Southern Alberta Hostelling Association and now houses standard hostel rooms and all the usual hostel facilities, including laundry machines and a common kitchen.

You can stay at the **Kosy Knest Kabins** *($39-44, ℂ, tv; Box 670, Coleman, TOK 0M0, ☎ 563-5155)*, looking out over Crowsnest Lake, from May 1 to November 1. The nine cabins are located 12 km west of Coleman on Hwy 3.

Also on the lake, the **Runner's Roost B&B** *($45; pb; ☎ 563-5111)*, a lovely country house, is a cosy place to enjoy a delicious hot breakfast.

Waterton Townsite

Things slow down considerably during the winter months, when many hotels and motels close and others offer winter rates and packages.

The **Northland Lodge** *($50; sb or pb, ℂ, tv; on Evergreen Ave., Waterton Lakes National Park, TOK 2M0, ☎ 859-2353)*, open from mid-May to mid-October, is a converted house with eight cosy rooms. Kitchenettes are available for an extra charge.

The small **Crandell Mountain Lodge** *($79-119; ℂ, tv; 102 Mountview Rd, Box 114, Waterton Lakes National Park, TOK 2M0, ☎ and ⇄ 859-2288)* is one of the few hotels in Waterton that is open year-round. Its rustic, cosy country inn atmosphere fits right in with the setting, and is a nice change from the motel scene. Two suites with kitchenettes are available. In the winter cross-country ski packages (including equipment) are offered; other winter activities include ice-fishing, snowshoeing, ice-climbing and telemark skiing.

The **Kilmorey Lodge** *($87-115; tv, ℜ, ℂ, 117 Evergreen Ave., Box 100, Waterton Lakes National Park, TOK 2M0, ☎ 859-2334, ⇄ 859-2349)* is also open year-round. It is ideally located overlooking Emerald Bay, and many rooms have great views. Antiques and duvets contribute to the old-fashioned, homey feel. The Kilmorey also boasts one of Waterton's finest dining spots, The Lamp Post Dining Room (see p 354).

The venerable **Prince of Wales Hotel** *($135 economy room, $280 suite; pb, ℜ; Waterton Lakes National Park, TOK 2M0, ☎ 236-3400, reservations in Calgary ☎ 236-3400, off-season ☎ (602) 207-6000)* is definitely the grandest place to stay in Waterton, with bell-hops in kilts, and high tea in Valerie's Tea Room, not to mention the unbeatable view. The lobby and rooms are all adorned with original wood panelling. The rooms, are actually quite small and unspectacular, however, with tiny bathrooms and a rustic feel. Those on the third floor and higher have balconies. Try to request a room facing the lake, which is after all, what people stay here for. Things will certainly change here, and possibly for the worse, if the rumours about expanding the Prince of Wales are true (see p 333).

Fort Macleod

Rooms are available at the historic **Queen's Hotel** *($25; 207 24th St., ☎ 553-4343)* for those who insist on experiencing the real Fort Macleod, but there is little beyond history to recommend these rooms.

The **Red Coat Inn** *($46; ℭ, ≈, ⊛, △, tv; 359 Col. Macleod Tr., Fort Macleod, TOL OZO ☎ 553-4434)* is one of the most reliable motel choices in Fort Macleod. Clean, pleasant rooms, kitchenettes and a pool make this a good deal.

The **Mackenzie House Bed and Breakfast** *($55; sb; 1623 3rd Ave., Fort Macleod, TOL OZO, ☎ and ⇌ 553-3302)* is located in a historic house built in 1904 for an Alberta member of the Legislative Assembly at the time the province was founded, in 1905. Tea and coffee are served in the afternoon, and guests are greeted in the morning with a delicious home-made breakfast.

Lethbridge

Built in 1937, the Art Deco **Heritage House B&B** *($45; sb; 1115 8th Ave. S, Lethbridge, ☎ 328-9011)* is located on one of Lethbridge's pretty tree-lined residential streets, only a few minutes' walk from downtown. The guest rooms are uniquely decorated in concordance with the design of the house, and generous breakfasts are served.

Motel Magic *($53; ≡, ⊛, ℭ, ☉, tv; 100 3rd Ave. S, Letbridge, T1J 4L2, ☎ 327-6000, or 1-800-661-8085, ⇌ 320-2070)* is the best motel choice downtown. The typical motel-style rooms are non-descript, but are modern and clean. A free continental breakfast is served. Coin laundry available.

The **Best Western Heidelberg Inn** *($62; ≡, △, ℜ, bar, tv; 1303 Mayor McGrath Dr. S, Lethbridge, T1K 3R1, ☎ 329-0555 or 1-800-528-1234, ⇌ 328-8846)* is an inexpensive, reliable option along the motel strip south of the city. Though the decor is a bit dated, the rooms are spotless, the staff is friendly and you get a complimentary newspaper in the morning.

The **Sandman Inn** *($71; ≡, ≈, ℜ, ⊛, △, ☉, tv, bar; 421 Mayor McGrath Dr. S, Lethbridge, T1J 3LB, ☎ 328-1111 or 1-800-726-3626, ⇌ 329-9488)* is another safe bet, with a nice indoor pool and clean, modern rooms.

The best hotel accommodation in Lethbridge is found at the **Lethbridge Lodge Hotel** *($74; ≡, ≈, ℜ, ⊛, tv, bar; 320 Scenic Dr., Lethbridge, T1J 4B4, ☎ 328-1123 or 1-800-661-1232, ⇌ 328-0002)*, overlooking the river valley. The comfortable rooms decorated in warm and pleasant colours seem almost luxurious when you consider the reasonable price. The rooms surround an interior tropical courtyard where small footbridges lead from the pool to the lounge and Anton's Restaurant (see p 355).

Medicine Hat

Besides the one central hotel, there is actually another, very pleasant place to stay that is close to downtown, along pretty 1st St. SE. After major renovations, the **Sunny Holme B&B** *($55; sb; 271 1st St. SE, Medicine Hat T1A 0A3, ☎ 527-9853)* has so far opened one guest room, and expects to have two more ready by spring 1996. The grand western Georgian-style house has a Victorian interior, and the room is decorated in the arts and crafts style. A large leafy lot surrounds the house. Sourdough pancakes are just one of the breakfast possibilities. Be sure to call ahead.

The only hotel right downtown is the little **Medicine Hat Inn** *($62; ≡, ℜ, tv; 530 4th St. SE, Medicine Hat, T1A 0K8, ☎ 526-1313, ⇄ 526-4189)*, which only has 34 rooms. The decor could use a little freshening up, but the rooms are clean.

For about the same price, you can stay along the motel strip at the **Best Western Inn** *($63; ≡, ≈, △, ◉, C, tv; Medicine Hat, ☎ 527-3700 or 1-800-528-1234, ⇄ 526-8689)*, where the surroundings may not be as pleasant, but the facilities and rooms are more modern. Guests have access to an indoor pool and laundry facilities.

Brooks

About 30 minutes down the highway from Dinosaur Provincial Park is the town of Brooks and the **Tel-Star Motor Inn** *($46; ≡, ℛ, C, tv; on Hwy 1, on the way into town, Box 547, Brooks, T1R 1B5, ☎ 362-3466, ⇄ 632-4067)*. The rooms don't have much to recommend them aside from the fact that they are clean and each one has a microwave and a refrigerator. The hotel also doesn't charge for local calls and has freezer facilities for your catch.

Six and a half kilometres north of town on Hwy 873 is the **Douglas Country Inn** *($77 bkfst incl.; ≡, pb; Box 463, Brooks, T1R 1B5, ☎ 362-2873, ⇄ 362-2100)*. A casual country atmosphere is achieved in each of the seven beautifully appointed rooms and throughout the rest of the inn. The only television is in the small tv room, which hardly ever gets used. Enjoy your complimentary sherry by the fire in the sitting room. The special occasion room ($99) boasts a divine Japanese soaker tub with a view.

Drumheller

A converted downtown hotel now houses the **Alexandra International Hostel** *(members $13.65, non-members $18.65; 30 Railway Ave. N, Drumheller, T0J 0Y0, ☎ 823-6337)*. It opened in 1991 after renovations and is independently operated in cooperation with Hostelling International. Most dorm rooms have eight beds, though there are some with fewer, and several even have private bathrooms. There are kitchen and laundry facilities on the premises, as well as all sorts of information brochures and a mountain-bike rental service.

The **Badlands Motel** *($44; ≡, ℜ, ℛ, C, tv; on the Dinosaur Trail, Box 2217, Drumheller, T0J 0Y0, ☎ 823-5155)* lies outside of town, along the scenic Dinosaur Trail. Rooms are typical, but the pancake restaurant next door is particularly noteworthy.

The fittingly name **Taste the Past B&B** *($60; sb; 281 2nd St. W, Drumheller,*

T0J 0Y0, ☎ 823-5889) is a 1911 Victorian house decorated with antiques. Guests enjoy a large yard and veranda and a choice of breakfasts come morning.

The **Rockhound Inn** ($70; ≡, ℜ, tv, tv; 105 Grove Place, on Hwy 9 north just across the bridge, Box 2350, Drumheller, T0J 0Y0, ☎ 823-5302, ⇄ 823-5342) is a step up from the Badlands, with a riverside location and spacious rooms.

By far, the prettiest place to stay in town is the **Heartwood Manor** ($75-110; pb, ✺, ≡, tv; 356 4th St. W, Drumheller, T0J 0Y3, ☎ and ⇄ 823-6495), a bed and breakfast in a restored heritage building, where a striking use of colour creates a cosy and luxurious atmosphere. Eight of the nine rooms have jet-tubs, and one even boasts a fireplace. A spacious cottage is also available. Yummy home-made fruit syrups are served with the pancake breakfast. French and English spoken.

■ Tour C: Central Alberta

Trochu

Once the ranch of French cavalry men, the **St. Ann Ranch Trading Co.**'s country bed and breakfast ($55-75; Box 249, Trochu, T0M 2C0, ☎ 442-3924) offers travellers the chance to experience a true French gîte. Guests of the B&B have the choice of seven private, antique-furnished rooms (five with private bath) in the rambling 30-room ranch house or in the Pioneer Cottage, and the use of a parlour with a fireplace, a library and patios. While you're here visit the tea house and museum (see p 308).

Red Deer

Many conventions are held in Red Deer, and as a result weekend rates in the many hotels are often less expensive.

The **Renford Inn** ($51; ≡, ℜ, ℂ, tv; 2803 Gaetz Ave., Red Deer, T4R 1H1, ☎ 343-2112 or 1-800-661-6498, ⇄ 340-8540) is one of many hotels and motels along Gaetz Avenue. It houses pleasant, simple rooms. Kitchenette units are available for a surcharge.

In Red Deer you can stay in the **McIntosh House Bed and Breakfast** ($60; pb; 4631 50th St., Red Deer, T4N 1X1, ☎ 346-1622), the former home of the great grandson of the creator of the McIntosh apple. Each of the three upstairs rooms of the red-brick historic Victorian is decorated with antiques. Guests can enjoy a game of apple checkers in the private parlour. Tea and sweets are served in the evening and a full breakfast in the morning.

The **Red Deer Lodge** ($80; ≡, ≈, ℜ, bar, ✺, tv; 4311 49th Ave., Red Deer, T4N 5Y7, ☎ 346-8841 or 1-800-661-1657, ⇄ 341-3220) is a favourite with convention-goers because of its modern and extensive amenities. As one would expect, the rooms are comfortable and spotless.

Wetaskiwin

Close to the Reynolds-Alberta Museum, on 56th St., the **Rose Country Inn** ($49; ≡, ℜ, ℝ, ℂ, bar, tv; 4820 56th St., Wetaskiwin, T9A 2G5, ☎ 352-3600, ⇄ 352-2127) is one of the best deals in town. Each of the newly renovated rooms has a refrigerator and microwave oven.

If you're looking for one of the prettiest places available, however, try the **Heritage House B&B** *($55; pb; 4714 48th Ave., Wetaskiwin, T9A 0M3,* ☎ *352-3025,* ⇄ *352-2667)*. This registered historic site is identifiable by the antique lamp standard out front. Guests can stroll about the lovely English garden or enjoy breakfast on the pretty terrace adjoining the house. The single private *en suite* is a cosy spot to enjoy a book by the fire.

Rocky Mountain House

The **Voyageur Motel** *($44, C, R, tv; on Hwy 11, Box 1376, Rocky Mountain House, T0M 1T0,* ☎ *845-3381,* ⇄ *845-6166)* is a practical choice with spacious, clean rooms, each equipped with a refrigerator. Kitchenettes are also available for a surcharge.

The log exterior of the **Walking Eagle Motor Inn** *($63; ≡, R, tv, bar; on Hwy 11, Box 1317, Rocky Mountain House, T0M 1T0,* ☎ *845-2804,* ⇄ *845-3685)* encloses 63 clean and large rooms, decorated in keeping with the hotel's name.

Nordegg

Set against the stunning backdrop of the Rocky Mountains in David Thompson Country, and surrounded by countless opportunities for outdoor activities, is the **Shunda Creek Hostel** *(members $14, non-members $19; west of Nordegg, 3 km north of Hwy 11, on Shunda Creek Recreation Area Road,* ☎ *721-2140)*. The two-story lodge encloses kitchen and laundry facilities, a common area with a fireplace and 10 rooms able to accommodate a total of 48 people; it

Accommodations 347

also adjoins an outdoor hot tub. Hiking, mountain biking, fishing, canoeing, cross-country skiing and ice-climbing are possible nearby.

Cochrane

Take in the panoramic views of the mountains from the **Dickens Inn** *($65; 2 km west of Cochrane on the 1A, turn right on Horse Creek Road and continue for 7 km, driveway to the right, R.R. 1, Cochrane, T0L 0W0,* ☎ *932-3945)*, a Victorian-style house, built as a B&B. Enjoy peaceful slumber in one of three guest rooms with queen-size four-poster beds and private bathrooms and then awaken to a copious breakfast featuring home-made preserves and fresh bread.

■ Tour D: Edmonton

The **Edmonton International Hostel** *(members $12.50, non-members $17.50; ≡; 10422 91st St., Edmonton, T5H 1S6,* ☎ *429-0140)* is located close to the bus terminal, in a questionable area, so take care. The usual hostel facilities, including laundry machines, common kitchen and a common room with a fireplace are rounded out by a small grocery store and bike rentals. There is a midnight curfew.

Student residences at the **University of Alberta** *($35-40; 116th St. at 87th Ave., Edmonton, T6G 2H6,* ☎ *492-4281,* ⇄ *492-7032)* are available year-round. Single and twin rooms with shared bathrooms can be rented in the summer, while hotel-like guest suites are available throughout the year. Reservations recommended.

Downtown (Edmonton)

The **Quality Inn Downtown** *($54 bkfst incl.;* ≡, ℜ, ⊛, *tv, bar; 10209 100th Ave., Edmonton, T5J 0A1,* ☎ *428-6442 or 1-800-661-6498)* has 73 rooms including some suites featuring whirlpool baths. Parking and an airport shuttle service make this a good deal for those looking for lodging downtown. Rooms are nothing special, however.

The **Renford Inn at 5th** *($59;* ≡, ≈, ℜ, ⊛, △, *tv, bar; 10041 106th St., Edmonton, T5J 1G3,* ☎ *423-1925 or 1-800-267-2191,* ⇄ *424-5302)* boasts comfortable modern rooms and a swimming pool with a wet-bar. This is another downtown spot with a good quality price ratio.

The **Edmonton House Suite Hotel** *($62;* ℜ, ₵, ≈, △, *tv; 10205 100th Ave., Edmonton, T5J 4B5,* ☎ *420-4000 or 1-800-661-6562,* ⇄ *420-4008)* is actually an apartment-hotel with suites that boast kitchens and balconies. This is one of the better apartment-hotel options in town. Reservations are recommended.

The **Best Western City Centre** *($68;* ≡, ≈, ℜ, ⊛, *tv, bar; 11310 109th St., Edmonton, T5G 2T7,* ☎ *479-2042 or 1-800-528-1234,* ⇄ *474-2204)* is not quite in the city centre and has a rather dated exterior. The rooms are nevertheless very comfortable and pleasantly decorated with wood furniture.

Fifteen of the close to 200 clean and modern rooms at the **Inn on Seventh** *($75;* ≡, ℜ, ⊛, *tv, bar; 10001 107th St., Edmonton, T5J 1J1,* ☎ *429-2861 or 1-800-661-7327,* ⇄ *426-7225)* are "environmentally safe", though this just means they are non-smoking rooms on non-smoking floors. Weekend rates are available. Facilities include coin-laundry machines.

The **Delta Edmonton Centre Suite Hotel** *($85-225;* ℜ, ⊛, △, ₵, *tv, bar; 1022 102nd St., Edmonton, T5J 4C5,* ☎ *429-3900 or 1-800-661-6655,* ⇄ *426-0562)* is part of the downtown Eaton Centre shopping centre. This means that apart from the hotel's extensive facilities, guests have access to shops and cinemas. Rooms are comfortable and the suites are lavishly decorated.

Edmonton's grand chateau-style **Hotel MacDonald** *($129-189;* ≡, ℜ, ≈, ⊛, △, ◉, *tv, bar; 10065 100th St., Edmonton, T5J 0N6,* ☎ *424-5181 or 1-800-441-1414,* ⇄ *424-8017)* is stunning. Classic styling from the guest rooms to the dining rooms make this an exquisite place to stay. A variety of weekend packages are available including golf packages and romantic getaways. Call for details.

Northwest and West (Edmonton)

For those who want to be close to the shopping, but aren't necessarily big-spenders, the **Travelodge West** *($50;* ≡, ℜ, ⊛, *tv; 18320 Stony Plain Rd., Edmonton, T5S 1A7,* ☎ *483-6031 or 1-800-578-7878,* ⇄ *484-2358)* is one of two relatively inexpensive hotels located close to the West Edmonton Mall. The rooms were recently redone and there is a big indoor pool.

The **West Harvest Inn** *($63;* ≡, ℜ, ⊛, *tv; 17803 Stony Plain Rd., Edmonton, T5S 1B4,* ☎ *484-8000 or 1-800-661-6993,* ⇄ *486-6060)* is the other inexpensive choice within striking distance of the mall. This hotel is relatively quiet and receives quite a few business travellers.

The **Best Western Westwood Inn** *($74; ≡, ≈, ℜ, tv; 18035 Stony Plain Rd., Edmonton, T5S 1B2, ☎ 483-7770 or 1-800-528-1234, ⇌ 486-1769)* is also close to the mall. The rooms are more expensive here but they are also much larger and noticeably more comfortable and more pleasantly decorated.

Travellers on a shopping vacation will certainly want to be as close to the West Edmonton Mall as possible, making the **Fantasyland Hotel & Resort** *($138-188; ≡, ℜ, ⊛, △, tv, bar; 17700 87th Ave., Edmonton, T5T 4V4, ☎ 444-3000 or 1-800-661-6454, ⇌ 444-3294)* the obvious choice. Of course, you might also choose to stay here just for the sheer delight of spending the night under African or Arabian skies, or in the back of a pick-up!

South (Edmonton)

For a very reasonable rate, guests can stay at the **Southbend Motel** *($37; C, tv; 5130 Calgary Tr. Northbound, T6H 5C3, ☎ 434-1418)*, where rooms are admittedly a bit dated, and for no extra charge use all the facilities at the Best Western Cedar Park Inn next door (see below). These include pool, sauna, exercise room and West Edmonton Mall shuttle.

Set in the heart of Old Strathcona is one of Edmonton best-located hotels, the **Renford Inn on Whyte** *($62; ≡, ℜ, △, tv, bar; 10620 Whyte Ave., Edmonton, ☎ 433-9411 or 1-800-661-6498, ⇌ 439-1195)*. Rooms are comfortable and nicely decorated with a few classic touches.

The **Best Western Cedar Park Inn** *($72; ≡, ℜ, ≈, △, ⊛, tv; 5116 Calgary Tr. Northbound, ☎ 434-7411 or 1-800-528-1234, ⇌ 437-4836)* is a large hotel with 190 equally spacious rooms. Some of these are called theme rooms ($109), which essentially means there is a hot-tub for two, a king-size bed, a living room and a fancier decor. Weekend and family rates are available, and there is a courtesy limo service to the airports or the West Edmonton Mall.

East (Edmonton)

Set on the second floor of the historic Gibbard Building and upstairs from the restaurant of the same name, **La Boheme B&B** *($50-75; pb, C; 6427 112th Ave., Edmonton, ☎ 474-5693)* occupies the rooms of a former luxury apartment building. All the rooms are charmingly decorated and equipped with a kitchenette, but you will find it hard to resist the gastronomical delights at the restaurant downstairs.

Located nearby in the historic Highlands district is the **Holgate Edwardian-Style B&B** *($85-100; ≡, pb; 6210 Ada Blvd, Edmonton, T5W 4P1, ☎ 448-0901)*. Two exquisite rooms decorated in the arts and crafts style each boast a private *en suite* bathroom complete with a six-foot soaker tub. After exploring the scenic streets that surround the house and overlook the Saskatchewan River Valley, guests can relax on the lovely front verandah, in the sitting room by a roaring fire or in the morning room with a good book.

Tour E: Northern Alberta

St. Paul

King's Motel and Restaurant *($46; ≡, ℜ, ℝ, tv; Box 1685 St. Paul, T0A 3A0, ☎ 645-5656 or 1-800-265-7407, ⇄ 645-5107)* offers decent, clean rooms, most of which have refrigerators. Breakfast at the restaurant is included in the price.

Smoky Lake

Each of the six rooms at the **Countrylane Bed & Breakfast** *($55; sb; Box 38, Smoky Lake, T0A 3C0, off Hwy 855, watch for signs, ☎ 656-2277)* are named after the original six girls that were born in the house. Each room has a shared bathroom, except "Mary's House" which is a self-contained unit that is part of the original homestead. The sound of birds chirping, and a sunny balcony are among the extras found throughout the rest of the house. An evening meal can be arranged with advance notice and group rates are available.

Smoky Lake is home to another charming bed and breakfast, the **Inn at the Ranch** *($65; pb; Box 562, Smoky Lake, T0A 3C0, Hwy 855, 22 km north of Hwy 28, follow the signs, ☎ 656-2474 or 1-800-974-2474, ⇄ 656-3094)*. This working bison-elk ranch has 2 lovely rooms. The newly-built mansion is surrounded by a veritable bird-watcher's paradise.

Athabasca

The **Athabasca Inn** *($58; ≡, ℜ, ☯, tv; 5211 41 Ave., Athabasca, T9S 1A5, ☎ 675-2294 or 1-800-567-5718, ⇄ 675-3890)* features non-smoking rooms with filtered air. Business people make up the bulk of this hotel's residents. Rooms are clean and spacious.

Donatville

Located about halfway between Lac La Biche and Athabasca on Hwy 63 is the small town of Donatville, home of the **Donatberry Inn B&B** *($69.50; pb, ☯; R.R. 1, Boyle, T0A 0M0, ☎ 689-3639)*. This newly-built house is set on a large property with a northern berry orchard nearby (home-made preserves made with these berries are served at breakfast). The large and bright rooms all have a private bathroom, and guest also have access to a whirlpool and steam room.

Lac La Biche

The **Parkland Motel** *($51; ≡, ℂ, tv; Box 659, Lac La Biche, T0A 2C0, ☎ 623-4424, ⇄ 623-4599)* features regular rooms and kitchenette suites some of which have fireplaces and lofts. Good quality/price ratio.

Fort McMurray

With a good restaurant and lounge as well as a pool, the **Mackenzie Park Inn** *($64; ≡, ≈, ℜ, ☯, tv, bar; 424 Gregoire Dr., Fort McMurray, T9H 3R2, ☎ 791-7200 or 1-800-582-3273, ⇄ 790-1658)* is the most reliable hotel or motel choice in town. It is located about 4 km south of the centre of town.

Slave Lake

The rather interesting exterior of the **Sawridge Hotel** *($60; ≡, ℜ, △, ☻, ℝ, tv; Box 879, Slave Lake, TOG 2A0, just off Hwy 2 on Main St., ☎ 849-4101 or 1-800-661-6657, ⇄ 849-3426)* houses some rather ordinary rooms that are just a tad outdated. Several of the rooms have a refrigerator.

Farther along Main St. towards town, is the newest hotel in town, the **Northwest Inn** *($67; ≡, ℜ, ℂ, ☻, △, ☺, tv; Box 2459, Slave Lake, TOG 2A0, ☎ 849-3300, ⇄ 849-2667)*. The rooms, though clean and modern, are unfortunately very plain and bare. Some of the rooms are equipped with refrigerators.

Peace River

The **Crescent Motor Inn Best Canadian** *($45; ≡, ℂ, tv; 9810 98th St., Peace River, T8S 1J3, ☎ 624-2586, ⇄ 624-1888)* is located close to the centre of town and offers clean, rather ordinary rooms. Waterbeds are available in some. Family suites with kitchenettes are certainly an economical choice.

The **Kozy Quarters B&B** *($55; 1105 99th St., Box 7493, Peace River, T8S 1T1, ☎ 624-2807)* is an historic 2-story structure on the waterfront. It was built by the R.C.M.P., but today houses cosy and spacious guest rooms. A choice of breakfasts is offered each morning.

The **Traveller's Motor Hotel** *($55-75; ≡, ℜ, ℂ, △, tv, bar; Box 7290, Peace River, T8S 1S9, ☎ 624-3621 or 1-800-661-3227, ⇄ 624-4855)* offers ordinary hotel-motel rooms as well as suite rooms. With a night club in the hotel, this isn't the quietest place in town.

Grande Prairie

The **Golden Inn** *($60; ≡, ℜ, ℂ, tv, bar; 11201 100th Ave., Grande Prairie, T8V 5M6, ☎ 539-6000 or 1-800-661-7959, ⇄ 532-1961)* lies north of the city centre with services and shops nearby. The decor of the rooms and lobby is slightly outdated. There is a pool, but it seems to be indefinitely closed for repairs.

Grande Prairie's best hotel and motel bet is the **Canadian Motor Inn** *($53; ≡, ℜ, ℝ, ≈, ℂ, tv, ☻; 10901 100th Ave., Grande Prairie, T8V 3J9, ☎ 532-1680, ⇄ 532-1245)* where each room has two queen-sized beds, a refrigerator and large-screen television. Rooms with fully-equipped kitchenettes are available ($58) and there is also an executive suite with a whirlpool bath ($100-150). The hotel was recently completely renovated and the result is spotless, modern, yet very comfortable accommodations.

Set on a secluded lakeside property, the **Fieldstone Inn B&B** *($70; pb; Box 295, Grande Prairie, T8V 3A4, ☎ 532-7529)* is such a great find, you'll want to keep it to yourself. This newly-built fieldstone house has a homey feel thanks to the old-fashioned decor and classic styling. Some rooms have whirlpool baths or fireplaces. The balcony is an ideal the spot to contemplate the rose garden, and if you're lucky the northern lights.

Restaurants

Tour A: Calgary

The interior of **Jenny's Jamaican Cuisine** (*$-$$; 2015 4th St. SW, ☎ 228-6966*) is decorated with a huge ocean mural to get you in the mood for a rum cocktail, some pepper pot soup and jerk chicken. This neat, family-run restaurant is located in the old art deco Tivoli Theatre.

Good Earth Café (*$; at Eau Claire Market, 200 Barclay Parade SW, ☎ 237-8684*) is a wonderful coffee shop with tasty wholesome goodies all made from scratch. Besides being a choice spot for lunch, this is also a good source of picnic fixings.

The **Croissant Company** (*$; at the corner of 9th St. SW and 4th Ave. SW*) serves real French butter croissants and great big bowls of *café au lait*, as well as hearty soups and sandwiches.

The **Chocolate Bar** (*$; in the Eau Claire Market*) is the ideal spot for a heavenly finish to a good meal. The scrumptious desserts are all on display so you can make an informed choice.

Right next door to the market is **Cafe 1886** (*$-$$; every day 7am to 3pm; breakfast only; ☎ 269-9255*), located in the old Eau Claire & Bow River Lumber Company building. Buffalo heads and a large collection of old clocks decorate the interior. Huge breakfast portions are served all day long.

Everything is made from scratch at the informal **Nellie's Kitchen** (*$; 17th Ave. SW between 7th and 6th St. SW*), a neat little rendez-vous for lunch and people-watching.

The European-style wine bar, **Buzzard's Café** (*$$; 140 10th Ave. SW, ☎ 264-6959*) may serve a wide variety of main dishes from chicken to pasta, beef and sandwiches, but the local brew, Buzzard's Breath Ale, and the 70-plus wines are the main attractions here.

The open concept at **Joey Tomato's** (*$$; 208 Barclay Place SW, ☎ 263-6336, next to the Eau Claire Market; ☎ 263-6336*) makes for a lively atmosphere. The food is Italian and includes a great selection of pastas, topped, among other things, by original tomato sauces.

The **Silver Dragon** (*$$; 106 3rd Ave. SE, ☎ 264-5326*) is one of the best of the many Chinese restaurants in Chinatown. The staff are particularly friendly and the dumplings particularly tasty.

The **Mongolie Grill** (*$$; 1108 4th St. SW, ☎ 262-7773*) is truly a culinary experience. Diners choose meats and vegetables from a fresh food bar, the combination is then weighed (to determine the cost) and grilled right before your eyes. Roll it all up in a Mongolian wrap with some rice and *hoisin* sauce and there you go!

Señor Frog's (*$$; 739 2nd Ave. SW, ☎ 264-5100*), formerly known as Solé Luna, is not just one of Calgary's most popular night clubs, but is also a terrific Latin American cantina. The homemade bread and desserts are particularly appetizing.

The **Barley Mill** (*$$; 210 Barclay Parade SW, next to the Eau Claire Market, ☎ 290-1500*) is located in what appears to be an historic building, but is actually a new construction. An old-fashioned interior is successfully achieved with worn-down hardwood floors, a grand fireplace, an old cash register and a bar that comes all the way from Scotland. The menu includes pasta, meat and chicken dishes as well as several imported beers on tap.

The King & I Thai Restaurant *($$; 822 11th Ave. SW, ☎ 264-7241)* features an extensive menu of exotic dishes including delicious *ChuChu Kai*. The ambience is modern and elegant.

The historic **Deane House Restaurant** *($$; year-round, Wed to Sun 11am to 2pm; 9th Ave. SE, just across the bridge from Fort Calgary, ☎269-7747)* is a pleasant tea house located in the house of former commanding RCMP officer Richard Burton Deane. Soups and salads figure prominently on the menu.

Baja Billy's Border Grille *($$; in the Eau Claire Market)* is a new restaurant in the market that serves delicious Mexican food. The funky colourful decor is reminiscent of a bright southern sunset. All of the ingredients are fresh, including those that go into the extensive salsa bar. There is an outdoor terrace.

Also in the market, **Cajun Charlie's** *($$; Eau Claire Market, ☎ 233-8101)*, with its Mardi Gras masks, trombone and giant iguana crawling out of the wall, is a real hoot. Gumbo and jambalaya are, of course, among the offerings, but so are "gator" eggs and Po'Boy sandwiches. Blues music adds to the ambience.

The **Naturbahn Teahouse** *($$; in the summer, lunch and tea 11am to 4pm; in the winter, Sunday brunch only; Canada Olympic Park, ☎ 247-5465)*, located at the top of the luge track at Canada Olympic Park, is actually the former start-house. The *Naturbahn*, which means natural track, no longer serves up luges; nowadays the menu features an interesting Sunday brunch. Reservations are recommended.

Entre Nous *($$-$$$; 2206 4th St. SW, ☎ 228-5525)* which means between us, boasts a friendly and intimate bistro atmosphere, perfect for savouring some good French food. Special attention to detail, from the hand-selected ingredients to the *table d'hôte* menu, make for a memorable dining experience. Reservations recommended.

The **River Café** *($$-$$$; summer only; Prince's Island Park, ☎ 261-7670)* is only open during the warm summer months, when brunch or lunch can be enjoyed outdoors in beautiful Prince's Island Park. Located in an old boathouse, this gem of a restaurant is the perfect escape from urban downtown Calgary, just across the Bow River. Reservations are recommended.

Teatro *($$$; 200 8th Ave. SE, ☎ 290-1012)*, right next to Olympic Plaza in the old Dominion Bank Building, boasts a great setting and stylish atmosphere. Traditional "Italian Market Cuisine" prepared in a wood-burning stove becomes innovative and exciting at the hands of Teatro's chef Dany Lamote. (Yes, this is the place in the Nescafé advertisement, but they serve both Nescafé and fresh-brewed coffee.)

Cannery Row *($$$; 317 10th Ave. SW, ☎ 269-8889)* serves this landlocked city's best seafood. An oyster bar and casual atmosphere is intended to make you feel like you're by the sea, and it works. Fresh halibut, salmon and swordfish are prepared in a variety of ways. **McQueen's Upstairs**,

($$$; ☎ 269-4722) appropriately located upstairs, has a similar seafood-oriented menu but is slightly more upscale.

The Casablancan chef at the **Sultan's Tent** ($$$; 909 17th Ave. SW, ☎ 244-2333) prepares fine authentic Moroccan cuisine. In keeping with tradition, guests are greeted upon arriving with a basin of scented water with which to wash their hands. The room is decorated with a myriad of plush cushions and tapestries and the mood is set with lanterns and soft Arabic music. The friendly hosts also speak French. (Remember it is traditional to eat with your right hand as your left one is impure.)

Caesar's Steakhouse ($$$$; 512 4th Ave. SW; ☎ 264-1222 and 10816 Macleod Tr. S, ☎ 278-3930) is one of Calgary's most popular spots to dig in to a big juicy steak, though they also serve good seafood. The elegant decor features Roman columns and soft lighting.

Hy's ($$$$; 316 4th Ave. SW, ☎ 263-2222), around since 1955, is the other favourite for steaks. The main dishes are just slightly less expensive than Caesar's and the atmosphere is a bit more relaxed with wood panelling. Reservations are recommended.

The **Inn on Lake Bonavista** ($$$$; 747 Lake Bonavista Dr. SE, ☎ 271-6711) is one of Calgary's finest dining rooms with fine menu selections like filet mignon and Châteaubriand, complemented by fine views over the lake.

Fine French and European dishes are artfully prepared at the **Owl's Nest** ($$$$; in the Westin Hotel, 4th Ave. and 3rd St. SW, ☎ 266-1611). Some are even prepared at your table and flambéd right in front of you. All the ladies get a rose and the men, a cigar, at this fancy dining establishment.

The Palliser Hotel's **Rimrock Room** ($$$$; 133 9th Ave. SW, ☎ 262-1234) serves a fantastic Sunday brunch and of course healthy portions of prime Alberta beef. The Palliser's classic surroundings and fine food coalesce into one of Calgary's most elegant dining experiences.

■ **Tour B: Southern Alberta**

Okotoks

Ginger Tea Room and Gift Shop ($-$$; 43 Riverside Dr.; ☎ 938-2907) is a fanciful mix of sensible lunch fare and two floors of unique antiques and gifts. The menu includes sandwiches, soups, salads and an afternoon country tea with hot biscuits with jam. You can eat in or take out. A "Romantic Dinner for Two" is also available.

Waterton

Pearl's Patio Café and Deli ($; 305 Windflower Ave., ☎ 859-2284) is a friendly place for a hearty breakfast. The home-made soups and breads are delicious. Take-out lunches are available. The place stays busy throughout the day, both inside and outside on the terrace.

The **Waterton Park Café** ($; Waterton Ave., ☎ 859-2393) is popular with the seasonal workers in the park as a place to eat and drink. Good sandwiches and lunch fare.

The **Lamp Post Dining Room** ($$$; in Kilmorey Lodge, ☎ 859-2334) offers what some argue is the best dining in Waterton. The traditional charm, coupled with award-winning food and a relatively reasonable price, definitely make it one of the best.

The atmosphere at the **Garden Court Dining Room** *($$$$;* ☎ *859-2231)* in the Prince of Wales Hotel, however, is unbeatable. This formal dining room serves a complete menu and a daily *plat du jour* that often includes delicious seafood or pasta. Reservations are required. Also in the Prince of Wales, and enjoying an equally elegant ambience and stunning view are the **Windsor Lounge** and **Valerie's Tea Room**, where afternoon tea and continental breakfast are both served.

Lethbridge

The **Penny Coffee House** *($; 351 5th St. S,* ☎ *320-5282)*, located next to B. Maccabee's bookseller is the perfect place to enjoy a good book; don't worry if you haven't got one, there is plenty of interesting reading material on the walls. This café serves delicious hearty soups and chilis, filling sandwiches, a wonderful cheese and tomato scone, sodas and of course a great cup of Jo.

The **Union Coffee Roasting Co.** *($; at the corner of 3rd Ave. S at 5th St. S)* serves interesting sandwiches and other simple dishes up until 4pm. From 4pm to 10pm, this bright café sticks to coffee and desserts.

For a change from Alberta beef try the **O'Sho Japanese Restaurant** *($$; 1219 3rd Ave. S,* ☎ *327-8382)* where traditional Japanese fare is enjoyed in traditional style from low tables set in partitioned rooms.

Showdowns Eatin' Adventures *($$; 329 5th St. S,* ☎ *329-8830)* is indeed an adventure with a gun-toting, can-can girl act. Steaks and ribs figure prominently on the menu, which is rather ordinary.

Billy MacIntyre's Cattle Company *($$-$$$; 1621 3rd Ave. S,* ☎ *327-2727)* serves up everything from pasta, chicken, seafood and of course steak. In keeping with the cattle company theme, the decor is classically western.

The Lethbridge Lodge is home to **Anton's** *($$$$; Lethbridge Lodge,* ☎ *328-1123)*, the city's finest restaurant. The pasta dishes are particularly well-received, as is the setting, amidst the hotel's tropical indoor courtyard. Reservations recommended. The **Garden Café** *($$)* is a less expensive alternative in the Lethbridge Lodge, with the same lovely surroundings. It is open from 6:30am to 11:30pm and serves a hearty breakfast, as well as truly divine desserts.

Fort Macleod

The **Silver Grill** *($; 24th St. between 2nd and 3rd Ave.)* is an interesting alternative to the couple of fast food joints near the motels. This historic saloon serves a mediocre Chinese buffet, called a "Smorg", and typical North American dishes, but it is the interior that makes it worth a stop. The original bar and a bullet-pierced mirror will make you feel like you should be watching your back!

Medicine Hat

The **City Bakery** *($; 5th Ave. SW, between 3rd and 4th St. SW)* bakes up wonderful fresh breads and New York bagels.

Full O' Beans Cappuccino Bar *($; 453 3rd St. SW)* is a good place to pick up a good steaming cup of coffee to go with one of the muffins, cakes and sandwiches on the menu, or maybe with a bagel from the City Bakery, which is just around the corner.

For lunch, try **Caroline's Pub & Eatery** *($-$$; 101 4th Ave. SE, ☎ 529-5300)*, a big and airy place that lacks a bit of ambience, but serves good inexpensive food.

Rustler's *($$; 901 8th St. SW, ☎ 526-8004)* is another spot that transports you back to the lawless wild west — the restaurant boasts a blood-stained card table preserved under glass for all to gawk at! The menu features steaks, chicken, ribs, pasta and several Mexican dishes. Breakfasts are particularly busy and copious.

Brooks

Peggy Sue's Diner *($; 603 2nd St. W, ☎ 362-7737)* is neat little family-run eatery. Smoked meat, burgers, great fries and delicious mud pie can be eaten in or taken out.

Drumheller

The **Bridge Greek Restaurant, Steak and Pizza House** *($$; 71 Bridge St. N, ☎ 823-2225)* serves a bit of everything, but you should definitely choose one of the Greek dishes. The home-made dishes, including the lamb specialty, all contain fresh ingredients.

The **Sizzling House** *($$; 160 Centre St. ☎ 823-8098)* serves up equally good Sichuan-style cuisine. A good place for lunch.

■ Tour C: Central Alberta

Rosebud

The **Rosebud Dinner Theatre**, is an entertaining way to spend an evening. The food is simple, but the plays are always well presented. Reservations are mandatory; for a schedule and information call ☎ 677-2001 or 1-800-267-7553 (see p 363).

Red Deer

City Roast Coffee *($; 4940 50th St.)* serves hearty soup and sandwich lunches and good coffee. The walls are decorated with posters announcing local art shows and events.

The **Good Food Company** *($-$$; at the corner of 50th St. and Gaetz Ave.)* is located in the old Greene Block, an historic building in downtown Red Deer. Healthy meals including borscht and a peasant's platter are all served with home-made bread.

Wetaskiwin

The **MacEachern Tea House & Restaurant** *($-$$; Mon to Sat until 4pm; 4719 50th Ave., ☎ 352-8308)* serves specialty coffees and over 20 teas. The menu boasts hearty home-made soups and chowders, as well as sandwiches and salads.

Rocky Mountain House

The **Sandwich Drive-in** *($)* is the only place in town with the least bit of character. The menu includes the usual soups, sandwiches and desserts. The place is a bit hard to find: it is off 50th Ave., behind Kiko's video store and between the Kentucky Fried Chicken and the National Bank.

Cochrane

Mackay's Ice Cream *($)* scoops up what many claim is the best ice cream in the country. Be sure to stop in to see for yourself!

Cochrane's friendly **Home Quarter Restaurant & Pie Shoppe** *($$; 216 1st St. W, ☎ 932-2111)* is the home of the ever-popular Rancher's Special breakfast with eggs, bacon and sausage. Home-made pies are available all day long to eat in or take out. The lunch and dinner menu boasts filet mignon and chicken parmesan.

■ **Tour D: Edmonton**

Among the many cafés in Old Strathcona, the **Café La Gare** *($; 10308 81st Ave.)* seems to be the place to be. Outdoor chairs and tables are reminiscent of a Parisian café. The only food available is bagels and scones. An intriguing intellectual atmosphere prevails.

Bee-Bell Health Bakery *($; 10416 80th Ave., ☎ 439-3247)* sells wonderful breads and pastries.

Barb and Ernie's *($; 9906 72nd Ave., ☎ 433-3242)* is an exceptionally popular diner-style restaurant with good food, good prices and a friendly unpretentious ambience. Breakfast is a particularly busy time, expect to have to wait a bit for a table.

Cheesecake Café Bakery Restaurant *($; 17011 100th Ave., ☎ 486-0440 or 10390 51st Ave., ☎ 437-5011)* serves a huge variety of cheesecakes — need we say more?

Block 1912 *($; 10361 Whyte Ave., ☎ 433-6575)* is a European café that won an award for its effort to beautify the Strathcona area. The interior is like someone's living room with an eclectic mix of tables, chairs and sofas. Lasagna is one of the simple menu's best offerings. Soothing music and a relaxed mood are conducive to a chat with friends, or the enjoyment of a good book.

As one would expect the **Bagel Tree** *($; 10354 Whyte Ave., ☎ 439-9604)* makes their own bagels, but they also sell bagels imported from Fairmount Bagels in Montréal, arguably the best bagels around.

The **Mongolian Food Experience** *($$; 10160 100A St., ☎ 426-6806)* involves choosing meat, vegetables and sauce from a large buffet, having it weighed to determine the price and then cooked up right before your eyes. All this is then rolled into a Mongolian wrap and savoured. There is also a regular menu for those who prefer to remain inexperienced!

Stone Age Wood Fired Food *($$; 10338 81st Ave., ☎ 433-4343)* serves delicious pizzas (including one with eight kinds of cheese), cooked in a wood stove that rises in the middle of the restaurant. The funky, hangar-like interior features cast-iron chandeliers and exposed brick walls.

Casual French dining is the theme at **Café Soleil** *($$; 10360 Whyte Ave., ☎ 438-4848)*, where the menu includes a good selection of stuffed dinner and dessert crepes.

Julio's Barrio *($$; 10450 82nd Ave., ☎ 433-6575)* boasts an original Mexican-Southwest decor with piñatas hanging from the ceiling, cactus coat racks and soft leather chairs. The menu features a good selection of nachos and soups, plus all the regular Mexican fare. Servings are huge and the service is quick.

Packrat Louie Kitchen & Bar *($$; 10335 83rd Ave., ☎ 433-0123)* has a good selection of wines and a nice atmosphere with interesting music. The menu offerings are varied and generally well-prepared.

More than 20 varieties of pasta are served at **Chianti Café** *($$; 10501 82nd Ave., ☎ 439-9829)* located in Old Strathcona's former post office. They don't take reservations so be prepared to wait.

Vi's *($$; 9712 111th St., ☎ 482-6402)* is located in a converted house overlooking the North Saskatchewan River Valley. Innovative and delicious dishes are served in the several small dining rooms, and, in the summer, on the terrace from which you can enjoy great views and spectacular sunsets. Service can be slow if they are really busy, but the chocolate pecan pie on the dessert menu is worth the wait!

The whitewashed and blue decor of the **Syrtaki Greek Restaurant** *($$-$$$; 16313 111th Ave., ☎ 484-2473)* is enough to make you forget you are in Edmonton. Belly dancers animate the evening on Fridays and Saturdays. Fresh game, seafood, meat, chicken and vegetables are all prepared according to authentic Greek recipes.

The **West Edmonton Mall**'s Bourbon Street harbours a collection of moderately priced restaurants. **Café Orleans** *($$)* serves Cajun and Creole specialties; **Sherlock Holmes** *($$)* serves typical English pub grub; and **Albert's Deli** *($)* serves Montréal smoked meat. Finally **Pacific Fish** *($$-$$$)* also has an outlet here. Perhaps Edmonton's best seafood restaurant, fresh fish arrives here daily. Other locations include 10020 101A Ave., ☎ 422-0282. Reservations are recommended.

The posh ambience at the **Café Select** *($$$; 10018 106th St., ☎ 423-0419)* is deceiving. The atmosphere is actually elegantly unpretentious, all the better to enjoy the chicken breast Select stuffed with parmesan, mushrooms and smoked ham, or one of the other delicious entrées. With a 2am closing time, this is the place for a fashionably late meal.

Edmonton's first European bistro, **Bistro Praha** *($$$; 10168 100A St., ☎ 424-4218)* is very popular and charges in accordance. Favourites like cabbage soup, Wiener schnitzel, filet mignon, tortes and strudels are served in a refined but comfortable setting.

La Bohème *($$$; 6427 112th Ave., ☎ 474-5693)* is set in the splendidly restored Gibbard Building. A delicious variety of classic yet original French appetizers and entrées are enjoyed in a romantic setting complete with cosy fire. Bed and breakfast are also offered upstairs (see p 349).

Claude's on the River *($$$$; 9797 Jasper Ave., ☎ 429-2900)* is one of Edmonton's finest. An exceptional river valley view, menu offerings like Australian rack of lamb in a provençale crust and other distinguished French dishes as well as an extensive wine list explain why.

Like its Calgary counterpart, **Hy's Steakloft** *($$$$; closed Sun; 10013 101A Ave., ☎ 424-4444)* serves up juicy Alberta steaks done to perfection. Chicken and pasta dishes round out the menu. A beautiful skylight is the centrepiece of the restaurant's classy decor.

The Unheardof Dining Lounge *($$$$; 9602 82nd Ave., ☎ 432-0480)*: the name fits and it doesn't. This restaurant is no longer unheard of, yet it is an exception to Edmonton's dining norm. A seven-course set menu is served every evening except Sunday and Monday in a restored house full of antiques. The *table d'hôte* usually features fresh game in the fall and chicken or beef the rest of the year. The food is exquisite and refined. Reservations are required.

■ **Tour E: Northern Alberta**

St. Paul

The **King's Motel** *($; 5638 50th Ave.)* restaurant serves hot pancakes and French toast breakfasts, as well as lunch and dinner. The atmosphere is nothing special, but the food is good and inexpensive (breakfast is free if you're staying at the motel).

Corfou Restaurant *($ $; 5010 50th Ave., ☎ 645-2948)* serves Greek food, as its name suggests, but also dishes up Italian and Spanish specialities.

Athabasca

Green Spot *($; 4820 51st St., ☎ 675-3040)* is open from breakfast to dinner and serves a bit of everything, from healthy soups and sandwiches (as its name suggests) to big juicy burgers.

Fort McMurray

The **Garden Café** *($; 9924 Briggs Ave., ☎ 791-6665)* is a fresh and cheery place to enjoy soups, sandwiches and good desserts. It is open all day and all night.

The **Mapletree Pancake House** *($$; 424 Gregoire Dr., ☎ 791-7200)* in the Mackenzie Park Inn is known for its huge Sunday brunch and of course, its pancakes.

Slave Lake

Joey's Incredible Edibles *($-$$; at the corner of 3rd Ave. and Main St., ☎ 849-5577)* is a pleasant family-style restaurant with a complete menu including a big choice of juicy hamburgers.

Widewater

Rita's Boutique and Teahouse *($; Widewater)* is located about 15 minutes from the town of Slave Lake. Simple soups and sandwiches are served in a quaint setting of antiques and soothing music, though afternoon tea with a chunk of one of the eight flavours of fudge are reason enough to stop. Open for lunch and tea.

Peace River

The **Peace Garden** *($$; 10016 100th St., ☎ 624-1048)* is the best of the handful of Chinese restaurants in town. Besides good seafood dishes, they also serve North American dishes like steak and pizza.

The **Villa Bokou** *($$; 9703 100th St., ☎ 624-5590)* also serves traditional North American fare, but specializes in Greek food. The atmosphere and staff are friendly.

Grande Prairie

Java Junction *($; 9931 100th Ave., ☎ 539-5070)* is a funky spot in the small downtown area with hearty and inexpensive muffins, soups and sandwiches.

The **Bear Creek Cattle Company** *($$; on 100th Ave. between 106th and 108th St.)* is a new addition to the restaurant possibilities in town. Its great decor features ranching paraphernalia and an open kitchen. The interesting menu lists tasty Mexican and southwestern-style dishes including mesquite-broiled Alberta beef or something from the coup (chicken) or the creek (fish and seafood); the menu also gives an interesting history of some of the dishes.

Grande Prairie is home to one of Alberta's several **Earl's** *($$; 100th St.)* restaurant outlets. With its outdoor terrace and reliable and varied menu, it is a favourite in town.

Entertainment

■ Tour A: Calgary

Cityscope and **The Avenue** are two monthly publications that list what's on throughout Calgary, including live acts around town and theatre offerings. They are both available free of charge throughout the city. **The Mirror** is a free news and entertainment weekly.

Bars and Nightclubs

The majority of Calgary's dance bars are found along 11th Ave., known, as a result, as Electric Avenue. These include **The Bank**, **Bandito's** and **Coconut Joe's** which attract younger crowds; **Señor Frog's** is the place to be seen by young professionals with constant dance music (see also "Restaurants" p 352); **Crazy Horse** is another popular yuppie hang-out, classic rock and roll tunes keep things hopping here. **The Republic** and **The Warehouse** offer a more "alternative" alternative.

Boystown *(213 10th Ave. SW, ☎ 228-7999)* attracts a gay crowd, while **The 318** and **Victoria's Restaurant** *(17th Ave. at 2nd St. SW)* both located in the same building, cater to a mixed crowd.

Kaos Café *(718 17th Ave. SW, ☎ 228-9997)* is a popular jazz club with live shows Thursday to Saturday, it is also a fun café with an interesting menu.

If you're itchin' to two-step then you're in luck. Calgary has two great country bars. At **The Ranchman's** *(9615 Macleod Tr. SW, ☎ 253-1100)*, the horseshoe-shaped dance flor is the scene of two-step lessons on Tuesdays and line-dancing lessons on Wednesday; the rest of the week it is packed. The **Rockin' Horse Saloon** *(7400 Macleod Tr. SE, ☎ 255-4646)* is where the real cowboys and cowgirls hang out.

Theatre

Alberta Theatre Projects *(☎ 294-7475)* is an excellent troupe that performs great contemporary plays.

Those in need of some culture may want to inquire about performances of the **Calgary Opera** *(☎ 262-7286)*, the **Calgary Philharmonic Orchestra** *(☎ 294-7420)* and the **Alberta Ballet** *(☎ 245-4222)*.

Calgary has an **IMAX** theatre in the Eau-Claire Market *(☎ 263-4629)*.

Uptown Screen *(612 8th Ave., ☎ 265-0120)* shows foreign films in an old revamped theatre downtown. First-run movies can be seen at movie theatres throughout the city. Pick up a newspaper for schedules and locations, or call the Talking Yellow Pages ☎ 521-5222 (see p 282).

THE RODEO

Rodeos are serious stuff in Alberta. In some schools cowboy skills are part of the sports program and are on a par with football and hockey. There are essentially six official events in a rodeo. In the **bareback riding**, **saddle bronc riding**, and **bull riding** events, the cowboy must stay on the bucking animal for eight seconds to even qualify, at which point he is given a score based on style, rhythm and control. In the bareback and saddle bronc riding, the animal is a horse, and in all three cases a cinch is placed around the animal's hind quarters which causes him to buck. The bull riding event is of course the most exciting, with the bulls weighing in at around 1,800 pounds. In the **calf roping** event the cowboy must lasso the calf from his horse, race to the animal and tie three of its legs. This is a timed event, and the time includes a final six seconds during which the calf must remain tied. Big cowboys are the usual participants in the **steer wrestling** event where the cowboy slides off his horse onto the steer, grabs its horns, twists them and throws the steer to the ground. Again the fastest time wins. The **barrel racing** event is the only one for cowgirls. Riders must circle three barrels in a clover-leaf pattern, and there is a five-second penalty for knocking one over. The fastest time wins. Other entertaining events and the rodeo clown keep the crowd happy in between the official events. One of the most amusing crowd-pleasers is the **mutton busting**, where young cowpokes are strapped to sheep and sent flying around the corral.

Festivals and Events

The **Calgary Exhibition and Stampede** is deservedly called the "Greatest Show on Earth". It began in 1912, at a time when many people expected that the wheat industry would eventually supersede the cattle industry and was intended to be a one-time showcase for traditional cowboy skills. Of course the cattle industry thrived and the show has been a huge success ever since. Every July, around 100,000 people descend on Stampede Park for the extravaganza. It begins with a parade, which starts at 6th Ave. SE and 2nd St. SE at 9am, but get there early (by 7am) if you want to see anything. The main attraction is of course the rodeo where cowboys and cowgirls show off their skills. The trials take place every afternoon at 1:30pm and the big final is held on the last weekend. Reserved seats for this event sell out quickly and you are better off ordering tickets in advance if you have your heart set on seeing the big event. There are also chuck wagon races; heats for the Rangeland Derby are held every evening at 8pm, and the final on the last weekend. Downtown's Olympic Plaza is transformed into Rope Square, where free breakfast is served every morning from the back of chuck wagons. Festivities continue throughout the day in the Plaza. Back at Stampede Park, an Indian Village and agricultural fair are among the exhibits to explore. Evening shows often showcase some of the biggest stars in country music. A gate admission fee of $8 is charged and allows access to all live entertainment, except shows at the Saddledome, for which tickets must be purchased in advance. For information on the good rodeo seats write to Calgary Exhibition and Stampede, Box 1860, Station M, Calgary, Alberta, T2P 2L8, or call ☎ 261-0101 or 1-800-661-1260.

The **Calgary International Jazz Festival** *(☎ 233-2628)* takes place the last week in June. The **International Native Arts Festival** *(☎ 233-0022)* and **Afrikadey** *(☎ 283-7119)* both take place the third week in August, and both highlight entertainment and art from a variety of cultures from all over the world. The **Calgary Winter Festival** *(☎ 268-2688)* takes place in late January.

Spruce Meadows, located southwest of the city, is Canada's premier equestrian facility. There are actually three yearly events here, the **National** in early June, the **North American** in July (same time as Stampede) and the **Spruce Meadows Masters** during the second week in September. The winner of the Du Maurier International during this last event takes home the biggest purse of any equestrian event anywhere. For information call ☎ 254-3200.

The Canadian Football League's **Calgary Stampeders** play their home games in McMahon Stadium *(1817 Crowchild Tr. NW, ☎ 289-0258)* from July to November. The National Hockey League's **Calgary Flames** play at the Olympic Saddledome *(17th Ave. and 2nd St. SE, ☎ 261-0475 or 270-6700)* from October to April.

■ **Tour B: Southern Alberta**

Lethbridge

The first week in July is time for **Whoop-Up Days** in Lethbridge. Parades, festivities in the streets, a casino, performances every night and, of course, a rodeo are just some of the highlights. For information call ☎ 328-4491.

Medicine Hat

The **Medicine Hat Exhibition and Stampede**, held the last weekend in July, is second only to Calgary's Stampede in grandeur and extravagance. For information call ☎ 527-1234.

Fort Macleod

Main Street's **Empress Theatre** *(235 24th St.)* is the original theatre from the early 19th century. Recent big-named movies are shown and plays are put on regularly.

Every year in mid-July the **Annual Pow-wow** is held at Head-Smashed-In Buffalo Jump. A large teepee is set up on the grounds where visitors can see traditional native dancing and sample some native food. For information ☎ 553-2731).

■ Tour C: Central Alberta

The **Rosebud Dinner Theatre**, in Rosebud, is a splendid way to spend a fun evening with friends. Amusing plays are presented every day except Sunday, alternating from one day to the next between matinee and evening performances. Reservations are mandatory; for a schedule and information call ☎ 677-2001 or 1-800-267-7553. Rosebud is located about an hour from Calgary on Hwy 840 about halfway to Drumheller.

■ Tour D: Edmonton

See Magazine is a free news and entertainment weekly that outlines what's on throughout the city.

Bars and Nightclubs

Barry T's on 104th St. is a sports pub that attracts a young crowd with a mix of country and popular music. **Club Malibu** has two locations at 10310 85th Ave. and 10045 109th St.; both places attract crowds of young professionals. The **Thunderdome** is another hot spot with top name rock and roll acts. There is always something happening at the **Sidetrack Cafe** *(10333 112th Ave., ☎ 433-3663)* resto-bar with its mix of comedy, rock and jazz acts.

The **Sherlock Holmes** *(10012 101A Ave., ☎ 433-9676)* has an impressive choice of British and Irish ales on tap. The relaxed atmosphere seems to attract a mixed crowd. The **Yardbird Suite** *(10203 86th Ave., ☎ 432-0428)* is the home base of the local Jazz Society, with live performances every night of the week. A small admission fee is charged. **Blues on Whyte** *(10329 82nd Ave., ☎ 439-3981)* showcases live acts.

The Roost *(10345 104th St., ☎ 426-3150)* is one of the few gay bars in Edmonton.

Well-known as Edmonton's premiere country bar, the **Cook Country Saloon** *(8010 103rd St., ☎ 432-2665)* offers lessons for amateur line-dancers and a mechanical bull for those closet cowboys looking for a wild eight seconds.

Theatre

The **Citadel Theatre** is a huge facility with five theatres inside. A variety of shows are put on from children's theatre to experimental and major productions. For information contact the box office at ☎ 426-4811 or 425-1820.

The **Phoenix Theatre Company** (☎ 429-4015) and the **Northern Light Theatre** (☎ 471-1586) both stage innovative and interesting works.

For some more classical culture, check out the offerings of the **Edmonton Opera** (☎ 429-1000), the **Edmonton Symphony Orchestra** (☎ 428-1414) and the **Alberta Ballet** (☎ 428-6839).

First-run movies are shown throughout the city, for locations and schedules pick up a newspaper or call the Talking Yellow Pages ☎ 493-9000 (see p 282).

Festivals and Events

Edmonton is touted as a city of festivals, and **Edmonton's Klondike Days** is possibly the city's biggest event. During the Yukon gold-rush, gold diggers were attracted to the "All-Canadian Route" which departed from here. The route proved almost impassable and none of the prospectors made it to the Yukon before the rush was over. This albeit tenuous link to the gold rush is, however, reason enough for Edmontonians to celebrate for 10 days in July. Starting the third Thursday in July, festivities, parades, bathtub road races, sourdough raft races and a casino bring the city to life. Every morning, free pancake breakfasts are served throughout the city. For information call ☎ 471-7335.

Other festival highlights include the **Jazz City International Festival** (☎ 432-7166), which takes place during the last week in June. In early June, **The Works: A Visual Arts Celebration** (☎ 426-2122) sees art exhibits take to the streets. The **Edmonton Heritage Festival** (☎ 433-3378) features international singing and dancing during the last week in July. The **Edmonton Folk Music Festival** (☎ 429-1899) takes place the last week in August and tickets are recommended. The **Fringe Theatre Festival** (☎ 448-9000) is one of North America's largest alternative-theatre events; it takes place throughout Old Strathcona starting the second Friday in August for ten days. The **Dream-Speakers Festival** at (☎ 439-3456) the end of August celebrates native arts and culture.

The National Hockey League's **Edmonton Oilers** play at the Northland Coliseum (118th Ave. and 74th St., ☎ 471-2191); the season lasts from October to April.

■ **Tour E: Northern Alberta**

Grande Prairie

The **Grande Prairie Little Theatre** is a small, but popular, theatre company. For information call ☎ 538-1616.

Snapper's Party House (corner of 100th St. and 101st Ave.) is exactly that, a party house. All weekend-long crowds of young partyers frequent this large dance bar and its upstairs terrace (when it's not too cold!).

Peace River

River Daze takes place the second weekend in August and is marked by all sorts of activities along the river.

Shopping

■ Tour A: Calgary

The **Eaton Centre, TD Square, Scotia Centre** and **The Bay** department store line 8th Ave. SW, as does a collection of swanky upscale shops including **Holt Renfrew** and the boutiques in **Penny Lane Hall**.

The **Eau-Claire Market** is a wonderful spot to pick up just about anything. Imported goods including Peruvian sweaters, and southwestern style decorating items are all sold right next to the fresh fish and produce. **Sandpiper Books** on the upper level is a marvellous bookshop with a good collection of books on Alberta.

Not only are **Kensington Avenue** and the surrounding streets a pleasant place to stroll, but the area is also full of interesting specialty shops that are worth a look. One of these is **Heartland Country Store** *(940 2nd Ave. NW)* which sells beautiful pottery. **Uptown 17** is a collection of shops, cafes and galleries along 17th Ave. SW, with a distinctly upbeat atmosphere. Along 9th Ave. SE, east of the Elbow River, is an area known as **Atlantic Avenue**, where gentrified houses now contain shops and cafés.

The **Alberta Boot Co.** *(614 10th Ave. SW)* is the place to outfit yourself for the Stampede, with boots in all sizes and styles, just to make sure you fit in!

Mountain Equipment Co-op *(1009 4th Ave. SW)* is a co-operative that is essentially open only to its members, but it only costs $5 to join and is well worth it. High-quality camping and outdoor equipment, clothing and accessories are sold at very reasonable prices.

■ Tour B: Southern Alberta

Lethbridge

B Macabee's Bookseller *(4th Ave. S at 5th St. S)* is a cosy little bookstore adjoining the Penny Coffee House (see p 355). Choose from among an extensive selection of books by local writers and about local issues. Not only is this a great place to pick up a good book, but its also a great place to peruse your purchase.

Medicine Hat

The **Clay Interpretive Centre** (see p 306) sells replicas and originals of Hycroft China and Medalta potteries. Copies of the Medalta cauldrons that are prized by antique collectors are available.

■ Tour C: Central Alberta

Markerville

Three gift shops can be found in the vicinity of the Markerville Creamery (see p 315), the **Gallery and Gift Shop** adjoins the creamery and sells pretty bric-a-brac and gifts. Next door the **Butterchurn** features a remarkable collection of wood-worked items, from small shelves to benches and tables. Just down the road, **Blacksmith** has a little something for everyone, in a country store atmosphere.

Carstairs

Pa-Su Farm *(9 km west of Carstairs on Hwy 580, follow the signs, ☎ 337-2800)* is a working sheep farm with a collection of rare and endangered breeds of sheep. A 280 m^2 gallery displays weavings from Africa and local sheepskin and woolen products. The working part of the farm is only open to scheduled tours. The Devonshire Tea Room serves delicious warm scones with tea.

On the other side of Carstairs, the **Custom Woolen Mills** *(21 km east of Carstairs on Hwy 581, then 4.5 km north on Hwy 791, ☎ 337-2221)* is a curious little spot. Raw wool is processed on machines that in some cases are more than a hundred years old. Yarns and ready-made knitted articles can be purchased.

■ **Tour D: Edmonton**

Besides the obvious, the **West Edmonton Mall** (see "Exploring" section p 323) and its 800 shops and services located at 87th Ave. and 170th St., there are regular malls scattered north, south and west of the city centre.

Downtown, the **Eaton Centre** and **The Bay** boast the usual department store and mall offerings.

Old Strathcona makes for a much more pleasant shopping experience, with some funky specialty shops, bookstores and women's clothing stores along Whyte Ave. (82nd Ave.) including **Avenue Clothing Co.** and **Etzio**, and along 104th St. **Strathcona Square** *(8150 105th St)* is located in an old converted post office and boasts a bright assortment of cafes, boutiques all set in a cheery market atmosphere. The **Treasure Barrel** *(8216 104th St.)* is like a permanent craft fair showcasing arts and crafts of all kinds and for all tastes.

High Street at 124th Street *(124th St. and 125th St. between 102nd Ave. and 109th Ave.)* is an outdoor shopping arcade with galleries, cafes and shops located in a pretty residential area.

■ **Tour E: Northern Alberta**

Widewater

Fifteen minutes east of Slave Lake, in the town of Widewater is **Rita's Boutique and Teahouse**, a wonderful little treasure just waiting to be discovered. All sorts of crafts and antiques create a divine atmosphere in which to enjoy a light lunch and one (or maybe more) of the eight flavours of fudge.

INDEX

17 Mile House (Victoria) 94
1940's Canteen Show (Watson Lake,
　　Yukon) 176
Accidents 33
Accommodations 39, 40
　　Bed and Breakfasts 39
　　Hotels 39
　　Inns 39
　　Motels 39
　　Youth Hostels 39
Active Pass Lighthouse (Mayne
　　Island) 112
Aerial tramway (Vancouver) 71
Ainsworth Hot Springs (Kaslo) 132
Ainsworth Hot Springs (Southern BC)
　　Accommodations 153
Airports 34
Akamina Highway (Waterton Park) .. 333
Alaska Highway Interpretive Centre
　　(Watson Lake, Yukon) 176
Alaska Highway Signpost Forest
　　(Watson Lake, Yukon) 176
Alberta 275
　　Accommodations 340
　　Entertainment 360
　　Exploring 284
　　Finding Your Way Around 278
　　Outdoor Activities 338
　　Parks 331
　　Practical Information 282
　　Restaurants 352
　　Shopping 365
　　Tour A: Calgary 284
　　Tour B: Southern Alberta 293
　　Tour C: Central Alberta 308
　　Tour D: Edmonton 316
　　Tour E: Northern Alberta 324
Alberta Legislature Building
　　(Edmonton) 321
Alberta Prairie Railway Excursions
　　(Stettler) 310
Alcan aluminum factory (Kitimat) ... 183
Alder Flats (Central Alberta)
　　Exploring 312
Alert Bay (Vancouver Island)
　　Exploring 110
Alexandria Bridge (Yale) 128
Alpha Lake (Southern BC) 147
Alta Lake (Southern BC) 147
Amerindian Culture 22
Amerindians 21
Amphitrite Point Lighthouse (Ucluelet) 108

Andrew Wolf Wine Cellar (Stony
　　Plain) 312
Angel Glacier (Jasper National Park) . 230
Animal Lick (Kootenay National Park) . 235
Architectural Institute of British
　　Columbia (Vancouver) 60
Artwalk (Nelson) 133
Ashcroft (Southern BC)
　　Accommodations 152
　　Exploring 129
Asian Centre (Vancouver) 68
Athabasca (Northern Alberta)
　　Accommodations 350
　　Exploring 327
　　Restaurants 359
Athabasca Falls (Icefields Parkway) .. 228
Athabasca Glacier (Icefields Parkway) 227
Atlas Coal Mine Museum (East
　　Coulee) 308
Aylmer Lookout Viewpoint (Banff
　　National Park) 220
B.C. Museum of Mining (Britannia
　　Beach) 141
Baker Street (Nelson) 132
Balance Rock (Skidegate) 186
Banff Centre of the Arts (Banff) 219
Banff Festival of the Arts (Banff) 219
Banff National Park
　　Accommodations 252
　　Entertainment 271
　　Exploring 214
　　Finding Your Way Around 210
　　Practical Information 213
　　Restaurants 265
　　Shopping 272
Banff Park Museum (Banff) 216
Banff Public Library (Banff) 216
Banff Springs Hotel (Banff) 219
Bankhead (Banff National Park) 220
Banks 37
Bar U Ranch National Historic Site
　　(Longview) 296
Bars 41
Bastion (Nanaimo) 107
Bastion Square (Victoria) 90
Battle Hill (Kitwanga) 177
BC Place Stadium (Vancouver) 66
Beaches 47
　　Agate Beach 191
　　Botanical Beach 95
　　Cadboro Bay Beach 95
　　China Beach 95

368 Index

East Beach 191
First Beach 73
French Beach 95
Long Beach 108
Ma-Me-O Beach 338
North Beach 191
Second Beach 73
Slave Lake 338
South Beach 191
Sunset Beach 73
Sylvan Lake 338
Third Beach 73
Willows Beach 95
Wreck Beach 73
Beacon Hill Park 93, 95
Bear Glacier (Northern BC) 179
Bed and Breakfasts (Alberta) 283
Bellevue Mine (Bellevue) 298
Bicycling 46
    Alberta 340
Big Rock (Okotoks) 296
Bird-watching 47
    Alberta 339
    Northern British Columbia 192
    Vancouver 75
Birds of Prey Centre (Coaldale) 304
Black Diamond (Southern Alberta)
    Exploring 294
Blackcomb Mountain (Southern BC) . . 151
BlackJack Cross Country Trails
    (Southern BC) 150
Bleriot Ferry (Drumheller) 307
Bluffs Park 114
Bonnyville (Northern Alberta)
    Exploring 326
Botanical Beach 95
Bow River Falls (Banff) 219
Bow Summit (Icefields Parkway) 225
Bow Valley Parkway (Banff National
    Park) 220
Britannia Beach (Southern BC)
    Exploring 141
Brooks (Southern Alberta)
    Accommodations 345
    Exploring 306
    Restaurants 356
Brooks Aqueduct (Brooks) 306
Buddhist Temple (Vancouver) 73
Buffalo Paddock (Banff National Park) 219
Buffalo Paddock (Waterton National
    Park) 333
Bulkley Valley Art Gallery and
    Museum (Smithers) 181
Bulkley Valley Fall Fair (Smithers) . . . 181

Bungee Jumping
    Vancouver Island and the Gulf
        Islands 115
Burgess Shale (Yoho National Park) . . 236
Burns Lake (Northern BC)
    Exploring 181
Bus 33
Business Hours 35
    Banks 35
    Post Offices 35
    Stores 35
Butchart Gardens (Victoria) 94
C&E Railway Museum (Edmonton) . . . 322
Cablehouse Restaurant (Sayward) . . . 110
Cadboro Bay Beach 95
Calgary
    Accommodations 340
    Entertainment 360
    Exploring 284
    Finding Your Way Around 278
    Parks 331
    Restaurants 352
    Shopping 365
Calgary International Airport 34
Calgary Tower (Calgary) 286
Calgary Zoo, Botanical Gardens and
    Prehistoric Park (Calgary) . . 291
Campbell River (Vancouver Island)
    Accommodations 117
    Exploring 109
    Restaurants 119
Campbell River & District Museum &
    Archives (Campbell River) . 109
Camping
    Alberta 340
Canada Olympic Park (Calgary) 293
Canada Place (Vancouver) 70
Canada's Aviation Hall of Fame
    (Wetaskiwin) 311
Canadian Country Music Hall of Fame
    (Edmonton) 320
Canadian Craft Museum (Vancouver) . . 65
Canadian Forest Products (Prince
    George) 170
Canadian Pacific Railway Museum
    (Revelstoke) 130
Canadian Pacific Railway Station
    (Vancouver) 70
Canmore (Banff National Park)
    Accommodations 257
    Exploring 223
    Restaurants 267
Canmore Centennial Museum
    (Canmore) 224

Index

Canmore Nordic Centre (Canmore) .. 224
Canmore Recreation Centre
    (Canmore) 224
Canoeing 46
    Alberta 338
    Southern British Columbia 147
Cape Scott Provincial Park 113
Capilano fish hatchery (Vancouver) ... 71
Capilano Suspension Bridge and Park
    (Vancouver) 70
Car 31
Car Rentals 33
Cardston (Southern Alberta)
    Exploring 299
Carr House (Victoria) 93
Carr, Emily (Vancouver) 65
Carstairs (Central Alberta)
    Exploring 315
    Shopping 366
Cascade Gardens (Banff) 216
Castlegar (Southern BC)
    Exploring 133
Castleguard Cave (Icefields Parkway) 227
Cathedral Provincial Park (Southern
    BC) 146
    Accommodations 155
Cave and Basin (Banff) 214, 216
Cedar Creek Winery (Kelowna) 139
Cedarvale (Northern BC)
    Restaurants 201
Centennial Museum (Kitimat) 183
Central Alberta
    Accommodations 346
    Entertainment 363
    Exploring 308
    Finding Your Way Around 278
    Parks 336
    Restaurants 356
    Shopping 365
Chain Lakes Provincial Park 296
Chateau Lake Louise (Lake Louise) .. 223
Chemainus (Vancouver Island)
    Exploring 105
Chetwynd (Northern BC)
    Accommodations 193
    Exploring 171
    Restaurants 198
Chief Mountain International Highway
    (Waterton Park) 333
Children 41
China Beach 95
Chinatown (Calgary) 290
Chinatown (Victoria) 90
Chinatown Gate (Edmonton) 320

Chinese Cultural Centre (Calgary) ... 290
Chinook Wind 297
City Hall (Calgary) 288
City Hall (Edmonton) 318
City Hall Park (Red Deer) 310
Clay Interpretive Centre (Medicine
    Hat) 306
Cleveland Dam Park (Vancouver) 71
Climate 37
Coalbanks Interpretive Site
    (Lethbridge) 302
Coaldale (Southern Alberta)
    Exploring 304
Coast Mountains (Northern BC) 183
Cochrane (Central Alberta)
    Accommodations 347
    Exploring 316
    Restaurants 357
Cochrane Ranche Historic Site
    (Cochrane) 316
Coldwater Hotel (Merritt) 139
Columbia Icefield (Glacier Parkway) .. 227
Commercial Drive (Vancouver) 62
Commodore (Vancouver) 65
Connaught Hill Park 189
Consulates 26
Coombs (Vancouver Island)
    Exploring 107
Copper Maker (Port Hardy) 111
Copper Valley (Southern BC) 129
Cornfest (Taber) 304
Cottonwood Island Nature Park 189
Cow Bay (Prince Rupert) 185
CPR Roundhouse (Vancouver) 66
Craigdarroch Castle (Victoria) 92
Credit Cards 36
Crescent Road Viewpoint (Calgary) .. 290
Crimson Lake Provincial Park 336
Cross-country Skiing 48
    Alberta 339
    Rocky Mountains 250
Crowsnest Museum (Coleman) 298
Crowsnest Pass (Southern Alberta)
    Accommodations 343
    Exploring 297
Crystal Garden (Victoria) 92
Culture 22
    Amerindian Culture 22
    Literature 23
    Music 24
    Visual Arts 23
Currency 37
Custom Woolen Mills (Carstairs) 315
Customs 29

Cycling
  Vancouver 75
Cypress Bowl Provincial Park
  (Vancouver) 75
Cypress Hills Provincial Park ... 306, 335
Cypress Provincial Park (Vancouver) . 71, 75
Dawson Creek (Northern BC)
  Accommodations 193
  Exploring 171
  Finding Your Way Around 164
  Practical Information 167
  Restaurants 199
  Shopping 202
Dawson Creek Art Gallery (Dawson
  Creek) 172
Dawson Creek Farmer's Market
  (Dawson Creek) 172
Deane House (Calgary) 291
Dease Lake (Northern BC)
  Accommodations 195
  Exploring 178
  Practical Information 167
  Restaurants 200
Deep Cove (Vancouver) 71
Den Wildlife Museum (Japser) 230
Desolation Sound (Lund) 145
Desolation Sound Marine Park 147
Devonian Gardens (Calgary) 288
Dickinson Family Farm (Penticton) ... 136
Dingman No. 1 (Turner Valley) 294
Dinosaur Provincial Park 306, 335
Dinosaur Trail (Drumheller) 307
Dionisio Point Provincial Park 113
Discos 41
Discovery Pier (Campbell River) 109
Dogsledding
  Rocky Mountains 251
Domaine Combret (Osoyoos) 135
Dominion Building (Vancouver) 63
Dominion Radio Astrophysical
  Observatory (Kaleden) 139
Donatville (Northern Alberta)
  Accommodations 350
Donnelly (Northern Alberta)
  Exploring 329
Douglas Channel (Kitimat) 183
Doukhobor Museum (Castlegar) 133
Downhill Skiing 48
  Rocky Mountains 249
  Vancouver Island and the Gulf
    Islands 115
Driftwood Canyon Provincial Park
  (Northern BC) 181

Drugs 42
Drumheller (Southern Alberta)
  Accommodations 345
  Exploring 307
  Restaurants 356
Dry Island Buffalo Jump Provincial
  Park 308
Duncan (Vancouver Island)
  Exploring 105
Dunvegan (Northern Alberta) 330
East Coulee (Southern Alberta)
  Exploring 308
East Coulee Drive (Drumheller) 308
East Sooke Park 94
Eau Claire Market (Calgary) 290
Economy 20
Edmonton
  Accommodations 347
  Entertainment 363
  Exploring 316
  Finding Your Way Around 280
  Parks 336
  Restaurants 357
  Shopping 366
Edmonton Airport 35
Edmonton Art Gallery (Edmonton) ... 318
Edmonton Police Museum (Edmonton) 320
Electricity 42
Elk Island National Park 324, 336
Em-Te Town (Alder Flats) 312
Embassies 26
Emerald Lake (Yoho National Park) .. 236
Emergencies 33, 38
Empress Hotel (Victoria) 92
Empress Theatre (Fort Macleod) 300
Energeum (Calgary) 289
English Village and Anne Hathaway's
  Cottage (Victoria) 93
Entrance Formalities 25
Etzikom Museum (Etzikom) 305
Eurocan Pulp paper mill (Kitimat) 183
Exchange Rates 37
Extended Visits 25
Fan Tan Alley (Victoria) 92
Fantasyland Hotel (Edmonton) 324
Farmer's Market (Millarville) 294
Father Lacombe Chapel (St. Albert) .. 326
Father Pandosy mission (Kelowna) ... 138
Fauna 12
Field (Yoho National Park)
  Exploring 236
Field Station of the Tyrell
  Museum 307, 335

Index

Finding Your Way Around
    By Bus 33
    By Car 31
    By Ferry 33
    By Plane 29
    By Train 30
Fire Hall (Stewart) 179
Fire station (Nelson) 132
Fish Creek (Hyder, Alaska) 180
Fish Creek Provincial Park 331
Fishing 47
    Alberta 339
    Northern British Columbia 191
    Rocky Mountains 245
    Vancouver Island and the Gulf
        Islands 115
    Victoria 96
Flora 12
Flying
    Southern British Columbia 151
Former Canadian Pacific Railway
    station (Vancouver) 70
Fort Calgary (Calgary) 290
Fort Edmonton Park (Edmonton) 322
Fort Langley (Southern BC)
    Exploring 126
Fort Langley National Historic Site
    (Fort Langley) 126
Fort Macleod (Southern Alberta)
    Accommodations 344
    Entertainment 363
    Exploring 300
    Restaurants 355
Fort McMurray (Northern Alberta)
    Accommodations 350
    Exploring 328
    Restaurants 359
Fort McMurray Oil Sands Interpretive
    Centre (Fort McMurray) ... 328
Fort Museum (Fort Museum) 300
Fort Nelson (Northern BC)
    Accommodations 194
    Exploring 174
    Finding Your Way Around 164
    Practical Information 167
    Restaurants 199
Fort Nelson Heritage Museum (Fort
    Nelson) 174
Fort Normandeau (Red Deer) 310
Fort St. James (Northern BC)
    Accommodations 196
    Exploring 180
    Practical Information 168

Fort St. James National Historic Park
    (Northern BC) 180
Fort St. John (Northern BC)
    Accommodations 194
    Exploring 174
    Finding Your Way Around 164
    Practical Information 167
    Restaurants 199
Fort Vermillion (Northern Alberta) ... 330
Fort Whoop-Up (Lethbridge) 302
Fortress Mountain ski resort
    (Kananaskis Country) 238
Franchère (Northern Alberta)
    Exploring 326
Frank Slide Interpretive Centre (Frank) 298
Fraser Fort George Regional Museum
    (Prince George) 170
French Beach 95
Galiano (Gulf Islands)
    Accommodations 118
    Entertainment 120
    Exploring 112
    Restaurants 120
Garibaldi Provincial Park 146
Geography 11
    Flora and Fauna 12
George C. Reifel Bird Sanctuary
    (Vancouver) 75
Georgia Cannery (Vancouver) 73
Gibsons (Southern BC)
    Accommodations 156
    Exploring 144
    Practical Information 126
Gitwangak Indian Reserve (Kitwanga) 177
Glacier National Park 146
Glaciers 204
Glenbow Museum (Calgary) 286
Golden (Rocky Mountains)
    Accommodations 264
    Restaurants 270
Golden Spruce (Port Clements) 188
Golf 48
    Alberta 338
    Rocky Mountains 248
    Southern British Columbia 148
Good Hope Lake (Northern BC)
    Exploring 179
Graham Island (Northern BC) 185
Grain Academy (Calgary) 292
Grand Canyon of the Stikine
    (Telegraph Creek) 179
Grand Forks (Southern BC)
    Exploring 134

Grande Prairie (Northern Alberta)
    Accommodations 351
    Entertainment 364
    Exploring 330
    Restaurants 360
Grande Prairie Regional College
    (Grande Prairie) 331
Granville Island (Vancouver) 64
Granville Island Brewing Company
    (Vancouver) 64
Granville Street (Vancouver) 65
Grimshaw (Northern Alberta) 330
Grist Mill (Keremeos) 139
Grouard (Northern Alberta)
    Exploring 329
Grouard Native Art Museum (Grouard) 329
Grouse Mountain (Vancouver) 71, 75
Gwaii Haanas National Park 190
Haida Arts and Jewellery (Old
    Masset) 189
Haig-Brown Kingfisher Creek Heritage
    Property (Campbell River) . 113
Hamilton Falls (Yoho National Park) . . 236
Harbour Quay (Port Alberni) 108
Harbourside Walkway (Nanaimo) 107
Harrison Hot Springs (Southern BC)
    Accommodations 152
    Exploring 128
    Practical Information 124
Hay River (Northern Alberta) 330
Hazelton (Northern BC)
    Exploring 182
He Tin Kis Park (Ucluelet) 108
Head-Smashed-In Buffalo Jump (Fort
    Macleod) 300
Health 38
Hector Lake (Icefields Parkway) 225
Helen Schuler Coulee Centre
    (Lethbridge) 302
Heliskiing
    Rocky Mountains 250
Hell's Gate (Yale) 128
Heritage Park Historical Village
    (Calgary) 292
Heritage Park Museum (Terrace) 182
Heritage Square (Red Deer) 310
Heritage Trail (Edmonton) 321
Heritage Walking & Driving Tour
    (Revelstoke) 130
High Level (Northern Alberta) 330
High River (Southern Alberta)
    Exploring 296
Hiking 46
    Alberta 339

Northern British Columbia 191
Rocky Mountains 238
Southern British Columbia 148
Vancouver 75
Vancouver Island and the Gulf
    Islands 114
Victoria 95
Hillcrest (Southern Alberta)
    Exploring 297
Hinton (Rocky Mountains)
    Accommodations 262
    Restaurants 269
Historic Dunvegan 330
Historic O'Keefe Ranch (Vernon) 139
Historical Museum (Bonnyville) 326
History 14
Hog's Breath Coffee Co. (Penticton) . 136
Holidays 35
Hollyburn Ridge (Vancouver) 76
Honey Place (Fort St. John) 174
Hoodoos (Yoho National Park) 236
Hope (Southern BC)
    Accommodations 152
    Exploring 140
    Practical Information 124
Horseback Riding
    Rocky Mountains 247
Horseshoe Bay (Langdale) 144
Horsethief Canyon Lookout
    (Drumheller) 307
Hot Springs Island (Northern BC) 188
Hotel Europe (Vancouver) 60
Hotel Macdonald (Edmonton) 320
House of Hewhiwus (Sechelt) 144
House of Himwitsa (Tofino) 109
Houston (Northern BC)
    Exploring 181
    Practical Information 168
Hudson Bay Mountain (Smithers) 181
Hudson's Hope (Northern BC)
    Accommodations 193
    Exploring 173
    Practical Information 167
    Restaurants 199
Hudson's Hope Museum (Hudson's
    Hope) 173
Hyder, Alaska (Northern BC)
    Accommodations 195
    Exploring 179
    Practical Information 168
    Restaurants 200
Icefields Parkway
    Accommodations 258
    Exploring 225

Index

Finding Your Way Around 212
Practical Information 213
Restaurants 268
IMAX (Calgary) 290
Indian Battle Park (Lethbridge) 301
Indian Cabins (Northern Alberta) 330
Ink Pots (Banff National Park) 221
Ironman triathlon (Penticton) 136
Iskut (Northern BC)
    Accommodations 195
    Exploring 178
    Restaurants 200
Jasper Aquatic Centre (Jasper) 230
Jasper National Park
    Accommodations 259
    Entertainment 272
    Exploring 228
    Finding Your Way Around 212
    Practical Information 213
    Restaurants 268
    Shopping 274
Jasper Park Lodge (Japser National
    Park) 230
Jasper Tramway (Jasper National
    Park) 230
Jasper-Yellowhead Museum and
    Archives (Jasper) 228
Jensen's Trading Post (Aetna) 300
John Janzen Nature Centre
    (Edmonton) 323
John Walter Museum (Edmonton) ... 321
Johnston Canyon (Banff National
    Park) 221
Joy's Island Jewellers (Queen
    Charlotte City) 186
Junction 37 (Northern BVC) 176
Kaleden (Southern BC)
    Exploring 139
Kamloops (Southern BC)
    Accommodations 153
    Exploring 129
    Practical Information 124
    Restaurants 157
Kananaskis Country
    Accommodations 264
    Exploring 237
    Finding Your Way Around 212
    Practical Information 213
    Restaurants 271
Kananaskis Village
    Accommodations 265
    Exploring 265
Kaslo (Southern BC)
    Exploring 132

Kelowna (Southern BC)
    Accommodations 155
    Exploring 138
    Practical Information 125
    Restaurants 158
Kensington (Calgary) 289
Keremeos (Southern BC)
    Exploring 139
Kettle Valley Railway (Hope) 140
Kettle Valley Railway (Kelowna) 138
Kettle Valley Railway (Penticton) 136
Kicking Horse River (Yoho National
    Park) 236
Kitimat (Northern BC)
    Accommodations 197
    Exploring 183
    Practical Information 168
    Restaurants 201
Kitwancool (Northern BC)
    Exploring 177
Kitwanga (Northern BC)
    Exploring 177
    Practical Information 167
Knox Mountain Park 146
Kokanee Glacier Provincial Park 146
Kootenay National Park
    Accommodations 263
    Exploring 233
    Finding Your Way Around 212
    Practical Information 213
    Restaurants 270
Kootenay Valley Viewpoint (Kootenay
    National Park) 235
Ksan Indian Village (Hazelton) 182
Kwinitsa station (Prince Rupert) 185
La Corey (Northern Alberta)
    Exploring 326
Lac La Biche (Northern Alberta)
    Accommodations 350
    Exploring 327
Lac La Biche Mission (Lac La Biche) .. 328
Lake Louise (Banff National Park)
    Accommodations 255
    Entertainment 272
    Exploring 221
    Restaurants 266
    Shopping 273
Lake Minnewanka (Banff National
    Park) 220
Lakelse Lake Provincial Park ... 190, 183
Landing (Vancouver) 60
Langdale (Southern BC)
    Exploring 144
Language 22

374 Index

Laskeek Bay (Northern BC) 188
Laurel Point Park (Victoria) 93
Le Roi mine (Rossland) 134
Leduc (Central Alberta)
    Exploring 311
Leland Hotel (Southern BC) 131
Lethbridge (Southern Alberta)
    Accommodations 344
    Entertainment 362
    Exploring 301
    Restaurants 355
    Shopping 365
Liard Hot Springs Provincial Park
    (Northern BC)
    Accommodations 194
    Exploring 176, 190
    Restaurants 200
Lietch Collieries (Crowsnest Pass) 297
Lighthouse Park (Vancouver) 71, 75
Literature 23
Long Beach (Vancouver Island) 108
    Restaurants 119
Longview (Southern Alberta)
    Exploring 296
Lonsdale Quay Market (Vancouver) ... 70
Lower Kananaskis Lake (Kananaskis
    Country) 238
Lund (Southern BC)
    Accommodations 157
    Exploring 145
    Restaurants 159
Luxton Museum (Banff) 216
Lytton (Southern BC)
    Exploring 129
    Practical Information 124
M.V. Lady Rose (Port Alberni) 108
Ma-Me-O Beach Provincial
    Park 312, 336
Mackenzie (Northern BC)
    Accommodations 193
    Exploring 171
    Practical Information 167
    Restaurants 198
Mail 36
Maligne Canyon (Jasper National
    Park) 230
Maligne Lake (Jasper National Park) .. 232
Mallaig (Northern Alberta)
    Exploring 326
Manning (Northern Alberta) 330
Manning Provincial Park 146
Marble Canyon (Kootenay National
    Park) 233
Marine Building (Vancouver) 68

Maritime Museum (Vancouver) 68
Maritime Museum of British Columbia
    (Victoria) 90
Markerville (Central Alberta)
    Exploring 314
    Shopping 365
Markerville Creamery (Markerville) ... 315
Market Square (Victoria) 90
Masset (Northern BC)
    Accommodations 197
    Exploring 188
    Practical Information 168
    Restaurants 202
Masset Sound (Old Masset) 188
Maverick Cattle Drives Ltd.
    (Princeton) 140
Mayne Island (Gulf Islands)
    Accommodations 118
    Exploring 112, 114
McBride (Northern BC)
    Exploring 180
    Practical Information 168
McDougall Centre (Calgary) 289
Meander River (Northern Alberta) ... 330
Measures 41
Medicine Hat (Southern Alberta)
    Accommodations 345
    Entertainment 363
    Exploring 305
    Restaurants 355
    Shopping 365
Medicine Hat Museum and Art Gallery
    (Medicine Hat) 305
Medicine Lake (Jasper National
    Park) 232
Memorial Totems (Alert Bay) 111
Merritt (Southern BC)
    Accommodations 155
    Exploring 139
    Practical Information 125
    Restaurants 158
Methanex petrochemical plant
    (Northern BC) 183
Mewata Armoury (Calgary) 289
Meziadin Junction (Northern BC)
    Exploring 177
Miette Hot Springs (Jasper National
    Park) 232
    Accommodations 262
Mile 0 Post (Dawson Creek) 172
Millarville (Southern Alberta)
    Exploring 294
Mineral Lick (Icefields Parkway) 228
Miracle Beach Park 113

Index 375

Mission (Southern BC)
   Exploring 126
Molly's Lane (Southern BC) 144
Molly's Reach Café (Southern BC) ... 144
Montague Harbour Provincial Park ... 113
Moraine Lake (Banff National Park) .. 223
Moresby Island (Northern BC) 185
Moricetown Canyon and Falls
   (Northern BC)
   Exploring 181
Morinville (Northern Alberta)
   Exploring 327
Mormon Temple (Cardston) 299
Mosquito Creek (Icefields Parkway) .. 225
Motorcycling
   Rocky Mountains 245
Mount Cirrus (Icefields Parkway) ... 227
Mount Douglas Park 94
Mount Edith Cavell (Jasper National
   Park) 230
Mount Edziza Provincial Park ... 178, 190
Mount Kidd (Kananaskis Country) ... 238
Mount Lorette (Kananaskis Country) . 238
Mount Mackenzie Ski (Southern BC) . 149
Mount Maxwell Provincial Park 113
Mount Norquay Ski Centre (Banff
   National Park) 220
Mount Seymour Provincial Park
   (Vancouver) 71, 75
Mount Whistler (Japser National Park) 230
Mountain Biking
   Rocky Mountains 243
   Southern British Columbia 151
Mountain Climbing
   Rocky Mountains 251
   Southern British Columbia 151
Muncho Lake Provincial Park
   (Northern BC)
   Accommodations 194
   Exploring 186, 175
   Restaurants 199
Musée Heritage Museum (St. Albert) . 327
Museum (Hyder, Alaska) 179
Museum of Anthropology (Vancouver) . 68
Museum of Northern British Columbia
   & Art Gallery (Northern BC) 185
Museum of the Highwood (High
   River) 296
Museum of the Regiments (Calgary) . 292
Music 24
Muskoseepi Park (Grande Prairie) 330
Muttart Conservatory (Edmonton) ... 322
Myra Canyon (Kelowna) 138
Naikoon Provincial Park 190

Nakiska ski resort (Kananaskis
   Country) 237
Nakusp (Southern BC)
   Exploring 131
   Practical Information 125
Nanaimo (Vancouver Island)
   Accommodations 116
   Exploring 105
   Restaurants 118
National Parks 45
Native Burial Grounds (Alert Bay) 111
Native Heritage Centre (Duncan) 105
Natural Bridge (Yoho National Park) .. 236
Natural harbour (Prince Rupert) 183
Natural History Museum (Banff) 214
Naval Museum of Alberta (Calgary) .. 293
Nelson (Southern BC)
   Accommodations 153
   Exploring 132
   Practical Information 125
Nelson Brewing Company (Nelson) .. 133
Nelson Congregational Church
   (Nelson) 132
Nelson Electric Tramway Company
   (Nelson) 133
New Denver (Southern BC)
   Exploring 131
Newcastle Island (Vancouver Island
   and the Gulf Islands) 107
Newcastle Island Provincial Park 112
Newspapers 42
Nikka Yuko Japanese Garden
   (Lethbridge) 303
Nikkei Internment Memorial Centre
   (New Denver) 131
Ninstints (Northern BC) 188
Nootka Sound (Vancouver Island)
   Exploring 109
Nordegg (Central Alberta)
   Accommodations 347
   Exploring 312
North Pacific Cannery Village
   Museum (Prince Rupert) .. 185
North Peace Museum (Fort St. John) . 174
North Vancouver (Vancouver) 70
Northern Alberta
   Accommodations 350
   Entertainment 364
   Exploring 324
   Finding Your Way Around 280
   Parks 336
   Restaurants 359
   Shopping 366

Index

Northern British Columbia 161
    Accommodations 192
    Exploring 168
    Finding Your Way Around 162
    Outdoor Activities 191
    Parks and Beaches 189
    Practical Information 166
    Restaurants 198
    Shopping 202
Northern Light Studio & Gardens
    (Terrace) 182
Northwood Pulp & Timber and North
    Central Plywoods (North
    BC) 170
Num-Ti-Jah Lodge (Icefields Parkway) 225
Okotoks (Southern Alberta)
    Exploring 294
    Restaurants 354
Okotoks Bird Sanctuary (Okotoks) ... 296
Old Country Market (Coombs) 107
Old Masset (Northern BC)
    Exploring 188
Old Strathcona (Edmonton) 321
Old Strathcona Model and Toy
    Museum (Edmonton) 322
Olympic Hall of Fame (Calgary) 293
Olympic Plaza (Calgary) 288
Orkney Hill Lookout (Drumheller) 308
Orpheum Theatre (Vancouver) 65
Osoyoos (Southern BC)
    Accommodations 154
    Exploring 135
    Practical Information 125
Othello Tunnels (Hope) 140
Outdoor Activities
    Beaches 47
    Bicycling 46
    Bird-watching 47
    Canoeing 46
    Cross-country Skiing 48
    Downhill Skiing 48
    Fishing 47
    Golf 48
    Hiking 46
    Parks 43
    Seal-watching 48
    Snowmobiling 49
    Summer Activities 46
    Whale-watching 48
    Winter Activities 48
Outdoors 43
Pa-Su Farm (Carstairs) 315
Pacific Rim National Park 95
    Long Beach section 112

Pacific Space Centre (Vancouver) 66
Pacific Undersea Gardens (Victoria) ... 93
Paint Pots (Kootenay National Park) .. 233
Parker Ridge (Icefields Parkway) 227
Parks 43, 331
    Banff National Park 214
    Beacon Hill Park 93, 95
    Bluffs Park 114
    Cape Scott Provincial Park 113
    Cathedral Provincial Park 146
    Chain Lakes Provincial Park 296
    Connaught Hill Park 189
    Cottonwood Island Nature Park . 189
    Crimson Lake Provincial Park ... 336
    Cypress Hills Provincial
        Park 306, 335
    Desolation Sound Marine Park .. 147
    Dinosaur Provincial
        Park 306, 335
    Dionisio Point Provincial Park ... 113
    Dry Island Buffalo Jump
        Provincial Park 308
    East Sooke Park 94
    Elk Island National
        Park 324, 336
    Fish Creek Provincial Park 331
    Garibaldi Provincial Park 146
    Glacier National Park 146
    Gwaii Haanas National Park 190
    Indian Battle Park 301
    Jasper National Park 228
    Knox Mountain Park 146
    Kokanee Glacier Provincial Park . 146
    Kootenay National Park 233
    Lakelse Lake Provincial Park 190
    Liard Hot Springs Provincial Park 190
    Ma-Me-O Beach Provincial
        Park 312, 336
    Manning Provincial Park 146
    Miracle Beach Park 113
    Montague Harbour Provincial
        Park 113
    Mount Douglas Park 94
    Mount Edziza Provincial Park ... 190
    Mount Maxwell Provincial Park .. 113
    Muncho Lake Provincial Park ... 189
    Muskoseepi Park 330
    Naikoon Provincial Park 190
    National Parks 45
    Newcastle Island Provincial Park . 112
    Pacific Rim National Park ... 95, 112
    Peter Lougheed Provincial Park .. 238
    Pigeon Lake Provincial
        Park 312, 336

Index

Police Outpost Provincial Park .. 300
Prince's Island Park 331
Provincial Parks 45
Revelstoke National Park 146
River Valley Park System 336
Saltery Bay Provincial Park 147
Sasquatch Provincial Park 146
Spatsizi Plateau Wilderness Park . 190
Stone Mountain Provincial
    Park 189
Strathcona Park 113
Sylvan Lake Provincial Park 314
Tseax Lava Beds 190
Waskasoo Park System 310
Waterton Lakes National
    Park 299, 331
Wokkpash Recreation Area 189
Wood Buffalo National
    Park 328, 337
Writing-on-Stone Provincial
    Park 304, 334
Yoho National Park 236
Parliament Buildings (Victoria) 92
Passport 25
Patricia Lake (Jasper National Park) .. 232
Peace Canyon (Hudson's Hope) 173
Peace Gallery North (Fort St. John) .. 174
Peace River (Northern Alberta)
    Accommodations 351
    Entertainment 365
    Restaurants 360
Peace River Centennial Museum
    (Peace River) 329
Peachland (Southern BC) 138
Pender Harbour (Southern BC)
    Exploring 145
Penticton (Southern BC)
    Accommodations 154, 155
    Exploring 135
    Practical Information 125
    Restaurants 158
Peter Lougheed Provincial Park
    (Kananaskis Country) 238
Peyto Lake (Icefields Parkway) 225
Pigeon Lake Provincial Park ... 312, 336
Pioneer Village (Grande Prairie) 330
Plane 29
    From Asia 30
    From Europe 29
    From the United States 30
    Within Canada 30
Pocahontas (Jasper National Park) ... 232
Police Outpost Provincial Park 300
Politics 19

Population 21
Port Alberni (Vancouver Island)
    Exploring 107
Port Clements (Northern BC)
    Accommodations 197
    Exploring 188
Port Hardy (Vancouver Island)
    Accommodations 117
    Exploring 111
    Restaurants 119
    Shopping 120
Port McNeill (Vancouver Island)
    Exploring 110
Port Renfrew (Victoria) 94
Portland Canal (Stewart) 179
Portrait 11
    Amerindians 21
    Canadian Political System 19
    Culture 22
    Economy 20
    Geography 11
    History 14
    Language 22
    Population 21
Powell Forest Canoe Route (Southern
    BC) 147
Powell River (Southern BC)
    Accommodations 156
    Exploring 145
    Practical Information 126
    Restaurants 159
Practical Information 25
    Accommodations 39
    Advice for Smokers 41
    Airports 34
    Business Hours and Public
        Holidays 35
    Children 41
    Climate and Clothing 37
    Customs 29
    Embassies and Consulates 26
    Entrance Formalities 25
    Finding Your Way Around 29
    Health 38
    Mail and Telecommunications ... 36
    Money and Banking 36
    Restaurants and Bars 40
    Safety 41
    Shopping 38
    Taxes and Tipping 40
    Time Difference 35
    Tourist Information 28
    Weights and Measures 41
    Wine, Beer and Alcohol 41

Index

Prairie Gallery (Grande Prairie) 331
Prince George (Northern BC)
    Accommodations 192
    Exploring 169
    Finding Your Way Around 162
    Practical Information 166
    Restaurants 198
Prince George Art Gallery (Prince
    George) 170
Prince George Native Art Gallery
    (Prince George) 170
Prince of Wales Hotel (Waterton Park) 333
Prince Rupert (Northern BC)
    Accommodations 197
    Exploring 183
    Finding Your Way Around 166
    Practical Information 168
    Restaurants 201
Prince's Island (Calgary) 290, 331
Princeton (Southern BC)
    Exploring 140
    Practical Information 125
Princeton Museum and Archives
    (Princeton) 140
Protection Island (Vancouver Island
    and the Gulf Islands) 107
Provincial Law Courts (Vancouver) ... 65
Provincial Museum and Archives of
    Alberta (Edmonton) 322
Provincial Parks 45
Public Holidays 35
Pyramid Lake (Jasper National Park) . 232
Qualicum Beach (Vancouver Island)
    Accommodations 117
    Exploring 109
Queen Charlotte and San Christoval
    Mountains (Northern BC) .. 185
Queen Charlotte City (Northern BC)
    Accommodations 197
    Exploring 186
    Practical Information 168
    Restaurants 201
Queen Charlotte Islands Museum
    (Skidegate) 186
Queen Elizabeth Park (Vancouver) 71
Quilchena Hotel (Merritt) 139
Quinsam Salmon Hatchery (Campbell
    River) 109
Radium Hot Springs (Kootenay
    National Park) 235
    Accommodations 263
Rafting
    Alberta 338

Railway & Forest Industry Museum
    (Prince George) 170
Rectory (St. Paul) 326
Red Deer (Central Alberta)
    Accommodations 346
    Exploring 310
    Restaurants 356
Red Deer and District Museum (Red
    Deer) 310
Red Mountain (Southern BC) 150
Red Rock Canyon Parkway (Waterton
    Park) 333
Remington-Alberta Carriage Centre
    (Cardston) 299
Restaurants 40
Revelstoke (Southern BC)
    Accommodations 153
    Exploring 130
    Practical Information 125
    Restaurants 157
Revelstoke Dam (Revelstoke) 130
Revelstoke National Park 146
Reynolds-Alberta Museum
    (Wetaskiwin) 311
River Rafting
    Rocky Mountains 246
    Southern British Columbia 147
River Valley Park System (Edmonton) 336
Robson Square (Vancouver) 65
Rocky Mountain House (Central
    Alberta)
    Accommodations 347
    Exploring 312
    Restaurants 356
Rocky Mountain House National
    Historic Park 313
Rocky Mountains 203
    Economy 209
    Entertainment 271
    Exploring 214
    Fauna 206
    Finding Your Way Around 209
    Flora 205
    Geography 203
    History 208
    Outdoor Activities 238
    Parks 214
    Practical Information 213
    Restaurants 265
    Shopping 272
Rodeo 361
Rogers Pass (Revelstoke) 130
Rogers Pass Centre (Revelstoke) 131
Roonay Bay (Skidegate) 186

Rosebud (Central Alberta)
　　Restaurants 356
Rosedale (Southern Alberta)
　　Exploring 308
Rossland (Southern BC)
　　Accommodations 154
　　Exploring 133
　　Practical Information 125
　　Restaurants 158
Rossland Historical Museum
　　(Rossland) 134
Royal British Columbia Museum
　　(Victoria) 92
Royal Hudson Steam Train
　　(Squamish) 142
Royal Tyrell Museum of Paleontology
　　(Drumheller) 307
Rutherford House (Edmonton) 321
Saamis Archaeological Site (Medicine
　　Hat) 306
Saamis Tepee (Medicine Hat) 305
Saddledome (Calgary) 291
Safety 41
Sagitawa Lookout (Peace River) 329
Sailing
　　Southern British Columbia 147
　　Vancouver Island and the Gulf
　　　　Islands 115
Salmon Glacier (Northern BC) 180
Salt Spring (Gulf Islands)
　　Accommodations 118
　　Exploring 111
Saltery Bay Provincial Park 145, 147
Sandon (Southern BC)
　　Exploring 131
Sandspit (Northern BC)
　　Accommodations 198
　　Exploring 188
Sasquatch Provincial Park 146
Sayward (Vancouver Island)
　　Exploring 110
　　Restaurants 119
Science Centre (Calgary) 289
Science World (Vancouver) 66
Scuba Diving
　　Rocky Mountains 245
　　Vancouver Island and the Gulf
　　　　Islands 114
Sea Kayaking
　　Victoria 96
Seafest (Prince Rupert) 185
Seal-watching 48
Seaplane Base (Prince Rupert) 185

Sechelt (Southern BC)
　　Exploring 144
Set Foot for UBC (Vancouver) 68
Shaftesbury Trail (Peace River) 329
Shopping 38
Siding General Store (Field) 236
Silver City (Banff National Park) 221
　　Accommodations 255
Silver Grill (Fort Macleod) 300
Silvery Slocan Museum (New Denver) 131
Simon Fraser University (Vancouver) . . 66
Sir Alexander Galt Museum
　　(Lethbridge) 303
Skating
　　Alberta 339
Skeena River (Northern BC) . . . 182, 183
Ski Hall of Fame (Rossland) 134
Ski Whitewater (Southern BC) 150
Skidegate (Northern BC)
　　Exploring 186
Skiing
　　Southern British Columbia 149
Skydiving
　　Rocky Mountains 248
Slave Lake (Northern Alberta)
　　Accommodations 351
　　Exploring 328
　　Restaurants 359
Smithdorien Trail (Kananaskis
　　Country) 238
Smithers (Northern BC)
　　Accommodations 196
　　Exploring 181
　　Practical Information 168
　　Restaurants 201
Smokers 41
Smoky Lake (Northern Alberta)
　　Accommodations 350
　　Exploring 326
Snowmobiling 49
　　Rocky Mountains 251
Société Historique et Généalogique
　　(Donnelly) 329
Soo Coalition for Sustainable Forests
　　(Squamish) 141
Southern Alberta
　　Accommodations 343
　　Entertainment 362
　　Exploring 293
　　Finding Your Way Around 278
　　Parks 331
　　Restaurants 354
　　Shopping 365

Index

Southern British Columbia 121
   Accommodations 152
   Entertainment 160
   Exploring 126
   Outdoor Activities 147
   Parks and Beaches 146
   Practical Information 124
   Restaurants 157
   Shopping 160
Spatsizi Plateau Wilderness Park 177, 190
Spirit Island (Jasper National Park) . . . 232
Spotted Lake (Osoyoos) 135
Squamish (Southern BC)
   Exploring 141
   Practical Information 125
SS Sicamous (Penticton) 136
St. Albert (Northern Alberta)
   Exploring 326
St. Ann Ranch and Trading Company
   (Trochu) 308
St. Jean Baptiste Church
   (Morinville) 327
St. Josephat's Ukrainian Catholic
   Cathedral (Edmonton) 320
St. Paul (Northern Alberta)
   Accommodations 350
   Exploring 326
   Restaurants 359
St. Paul Culture Centre (St. Paul) . . . 326
St. Paul's Anglican Church (Kitwanga) 177
St. Peter's United Church (Hudson's
   Hope) 173
Stampede Park (Calgary) 291
Stanley Park (Vancouver) 63
Station Museum (Dawson Creek) . . . 171
Stawamus Chief Mountain
   (Squamish) 142
Steen River (Northern Alberta) 330
Stephansson House (Markerville) 315
Stephen Avenue Mall (Calgary) 288
Stettler (Central Alberta)
   Exploring 310
Stewart (Northern BC)
   Accommodations 195
   Exploring 179
   Finding Your Way Around 165
   Practical Information 167
   Restaurants 200
Stikine RiverSong (Telegraph Creek) . 179
Stone Mountain Provincial Park . 174, 189
Stone Storehouse (Stewart) 179
Stony Plain (Central Alberta)
   Exploring 312

Strathcona Farmer's Market
   (Edmonton) 322
Strathcona Park 113
Streetcar no. 23 (Nelson) 133
Strohn Lake (Northern BC) 179
Studio West Art Foundry (Cochrane) . 316
Stutfield Glacier (Icefields Parkway) . . 227
Sulphur Mountain Gondola (Banff) . . . 218
Summer Activities 46
Summerland (Southern BC) 138
   Accommodations 154
Sun Peaks (Southern BC) 149
Sun Tower (Vancouver) 63
Sun Yat-Sen Garden (Vancouver) 62
Suncor/Syncrude Sand Plant (Fort
   McMurray) 328
Sunmore company (Kamloops) 129
Sunshine Coast Maritime Museum
   (Southern BC) 144
Sunwapta Falls (Icefields Parkway) . . 228
Sunwapta Pass (Icefields Parkway) . . 227
Sylvan Lake Provincial Park (Central
   Alberta) 314
Taber (Southern Alberta)
   Exploring 304
Tahltan-Stikine lava beds (Telegraph
   Creek) 179
Takakaw Falls (Yoho National Park) . . 237
Tax Refunds for Non-Residents 40
Taxes 40
Tear Mountain overlook (McBride) . . . 180
Telecommunications 36
Telegraph Cove (Vancouver Island)
   Accommodations 117
   Exploring 110
Telegraph Creek (Northern BC)
   Accommodations 195
   Exploring 178
   Practical Information 167
   Restaurants 200
Telephone Historical Information
   Centre (Edmonton) 322
Terrace (Northern BC)
   Accommodations 196
   Exploring 182
   Restaurants 201
The Crossing (Icefields Parkway) 227
Therien (Northern Alberta)
   Exploring 326
Thompson, David 313
Time Difference 35
Tipping 40

Index 381

Tlell (Northern BC)
   Accommodations 197
   Exploring 188
   Restaurants 202
Tlell River (Tlell) 188
Tofino (Vancouver Island)
   Accommodations 116
   Exploring 108
   Restaurants 119
   Shopping 120
Totem poles (Kitwanga) 177
Totem poles (Kitwancool) 177
Tourist Information 28
Town hall (Nelson) 132
Trail (Southern BC)
   Exploring 134
Train 30
Traveller's Cheques 36
Tree-chipper (Mackenzie) 171
Trochu (Central Alberta)
   Accommodations 346
   Exploring 308
Tseax Lava Beds (Northern BC) . 182, 190
Tsuu T'ina Museum (Calgary) 292
Turner Valley (Southern Alberta)
   Exploring 294
Tuya River (Telegraph Creek) 179
Twelve Foot Davis (Peace River) 329
Ucluelet (Vancouver Island)
   Accommodations 116
   Exploring 108
   Restaurants 119
   Shopping 120
Ukrainian Canadian Archives and
   Museum of Alberta
   (Edmonton) 320
Ukrainian Cultural Heritage Village
   (Northern Alberta) 324
Ukrainian Museum of Canada
   (Edmonton) 320
University of British Columbia
   (Vancouver) 68
Upper Hot Spring (Banff) 218
Upper Kananaskis Lake (Kananaskis
   Country) 238
Upper Spiral Tunnel Viewpoint (Yoho
   National Park) 237
U'mista Cultural Center (Alert Bay) . . 110
Valley Zoo (Edmonton) 323
Van Dusen Botanical Garden
   (Vancouver) 71
Vancouver 51
   A brief history 52
   Accommodations 76
   Entertainment 81
   Exploring 60
   Finding Your Way Around 56
   Harbour Centre 60
   Outdoor Activities 75
   Parks and Beaches 73
   Practical Information 59
   Restaurants 78
   Shopping 82
   Vancouver today 51
Vancouver Art Gallery (Vancouver) . . . 65
Vancouver International Airport 56
Vancouver Island and the Gulf Islands 101
   Accommodations 116
   Exploring 105
   Finding Your Way Around 102
   Parks and Beaches 112
   Practical Information 104
Vancouver Museum (Vancouver) 66
Vancouver Public Aquarium and Zoo
   (Vancouver) 63
Vancouver Public Library (Vancouver) . 65
Vanderhoof (Northern BC)
   Accommodations 196
   Exploring 180
   Practical Information 168
Vanderhoof International Airshow
   (Vanderhoof) 180
Vegreville (Northern Alberta)
   Exploring 324
Vermillion Pass (Kootenay National
   Park) 233
Vernon (Southern BC)
   Exploring 139
Victoria 85
   Accommodations 96
   Entertainment 99
   Exploring 90
   Finding Your Way Around 86
   Outdoor Activities 95
   Parks and Beaches 95
   Practical Information 89
   Restaurants 98
   Shopping 100
Victoria Airport 34
Victoria Settlement (Smoky Lake) . . . 326
Victory Square (Vancouver) 63
Visual Arts 23
Vogue Theatre (Vancouver) 65
Volcanic craters (Tseax Lava Beds) . . 182
WAC Bennett (Hudson's Hope) 173
Wanda-Sue (Kamloops) 129
Wapta Falls (Yoho National Park) 236

Warner (Southern Alberta)
    Exploring 304
Waskasoo Park System (Red Deer) . . 310
Waterton Lakes National Park . . 299, 331
    Accommodations 343
    Restaurants 354
Watson Lake (Yukon)
    Accommodations 194
    Exploring 176
    Finding Your Way Around 164
    Practical Information 167
    Restaurants 200
Wayne (Southern Alberta)
    Exploring 308
Weeping Wall (Icefields Parkway) . . . 227
Weights 41
West Coast Trail (Victoria) 95
West Edmonton Mall (Edmonton) 323
West End (Vancouver) 64
West Summerland Station of the
    Kettle Valley Steam
    Railway 138
West Vancouver (Vancouver) 71
Western Heritage Centre (Cochrane) . 316
Wetaskiwin (Central Alberta)
    Accommodations 346
    Exploring 311
    Restaurants 356
Whale-watching 48
    Vancouver Island and the Gulf
        Islands 115
Whistler (Southern BC)
    Accommodations 156
    Entertainment 160
    Exploring 142
    Practical Information 125
    Restaurants 159
    Shopping 160
Whistler Mountain (Southern BC) 150
Whyte Museum of the Canadian
    Rockies (Banff) 216
Widewater (Northern Alberta)
    Restaurants 359
    Shopping 366
William Watson Lodge (Kananaskis
    Country) 238
Williston Lake (Mackenzie) 171
Willows Beach 95
Wokkpash Recreation Area (Northern
    BC) 174, 189
Wood Buffalo National Park . . . 328, 337
Wreck Beach (Vancouver) 68
Writing-on-Stone Provincial
    Park 304, 334
Xa:ytem Long House Interpretive
    Centre (Mission) 126
Yale (Southern BC)
    Exploring 128
Yaletown (Vancouver) 65
Yoho National Park
    Accommodations 263
    Exploring 236
    Finding Your Way Around 212
    Practical Information 213
    Restaurants 270
Zoo (Vancouver) 63

■ ULYSSES TRAVEL GUIDES

☐ Affordable Bed & Breakfasts in Québec .... $11.95 CAN $9.95 US
☐ Canada's Maritime Provinces .... $24.95 CAN $14.95 US
☐ Dominican Republic 2nd Edition .... $24.95 CAN $16.95 US
☐ El Salvador .... $22.95 CAN $14.95 US
☐ Guadeloupe .... $24.95 CAN $16.95 US
☐ Honduras .... $24.95 CAN $16.95 US
☐ Martinique .... $24.95 CAN $16.95 US
☐ Montréal .... $19.95 CAN $13.95 US
☐ Ontario .... $24.95 CAN $14.95 US
☐ Panamá .... $24.95 CAN $16.95 US
☐ Portugal .... $24.95 CAN $16.95 US
☐ Provence - Côte d'Azur .... $24.95 CAN $14.95 US
☐ Québec .... $24.95 CAN $14.95 US
☐ Toronto .... $19.95 CAN $13.95

☐ Vancouver .... $14.95 CAN $9.95 US
☐ Western Canada .... $24.95 CAN $16.95 US

■ ULYSSES GREEN ESCAPES

☐ Hiking in the Northeastern United States .... $19.95 CAN $13.95 US
☐ Hiking in Québec ..... $19.95 CAN $13.95 US

■ ULYSSES DUE SOUTH

☐ Cartagena (Colombia) . $9.95 CAN $5.95 US
☐ Montelimar (Nicaragua) $9.95 CAN $5.95 US
☐ Puerto Plata - Sosua - Cabarete (Dominican Republic) .. $9.95 CAN $5.95 US
☐ St. Barts .... $9.95 CAN $7.95 US
☐ St. Martin .... $9.95 CAN $7.95 US

■ ULYSSES TRAVEL JOURNAL

☐ Ulysses Travel Journal $9.95 CAN $7.95 US

QUANTITY	TITLES	PRICE	TOTAL

NAME:_____
ADDRESS:_____
_____
_____

	Sub-total	
	Postage & Handling	$4.00
	Sub-total	
	G.S.T.in Canada 7%	
	TOTAL	

Payment: ☐ Money Order ☐ Visa ☐ MasterCard
Card Number:
Expiry Date:
Signature

ULYSSES TRAVEL PUBLICATIONS
4176 Rue Saint-Denis, Montréal, Québec, H2W 2M5
☎(514) 843-9447 fax (514) 843-9448